Lecture Notes of the Institute for Computer Sciences, Social Informatics and Telecommunications Engineering   96

Editorial Board

Ozgur Akan
Middle East Technical University, Ankara, Turkey

Paolo Bellavista
University of Bologna, Italy

Jiannong Cao
Hong Kong Polytechnic University, Hong Kong

Falko Dressler
University of Erlangen, Germany

Domenico Ferrari
Università Cattolica Piacenza, Italy

Mario Gerla
UCLA, USA

Hisashi Kobayashi
Princeton University, USA

Sergio Palazzo
University of Catania, Italy

Sartaj Sahni
University of Florida, USA

Xuemin (Sherman) Shen
University of Waterloo, Canada

Mircea Stan
University of Virginia, USA

Jia Xiaohua
City University of Hong Kong, Hong Kong

Albert Zomaya
University of Sydney, Australia

Geoffrey Coulson
Lancaster University, UK

Muttukrishnan Rajarajan   Fred Piper
Haining Wang   George Kesidis (Eds.)

Security and Privacy in Communication Networks

7th International ICST Conference, SecureComm 2011
London, UK, September 7-9, 2011
Revised Selected Papers

 Springer

Volume Editors

Muttukrishnan Rajarajan
City University London
10 Northampton Square, London EC1V 0HB, UK
E-mail: r.muttukrishnan@city.ac.uk

Fred Piper
Royal Holloway University of London
Egham Hill, TW20 0EX, UK
E-mail: f.piper@rhul.ac.uk

Haining Wang
College of William and Mary
P.O. Box 8795, Williamsburg, VA 23187, USA
E-mail: hnw@cs.wm.edu

George Kesidis
Pennsylvania State University
338J IST Building, University Park, PA 16802, USA
E-mail: kesidis@cse.psu.edu

ISSN 1867-8211   e-ISSN 1867-822X
ISBN 978-3-642-31908-2   e-ISBN 978-3-642-31909-9
DOI 10.1007/978-3-642-31909-9
Springer Heidelberg Dordrecht London New York

Library of Congress Control Number: Applied for

CR Subject Classification (1998): K.6.5, C.2.2, C.2, D.4.6, E.3, H.4

© ICST Institute for Computer Science, Social Informatics and Telecommunications Engineering 2012
This work is subject to copyright. All rights are reserved, whether the whole or part of the material is
concerned, specifically the rights of translation, reprinting, re-use of illustrations, recitation, broadcasting,
reproduction on microfilms or in any other way, and storage in data banks. Duplication of this publication
or parts thereof is permitted only under the provisions of the German Copyright Law of September 9, 1965,
in its current version, and permission for use must always be obtained from Springer. Violations are liable
to prosecution under the German Copyright Law.
The use of general descriptive names, registered names, trademarks, etc. in this publication does not imply,
even in the absence of a specific statement, that such names are exempt from the relevant protective laws
and regulations and therefore free for general use.

Typesetting: Camera-ready by author, data conversion by Scientific Publishing Services, Chennai, India

Printed on acid-free paper

Springer is part of Springer Science+Business Media (www.springer.com)

Preface

On a daily basis, we see cyber attacks getting more powerful than before. Lately we have witnessed security failures at a host of commercial enterprises like Sony (their Playstation network and later their Web services) that have made international news. Thus, it becomes essential to understand why such systems fail. Depending on the industrial sector, the company policy, national customs, laws and regulations, the reaction after a failure varies. Indeed, revelation of the cyber-theft at Citibank in 1995, made stocks drop. In general, companies, engineers, individuals, prefer to avoid talking about failures. This is often motivated by commercial interest, nationalistic reasons, people's self-esteem, etc. The resulting overconfidence may have dramatic consequences. The Fukushima accident seems to have been such an example. Although we often do not have access to detailed information about why security engineering failed, in the case of Electronic Passports and E-Voting, we have clear evidence. These examples will be used to analyze why (information) security engineering fails.

September 2011   Yvo G. Desmedt

Organization

SecureComm 2011 was organized by the School of Engineering and Mathematical Sciences at City University London, in cooperation with European Alliance for Innovation (EAI), Italy.

Organizing Committee

General Chairs
Muttukrishnan Rajarajan   City University London, UK
Fred Piper   Royal Holloway, University of London, UK

Program Chairs
George Kesidis   Pennsylvania State University, USA
Haining Wang   College of William and Mary, USA

Workshops Chair
Morley Mao   University of Michigan, USA

Publicity Chair
Syed Ali Khayam   NUST, Pakistan

Panels Chair
Veselin Rakocevic   City University London, UK

Demos Chair
Dhiren Patel   NIT Surat, India

Exhibits Chair
Theo Dimitrakos   BT, UK

Posters Chair
Divya Bansal   Punjab Engineering College, India

Local Chair
Steve Furnell   University of Plymouth, UK

Publications Chair
Ali Sajjad   City University London, UK

Web Chair

Pramod Pawar   City University London, UK

Conference Manager

Anna Sterzi   European Alliance for Innovation (EAI), Italy

Technical Program Committee

Ehab Al-Shaer	University of North Carolina at Charlotte, USA
Kun Bai	IBM T.J. Watson Research Center, USA
Raheem Beyah	Georgia Institute of Technology, USA
Kevin Butler	University of Oregon, USA
David Chadwick	University of Kent, UK
Aldar Chan	Institute for Infocomm Research, Singapore
Hao Chen	University of California at Davis, USA
Songqing Chen	George Mason University, USA
Yan Chen	Northwestern University, USA
Mihai Christodorescu	IBM T.J. Watson Research Center, USA
Mauro Conti	Vrije Universiteit Amsterdam, The Netherlands
Jedidiah Crandall	University of New Mexico, USA
Michel Cukier	University of Maryland, USA
Tassos Dimitriou	Athens Information Technology, Greece
Wenliang Du	Syracuse University, USA
Zhenhai Duan	Florida State University, USA
Xinwen Fu	University of Massachusetts at Lowell, USA
Vinod Ganapathy	Rutgers University, USA
Matthew Green	Johns Hopkins University, USA
Yong Guan	Iowa State University, USA
Peter Gutmann	University of Auckland, New Zealand
Chris Hankin	Imperial College London, UK
Thorsten Holz	Ruhr University Bochum, Germany
Xuxian Jiang	North Carolina State University, USA
Loukas Lazos	University of Arizona, USA
Adam J. Lee	University of Pittsburgh, USA
Jun Li	University of Oregon, USA
Qun Li	College of William and Mary, USA
Alex Liu	Michigan State University, USA
Wenjing Lou	Worcester Polytechnic Institute, USA
John C.S. Lui	The Chinese University of Hong Kong, China
Ludovic Me	SUPELEC, France
Chris Mitchell	Royal Holloway University of London, UK
Yi Mu	University of Wollongong, Australia
David Nicol	University of Illinois at Urbana-Champaign, USA
Panos Papadimitratos	KTH at Stockholm, Sweden

Joachim Posegga   University of Passau, Germany
Atul Prakash   University of Michigan, USA
Geraint Price   Royal Holloway University of London, UK
Radha Provendran   University of Washington, USA
Douglas Reeves   North Carolina State University, USA
Peter Reiher   University of California at Los Angeles, USA
Kui Ren   Illinois Institute of Technology, USA
William Robertson   University of California at Berkeley, USA
Luca Salgarelli   University of Brescia, Italy
Pierangela Samarati   Università degli Studi di Milano, Italy
Micah Sherr   Georgetown University, USA
Mukesh Singhal   University of Kentucky, USA
Angelos Stavrou   George Mason University, USA
Paul Syverson   Naval Research Laboratory, USA
Patrick Tague   Carnegie Mellon University, USA
Xiaofeng Wang   Indiana University, USA
Xinyuan Wang   George Mason University, USA
Andreas Wespi   IBM Zurich Research Laboratory, Switzerland
Susanne Wetzel   Stevens Institute of Technology, USA
Mengjun Xie   University of Arkansas at Little Rock, USA
Dong Xuan   Ohio State University, USA
Danfeng Yao   Virginia Tech, USA
David Yau   Purdue University, USA
Vinod Yegneswaran   SRI International, USA
Heng Yin   Syracuse University, USA
Chuan Yue   University of Colorado at Colorado Spring,
                                USA
Xiaolan Zhang   IBM T.J. Watson Research Center, USA
Sencun Zhu   Pennsylvania State University, USA
Andrea Zisman   City University London, UK
Cliff Zou   University of Central Florida, USA

Steering Committee

Peng Liu (Chair)   Pennsylvania State University, USA
Imrich Chlamtac   Create-Net, Italy
Andreas Schmid   Novalyst, Italy

Table of Contents

System Security

Anonymity and Privacy (II)

DNS and Routing Security

Key Management

Wireless Security (II)

Short Papers

Designing Scalable and Effective Decision Support for Mitigating Attacks in Large Enterprise Networks

Zhiyun Qian[1], Z. Morley Mao[1], Ammar Rayes[2], and David Jaffe[2]

[1] University of Michigan, Ann Arbor, MI 48105, USA
{zhiyunq,zmao}@umich.edu
[2] Cisco Systems, Inc. San Jose, CA 95134, USA
{rayes,djaffe}@cisco.com

Abstract. Managing numerous security vulnerabilities has long been a difficult and daunting task especially due to the complexity, heterogeneity, and various operational constraints of the network. In this paper, we focus on the task of mitigating and managing network-device-specific vulnerabilities automatically and intelligently. We achieve the goal by a scalable, interactive, topology-aware framework that can provide mitigation actions at selectively chosen devices. The intuition behind our work is that more and more network devices are becoming security-capable so that they can be collectively used to achieve security goals while satisfying certain network policies.

The intelligence utilizes integer programming to optimize a quantifiable objective conforming to the policy of a given network. An example would be to find the minimum number of network devices to install filters to effectively protect the entire network against potential attacks from external untrusted sources. The constraints of the integer programming are mainly based on the network topology and settings of vulnerable devices and untrusted sources. Our novel implementation uses an iterative algorithm to scale to networks of tens of thousands of nodes, and we demonstrate the effectiveness of our framework using both synthetic and realistic network topologies. Besides scalability, our tool is also operationally easy to use by enabling interactivity to input additional constraints during runtime.

Keywords: vulnerability management, optimization, integer programming.

1 Introduction

With the increasing complexity of the Internet, enterprise networks have grown in both size and complexity, so have associated network devices which not only perform packet routing and forwarding but are also equipped with network management and security functionalities such as packet filtering. These devices can act as firewalls to partition the network into distinct groups and prevent intrusions by filtering unwanted traffic based on attributes such as source/destination IP address, source/destination port, TTL values, *etc.* These can provide intermediate or temporary solutions to defend the network, for instance, by limiting access to potentially vulnerable services only to trusted/valid IPs through the use of ACLs (Access Control List).

Given the broad range of security vulnerabilities in existing networks ranging from buffer overflow, code injection [1] to denial of service [2], it may not be sufficient to

M. Rajarajan et al. (Eds.): SecureComm 2011, LNICST 96, pp. 1–18, 2012.
ⓒ Institute for Computer Sciences, Social Informatics and Telecommunications Engineering 2012

rely on simple firewalls. However, many of such vulnerabilities can be mitigated at the network level due to significant advance in network security technology manifested in devices such as Network Intrusion Detection System (NIDS) and Network Intrusion Prevention System (NIPS).

If a network device, *e.g.,* Cisco Intrusion Prevention System (IPS) device [3], has advanced Deep Packet Inspection (DPI) capability, packet filters can be set up based on payload. They are capable of detecting and preventing a variety of intrusions. For example, the *DNS Implementations Insufficient Entropy Vulnerability* can be mitigated by installing a signature on the DPI-capable device to detect a DNS flood possibly leading to DNS cache poisoning, reflection, or amplification attacks [4].

Note that network level defense suffers from the shortcoming by assuming where attacks can enter the network. Thus our proposed framework shares the same assumption, revealing the difficulties of fully defending against internal attacks. Nevertheless, network level defense complements well other types of defense such as host-based intrusion detection system. The alternative of applying a patch to fully fix the vulnerability may not be immediately adopted because of several reasons. First, a patch for the vulnerable software may not be available. Second, the patch may not be fully tested and may introduce unwanted side-effects. Finally, applying the patch may require rebooting the device, introducing network disruption. Since the basic firewall capability is built-in for virtually every modern router and switch (*e.g.,* Access Control List), various choices with different tradeoffs exist in terms of how to temporarily protect the network.

For those vulnerabilities that cannot be prevented at the network level, applying the patch directly to the vulnerable software is preferred since patching only incurs one-time overhead and provides the best protection. However, considering the number of devices in the network that are potentially very diverse (as shown in the next section), knowing what to patch first without causing much disruption can be very challenging, let alone consider the case when the options of patching vs. network-level defense are both available. Finding the best strategy considering various tradeoffs can be a daunting task. For that purpose, we have developed *a framework using integer programming that considers various tradeoffs and makes optimal suggestions on which routers to reconfigure/patch to prevent intrusions based on the topology of the network and policies/preference of network/sys admin.* In what follows, we will use the term *filter* as a general term for network-level defense.

Our work is quite applicable as large networks today often deploy DPI capable security systems not only at a few external gateways but also internally to defend against internal threats. Furthermore, it is the trend that more network devices will have such security capabilities built-in. There is however no prior work to thoroughly analyze how to plan or utilize these resources wisely. More specifically, decision has to be made to determine which devices and what operations are to be performed to address known vulnerabilities while minimizing overhead without compromising security protection. The overhead includes management complexity, as well as performance penalty introduced by the size of DPI signatures or firewall rules [5].

We develop a prototype framework to help network/sys admin manage security vulnerabilities at the network level by integrating two main primitive operations – filter and patch. Our novel iterative implementation allows the system to easily scale to networks of thousands of network devices. Furthermore, we build operational interactivity into the design to facilitate constraint modification during run time. As with any model-based approach, the guarantees offered depend on the model accuracy. Despite the simplicity of the abstraction used in our model, it is sufficient for our purpose as shown later. Furthermore, our approach has the benefit of being independent of low-level implementations, *e.g.,* how to configure the filtering rules. Our framework also complements existing work in formal analysis [6] to ensure the correctness of rule configurations.

The paper is organized as follows. §2 motivates our work by revealing the heterogeneity and complexity of real networks. §3 introduces our framework. §4 then focuses on how we translate the security management problem into an optimization problem illustrated using a simple example. We evaluate our tool against several real networks to demonstrate its effectiveness in §6. §7 describes several related work. Finally we conclude with discussions in §8 and §9.

2 Network Device Diversity in Real Networks

To motivate the need for a framework to deal with complex network goals and constraints, we first want to understand how diverse real networks are. We leverage the inventory data from Cisco's remote router management system (formally known as Cisco Inventory and Reporting or IR [7]). In a nutshell, Cisco IR allows Cisco to remotely manage the network of a company that chooses to use the service (many big companies from different industrials use the service).

Interestingly, from these real networks, we found there are many different versions of operating systems running on their network devices (*e.g.,* shown in Figure 1). The Y-axis is $\frac{\#\ of\ different\ IOS\ version}{\#\ of\ devices/chassis}$ which indicates the degree of variety of the network devices. The X-axis is different organizations whose networks are managed by Cisco's Inventory Reporting application. The number of devices for each of the organizations range from hundreds to a thousand. Surprisingly, the most diverse network has more than 180 different OS versions. This many different OS versions cause complex many-to-many relationships between OS versions and corresponding vulnerabilities as shown in Table 1, securing the entire network taking into account all OS versions and device vulnerabilities in an optimized fashion is quite challenging. Furthermore, some of the vulnerability may be more critical than others, some incur more overhead (*e.g.,* downtime). The surprisingly diverse and complex network devices motivate the need to mitigate and manage their vulnerabilities automatically and intelligently. To ensure practical relevance, we design our framework to handle multiple vulnerabilities, allowing users to specify these in a quantifiable metric.

3 The Framework

In this section, we first describe the high-level framework and the building blocks to support our objective of providing intelligent attack mitigation decision support. As example mitigation support of interest to network/sys admin could be "finding the minimum number of network devices to install filters to prevent attack X". This work is based on the observation that many of the security management problems can be

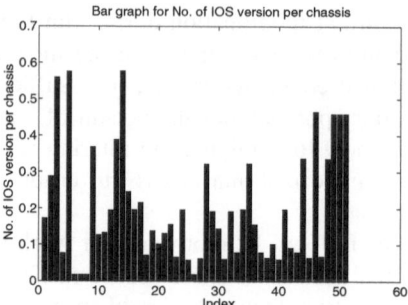

Fig. 1. The number of unique OS version per chassis in different real networks

Table 1. An example of multiple vulnerabilities on various versions of Cisco IOS

Vulnerability ID / IOS version	1 2 3 4
11.0(11)BT	x x
12.0(10)ST	x x x x
12.0(11)S4	x x

modeled as optimization problems. We present our simple and elegant method based on integer programming to help solve this class of problems.

Our framework is designed to be built on top of existing network information including network topology, configuration files of the network devices, the security alert data and the network/sys admin's objective and requirements. We describe the inputs below, also illustrated in Figure 2.

Inventory and vulnerability information contains data such as device type and running services (including PCs and routers/switches). IT departments in companies often track a subset, if not all, of such information already. For instance, Cisco offers remote router management that tracks the inventory and vulnerability information of all the routers. The information can be automatically collected using both open source and commercial tools [8, 9]. As an open standard, Open Vulnerability Assessment Language (OVAL) [9] is an XML-based language for specifying machine configuration tests. OVAL-compatible scanners can be used to gather vulnerability information of the devices given OVAL definitions. For network devices, the network/sys admin typically runs the scanner via SNMP to collect the device info as well as the OS version and its patch level. We ran the similar test on our local network which has several hundreds of network devices and it takes only less than a minute to finish.

Security alerts contain vulnerability information for software on different platforms (both PCs and routers/switches) and provides the basic prevention or detection recommendations. For example, the alerts may disclose whether a patch is available for a particular piece of software. Such information or service is published by various vendors such as Cisco Intellishield [10]. For instance, we can easily tell, according to the security alert service, that the *Multiple SNMPv3 Implementations Hash-Based Message Authentication Code Manipulation Vulnerability* can be mitigated by either applying patches, configuring ACLs, or installing IPS signatures on DPI-capable devices.

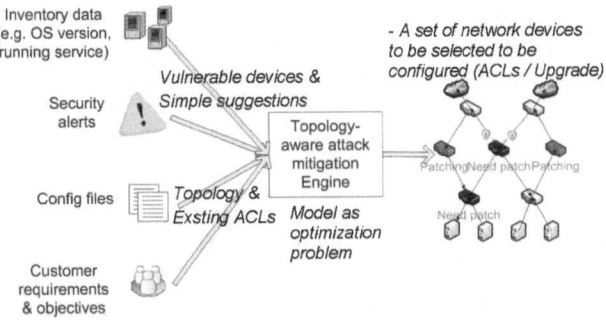

Fig. 2. Our framework for making attack mitigation suggestions

Network Topology. Typically, this information is maintained by IT department already. If not, there are techniques to reconstruct layer-three topology based on their IP addresses [11] from router configuration files. The topology information can also be obtained by probing the network [8, 11], typically, by real network management tools such as NetMRI [12].

Objective is used to describe the network-dependent properties that can either be specified by the network/sys admin or inferred automatically discussed later.

Here we assume that different kinds of attack mitigation building blocks can be used on each network device depending on its unique capability:

- Configure the ACL (Access Control List) to guard against certain (untrusted) IP range and/or ports.
- Configure the firewall to stop unwanted traffic.
- Install an appropriate packet filter based on signatures for identifying malicious payload if the device is IDS or IPS-enabled.
- Apply the patch on the devices or the end-hosts.
- Other network device built-in capabilities such as IP Source Guard enabled on many Cisco devices.

4   Problem Formulation - Optimization

From the input of the framework, we can extract the network settings, the vulnerable nodes (PCs or routers/switches), and more importantly, the goals and constraints. For example, network/sys admin may want to balance the number of filtering rules on a particular router (due to processing overhead) and the overall number of interfaces to be reconfigured (due to management overhead). The constraint can be, for example, to protect all of vulnerable nodes or to protect only nodes with the most severe vulnerability. Based on the problem requirement, it is natural to cast it as an optimization problem which we can model using integer programming. The reason for this choice is that integer programming is not only very simple and intuitive to use, but also provides a small and well-defined interface, thus allowing various Integer Programming Solvers to be optimized separately. We will illustrate how these variables are defined and how to use different objective functions and constraints to solve several types of realistic security management problems.

Note that our framework aims to provide intelligent suggestions for various security management problems. More specifically, the framework supports filtering and patching decisions based on various constraints/tradeoffs for multiple vulnerabilities.

4.1 Overview

Variables. For each interface in the network, we define a binary integer variable x_i, which can either be 0 or 1 indicating whether this interface is configured with a filter (for normal switch/router) or a signature (for NIDS/NIPS). Alternatively, a variable can be defined for each node (PC or switch/router) rather than an interface indicating whether a node has filters installed (regardless of the interfaces). Similarly, for each node, we define a binary integer variable y_i which indicates whether this particular node is to be patched.

Note here we can omit a variable or always assign the variable to zero if a network device or interface does not support the basic mitigation support (*e.g.*, an older version of router without ACL support). To address multiple vulnerabilities, we define different sets of variables $x_i^{(k)}$, $x_{i+1}^{(k)}$ *etc.* for the k_{th} vulnerability. In comparison, we also define a special patch variable y_i. Since patching one node usually eliminate all the vulnerabilities under consideration, either all k vulnerabilities are protected by filters or the node is patched suffices the security requirement. In the following discussions, any variables defined will be a binary integer variable unless otherwise specified.

Objective function can express many different goals but with the limitation that it has to be linear function of the variables of the form $\sum_i a_i x_i$. Despite this apparent limitation, it is sufficient to solve many of the security management problems. For example, the objective function could be $\sum_i x_i$ which is the total number of interfaces that are configured to install filters or NIDS/NIPS signatures. The goal would be to minimize this value.

Constraint is of the form $\sum_i a_i x_i <= b$ where a_i and b are constants. A sample constraint would be defined as $x_1 + x_2 + x_3 + y_1 >= 1$ where x_1 is an untrusted interface and x_3 is an interface that belongs to a vulnerable device y_1. This constraint means that there has to be at least one filter along this path to protect the vulnerable device or the device can be patched by assigning variable y_1 to 1. If there is no patch available yet for the vulnerability or due to other business reasons (*e.g.*, downtime), we can simply remove the variable y_1.

4.2 An Example

A simple example that illustrates how integer programming can be set up is shown in Figure 3. We do not consider patch in this example for simplicity. The topology consists of a set of routers (from x_1 to x_7) and a set of servers that are vulnerable to a newly discovered vulnerability in an enterprise network. Assuming that the operator prefers not to simply patch these servers due to reasons such as possible downtime to their customers, so we remove all the patch variables y_i. The alternative is to install a corresponding signature for this vulnerability to filter malicious incoming packets on the routers (or any other mitigation building blocks such as ACLs), assuming the signature is available. The question is where to install such filters. A simple solution would be to

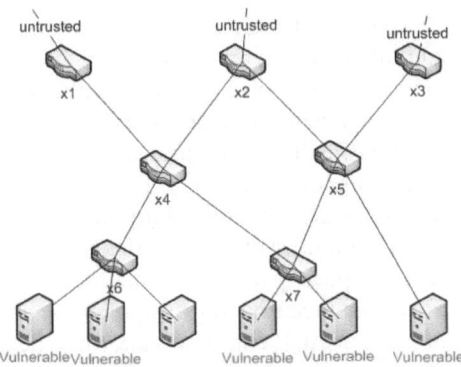

Fig. 3. Example 1 - topology

install it on every gateway (x_1, x_2 and x_3), but it is not an optimal solution in terms of the number of devices involved (assuming a desirable goal is minimal complexity).

A better strategy is to install the filters on x_4 and x_5 only. This optimal solution can be found by solving the corresponding integer programming problem that is translated from the current network setting (network topology, untrusted source interfaces and vulnerable nodes). Below are the definitions of objective functions and constraints for this example.

Objective Function. Since we are trying to minimize the number of nodes that are installed with filters, the objective function is defined as $\sum_{i=1}^{7} x_i$.

Constraints:
$$x_1 + x_4 + x_6 >= 1$$
$$x_1 + x_4 + x_7 >= 1$$
$$x_2 + x_4 + x_6 >= 1$$
$$x_2 + x_4 + x_7 >= 1$$
$$x_2 + x_5 >= 1$$
$$x_3 + x_5 >= 1$$
$$x_i >= 0 \text{ for each } 1 <= i <= 7$$

We can easily get the answer from this integer programming setup: $x_4 = x_5 = 1$, $x_i = 0$ for $i \neq 4$ and $i \neq 5$. Sometimes, however, the number of filters on x_4 and x_5 may be too large so that the network/sys admin may want to avoid using them. This can either be solved by setting a different objective function (§4.3) or allow the user to interact with the tool and provide feedback to the tool (§6.3).

4.3 Objectives

Network/sys admins may specify different kinds of objective functions that they want to optimize based on a given set of constraints. Here we describe some common objective functions of interest:

Minimal involvement - minimum number of network device configuration changes. The objective function is defined as $\sum_i x_i$ where x_i is the variable for each node indicating whether a particular node has been configured for filters as discussed before.

Note here once the node is configured, then it can be applied to any number of interfaces on that device without additional cost in our formulation. The reason for this policy is that network operators may want to involve smallest number of devices to defend their network for simplicity or management overhead considerations.

Minimal management complexity - minimum amount of management complexity imposed. The objective function is defined as $\sum_i (((n_i + 1)^2 - n_i^2) \times x_i)$ where $(n_i + 1)^2 - n_i^2$ is the amount of management complexity increased by adding a new ACL entry on an interface, n_i as the number of ACL entries for the corresponding interface and n_i^2 is the management complexity of a given interface where n is the number of entries of ACLs configured. The incentive for this policy is that due to complex ACL matching rules, a large number of ACL entries are known to be difficult to manage.

Minimal number of devices involved - minimum number of devices that are either to be configured for filters or patches. The objective function is defined as $\sum_{i,j} x_i^{(j)} + \alpha \sum_m y_m$, where $x_i^{(j)}$ is the variable for node i and vulnerability j indicating whether this node has been configured for filters to prevent vulnerability j, y_m is the variable for node m indicating whether this node is to be patched (multiple real patches for different vulnerabilities are combined into this single variable). α is the constant coefficient which balances the choice between installing filtering and patching. Normally it is larger than the cost of installing filters. However, as previously stated, if patching one node can eliminate the need for filters on many nodes, then it may be a preferred choice. This is the case given multiple vulnerabilities in one or more nodes, patching them obviates any other filters. In fact, modern routers tend to have multiple vulnerabilities due to their complexities [13]. §2 describes how to set up the constraints for multiple vulnerabilities and patch operation. We can also define the objective function in terms of interfaces instead of nodes.

Minimal network performance overhead - minimize possible throughput and latency performance overhead imposed by installing filters. The idea is that although most network devices support ACL or firewall rules, they come with a cost. Even for modern devices where hardware support has been widely applied to optimize the ACL or firewall rules, for example, by using Content-addressable memory (CAM), the throughput can drop significantly [14] when the number of ruleset exceeds certain threshold (depending on vendors and models). The same also applies to DPI devices. As a result, the objective function can be defined as $\sum_i k_i$ where k_i is defined based on the number of existing filters (denoted by n_i) on interface i. $k_i = 0$ when $n_i <= s$ and $k_i = x_i{}^j + n_i - s$ when $n_i > s$.

Intuitively, the objective function captures the performance penalty imposed on each interface due to filters and the overall impact. Note that $k_i = 0$ when $n_i <= s$ is approximated because s is relatively larger than the number of filters to be placed on a single interface. Typical s for modern routers is in the order of hundreds. An alternative objective function would be to minimize $\max(k_i)$ because usually the overall network performance is determined by the bottleneck component. This policy is to help eliminate the scenario where filters are installed only on few core routers which may deeply impact the network performance.

Note that these objective functions can be combined to achieve a balance between different goals. Here in many cases the cost of placing filter is to be set identically for simplicity. However, we do offer some simple heuristics on how the cost can be selected. For example, a network device with high capability and low overhead for installing filters should generally be considered low cost. Another example is that when the number of existing filters on the device is already large, it should be considered high cost. Further, we allow the users to tune the result in an interactive fashion which provides much better usability as shown in § 6.3.

4.4 Constraints

Below are some examples of useful constraints.

Installing Filters to Protect Vulnerable Nodes. For each vulnerable node j and untrusted node i, enumerate all possible paths from i to j. For each path, consider the constraint $x_i + .. + x_j >= 1$ where each variable can be the variable for the node or the interface, depending on the problem setup. If this constraint is satisfied, then a vulnerable node is guaranteed to be protected on this particular path (since at least one interface/router along the way will be configured to filter malicious packets). Similarly, we can apply this for every vulnerable node and untrusted node pair to ensure global safety. There are variants where one can specify the constraint to be $x_i + .. + x_j >= 2$ to increase defense redundancy.

Filters or Patch. Given a particular vulnerability for which a patch is available, a vulnerable node j and an untrusted node i, enumerate all possible paths from i to j. For each path, consider the constraint $x_i + .. + x_j + y_j >= 1$ where x_i to x_j can be the variables for the node or the interface. y_j is the additional variable (defined in objective functions) indicating whether this node will be patched. This constraint will be satisfied either when there is a filter along the path or it is patched. Note that in practice, we might need several different patches to be installed for diverse vulnerabilities, but generally we consider them logically as one aggregate patch in our abstraction. Exceptions are made when some vulnerabilities have corresponding patches but some do not. We can also support this case by partitioning the vulnerabilities into patchable ones and un-patchable ones, as discussed in §4.3 and §4.4.

Latency Constraint. For simplicity, we can model the latency constraint using filtering rules. Intuitively, with more rules, the router needs to spend more time processing them. For a beginning node i and an ending node j on a path, consider the constraint $x_i^{(1)} + .. + x_j^{(1)} + x_i^{(2)} + ... + x_j^{(2)} + ... + x_i^{(n)} + ... + x_j^{(n)} <= c$, where each $x_l^{(k)}$ is the variable defined for each interface along the path, assuming that $x_l^{(k)} = 1$ is equivalent of adding one filtering rule on an interface. c is a constant describing the maximum number of increased filtering rules allowed. $x_i^{(k)} + ... + x_j^{(k)}$ is the number of filtering rules added for k_{th} vulnerability along the path from node i to node j. Obviously, $\sum_k x_i^{(k)} + ... + x_j^{(k)}$ is the overall filtering rules added for the path.

5 Implementation

The Integer Programming Solver we use is CPLEX-11.0 [15]. We first implement our tool in a brute-force, naive manner, by calculating all possible constraints through the

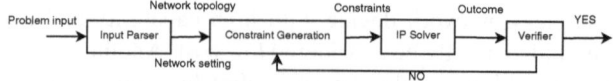

Fig. 4. Logic flow of iterative implementation

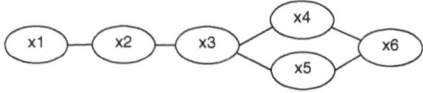

Fig. 5. An example topology that shares common path

enumeration of all paths between untrusted node and vulnerable node. The problem is that when the graph is dense enough, the number of paths between two nodes could be exponential with respect to the number of nodes. We may argue that most real topologies are usually not dense graphs, but many large networks usually have redundant links/backup nodes to provide availability and failure resilience. To address this problem, we have proposed the novel implementation that uses *an iterative approach* to incrementally add constraints to reduce the search space for all possible paths between two nodes. Further, the iterative implementation produces the same optimal result as the naive implementation.

Formally, our problem is $min\ c^T x$, under a set of constraints I. Note that the size of I can be very large. We propose to iteratively add a subset of I and generate a temporary result for the subset of constraints. The hope is that the outcome computed based on the subset of I will satisfy the ultimate constraint that all of the vulnerable nodes are protected before all of the constraints in I are added. It is illustrated in Figure 4.

This approach is based on the following observations:

1. We may not need all the constraints in I to compute the optimal solution because there are many redundant constraints. It is unnecessary to go through all of them. For example, $x_1 + x_2 + x_3 >= 1$ is redundant if there is a constraint $x_1 + x_2 >= 1$. These cases should be handled automatically by standard linear programming or integer programming solver. However, there are many other constraints that can share common variables while neither one of them is redundant. See Figure 5 as an example, there are two paths from x_1 to x_6 whose corresponding constraints look like $x_1 + x_2 + x_3 + x_4 + x_6 >= 1$ and $x_1 + x_2 + x_3 + x_5 + x_6 >= 1$. They share four common variables. It is highly likely, although not always the case, that one satisfied constraint will lead to others being satisfied as well. In real networks, it is not uncommon that several paths share common devices or links. By iteratively adding constraints (in a certain order), we are able to take advantage of such properties.

2. It is relatively easy to verify whether a given set of filters and patch operations will protect all vulnerable devices. This allows us to quickly iterate several times. To check if all vulnerable devices are protected, we perform a breadth-first search in the graph from the untrusted nodes to the vulnerable nodes. The search stops when it encounters a filter or the reached vulnerable node on the edge will be patched.

3. The ordering of added constraints can be determined relatively easily – first add the ones that are less likely to be redundant. Specifically, we pick those shortest attack paths to be the constraints. In general, fewer variables result in less redundancy. If a constraint

---

Algorithm 1. The iterative algorithm

Initialization: $I' = \{\}$,
$\qquad$ filter set $F_0 = \{\}$,
$\qquad$ patch set $P_0 = \{\}$,
$\qquad$ objective function f.
repeat {iteration i from 0 to ...}
$\quad$ 1. Given F_i and P_i, compute the set of shortest attack paths and its corresponding
$\quad$ I_i based on the topology.
$\quad$ 2. $I' = I' \cup I_i$.
$\quad$ 3. Run the IP solver for objective function f under constraints I', get the solution
$\quad$ F_{i+1} and P_{i+1}.
until F_{i+1} and P_{i+1} protects all vulnerable nodes

---

with fewer variables is satisfied, the constraints with more variables that share common variables are also likely satisfied.

Formally, the algorithm works as shown in Algorithm 1. It is easy to see that when we select a set of constraints, it limits the search space of the IP solver. The complete set of constraints I will produce the smallest search space. Given a subset of I, we essentially enlarge the search space for the IP solver.

We illustrate the iterative algorithm in Figure 6. The oval here represents the search space of corresponding constraint set. Initially, the search space of the constraint set I'' is generated for the first iteration and then I' is generated in the second iteration. Suppose the initial search space by I'' is too large and causes an incorrect solution (*i.e.*, some nodes will not be protected), while the search space by I' is smaller and the solution can be found within the same range, then there is no need to go to the next iteration and use constraints I to re-compute. The reasoning is that if we found a minimum value in a larger search space (suppose the objective is to minimize), it is guaranteed that we can only find the same minimum or bigger value in a smaller search space too. Since we also check if the result in larger search space satisfies all the constraints, a satisfying result can guarantee that the same minimum value can be found in the final smaller search space.

Note that we are able to approach a good subset quickly and wisely by adding the constraints that are represented by shortest attack path in each iteration. It is essentially an optimistic method by assuming a smaller number of constraints are needed to find the optimal solution which in reality is often the case. By reducing the exponentially large number of constraints, the execution time is significantly improved shown in §6 where most cases take 2 to 5 iterations only.

5.1 Correctness Verification

Note that by the above reasoning, the iterative algorithm is equivalent to the naive approach. To further verify the correctness of our implementation, we ran more than 100 tests up to hundreds of nodes to check that the results generated by naive implementation indeed matches the results generated by the iterative algorithm.

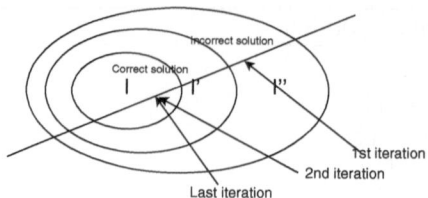

Fig. 6. Illustrating why results computed under a subset of the complete constraint set I are the same as the one under I

6   Evaluation

We describe the evaluation of our framework using both realistic and synthetic network data.

6.1   Real Network Based Evaluation

We have evaluated our tool for a small real network, as shown in Figure 7. The problem setting is as follows (based on a real topology and vulnerabilities): In this network, each node is a router. Node 15 - 18 and 19 - 22 are the untrusted nodes (For simplicity, we do not consider internal nodes as potentially untrusted), and nodes 1 and 2 are the vulnerable nodes. These two vulnerable nodes are installed with different OS versions on the router with a different set of vulnerabilities. Node 1 has vulnerability 1 while Node 2 has vulnerability 1 and 2. All of the vulnerabilities can either be patched or temporarily protected by installing filters. The cost of patch operation is set to be 3 here. The variables are defined in terms of the interfaces visible in the figure.

Our first attempt to set up the problem is to only consider installing filters. Thus the objective function can be setup as:

$$\sum_i x_i^{(1)} + \sum_i x_i^{(2)}$$

where two vulnerabilities are considered together in the objective function.

Alternatively, we can examine each vulnerability independently. These two approaches yield the same solution since the variables in different set of constraints for each vulnerability happen to be disjoint. We first consider vulnerability 1.

The goal is to minimize the objective function defined as $\sum_i x_i^{(1)}$. The constraints are to protect every possible attack path and the solution would be 3 according to the integer programming solver which means only three interfaces need to be configured for filters. Similarly we can obtain the solution for vulnerability 2, which is 2. So it takes $3 + 2 = 5$ interfaces to be configured in order to protect from all of the vulnerabilities.

Our next step is to set up the problem by allowing patch operation, and the objective function is slightly tuned to include the patch variables for the two nodes:

$\sum_i x_i^{(1)} + \sum_i x_i^{(2)} + 2 \times (y_1 + y_2)$

The $2 \times (y_1 + y_2)$ is added to include the cost of patching vulnerable nodes. y_1 and y_2 indicate whether Node 1 and 2 will be patched respectively.

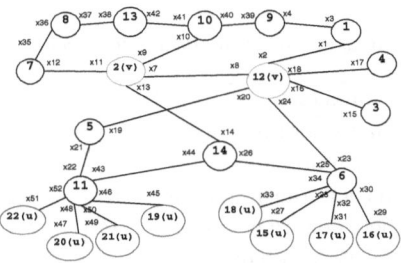

Fig. 7. A small real network for evaluation

The constraints are similar as before, namely to protect every possible attack paths. The difference is that the patch variable y_1 and y_2 are added respectively into each previous constraint depending on the destination node. For example, y_1 will be added to the original constraint $x_{33} + x_{34} + x_{23} + x_{24} + x_2 + x_1 >= 1$ such that $x_{33} + x_{34} + x_{23} + x_{24} + x_2 + x_1 + y_1 >= 1$ forms a new constraint. Since x_4 belongs to Node 1, this means that if the vulnerable node is patched, all the constraints associated with protecting this node can be automatically satisfied.

We obtain the value 4 as the optimal solution where $x_4^{(1)} = x_3^{(1)} = x_5^{(2)} = y_2 = 1$ with every other variable equals to zero.

6.2 Simulation-Based Evaluation

To illustrate the performance of our tool, we simulate various random topologies using the transit-stub model in GT-ITM [16] and randomly select malicious nodes and vulnerable nodes for the problem setup.

In the simulation, we first measure the average running time of our tool against various topologies using our iterative implementation compared with the naive implementation. Then, we measure the number of paths generated and compare with that of the naive implementation. The parameters can be found in Table 2 and Table 3. The sizes of the topologies are approximately 100, 500, 1000, 3000, 5000, 7000 and 10000 respectively.

It can be seen from Figure 8 that the running time (average for ten runs) for naive implementation increases much more quickly with network size compared with the iterative approach. We also verified that they indeed produce the same optimal value. It is quite evident that our iterative approach scales very well. Similarly, Figure 9 shows the overall number of paths for the naive implementation is much larger. This clearly implies much information in the complete constraint set I is quite redundant.

We also illustrate how performance changes when the problem becomes more complex (*e.g.*, with increasing number of untrusted devices and vulnerabilities). We fix a topology with 200 nodes and set up the problem so that the number of untrusted nodes grows together with the number of vulnerable nodes and the types of vulnerabilities. We execute our tool 10 times to measure the average running time and the number of paths/constraints generated. In Figure 10, we can see that our tool can efficiently handle networks of large size.

Table 2. Parameter in the topology generation

Parameters	Variable	Values
# stubs domains per trans node	$F_{s/t}$	4,4,5,7,8,10
# of transit domains	N_t	4,5,6,8,8,8
# of nodes in each transit domain	n_t	5,8,10,10,10,11
Edge prob. between transit nodes	P_t	0.6
# of nodes in each stub domain	N_s	6,6,10,10,11,11
Edge prob. between stub nodes	P_s	0.42

Table 3. Parameter in the problem setup

Parameters	Variable	Value
# of untrusted/malicious node	N_u	10
# of vulnerable node	N_v	10
# of vulnerability	V	3

6.3 Enabling User Interactivity

From the large simulation result, we know that the execution time increases with the problem size (*i.e.*, network size, the number of untrusted/vulnerable nodes, and the number of vulnerability). To understand the bottleneck of the iterative algorithm, we compare the time spent on calculating constraints vs. that on the solver, and observe that the former consumes more than 90% of the execution time. This leads us to develop the heuristic of reusing already calculated constraints. One of the interesting applications it enables is allowing network/sys admin to modify the constraint after he/she sees the result. This effectively turns the tool into an *interactive* one, which is very useful in operational settings. Although theoretically the result computed is the global optimal in terms of the objective function and constraints, the network/sys admin may not have given sufficient input to the tool initially. So allowing changes to the initial result in an

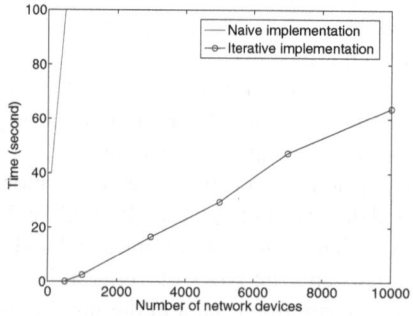

Fig. 8. Execution time for networks of different sizes

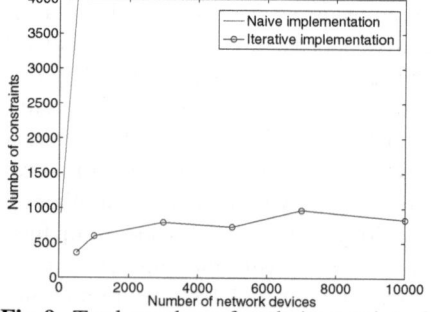

Fig. 9. Total number of paths/constraints for networks of different sizes

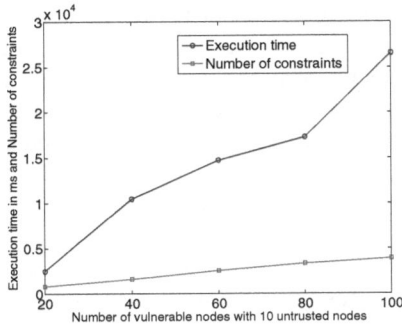

Fig. 10. Number of vulnerable nodes vs. Execution time and number of paths/constraints for size of 1000 network devices

interactive fashion is useful to further tune based on the network/sys admin's domain knowledge of the network. For example, the network/sys admin may want to manually tune the result slightly (*e.g.*, remove filters from some network devices and/or give preference to other devices).

We implemented two types of primitives to allow interactive changes and evaluate their performance. The first primitive is removing a filter assigned on an interface, and the second one is giving preference to a network device for installing filters. The implementation of the first one is straightforward – adding another constraint $\sum_j x_i^{(j)} == 0$ where $x_i^{(j)}$ is the variable indicating whether there should be a filter for vulnerability j on interface x_i. The implementation of second primitive is also simple, *i.e.*, reducing the cost of installing a filter on the specified network device in the objective function (*e.g.*, halving the cost). Given such simplicity, the performance overhead is minimal for supporting interactivity.

7   Related Work

There is a significant amount of research focusing on describing, analyzing and verifying firewall rules [17, 18, 19, 6] to achieve specific global policy. Work on developing a higher level language to describe the firewall rules can be useful, but orthogonal to our work. Investigating issues after the rules are set is complementary to our goal of designing the rules in advance.

Several related work tries to enforce the global policy by distributing policies at different places in the network. An extreme is to distribute the policy to end-hosts instead of to network nodes [20, 21]. This method is topology-ignorant and can be easy to deploy since end-host is easier to change. However, if every policy is to be checked at the end-host (for each packet), it could incur non-trivial overhead. There is additional complexity and security measure introduced to ensure end-host identity, which can potentially lead to another set of security holes; While our solution is leveraging existing security measures and does not introduce new mechanisms. Further, their solution focuses on the access control policy issues rather than protecting vulnerable nodes in general. For example, routers may also be vulnerable and require protection.

There are many reasoning systems specific to firewall or NIDS. For example, filtering Postures [22] uses heuristics to automatically compute the set of filters for individual routers to enforce a particular global policy. The solution they found, however, may not be optimal. Further, they are only limited to the problem of network access control, rather than our broader goal of leveraging both filter and patch operations to mitigate network vulnerabilities. A follow-up work in [23] includes NIDS behavior into the reasoning system and differ from our work by neither considering patch operation nor trade-offs among various defense strategies.

Similar but more powerful, MulVal [24] uses formal methods to reason about the security properties which can easily enable what-if analysis such as verifying "if router A is patched, machine B will be free of attack." Our proposed framework tackles a different problem by going a step further that not only verifies that machine B is free of attack, but also computes the optimal way to stop such attack. In fact, our work complements theirs in the sense that once they finish reasoning about the vulnerabilities and identify the available options to fix the network, it can be abstracted into our model which performs the subsequent optimization.

Other works including [25, 26, 11] have somewhat similar goals though without considering patch operation either. For example, one of their goals is to find the *virtual border* - minimum number of filters or nodes to install filters. We can easily capture this goal by our *Minimal disruption* objective function. Further, we can also express other goals by using different objective functions as those listed in §4.3. The use of integer programming allows us to easily accommodate new objective functions and constraints. As a result, our framework is more general and extensible compared to previous work, as it can solve not only one particular problem but also many other problems by tuning the objective functions and taking various constraints into account.

8   Discussion

Different Types of Network-Level Defense. Different types of network defense have different capabilities (some may be able to defend against more sophisticated attacks). It is possible to distinguish different network-level defense (*e.g.*, ACL and NIDS) in our framework by assigning different cost for different types of network defense. Alternatively, we can simply always choose the most powerful defense mechanism available.

Incremental Deployment. While it is easy to use our tool to provide a new protection suggestion, our tool also fits in the scenario where the network has been partially protected and we can provide incremental suggestions in terms of additional protection based on existing setups.

Appropriate Abstraction? Note that the abstraction we have still support many of the existing abstractions. For example, to solve similar problems a human expert may use abstractions such as *the network of department x* or *the unsecured wireless network* or *the group of servers holding financial records*. We can easily support these abstractions by understanding the mapping between the group and a number of network devices or IP addresses.

Path Selection. Currently we are conservatively assuming that any path could be traversed from untrusted devices to the vulnerable device while it may not be the case in reality. One may desire to pick only paths that are in greater need of protection by ranking each path by the probability that it is selected as the actual forwarding path. This can be done by enumerating all possible failures in the network and simulate the routing algorithm to find the path [25].

9   Conclusions and Future Work

We have presented a simple and novel way of modeling the vulnerability mitigation and management problem using integer programming. We have given examples about how to model the problem. More specifically, our framework provides intelligent suggestions in terms of where to deploy filtering or where to patch which are the two main mechanisms in network defense. Further, optimal solutions can be computed by considering multiple vulnerabilities jointly which is of practical need. Our prototype suggestion tool has been evaluated using several examples based on real network topologies with demonstrated efficiency and effectiveness.

For future work, we plan to consider other objective functions and constraints. Our framework is fairly easy to extend since integer programming has a plain and clean interface. We plan to add more objective functions and constraints into our framework based on real user needs. In addition, we also plan to evaluate our tool more extensively with real usage scenarios.

References

1. Cisco IOS HTTP Server Code Injection Vulnerability,
   http://tools.cisco.com/security/center/
   viewAlert.x?alertId=10102
2. Cisco IOS Software UDP Packet Processing Denial of Service Vulnerability,
   http://tools.cisco.com/security/center/
   viewAlert.x?alertId=17765
3. Cisco Intrusion Prevention System,
   http://www.cisco.com/en/US/products/sw/
   secursw/ps2113/index.html
4. Multiple Vendor DNS Implementations Insufficient Entropy Vulnerability,
   http://tools.cisco.com/security/center/
   viewAlert.x?alertId=16183
5. Grote, A., Funke, R., Heiss, H.-U.: Performance evaluation of firewalls in gigabit-networks. In: Proc. 1999 Symposium on Performance Evaluation of Computer and Telecommunication Systems (1999),
   http://www.kbs.cs.tu-berlin.de/publications/
   fulltext/GFH99.pdf
6. Capretta, V., Stepien, B., Felty, A., Matwin, S.: Formal correctness of conflict detection for firewalls. In: FMSE 2007: Proceedings of the 2007 ACM Workshop on Formal Methods in Security Engineering, pp. 22–30 (2007)

7. Introduction to Cisco Inventory and Reporting,
   http://www.cisco.com/en/US/docs/net_mgmt/
   inventory_and_reporting/User_Guides/Introduction_
   to_Cisco_Inventory_and_Reporting.html
8. David System, a network management system (nms),
   http://www.hadden.pl/en/index.php
9. Introduction to OVAL: A new language to determine the presence of software vulnerabilities
   (2003), http://oval.mitre.org/documents/docs03/intro/intro.html
10. Cisco Intellishield, http://www.cisco.com/security/
11. Todtmann, B., Rathgeb, E.P.: Integrated management of distributed packet filter configura-
    tions in carrier-grade ip networks. In: International Conference on Networking, p. 44 (2007)
12. NetMRI, http://www.netcordia.com/
13. Cisco Multiple Vulnerabilities, http://secunia.com/advisories/23867/
14. Old, J.L., Buchanan, W., Graves, J., Saliou, L.: Performance analysis of network based
    forensic systems for in-line and out-of-line detection and logging. In: 5th European
    Conference on Information Warfare and Security, ECIW (2006)
15. CPLEX, High-performance software for mathematical programming and optimization,
    http://www.ilog.com/products/cplex/
16. GTITM, Modeling Topology of Large Internetworks,
    http://www.cc.gatech.edu/projects/gtitm/
17. Bartal, Y., Mayer, A., Nissim, K., Wool, A.: Firmato: A novel firewall management toolkit.
    ACM Trans. Comput. Syst. 22(4), 381–420 (2004)
18. Mayer, A., Wool, A., Ziskind, E.: Fang: A firewall analysis engine. In: SP 2000: Proceedings
    of the 2000 IEEE Symposium on Security and Privacy, p. 177 (2000)
19. Al-shaer, E., Hamed, H., Boutaba, R., Hasan, M.: Conflict classification and analysis of
    distributed firewall policies. IEEE Journal on Selected Areas in Communications 23, 2069–
    2084 (2005)
20. Bellovin, S.M.: Distributed firewalls. Login, 37–39 (1999)
21. Ioannidis, S., Keromytis, A.D., Bellovin, S.M., Smith, J.M.: Implementing a distributed
    firewall. In: CCS 2000: Proceedings of the 7th ACM Conference on Computer and
    Communications Security, pp. 190–199 (2000)
22. Guttman, J.D.: Filtering postures: local enforcement for global policies. In: SP 1997:
    Proceedings of the 1997 IEEE Symposium on Security and Privacy, p. 120. IEEE Computer
    Society (1997)
23. Uribe, T.E., Cheung, S.: Automatic analysis of firewall and network intrusion detection
    system configurations. In: FMSE 2004: Proceedings of the 2004 ACM Workshop on Formal
    Methods in Security Engineering, pp. 66–74 (2004)
24. Ou, X., Govindavajhala, S., Appel, A.W.: Mulval: a logic-based network security analyzer.
    In: SSYM 2005: Proceedings of the 14th Conference on USENIX Security Symposium
    (2005)
25. Tödtmann, B., Rathgeb, E.P.: Anticipatory distributed packet filter configurations for carrier-
    grade ip networks. Comput. Netw. 51(10), 2565–2579 (2007)
26. Todtmann, B., Rathgeb, E.P.: Advanced packet filter placement strategies for carrier-
    grade ip-networks. In: AINAW 2007: Proceedings of the 21st International Conference on
    Advanced Information Networking and Applications Workshops, vol. 1, pp. 415–423 (2007)

An On-Line Learning Statistical Model to Detect Malicious Web Requests

Harald Lampesberger[1,2], Philipp Winter[1], Markus Zeilinger[1],
and Eckehard Hermann[1]

[1] Upper Austria University of Applied Sciences, Department Secure Information
Systems, Softwarepark 11, A-4232 Hagenberg, Austria
[2] Johannes-Kepler-University Linz, Christian-Doppler Laboratory for Client-Centric
Cloud Computing, Softwarepark 21, A-4232 Hagenberg, Austria
h.lampesberger@cdcc.faw.jku.at

Abstract. Detecting malicious connection attempts and attacks against web-based applications is one of many approaches to protect the World Wide Web and its users.

In this paper, we present a generic method for detecting anomalous and potentially malicious web requests from the network's point of view without prior knowledge or training data of the web-based application. The algorithm assumes that a legitimate request is an ordered sequence of semantic entities. Malicious requests are in different order or include entities which deviate from the structure of the majority of requests. Our method learns a variable-order Markov model from legitimate sequences of semantic entities. If a sequence's probability deviates from previously seen ones, it is reported as anomalous.

Experiments were conducted on logs from a social networking web site. The results indicate that that the proposed method achieves good detection rates at acceptable false-alarm rates.

Keywords: intrusion detection, anomaly detection, on-line learning, Markov model, web security.

1 Introduction

The popularity of the Web is continuously rising and our daily lives are more and more dependent on this source of information. Accordingly, the *Hypertext Transfer Protocol* (HTTP) has evolved to one of the most employed application layer protocols in the Internet. But with increasing global dependence on the Web, attackers are even more interested in tampering with those systems.

The paper is structured as follows: The remaining introduction deals with HTTP, its security challenges and related work in this area. Section 2 explains the concept of the proposed anomaly detection method. Section 3 outlines implementation details, evaluation results are listed in Section 4 and Section 5 draws the conclusion.

M. Rajarajan et al. (Eds.): SecureComm 2011, LNICST 96, pp. 19–38, 2012.
© Institute for Computer Sciences, Social Informatics and Telecommunications Engineering 2012

1.1 HTTP and Web Security

The HTTP protocol [11] defines stateless and generic exchange of information. The communication is initiated by a client who requests a specific resource, identified by the Unified Resource Identifier (URI) path, from the server. The response assembles server status codes, meta information and possible entity content.

A fundamental security problem of web-based applications is that the client is out of the application's scope of control. The protocol was originally designed for static resources and stateless interaction, but today's web applications employ it for dynamic content and stateful sessions. Consequently, data sent from the client must be somehow interpreted by the server. Semantic client data can be found in the request-URI path, header fields and possible request entity content.

Request-URI Path. The path is a hierarchically structured sequence of string segments and an optional query component. The grammar is defined in [5] and traditionally, the path references a static resource, or in dynamic web applications a content generating process. A segment only allows a subset of printable characters; others must be escaped by using the URI percent-encoding.

The '?' character introduces the query component of a path and parameters are supposed to be in field-value pairs. But real-world implementations tend to break this convention because expressive path names in URLs are preferred by developers and users. This is called *URL Rewriting* and a representative example is the widely used Apache web server module *mod_rewrite* [2] which allows mapping of path segments into queries. As a result, a client can never conclude from a path whether segments are interpreted as static resources or parameters in a web-based application.

Request Headers. In a request, headers represent meta data from the client in an unordered field-value structure. For example, headers inform the server which kind of content and encoding is understood by the client. The best example for client data processed by the web application is the so-called *cookie*. Many applications use the cookie to track states in the stateless HTTP protocol.

Request Entity Content. A typical GET request can transport parameters in the URI path, but the size of the query part is restricted by server's implementation. For high-volume transmissions or forms, the POST method allows query-style or MIME-encoded data in the request entity content. Additional headers are necessary to describe type and length of this entity content.

Weaknesses. Wrong handling of client data in any function of the web application introduces a security weakness which can probably be exploited by an attacker. To name a few, attack vectors like buffer overflows, SQL or code injections, Cross-Site Scripting, Cross-Site Request Forgery or HTTP parameter pollution emerge from few common pitfalls. These classic flaws are gathered in the Common Weakness Enumeration database [22] and, in this paper, attacks

```
Legitimate Request:
  GET /fotos.php?action=view HTTP/1.1
Code Injection:
  GET /fotos.php?action=http://195.33.221.4:8081/bot.txt? HTTP/1.1
SQL Injection:
  GET /userportal.php?id=4518-999.9+union+select+0-- HTTP/1.1
Cross-Site Scripting:
  GET /fotos.php?action=search&album=%22%2F%3E%3Cscript%3Ealert%281%29
  %3B%3C%2FScript%3E HTTP/1.1
Path Traversal:
  GET /images/../../../../../../../../../etc/passwd HTTP/1.1
```

Fig. 1. Examples for legitimate and malicious URI paths in HTTP requests

are grouped by their common weakness. Some examples are given in Figure 1 for a better understanding.

Protecting a web-based application implicitly protects its users. Drive-by downloads to create botnets are on the rise as noted by Provos et al. [25]. In addition to disturbing the service availability or stealing information from a high-volume web site, an attacker might consider planting drive-by malware to infect visitors.

1.2 Intrusion Detection

Another approach in protecting web-based applications, besides writing robust code, is the domain of payload-based intrusion detection systems (IDS) to enable prevention mechanisms or early warning. IDS techniques can be distinguished into *misuse detection* and *anomaly detection* based on the style of detection. While misuse detection relies on proper signatures of malicious behavior, anomaly detection tends to use methods such as machine learning or statistics to construct a profile of normal behavior and report deviating interactions as anomalies.

As stated by Sommer and Paxson [29], both concepts are challenged in different ways. The detection performance of misuse detection completely depends on currentness and coverage of signatures, but false-alarm rates are accordingly low. Anomaly detection is prone to costly false-alarm rates, but it is more probable by design to recognize novel attacks. To succeed in real-world scenarios, anomaly detection must consider a) the variability of input data, b) the lack of training data, c) a very high cost of errors, d) the difficulty of sound evaluation and e) descriptiveness of detection results.

Detecting malicious web requests is challenging. Encodings, especially polymorphic ones as used in attack frameworks like Metasploit [20], make it almost impossible to induce valid signatures for misuse detection. Additionally, web applications are very dynamic and constantly change over time. This *concept drift* [19] handicaps the process of learning normal behavior in anomaly detection.

1.3   Related Work

Anomaly detection in network data is not new. Over the past years, different strategies for extracting representative features from network payload were presented. The payload-based anomaly detector (*PAYL*) by Wang and Stolfo [34] uses byte frequencies for payload profiling. *Anagram* [33] is an advancement of PAYL using n-grams instead of single byte frequencies. Perdisci et al. [24] further pursue this approach and introduce McPAD, a method based on 2_ν-grams. PAYL, Anagram and McPAD are rather generic concepts to analyze application layer network traffic, but their evaluation focuses on HTTP. Also, the three methods rely on training data sets.

Kruegel and Vigna [16] introduce the first detection system focused on web applications. It uses a linear combination of six different anomaly detection measures like attribute character distributions, structural information or attribute lengths. This concept establishes the foundation for follow-up research: grouping similar anomalies [26], addressing concept drift [19] and dealing with scarce training data [27].

Ingham et al. [14] define an approach where finite automaton representations are learned from HTTP tokens. Another method customized to protocol syntax using an attributed token kernel in One-Class Support Vector Machines is shown by Duessel et al. [9]. *Spectogram* is a model of multiple Markov chains proposed by Song et al. [30]. Ma et al. [18] define a model based on compression for web anomaly detection which tolerates concept drift to a certain degree. The HTTP reverse proxy *TokDoc*, presented by Krueger et al. [17], uses an ensemble of anomaly detection methods to detect, and automatically repair, malicious web requests.

All previously listed algorithms achieve good evaluation results, but they depend on training data. Especially for a fast-paced large-scale web application it is hardly possible to create an up-to-date and representative training data set. Görnitz et al. [12] realize this problem and present an active learning strategy based on methods such as PAYL, Anagram and McPAD. Their solution actively queries for labels to reduce the need for training, but context drift is not addressed.

1.4   Scope of This Work

As outlined in 1.1, a client or network device cannot conclude which elements of a web request will be processed in weakness-prone functions of the web application. Furthermore, URL Rewriting is not mentioned in previous work, but it is actively used in practical scenarios. So, RFC-compliant queries in URI paths cannot be assumed. The only possible assumption is that during normal operation of a web site, the application is probably receiving more legitimate web requests than malicious ones.

This paper explores the question of whether potentially malicious web requests can be detected from the network's point of view without prior knowledge at decent performance levels. An exemplary implementation scenario is a network-based IDS system for providers to monitor high-volume web sites and provide early warning mechanisms. Considering Sommer and Paxson's conclusions [29], the following requirements were defined:

- No explicit training data is necessary,
- The model considers concept drift of the web application,
- The model accepts URL Rewriting,
- False-alarm rates are minimized,
- Details on an alert's cause are available and
- Throughput performance is kept in mind.

2 Methodology

Our approach is formed by two assumptions:

- A legitimate web request is a series of semantic entities in specific order and
- Normal requests are more probable than malicious ones.

Within a web request, the data, especially the URI path, is in some kind of order as the result of design principles. For example, if the request is processed as stream and the first bytes indicate request method POST, then entity content is to be expected. It might come natural to say that a web request is *Markovian*. A conjecture of our detection method is that malicious requests have unexpected order of data or include entities which differ from the common structure. Consequently, Markov modeling seems to be a suitable approach for prediction.

It is important to mention that web-based applications actually use random strings in requests, for example session identifiers, random file names of image thumbnails, random transaction codes and so on. If transition probabilities purely rely on single byte frequencies, a single Markov model will get falsified by random strings. But Markov chains and Hidden Markov Models have successfully been employed for modeling web requests [19, 16, 26, 30, 18, 17, 27]. These concepts use multiple models to cope with high-entropy content.

Our method was inspired by Begleiter et al. [4] and their work on sequence prediction using compression models. The core idea is to deduce a variable-order Markov model (VMM) from legitimate web requests and use this model to classify novel web requests based on their probability. To increase robustness and handle high-entropy content, the grammar of HTTP is exploited to transform a web request into a sequence of abstract symbols beforehand. A novel web request is classified whether it is normal or not by comparing its probability to the distribution of ones. Therefore, the algorithm maintains a sliding window over recent sequence probabilities.

Based on Vovk et al. [31, pp. 3–7], we consider learning in our scenario as *transductive on-line learning*: Instead of inducing a general rule from training data, samples are presented one by one to the model, it predicts the sample's label and adds it to a bag of training examples. In our case, a so-called sample equals a web request and the VMM represents the bag of training examples. Each new prediction relies on previously seen samples, no induction is needed and the quality of predictions should improve over time. Finally, the model predicts whether a sample is normal or anomalous.

On-line learning requires somehow feedback of the truth. Following Vovk's definitions [31, p. 107], our scenario has two so-called *lazy teachers* who occasionally reveal the true label of a sample. The first lazy teaching mechanism is a constrained randomness assumption: the majority group of similar samples is probably normal. The second lazy and slow teacher is the human expert who works with and maintains the system. The expert intervenes after possible delay if false positive or false negative detections were realized. To sum up, our proposed algorithm processes a web request in four steps:

1. The web request is converted into a sequence of symbols,
2. A VMM estimates a probability of the sequence,
3. The sequence probability is assigned to a confidence interval in the sliding window probability distribution and
4. Depending on the confidence interval, the sequence is learned, ignored or reported.

2.1 A Request is a Sequence of Symbols

RFC 2616 [11] defines the grammar of the US-ASCII-oriented HTTP. The fundamental grammar entity is one byte. A class of characters called *separators* has special meaning in the protocol. So, in context of this work, a symbol $\sigma \in \mathbb{N}_0^{16}$ is the statistical representation of bytes between two separators. These 16 occurrence counters of a symbol are a computationally optimized heuristic to model the appearance of a variable-length string token in fixed-length memory while simultaneously handling high-entropy content. The counter definitions are based on HTTP character classes defined in the RFC and some additional counters capture structural characteristics of the content:

$$\sigma \Rightarrow \begin{cases} \sigma[0] & \text{amount of printable ASCII characters,} \\ \sigma[1-4] & \text{lexical letter index} \in \{a..z, A..Z\} \mod 4, \\ \sigma[5-6] & \text{digit index} \in \{0..9\} \mod 2, \\ \sigma[7] & \text{uppercase letters} \in \{A..Z\}, \\ \sigma[8] & \text{lowercase letters} \in \{a..z\}, \\ \sigma[9] & \text{US-ASCII control characters,} \\ \sigma[10] & \text{protocol-specific bytes} \in \{\text{CR LF SPACE TAB}\}, \\ \sigma[11] & \text{path-specific characters} \in \{./\}, \\ \sigma[12] & \text{protocol separators} \in \{\texttt{?\&;()<>@,:[]\{\}=\textbackslash}\}, \\ \sigma[13] & \text{single and double quotes,} \\ \sigma[14] & \text{percent character,} \\ \sigma[15] & \text{non-US-ASCII character.} \end{cases} \quad (1)$$

A web request is transformed into an n-tuple or sequence of symbols $q_1^n = (\sigma_1, \sigma_2, \ldots, \sigma_n)$. For precise tokenization of URI paths, the class of separators is split up in pre- and post-separators:

$$\begin{aligned} \text{pre-separators} &= \{\text{SPACE TAB}\}, \\ \text{post-separators} &= \{\texttt{/?\&;()<>@,:"[]\{\}=\textbackslash}\}. \end{aligned} \quad (2)$$

In a data stream, the observation of a pre-separator triggers the allocation of a new symbol in the sequence before the observed byte increments the occurrence counter in the symbol. Given the previous definitions, Figure 2 shows part of an exemplary HTTP GET request and how it is transformed into a sequence of symbols.

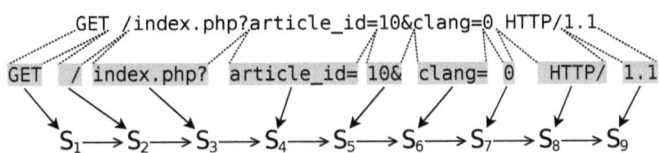

Fig. 2. Transformation of a web request data into a sequence of symbols

The dynamic alphabet $\mathcal{A}$ consists of all the symbols the anomaly detection model is currently aware of. The initial alphabet is empty and as a result of learning, symbols are added or removed over time. For prediction, the symbols of the web request are mapped to similar symbols in $\mathcal{A}$ if possible. This mapping function Φ requires a metric to compare symbols. A similarity measure between two sets is the *Tanimoto coefficient* τ [13, p. 398] which estimates the intersection of two symbols:

$$\tau(\sigma_1, \sigma_2) = \frac{\sigma_1 \cdot \sigma_2}{\|\sigma_1\|^2 + \|\sigma_2\|^2 - \sigma_1 \cdot \sigma_2} . \tag{3}$$

Let $T_{\mathcal{A}}$ be the similarity threshold for alphabet $\mathcal{A}$ and also an anomaly detection model parameter. Two symbols σ_1 and σ_2 are considered identical if $\tau(\sigma_1, \sigma_2) > T_{\mathcal{A}}$. So, the mapping function Φ is defined as:

$$\Phi(\sigma, \mathcal{A}, T_{\mathcal{A}}) = \begin{cases} \arg\max_{\nu \in \mathcal{A}} \tau(\sigma, \nu) & \text{if } \exists \nu \in \mathcal{A} : \tau(\sigma, \nu) > T_{\mathcal{A}}, \\ \sigma & \text{otherwise.} \end{cases} \tag{4}$$

2.2   Prediction by Partial Matching

The idea of *Prediction by Partial Matching* (PPM) is to predict the next symbol $\sigma \in \mathcal{A}$ in a stream based on the previously seen symbols, the so-called context $s \in \mathcal{A}^n$ of order n. Probability estimates are based on symbol counts in the data.

Cleary and Witten [7] present PPM as a concept of statistical modeling for lossless compression. PPM belongs to the group of variable-order Markov models which are able to capture both large and small order Markov dependencies in observed data, as stated by Begleiter et al. [4]. To handle the zero-frequency problem when novel symbols are encountered, PPM provides the *escape* and *exclusion* mechanisms. In this work, exclusion is ignored due to the computational overhead and escape follows 'Method C' proposed by Moffat [23].

PPM requires an upper Markov order bound D for VMM construction. A data structure to model PPM is a *trie* of depth $D + 1$. A trie node references a symbol from alphabet $\mathcal{A}$ and maintains a frequency counter. Each path from root to node represents a subsequence in the already processed stream and the node's count indicates, how often this subsequence appeared. Figure 3 shows an exemplary trie for Markov order $D = 2$ constructed from a single sequence.

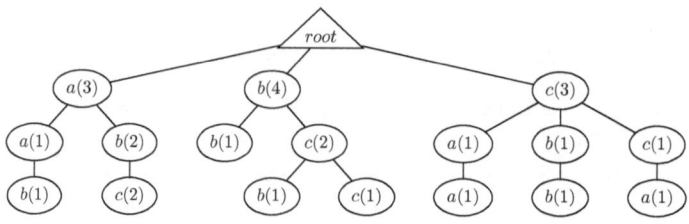

Fig. 3. PPM trie (order $D = 2$) for simplified sequence $q_1^{10} = abccaabcbb$

Let k be the length of the current context and $k \leq D$. Estimating the probability $\hat{P}$ of symbol σ considering its context s follows a recursive relation, where s' is a one-symbol-shorter context and $k < 0$ ends the recursion:

$$\hat{P}(\sigma|s) = \begin{cases} \hat{P}_k(\sigma|s) & \text{if } s\sigma \text{ exists in the VMM,} \\ \hat{P}_k(escape|s) \cdot \hat{P}(\sigma|s') & \text{otherwise.} \end{cases} \quad (5)$$

Let $\mathcal{A}_s$ be the specific alphabet of context s and $N(s\sigma)$ be a count value of the node in context s referencing symbol σ. Then the probability estimates based on 'Method C' [23] are:

$$\hat{P}_k(\sigma|s) = \frac{N(s\sigma)}{|\mathcal{A}_s| + \sum\limits_{\sigma' \in \mathcal{A}_s} N(s\sigma')} \quad \text{if } \sigma \in \mathcal{A}_s , \quad (6)$$

$$\hat{P}_k(escape|s) = \frac{|\mathcal{A}_s|}{|\mathcal{A}_s| + \sum\limits_{\sigma' \in \mathcal{A}_s} N(s\sigma')} \quad \text{otherwise.} \quad (7)$$

The escape probability depends on the entropy within a specific context and the alphabet size is not assumed finite. The following examples based on Figure 3 are for a better understanding of the estimation process: The probability that a sequence starts with b is $\hat{P}(b) = \frac{4}{3+10} = 0.308$. The chance that c occurs after 'ab' is $\hat{P}(c|ab) = \frac{2}{1+2} = 0.667$. But a after 'bc' has not been seen before, so $\hat{P}(a|bc) = \hat{P}(escape|bc) \cdot \hat{P}(a|c) = \frac{2}{2+2} \cdot \frac{1}{3+3} = 0.083$.

Finally, the average probability of a sequence q_1^n is the arithmetic mean of all its symbol probabilities:

$$\hat{P}(q_1^n) = \frac{1}{n} \sum_{i=1}^{n} \hat{P}(q_i|q_{i-D}^{i-1}) . \quad (8)$$

In context of web-based applications, a perfect VMM that learned all possible web requests delivers approximately high mean probability scores for legitimate sequences. A malicious web request will likely contain symbols that are unknown to the VMM's alphabet or symbol arrangements in an unexpected order. This results in a low mean probability score of the sequence. The distribution of probabilities depends on the web application and its dynamics. Accordingly, a static threshold for classification of outliers is insufficient.

2.3 Detecting Outliers

The proposed outlier detection method assumes that mean sequence probabilities of all legitimate web requests are somehow similar distributed in a perfect VMM. Different quantiles of the estimated distribution represent confidence intervals. Outliers are found in intervals distant to the mean.

Algorithm 1. Sliding window mean and sample variance estimator in $O(1)$

Require: $w_{size} > 0$
  empty queue $W \leftarrow [\,]$
  sum-of-squared residuals $M_2 \leftarrow 0$
  fill count $n \leftarrow 0$
  $\bar{P} \leftarrow s^2 \leftarrow 0$
  while $P_{new} \leftarrow Input$ **do**
    if $n < w_{size}$ **then**
      $n \leftarrow n + 1$
    else
      $P_{old} \leftarrow Dequeue(W)$
      $\delta \leftarrow P_{old} - \bar{P}$
      $\bar{P} \leftarrow \bar{P} - \delta/(n-1)$
      $M_2 \leftarrow M_2 - \delta * (P_{old} - \bar{P})$
    end if
    $\delta \leftarrow P_{new} - \bar{P}$
    $\bar{P} \leftarrow \bar{P} + (\delta/n)$
    $M_2 \leftarrow M_2 + \delta * (P_{new} - \bar{P})$
    $Enqueue(W, P_{new})$
    if $n > 1$ **then**
      $s^2 \leftarrow M_2/(n-1)$
    end if
    print $\bar{P}, s^2${mean and sample variance of previous w_{size} entities}
  end while

The bounded probability space $[0,1]$ is supported by the Beta distribution $Beta(\alpha, \beta)$. The parameters for this distribution are estimated from the mean $\bar{P}$ and sample variance s^2 of recent sequence probabilities by the method-of-moments [10, p. 40]:

$$\hat{\alpha} = \bar{P}\left(\frac{\bar{P}(1-\bar{P})}{s^2} - 1\right), \qquad \hat{\beta} = (1-\bar{P})\left(\frac{\bar{P}(1-\bar{P})}{s^2} - 1\right). \qquad (9)$$

Due to numerical and complexity boundaries, it is challenging to calculate the mean and sample variance in a streaming scenario, where each new sequence causes an update of the values. Maintaining a sliding window over the recent w_{size} sequence probabilities reduces the computational complexity. Also, a sliding window forgets values over time and allows better adaption to concept drift of the underlying application. The size of the sliding window affects how strong the mean and sample variance are affected by outliers in the data.

For computational efficiency, the algorithm for one-pass mean and sample variance estimation proposed by Welford [35], and recommended by Knuth [15, p. 216], has been modified for sliding windows. Algorithm 1 updates the sliding window mean $\bar{P}$ and sample variance s^2 in constant time. All probability values stay in a FIFO queue for w_{size} updates and before discarding them, their moments are withdrawn from the mean and sample variance to attain the sliding window.

The confidence c_q of a web request's mean sequence probability $\hat{P}(q)$ is estimated by the Beta distribution's cumulative distribution function:

$$c_q = I_{\hat{P}(q)}(\hat{\alpha}, \hat{\beta}). \tag{10}$$

We define three confidence thresholds as model parameters: base confidence T_{base}, warn confidence T_{warn} and alert confidence T_{alert}. As a result, four confidence intervals are formed in the distribution and Figure 4 outlines them. A web request is classified according to its confidence c_q:

$$classify(c_q) = \begin{cases} Normal \text{ (learning)} & \text{if } c_q > 1 - T_{base}, \\ Normal \text{ (ignore)} & \text{if } 1 - T_{base} > c_q > 1 - T_{warn}, \\ Anomalous \text{ (warn)} & \text{if } 1 - T_{warn} > c_q > 1 - T_{alert}, \\ Anomalous \text{ (alert)} & \text{otherwise.} \end{cases} \tag{11}$$

To sum up outlier detection, a Beta probability distribution over previous VMM prediction results is estimated. Depending on a web request's confidence, the grade of abnormality is known, it is assigned to one of four confidence intervals and further learning or reporting actions are taken.

2.4   On-line Learning Strategy

The VMM requires learning of legitimate sequences to reduce VMM escapes and to increase prediction precision over time. Better predictions result in higher mean and lower sample variance, the distribution and its confidence intervals get more and more distinct and anomaly detection performance improves.

Learning. The first lazy teacher in the on-line learning scenario is a constrained randomness assumption: most of the web requests are probably normal. Consequently, sequences in the learning interval are automatically fed back, the VMM trie grows and new symbols are added to alphabet $\mathcal{A}$.

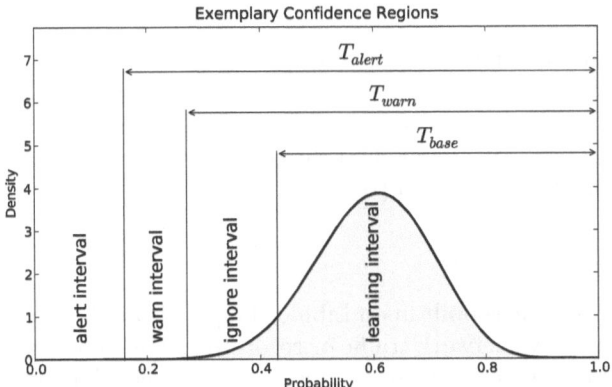

Fig. 4. Exemplary Beta probability-density function graph where the four confidence intervals (*alert, warn, ignore* and *learning interval*) are marked

The second lazy and slow teacher is a human expert who eventually recognizes a false positive or false negative with possible delay. In the case of false positive, the sequence and novel symbols are added into the VMM trie and alphabet. The according node counters are incremented until the sequence resides in the learning interval. If a false negative detection is corrected, the trie nodes related to the sequence are decremented or removed from the trie. Unreferenced alphabet symbols are deleted.

Especially during the first hundred web requests, a malicious attempt may unintentionally be learned. Also because of concept drift, the web-based application might change, new resources appear or old resources fade to exist. The web application matures and the detection model must *forget* outdated information over time too.

Pruning. Due to concept drift and numerical limits in computers, the VMM trie and its counters cannot grow indefinitely. The model parameter T_{prune} is a threshold for the most frequent node counter in the trie. If the most frequent node exceeds T_{prune}, pruning is performed. All node counters in the trie are integer divided by two, zero nodes or branches are removed and unreferenced symbols are deleted from the alphabet.

So, VMM escape probabilities increase again, the model is able to adapt to a certain degree of concept drift and malicious sequences learned by mistake will be dropped over time.

To sum up all introduced model parameters, the proposed anomaly detection model M is parameterized by:

$$M\langle T_{\mathcal{A}}, D, w_{size}, T_{base}, T_{warn}, T_{alert}, T_{prune}\rangle \; .$$

3   Implementation

The proposed methodology is implemented in two independent prototypes with the same algorithmic background: an off-line log file analyzer for performance evaluation and a passive network analysis tool. For performance reasons, all implementations are written in C and the efficient trie data structure follows the recommendations from Salomon [28, pp. 150–155].

3.1   Network Operation

The network prototype is built upon Libnids [36], a library for payload inspection of TCP sessions in live network traffic or recordings. Due to full decoding of TCP sessions, the library is resistant to fragmentation attacks. Furthermore, it allows intervening in established TCP sessions by sending forged reset segments to both communication partners. Reset segments are an unreliable third-party method for killing connections because of possible network delays, but it still gives this prototype some intrusion prevention abilities.

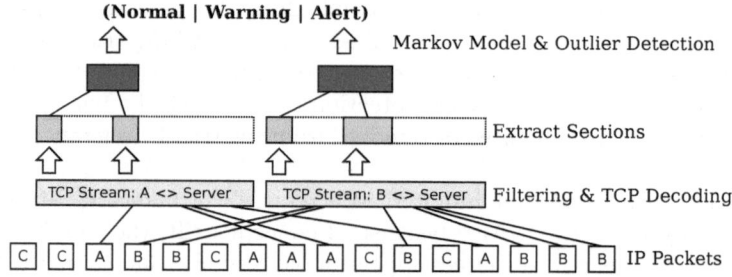

Fig. 5. Analysis concept for network data processing

Figure 5 outlines the concept of network data processing. Libnids decodes TCP sessions for a configured subset of destination hosts, other sessions are ignored. Packet payload is handed to the *Protocol State Machine* (PSM). The PSM is a TCP session-specific deterministic finite automaton, where state transitions are triggered by payload byte tokens. A transition also performs user-specified actions. This includes starting and finalizing of anomaly detection, reporting, killing connections or canceling further analysis of the session.

The PSM states, transition tokens and actions are defined in XML by the user and Aho-Corasick pattern matching [1] enables the search for these tokens in the payload stream. So, the computationally intensive anomaly detection can be limited to weakness-prone sections in the protocol, for example the HTTP request and response headers.

A TCP session is reported if it is anomalous. The raw analyzed data and prediction results are kept in a ring-buffer for a certain amount of time. In case of a detection error, an expert can see which symbols in the payload stream are responsible for the anomaly.

At last, all anomaly detection model parameters are changeable during operation. The network prototype features an XML-RPC interface for parameter modifications or teaching of false positive or false negative detections.

4   Experiments

For evaluation of detection performance, we assume a binary classification case where legitimate requests represent class *Normal* and warnings or alerts are considered as class *Attack*. A labeled data set is required to construct a confusion matrix as shown in Table 1. The values in the matrix are mandatory for estimating performance metrics.

Table 1. Confusion matrix for the binary classification case

		Actual	
		Attack	**Normal**
Predicted	**Attack**	True Positive (TP)	False Positive (FP)
	Normal	False Negative (FN)	True Negative (TN)

The Receiver Operator Characteristic (ROC) curve and its area under the curve (AUC) are commonly used metrics to describe detection performance of a classification algorithm. But in the intrusion detection area, normal and malicious examples are not equally distributed. So, false positives cause a much higher cost and impact in the IDS area, as already shown by Axelsson [3]. We assume that ROC is not an optimal choice in this case.

Performance evaluation in this paper uses the metrics *Precision* and *Recall* as recommended by Davis and Goadrich [8] for skewed data sets. For intrusion detection, Recall is equivalent to detection rate and Precision indicates how reliable the detections are. The Precision-Recall (PR) curve and its area under the curve (PR-AUC) give better information on the algorithm's performance in a scenario, where examples are not equally distributed. Also, Precision and the false positive rate (FPR) are interdependent. Maximizing Precision implicitly minimizes the FPR.

$$Precision = \frac{TP}{TP+FP}, \quad Recall = \frac{TP}{TP+FN}, \quad FPR = \frac{FP}{FP+TN}. \quad (12)$$

In PR space, a perfect algorithm has maximum Precision for the complete Recall range, the curve is in the upper-right corner and PR-AUC = 1. The PR-AUC represents the capability of an algorithm to correctly separate the two classes in the binary classification case.

4.1   Evaluation Data

Realistic data is mandatory for sound evaluation. As logs contain a part of the web request, the presented evaluation results are based on anonymized web site log files. A data set is neither partitioned for training nor ordered, the analysis starts with an empty model and the first sample, and ends with the last sample in the data set. So, these experiments are kept as realistic as possible.

Manifesting attacks are planted randomly in the data sets. Table 2 shows a pool of 57 unique attack vectors and their CWE classes. Custom attacks are adapted to the web application in use; others are referenced either by their Common Vulnerability and Exposures (CVE) [21] identifier or worm name.

Table 2. Unique CWE weaknesses for a total of 57 attack vectors

CWE	Name	Num	CVE or Other References
20	Input Validation	16	worm:Nimda worm:CodeRed
22	Path Traversal	3	custom:2 2010-2334
78	OS Command Injections	5	custom:3 2005-0116 2005-2847
79	Cross-Site Scripting	8	custom:5 2010-0804 2010-2356 2010-4366
89	SQL Injection	9	custom:3 2005-1810 2008-0397 2008-1982 2009-0968 2010-3601 2011-0519
94	Code Injection	5	custom:3 2005-0511 2007-1599
119	Buffer Errors	11	1999-0874 2001-0241 2001-0500 2003-0109 2003-1192 2004-1374 2004-1561 2004-1134 2006-1148 2006-5216 2007-0774

CMS Data Set. The data is from a PHP-based content management system named Redaxo and samples were collected within several months. The original data contains 108 malicious attempts, basically automated scans and code injections. The final set consists of 3,279 log lines where additional 29 attacks are added.

CACTI Data Set. Samples are from the web front-end of a Cacti monitoring solution deployed in a hosting environment and were collected within approximately one month. There is one code injection attempt in the original data and it is free of scanning events. The final set with planted attacks has 25,057 request samples where 126 requests are malicious.

SOCIAL Data Set. The log data is from a social networking site which is a hybrid solution of different web applications. From the analyst's point of view, the data is a worst-case scenario because there is a) concept drift, b) user data like events or names in the URI path, c) URL Rewriting, d) lots of random data like names of image thumbnails and e) an advertising system that transmits the encoded referee URL within the URI path.

The original set has 12,515,970 log lines and contains 1,922 attacks where 1,392 are scanning attempts. Also, 115 suspicious requests are the result of a JavaScript fault in the application and marked as CWE-0 in this paper. This data was collected in a timespan of about two weeks. The final data set for evaluation has 12,528,513 samples where a total of 14,465 are considered anomalous.

Table 3. Distribution of weaknesses in the data sets

CWE	0	20	22	78	79	89	94	119	200	total	fraction
CMS	0	7	1	2	6	6	58	5	52	137	4.178%
CACTI	0	26	7	18	30	15	8	22	0	126	0.503%
SOCIAL	115	3464	611	1137	1794	2076	1416	2460	1392	14465	0.115%

4.2   Results

To keep experiments as realistic as possible, we assume that a virtual expert gives feedback to the algorithm occasionally. This expert randomly recognizes 66.6% of false positives and 10% of false negatives and triggers a learning function. All experiments were performed on one core of a consumer-grade Intel i5-760 CPU.

The advantage of the chosen scenario is that it is oriented on practical deployment. Due to the constant on-line learning and varying detection performance, results cannot be directly compared to solutions that are pre-trained on existing training data.

CMS Results. The CMS data set is a toy example to visualize outlier detection and learning. Figure 6 shows the time-series of evaluated samples. Within the first 500 requests, the confidence intervals stabilize. As visible at about sample 1,000, only few values are in the sliding window, the distribution is not yet robust against outliers.

A model with parameters $\langle 0.7, 2, 10000, 0.99, 0.999, 0.9999, 50000 \rangle$ minimizes false positives to one and achieves Recall = 97.08% and Precision = 99.25%. The final model has 119 trie nodes, alphabet size $|\mathcal{A}| = 15$ and reaches throughput of 91,083 logs/second due to the simpleness of the underlying web application.

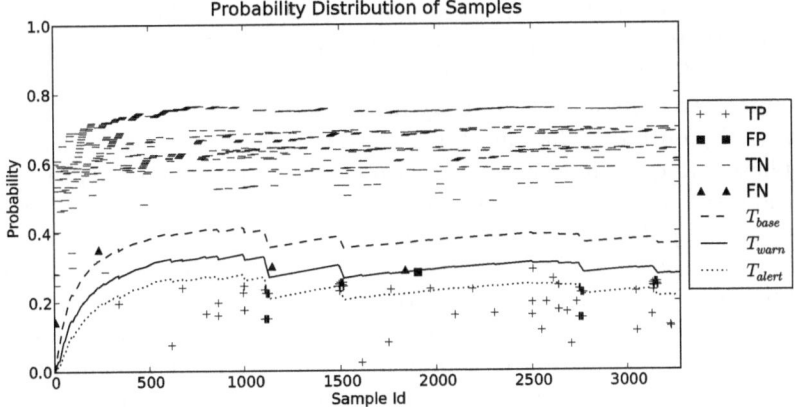

Fig. 6. Time-series of sequence probabilities and evolution of confidence intervals in the CMS data set

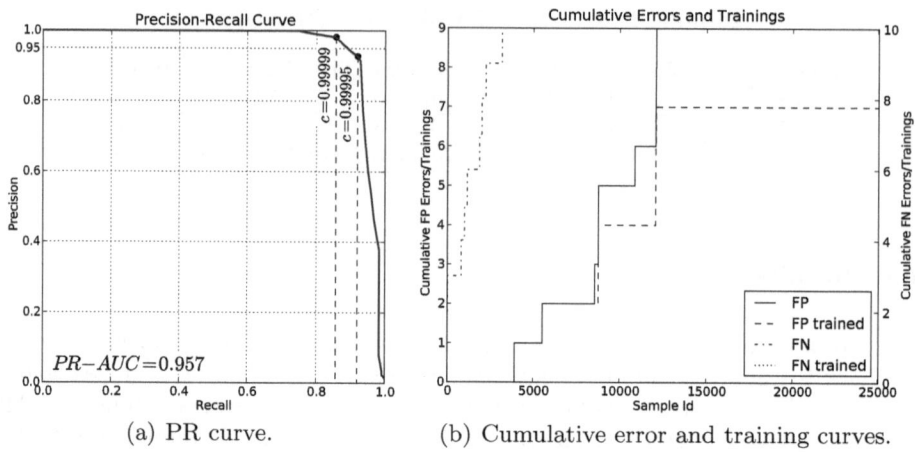

(a) PR curve.   (b) Cumulative error and training curves.

Fig. 7. Performance metrics for the CACTI data set

CACTI Results. This data set is more realistic and performance curves are displayed in Figure 7. Here, Recall = 92.06% and Precision = 92.8% are achieved by parameters $\langle 0.82, 2, 10000, 0.995, 0.99995, 0.99995, 10000 \rangle$, only nine false positives take place in the simulated timespan.

Figure 7(a) outlines the PR curve and two different confidence thresholds are marked. It is visible that an increased threshold also increases the precision at the expense of detection rate. The cumulative curves in Figure 7(b) show that false negatives only occur in the initial phase and after about sample 13,000 the growth of false positives stagnates. This stagnation indicates that the statistical model adepts to the data. After the last sample processed, the model has 225 trie nodes, alphabet size $|\mathcal{A}| = 20$ and still achieves throughput of 65,083 logs/second.

SOCIAL Results. The last data set represents the worst case experiment and resulting performance curves are shown in Figure 8. A model with parameters $\langle 0.8, 4, 20000, 0.995, 0.99995, 0.99995, 5000000 \rangle$ achieves the best performance with Recall = 74.15% and Precision = 93.76%. A total of 714 false positives yield FPR = $5.71 \cdot 10^{-5}$. The two least-recalled classes of weaknesses are scanning attempts and the already mentioned JavaScript fault.

Figure 8(b) outlines, that most false positive detections take place in the initial phase and growth decreases over time. Due to the complexity of this web application, the final model has 19,650 trie nodes, alphabet size $|\mathcal{A}| = 100$ and permits throughput of 29,200 logs/second.

To sum up, the results of all three data sets are promising considering the on-line scenario and evaluation data. Also, the search for optimal performance has shown that initial parameters $\langle 0.7, 2, 10000, 0.99, 0.9999, 0.9999, 500000 \rangle$ are a good start. For each data set there are several parameter combinations with comparable performance results and the presented ones in this paper maximize throughput. The parameter $T_{\mathcal{A}}$ has direct impact on the size of the alphabet and accordingly, the throughput performance.

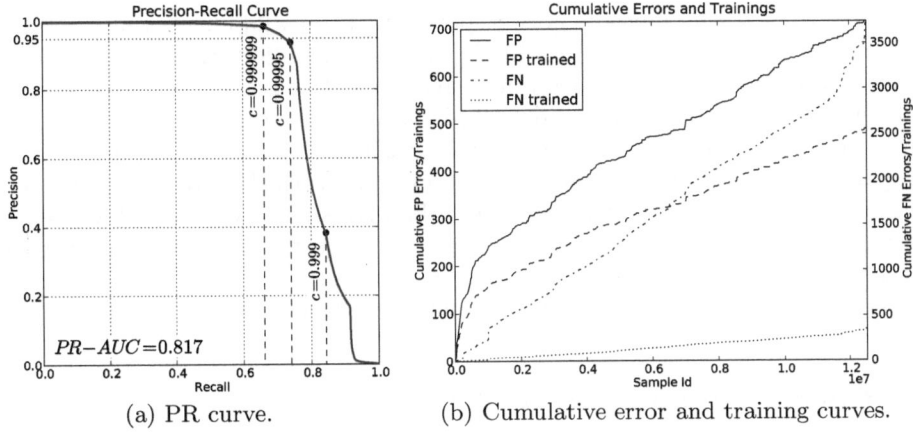

(a) PR curve.   (b) Cumulative error and training curves.

Fig. 8. Performance metrics for the SOCIAL data set

4.3   Evasion Strategies

The proposed concept relies on statistical features collected over time to detect deviating web requests. Due to the nature of the problem domain, an attacker with detailed knowledge about the algorithm might be able to evade detection under certain conditions. Three potential evasion strategies, which apply to the proposed algorithm, have been studied in theory.

Initial Phase Attack. During the initial phase of deployment, the algorithm might unintentionally learn an attack. If this attack keeps undetected and similar attacks occur regularly, the algorithm will assume them as normal too. In the best case, the attack is a single incident and the pruning mechanism will clean the VMM and symbol alphabet over time. In the worst case, the web application constantly receives a high amount of similar malicious requests. This scenario needs lower T_{base} and T_{prune} thresholds to limit the feedback of sequences into the VMM. As a side-effect, these parameters will produce more false positive detections and require more human expert feedback, especially during the initial phase.

Mimicry Attack. A skilled attacker might be able to craft malicious data which undergoes detection [32]. The presented algorithm has shown to be resistant against classic polymorphic attacks, but a potential weakness is the decision-making based on the arithmetic mean sequence probability. In a malicious request, some symbols have a very low probability, and so, the mean sequence probability is lowered towards zero. But if the attacker is able to extend the malicious request with additional highly probable symbols, the impact of low-probable symbols on the mean decreases and the attack might not be recognized. A possible countermeasure is to increase the algorithm's sensitivity by increasing order D and T_A while reducing T_{warn} and T_{alert}.

Frog-Boiling Attack. This category of poisoning attack [6] affects the presented detection mechanism. It aims to falsify the statistical detection model by continuously sending borderline legitimate requests. At some point, the detection model will be too inaccurate to detect real attacks. A possible countermeasure, in addition to increasing the algorithm's sensitivity, is to include the server's response into the analysis. For example, tampering with the URI path will likely produce invalid requests, and accordingly, bad response codes. The downside of using response codes for decision-making is the limitation of prevention capabilities, because the malicious data has already been sent. This concept has been implemented in the network prototype, but more testing is still required.

5   Conclusion and Future Work

We propose an on-line learning approach to detect malicious web requests. The main contribution of this paper is a concept that addresses both concept drift of web applications and the problem of representative training data. Also by design, the algorithm copes with URL Rewriting which is popular in realistic web deployments. In experiments with realistic log data the implemented log analyzer prototype shows decent detection and throughput performance.

To sum up, our presented method transforms the HTTP request into a sequence of symbols, where one symbol is the statistical representation of bytes between HTTP separator characters. A variable-order Markov model assigns a probability of occurrence to the sequence. An estimated Beta distribution over recent sequence probabilities is used to detect deviating sequences. In case of an detected anomaly, an expert can trace the responsible section in the web request according to the individual symbol probabilities. Feedback of highly probable sequences into the model achieves lazy teaching in context of on-line learning, also, the human expert can intervene in case of erroneous detections.

For future research, testing the network prototype implementation on realworld network data is necessary. This includes comparison to other existing methods and long-term testing. Also, binary classification is insufficient for practical scenarios because the abnormality of an alert does not reflect its potential impact. For example, scanning attempts are not as harmful as successful code injections. Clustering of similar alerts is a reasonable approach here. Furthermore, throughput performance can still be optimized if parallelization or GPU-offloading is considered.

References

1. Aho, A.V., Corasick, M.J.: Efficient string matching: an aid to bibliographic search. Commun. ACM 18(6), 333–340 (1975)
2. Apache 2.0 Documentation: Apache Module mod_rewrite (2011), http://httpd.apache.org/docs/2.0/mod/mod_rewrite.html (Online; accessed April 28, 2011)

3. Axelsson, S.: The base-rate fallacy and its implications for the difficulty of intrusion detection. In: CCS 1999: Proceedings of the 6th ACM Conference on Computer and Communications Security, pp. 1–7. ACM, New York (1999)
4. Begleiter, R., El-Yaniv, R., Yona, G.: On prediction using variable order markov models. J. Artif. Int. Res. 22(1), 385–421 (2004)
5. Berners-Lee, T., Fielding, R., Masinter, L.: Uniform Resource Identifier (URI): Generic Syntax. RFC 3986 (Standard) (January 2005), http://www.ietf.org/rfc/rfc3986.txt
6. Chan-Tin, E., Feldman, D., Hopper, N., Kim, Y.: The Frog-Boiling Attack: Limitations of Anomaly Detection for Secure Network Coordinate Systems. In: Chen, Y., Dimitriou, T.D., Zhou, J. (eds.) SecureComm 2009. LNICST, vol. 19, pp. 448–458. Springer, Heidelberg (2009)
7. Cleary, J.G., Witten, I.H.: Data compression using adaptive coding and partial string matching. IEEE Transactions on Communications 32, 396–402 (1984)
8. Davis, J., Goadrich, M.: The relationship between precision-recall and roc curves. In: ICML 2006, pp. 233–240. ACM, New York (2006)
9. Düssel, P., Gehl, C., Laskov, P., Rieck, K.: Incorporation of Application Layer Protocol Syntax into Anomaly Detection. In: Sekar, R., Pujari, A.K. (eds.) ICISS 2008. LNCS, vol. 5352, pp. 188–202. Springer, Heidelberg (2008)
10. Evans, M., Hastings, N., Peacock, B.: Statistical Distributions, 3rd edn. Wiley-Interscience (2000)
11. Fielding, R., Gettys, J., Mogul, J., Frystyk, H., Masinter, L., Leach, P., Berners-Lee, T.: Hypertext Transfer Protocol – HTTP/1.1. RFC 2616 (Draft Standard) (June 1999), http://www.ietf.org/rfc/rfc2616.txt, updated by RFCs 2817, 5785
12. Görnitz, N., Kloft, M., Rieck, K., Brefeld, U.: Active learning for network intrusion detection. In: Proceedings of the 2nd ACM Workshop on Security and Artificial Intelligence, AISec 2009, pp. 47–54. ACM, New York (2009)
13. Han, J., Kamber, M.: Data Mining: Concepts and Techniques, 2nd edn. Morgan Kaufmann Publishers Inc., San Francisco (2006)
14. Ingham, K.L., Somayaji, A., Burge, J., Forrest, S.: Learning dfa representations of http for protecting web applications. Comput. Netw. 51, 1239–1255 (2007)
15. Knuth, D.E.: The Art of Computer Programming. Seminumerical Algorithms, 2nd edn., vol. II. Addison-Wesley (1981)
16. Kruegel, C., Vigna, G.: Anomaly detection of web-based attacks. In: CCS 2003: Proceedings of the 10th ACM Conference on Computer and Communications Security, pp. 251–261. ACM, New York (2003)
17. Krueger, T., Gehl, C., Rieck, K., Laskov, P.: Tokdoc: a self-healing web application firewall. In: SAC 2010: Proceedings of the 2010 ACM Symposium on Applied Computing, pp. 1846–1853. ACM, New York (2010)
18. Ma, J., Liu, X., Wang, Q., Dai, G.: Compression-based web anomaly detection model. In: 2010 IEEE 29th International Performance Computing and Communications Conference (IPCCC) (December 2010)
19. Maggi, F., Robertson, W., Kruegel, C., Vigna, G.: Protecting a Moving Target: Addressing Web Application Concept Drift. In: Kirda, E., Jha, S., Balzarotti, D. (eds.) RAID 2009. LNCS, vol. 5758, pp. 21–40. Springer, Heidelberg (2009)
20. Metasploit: The Metasploit Project (2011), http://www.metasploit.com/ (Online; accessed April 30, 2011)
21. MITRE Corporation: Common Vulnerabilites and Exposures (2011), http://cve.mitre.org/ (Online; accessed May 12, 2011)
22. MITRE Corporation: Common Weakness Enumeration (2011), http://cwe.mitre.org/ (Online; accessed April 28, 2011)

23. Moffat, A.: Implementing the ppm data compression scheme. IEEE Transactions on Communications 38(11), 1917–1921 (1990)
24. Perdisci, R., Ariu, D., Fogla, P., Giacinto, G., Lee, W.: Mcpad: A multiple classifier system for accurate payload-based anomaly detection. Computer Networks 53(6), 864–881 (2009); traffic Classification and Its Applications to Modern Networks
25. Provos, N., McNamee, D., Mavrommatis, P., Wang, K., Modadugu, N.: The ghost in the browser analysis of web-based malware. In: Proceedings of the First Conference on First Workshop on Hot Topics in Understanding Botnets. USENIX Association, Berkeley (2007)
26. Robertson, W., Vigna, G., Kruegel, C., Kemmerer, R.: Using generalization and characterization techniques in the anomaly-based detection of web attacks. In: Proceedings of the Network and Distributed System Security Symposium (NDSS), San Diego, CA (February 2006)
27. Robertson, W., Maggi, F., Kruegel, C., Vigna, G.: Effective anomaly detection with scarce training data. In: Proceedings of the Network and Distributed System Security Symposium (NDSS), San Diego, CA (February 2010)
28. Salomon, D.: Data Compression: The Complete Reference. Springer, Heidelberg (2007)
29. Sommer, R., Paxson, V.: Outside the closed world: On using machine learning for network intrusion detection. In: IEEE Symposium on Security and Privacy, pp. 305–316 (2010)
30. Song, Y., Keromytis, A.D., Stolfo, S.J.: Spectrogram: A mixture-of-markov-chains model for anomaly detection in web traffic. In: Proc. of Network and Distributed System Security Symposium, NDSS (2009)
31. Vovk, V., Gammerman, A., Shafer, G.: Algorithmic Learning in a Random World. Springer-Verlag New York, Inc., Secaucus (2005)
32. Wagner, D., Soto, P.: Mimicry attacks on host-based intrusion detection systems. In: Proceedings of the 9th ACM Conference on Computer and Communications Security, CCS 2002, pp. 255–264. ACM, New York (2002)
33. Wang, K., Parekh, J.J., Stolfo, S.J.: Anagram: A Content Anomaly Detector Resistant to Mimicry Attack. In: Zamboni, D., Kruegel, C. (eds.) RAID 2006. LNCS, vol. 4219, pp. 226–248. Springer, Heidelberg (2006)
34. Wang, K., Stolfo, S.J.: Anomalous Payload-Based Network Intrusion Detection. In: Jonsson, E., Valdes, A., Almgren, M. (eds.) RAID 2004. LNCS, vol. 3224, pp. 203–222. Springer, Heidelberg (2004)
35. Welford, B.P.: Note on a method for calculating corrected sums of squares and products. Technometrics 4(3), 419–420 (1962)
36. Wojtczuk, R.: Libnids (2011), http://libnids.sourceforge.net/ (Online; accessed May 9, 2011)

Secure Configuration of Intrusion Detection Sensors for Changing Enterprise Systems

Gaspar Modelo-Howard, Jevin Sweval, and Saurabh Bagchi

Dependable Computing Systems Laboratory, Purdue University
465 Northwestern Avenue, West Lafayette, IN 47907, USA
{gmodeloh,jsweval,sbagchi}@purdue.edu

Abstract. Current attacks to distributed systems involve multiple steps, due to attackers usually taking multiple actions to achieve their goals. Such attacks are called multi-stage attacks and have the ultimate goal to compromise a critical asset for the victim. An example would be compromising a web server, then achieve a series of intermediary steps (such as compromising a developer's box thanks to a vulnerable PHP module and connecting to a FTP server with gained credentials) to ultimately connect to a database where user credentials are stored. Current detection systems are not capable of analyzing the multi-step attack scenario. In this document we present a distributed detection framework based on a probabilistic reasoning engine that communicates to detection sensors and can achieve two goals: (1) protect the critical asset by detecting multi-stage attacks and (2) tune sensors according to the changing environment of the distributed system monitored by the distributed framework. As shown in the experiments, the framework reduces the number of false positives that it would otherwise report if it were only considering alerts from a single detector and the reconfiguration of sensors allows the framework to detect attacks that take advantage of the changing system environment.

Keywords: Distributed intrusion detection, multi-stage attacks, Bayesian reasoning, sensor reconfiguration.

1 Introduction

Current computer attacks against distributed systems involve multiple steps, thanks to attackers usually taking multiple actions to achieve their ultimate goal to compromise a critical asset. Such attacks are called multi-stage attacks (MSA). As today's enterprise systems are structured to protect their critical assets, such as, a mission-critical service or private databases, by placing them inside the periphery, MSAs have gained prominence. Examples include the breach of a large payment processing firm [1] and the breaches published by the U.S. Department of Health & Human Services [24]. MSAs are characterized by progressively achieving intermediate attack steps and progressing using these as stepping stones to achieve the ultimate goal(s). Thus, prior to the critical asset being compromised, multiple components are compromised. Logically, therefore,

M. Rajarajan et al. (Eds.): SecureComm 2011, LNICST 96, pp. 39–58, 2012.
© Institute for Computer Sciences, Social Informatics and Telecommunications Engineering 2012

to detect MSAs, it would be desirable to detect the security state of various components in an enterprise distributed system—the outward facing services as well as those placed inside the periphery. Further, the security state needs to be inferred from the alerts provided by intrusion detection sensors (henceforth, shortened as "sensors") deployed in various parts of the system.

In the context of MSAs against distributed systems, this is challenging because sensors are designed and deployed without consideration for assimilating inputs from multiple detectors to determine how an MSA is spreading through the protected system. Prior work has shown that it is possible to determine the choice and placement of sensors in a systematic manner and at runtime, perform inferencing based on alerts from the sensors to determine the security state of the protected system components [7][1]. In achieving this, the solutions have performed characterization of individual sensors prior to deployment, in terms of their capability to detect specific attack step goals. At runtime, inferencing has been performed on the basis of the evidence—the alerts from the sensors—to determine the unobservable variables—the security state of the different components of the protected system. The sensors may be either network-based sensors, which observe incoming or outgoing network traffic, or host-based sensors, which observe activities within a host.

However, no existing solution has handled the various sources of dynamism that are to be expected in large-scale protected systems deployed in enterprise settings. The underlying protected system itself changes with time, with the addition or deletion of hosts, ports, software applications, or changes in connectivity between hosts. A static solution is likely to miss new attacks possible in the changed configuration of the protected system as well as throw off false alarms for attack steps that are just not possible under the changed configuration. The nature of attacks may also change with time or the anticipated frequencies of attack paths may turn out to be not completely accurate based on attack traces observed at runtime. Existing solutions cannot update their "beliefs" in an efficient manner and are therefore likely to be less accurate. Finally, when the compromise of a critical asset appears imminent, fast reconfiguration of existing sensors (such as, turning on some rules) may be needed to increase the certainty about the security state of the critical asset. Our contribution in this paper is to show how the choice and placement of sensors can be updated through incremental processing when the above kinds of dynamism occur.

The solution we propose in this paper called **D**istributed **I**ntrusion and **A**ttack **D**etection **S**ystem *(DIADS)* is to have a central inferencing engine, which has a model of MSAs as attack graphs. DIADS creates a Bayesian Network (BN) out of an attack graph and observable (or evidence) nodes in the attack graph are mapped from sensor alerts. It receives inputs from the sensors and performs inferencing to determine whether a rechoosing or replacement of sensors is needed. Further, it can reconfigure existing sensors, by turning on or off rules or event

---

[1] In this paper, we will refer to the distributed enterprise system that is being protected as the *protected system* and the set of sensors embedded in various components of the protected system as the *sensor system*.

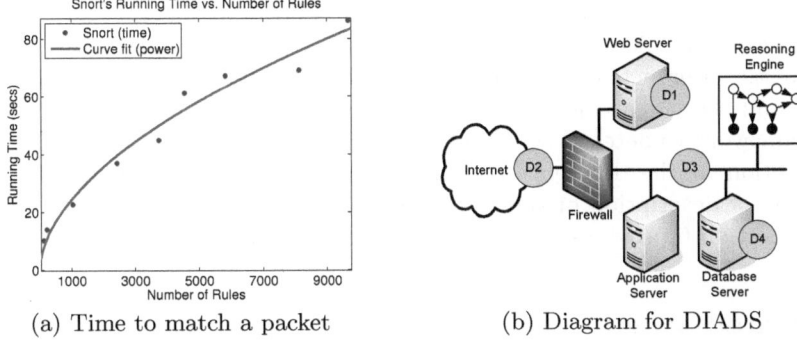

(a) Time to match a packet   (b) Diagram for DIADS

Fig. 1. (a) Results from curve fitting the data points from the Snort experiment. (b) General block diagram of the proposed DIADS. A wrapper (software) is used to allow communication from the sensors (circles labeled D1 to D4) and firewall to the reasoning engine and viceversa (only for sensors).

definitions based on the changed circumstances. Thus, the inferencing engine has a two-way communication path with the sensors. DIADS determines changes to the protected system by parsing changes to firewall rules at network points as well as at individual hosts and updates the BN accordingly. If on the basis of current evidence, it determines that a critical asset (also synonymously referred to as a crown jewel) will imminently be compromised, it determines what further sensors close to the asset should be chosen, or equivalently, what further rules in an already active sensor should be turned on.

One may think that a perfectly acceptable, and a much simpler, solution is to activate all the available sensors and turn on all the available rules at any sensor. Thus, there will be no reason to react to dynamic changes of the three types mentioned above. However, this will impose too high an overhead on the protected system in terms of the amount of computational resources that will be required and the frequency of false alerts that will be generated. For example, we determine empirically that for the popular Snort IDS [19] turning on the default set of rules will cause it to potentially take 85 seconds to match a single packet (corresponding to 9700 rules in Figure 1a). Therefore there is the motivation to dynamically reconfigure the sensors according to the activity observed in the network.

To sum up, in this paper we make the following contributions:

1. We design a distributed intrusion detection system that can choose and place sensors in a distributed system to increase the certainty of knowledge about the security state of the critical assets in the system.
2. We imbue our solution with the ability to evolve with changes to the protected system as well as the kinds of attacks seen in the system.
3. Through domain-specific optimizations, we make our reasoning engine fast enough that it can perform reconfiguration of existing sensors while a multi-stage attack (MSA) is coursing through the protected system.

We structure the remainder of this paper as follows. In Section 2 we review previous work on distributed intrusion detection systems (DIDS), MSA, and probabilistic approaches to intrusion detection. Section 3 states the problem studied and the threat model considered. Section 4 presents the proposed DIADS framework to detect MSAs and to reconfigure detection sensors, including a description of the different components and algorithms used. In Section 5 we provide a description of the experiments performed along with the results. Finally, Section 6 provides conclusions and future work.

2   Related Work

There has been previous work on developing and proposing DIDSs. Early examples of these systems are [20], [17], [26], and [21]. A starting point for DIDSs is the collaboration between Lawrence Livermore National Labs, U.S. Air Force and other organizations [20]. It represented the first attempt to physically distribute the detection mechanism, while centralizing the analysis phase in a single component, running a rule-based system.

Another distributed IDS is EMERALD [17]. It is a signature- and anomaly-based distributed IDS with statistical analysis capabilities (rule-based and Bayesian inference). The communication among sensors and monitors is structured in a hierarchy. NetSTAT [26] is a network-based IDS modeling intrusions as state transition diagrams and the target network as hypergraphs. By using both models, the system prioritizes which network events to monitor. AAFID [21] is a distributed framework based on software agents to collect and analyze data and used as a platform to develop intrusion detection techniques. An interesting policy-based proposal based on the popular Bro IDS [15] was presented in [6], using intrusion detection sensors in a distributed, collaborative manner.

Unfortunately there has not been much discussion about DIDS in the last few years so the impact of more complex distributed systems on the detection capabilities of IDS as well as the evolution of MSAs has been somewhat neglected. Previous work has primarily concentrated on increasing the accuracy of IDSs by improving their true positive (TP) rate on single step attacks. Additionally, it does not consider the dynamic nature of the protected system, one of our focus areas.

Previous work has considered MSAs [9], [10] but within a limited scope. [9] proposes an offline-method to correlate alerts using an attack graph, to improve detection rate, while reducing false positive (FP) and false negative (FN) rates. It is a rule-based method and does not consider a probabilistic approach. [10] presents a formal conceptual model based on Interval Temporal Logic (ITL) to express the temporal properties of MSAs.

A principal component for our framework is an attack graph, from which to create a corresponding Bayesian network. An example of previous work on using attack graphs for intrusion detection is found in [4]. Other works have previously focused on using attack graphs to evaluate (offline) the vulnerability state of the computer system [27].

Bayesian networks have been used for intrusion detection, examples include [7] and [5]. [7] models the potential attacks to a target network using a Bayesian network to determine (off-line) a set of detectors to protect the network. [5] presents a method based on Dynamic Bayesian networks to include the temporal properties of attacks in a distributed system.

Alert correlation is an area related to intrusion detection, that has received the attention of the research community. Schemes in this area can be classified under two basic groups: schemes that require patterns of actual attacks and/or alert interdependencies, and schemes that do not. Members of the first group include [11], [12], and [13]. Our proposed framework, can be classified as part of the first group. The second group of correlation schemes works without any specific knowledge of attacks. Examples include [25], [18].

In [11], the authors present a formal framework for alert correlation that constructs attack graphs by correlating individual alerts on the basis of the prerequisites and consequences manually associated to each alert. [12] presents techniques to learn attack strategies from correlated attack graphs. The basic idea is to compute how similar different attack graphs are by using error tolerant subgraph isomorphism detection. In [13] the authors built on the results from the previous two papers, integrating two alert correlation methods: correlation based on prerequisites and consequences of attacks and those based on similarity between alert attribute values. They used the results to hypothesize and reason about single attacks possibly missed by the IDSs. There are several similarities between their approach and ours. We both represent attack scenarios as graphs, assume attack steps are usually not isolated but rather part of an MSA. Still, there are also several differences between their alert correlation approach and ours. In a nutshell, our approach is adaptive, provides a larger visibility of the target network, follows a probabilistic model, and works online, while theirs is not.

3   Problem Statement and Threat Model

In this paper, we answer two fundamental questions:

(1) How to update the configuration of sensors in an enterprise distributed system (i.e., one with many hosts and software applications and hence attack injection points) based on updated information that is obtained after the protected system and the sensor system have been deployed.

(2) When the imminent threat to a critical asset(s) is high, how to reconfigure existing sensors (such as, by activating new rules) to increase confidence in the estimate of the security state of the critical asset(s).

In terms of the model for the protected system, all the components fall target network under a single administrative domain and therefore, there is complete trust between the owners of the different assets.

The profile of the attackers includes highly motivated individuals that might have an economical incentive to compromise the distributed system. Attackers follow a multi-step approach to compromise a resource or acquire data. It could start with some reconnaissance, followed by exploitation of different hosts or services in the target network. This description also fits the cases where attack sources are botnets and malware, that does not include human intervention. We do not address intruders who steal data by physically connecting to a host (for example, an insider's attack using a USB memory stick).

In our framework, one or more *critical assets* are identified in the protected system by the system owner and become the main protection objective of our DIADS framework. Each critical asset is represented in the BN as a leaf node. An example of a critical asset is a database that contains personally identifiable information (PII). The above statement does not preclude having sensors that detect attacks at other assets (such as, at a network ingress point), but our inferencing uses such sensors to provide evidence of attacks leading up to a potential compromise of the critical assets. Also, our DIADS framework is not attempting to create better intrusion detection sensors; rather it is seeking to use existing sensors intelligently to obtain a better estimate of the security state of critical assets in an enterprise distributed system.

We consider only multi-stage attacks (MSAs) to distributed systems. An important example is an MSA to a three-tier system (web / application logic / database) which might allow an attacker to launch HTTP-based attacks to ultimately reach the database and the information stored in it.

4   DIADS Framework

In this document we propose a distributed intrusion detection framework that includes two components: (1) a probabilistic reasoning engine and (2) a network of detection sensors to detect various stages of MSAs, as shown in Figure 1b. The second component comprises off-the-shelf sensors, augmented with a standard wrapper that allows the sensor to send alerts to the reasoning engine and receive commands back from the reasoning engine. The architecture is able to alert intrusion events related to potential MSAs and determine if any critical asset has been compromised, or is under imminent likelihood of being compromised based on current evidence of the spread of the attack. It also allows for reconfiguration of sensors according to changes to the protected system that is being monitored by the DIADS. Through this architecture, the DIADS can reduce the number of false positives that it would report if it were independently considering each step of the MSA. A block diagram of the proposed architecture is shown in Figure 2.

The reasoning engine represents different possible MSAs as a single Bayesian network, which is updated according to events reported by the detection sensors and the changing network configuration. The probabilistic engine can also request more information from sensors when necessary. The reasoning engine can estimate the security state of the critical assets given partial information about multi-stage attacks and from imperfect or noisy sensors.

The reasoning engine also collects background information about the distributed system so the model can be updated. As a starting point, we should consider the network and policy configurations stored in a firewall. The firewall can be at a network ingress-egress point as well as at individual hosts. The

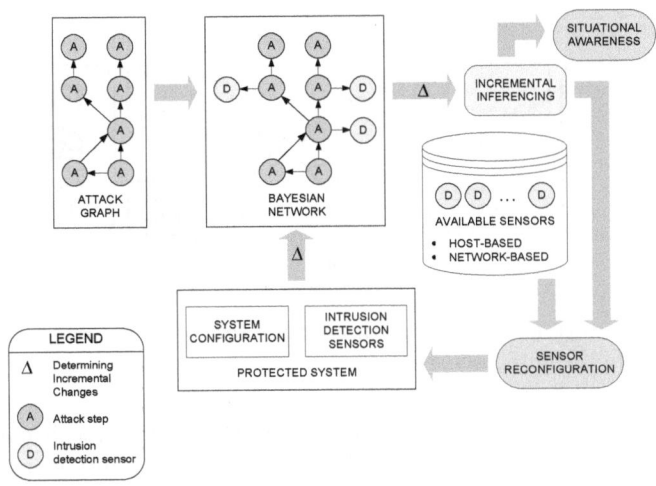

Fig. 2. Diagram of the proposed framework, providing details on the components of the reasoning engine

firewall configuration indicates which components are allowed to communicate with which components and thus has an important determining effect on the structure of the attack graph, and consequently, on the structure of the BN.

4.1 Probabilistic Reasoning Engine

To build our reasoning engine, we use Bayesian Network (BN), which is a popular probabilistic graphical model. It is a macro-language, representing joint distributions compactly by using a set of local relationships between random variables and specified by a graph. A key point is that the missing edges in the graph imply the conditional independence between the corresponding nodes. BN captures the characteristic in real-world data of *locality of influence*, the idea that most variables are influenced by only a few others. [7] shows the implications of this.

Bayesian networks combine graph theory with statistical techniques to model MSA scenarios. In our framework, we use an attack graph to create the structure of the BN, a directed acyclical graph. Each node in the graph represents a vulnerability, more specifically, a 3-tuple: *host* × *port* × *vulnerability* existing in the target network. This means that the service running on that host and listening on that port has that vulnerability. The edges between nodes represent the direct precondition relationship between the attack steps. The BN also includes nodes to represent intrusion detection sensors. An edge $A \rightarrow D$ from an attack step node to a sensor node represents the possibility of the sensor detecting that attack step, with the CPT quantifying the accuracy and precision of the detection. Each node is parametrized by a set of probability values and represented as a *conditional probability tables (CPT)*. Proposed in previous work [7] and also suggested by [5], the Bayesian network representation can unify the information available from multiple sensors, in order to determine if an MSA is occurring.

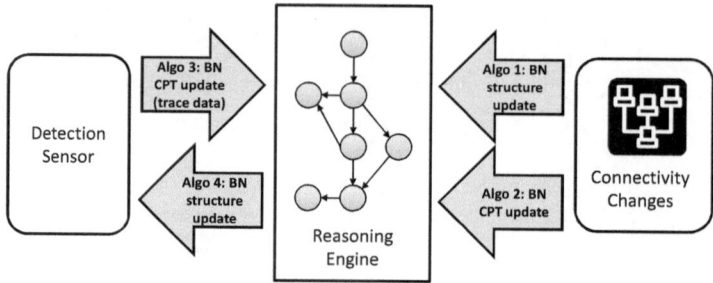

Fig. 3. The framework uses four algorithms, three to update the reasoning engine and one to reconfigure the detection sensors

There are several benefits of using Bayesian networks. First, it can be a more appropriate representation of reality than deterministic approaches, accounting for several sources of uncertainty—noisy sensors, unknown intentions of the adversary affecting the path of the MSA, and unknown difficulty of transitioning from one attack step node to the next. A potential drawback of probabilistic models is the combinatorial explosion faced when computing a joint probability distribution. In our work, we address this issue by using the Noisy-OR model [16] to represent the CPTs. Further details are provided in section 4.5. Our DIADS framework is composed of four algorithms, which are schematically shown in Figure 3. Pseudo-code for algorithms 1, 2, and 4 are provided in the Appendix.

4.2   Algorithm 1: BN Update to Structure Based on Firewall Rule Changes

The algorithm produces a list of nodes and edges that should be added to (V_a, E_a) or deleted from (V_d, E_d) the Bayesian network to represent changes to the protected system. We use changes to firewall rules as a proxy for the changes to the protected system. The firewalls can be at a network ingress-egress point or at individual hosts in the system.

The message passed from the Firewall to the reasoning engine has the following structure: $message = < number, srcIPaddr, destIPaddr, portnumber, action, ruletype >$ where $number$ refers to the order of the rule in the firewall table. $srcIPaddr$ and $destIPaddr$ are the IP addresses for the source and destination of communication; $portnumber$ is the TCP or UDP port number (16-bits in IPv4); $action$ is one of three options: allow, deny or drop; and $ruletype$ refers to the change made to the rule table: adding a new rule, modifying an existing rule or deleting an existing rule. For the purposes of our experiments, we only considered firewall rule tables composed of $allow$ rules followed by a $denyall$ rule. So effectively, the rule table creates a policy where allowed communication is explicitly defined and everything else not defined, is denied.

The algorithm can be divided into four parts: how to select the nodes and edges to be added, if the rule has type add (lines 1 to 11); how to select the nodes and edges to be deleted, if the rule has type $delete$ (lines 13 to 29); checking for

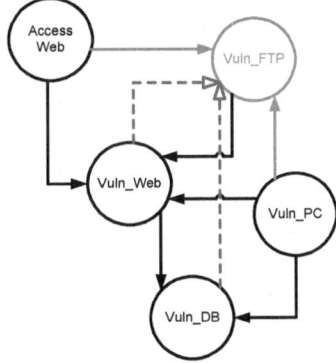

No.	Source	Destination	Action
1	Any	Web:80	Allow
2	Web	DB:3306	Allow
3	Web	DB:22	Allow
4	DB	Web:22	Allow
5	PC	DB:3306	Allow
6	PC	DB:22	Allow
7	Any	FTP:21	Allow
8	Any	Any	Deny

(a) Firewall rule table   (b) Bayesian network

Fig. 4. Impact of changes to a firewall rule. A new rule (No.7) in the firewall table changes the topology of the Bayesian network. Two of the four new edges, shown as dashed lines, will be removed by the algorithm since they lead to a cycle. A BN node is actually host × port × vulnerability, but here for simplicity, we have a single vulnerability per service (i.e. per host × port).

the resulting changes to the BN to not introduce cycles and to confirm that the resulting nodes are part of a path to the nodes representing the critical assets (lines 31 to 37); and finally, the converting the *destIPaddr:port* nodes into their corresponding *address:port:vulnerability* nodes in the BN.

When a rule has type *add* or *delete*, the algorithm checks if the source and destination addresses are new to the BN or already exist. If a node exists, then the edges shared with its parents (line 4) or its children (line 7) should be included to the set of edges to add (E_a). Also, the edge explicitly defined by the rule is included in (E_a). If a node is new, then it should be added to the set of nodes to add (V_a). A similar approach (but with opposite results) is used for case when a rule has type *delete*.

The algorithm then checks the nodes and edges in the resulting BN by running *Depth First Search* (DFS) to determine if the nodes have a path to the critical assets. If the nodes do not, then they are pruned. DFS also checks if the addition creates any cycles and if so, the back edges are deleted. The first is an important optimization focusing the attention of DIADS to the critical assets and limiting the growth of the BN.

Finally, the algorithm transforms the nodes in the sets V_a and V_d to nodes in the BN. It does this by doing a lookup in a matrix R that maps the *host × port* to the vulnerability. It acquires the raw data for this from the *National Vulnerability Database* (NVD) [23], a public repository of vulnerability management data.

As an example, consider a distributed system connected to the Internet, with three computers: a web server (accessible from the Internet), a database server and a desktop computer. The database server and the desktop computer are connected to the same subnet, while the web server is connected to a separate

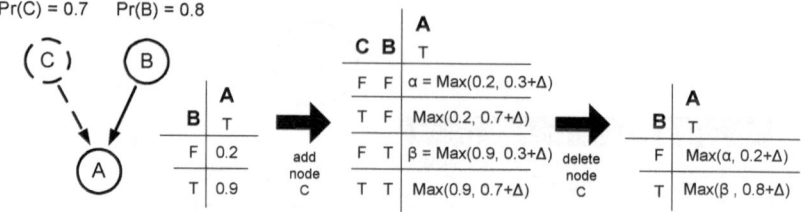

Fig. 5. Example for algorithm 02: initialization of BN CPT. To add a new parent (C) to an existing node (A), we create the marginal probability $Pr(C)$ from its CVSS (base metric) value and use it to update the new CPT of A.

subnet (DMZ). All computers are protected by a network-based firewall and the rule table is shown in Figure 4a. A Bayesian network can be built from the table, as shown in Figure 4b. The critical asset is the database server and for simplicity purposes, we have assumed one existing vulnerability per host.

If the rule `any −− > FTP:21 allow` is now added to the network firewall because a new FTP server has been deployed and connected to the DMZ network, the resulting Bayesian network is shown in Figure 4b. A new node, `Vuln_FTP`, is added and will have five edges. Four are inbound, created from the added rule and one outbound, from rule No. 1 in the table. The inbound edges from nodes `Vuln_Web` and `Vuln_DB` are not included in the final Bayesian network as they make the graph cyclical.

4.3   Algorithm 2: Initialization of BN CPTs Based on Firewall Changes

Algorithm 2 produces a list of CPTs for the changed nodes, i.e., nodes for which there is an increase or reduction in the number of parents of the nodes, according to the output from Algorithm 1. To update the CPT, we use the base metric value of the $CVSS$ score [3] of the node (corresponding to a vulnerability) to be added or removed and divide it by 10 to use it as its marginal probability value. Then if the resulting CPT is for an existing node, we take $max(newProb(v_i) + \Delta, oldProb(v_i))$. Figure 5 shows an example of how we use the formula.

In figure 5, first a new parent node C is added to an existing node A in the BN. We take the base metric score (7) of the vulnerability corresponding to node C and divide it by 10. Then use the formula $max(Prob(C)+\Delta, oldProb(A|\text{previous evidence}))$ to create the new CPT. In our experiments, we use $\Delta = 0.05$. Figure 5 also shows the CPT when node C is later removed. The base metric score of the other parent node (B) is used to update the CPT.

4.4   Algorithm 3: BN Update of CPT Based on Incremental Trace Data

The alerts received by the reasoning engine from the individual sensors are used to update the CPTs in the Bayesian network in an incremental manner. To achieve this, this algorithm uses the set of alerts received during a window of time and the matrix R, that maps the existing vulnerabilities in the system to their corresponding hosts and ports. The output of the algorithm is the set of CPTs with the updated values.

The algorithm uses a popular and powerful model known as Noisy-OR [16] to represent each CPT. Noisy-OR allows us to specify the CPT of a node with n parents, using with $n + 1$ parameters as opposed to 2^n for binary nodes. This prevents the exponential growth experienced by the CPT of a node when the number of parents (n) is large. The Noisy-OR model assumes that effect of each parent on the CPT of the edge to the child node (v_i) is independent from that of the other parents and is sufficient to produce the effect (represented by the child node) in the absence of all other parents. An additional parent node is added to capture all other causes that were not modeled explicitly. The marginal probability of this node is $1 - p_0$. Then the CPT can be built with the following formula, where C represents a combination of the values for the parents of the child node:

$$Prob(v_i|C) = 1 - (1 - p_0) \prod_{A=parent(v_i) \in C} \left(\frac{1 - Prob(v_i|A = T, \text{Others} = F)}{1 - p_0} \right) \quad (1)$$

4.5   Algorithm 4: Update Choice of Sensors Based on Runtime Inference

The final algorithm of our framework is used to reconfigure the detection sensors. This includes adding and removing sensors, as well as reconfiguring existing ones. The high level objective is to reduce the uncertainty of knowing if the critical asset has been achieved or not. The algorithm works by looking at the alerts received and uses them as evidence to compute the posterior probability of each Bayesian network node that corresponds to the critical asset.

The first step of the algorithm (line 1) is to compute the posterior probability for the critical asset, given the evidence received from the currently enabled sensors in the system. If the value is larger than a threshold (determined by the system administrator), this is taken as indication that the critical asset is likely to be compromised and therefore greater certainty is needed in the determination of the security state. Therefore, the algorithm measures (lines 3 and 4) the impact of candidate sensors, which are close to the detected alerts and the critical asset. A radius can be set a priori in terms of the number of edges away from a particular node to determine the candidate set of sensors. Previous work [7] has shown that the effect of a sensor on a Bayesian network node fades beyond 2-3 hops and thus this restriction appears reasonable.

The algorithm determines a new set of detectors by using the *Fully Polynomial Time Approximation Scheme* (FPTAS) presented in [8] for the problem of determining the placement of intrusion detection sensors. The same cost bound is maintained which will prevent the algorithm from blissfully adding new sensors. This problem has been mapped to the *0-1 Knapsack* problem for which a

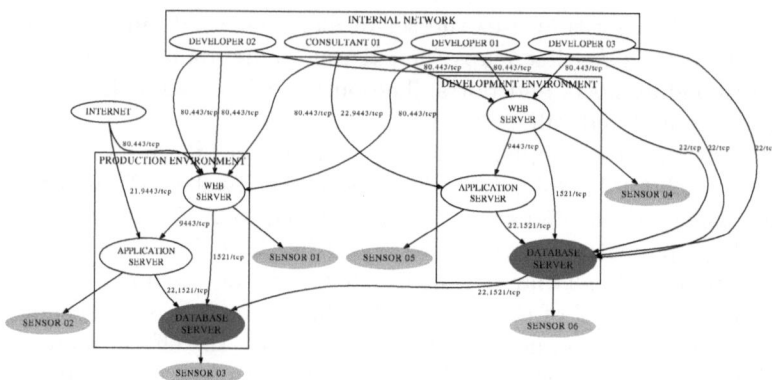

Fig. 6. Connectivity graph for testing scenario, showing the TCP ports enabled for communication between different hosts. The shaded nodes represent the critical asset (databases) in the protected system.

dynamic programming solution (FPTAS) exists that runs in *pseudo-polynomial* time (running time scales up as the solution approaches the optimal). The algorithm finishes by comparing the set of current detectors with the new set. The delta between the sets indicates the set of detectors to be disabled or enabled, which is output by the algorithm.

5   Experiments and Results

5.1   Experimental Setup

For our experiments, we used attacks against a real-world distributed system which is part of an NSF Center at our university and serves content and simulation tools for an engineering domain for thousands of users. The system includes fifteen hosts that include two environments, one for production and another for development of applications and staging prior to moving them to the production environment. Each environment includes a web server, an application server and a database server. A team of developers' and consultants' computers have access to subsets of both environments. Communication between all hosts is controlled by firewall rules at each host. The corresponding connectivity graph is shown in Figure 6.

In our experiments, the database servers are the critical assets to protect. A strong motivation to pick the databases is their role to store critical information for the organization. We created a Bayesian Network (BN) from the distributed system by first generating a list of the vulnerabilities found by the OpenVAS [14] vulnerability scanner on servers and client machines. Each vulnerability was then mapped to a node in the BN by associating it to the host and service(port) where the vulnerability was found. Finally, the nodes were connected according to the connectivity information for the distributed system. The BN had 345 nodes and

1948 edges. We then pruned the BN to only include high risk vulnerabilities, according to OpenVAS, as these ones are the primary vectors used by attackers to compromise systems. The final BN had 90 nodes and 582 edges.

We provide comparative results between DIADS (our algorithms presented in this paper) and a static and heuristic-driven choice of sensors. All results are presented as *Receiver Operating Characteristics* or *ROC curves* [22]. The curve is a graphical plot of the tradeoff between true positive rate (TPR, detection rate) and the false positive rate (FPR, false alerts) for a detector. The different points in the ROC curves are generated by varying the threshold for the probability value for the BN nodes corresponding to the critical assets.

We had a total of 18 possible sensors; 3 sensors for each of the web server, application server, and database server, in both the development and the production environments. They are all generic sensors with signatures customized to detect the class of attack into which the corresponding (vulnerability) node can be categorized. For all experiments, for both baseline and DIADS, we constrain the algorithms to pick a set of 6 from 18 possible detectors.

It is important to note that DIADS' goal is to improve the performance of a set of detectors, by considering temporal information (i.e. when detectors are sending alerts about a progressing attack or when changes occur to the distributed system). For our experiments, we defined detectors with adequate but not perfect performance (in terms of TP and FP). It is not our goal to improve the performance of individual detectors.

5.2   Experiment 1: Dynamic Reconfiguration of Detection Sensor

The first experiment compared the performance between a dynamic reconfiguration of sensors and an static set of sensors, all close to the database servers. The static setup follows the intuitive decision of turning on all the sensors at the critical assets, in this case the database servers. To test both setups, we use an attack scenario that had the following progress: the attack started from the Internet, compromised the production web server, from where to compromise the applications server and then elevate permissions, and finally compromise the database server. Further details for all attack scenarios and the Bayesian network used in all experiments, are provided in [2].

In this experiment, a set of alerts are generated for the first three steps of the attack scenario. This set serves as evidence and is provided to the reasoning engine for DIADS to recompute the set of sensors. As shown in Figure 7, the dynamic reconfiguration setup outperforms the static configuration of sensors. The area under the continuous line (dynamic) is greater than the area under the dotted line (static) by 16% ($Area_{DIADS} = 0.7810$ and $Area_{baseline} = 0.6728$). This also means, the dynamic setup provides a higher detection rate at points when both setups have the same false alarm rate.

A notable point is that the difference between both setups is not large. This should be expected as the static setup is concentrated around the database servers (the critical asset and final setup in the attack scenario) while the dynamic setup is scattered around the protected system.

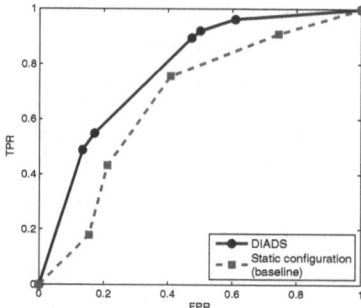

Fig. 7. Performance comparison between dynamic configuration of DIDS and a set of detectors monitoring only DB servers

5.3   Experiment 2: Dynamism from Firewall Rules Changes

Experiment 2 tested the performance of the dynamic and static setups as changes were made to the firewall rule table of the protected system. We considered two real scenarios: (1) removing from the system a host belonging to a developer and (2) adding a direct communication path is created from a consulant's host to the database server, in the development environment (in this case, the consultant determined some changes to the database schema had to be tried out in the development environment prior to unveiling it on production). For the static configuration, one sensor was deployed on each host in both development and production environments.

For the first firewall change where a developer's host was removed, we tested both setups using an attack scenario starting from another developer's host. This represents the increasingly common client-side attacks. The attack starts as the developer visits a malicious website that installs some malware on the host. Then permissions are elevated thanks to another existing vulnerability in the developer's host. Then a vulnerability in the database server (production) is exploited and finally another vulnerability is used to access the data in the database. For the second firewall change where a direct communication path is created, we used a different attack scenario. The attack starts from another developer's host that also visits a malicious website and malware is installed in the host. Then a vulnerability in the web server (development) is exploited, after which the application server and finally the database server, all part of the development environment, are compromised.

For DIADS, the BN was modified based on the firewall rule changes and the dynamic programming algorithm picked the set of detectors after receiving the alerts at the start of the attack - the starting point being the same as in the static case.

Results from this experiment are shown in Figures 8a and 8b. The dynamic reconfiguration setup performs better under both attack scenarios than the static configuration. The area under the curve is greater by 32.7% ($Area_{DIADS} =$

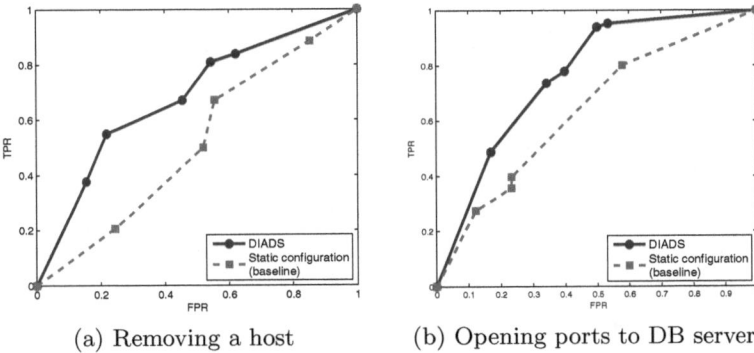

(a) Removing a host   (b) Opening ports to DB server

Fig. 8. Impact on topology changes. (a) Removing a host (developer) from network. (b) Allowing direct access between the consultant box and the DB development server.

0.6809 and $Area_{baseline} = 0.5132$) in the scenario when a host is removed and 20% ($Area_{DIADS} = 0.7659$ and $Area_{baseline} = 0.6383$) in the scenario when a direct access is set up between a consultant box and the DB development server. We consider the most interesting result to be in Figure 8b, where both setups show similar performance at the start. Both lines in the ROC curve have similar slopes, which is expected as the dynamic and static setups share 4 out of the 6 initial sensors. But as the alerts from the first three attack steps are provided to the reasoning engine in the dynamic setup, three sensors are reconfigured. This is the cause of the difference in performance, as shown in the ROC cuve.

5.4 Experiment 3: Dynamism with Attack Spreading

The goal of this experiment was to see if DIADS can reconfigure sensors on the fly as an attack spreads through the protected system. We used two different attack scenarios: (1) one starting from the Internet and (2) another starting from the internal network, a developer's host. An attack starting from the internal network usually requires less steps to reach the critical asset than attacks starting from the Internet. The static configuration picks sensors as in the earlier experiment 2 (one for each host).

The results are presented in Figures 9a and 9b for the two attack scenarios. In the attack starting from the Internet, the static setup shows a lower false alerts rate than the dynamic setup. But as evidence is provided, the ROC curve shows that the dynamic setup improves its performance. The curve shows the importance of taking into account the alerts from the initial stages of the attack to improve the performance of detection system. The improvement over the static setup, in terms of the area under the curve, is 23% ($Area_{DIADS} = 0.7845$ and $Area_{baseline} = 0.6366$). During the experiments, 4 of the 6 original sensors are replaced by the reasoning engine.

For the attack starting from internal network, the ROC curve in Figure 9b shows a similar performance between both setups. Three of the six

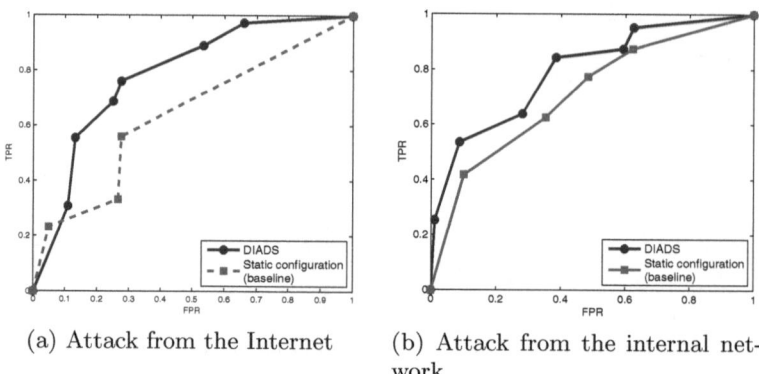

(a) Attack from the Internet   (b) Attack from the internal network

Fig. 9. Comparison between our dynamic technique and a static setup for two attacks scenarios. The dynamic reconfiguration technique allows to reconfigure the detection sensors as alerts from the initial steps of the attacks are received.

sensors selected for the static setup are on the attack path and are quite accurate. Therefore, though DIADS outperforms the static setup, the advantage is not very large (11% where $Area_{DIADS} = 0.7964$ and $Area_{baseline} = 0.7128$). This experiment shows promise that inferencing in BN can be done fast enough relative to the speed of attacks. Of course, further experimentation is needed with a variety of attacks (and attack speeds).

6   Conclusions and Future Work

Current attacks to distributed systems involve multiple steps, with the ultimate goal of compromising a critical asset such as a database where important data is stored for an organization. In this paper, we presented a distributed intrusion detection system called DIADS that picks and places sensors in a protected system, decreasing the uncertainty inherent in estimating the security state of the critical assets in the system. DIADS has the ability to evolve when changes are made to the topology of the protected system and with further evidence coming in the form of alers while the deployed system is operational.

Future work will include experimenting further with the size of the Bayesian network. We consider we made reasonable assumptions when pruning the Bayesian network, such as only including high risk vulnerabilities as nodes. Still, as the size of the CPTs for the nodes in the Bayesian network grows exponentially in terms of the number of nodes' parents, we would like to answer the question of whether inferencing can be done fast enough. Another area to explore is the impact of evasion techniques or attacks directly targeted against DIADS. If an attacker has complete knowledge of our model, she might launch attacks to falsely cause reconfiguration of our sensors away from the attack paths.

Acknowledgment. The work described in this paper was conducted under partial funding by Northrop Grumman Information Systems under the Northrop Grumman Cybersecurity Research Consortium. We acknowledge the help of Dr. Kenneth Brancik and Dr. Donald Steiner of Northrop Grumman in formulating the problem and identifying how the solution integrates in an enterprise security architecture.

References

1. Acohido, B.: Hackers breach Heartland Payment credit card system. USA Today (January 2009)
2. Addendum: Secure Configuration of Intrusion Detection Sensors, `http://sites.google.com/site/securecomm11msa/`
3. Forum of Incident Response and Security Teams: Common Vulnerability Scoring System (CVSS), `http://www.first.org/cvss/`
4. Foo, B., Wu, Y., Mao, Y., Bagchi, S., Spafford, E.: ADEPTS: Adaptive Intrusion Response Using Attack Graphs in an E-Commerce Environment. In: International Conference on Dependable Systems and Networks, pp. 508–517. IEEE Computer Society (2005)
5. Frigault, M., Wang, L., Singhal, A., Jajodia, S.: Measuring network security using dynamic bayesian network. In: 4th ACM Workshop on Quality of Protection, pp. 23–30. ACM, New York (2008)
6. Kreibich, C., Sommer, R.: Policy-controlled Event Management for Distributed Intrusion Detection. In: 4th Int. Workshop on Distributed Event Based Systems (2005)
7. Modelo-Howard, G., Bagchi, S., Lebanon, G.: Determining Placement of Intrusion Detectors for a Distributed Application through Bayesian Network Modeling. In: Lippmann, R., Kirda, E., Trachtenberg, A. (eds.) RAID 2008. LNCS, vol. 5230, pp. 271–290. Springer, Heidelberg (2008)
8. Modelo-Howard, G., Bagchi, S., Lebanon, G.: Approximation Algorithms for Determining Placement of Intrusion Detectors. CERIAS Tech. Report 2011-01 (2011)
9. Noel, S., Robertson, E., Jajodia, S.: Correlating Intrusion Events and Building Attack Scenarios Through Attack Graph Distances. In: 20th Annual Computer Security Applications Conference, pp. 350–359. IEEE Computer Society, New York (2004)
10. Nowicka, E., Zawada, M.: Modeling Temporal Properties of Multi-event Attack Signatures in Interval Temporal Logic. In: IEEE/IST Workshop on Monitoring, Attack Detection and Mitigation (2006)
11. Ning, P., Cui, Y., Reeves, D.: Constructing attack scenarios through correlation of intrusion alerts. In: 9th ACM Conf. Computer and Communications Security, pp. 245–254. ACM Press, New York (2002)
12. Ning, P., Xu, D.: Learning attack strategies from intrusion alerts. In: 10th ACM Conf. Computer and Communications Security, pp. 200–209. ACM Press, New York (2003)
13. Ning, P., Xu, D., Healey, C., St. Amant, R.: Building Attack Scenarios through Integration of Complementary Alert Correlation Method. In: Network and Distributed System Security Symposium (2004)
14. OpenVAS. The Open Vulnerability Assessment System, `http://www.openvas.org`

15. Paxson, V.: Bro: a system for detecting network intruders in real-time. J. Comp. Net. 31, 2435–2463 (1999)
16. Pearl, J.: Probabilistic reasoning in intelligent systems: networks of plausible inference. Morgan Kaufmann Publishers Inc., San Francisco (1988)
17. Porras, P., Neumann, P.: EMERALD: Event monitoring enabling responses to anomalous live disturbances. In: 20th National Information Systems Security Conference, pp. 353–365 (1997)
18. Qin, X., Lee, W.: Statistical Causality Analysis of INFOSEC Alert Data. In: Vigna, G., Krügel, C., Jonsson, E. (eds.) RAID 2003. LNCS, vol. 2820, pp. 73–93. Springer, Heidelberg (2003)
19. Roesch, M.: Snort: Lightweight Intrusion Detection for Networks. In: 13th Conference on Systems Administration, pp. 229–238. USENIX (1999)
20. Snapp, S., et al.: DIDS (Distributed Intrusion Detection System) - Motivation, Architecture, and An Early Prototype. In: 14th National Computer Security Conferenc, pp. 167–176 (1991)
21. Spafford, E., Zamboni, D.: Intrusion detection using autonomous agents. J. Comp. Net. 34, 547–570 (2000)
22. Swets, J.: The Relative Operating Characteristic in Psychology. Science 182, 990–1000 (1973)
23. U.S. Department of Commerce. National Vulnerability Database, http://nvd.nist.gov/
24. U.S. Department of Health & Human Services: Health Information Privacy: Breaches Affecting 500 or More Individuals, http://www.hhs.gov/ocr/privacy/hipaa/administrative/ breachnotificationrule/postedbreaches.html
25. Valdes, A., Skinner, K.: Probabilistic Alert Correlation. In: Lee, W., Mé, L., Wespi, A. (eds.) RAID 2001. LNCS, vol. 2212, pp. 54–68. Springer, Heidelberg (2001)
26. Vigna, G., Kemmerer, R.: NetSTAT: A Network-based Intrusion Detection System. J. Comp. Sec. 7, 37–71 (1999)
27. Wing, J.: Scenario graphs applied to network security. In: Qian, Y., Tipper, D., Krishnamurthy, P., Joshi, J. (eds.) Information Assurance: Dependability and Security in Networked Systems. Morgan Kaufmann, San Francisco (2007)

Appendix: Algorithms

Algorithm 1. BN-Structure-Update $(message, A)$

Input: message $m = (number, srcIPaddr, destIPaddr, portnumber, action,$ $ruletype)$. This input represents an addition, change, or deletion of a firewall rule; Adjacency matrix representation of Bayesian network $BNet = (V, E)$ consists of a $|V|x|V|$ matrix $A = (a_{ij})$ such that $a_{ij} = 1$ if $(i, j) \in E$ otherwise $a_{ij} = 0$

Output: $V_a =$ set of nodes to add, $V_d =$ set of nodes to delete, $E_a =$ set of edges to add, $E_d =$ set of edges to delete

1: //case when a rule is added
2: **if** $ruletype =$ add **then**
3:    **if** $srcIPaddr : *$ in A **then**
4:       add all $(parents(srcIPaddr : *), srcIPaddr : *)$ to E_a
5:    **end if**
6:    **if** $destIPaddr : port$ in A **then**
7:       add all $(destIPaddr : port, children(destIPaddr : port))$ to E_a
8:    **else**
9:       add $E_a \leftarrow (srcIPaddr : *, destIPaddr : port)$
10:    **end if**
11: **end if**
12: // case when a rule is deleted
13: **if** $ruletype =$ delete **then**
14:    add $E_d \leftarrow (srcIPaddr : *, destIPaddr : port)$
15:    **if** $srcIPaddr : *$ in A **then**
16:       **if** $notparents(srcIPaddr : *)$ **then**
17:          add $V_d \leftarrow srcIPaddr : *$
18:       **else**
19:          add all $(parents(srcIPaddr : *), srcIPaddr : *)$ to E_d
20:       **end if**
21:    **end if**
22:    **if** $destIPaddr : port$ in A **then**
23:       **if** $notchildren(destIPaddr : port)$ **then**
24:          add $V_d \leftarrow destIPaddr : port$
25:       **else**
26:          add all $(destIPaddr : port, children(destIPaddr : port))$ to E_d
27:       **end if**
28:    **end if**
29: **end if**
30: // check if new edge creates a path to the end goal and if node creates a cycle
31: **for all** $address : port \in V \cup V_a$ **do**
32:    run DFS from $address : port$
33:    **if** $not(address : port \rightsquigarrow V_{CA})$ **then**
34:       remove $address : port$ from V_a
35:    **end if**
36:    add $backedges$ to E_d
37: **end for**
38: // convert address:port node to address:port:vulnerability node
39: **for all** $address : port \in V_a$ **do**
40:    **if** $vulnerability(address : port) \in NVD$ **then**
41:       update $address : port$ to $address : port : vulnerability(v_i)$ in V_a and E_a
42:    **else**
43:       remove $address : port$ from V_a
44:    **end if**
45: **end for**
46: **for all** $address : port \in V_d$ **do**
47:    search BNET and replace for corresponding $address : port : vulnerablity(v_i)$
48: **end for**
49: return V_a, V_d, E_a, E_d

Algorithm 2. BNet-CPT-Update (V_a, V_d, E_a, E_d)

Input: V_a = set of nodes to add, V_d = set of nodes to delete, E_a = set of edges to add, E_d = set of edges to delete
Output: S_{CPT} = set of CPTs to update
1: **for all** $v_i \in V_a$ **do**
2:      new $Prob(v_i) = CVSS(v_i)/10$
3:      add each $outedge(v_i) \in E_a$
4:      **for all** $children(v_i)$ **do**
5:          update CPT using $max(newProb(v_i) + \Delta, oldProb(v_i))$
6:      **end for**
7: **end for**
8: **for all** $(v_i, v_j) \in E_a$ **do**
9:      new $Prob(v_i) = CVSS(v_i)/10$
10:     add each $(v_i, v_j) \in E_a$
11:     **for all** $children(v_i)$ **do**
12:         update CPT using $max(newProb(v_i) + \Delta, oldProb(v_i))$
13:     **end for**
14: **end for**
15: **for all** $v_i \in V_d$ **do**
16:     new $Prob(v_i) = CVSS(v_i)/10$
17:     remove all $inedge(v_i)$ and $outedge(v_i)$
18:     **for all** $children(v_i)$ **do**
19:         update CPT using $max(newProb(v_i) + \Delta, oldProb(v_i))$
20:     **end for**
21: **end for**
22: **for all** $(v_i, v_j) \in E_d$ **do**
23:     new $Prob(v_i) = CVSS(v_i)/10$
24:     remove all $(v_i, v_j) \in E_d$
25:     **for all** v_j **do**
26:         update CPT using $max(newProb(v_i) + \Delta, oldProb(v_i))$
27:     **end for**
28: **end for**

Algorithm 3. Sensor-Reconfiguration $(E, Detectors_{existing})$

Input: $E = evidence$, represented by set of alerts received; $Detectors_{existing}$ = set of detectors currently enabled
Output: set of nodes to enable/disable. Nodes correspond to $< address, port, vulnerability >$ tuple so can be mapped to a detection sensor
1: compute $a = Prob(critical\ asset\ |E)$
2: **if** $a > threshold$ **then**
3:      Create set of candidate sensors close to E and $critical\ asset$
4:      Run $FPTAS(BN)$
5: **end if**
6: $Detectors_{disable} = |Detectors_{existing} - Detectors_{FPTAS}|$
7: **return** $Detectors_{FPTAS}, Detectors_{disable}$

K2C: Cryptographic Cloud Storage with Lazy Revocation and Anonymous Access [*]

Saman Zarandioon[1], Danfeng (Daphne) Yao[2], and Vinod Ganapathy[1]

[1] Department of Computer Science, Rutgers University,
Piscataway, NJ 08854
`samanz,vinodg@cs.rutgers.edu`
[2] Department of Computer Science, Virginia Tech,
Blacksburg, VA 24060
`danfeng@cs.vt.edu`

Abstract. Security and privacy concerns hinder the adoption of cloud storage and computing in sensitive environments. We present a user-centric privacy-preserving cryptographic access control protocol called *K2C* (Key To Cloud) that enables end-users to securely store, share, and manage their sensitive data in an untrusted cloud storage anonymously. *K2C* is scalable and supports the lazy revocation. It can be easily implemented on top of existing cloud services and APIs – we demonstrate its prototype based on Amazon S3 API.

K2C is realized through our new cryptographic key-updating scheme, referred to as *AB-HKU*. The main advantage of the *AB-HKU* scheme is that it supports efficient delegation and revocation of privileges for hierarchies without requiring complex cryptographic data structures. We analyze the security and performance of our access control protocol, and provide an open source implementation. Two cryptographic libraries, Hierarchical Identity-Based Encryption and Key-Policy Attribute-Based Encryption, developed in this project are useful beyond the specific cloud security problem studied.

Keywords: Cloud, Untrusted Storage, Access Control, Mashup, Security, Web.

1 Introduction

In industries such as health-care, insurance and financial organizations, which deal with sensitive data, the question of how to ensure data security and privacy in cloud environments is crucial [19,28] and even of legal concerns. For example, in the health-care industry the privacy and security of protected health information (PHI) need to be guaranteed according to HIPAA (Health Insurance Portability and Accountability Act)[1] requirements.

To take advantage of public clouds, data owners must upload their data to commercial cloud providers which are usually outside of their trusted domain. Therefore, they need a way to protect the confidentiality of their sensitive data from cloud providers. Moreover, in many cases, data owners also play the role of content provider for other parties. Following the naming convention used in [29,31], we refer to the parties that

---

[*] This work has been supported in part by DHS CCICADA and NSF grants CNS-0831186, CNS-0953638, CNS-0831268, CNS-0915394, CNS-0931992, and CNS-0952128.

M. Rajarajan et al. (Eds.): SecureComm 2011, LNICST 96, pp. 59–76, 2012.
© Institute for Computer Sciences, Social Informatics and Telecommunications Engineering 2012

consume data owner's data as *data consumers* or *end-users*. For example, a healthcare provider (data owner) may need to let a medical doctor (data consumer) access medical record of his patient. Even a data consumer may recursively play the role of data owner on its own. A medical doctor may want to share part of his patient's medical record with his secretary or nurse. Therefore, there is a need for a decentralized, scalable and flexible way to control access to cloud data without fully relying on the cloud providers.

In this paper we design and implement a scalable, user-centric, and privacy-preserving access control framework for untrusted cloud storage. Our framework protects the confidentiality and integrity of stored data as well as the privacy of end-users. It is also implementable on top of existing cloud services and APIs. (Design goals in more details are presented in Section 3.1) .

Traditional access control techniques are based on the assumption that the server is in the trusted domain of the data owner and therefore an omniscient reference monitor can be used to enforce access policies against authenticated users. However, in cloud-based services this assumption usually does not hold and therefore these solutions are not applicable. Cryptographic access control techniques designed for shared/untrusted file systems are potential candidates for clouds. In these approaches, the data stored on untrusted storage is encrypted and the corresponding decryption keys are disclosed only to the authorized users. Therefore, the confidentiality of data is protected against untrusted storage as well as unauthorized users.

However, the existing solutions [23,24,25] have scalability limitations that hinder their adoption in the cloud-storage settings. For example, until recently finding a cryptographic approach that simultaneously supports fine-granularity, scalability, and data confidentiality was an open problem. In [31], Shucheng Yu et al addressed this open problem by introducing a novel protocol which closes this gap. Another scalability issue, which we address in this paper, is related to access revocation. To eliminate re-encryptions required as part of access revocation, a technique called *lazy revocation* is widely adopted by existing cryptographic filesystems [12,26,27]. Lazy re-encryption delays required re-encryptions until the next write access [1]. In practice, lazy revocation eliminates extra re-encryptions as write access requires the client to re-encrypt the data anyway. Therefore, lazy revocation significantly improves the performance at the cost of slightly lowered security. To support lazy revocation, cryptographic access control protocols need to use a *key-updating scheme* which provides *key regression*. Key regression enables a user holding a new key to derive an older key.

Despite the recent developments on untrusted cloud storage, current key-updating schemes are still inadequate in terms of usability and efficiency. Specifically, existing key-updating schemes [12], especially for access hierarchies, are not scalable as they require complex data structures such as cryptographic trees [23] or linked lists [25] (section 2). These cryptographic data structures need to be updated after each revocation. Since most of the existing cloud storage services have very simple APIs which allow only storing and updating key-value pairs, implementation of existing key-updating schemes on top of existing commercial clouds is inefficient and unscalable.

---

[1] Lazy re-encryption, adopted by [31], delays re-encryptions till next (read or write) access. Since in regular workloads read accesses are significantly more than write accesses, the performance gain by lazy revocation is drastically more than that of lazy re-encryption.

We introduce a new key-updating scheme called *AB-HKU* which is scalable and also supports access hierarchies without requiring complex data structures. Our *AB-HKU* scheme enables us to support lazy revocation without requiring any change in the existing cloud APIs. We also introduce a new signature scheme for Key-Policy Attribute-Based Encryption [22] called *AB-SIGN*. We then apply these new cryptographic schemes to achieve scalable and anonymous information sharing in existing commercial cloud storage services. We provide an implementation of the proposed protocols and perform extensive experimental evaluation on cloud storage environments. Our technical contributions are summarized as follows:

- We introduce a new scalable and secure key-updating scheme for access hierarchies.
- We design and implement a scalable and privacy-preserving access control framework for existing untrusted cloud services. Our framework supports lazy revocation and access hierarchies.
- We present a signature scheme for Key-Policy Attribute-Based Encryption [22]. Using our signature scheme, users can prove that they own a key that its policy satisfies with a set of attributes, without revealing their identity or credentials.
- We provide the first open source implementation of cryptographic libraries for Hierarchical Identity-Based Encryption [6] and Key-Policy Attribute-Based Encryption [8] schemes. They are useful beyond the specific cloud storage problem studied.

Our paper is organized as follows. In Section 2 we introduce our new key-updating scheme and prove its security. In Section 3 we explain our access control protocol and discuss its features and security guarantees. Then, in Section 4 we discuss the implementation details of our cryptographic libraries and access control framework and evaluate its performance. In Section 5 we discuss the related work. Conclusions and future work are given in Section 6.

2   Key Updating Schemes for Access Hierarchies

In this section we present an efficient secure key-updating scheme that supports hierarchies. First, we provide a formal definition for secure key-updating schemes for hierarchical access. Then, we give a concrete construction of a key-updating scheme based on the use of attribute-based encryption scheme. Our solution supports both key revocation and hierarchical delegation of secret access keys. Our secure cloud storage framework for easy sharing and revocation, described in Section 3, is built based on those two key properties.

2.1   Background

Lazy revocation, first introduced in Cephues [20], is a technique which reduces the overhead of revocation at the price of slightly lowered security [23]. When a user's read access right on a file is revoked, lazy revocation allows to postpone re-encryption of that file until the next change. Lazy revocation has been adopted by all majors cryptographic file systems [12,26,27]. However, it also causes fragmentation of encryption keys in access hierarchies. Therefore, a user receiving the most recent key of an access hierarchy should be able to compute the older keys in order to decrypt files that are not yet re-encrypted by the most recent key, a capability that is referred to as *key regression* [21]. *Key-updating schemes* [12] are cryptographic schemes which support *key regression*.

Another key management issue that we need to address is related to access hierarchies. A user owning access key of a specific hierarchy class should be able to decrypt all objects belonging to that hierarchy as well as all lower hierarchies. Key management schemes for hierarchies generate keys that satisfy this requirement. Key-updating schemes enable users to move backward in time dimension and decrypt data objects encrypted by older keys, whereas key management schemes for hierarchies let users traverse space forward and decrypt data objects encrypted by keys which correspond to lower hierarchies. Access control protocols that are coupled with folder structure of file system ([23]) and need support for lazy revocation, require schemes that let the users simultaneously traverse time backward and space forward. For example, a user holding the most recent version of an access key for folder /a should be able to decrypt a file located at /a/b/c which is encrypted by an older key.

In [12], Backes et al formalize key-updating schemes. They also analyze and evaluate existing protocols that support key regression, but none of these protocols support hierarchies. In [15,16], Blanton et al formalize key management schemes for hierarchies, study existing protocols and introduce an efficient protocol for managing keys in hierarchies. But all of these schemes and protocols are static with respect to time, as they do not support key-updating/regression. *Therefore, none of these schemes are capable of handling key regression and hierarchies simultaneously.*

To our knowledge, the only work on key regression (lazy revocation) in hierarchies is [23], in which Grolimund et al introduced the concept of Cryptree, a tree constructed by symmetric and asymmetric cryptographic links. In Cryptree, a user holding a clearance key pointing to a folder can traverse a sequence of cryptographic links to derive access keys to all of its sub-folders and files. Moreover, the structure of the Cryptree lets the protocol delay re-encryption of data until the next update; thus supports lazy revocation. However, for the reasons that we explain in Section 5, the complexity of required data structure and its high performance cost for large volume of data makes its implementation on top of existing cloud services unscalable and inefficient.

2.2   Model and Definitions in HKU Scheme

In this section we present a formal definition for Hierarchical Key Updating (HKU) Schemes and its security. Let $T = (V, E, O)$ be a tree that represent a hierarchical access structure. More general access class hierarchies in which partially ordered access classes are represented by a DAG are studied in [16]. In our work, we are only interested in a special case where DAG is a tree. Each vertex v_i in $V = \{v_0, v_1, ..., v_n\}$ corresponds to an access class. v_0 is the root and an edge $e = (v_i, v_j) \in E$ implies that v_i class is the parent of class v_j.

For example, *top secret*, *secret*, *confidential*, and *unclassified* form a hierarchy of access classes, where the root *top secret* access class is the parent of the *secret* access class. In a more complex access tree, a parent access class may have two or more child access classes. For example, a root *Enterprise* access class may have *Marketing, Manufacturing*, and *R & D* as its child access classes. We sometimes refer to access class as class, and use terms *node, vertex* and *access class* interchangeably.

O is a set of sensitive data objects, each object o is associated with exactly one access class $\mathcal{V}(o)$. In this model, any subject that can assume access rights at class v_i is also permitted to access any object assigned to a vertex that is a descendant of v_i.

The following definitions introduce the concept of time into our model.

Definition 1. *The local time at vertex v_i is an integer t_i that increases (elapses) every time access rights of a subject to that class is revoked.*

Definition 2. *The global time associated with node v_i is a vector $\tau_i = (t_0, ..., t_j, .., t_i)$ where t_j is the local time of jth vertex on the path from root to vertex v_i on the access tree T.*

Two instances of global time are comparable only if the vertices that they belong to are identical or one of them is the ancestor of the other one; We say $\tau_i < \tau_j$ iff τ_i and τ_j are comparable and all common components of τ_i are less then the corresponding components in τ_j. Similarly, we define comparative operators $=, >, \leq$, and $\geq$.

Definition 3. *A Hierarchical Key-Updating (HKU) Scheme consists of a root user and end users. An end user may be a reader, a writer, or both. There are five polynomial time algorithms HKU = (Init, Derive, Encrypt, Decrypt, Update) defined as follows.*

- *Init($1^k, T$) is a randomized process run by the root user which takes as inputs a security parameter k and an access hierarchy tree T and then generates and publishes a set of public parameters Pub and outputs the root key $K_{v_0, \perp}$. It also initializes the state parameters including the value of local time at each vertex.*
- *Derive($T, K_{(v_i, \tau_i)}, v_j$) is a randomized process run by the root user, reader or writer which using the private key $K_{(v_i, \tau_i)}$ of v_i at time τ_i derives a private key of target class v_j at its current global time τ_j according to T. Derive computes the requested key only if v_i is an ancestor of v_j and $\tau_j = \tau_i$; otherwise, it outputs null ($\perp$).*
- *Revoke(T, v_i) run by the root user, reader or writer, increments the local time t_i of v_i by one, updates other state variables, and returns the updated tree T'.*
- *Encrypt(T, o_k) is a randomized algorithm called by writer that encrypts the data object o_k and returns the encrypted object C.*
- *Decrypt($K_{(v_i; \tau_i)}, C$) is a deterministic process run by reader which takes a key and an encrypted object as inputs and returns the corresponding object in plaintext. This function can decrypt C only if it belongs to the same or a descendant of the access class that the key belongs to and the time that o_k is encrypted at is less than or equal to τ_i; otherwise, it outputs null ($\perp$).*

Definition 3 is a generalization of the definition of key-updating schemes in [12] and the definition of key allocation schemes for hierarchies in [16]. If we assign to T a tree of depth 1 where its leaves are a set of groups (i.e, remove heirarchies), our definition reduces to a key-updating scheme defined in [12] and if we remove the update process and the time dimension, our scheme reduces to key allocation scheme for hierarchies defined in [16]. Intuitively, a hierarchical key-updating scheme is secure if all polynomial time adversaries have at most a negligible advantage to break the ciphertext encrypted with the current-time key of a target class, assuming that the adversaries do not belong to higher (ancestor) target classes in the hierarchy, or possess keys for earlier time periods. The formal definition of the security model of hierarchical key-updating schemes is provided in the technical report [32]. In this model the adversary chooses her target at the beginning of the game and then adaptively queries the scheme.

2.3 AB-HKU Scheme

In this section, we present a concrete construction for *HKU* scheme called *AB-HKU*. This scheme is based on the use of bilinear map and the difficulty of the Bilinear Diffie-Hellman problem. Our solution is realized on top of the Key-Policy Attribute-Based Encryption scheme (KP-ABE) [22] and invokes KP-ABE operations including SETUP_ABE, KEYGEN_ABE for private key generation, ENCRYPT_ABE for data encryption, and DECRYPT_ABE for decryption.

- *Init*$(1^k, T)$
    1. The root user runs the SETUP_ABE process with 1^k as security parameter to generate ABE public parameters and the master key MK. Publishes the ABE public parameters as Pub$_{abe}$.
    2. Calls KEYGEN_ABE procedure using MK as the secret key and "$L_0 = v_0$" as its policy. Outputs the result as the root key $(K(v_0, \perp) = $ KEYGEN_ABE(MK, $L_0 = v_0$)).
    3. To each vertex in T adds a local time variable t_i initialized to zero.
- *Derive*$(T, K(v_i; \tau_i), v_j)$ is run by a user (root user, reader, or writer) with secret key $K(v_i; \tau_i)$ at time τ_i to obtain the private key for node v_j.
    If class v_j is not a descendant of class v_i, or the time τ_i is not equal to current time τ_j associated with v_j, then return null. Otherwise, denote $(u_1, u_2, ..., u_n)$ as the list of vertices in the path from v_i to v_j; denote $(t_{u_1}, t_{u_2}, ..., t_{u_n}, t_{v_j})$ on T as the list of current local time values of intermediate vertices (including v_j); and let d represent the depth of v_i.
    The user performs the following operations.
    1. Construct the access tree $\mathcal{T}'$ which corresponds to the following Boolean expression: ($L_d.v$ attribute represents vertex in d-th level, $L_d.t$ represents its current local time and $\wedge$ is conjunction operator.)

$$\begin{aligned}
(L_{(d+1)}.v = u_1 \wedge ... \wedge L_{(d+n)}.v = u_n \\
\wedge L_{(d+n+1)}.v = v_j) \wedge \\
(L_{(d+1)}.t \leq \tau_{u_1} \wedge ... \wedge L_{(d+n)}.t \leq \tau_{u_n} \\
\wedge L_{(v_j)}.t \leq \tau_{v_j})
\end{aligned} \tag{1}$$

This Boolean expression restricts access to objects that belong to node v_j or its descendants and are created at current time or before.

2. Denote the access tree of $K_{(v_i,\tau_i)}$ by $\mathcal{T}$. Using the procedure for delegation of private key in [22], add the access tree $\mathcal{T}'$ to the root of $K(v_i, \tau_i)$, increase its threshold by one, update and calculate the private parameters associated to the root according the protocol. In implementation section we provide more details on this procedure.

3. Output the resulting access tree and parameters as a private key $K(v_j, \tau_j)$ for v_j.

- *Encrypt(T, o_k)*: Denote v_i as the access class that object o_k belongs to. $(v_i = \mathcal{V}(o_k))$. Denote $(v_0, u_1, u_2, ..., u_n, v_i)$ as v_i's path and $\tau_i = (t_{v_0}, t_{u_1}, t_{u_2}, ..., t_{u_n}, t_{v_i})$ as its current time according to T. A writer encrypts o_k as follows.

  1. Set the attribute set γ as follows. The attribute set is used as the public key for encryption.

$$\gamma = \{L_0.v = v_0, ..., L_n.v =_n, L_{n+1}.v = v_i,$$
$$L_0.t = t_{v_0}, ..., L_n.t = t_{u_n}, L_{n+1}.t = t_{v_i}\} \tag{2}$$

  2. Use ABE encryption procedure to encrypt o_k with attribute set γ and return the resulting encrypted object. $(C = \text{ENCRYPT\_ABE}(\text{Pub}_{\text{abe}}, \gamma, o_k))$.

- *Decrypt($K_{(v_i,\tau_i)}$, C)*. The reader decrypts as follows.

  1. If the encrypted object C does not belong to the same access class v_i as the key $K_{(v_i,\tau_i)}$ or one of its descendants, or the time when C is encrypted is later than the time τ_i when the key is generated, then return null ($\perp$).

  2. Otherwise, run ABE decryption procedure and return its result as output ($o_k = \text{DECRYPT\_ABE}(K_{(v_i,\tau_i)}, C)$).

- *Revoke* (T, v_i) is run by a user to increment the local time of v_i by one and then returns the updated tree T'.)

The correctness of our HKU scheme follows the correctness of the key policy ABE scheme [22] and is omitted here.

Theorem 1. *Assuming the hardness of the Decisional BDH, AB-HKU is a secure hierarchical key-updating scheme.*

Proof. Proof is presented in the technical report [32].

3   K2C Protocol

We describe the application of our hierarchical key-updating scheme in realizing a secure and scalable cloud access control protocol that supports easy sharing and revocation on hierarchically organized resources. We also analyze the security of our protocol.

3.1 Design Goals

Below we list the design goals of our *K2C* access control protocol:

- *Security:* Our protocol must protect the confidentiality and integrity of stored data against cloud providers and unauthorized end-users. Meaning that the stored data should be readable for authorized users only and any unauthorized change to the data should be prevented or detectable.
- *Privacy-preserving:* Access rights of a specific end-user as well as his usage trends should not be visible to other users or cloud service providers.
- *Efficiency and Scalability:* To avoid unjustified cost of re-encryption, the protocol should support lazy revocation. Also, the complexity of operations should be independent of number of data objects and users in the system. This ensures that the protocol will not affect the scalability of existing cloud services.
- *Flexibility:* The protocol should allow data owners and end-users to organize and manage their data in hierarchies similar to conventional file systems. Directories also represent access class hierarchies, users who have access to a directory/folder also assume the same access to all files and directories below that directory. Also, they should be able to grant/revoke part of their access rights to/from other users in a decentralized and scalable manner.
- *Simplicity and Extensibility:* Last but not the least, the protocol should be simple enough to be efficiently implementable on top of existing commercial cloud APIs.

We assume end-users have secure communication channels, limited computation power and storage required for authenticating each other and performing client-side key distribution in a synchronous or asynchronous manner.

Security Model. We assume that the root user, representing the data owner, is trusted. The cloud providers are honest-but-curious (aka semi-honest), who follow the protocol and faithfully execute the operations, but may actively attempt to gain additional knowledge, such as the sensitive data stored in the cloud. An adversary may attempt to perform unauthorized read or write access against the stored data, or attempt to learn the identities of readers or writers. For example, end-users may try to perform unauthorized read or write operations on stored data objects. To perform their attacks, unauthorized users may use their existing access keys for other objects and categories or cooperate with other unauthorized users and cloud providers to derive/guess credentials required to perform unauthorized access. Similarly, cloud providers may try to read or modify stored data or learn about the identities of the end uers. Cloud providers may collude with each other or some unauthorized end-users to break the security of *K2C*. We assume communication channels between participants are secure (e.g., SSL).

3.2 A Signature Scheme for KP-ABE

K2C requires a signature scheme to 1) enable the readers to verify the integrity of data and ensure that it is produced by an authorized writer, 2) enable the cloud service providers to validate incoming requests and block unauthorized accesses. However, the original paper which introduces KP-ABE [22] does not present any signature scheme. In this section we introduce an attribute-based signature scheme called *AB-SIGN* which enables the verifier to ensure that a signature is produced by a user whose access policy is satisfiable by a set of attributes without learning the signer's identity.

Definition 4. *AB-SIGN is a signature scheme for key-policy attribute-based encryption that its signing and verification methods are defined as follows. Let's say that the signer has a key K for policy P, and wants to sign message $\mathcal{M}$. The verifier needs to verify that the signature is generated by a signer whose key policy satisfies attribute set A.*

Signing: From K derive a key (K') which corresponds to a policy which is the concatenation of P and $(@S = \mathcal{M})$ ($@S$ is a reserved attribute for signatures). Send the derived key to the verifier as the signature.

Verification: Generate a random token and encrypt it using the attribute set $A \cup \{@S = \mathcal{M}\}$ and then decrypt the result using a key which is equal to the signature. If the result is equal to the original token the signature is valid (i.e. the attribute set A satisfies the signer's key policy.)

To prevent an attacker from using the signature method to derive a valid access key, we need to reserve the attribute '@S' for signature. The security of *AB-SIGN* scheme in terms of unforgeability follows immediately from the security of KP-ABE scheme.

3.3 Protocol Description

In this section we provide the details of *K2C* protocol. The protocol runs between the root user, end-user (reader or writer), and the cloud providers. The root user may be a system administrator in the data owner's organization, who can specify the access privileges of end-users. The end-users may further delegate their access privileges to other individuals for easy sharing. We achieve the revocation of privilege by encoding the validity period in the private keys of users and advancing time with respect to the target hierarchy or data object. Another advantage of our K2C framework for use in cloud storage is the support of anonymous access.

As illustrated in Figure 1, *K2C* requires three repositories: *Meta-data Directory*, *Data Store* and *Key-store*.

– **Meta-data Directory**: All meta-data associated with hierarchies and data objects are maintained in this repository. *K2C* requires two properties for each object: *Read Access Revision* (RAR) and *Write Access Revision* (WAR). These two properties play the role of local time in *AB-HKU* for read and write access, respectively. In order to compute Read/Write Access Revision Vectors (which correspond to global time instances in *K2C*), the cloud provider that hosts Meta-data Directory needs to provide an API for querying RAR and WAR values of multiple directories in a single request. All existing cloud-based databases such as Amazon SimpleDB [3], Microsoft Azure SQL [10], and Google's AppEngine [5] database (Bigtable [18])) satisfy this requirement and therefore qualify to host a *K2C* Meta-data Directory. For our experiments we use Amazon SimpleDB [3].

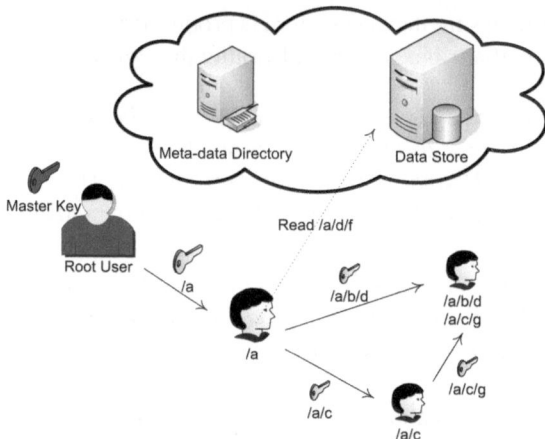

Fig. 1. Illustration of all major participants of *K2C*. Following *K2C* protocol, end-users can enforce access control on their own data without fully trusting or relying on the cloud providers. In *K2C*, keys are distributed and managed in a distributed fashion. Solid arrows represent access delegation.

- **Data Store**: This repository contains the actual content of each data object. Any cloud key-value based storage system such as Amazon S3 [2] can be used as *K2C* Data Store. In *K2C*, *keys* are hierarchical path name of data objects and *values* are the actual content of corresponding data objects. Cloud key-value storage providers are tuned for high throughput and low storage cost; these features make them a good candidate for *K2C* Data Store[2].
- **Key-store**: All read/write access keys of end-users are kept in their secure local repository called Key-store.

Initial Setup: To setup *K2C*, the root user needs to follow the steps listed below:

1. Sign up for cloud services required for hosting Meta-data Directory and Data Store.
2. Run $Init$ procedure according to *AB-HKU* scheme to generate public parameters and the master key.
3. Save the master key and public parameters in the root's Key-store.
4. Share the public parameters with the cloud service providers that support *K2C* request authorization.
5. Create an entry in Meta-date Directory that corresponds to the root directory. The WAR and RAR numbers of the root directory entry are initialized to zero.

Basic Operations: There are four basic operations in our protocol: write, read, delegate, and revoke. Each basic operation leads to calls to Meta-data directory and/or Data Store. We present the high-level steps involved in these operations below. Other operations such as create/remove/rename for directories and data objects can be defined

---

[2] Note that using key-value storage for Meta-data Directory is not efficient as computing WAR/RAR vector leads to multiple calls to the cloud storage system.

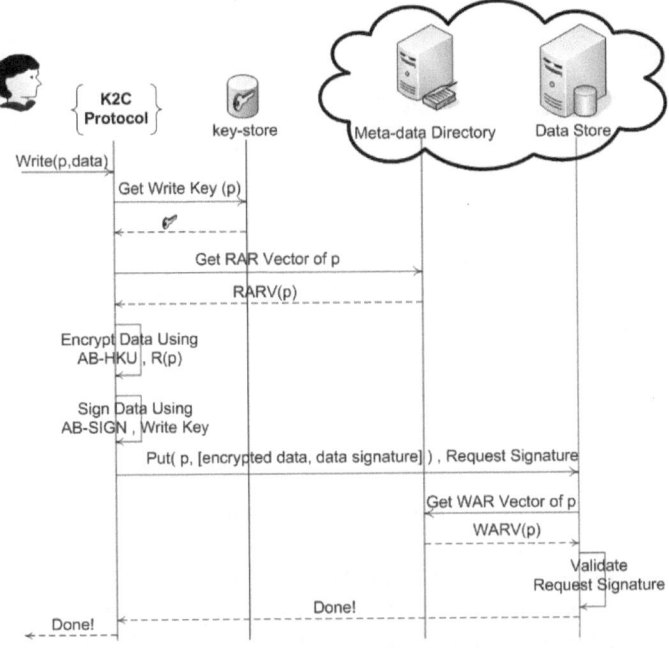

Fig. 2. Write operation

similarly. K2C requires that each request be signed by user's access key for the target object using our AB-SIGN operation. This requirement enables cloud providers which support K2C to block unauthorized request. We refer to this property as K2C request authorization.

- **Write**: To write into a specific data object, the end-user needs to perform the following steps (See also Figure 2).
  1. Retrieve the required write access key from the local Key-store.
  2. Query Meta-data directory to get read access revision (RAR) vector of the target object.
  3. Using *AB-HKU* scheme, encrypt the data by the retrieved RAR vector and its path.
  4. Using *AB-SIGN* scheme, sign the data by his write access key.
  5. Construct a key-value pair where the key is equal to the path of data object and the value is the encrypted data and corresponding signature. Store the pair in Data Store.
- **Read**: To read a specific data object stored using *K2C* protocol, the end-user needs to do the following (See also Figure 3). To ensure the data is produced by an authorized writer, the reader needs to validate the corresponding signature using *AB-SIGN* signature scheme. Then the reader can decrypt the data using its read access key and *AB-HKU* scheme.

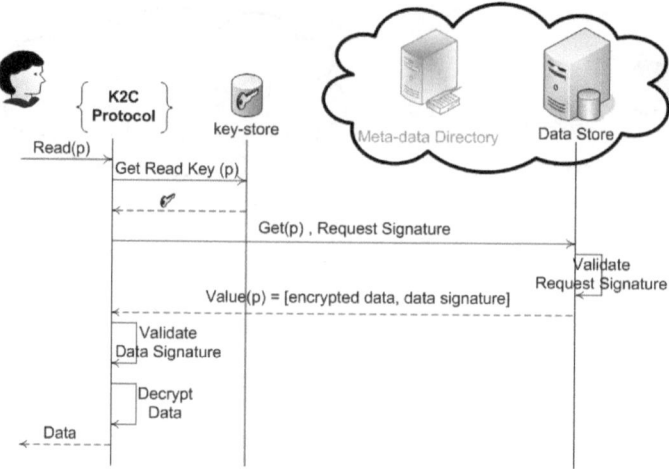

Fig. 3. Read Operation

1. Retrieve the required read access key from the local Key-store.
2. Using *AB-HKU* scheme and the read access key, decrypt the encrypted data.
3. Using *AB-SIGN* signature scheme, validate the signature to ensure that data is produced by a user who has the proper write access.
4. Return the decrypted data.

– **Delegation**: Delegation operation can be run by a user to authorize another user a subset of his access privileges. It requires three input parameters: the identity of the delegatee, the resource path, and access type (read/write). The steps required for this operation are listed below:
   1. From the local Key-store, get the access key that matches the target resource path and access type.
   2. Query Meta-date Directory to get the read/write access revision (RAR/WAR) vector of target resource.
   3. Run *Derive* operation, as defined in *AB-HKU* scheme, to generate the required access key.
   4. Send the generated access key to the delegatee through a secure communication channel.
– **Revocation**: To revoke a user's access on a specific directory or data object, the authorized user needs to make a signed request to the Meta-data Directory to increase the corresponding access revision number. To ensure the integrity of access revision numbers, these entries should be signed by the requester.

3.4   Security Analysis

In this section we state the security guarantees provided by *K2C* protocol. More detailed proofs and analysis can be found in our full version [32].

Confidentiality: Our solution ensures that only the users who have the most recent version of the access key of the data object or one of its ancestor directories can decrypt it. The confidentiality of stored data is protected under our protocol because writers always encrypt the data objects by their path and most recent read access revision (RAR) vector according to *AB-HKU* scheme. The cloud provider or other unauthorized users cannot gain any information that helps them to guess the access key of unauthorized data objects.

Collusion-resistance: of KP-ABE guarantees that unauthorized users and malicious cloud service providers cannot collude to guess access key to an unauthorized data object.

Integrity: The integrity of stored data is preserved. This guarantee is realized by requiring writers to sign the data by their write access key using *AB-SIGN* scheme. We require readers to validate writer's signature to ensure that it is produced by an authorized writer (i.e. a user with write access to that data object or on of its parent directories). Because meta-data entries stored in the Meta-data Directory are also required to be signed by the end-users, any unauthorized change in Meta-data Directory is detectable by the reader.

Anonymity: The end users are anonymous to each other and to the cloud providers. The signatures used in the our authorization do not contain any identify information. During the course of protocol, the end-users do not reveal any information about their credentials. *AB-SIGN* signatures bound to the data objects and requests, include only attributes related to the location and global time of those objects.

4   Implementation and Evaluation

We give our implementation of *K2C* framework and the required cryptographic libraries. We present our experimental results on accessing Amazon cloud storage [2,3] using *K2C* framework.

4.1   Key-Policy Attribute-Based Crypto Library

To support lazy-revocation and hierarchies, *K2C* uses our *AB-HKU* scheme that is based on Key-Policy Attribute-Based encryption scheme [22]. But, we were not able to find any implementation of KP-ABE [3]. Therefore, we develop a general KP-ABE cryptographic library and release it as an independent open source project [8]. In this section, we provide a short overview of this library.

Our library implements the KP-ABE scheme. We also fix a non-trivial limitation existed in the construction of [22]. KP-ABE is a *large universe construction*, meaning that it does not require the attributes to be fixed during the initialization process. However, the maximum number of attributes should be known in advance – a limitation which is not desirable in many practical cases. To overcome this limitation, we adopt the random oracle model [13] and replace function $T(X)$ (used in the *Setup* phase) by a secure hash function. This modification also improves the efficiency of the library. Therefore, our library does not put any limitation on the number of attributes that can be used in the system. We support numerical attributes and comparisons [14].

---

[3] The open source implementation of Ciphertext-Policy Attribute-Based Encryption (CP-ABE) [14] which was presented in the original paper [14] is available at [9]. However, CP-ABE is not applicable in our protocol.

In our library, policies are defined recursively and represented using an S-Expression (LISP-like expression) as follows:

$$
\begin{cases}
a = v & a \text{ is a symbolic attribute} \\
(c\ a\ v) & a \text{ is a numerical attribute \&} \\
& c \text{ is a comparative operator} \\
([\ t\ |\ \texttt{and}\ |\ \texttt{or}\ ]\ p_1\ p_2\ \ldots\ p_n) & \text{Composite policy}
\end{cases}
$$

The first and second types correspond to a simple policy for symbolic and numerical attributes, respectively. The third type represents policies which are composed of a set of policies (i. e. $p_1, p_2, \ldots, p_n$) proceeded by a threshold. Composed polices get satisfied only if the number of satisfied polices in that list is more than or equal to the specified threshold. The threshold can be one of the following three items: an integer threshold $t \in [1, n]$, $\texttt{and}$, or $\texttt{or}$. For example, ($\texttt{and role=manager (> age 18)}$) is a composite policy which gets satisfied only when the value of attribute $\texttt{role}$ is equal to $\texttt{manager}$ and the value of the numerical attribute $\texttt{age}$ is greater than 18. More implementation details are presented in the technical report [32].

4.2   K2C Framework and Performance Evaluation

In this section we present the high-level architecture of *K2C* framework. We also provide some experimental results that show its performance in an existing commercial cloud storage.

Simplicity and extendability are two major design goals of *K2C* framework. *K2C* framework is independent of any specific cloud provider. It has two simple interfaces which abstract away the details of the cloud providers: $\texttt{IDataStore}$ and $\texttt{IMetadataDirectory}$. A new cloud service provider can be supported easily by implementing these interfaces. Out of the box, *K2C* framework comes with a data store driver for Amazon S3 and a meta-data directory driver which uses Amazon SimpleDB. To make it easier for the developers to learn and use our framework, we expose its services through a set of APIs which are very similar to the Java APIs for accessing the file system. The source code is published at [7].

To evaluate the performance of *K2C* framework/protocol, we used the default drivers (Amazon S3 [2] data store driver and Amazon SimpleDB [3] meta-data directory driver) and ran our experiments on a machine with the following configuration: Intel Core 2 CPU, 2.53GHz, 2.90 GB RAM, Microsoft Windows XP 2002 SP2.

Figure 4 shows the time required for users in different access levels to perform read and write operations against the data objects of size 1KB belonging to directories in different hierarchical levels. Reported costs for each operation include computational time required for cryptographic operations (Symmetric and KP-ABE) as well as round trip time for HTTP calls to the cloud servers. As these diagrams show, users with higher level access (e.g. the root user) can perform read and write operations more efficiently, a property which is normally desirable[4]. Access time increases linearly as the access level of users decreases. Also this figure shows that access time for both read and write

---

[4] In Cyptree, high-level users have higher access time as they have to traverse longer cryptographic lists to find the access key (See Section 5).

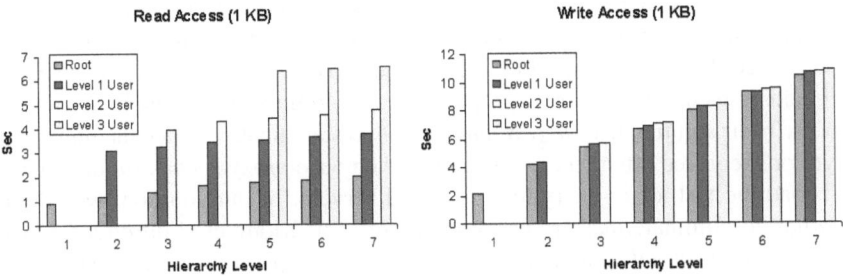

Fig. 4. Cost of read/write operation on objects which belong to different hierarchy levels performed by users with different access levels. The size of data objects are 1 KB.

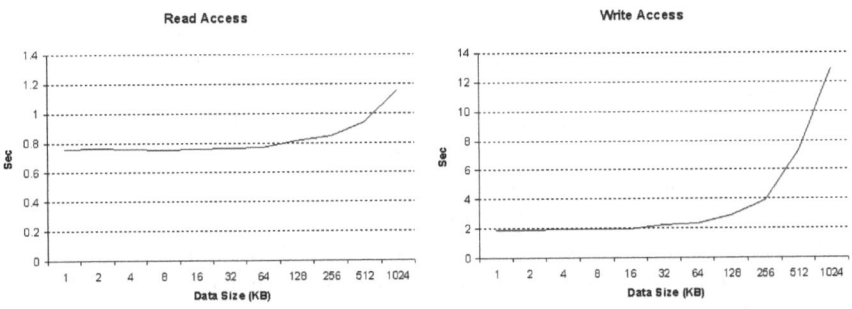

Fig. 5. Read/write access time for the root user as the size of data objects increase

operations increases linearly as the hierarchy level of object increases. The reason behind this linear increase is that encryption/deception time in KP-ABE is a function of number of attributes and the number of attributes associated with data objects linearly increases as their hierarchy level increases. Another observation is that write operations are more expensive than reads. This overload for write operations is partly due to an extra http call to Meta-data Directory required for retrieving the latest RAR vector.

Figure 5 shows the cost of read and write access as the size of data object increases. Since in our experiments the actual data is encrypted using the symmetric-key encryption scheme AES (Advanced Encryption Standard) and only the key is encrypted using KP-ABE, these statistics reflect the time required by AES to encrypt the data as the data size increases.

5   Related Work

There are two general key management approaches which are used in the existing cryptographic file systems: 1) classic access control list (e.g., [23,24]) requires maintaining a key list along with each file. This approach supports fine-granularity but is not scalable. 2) grouping files and assigning the same access key to each group (e.g., [25]). This approach is more scalable but provides coarse-grained access control. This trade-off makes these solutions unsuitable for clouds where we need a fine-grained and scalable access control mechanism. In [31], Shucheng Yu et al introduced a novel approach which addresses this trade-off by proposing a fine-grained and scalable access control protocol. Their solution uses *lazy re-encryption* to statistically reduce the number of re-encryptions required after access revocation. They use *proxy re-encryption* (PRE) [17] to off-load the task of re-encryption to cloud servers. In our solution, we adopt *lazy revocation* to eliminate these re-encryptions. In [30], Xiong et al introduce a protocol for securing end-to-end content distribution when delivery services are involved.

Lazy revocation was first introduced in Cephues [20] to eliminate re-encryption required for each revocation at the cost of slightly lowered security. Lazy revocation, which is widely being used in recent cryptographic file systems [25,26,27], requires a key-updating scheme to support key regression. Key-updating schemes are studied and formalized in [12]. In [23], Grolimund et al introduced Cryptree which can support access hierarchies and lazy revocation simultaneously. However, due to the explicit and physical dependency of these links, file system operations – especially revocations – require updating large number of these cryptographic links. For example, the revocation of write privilege requires updating $O(n)$ keys, where n is the number of data objects contained in that folder and its sub-folders. Therefore, revocation of write access for a folder containing many files is relatively slow as all the links that connect to the contained sub-folders and files need to be updated.

Moreover, in Cryptree, since key derivation requires traversing cryptographic links, key derivation time is a function of distance of data objects to the folder that the user has access to. Therefore, users with access to high-level folders (e.g. root user) have slower read access. For a specific user read access time depends on the location of the data object, but intuitively we expect the read access time to be independent of the location of the data object. Another limitation of this approach is that Cryptree does not support the delegation of administrative rights and assumes that granting and revoking access rights are done by a single administrator, an assumption which is usually unrealistic in the context of Cloud Storage, as we expect non-centralized administration of data. In this paper we introduced a scalable key updating scheme for hierarchies which addresses these shortcomings and enables us to build a cryptographic access control supporting lazy revocation.

6   Conclusion and Future Work

We presented a novel key-updating scheme that can be used to enhance the scalability and performance of cryptographic cloud storages by adopting lazy revocation. We also designed a new digital signature scheme that enables cloud providers to ensure that requests are submitted by authorized end-users, without learning their identities. Using our key-updating and signature scheme, we developed, implemented, and evaluated a scalable cryptographic access control protocol for hierarchically organized data. We plan to improve the efficiency of *K2C*, and to enhance our access control protocol by using proxy re-encryption [11] to off-load key distribution task to the cloud [31]. We are also investigating application of our key-updating scheme in existing cryptographic file systems and webtops [33].

Acknowledgments. The first author would like to thank the help of professors at Bahai Institute for Higher Education (BIHE [4]), Aidin Behroozi and Gurpreet Singh.

References

1. 104th United States Congress. Health Insurance Portability and Accountability Act of 1996 (HIPPA), http://aspe.hhs.gov/admnsimp/pl104191.html
2. Amazon S3, http://aws.amazon.com/s3/
3. Amazon SimpleDB, http://aws.amazon.com/simpledb/
4. BIHE, http://bihe.org/
5. Google App Engine, http://appengine.google.com
6. HIBE Crypto Library, https://sourceforge.net/projects/hibe
7. K2C Framework, https://sourceforge.net/projects/key2cloud/
8. KP-ABE Crypto Library, https://sourceforge.net/projects/kpabe.
9. Open Source Implementation of CP-ABE, http://acsc.cs.utexas.edu/cpabe/
10. SQL Data Services/Azure Services Platform, http://www.microsoft.com/azure/data.mspx
11. Ateniese, G., Fu, K., Green, M., Hohenberger, S.: Improved proxy re-encryption schemes with applications to secure distributed storage. In: NDSS, pp. 29–43 (2005)
12. Backes, M., Cachin, C., Oprea, A.: Secure Key-Updating for Lazy Revocation. In: Research Report RZ 3627, IBM Research, pp. 327–346. Springer, Heidelberg (2005)
13. Bellare, M., Rogaway, P.: Random oracles are practical: a paradigm for designing efficient protocols. In: Proceedings of the 1st ACM Conference on Computer and Communications Security, CCS 1993, pp. 62–73. ACM (1993)
14. Bethencourt, J., Sahai, A., Waters, B.: Ciphertext-policy attribute-based encryption. In: Proceedings of the 2007 IEEE Symposium on Security and Privacy, SP 2007, pp. 321–334. IEEE Computer Society, Washington, DC (2007)
15. Blanton, M.: Key Management in Hierarchical Access Control Systems, 2007. PhD Thesis, Purdue University (August 2007)
16. Blanton, M., Fazio, N., Frikken, K.B.: Dynamic and Efficient Key Management for Access Hierarchies. In: Proceedings of the ACM Conference on Computer and Communications Security (2005)
17. Blaze, M., Bleumer, G., Strauss, M.: Divertible Protocols and Atomic Proxy Cryptography. In: Nyberg, K. (ed.) EUROCRYPT 1998. LNCS, vol. 1403, pp. 127–144. Springer, Heidelberg (1998)
18. Chang, F., Dean, J., Ghemawat, S., Hsieh, W.C., Wallach, D.A., Burrows, M., Chandra, T., Fikes, A., Gruber, R.E.: Bigtable: A distributed storage system for structured data. In: Proceedings of the 7th Symposium on Operating Systems Design and Implementation, vol. 7, pp. 205–218 (2006)
19. Chow, R., Golle, P., Jakobsson, M., Shi, E., Staddon, J., Masuoka, R., Molina, J.: Controlling Data in the Cloud: Outsourcing Computation without Outsourcing Control. In: Proceedings of the 2009 ACM Workshop on Cloud Computing Security, CCSW 2009, pp. 85–90. ACM, New York (2009)
20. Fu, K.: Group sharing and random access in cryptographic storage file systems. Technical report, Masters thesis, MIT (1999)
21. Fu, K., Kamara, S., Kohno, T.: Key regression: Enabling efficient key distribution for secure distributed storage. In: NDSS (2006)
22. Goyal, V., Pandey, O., Sahai, A., Waters, B.: Attribute-based encryption for fine-grained access control of encrypted data. In: Proceedings of the 13th ACM Conference on Computer and Communications Security, CCS 2006, pp. 89–98. ACM, New York (2006)

23. Grolimund, D., Meisser, L., Schmid, S., Wattenhofer, R.: Cryptree: A folder tree structure for cryptographic file systems. In: Proceedings of the 25th IEEE Symposium on Reliable Distributed Systems, pp. 189–198. IEEE Computer Society, Washington, DC (2006)
24. Goh, E.J., Shacham, H., Modadugu, N., Boneh, D.: Sirius: Securing remote untrusted storage. In: NDSS, pp. 131–145 (2003)
25. Kallahalla, M., Riedel, E., Swaminathan, R., Wang, Q., Fu, K.: Plutus: Scalable secure file sharing on untrusted storage (2003)
26. Riedel, E., Kallahalla, M., Swaminathan, R.: A framework for evaluating storage system security. In: Proceedings of the 1st USENIX Conference on File and Storage Technologies, FAST 2002. USENIX Association, Berkeley (2002)
27. Stanton, P., Yurcik, W., Brumbaugh, L.: Protecting multimedia data in storage: A survey of techniques emphasizing encryption. In: IS and T/SPIE International Symposium Electronic Imaging/Storage and Retrieval Methods and Applications for Multimedia, pp. 18–29 (2005)
28. Takabi, H., Joshi, J.B.D., Ahn, G.-J.: Security and Privacy Challenges in Cloud Computing Environments. IEEE Security and Privacy 8, 24–31 (2010)
29. Wang, Q., Wang, C., Li, J., Ren, K., Lou, W.: Enabling Public Verifiability and Data Dynamics for Storage Security in Cloud Computing. In: Backes, M., Ning, P. (eds.) ESORICS 2009. LNCS, vol. 5789, pp. 355–370. Springer, Heidelberg (2009)
30. Xiong, H., Zhang, X., Zhu, W., Yao, D.: CloudSeal: End-to-End Content Protection in Cloud-Based Storage and Delivery Services. In: Rajarajan, M., et al. (eds.) SecureComm 2011. LNICST, vol. 96, pp. 483–492. Springer, Heidelberg (2012)
31. Yu, S., Wang, C., Ren, K., Lou, W.: Achieving secure, scalable, and fine-grained data access control in cloud computing. In: Proceedings of the 29th Conference on Information Communications, INFOCOM 2010, pp. 534–542. IEEE Computer Society Press, Piscataway (2010)
32. Zarandioon, S., Yao, D., Ganapathy, V.: K2C: Cryptographic Cloud Storage With Lazy Revocation and Anonymous Access. Technical report, Rutgers University. DCS-tr-688
33. Zarandioon, S.: Zaranux, http://zaranux.com/

Analyzing the Gold Star Scheme
in a Split Tor Network

Benedikt Westermann[1], Pern Hui Chia[1], and Dogan Kesdogan[1,2]

[1] Q2S*, NTNU, 7491 Trondheim, Norway
[2] Chair for IT Security, FB5, University of Siegen, 57068 Siegen, Germany
{westermann,chia,kesdogan}@q2s.ntnu.no

Abstract. Tor is an anonymity network and two challenges in Tor are (i) to overcome the scalability problems of Tor's current network information distribution scheme, and (ii) to motivate users to become operators of nodes. Several solutions have been proposed to address these challenges. We investigate the ramifications of combining two seemingly promising proposals, i.e., splitting the Tor network into several sub-networks (for better scalability), while using the Gold Star scheme (for motivating users to become node operators). Through simulation, we show that the sub-networks are likely to end up in a state of highly imbalanced division of size and bandwidth. This threatens the security and worsens the scalability problem of Tor. We identify the ratio of nodes given a gold star and the fact that a gold star is solely awarded based on a node's bandwidth, being highly skewed in practice, as two factors that contribute to an imbalanced split. We explore several potential mitigating strategies and discuss their strengths and shortcomings.

Keywords: Tor, Incentive Schemes, Gold Star, Split Network.

1 Introduction

Anonymous communication deals with concealing who is communicating with whom and is an important building block for privacy enhancing technologies. One of the most popular anonymity networks is Tor [6]. Here, two actively discussed problems are the issue of *scalability* and the challenge *to motivate more users to become operators of Tor relays*. The scalability problem of Tor stems from its current information distribution scheme, which provides every user the full view of the entire network. In [12], the authors predicted that more bandwidth will be used to distribute the network information than for the actual anonymization process in the near future. Various approaches have been proposed to improve the scalability of Tor, most often by limiting the number of relays a user needs to know (i.e., a partial view of the network). Danezis and Syverson investigated the impact of providing users only a partial view of the

---

* "Centre for Quantifiable Quality of Service in Communication Systems (Q2S), Centre of Excellence", appointed by the Research Council of Norway, is funded by the research council, NTNU and UNINETT. http://www.q2s.ntnu.no

M. Rajarajan et al. (Eds.): SecureComm 2011, LNICST 96, pp. 77–95, 2012.
© Institute for Computer Sciences, Social Informatics and Telecommunications Engineering 2012

anonymity network in [5] and highlighted the problems in doing so. They stated that *"[..] while scaling such systems [as Tor assuming a partial view] can maintain adequate anonymity in the face of route fingerprinting, splitting the network outright may be more desirable"* [5, p.156]

Interestingly, even though splitting the network seems to be a clean and straight-forward solution, there can be ramifications, such as an unintended competition among the sub-networks, e.g., for high bandwidth nodes, or, as pointed out in [5], a malicious entity trying to influence the split to take advantage of it.

In this paper, we analyze the consequences of splitting the Tor network in the presence of the gold star (GS) incentive scheme, proposed in [17] to motivate more users to operate a relay. We show that splitting the Tor network while using the GS scheme in individual sub-networks is likely to give a highly imbalanced division of relays and total available bandwidth. This threatens not only the users' anonymity, but also worsens the scalability of Tor. We identify the ratio of relays given a GS and the bandwidth based GS policy as two factors contributing to an imbalanced split. We explore several potential mitigation strategies and put forward some recommendations.

Our paper is structured as follows. In Section 2, we first detail on prior works related to the scalability issue and incentives schemes in Tor. Next, we describe our simulation design, scenarios, assumptions and dataset used in Section 3, and present the simulation results in Section 4 together with a series of robustness checks to our simulation model. We explore and discuss about several potential mitigation strategies in Section 5 before concluding.

2   Background and Related Work

The general idea of Tor is to hide a user within a large set of users, the so-called anonymity set [19], which is the set of all participants. Tor routes the data of an *Tor client* through several *Tor relays* using layered encryption, and thereby hides the relation between the Tor client and the data receiver from other parties, such as the ISPs. In Tor, a path through the network is known as a *circuit*. The relays used in a circuit are selected automatically by an Tor client. Each circuit is capable of anonymizing multiple TCP connections simultaneously.

2.1   Distributing the Network Information

Being an overlay network, Tor needs to inform the Tor client about different relays in the network. Tor does this currently by providing a global view of the network to all Tor clients. The global view, stored in a data structure called *consensus document*, is generated and distributed as follows. Each relay is required to upload a detailed description of itself (referred to as *descriptor*) to all known *directory authorities*. Every hour, the directory authorities agree on the state of the network based on the descriptors they received and publish an hourly consensus document. The document (together with new or updated descriptors of different relays) is downloaded by the *directory mirrors*. Each Tor client in turn downloads the consensus document and new (or updated) descriptors of individual relays from a directory mirror, or directly from a directory authority if no known directory mirror is available. This causes a quadratic distribution cost which does not scale [26,12].

To overcome the problem, several proposals have been made, mainly with the use of a *distributed hash table* (DHT). An early proposal, which use a DHT to distribute the network information, was presented in the first version of Tarzan [9]. In [8], however, the authors substituted the DHT with a gossip algorithm, which provides a full view of the network to the client applications. The importance of having a full view in Tarzan was later shown by Danezis and Clayton [4]. Nevertheless, having a full view, Tarzan faces a similar scalability issue as Tor. Another approach to distribute information using a DHT was proposed with Salsa [16] by Nambiar and Wright. But it was shown by Mittal and Borisov in [13] that Salsa is not as secure as claimed due to the information leakage introduced by redundant lookups in the DHT. Westermann et al. used a DHT based on Kademlia [11] to lookup nodes in an anonymity network [26]. Contrary to Salsa, only the servers are present in the DHT. The users use a small set of servers which they trust to perform node lookups. Additionally, the results are not immediately used to build a connection. This prevents timing correlations. In [18], Panchenko et al. showed that this approach does not provide enough security in big networks as an attacker can significantly bias the node selection.

A more recent approach, named Torsk, was proposed by McLachlan et al. [12]. Torsk is also based on a Kademlia DHT, but it uses additional certificates to verify that a node is the legitimate holder of a key based on the technique proposed in [22]. Furthermore, each node maintains a signed list of lookup buddies. A circuit is built by iteratively asking the buddies of the last node in a circuit to lookup a random ID. The lookup returns a list of verifiable nodes within the close neighborhood of the queried ID. The client then randomly selects a node from the list to extend the circuit. Another DHT based approach called Nisan was proposed by Panchenko et al. [18]. Nisan relies on a chord ring [21] for node lookups. Contrary to a classic chord lookup, nodes are asked for their finger table instead of the closest nodes to a given value. By doing so, a single node cannot learn about the ID a client is looking for. To provide more protection against active attacks by colluding nodes (e.g., by only returning a finger table with colluding malicious nodes), the authors proposed a bound check of the finger table. Yet, Wang et al. [23] showed that both Torsk and Nisan leak information, allowing the attacker to reduce the users' anonymity.

Mittal et al. [14] proposed ShadowWalker – another scheme to address the scalability problem in anonymity networks. The nodes for a circuit are selected by performing a random walk through the network. Only the last nodes in the random walk are used for circuit building so to improve performance and anonymity. Route capture attacks and manipulation to select malicious nodes are countered with the so-called *shadows*, which maintain and attest the finger table of shadowed nodes independently. But Schuchard et al. showed in [20] that ShadowWalker is not as secure as claimed. Yet, they noted that the impact of their attacks can be mitigated by modifying the parameters and the consensus requirements slightly.

In [15] Mittal et al. move towards a new direction to overcome the scalability problem with the use of *private information retrieval* (PIR) techniques. The authors suggested two different solutions based on PIR. The first solution utilizes the current directory servers for the distribution of the network information. Here, Tor clients download a small block of descriptors of (untrusted non-authoritative) directory server. Due to PIR, the directory server does not learn which block has been downloaded by the Tor client. The second solution relies on the client's *guards*, being the trusted entry points to the Tor network, to fetch the descriptors for a circuit. Both solutions have in common that a Tor client only downloads a small set of descriptors. Thereby, PIR ensures that only the Tor client knows which descriptor has been downloaded. The authors show that both solutions scale sufficiently to overcome the Tor's scalability problem.

An analytical study was performed by Danezis and Syverson in [5] extending from the work in [4]. The authors analyzed the impact of providing only a partial view to individual users in anonymity networks. Their analysis shows that with a partial view scheme, the anonymity set can be drastically reduced by just knowing two nodes in a path. They also discussed the potentials of splitting the Tor network (favoring it over a partial view scheme) but noted the importance of a secure split to avoid exploitation by malicious parties. Related to the problem of a secure split is a work of Dingledine and Syverson [7] where the authors worked on the problem of building reliable mix cascade networks. They suggested assigning mixes to cascades in an unpredictable but verifiable fashion based on random inputs from all mixes. This helps among others to prevent malicious mixes from targeting a specific cascade.

Considering the various approaches proposed, their complexity and the potential attacks, it seems that splitting the Tor network into several sub-networks is an interesting option to investigate more throughly.

2.2   Motivating the Users to become Relay Operators

Another challenge in anonymity networks is to motivate enough users to become a node operator. In Tor, relays are mostly operated by volunteers who hardly get any benefits for doing so. Despite a growing number of users, it is difficult to find enough independent relays and operators in Tor [17]. Several incentive schemes have been proposed to address this challenge and can be generally categorized into two classes: *incentive-by-money* and *incentive-by-performance*.

Incentive-by-money schemes include JonDonym's payment system [24,25], PAR [2] and XPay [3]. We omitted the details of these schemes here, instead, we focus on incentive-by-performance schemes.

Two incentive-by-performance schemes are the *gold star scheme* [17] and Braids [10]. The basic idea of the *gold star scheme* is to prioritize the traffic of useful relays by assigning a gold star (GS) to a fraction of the most useful relays. In [17] the authors assigned a GS to the 87.5% best performing relays. A relay having a GS (abbreviated as GS-relay) is entitled to extend a prioritized circuit to another GS-relay. If the whole circuit consists of only GS-relays, the traffic is prioritized resulting in an improved performance, e.g., lower response times or a higher bandwidth. One disadvantage of the GS scheme is that a prioritized circuit can only be initiated by a GS-relay. Therefore, the anonymity set for such a circuit is limited to the GS-relays only.

On the other hand, Braids proposes to distinguish the traffic in three different classes: *low latency, high throughput,* and *normal* [10]. In order to route the traffic in the low latency or the high throughput class, a client has to provide a relay with *tickets.* Tickets are distributed freely to all users, but the number is limited and bound to an expiry date. By enabling the relays to convert the collected tickets into new tickets, operators can route more of their own traffic in the low-latency or high-throughput class than the non-contributing Tor clients. Contrary to the GS scheme, prioritized traffic does not necessarily stem from a relay.

3   Simulation Design

In this paper, we investigate by simulations the outcomes of combining the two viable strategies: *splitting the Tor network* and *the GS scheme.* We detail on the simulation design, assumptions and dataset used in this section.

3.1   Basic Assumptions and Simulation Scenarios

We focus on the scenario where the Tor network is split into two sub-networks[1] and the relays are incentivized to contribute through separate GS schemes in individual sub-networks. Our simulation builds on two basic assumptions:

A1: GS Policy Is Publicly Known. Ngan et al. [17] suggested that the GSs are assigned (by directory authorities) in the consensus document. As the consensus document is publicly available, we assume that operators can learn about the details of the GS policy and can determine if he can obtain a relay in a particular sub-network reliably.

A2: GS Performance Is Estimable from Average Bandwidth of GS-Relays. We estimated the GS performance within a sub-network using the *average observed bandwidth* of GS-relays. We checked the suitability of the *average observed bandwidth,* obtainable from the descriptors of the relays, as a performance estimator by measuring its correlation with the *average download time*[2]. We obtained a Pearson correlation factor of -0.71 (with 280 data points corresponding to the daily average values from 03/27 to 12/31/2010), indicating a strong (negative) linear correlation.

We model the operators to decide if they should switch to another sub-network with the following decision rules:

---

[1] We present the results of splitting into more than 2 sub-networks in the appendix.
[2] Average download time measures the time Tor clients need to download files of different sizes and is available on the *Tor Metrics Portal* [1].

- If a relay has no GS and can become a GS-relay in a particular sub-network, it switches to this sub-network. We basically assume that the GS is an incentive for relays and they are eager to get one.
- If a relay can get a GS in multiple sub-networks, it chooses the sub-network that provides the best service according to its objective.

We distinguish between two different objectives: *performance-maximizing* and *anonymity-maximizing*. If a GS-relay is performance-maximizing, it chooses to join the sub-network that provides the best performance, i.e., one with the highest *average observed bandwidth*. If a GS-relay is anonymity-maximizing, it chooses to join the sub-network having the most GS-relays. It is important to note that a prioritized circuit can only be initiated by a GS-relay and therefore the sender anonymity set is limited only to the set of GS-relays.

We augment the simulation dynamics with two additional decision factors, which serve to test the robustness of our basic model. First, we consider the case where a relay switches to another sub-network only if the expected improvement, according to his objective is higher than a threshold γ. If the improvement is lower than γ, the relay will switch only with a probability equals to the ratio of improvement over γ. This models a cost for switching (e.g., extra configuration effort) and the reluctance to switch if the expected improvement in performance (or anonymity set) is small. We consider also a random decision factor, where an relay will with probability θ ignore the usual decision rules and switch to a random network (even when it cannot retrieve a GS there). This models the bounded rationality of the operators, especially in the event that the GS scheme is hard to predict in practice.

3.2 Simulation Details

Network State. To mimic the real life scenario, we ran our simulation based on Tor's actual network state as given in the consensus document published on 09/30/2010 at 6pm (GMT). The document describes 2136 active relays, each of which comes with a different *observed bandwidth*.

Figure 1(a) depicts the CDF of the observed bandwidth, that appears in the descriptors of the individual relays. The distribution is skewed: the top 17% of the relays actually provide 83% of the *total available bandwidth*.

To evaluate the effect of the skewed bandwidth distribution, we repeated most of our simulation scenarios assuming a uniform bandwidth distribution (see Figure 1). The uniform distribution was constructed such that the mean equals the *average observed bandwidth*. The number of relays equals 2136. We investigated also the effect of network size by scaling up the original network to have 10 times as many relays.

Simulation Flow. In the initialization phase of each simulation run, the relays are first ranked according to their *observed bandwidth* and assigned into different sub-networks in turns. Let $\{r_1, \ldots, r_N\}$ be the set of relays ranked in decreasing *observed bandwidth*, and let $\{S_1, \ldots, S_M\}$ be the set of sub-networks available,

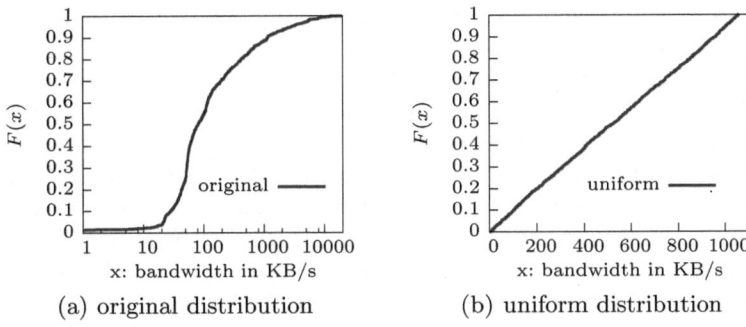

(a) original distribution   (b) uniform distribution

Fig. 1. Bandwidth distributions among the relays

repeat
    pick a random relay
    determine the sub-network relay is currently in, say S_k
    determine if relay will switch to another sub-network
    if relay switches **then**
        $stable_k \leftarrow 0$
    else
        $stable_k \leftarrow stable_k + 1$
    end if
    $round \leftarrow round + 1$
until $\forall j \in [1, M]$ $stable_j > STABILITY$, or $round > ROUND_{max}$

Fig. 2. The Simulation Flow

then the set of relays assigned to sub-network S_j is given by $\{r_i \mid i \mod M = j\}$. This gives us a near-balanced division of relays and bandwidth in the initial state. The simulation then proceeds as shown in Figure 2. Note that a relay is randomly selected per round (independent of the sub-networks) to check if it will switch to another sub-network given different objectives, θ and γ values. We repeated each simulation run 30 times to obtain the average outcomes.

4 Results

We present the findings from our simulation in the following.

4.1 Basic Simulation Model

We started our simulation by assuming that the operators are performance-maximizing, i.e., they will switch to another sub-network given a better performance, no matter the extent of improvement of the new sub-network. This simplistic scenario enables us to gauge the basic consequences of splitting the

Tor network while having the GS scheme in place. We investigate the robustness of our findings with several extended models in Section 4.3.

We first simulated the case where GS ratio (GSR) equals 87.5% as proposed in [17]. We assumed here that the Tor network is split into two sub-networks (A and B). Figure 3(a) depicts the size and total available bandwidth of sub-network A during the course of a simulation run. The simulation began with a near-balanced state in terms of size and total available bandwidth. In the first few thousand rounds, however, sub-network A started to attract more and more relays from sub-network B. This initial rush caused sub-network A to be highly dominating both in terms of size and bandwidth, and could lead to a collapse of sub-network B. At one point, sub-network B consisted of 875 relays (40%) and had mere 3% share of the total available bandwidth (35.45 MB/s). There is a considerable risk that sub-network B will stop to be functional. With a low share of bandwidth, it can only support few Tor clients. This in turn causes a small anonymity set and may drive away the Tor users.

The initial rush was followed by a reversal in switching direction. By inspecting the simulation log, we found that this was led by the low-to-medium bandwidth relays which began to realize that they could obtain a GS in the sub-network B. The migration of the low-to-medium bandwidth relays caused the medium bandwidth relays to gradually lose their GS (due to a fixed GSR), and thus followed suit. The simulation ended with the stability count being reached, i.e., when no relay switched for consecutive 2400 rounds. In the final state, sub-network A consisted of only 558 relays (26.12%) but had a large share of the total available bandwidth, 972.1 MB/s (87.9%). Meanwhile, sub-network B consisted of 1578 relays (73.88%) but was providing only 133.81 MB/s (12.1%). The distribution of relays and total available bandwidth was highly uneven. The distribution of exit bandwidth, considering the flags of the relays in the consensus document, corresponds roughly to the case of total available bandwidth. Sub-network A and B have 87.3% and 12.7% of the total exit bandwidth respectively. The situation is slightly different with respect to guard relays. Both sub-networks have a similar share of the total number of guard relays (sub-network A has a 51% share), but the division of guard bandwidth is again highly uneven (the guards in sub-network A actually provide 93.0% of the total guard bandwidth).

Figure 3(b) presents the CDFs of relays' bandwidth in separate sub-networks in the final state. Most notable is the absence of the medium bandwidth relays represented by the horizontal line in the mid area of the CDF of sub-network A.

Such an imbalanced split increases the risk of a user being deanonymized: the higher the fraction of bandwidth some relays provide, the higher is their probability of being selected as end-points of a circuit. Tor cannot provide any anonymity against an operator who holds the first and the last position in a circuit. An attacker with some high-bandwidth relays could enter sub-network B, where they can provide a higher fraction of bandwidth more easily, to attempt deanonymizing the users.

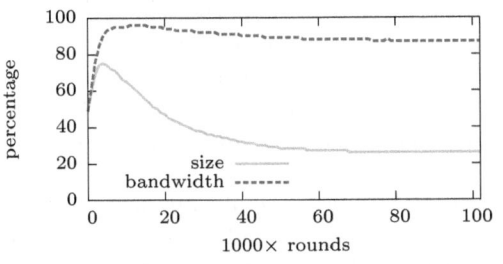 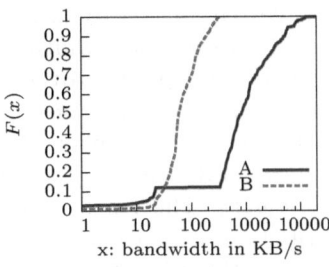

(a) Share of relays and total available bandwidth by sub-network A in the course of simulation

(b) Final bandwidth CDFs

Fig. 3. Simulating the basic model with GSR=87.5% as originally proposed in [17]

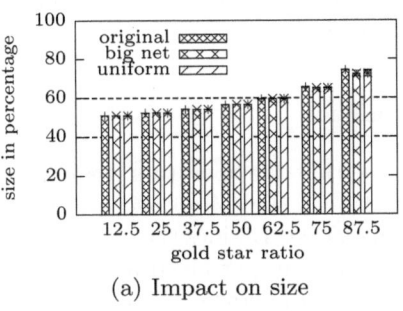 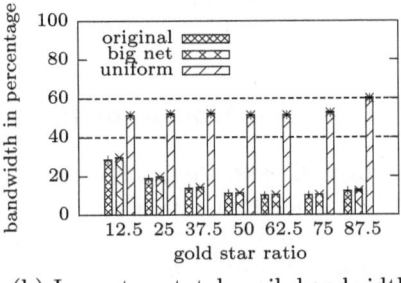

(a) Impact on size   (b) Impact on total avail. bandwidth

Fig. 4. The effect of GSR, number of relays and bandwidth distribution on the share of size and total available bandwidth. Both figures plot the state of the larger sub-network.

Independent of the risk to anonymity, the scalability problem is also worsened in sub-network B which has many relays, but on average provide only 87 KB/s (with a maximum of 330 KB/s).

4.2   Probing the Reasons of an Uneven Split

Different GSRs. We then simulated the basic model with other GSRs, ranging from 12.5% to 87.5%, to investigate the effect of GSR on the distribution of relays and total available bandwidth among the sub-networks. We found that the GSR has a significant effect on network size, as shown in Figure 4(a). The higher the GSR, the more uneven is the size of the sub-networks. This is mainly by the fact that the number of relays, which have a potential incentive to switch to a better sub-network, increases with a higher GSR.

Increased Number of Relays. We re-ran the simulation with a scaled-up Tor network with 10 times as many relays (following the same bandwidth distribution) as in the consensus document. As shown in the Figure 4, an increased number of relays has little or no effect to the simulation outcomes.

Bandwidth Distribution. Next, we considered a hypothetical set of relays where the relays' bandwidth follows a uniform distribution. The benefits of this can be seen in Figure 4. Although the sub-networks become more uneven in terms of size as the GSR increases, we see that with a uniform bandwidth distribution, the share of the total available bandwidth between the 2 sub-networks maintains at an even ratio (around 50%-60%).

Summary. The results show that the GSR has a significant impact on the distribution of relays among the sub-networks. The bandwidth distribution of relays, on the other hand, affects the share of the total available bandwidth.

As relays are rewarded solely based on the bandwidth they and their peers provide, we observed that the high-bandwidth relays prefer to gather in the same sub-network. Given the bandwidth distribution is skewed, the self-sorting of the high-bandwidth relays causes a highly uneven division of total available bandwidth. Interestingly also, an increased number of relays has only minimal effect on the distribution of relays and bandwidth.

4.3   Extended Models for Robustness Check

Switching Costs. Previously, we have assumed that the operators would prefer to switch to another sub-network whenever there is a slight improvement in performance. In practice, however, switching incurs a cost. Besides the configuration effort, other reasons, such as a good prior experience, perceived anonymity or trust for some specific set of relays, could render an operator to prefer remaining in his sub-network. To model such inertia, we simulated a threshold based switching strategy. Consider a threshold of γ, an operator switches to another sub-network (with certainty) if the improvement in performance δ is greater than or equal to γ. Meanwhile, if the improvement δ is smaller γ, we model that the operator to switch with a probability of δ/γ.

We plot the simulation outcomes in Figure 5. Comparing to the outcomes when GSR = 50% and 87.5% in Figure 4, we observe that the effect of having a switching threshold is minimal. A switching cost delays but does not deter the operators from switching for self-interests. Our previous findings on the effect of different GSR and bandwidth distribution also remain applicable. The counter-intuitive 'delays-but-does-not-deter' result could be partly due to the fact that we have used a probabilistic decision rule when the expected improvement in performance is below a specific threshold instead of a clear-cut switch or not decision. Yet, we note that the eventual switching of relays is also attributed to the dynamics of performance improvement. Specifically, the switching of a GS-relay (with either a deterministic or probabilistic decision) increases the bandwidth of the destined sub-network, while decreasing the performance of the origin sub-network. This increases the expected improvement in performance for relays remaining in the origin sub-network, inducing them to switch in turn.

Bounded Rationality / Complex GS Policy. Our basic model assumes that all operators could estimate the policy for GS-relays and determine if they can retrieve a GS in individual sub-networks. In practice, it may not be trivial

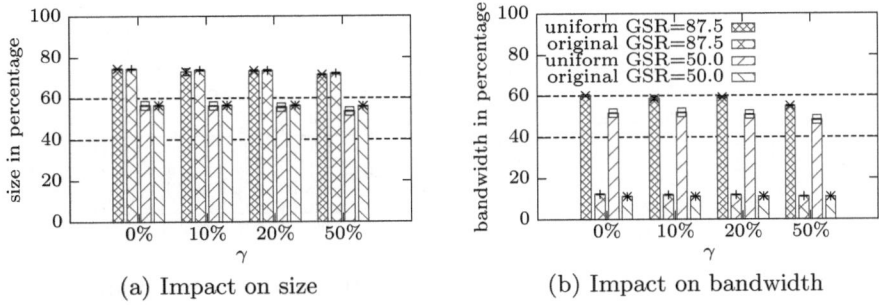

(a) Impact on size   (b) Impact on bandwidth

Fig. 5. The effect of threshold based switching on the distribution of relays and total available bandwidth. Both figures plot the state of the larger sub-network.

for all operators to do so (bounded rationality). A complex (or hidden) GS policy could also cause many operators to be uninformed (or indifferent) of the 'better' sub-network. We investigated whether the problem of uneven split remains considering a random decision factor where an operator ignores the usual decision rules and joins a sub-network randomly with probability θ.

Figure 6 shows that when a majority of relays decide randomly, the division becomes more even. A more even split is expected when θ is large, since the bigger sub-network has a higher chance to lose a relay due to the uniform selection of a relay from all relays. Additionally, if many relays decide randomly, the effect of self-sorting among the relays (high-bandwidth relays prefer to be with high-bandwidth peers) reduces. The relays in a sub-network become more heterogeneous in terms of bandwidth and this contributes to an even division of total available bandwidth.

While the problem of uneven split seems to disappear as θ increases, we note that this may not be desirable. A large θ in Tor translates into a GS policy that is hidden or too complex to be predictable by the relay operators. This in turn takes away the incentives for becoming a relay operator, defeating the purpose of implementing the GS scheme in the first place.

Anonymity-Maximizing Operators. So far we have assumed that Tor's users are performance-maximizing, not considering the anonymity that a sub-network provides. We regard this as a reasonable assumption for relays not having a GS (denoted as NGS-relays) and the Tor clients as long as the network split is not too extreme[3]. With several hundreds of thousands of users in today's Tor network, the anonymity set can be seen as sufficiently large. The situation is, however, different for GS-relays as their anonymity set is limited to only the GS-relays. When an attacker observes a prioritized circuit, he knows that one of the GS-relays in a particular sub-network has initiated it, thus it can be more critical for the GS-relays to consider the anonymity factor. We study the effect of the anonymity-maximizing objective of GS-relays here. For NGS-relays,

---

[3] When the distribution of relays is extremely uneven, there is a good chance that the smaller sub-network collapses as users see their anonymity threatened.

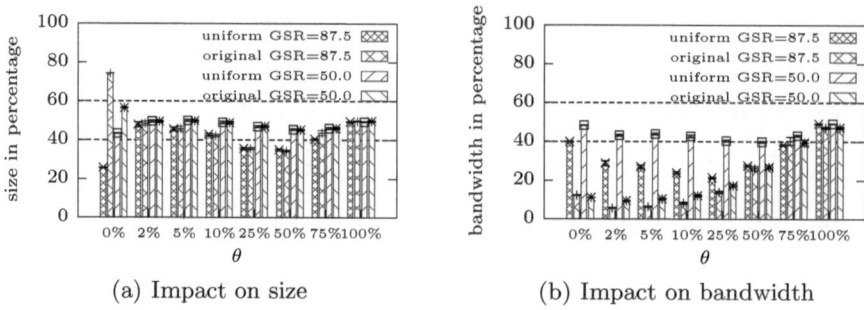

(a) Impact on size   (b) Impact on bandwidth

Fig. 6. The effect of random switching decision on the distribution of relays and total available bandwidth. The figures show the sub-network with the lower share of total available bandwidth.

the objective remains to switch to a sub-network where it can retrieve a GS. Meanwhile, we model the GS-relays to prefer switching to a sub-network with the largest anonymity set (i.e., one with the highest number of GS-relays). If two sub-networks have the same number of GS-relays, a GS-relay chooses the sub-network with the best performance.

Figure 7 depicts that the course of a simulation run where relays are all anonymity-maximizing. The simulation started with an initial rush to one sub-network (hereafter, sub-network A). The over-crowding in sub-network A caused the low-to-medium bandwidth GS-relays to lose their GS and to switch in the reverse direction in order to (re)gain a GS. The migration of low-to-medium bandwidth relays in turn caused the medium bandwidth relays to also gradually lose their GS (due to a fixed GSR) and thus followed suit. Thus far, this has been similar to the case as shown in Figure 3(a). The situation, however, started to differ when the migration of medium bandwidth relays caused sub-network B to have a higher number of GS-relays (i.e., a larger anonymity set). This made even the high bandwidth GS-relays to prefer joining sub-network B as it would provide better anonymity. However, the arrival of high bandwidth GS-relays in sub-network B caused the low-to-medium bandwidth GS-relays to start losing their GS again, and decided to return to sub-network A. The same process then repeated itself, which explains the oscillating nature of the share of total relays and total available bandwidth.

Notice that at the extreme cases during the course of simulation, the smaller sub-network has only a <5% share of total available bandwidth and can thus be expected to support only few Tor clients. This hints on a small anonymity set and may drive away the remaining Tor relays and Tor clients. Thus, the risk of a failed network split remains even with anonymity-maximizing relays.

Additionally, we simulated the case where there is a mix of performance- and anonymity-maximizing relays. Let the fraction of performance-maximizing relays be ϕ. With GSR = 87.5% and $\phi = 40\%$, we observed that the oscillating nature of the share of size and total available bandwidth disappeared. Meanwhile, when GSR = 50% and $\phi = 40\%$, we observed the oscillating outcomes occasionally

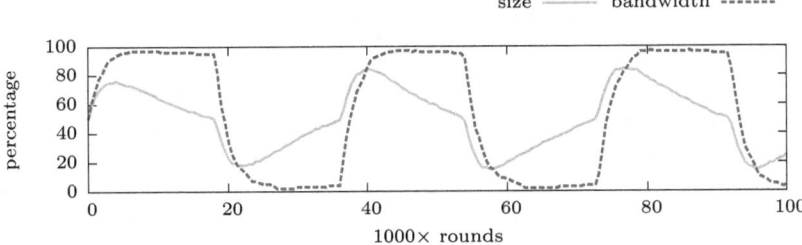

Fig. 7. The course of simulation where all relays are anonymity-maximizing

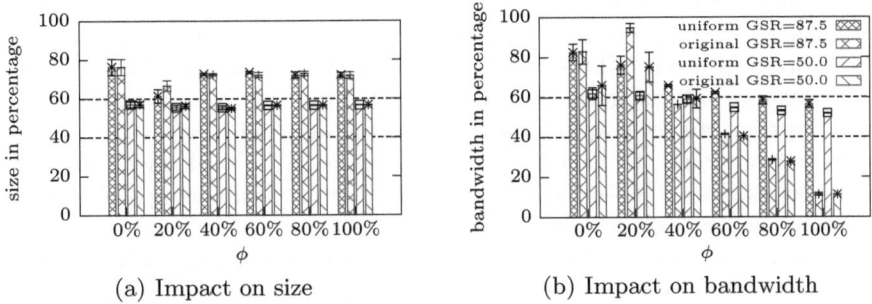

(a) Impact on size   (b) Impact on bandwidth

Fig. 8. The effect of having a mixture of performance- and anonymity-maximizing relays. ϕ denotes the fraction of performance-maximizing relays. With a low ϕ, the confidence intervals are big, indicating an oscillating nature of the simulation outcomes.

but not when $\phi \geq 60\%$. This holds for both simulation cases using the original bandwidth distribution and a uniform distribution. Most interestingly, when $40 \leq \phi \leq 60\%$, high bandwidth relays no longer gather in a single sub-network

5 Discussion

A highly imbalanced split of the Tor network has multiple serious implications. First, the scalability problem, being the original motivation for a split of the Tor network, can become worse in a sub-network that is large in size but has a low share of total available bandwidth. Secondly, the higher the fraction of bandwidth some relays provide, the higher is their chance of being the endpoints of a Tor circuit. In the event of an uneven split, the risk of a user being deanonymized is higher within the low-bandwidth sub-network as malicious relays can enter the sub-network, where they can provide a higher fraction of bandwidth more easily.

Global GS Scheme. An interesting question is whether an uneven split will still occur considering a global GS scheme, rather than separate GS schemes in individual sub-networks. In the worst case of an uneven split, all GS-relays will gather in one sub-network with the number of relays equals:

$$\lceil N \cdot GSR \rceil + \left\lfloor \frac{(1 - GSR) \cdot N}{M} \right\rfloor,$$

where N is the number of all relays and M is the number of sub-networks.

We observed the worst case outcome in our simulation as soon as one sub-network provides better performance and anonymity than the others, independent of the GSR, the relays' objective, and the underlying bandwidth distribution. A global GS scheme therefore does not help the situation.

Fixed Sub-network. We investigated the possibility of having a fraction of relays that do not switch from their assigned sub-networks (either by encouraging them to be cooperative or prohibiting them to switch at all). Figure 9 shows the outcomes where a fraction σ of Tor relays, selected in descending order of bandwidth or randomly from all Tor relays, do not switch from their assigned sub-networks. An even (40-60%) share of relays and total available bandwidth is only possible by fixing the sub-networks for the top 10% high-bandwidth relays. However, an even split is not achievable even with $\sigma = 50\%$ if relays are selected randomly to have fixed sub-networks. An alternative is to assign all Tor operators into sub-networks (randomly) while disallowing self-switching completely (see the case when $\sigma = 100r$).

Fixing the sub-networks for some percentage of the top high-bandwidth Tor relays, or (randomly) assigning all relays to sub-networks, are hence two possible solutions. These require an effective way to force a relay to stay in one sub-network. Additionally, assigning the ORs to one sub-network can raise multiple concerns. For instance, whether the Tor operators would be discouraged if their volunteering effort is 'punished' by not being able to choose their preferred sub-network freely. There may also be questions, e.g., on fairness, transparency, and security, if the assignment of sub-networks by a centralized authority is not completely random. A way to address such questions can be found in [7], where the authors proposed assigning mixes to cascades in a unpredictable but verifiable fashion. However, their approach deals mainly with mixes and cascades. Porting it to the problem of a fair and secure assignment of relays to sub-networks may warrant further investigation.

An Appropriate GSR. We note that a GSR of 87.5% is not optimal in a split network setup as it leads to an uneven share of relays. Our simulations indicate that a GSR of roughly $\frac{1}{M}$, where M equals the number of sub-networks, seems to be a good choice to avoid a uneven split.[4] A lower GSR trades off the risk of an uneven split with a reduced anonymity set for the GS-relays.

Alternative GS Criteria. On top of an even distribution of relays, it is also necessary to have the relays distributed across the sub-networks independently from the bandwidth they provide, to ensure an even distribution of total available bandwidth. This is, however, not possible if a GS is granted based on the relay's

---

[4] Simulation outcomes for $M = 3$ and 4 sub-networks are included in the appendix. For example, in Figure 11, one can see that for $M = 4$, the largest sub-network gets about 30% close to the $\frac{1}{4}$ share of relays.

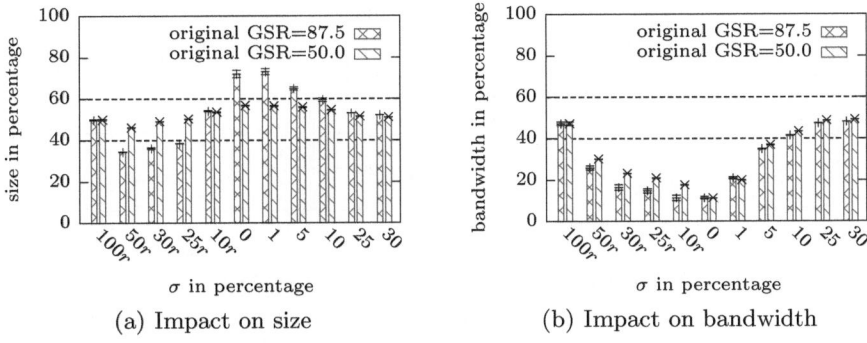

(a) Impact on size   (b) Impact on bandwidth

Fig. 9. The effect of having a fraction σ of relays, selected randomly (denoted with a suffix 'r') or in descending order of bandwidth, that do not switch from their assigned sub-network

bandwidth only, as high-bandwidth relays will gather in the same sub-network. Given that the GS scheme is introduced to motivate more users to become relay operators, using other requirements for awarding the GS will work. By having several independent requirements, relays in a sub-network can be more heterogeneous with respect to bandwidth.

To test our intuition, we re-ran the simulations using the basic model and assigned a value x_i to every relay r_i, which was sampled from a random variable X. In practice, x_i could be computed from any suitable properties, including the uptime, location or reputation of a relay. We then measured the *usefulness* of a relay by combining the relay's x_i value and its bandwidth, as shown in Equation 1, to decide if a relay r_i is eligible for a GS. In Equation 1, p_i denotes the fraction of relays providing less bandwidth as the relay r_i, and f_i is the fraction of relays that have a lower x value than r_i.

$$u_i = \omega \cdot p_i + (1 - \omega) \cdot f_i \qquad (1)$$

The weights for p_i and f_i was controlled using the variable ω. We used two different distributions of X: (i) a uniform distribution, $X \sim \mathcal{U}(0, N)$, and (ii) a heavy-tailed distribution constructed based on the skewed bandwidth distribution in Figure 1(a). We note that the x_i value of each relay is drawn independently of its bandwidth.

Figure 10 shows that when ω is low (i.e., when the usefulness of a relay depends largely on the random value x_i), the division of total available bandwidth is even. The sub-networks also have a similar share of guards and exit relays, both in terms of number and bandwidth (not depicted). Meanwhile, as ω increases (i.e., as the usefulness depends more on the bandwidth of a Tor relay), the problem of an uneven distribution of bandwidth arises. This highlights that the GS criteria should not be solely dependent on the bandwidth, which is highly skewed in practice. We suggest to assign a GS based on the usefulness of a relay which can be a combination of multiple bandwidth-independent properties to ensure a good mix of relays with heterogeneous bandwidth in each sub-network.

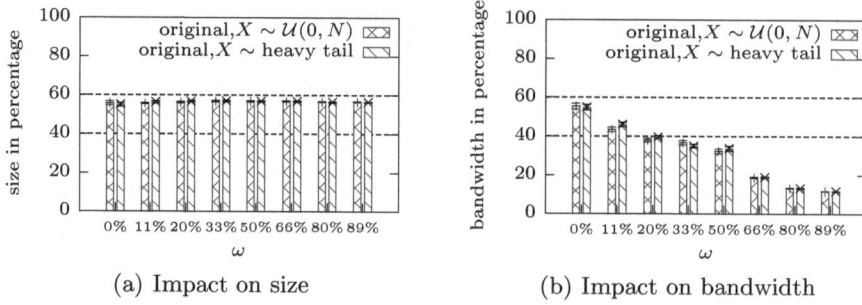

Fig. 10. Varying the dependence of the GS criteria (i.e., the usefulness measure) on the relay's bandwidth. With $\omega = 0\%$, the GS criteria is independent of the relay's bandwidth, while with $\omega = 100\%$ it depends on the relay's bandwidth only.

It is important to note that the relays with the highest u-values will again gather in one particular sub-network. However, the impact can be minimized with a careful selection of factors contributing to the usefulness, u measure. For example, by having a usefulness measure that is distributed uniformly among the relays, we can expect the effect of the self-sorting to be less prominent. This has been exemplified by the hypothetical scenario where there is a uniform distribution of bandwidth among the relays, as shown in Figure 4.

6   Conclusions

In this paper, we have analyzed the consequences of applying the Gold Star (GS) scheme in a split Tor network. While our simulation model has abstracted away the Tor clients, guards and exit relays for simplicity purposes, we have refrained ourselves from unrealistic assumptions besides taking into consideration a large number of different simulation scenarios.

We showed that applying the GS scheme directly in the setting of a split Tor network can lead to extremely imbalanced sub-networks both in terms of the share of relays and total available bandwidth. This threatens the users' anonymity and worsens the scalability problem of Tor.

In search of mitigation measures, we identified the ratio of relays given a GS (GSR) to be the main factor of an uneven distribution of relays across the sub-networks. By decreasing the GSR to $\frac{1}{M}$, where M is the number of sub-networks, we observed a near-balanced division of relays into the sub-networks.

Meanwhile, fixing the sub-network of some percentage of high-bandwidth relays or assigning all relays randomly, may represent two solutions for an even distribution of bandwidth across the sub-networks. Yet, while technically viable, fixing the sub-network of some or all relays can raise multiple concerns, including on respecting the contributors' choice and fairness.

A self-regulating solution can be achieved by changing how Tor would assign a GS to a relay. We showed that the imbalanced division of total available bandwidth can be addressed by designing a different set of GS criteria, for example by measuring the *usefulness* of a relay based on multiple bandwidth-independent properties, to improve the heterogeneity of relays in individual sub-networks.

References

1. Tor metric portal, `http://metrics.torproject.org` (last visited February 2011)
2. Androulaki, E., Raykova, M., Srivatsan, S., Stavrou, A., Bellovin, S.M.: PAR: Payment for Anonymous Routing. In: Borisov, N., Goldberg, I. (eds.) PETS 2008. LNCS, vol. 5134, pp. 219–236. Springer, Heidelberg (2008)
3. Chen, Y., Sion, R., Carbunar, B.: XPay: practical anonymous payments for tor routing and other networked services. In: WPES, pp. 41–50. ACM (2009)
4. Danezis, G., Clayton, R.: Route fingerprinting in anonymous communications. In: Peer-to-Peer Computing, pp. 69–72. IEEE Computer Society (2006)
5. Danezis, G., Syverson, P.F.: Bridging and Fingerprinting: Epistemic Attacks on Route Selection. In: Borisov, N., Goldberg, I. (eds.) PETS 2008. LNCS, vol. 5134, pp. 151–166. Springer, Heidelberg (2008)
6. Dingledine, R., Mathewson, N., Syverson, P.F.: Tor: The second-generation onion router. In: USENIX Security, pp. 303–320. USENIX (2004)
7. Dingledine, R., Syverson, P.F.: Reliable MIX Cascade Networks Through Reputation. In: Blaze, M. (ed.) FC 2002. LNCS, vol. 2357, pp. 253–268. Springer, Heidelberg (2003)
8. Freedman, M.J., Morris, R.: Tarzan: a peer-to-peer anonymizing network layer. In: CCS, pp. 193–206. ACM (2002)
9. Freedman, M.J., Sit, E., Cates, J., Morris, R.: Introducing Tarzan, a Peer-to-Peer Anonymizing Network Layer. In: Druschel, P., Kaashoek, M.F., Rowstron, A. (eds.) IPTPS 2002. LNCS, vol. 2429, pp. 121–129. Springer, Heidelberg (2002)
10. Jansen, R., Hopper, N., Kim, Y.: Recruiting new tor relays with braids. In: CCS, pp. 319–328. ACM (2010)
11. Maymounkov, P., Mazières, D.: Kademlia: A Peer-to-Peer Information System Based on the XOR Metric. In: Druschel, P., Kaashoek, M.F., Rowstron, A. (eds.) IPTPS 2002. LNCS, vol. 2429, pp. 53–65. Springer, Heidelberg (2002)
12. McLachlan, J., Tran, A., Hopper, N., Kim, Y.: Scalable onion routing with torsk. In: CCS, pp. 590–599. ACM (2009)
13. Mittal, P., Borisov, N.: Information leaks in structured peer-to-peer anonymous communication systems. In: CCS, pp. 267–278. ACM (2008)
14. Mittal, P., Borisov, N.: Shadowwwalker: peer-to-peer anonymous communication using redundant structured topologies. In: CCS, pp. 161–172. ACM (2009)
15. Mittal, P., Olumofin, F., Troncoso, C., Borisov, N., Goldberg, I.: PIR-Tor: Scalable anonymous communication using private information retrieval. In: USENIX Security (2011)
16. Nambiar, A., Wright, M.: Salsa: a structured approach to large-scale anonymity. In: CCS, pp. 17–26. ACM (2006)
17. "Johnny" Ngan, T.-W., Dingledine, R., Wallach, D.S.: Building Incentives into Tor. In: Sion, R. (ed.) FC 2010. LNCS, vol. 6052, pp. 238–256. Springer, Heidelberg (2010)
18. Panchenko, A., Richter, S., Rache, A.: Nisan: network information service for anonymization networks. In: CCS, pp. 141–150. ACM (2009)
19. Pfitzmann, A., Hansen, M.: Anonymity, unlinkability, undetectability, unobservability, pseudonymity, and identity management - a consolidated proposal for terminology, v0.31 (February 2008)

20. Schuchard, M., Dean, A.W., Heorhiadi, V., Hopper, N., Kim, Y.: Balancing the shadows. In: WPES, pp. 1–10. ACM (2010)
21. Stoica, I., Morris, R., Karger, D.R., Kaashoek, M.F., Balakrishnan, H.: Chord: A scalable peer-to-peer lookup service for internet applications. In: SIGCOMM, pp. 149–160 (2001)
22. Wang, P., Hopper, N., Osipkov, I., Kim, Y.: Myrmic: Secure and robust DHT Routing. Technical report, Uni. of Minnesota DTC Research (2006)
23. Wang, Q., Mittal, P., Borisov, N.: In search of an anonymous and secure lookup: attacks on structured peer-to-peer anonymous communication systems. In: CCS, pp. 308–318. ACM (2010)
24. Wendolsky, R.: A volume-based accounting system for fixed-route mix cascade systems. In: Bamberger Beiträge zur Wirtschaftsinformatik und angewandten Informatik, pp. 26–33 (February 2008)
25. Westermann, B.: Security Analysis of AN.ON's Payment Scheme. In: Jøsang, A., Maseng, T., Knapskog, S.J. (eds.) NordSec 2009. LNCS, vol. 5838, pp. 255–270. Springer, Heidelberg (2009)
26. Westermann, B., Panchenko, A., Pimenidis, L.: A Kademlia-Based Node Lookup System for Anonymization Networks. In: Park, J.H., Chen, H.-H., Atiquzzaman, M., Lee, C., Kim, T.-H., Yeo, S.-S. (eds.) ISA 2009. LNCS, vol. 5576, pp. 179–189. Springer, Heidelberg (2009)

Appendix

We simulated also the scenarios where the network is split into $M = 3$ or 4 sub-networks. As shown in Figure 11, the distribution of relays and total available bandwidth is uneven, same as the case when $M = 2$.

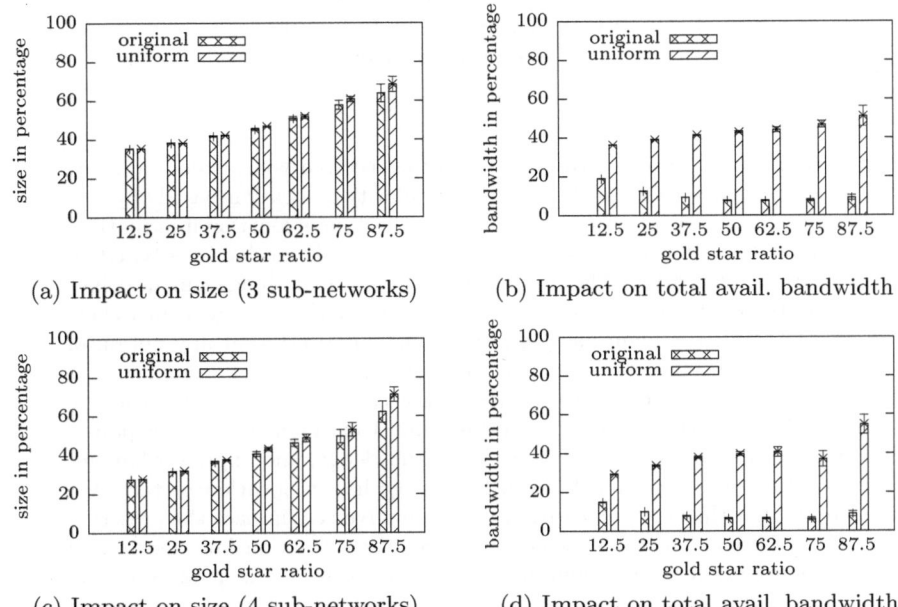

(a) Impact on size (3 sub-networks)   (b) Impact on total avail. bandwidth

(c) Impact on size (4 sub-networks)   (d) Impact on total avail. bandwidth

Fig. 11. The figures show the impact of different GSRs in the basic model when the network is split into $M > 2$ sub-networks. Figures a) and b) show the outcomes of a split into 3 sub-networks, while figures c) and d) show the outcomes of a split into 4 sub-networks. All of them plot the state of the largest sub-network at the end of simulation. The distribution of relays and total available bandwidth is uneven. The largest sub-network attracted more than $\frac{1}{M}$ of the relays but got less than 20% of the total available bandwidth.

Location Privacy and Attacker Knowledge: Who Are We Fighting against?

Rinku Dewri

Department of Computer Science
University of Denver, Denver CO 80208, USA
rdewri@cs.du.edu

Abstract. Location privacy research has received wide attention in the past few years owing to the growing popularity of location-based applications, and the skepticism thereof on the collection of location information. A large section of this research is directed towards mechanisms based on location obfuscation. The primary motivation for this engagement comes from the relatively well researched area of database privacy. Researchers in this sibling domain have indicated multiple times that any notion of privacy is incomplete without explicit statements on the capabilities of an attacker. The question we ask in the context of location privacy is whether the attacker we are fighting against exists or not. In this paper, we provide a classification of attacker knowledge, and explore what implication does a certain form of knowledge has on location privacy. We argue that the use of cloaking regions can adversely impact the preservation of privacy in the presence of approximate location knowledge, and demonstrate how perturbation based mechanisms can instead be useful.

Keywords: location privacy, differential privacy, query approximations.

1 Introduction

Location based applications are geared towards providing services tailored to the current location of a user. These applications utilize the positioning capabilities of a mobile device to determine the current location of the user, and customize query results to include neighboring points of interests. Wide acceptance of personal digital assistants and the advancements in wireless cellular technology have opened up countless possibilities in this business paradigm. Potential applications can range from proximity based notifications to tracking business resources. A wireless carrier typically serves as a channel between the user and the location content provider.

The potential advantages of location based applications is not difficult to realize. However, location knowledge is often perceived as personal information. It remains an open question whether the benefits of these applications can outweigh the underlying privacy risks. A similar question has been around for more than a decade in the field of database privacy. Databases hosting our personal information can serve as data mining grounds to facilitate research studies in

M. Rajarajan et al. (Eds.): SecureComm 2011, LNICST 96, pp. 96–115, 2012.
© Institute for Computer Sciences, Social Informatics and Telecommunications Engineering 2012

a variety of fields. At the same time, the same information in the hands of an adversary can have alarming ramifications. Database privacy preservation is an ongoing effort to design data sharing methods in order to prevent such an adversary from making personal inferences using the shared data [1,2,3]. Drawing inspiration from these efforts, location based applications have been argued to be usable without communicating precise location data to the content provider.

Location obfuscation is a widely researched technique to achieve location privacy. The fundamental idea here is to process location based queries relative to a sufficiently larger region, also known as a cloaking region, compared to one where a user can be uniquely located. For instance, a cloaking region can be generated to include k users, including the one making the query [4]. Multiple algorithms have been proposed to generate such a k-anonymous cloaking region [5,6]. However, as demonstrated in the case of database privacy, obfuscating private data without understanding the capabilities of the attacker can be unproductive [7,8,9]. A privacy preserving mechanism is not better or worse than another. It is the adversary who is weaker or stronger. The background knowledge of the attacker must be known (or at least assumed) in order to demonstrate the privacy guarantees of a mechanism.

We begin this work by identifying the primary form of attacker knowledge targeted by most location obfuscation techniques. This knowledge relates to an attacker being able to determine the true locations of a certain subset of users. Using a case by case analysis of what this attacker can achieve from queries made using true locations and queries made using cloaking regions, we argue that "location privacy" is a misused term in this context. The use of cloaking regions is motivated by the need to introduce ambiguity in correlating a user to a query. However, if an attacker does not have any location knowledge of the users, then location information in a query cannot be used to map it to a user. The attacker must posses at least approximate location knowledge about the user, to be able to exploit the location information in a query. On the other hand, if true location knowledge is present, then there is no location privacy. In fact, what is being offered is query privacy. We treat the two forms of privacy differently – location privacy meaning hiding the location and query privacy meaning preventing the mapping of a query to a user.

We also justify that cloaking regions are insufficient in preserving privacy when an attacker has approximate location knowledge. Although cloaking regions do not directly disclose the true locations, we believe that no privacy mechanism should enable an attacker to improve upon the existing background knowledge. The knowledge gain should be formally bounded in the worst case. Towards this end, we explore the possibility of using perturbed locations to issue queries and propose a perturbation method based on differential privacy [10]. Differential privacy works under the principle that the chances of being a victim of a privacy breach should not increase substantially due to the inclusion of ones private information in a shared data set. The perturbed location is differentially k-anonymous, in the sense that the probability ratio of any two of the k users is bounded. Empirical results are provided to demonstrate that such queries can retrieve a significantly large subset of the actual query results.

The remainder of the paper is organized as follows. Section 2 initiates our discussion on attacker capabilities, and the affect on location and query privacy. Section 3 presents our approach to address a form of attacker knowledge based on approximate locations of the users. Section 4 presents some empirical results on the effectiveness of the approach in generating useful query results. Section 5 lists some related work in this area, followed by references to future work in Section 6.

2   Attacker Class

Classification of attacker knowledge is crucial in order to provide a comprehensive statement on the privacy preserving properties of an obfuscation technique. To consider the extremes, location obfuscation in the presence of an "oracle" attacker, or an attacker with effectively no background knowledge, is only going to degrade the quality of service. Other intermediate scenarios also exist where location obfuscation cannot achieve one or both of location and query privacy. We begin with two forms of background knowledge that an attacker is likely to have.

The first form of background knowledge is related to the location of users. An adversary that has information on the locations of any individual(s) is referred to here as a *locator*. Further, a *perfect* locator knows exact coordinates of the users, while an *approximate* locator has approximate knowledge (an area instead of exact coordinates) on the locations. The second form of knowledge is related to the identity of users issuing the queries. We refer to any adversary that has access to the query database as a *holder*. A *perfect* holder in this case would be an adversary who knows the identity of the person who issued a query.

There are multiple permutations in which these two forms of knowledge may be present in an adversary. While each form in itself states how much an attacker knows about the locations or queries of the users, respectively, the objective is to avoid the inference or improvement of one form of knowledge using existing knowledge of the other form. Hence, given a certain level of background knowledge, we consider a privacy breach to have occurred if and only if the adversary gains additional knowledge. Gaining additional knowledge in this case refers to instances such as a perfect locator becoming a perfect holder (and vice versa), or an approximate locator improving its location approximations.

Location based service users communicate location information as part their queries. The location information can be in the form of precise GPS coordinates, the resulting query being processed thereafter with respect to a point in space. Such queries are also referred to as *point queries*. However, due to the implications on privacy, precise locations are obfuscated using a cloaking region. Queries in this case are processed on a geographic range, therefore referred to as *range queries*. We begin with point queries and put the two forms of attacker knowledge in perspective with respect to such queries. Some of the observations in the following section are well-known in the community. We present them here for the sake of completeness.

2.1   Point Queries

A point query is where exact geographic coordinates are communicated along with the query. A query database in this case contains the precise location of users, among other parameters of the queries. It is a straightforward observation that no location privacy can be achieved in the presence of a perfect locator, and no query privacy can be achieved in the presence of a perfect holder. Nonetheless, query privacy is preserved in the case of a perfect locator. However, as an immediate consequence of point queries, location privacy is violated even when the adversary is only a perfect holder. A perfect holder in this case performs a identity to location mapping using the location information in the query database. A perfect locator must also be at least a holder to effectuate a breach of query privacy. In this case, the adversary uses the location knowledge to determine the corresponding query of the user in the database. The perfect locator here covers situations such as restricted space identification and observation based identification [4]. A simple holder with access to the query database alone is no threat to either location or query privacy of the users.

The effectiveness of point queries in the presence of approximate locators has not been evaluated yet. Point queries can be potentially harmless depending on the extent of the adversary's approximation. For instance, an approximate locator with an approximation of a few hundred meters is stronger than one with an approximation of a city block. The exact extent of knowledge is difficult to estimate. We shall discuss later how point queries can still be effectively generated in the presence of approximate locators.

2.2   Range Queries

A range query is where a query region is associated with the query. Query results are generated assuming that the user may be located anywhere inside the region. The query region serves as a cloak for the user, and is generated following some established privacy principle. For instance, a k-anonymous cloaking region would encompass at least k users inside it. Large cloaking regions would potentially result in the communication of a larger result set and degrade the QoS levels of the system. Hence, the obfuscation algorithm tries to achieve the privacy principle within the smallest possible area. In the following, we present a case by case overview of which privacy aspect does a range query help preserve, and under what form of adversarial knowledge.

Perfect Locator. Since a perfect locator knows the location of a user, use of a cloaking region does not help hide the location of the user. Query privacy is preserved in the absence of access to the query database. This implies that no privacy breach (in the sense of gaining additional knowledge) can occur in the presence of this type of adversary. Point queries can in fact be used instead of a range query, in order to improve the quality of service.

Approximate Locator. Cloaking regions also do not help achieve better location privacy from an approximate locator. The approximation of the adversary on the user's location is what determines the location privacy level. Point queries can again be used here, given that the adversary has no access to the query database. In other words, no location privacy violation can occur as a side-effect of the user using the service.

Perfect Holder. No query privacy is possible in the presence of a perfect holder. Location privacy violation is certain since the cloaking regions present in the queries provide approximate location knowledge to the adversary. The cloaking regions can potentially reveal more precise information as well. Note that a privacy principle such as k-anonymity is meant to prevent the association of a user to the issued query – any of the k users could have issued the query. However, such a principle is irrelevant in the case of a perfect holder. A better principle to enforce would be location diversity [11,12]. This would guarantee that zones with multiple levels of sensitivity are present within the cloaking region, thereby preventing further location based inferences. Request locality is another issue to address. This situation occurs when different likelihoods can be estimated for issuing the query from different areas within the cloaking region.

Holder. A simple holder with no location based knowledge is unable to correlate a cloaking region to a specific user. Both location and query privacy are preserved. This is the weakest form of an adversary. Note that an adversary who is not a perfect or approximate locator cannot determine if a user is inside a cloaking region. Hence, a range query might as well be replaced with a point query.

Perfect Locator and Perfect Holder. As in the case of point queries, no level of obfuscation can hide the location and query of a user from this form of an adversary.

Perfect Locator and Holder. The location of a user is already known to this kind of an adversary. It is easy to determine the set of queries that could have potentially originated from a certain user. However, query privacy violation can be prevented if the cloaking region can generate an ambiguous mapping between a query and the user. This is achieved by anonymity principles such as k-anonymity. In fact, obfuscation methods that generate minimal k-anonymous cloaking regions assume the existence of a perfect locator with precise location knowledge of at least k users. This assumption implies that location obfuscation is used here to preserve query privacy, and not necessarily any form of location privacy. Query privacy, however, can also be preserved by issuing a point query using the true location of one of the k users. This can produce a relatively accurate result set if the bounding rectangle of the k users is not excessively large. The result sets would differ much for larger bounding rectangles, in which case the communication costs may itself be too high for acceptable range query processing.

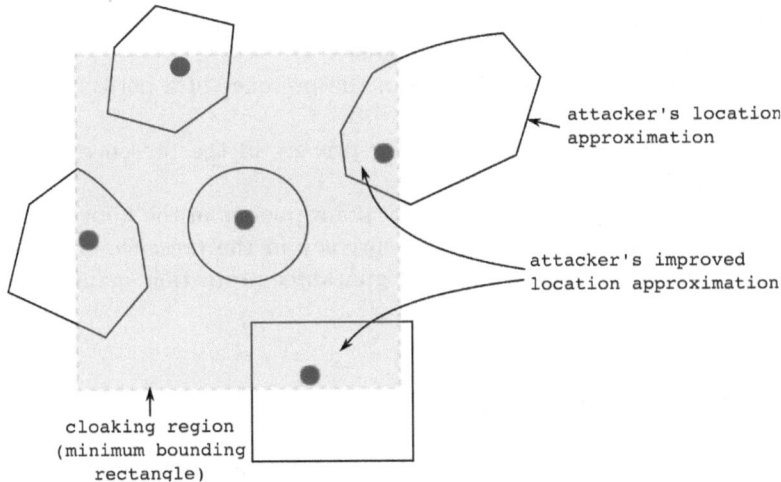

Fig. 1. Location privacy breach as a result of using cloaking regions

Approximate Locator and Perfect Holder. Approximate locators have the ability to correlate a user with a geographic region. The size of this region is not constant, and is an attribute related to the adversary's background knowledge. Under such a scenario, it becomes difficult to create a cloaking region that encompasses the entire area within the locator's approximation. Hence, it is possible that a perfect holder uses the cloaking region in a query to narrow down the geographic region where the user is located. Cloaking regions can therefore provide additional location knowledge to an adversary, thereby leading to a location privacy breach.

Approximate Locator and Holder. While cloaking regions are sufficient (although perhaps not always required) to handle a perfect locator and holder, their use starts to have a detrimental affect in the presence of approximate locators. As depicted in Fig. 1, a k-anonymous cloaking region may allow an approximate locator to improve upon the location knowledge of more than just the query issuer. The problem is eliminated only if the cloaking region is guaranteed to encompass the approximated regions corresponding to each of the k users. Unfortunately, it is difficult to judge the extent of knowledge that an adversary possesses. This case presents us with a situation where the obfuscation method helps preserve query privacy but can potentially lead to a breach in location privacy.

Note that most privacy preservation attempts address perfect locators and holders. Therefore, the term "location privacy" seems to have been misused, in the sense that true location knowledge is already assumed to be known to the adversary. Query privacy is a more appropriate term to use in this context.

We summarize below the conclusions that can be drawn from the discussion in the preceding sections.

1. Neither location privacy nor query privacy can be preserved in the presence of a perfect locator and a perfect holder.
2. Point queries pose privacy threats in the presence of a perfect locator and holder.
3. Cloaking regions help preserve query privacy in the presence of a perfect locator and holder.
4. Range queries may be replaceable by point queries in the above case.
5. Cloaking regions can provide query privacy in the presence of an approximate locator and holder, but do not guarantee protection against a location privacy breach.

3   Approximate Locators

Current location obfuscation techniques based on cloaking regions are insufficient, and undesirable, in location privacy preservation. This arises from the fact that perfect locators represent a very strong class of attackers. For instance, acquiring the exact geographic coordinates of a user would require satellite based monitoring capabilities. Further, not much can be done with location obfuscation once an adversary gains access to such information. A more plausible form of adversary is represented by an approximate locator. Approximate location knowledge can be obtained by a variety of means – device communication logs such as cell towers used, public records such as parking violations, or social engineering methods such as a "water-cooler conversation." Preserving location privacy in this context dwells upon the problem of preventing an attacker from reducing the margin of location error using external references of a user's activities (such as in a location based service log).

Recall that cloaking regions are insufficient in providing location privacy against an approximate attacker. Hence, we revert back to point queries and analyze if they can be used in a manner that preserves location privacy. Perturbation of user locations is the basis of this analysis. An attacker can identify common areas between a cloaking region and an approximate location in order to improve the approximation. This is possible because cloaking regions always cover the true location of the querying user (amongst others). However, a perturbed location is a single point in space that could have been generated by any user in a given set.

Queries based on perturbed locations can result in an inaccurate result set. However, if the perturbations are reasonably close to the actual location, then the query results can also be assumed to be close enough to the true set. There is definitely an inherent trade-off involved between the accuracy of the result set and the location perturbations. We postpone the analysis of this trade-off for a later stage and focus on the generation of the perturbations themselves.

A trivial method to perturb a user's location would be to use the centroid of a k-anonymous cloaking region while issuing the query. An adversary with exact location information can employ an inversion attack to determine the set of k locations used to arrive at the perturbed coordinates. An inversion attack would

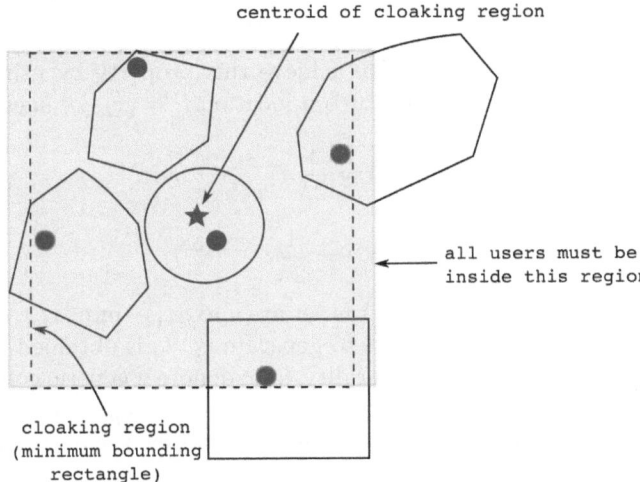

centroid of cloaking region

all users must be
inside this region

cloaking region
(minimum bounding
rectangle)

Fig. 2. Improving location approximations using the centroid of the cloaking region

involve re-computing the centroid of the bounding rectangle derived from different sets of k location coordinates, with the objective of matching the coordinate in the query. Note that we do not consider any privacy parameter (including k) to be hidden from the attacker. Executing an inversion attack is not straightforward for an approximate locator. Depending on the size of the k-anonymous cloaking region, the centroid can also serve as a good estimate of a user's location and possibly generate a significantly accurate set of results. However, as depicted in Fig. 2, owing to the equi-distance property of the centroid, its ability to prevent a location privacy breach is still questionable. In the figure, the grey area bounded by the solid line represents the largest possible region that can be a bounding rectangle (users can be anywhere in the approximate regions) and has a centroid same as the true minimum bounding rectangle. This improves the location approximation corresponding to two of the users. The applicability of other notions of a centroid remains to be explored.

Our approach is motivated by the requirement to provide probabilistic bounds on what an adversary can learn from the perturbed location. We adopt the differential privacy approach in statistical databases in this context [10].

3.1   Location Perturbation

Let l_p be the perturbed location corresponding to a true location l_t, denoted as $l_t \rightarrow l_p$. A location is assumed to have two components, denoted by the non-negative x and y coordinates. Let $l_1, ..., l_k$ be a set of k points, one of which is l_t. The method of choosing these k points is discussed in the next section. We would generate the perturbed location $l_p = (x_p, y_p)$ such that

$$Pr(x_i \rightarrow x_p) \leq e^{\epsilon} Pr(x_j \rightarrow x_p) \text{ and}$$

$$Pr(y_i \rightarrow y_p) \leq e^\epsilon Pr(y_j \rightarrow y_p)$$

where $\epsilon \geq 0$ and $i, j \in \{1, ..., k\}$. We achieve this property by using a Laplace distribution with scale $\lambda > 0$ to perturb a location $l_i = (x_i, y_i)$ such that

$$Pr(x_i \rightarrow x_p) = \frac{1}{2\lambda} e^{-\frac{|x_i - x_p|}{\lambda}} \text{ and}$$

$$Pr(y_i \rightarrow y_p) = \frac{1}{2\lambda} e^{-\frac{|y_i - y_p|}{\lambda}}.$$

Based on the following observation, λ is set at $(\max_n x_n - \min_n x_n)/\epsilon$ to generate x_p, and set at $(\max_n y_n - \min_n y_n)/\epsilon$ to generate y_p. l_p is obtained as (x_p, y_p).

Observation: Without loss of generality, let c denote a generic component of a location. Using the triangle inequality, we can write $|c_j - c_p| \leq |c_j - c_i| + |c_i - c_p|$. After rearrangement, dividing by λ, raising as a power of e and multiplying by $1/2\lambda$, we get

$$\frac{1}{2\lambda} e^{-\frac{|c_i - c_p|}{\lambda}} \leq \frac{1}{2\lambda} e^{-\frac{|c_j - c_p|}{\lambda}} e^{\frac{|c_j - c_i|}{\lambda}}, \text{ or}$$

$$Pr(c_i \rightarrow c_p) \leq Pr(c_j \rightarrow c_p) e^{\frac{|c_j - c_i|}{\lambda}}.$$

We therefore have

$$Pr(x_i \rightarrow x_p) \leq Pr(x_j \rightarrow x_p) e^{\frac{|x_j - x_i|}{\lambda}} \text{ and}$$

$$Pr(y_i \rightarrow y_p) \leq Pr(y_j \rightarrow y_p) e^{\frac{|y_j - y_i|}{\lambda}},$$

and the power of the exponent is bounded as

$$Pr(x_i \rightarrow x_p) \leq Pr(x_j \rightarrow x_p) e^{\frac{\max_n x_n - \min_n x_n}{\lambda}} \text{ and}$$

$$Pr(y_i \rightarrow y_p) \leq Pr(y_j \rightarrow y_p) e^{\frac{\max_n y_n - \min_n y_n}{\lambda}}.$$

Using the Laplace distributed noise also ensures that

$$Pr(c_i \rightarrow c_p) \geq e^{-\epsilon} Pr(c_j \rightarrow c_p).$$

The following inequalities verify that the desired property can be achieved for any component c in l_i and l_j.

$$e^{-\epsilon} \leq \frac{Pr(c_i \rightarrow c_p)}{Pr(c_j \rightarrow c_p)} \leq e^\epsilon$$

$$\iff e^\epsilon \geq \frac{Pr(c_j \rightarrow c_p)}{Pr(c_i \rightarrow c_p)} \geq e^{-\epsilon} \text{ with } \epsilon \geq 0.$$

Hence, the probability of a location coordinate generating a certain perturbed value is always within a factor e^ϵ of the probability of some other location (in the set of k points) generating the same perturbed value. In the k-anonymity sense, any of the k points could have been used to generate the perturbed location.

3.2   Selecting a Perturbation

A perturbed location for a query point can be chosen using the above method. However, the distribution of the k points can affect the proximity of the perturbed location to the true coordinates. Further, the k points should be chosen to preserve reciprocity [6,13]. In other words, the same set should be chosen irrespective of which of the k locations is the query point. This is achieved by dividing the users into buckets of size k, the set being chosen as the bucket to which the query point belongs. Each of the k points is subjected to perturbation, and the one having the minimum average distance to all points in the set is chosen as the location to issue the query. Given a perturbed location, the k points are probabilistically identical (within a factor of e^ϵ) irrespective of which one was used to perform the perturbation. Hence, choosing the one with minimum average distance to all points does not risk an inversion attack. Note that the context of the application still plays a crucial role. If the user base is relatively sparse, i.e. the k users are distributed over a significantly large area, then the generated perturbation will be far away from the true location. A cloaking region could also be unacceptably large in this case.

Algorithm 1 lists the pseudo code of the approach. The function returns a perturbed location of a user $\mathcal{U}$. Lines 1 to 11 determine the k size bucket to which the user belongs. The buckets are formed based on the Hilbert indices of the users. The locality preserving properties of Hilbert curves ensure (although not necessarily optimal) the formation of buckets with users that are at close proximity to each other. Error checks and boundary conditions are not shown

---

Algorithm 1. Location Perturbation

Require: User $\mathcal{U}$ with associated k.
Ensure: A perturbed location for $\mathcal{U}$.
 1: $\mathcal{H} = $ set of all users sorted by their Hilbert index
 2: **repeat**
 3:     $\mathcal{D} = \phi$
 4:     **for all** $(u \in \mathcal{H}$ in order) **do**
 5:         $\mathcal{D} = \mathcal{D} \cup \{u\}$
 6:         **if** $(|\mathcal{D}| = k)$ **then**
 7:             **break**
 8:         **end if**
 9:     **end for**
10:     $\mathcal{H} = \mathcal{H} - \mathcal{D}$
11: **until** $(\mathcal{U} \in \mathcal{D})$
12: $\mathcal{L} = \{$location of $u \in \mathcal{D}\}$
13: $\mathcal{L}_p = \phi$
14: **for all** $(l \in \mathcal{L})$ **do**
15:     $l_p =$ perturbed l
16:     $\mathcal{L}_p = \mathcal{L}_p \cup \{l_p\}$
17: **end for**
18: **return** $l_p \in \mathcal{L}_p$ such that l_p has minimum average distance from $\mathcal{L}$

---

in the code. For instance, if a user belongs to the last bucket and its size is less than k, then the last bucket should be merged with the previous one. Lines 14 to 17 compute a perturbed value corresponding to the location of every user in the bucket. Each component c of a location is perturbed to $c - \lambda \text{sign}(rnd) \ln(1 - 2|rnd|)$, where rnd is a random value between -0.5 and 0.5 drawn from a uniform distribution, and λ is set as described in the previous section. This makes the perturbation Laplace distributed around c.

3.3   Evaluating the Perturbation

Cloaking regions guarantee that the results generated for a location based query will contain the results corresponding to the location of the user. Such a claim cannot be made for queries issued with a perturbed location. However, it remains to be evaluated how different is the result set when generated with respect to the true location, compared to that generated with respect to a perturbed location. Differences in the result may or may not exist depending on the density of the queried objects, and the distance of the perturbed location from the true one. A Knn-query, for instance, on sparsely distributed objects (e.g. hospitals) is likely to generate a larger subset of common results. On the other hand, for densely distributed objects, this likelihood reduces. K here is the number of nearest neighbor objects to retrieve corresponding to a location. Note that we use a lower case k for the computation of a perturbed location.

Result set similarity can also be measured with respect to the distances to the retrieved objects. Under this measure, two result sets are considered similar if, corresponding to every object in one set, there exists an object in the other set that is equi-distant from the queried location. This perspective of result similarity applies well to proximity based queries – nearest gas stations, nearest restaurants, nearest friends – where the distance to the object carries more weight than attributes of the objects. Result set similarity using common subsets is relevant in queries where the retrieved objects must be ordered using user-stated preferences – nearest K cheapest gas stations.

A third measure is also possible using the distance of the perturbed location from the true location. Assuming that the service provider guarantees that the result set is accurate relative to the query point, a user wanting complete accuracy will have to travel from the current location to the perturbed point. It is therefore worth investigating how far is the generated perturbation from the current location of the user.

Although we are not stating any theoretical bounds on these metrics at this stage, intuition says that query processing relative to well-formed perturbed locations will not be futile. As the first step, the following three metrics are used to evaluate the effectiveness of our approach [14].

1. *Nearness:* Fraction of perturbations at close proximity to the true location.
2. *Displacement:* Let $\mathcal{O} = \{o_1, ..., o_K\}$ be the objects retrieved by a Knn-query relative to the true location of user $\mathcal{U}$, and $\mathcal{O}' = \{o'_1, ..., o'_K\}$ be the objects

retrieved relative to the perturbed location. The displacement is then given as

$$\sum_{i=1}^{K} dist(o'_i, \mathcal{U}) - \sum_{i=1}^{K} dist(o_i, \mathcal{U}),$$

$dist(\cdot)$ being a distance function. The minimum possible displacement is zero.

3. *Resemblance:* Fraction of common objects between $\mathcal{O}$ and $\mathcal{O}'$, given as

$$\frac{|\mathcal{O} \cap \mathcal{O}'|}{|\mathcal{O}|}.$$

4   Empirical Results

We have generated a trace data set using a simulator that operates multiple mobile objects based on real-world road network information available from the National Mapping Division of the US Geological Survey. We use an area of approximately $168\ km^2$ in the Chamblee region of Georgia, USA for this study (Fig. 3). Three road types are identified based on the available data – expressway, arterial and collector. Real traffic volume data is used to determine the number of users on the different road types [4]. The total number of users on a road type vary proportionately to the total length and traffic volume of the road type, and reciprocally to the average speed. The mean speed, standard deviation and traffic volumes on the road types are shown in the figure. Using the number of users on each road type, the simulator randomly places them on the network and moves them around. The users move with a speed drawn from a normal distribution, randomly making turns and changing speed at junctions. The simulator maintains the traffic volume statistics while moving the users.

The used traffic volume information results in 8,558 users with 34% on expressways, 8% on arterial roads and 58% on collector roads. The trace data consists of multiple records spanning one hour of simulated time. A record is made up of a time stamp, user identifier, and x and y coordinates of the user's location. The granularity of the data is maintained such that the Euclidean distance between successive locations of the same user is approximately 100 meters. Each user has an associated k value drawn from the range $[2, 50]$ by using a Zipf distribution favoring higher values and with the exponent 0.6. The trace data is sorted by the time stamp of records. The first minute of records is used for initialization. Location coordinates in each record thereafter are subjected to perturbation. Over 4,000,000 records are processed during a pass of the trace data.

Queried objects are distributed randomly over the entire map based on a density value (number of objects per km^2). A Knn-query is issued relative to every perturbed location. Displacement is measured using a Euclidean distance metric. The entire map is assumed to be on a grid of $2^{14} \times 2^{14}$ cells (a cell at every meter) while calculating the Hilbert indices [15]. Objects in the same cell have the same Hilbert index. All simulation results are obtained on a 2.8GHz Quad-Core Intel Xeon machine with 8GB memory and running Mac OSX 10.6.7.

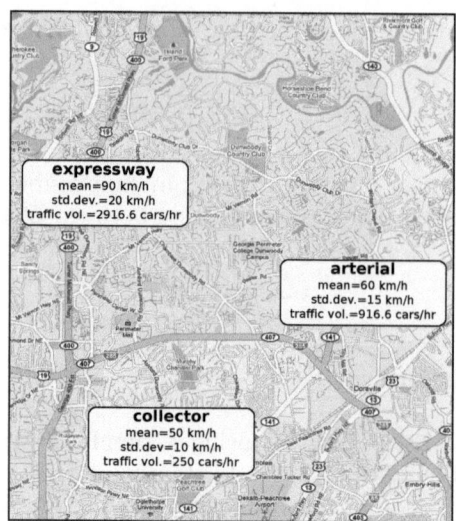

Fig. 3. Simulation performed over an area of Chamblee, GA, USA

Table 1. Percentage of anonymization attempts where perturbed location is at close proximity to true location

ϵ	$\leq 1000m$	$\leq 500m$	$\leq 100m$
0.01	1.05	0.37	0.01
0.1	36.61	13.70	1.00
0.3	84.16	48.33	4.64
0.5	93.79	64.53	7.81
1.0	97.41	76.10	11.89
2.0	98.11	79.91	14.42

Fig. 4 shows the number of perturbations that resulted in the perturbed point being generated within 5000 meters of the user's actual location. A value of $\epsilon = 0.01$ effectuates to saying that two users should effectively have the same probability of generating the perturbation ($e^\epsilon = 1.01$). This is difficult to achieve for most values of k. As the ϵ value approaches 0.5 ($e^{0.5} = 1.65$), we see a useful distribution. At this point, more than 90% of the perturbations are within 1000 meters of the true location (Table 1). 60% of the points are in a much closer proximity of 500 meters. The numbers increase favorably with increasing ϵ. However, higher values of ϵ reduce the practical significance of the approach. For instance, with $\epsilon = 2.0$, we are already willing to accept a factor of 7 difference in the probability estimates. Nonetheless, it is promising to see that significantly high nearness values are possible with smaller values of ϵ as well.

Fig. 5 shows the resemblance and displacement values corresponding to different values of K (the number of nearest neighbors to retrieve) and density. The values are averaged over the the total number of requests processed (4484683). A

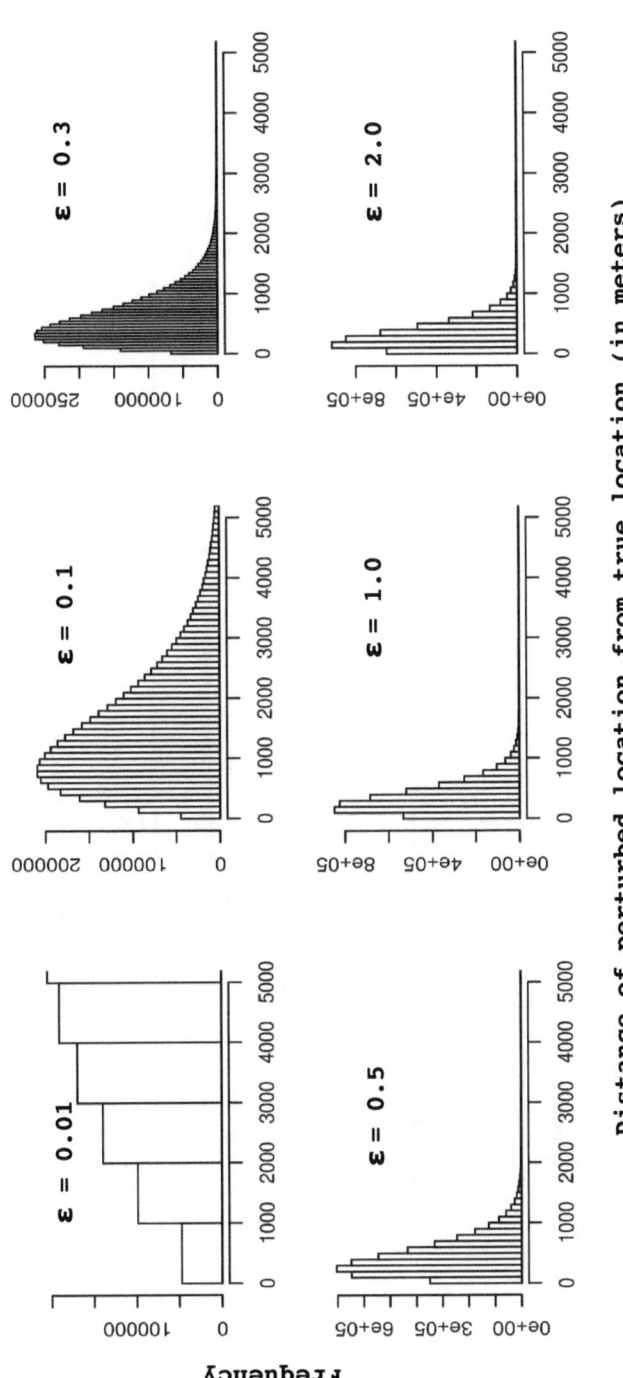

Fig. 4. Number of anonymization attempts where the perturbed location is within 5000 meters of the true location. Perturbed location is within 1000 meters for more than 90% of the attempts with $\epsilon = 0.5$. Total number of anonymization attempts = 4484683.

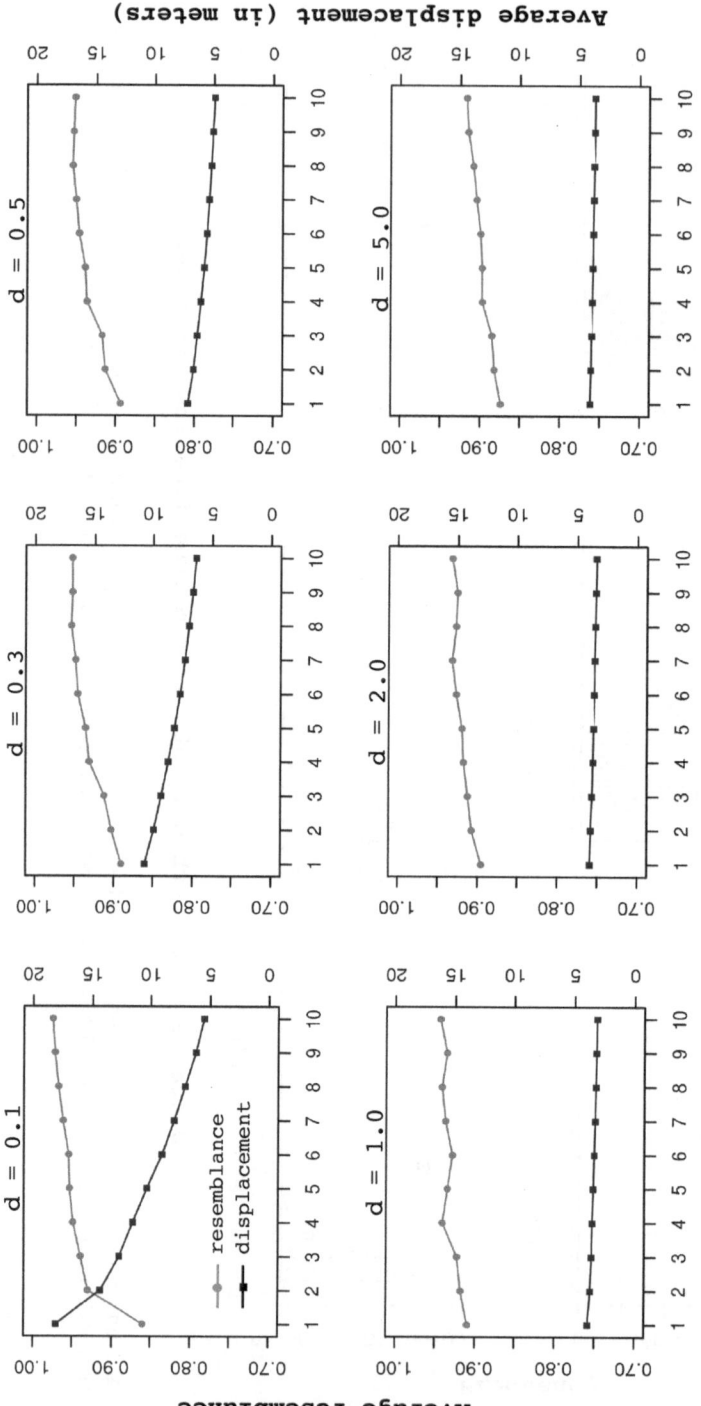

Fig. 5. Average resemblance and displacement values for *Knn*-queries on objects distributed with various density *d*. Perturbations are generated with $\epsilon = 0.5$

density of 0.1 results in 25 objects across the entire region (sparsely distributed), while a value such as 5 results in 980 objects (densely distributed). Subset similarity (resemblance) is over 80% on the average. However, the metric shows a slow decreasing trend as objects become more densely situated. The chances of finding points of interest in the neighborhood increases as they become more closely packed. The displacement is still minimal in this case. Differences in the distance are within a mere 5 meters for the simulated objects. Query results on sparse objects can be comparatively distant, but still acceptable. The number of objects to retrieve has an influence in this case. While the resemblance values are more or less similar, displacement is comparatively higher when a smaller number of objects are retrieved on sparse objects. A nearest neighbor search ($K = 1$) still retrieves the same object on more than 80% of the queries processed.

5   Related Work

Location obfuscation has been earlier achieved either through the use of dummy queries or cloaking regions. In the dummy query method, a user hides its actual query (with the true location) amongst a set of additional queries with incorrect locations [16,17]. The user's actual location is one amongst the locations in the query set. Using false dummies affect query privacy if user locations are known to the attacker. Cheng et al. propose a data model to augment uncertainty to location data using circular regions around all objects [18]. They use imprecise queries that hide the location of the query issuer and yield probabilistic results, modeled as the amount of overlap between the query range and circular region around the queried objects. Yiu et al. propose an incremental nearest neighbor processing algorithm to retrieve query results [19]. The process starts with an anchor, a location different from that of the user, and it proceeds until an accurate query result can be reported. Trusted third party based approaches rely on an anonymizer that creates spatial regions to hide the true location of users. The anonymizer communicates this region to the content provider and then filters the result set accordingly. Gedik and Liu develop a location privacy architecture where each user can specify a minimum anonymity level, and maximum temporal and spatial tolerances while creating the cloaking regions [5]. Ghinita et al. propose a decentralized architecture to construct an anonymous spatial region, and eliminate the need for the centralized anonymizer [20]. Kalnis et al. propose that all obfuscation methods should satisfy the reciprocity property [6]. This prevents inversion attacks where knowledge of the underlying anonymizing algorithm can be used to identify the actual object. Mokbel et al. explore query processing of different types on spatial regions – private queries over public data, public queries over private data, and private queries over private data [21]. Lee et al. explore privacy concerns in path queries where source and destination inputs may reveal personal information about users [22]. They propose the notion of obfuscated path queries where multiple sources and destinations are specified to hide the true inputs. Xu and Cai argue that the impact of a privacy parameter, such as k, on the level of privacy is often difficult to perceive. They treat privacy as a feeling-based property and propose using the popularity of a public region as the privacy level [23]. Each user specifies a spatial region as its privacy index, and the cloaking region for the user must at least have the same popularity as that of the specified region. An entropy based computation is used to define the popularity of a spatial region. Soriano et al. show that the privacy assurances of this model do not hold when the adversary possesses footprint knowledge on the spatial regions over time [24]. Shokri et al. propose a framework to quantify location privacy based on the expected estimation error of an adversary [25].

Data transformation is another method to prevent the inference of locations. Agrawal et al. propose an encryption technique called OPES (Order Preserving Encryption Scheme) that allows comparison operations to be directly applied on encrypted data [26]. Operand decryption is however required for computing SUM and AVG. Wong et al. overcome this drawback by developing an asymmetric scalar-product preserving encryption [27]. This allows the preservation of relative distances between database points. Khoshgozaran et al. employ Hilbert curves to transform the data points and then answer queries in the transformed space [14]. The parameters of the transformation, called the Space Decryption Key, is assumed to be not known to an adversary. A new paradigm in location privacy is based on private information retrieval (PIR) techniques. Khoshgozaran et al. propose K nearest neighbor queries that can be reduced to a set of PIR block retrievals [28]. These retrievals can be performed using a tamper-resistant processor located at the server so that the content provider is oblivious of the retrieved blocks. Papadopoulos et al. further warrant the need to retrieve the same number of blocks across queries [29].

6   Conclusions

Obfuscated locations can provide the means to access a location based service without risking privacy breaches. The strength of the obfuscation itself is dependent on the background knowledge of the attacker. Cloaking regions can be used to provide query privacy, but at the same time, can also enable an attacker with approximate location knowledge to improve its approximations. We propose a method based on location perturbation to address such attackers. Perturbed locations are generated using a Laplace distributed noise function in a way such that any user, from a set of k users, is likely to be the query issuer within a parameterized bound. Empirical evaluation shows that the perturbed locations can still serve as promising query points. A high fraction of the actual result set can be retrieved, or otherwise, similarity in distances to the points of interest can be achieved.

Resolution of bad perturbations is an issue that remains to be explored. These are perturbations that are significantly far away from the true locations. While their occurrence has not been found to be very high in the empirical study, it needs to be determined if they can be eliminated altogether. Reducing the value of k may have a positive impact, but at the expense of reduced anonymity. In addition, the k value is only used to determine a set of close neighbors that can be used to compute a noise level for the perturbations. Its may be possible to adaptively choose the value based on the proximity of the perturbations to the true locations. Further, the result set similarity could be improved upon by using queries from multiple perturbed locations. Decentralized computation of the perturbations should not be difficult, given a framework to determine the k users.

We have not considered another possible form of adversarial knowledge in this study. These adversaries, called *crossholders*, posses knowledge on the identity of individuals who did not issue a certain query. Consequently, a k-anonymous cloaking region in this case is $(k - n)$-anonymous, where n is the number of individuals that the adversary can eliminate. k-anonymity can still be achieved by ensuring the cloaking region is $(k + n)$-anonymous. As in the case of approximate locators, the difficulty lies in determining the attacker's extent of knowledge – the value of n. The perturbation based approach demonstrated here is also weak against such adversaries, specifically because of the underlying usage of k-anonymity. The dependence on k can be removed by using the maximum L_1-norm distance between all users in the variance computation. However, such high levels of variance can make the perturbed locations significantly distant from the true locations, and effectively useless in generating relevant results.

References

1. LeFevre, K., DeWitt, D.J., Ramakrishnan, R.: Incognito: Efficient Full-Domain k-Anonymity. In: Proceedings of the 2005 ACM SIGMOD International Conference on Management of Data, pp. 49–60 (2005)
2. LeFevre, K., DeWitt, D.J., Ramakrishnan, R.: Mondrian Multidimensional K-Anonymity. In: Proceedings of the 22nd International Conference in Data Engineering, p. 25 (2006)
3. Samarati, P.: Protecting Respondents' Identities in Microdata Release. IEEE Transactions on Knowledge and Data Engineering 13(6), 1010–1027 (2001)
4. Gruteser, M., Grunwald, D.: Anonymous Usage of Location-Based Services Through Spatial and Temporal Cloaking. In: Proceedings of the 1st International Conference on Mobile Systems, Applications, and Services, pp. 31–42 (2003)
5. Gedik, B., Liu, L.: Protecting Location Privacy with Personalized k-Anonymity: Architecture and Algorithms. IEEE Transactions on Mobile Computing 7(1), 1–18 (2008)
6. Kalnis, P., Ghinita, G., Mouratidis, K., Papadias, D.: Preventing Location-Based Identity Inference in Anonymous Spatial Queries. IEEE Transactions on Knowledge and Data Engineering 19(12), 1719–1733 (2007)
7. Machanavajjhala, A., Gehrke, J., Kifer, D., Venkitasubramaniam, M.: ℓ–Diversity: Privacy Beyond k–Anonymity. In: Proceedings of the 22nd International Conference on Data Engineering, p. 24 (2006)
8. Li, N., Li, T., Venkatasubramanian, S.: t–Closeness: Privacy Beyond k–Anonymity and ℓ–Diversity. In: Proceedings of the 23rd International Conference on Data Engineering, pp. 106–115 (2007)

9. Wong, R.C., Fu, A.W., Wang, K., Pei, J.: Minimality Attack in Privacy Preserving Data Publishing. In: Proceedings of the 33rd International Conference on Very Large Data Bases, pp. 543–554 (2007)

10. Dwork, C.: Differential Privacy. In: Bugliesi, M., Preneel, B., Sassone, V., Wegener, I. (eds.) ICALP 2006. LNCS, vol. 4052, pp. 1–12. Springer, Heidelberg (2006)

11. Bamba, B., Liu, L., Pesti, P., Wang, T.: Supporting Anonymous Location Queries in Mobile Environments with Privacy Grid. In: Proceedings of the 17th International World Wide Web Conference, pp. 237–246 (2008)

12. Xue, M., Kalnis, P., Pung, H.K.: Location Diversity: Enhanced Privacy Protection in Location Based Services. In: Choudhury, T., Quigley, A., Strang, T., Suginuma, K. (eds.) LoCA 2009. LNCS, vol. 5561, pp. 70–87. Springer, Heidelberg (2009)

13. Ghinita, G., Zhao, K., Papadias, D., Kalnis, P.: A Reciprocal Framework for Spatial k-Anonymity. Journal of Information Systems 35(3), 299–314 (2010)

14. Khoshgozaran, A., Shahabi, C.: Blind Evaluation of Nearest Neighbor Queries Using Space Transformation to Preserve Location Privacy. In: Papadias, D., Zhang, D., Kollios, G. (eds.) SSTD 2007. LNCS, vol. 4605, pp. 239–257. Springer, Heidelberg (2007)

15. Liu, X., Schrack, G.: Encoding and Decoding the Hilbert Order. Software-Practice and Experience 26(12), 1335–1346 (1996)

16. Kido, H., Yanagisawa, Y., Satoh, T.: An Anonymous Communication Technique Using Dummies for Location-Based Services. In: Proceedings of the IEEE International Conference on Pervasive Services, pp. 88–97 (2005)

17. Duckham, M., Kulik, L.: A Formal Model of Obfuscation and Negotiation for Location Privacy. In: Gellersen, H.-W., Want, R., Schmidt, A. (eds.) PERVASIVE 2005. LNCS, vol. 3468, pp. 152–170. Springer, Heidelberg (2005)

18. Cheng, R., Zhang, Y., Bertino, E., Prabhakar, S.: Preserving User Location Privacy in Mobile Data Management Infrastructures. In: Danezis, G., Golle, P. (eds.) PET 2006. LNCS, vol. 4258, pp. 393–412. Springer, Heidelberg (2006)

19. Yiu, M.L., Jensen, C.S., Huang, X., Lu, H.: SpaceTwist: Managing the Trade-Offs Among Location Privacy, Query Performance, and Query Accuracy in Mobile Services. In: Proceedings of the 24th International Conference on Data Engineering, pp. 366–375 (2008)

20. Ghinita, G., Kalnis, P., Skiadopoulos, S.: PRIVE: Anonymous Location-Based Queries in Distributed Mobile Systems. In: Proceedings of the 16th International Conference on World Wide Web, pp. 371–380 (2007)

21. Mokbel, M.F., Chow, C., Aref, W.G.: The New Casper: Query Processing for Location Services Without Compromising Privacy. In: Proceedings of the 32nd International Conference on Very Large Data Bases, pp. 763–774 (2006)

22. Lee, K.C.K., Lee, W.C., Leong, H.V., Zheng, B.: OPAQUE: Protecting Path Privacy in Directions Search. In: Proceedings of the 25th International Conference on Data Engineering, pp. 1271–1274 (2009)

23. Xu, T., Cai, Y.: Feeling-Based Location Privacy Protection for Location-Based Services. In: Proceedings of the 16th ACM Conference on Computer and Communications Security, pp. 348–357 (2009)

24. Marconi, L., Di Pietro, R., Crispo, B., Conti, M.: Time Warp: How Time Affects Privacy in LBSs. In: Soriano, M., Qing, S., López, J. (eds.) ICICS 2010. LNCS, vol. 6476, pp. 325–339. Springer, Heidelberg (2010)

25. Shokri, R., Theodorakopoulos, G., Boudec, J.Y.L., Hubaux, J.P.: Quantifying Location Privacy. In: Proceedings of the 32nd IEEE Symposium on Security and Privacy, pp. 247–262 (2011)

26. Agrawal, R., Kiernan, J., Srikant, R., Xu, Y.: Order Preserving Encryption for Numeric Data. In: Proceedings of the ACM SIGMOD International Conference on Management of Data, pp. 563–574 (2004)
27. Wong, W.K., Cheung, D.W., Kao, B., Mamouslis, N.: Secure kNN Computation on Encrypted Databases. In: Proceedings of the 35th SIGMOD International Conference on Management of Data, pp. 139–152 (2009)
28. Khoshgozaran, A., Shahabi, C., Shirani-Mehr, H.: Location Privacy: Going beyond k-Anonymity, Cloaking and Anonymizers. Journal of Knowledge and Information Systems 26(3), 435–465 (2011)
29. Papadopoulos, S., Bakiras, S., Papadias, D.: Nearest Neighbor Search with Strong Location Privacy. VLDB Endowment 3(1-2), 619–629 (2010)

Insecurity in Public-Safety Communications: APCO Project 25

Stephen Glass[1], Vallipuram Muthukkumarasamy[2],
Marius Portmann[1], and Matthew Robert

[1] NICTA, Queensland Research Laboratory, Brisbane, Australia
[2] Griffith University, Gold Coast, Australia
stephen.glass@nicta.com.au, marius.portmann@nicta.com.au,
v.muthu@griffith.edu.au, matt.robert@gmail.com

Abstract. *APCO Project 25* (P25) radio networks are perhaps the most widely-deployed digital radio technology currently in use by emergency first-responders across the world. This paper presents the results of an investigation into the security aspects of the P25 communication protocol. The investigation uses a new software-defined radio approach to expose the vulnerabilities of the lowest layers of the protocol stack. We identify a number of serious security flaws which lead to practical attacks that can compromise the confidentiality, integrity and availability of P25 networks.

Keywords: communications networks, wireless network security, security analysis.

1 Introduction

Emergency and public-safety communications systems are increasingly making use of digital technologies such as *Terrestrial Trunked Radio* (TETRA) and *APCO Project 25* (P25). Compared to the analogue land mobile radio systems that preceded them these digital systems claim improved radio spectrum use, increased geographical coverage, centralized channel management (trunking) and support for both voice and data services. A key advantage to digital systems is that they enable secure operation that ensures the confidentiality of voice and data traffic using proven cryptographic ciphers. As a result these systems have a reputation for being much more secure than analogue systems. In this paper we present the results of a critical security analysis of the P25 protocols and identify a number of flaws that lead directly to practical and effective attacks. These attacks include bypassing the authentication and access control mechanism, disabling specific nodes at will and the passive recovery of the encryption keys for some of the standard ciphers. We also describe in detail a widely-used proprietary P25 cipher system and show the encryption key can be recovered with only a relatively small effort. To the best of our knowledge this is the first time this cipher has been described.

M. Rajarajan et al. (Eds.): SecureComm 2011, LNICST 96, pp. 116–133, 2012.
© Institute for Computer Sciences, Social Informatics and Telecommunications Engineering 2012

1.1 Structure of the Paper

The structure of this paper is as follows: section 2 provides a brief background to P25 and the structure of P25 network traffic. Section 3 describes the motivation for the software radio approach used and describes the software tools we constructed for the investigation. Section 4 outlines the flaws we identified in the protocol. Section 5 the most effective attacks which result from these flaws. In section 6 we discuss related work and conclude in section 7.

2 APCO Project 25

P25-based systems are used by first-responder emergency services across the US, Canada, Australia and New Zealand. P25 radio systems may be used in simplex mode (i.e. without any infrastructure) but are typically used in infrastructure-based networks and consist of both fixed and mobile equipment as shown in figure 1. The *mobile radios* (MRs) are either hand-portable or vehicle-mounted and paired with a *mobile data terminal* (MDT) for accessing data services. The *fixed station* (FS) fulfills the roles of base station, *key management facility* (KMF), trunking controller and repeater. The FS may also provide data services and gateways to the public switched telephone network, automatic branch exchanges and other radio systems.

The P25 standard is jointly administered by the *Telecommunications Industry Association* (TIA) and the *American National Standards Institute* (ANSI)

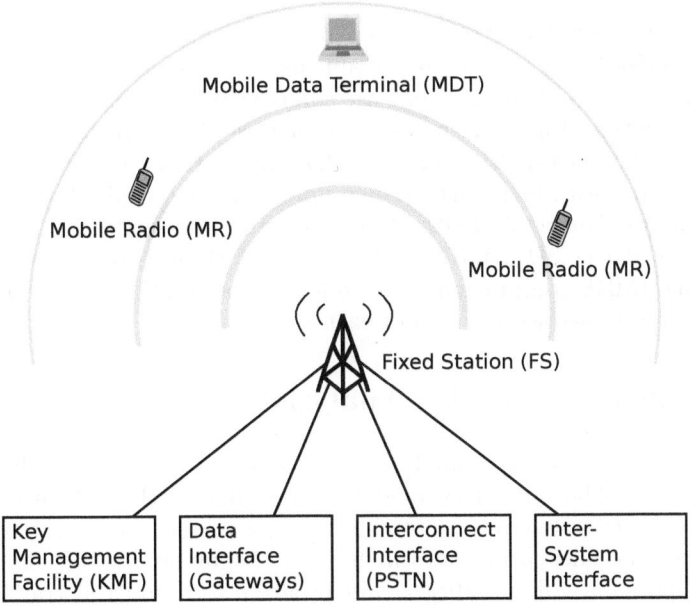

Fig. 1. P25 System Components

and ensures interoperability of equipment from different manufacturers. The
P25 *Common Air Interface* (CAI) defines the modulation techniques, frame
types and physical layer representations that must be implemented by all P25-
compliant radios [1]. In the existing P25 standard CAI traffic is exchanged
at 9600 bps using either 4-level *frequency-shift keying* (FSK) modulation in
a 12.5 kHz half-duplex channel or $\frac{\pi}{4}$ *differential quadrature phase-shift keying*
(DQPSK) modulation in a 6.125 kHz half-duplex channel. To accommodate the
limited data rate, voice transmissions make use of the IMBE vocoder to encode voice traffic into compressed voice codewords; where each 88-bit codeword
represents 20ms of uncompressed speech.

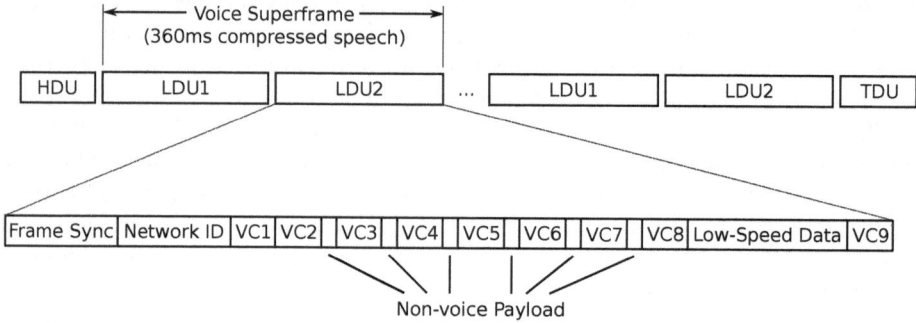

Fig. 2. P25 Voice Transmission Frame Structure

All P25 voice and data traffic is transported by data-link layer frames which
are known as *data units* (DUs). Data traffic uses variable-length *packet data units*
(PDUs) whereas voice transmissions use a variety of fixed-size frames that occur
in a fixed structure. Figure 2 shows the structure of a voice transmission. Each
voice transmission begins with a *header data unit* (HDU), followed by a number
of voice superframes which carry the compressed voice traffic. That is followed
by a *terminator data unit* (TDU). Each superframe is composed of alternating
logical data unit 1 (LDU1) and *logical data unit 2* (LDU2) frames; each of which
contains nine IMBE compressed voice codewords and differ only in the meaning
attached to the non-voice payload of each frame.

3   Approach to Security Analysis

The purpose of the security analysis is to identify any security flaws present
in the protocol. The adversary model we presume is that of an external attacker who has complete access to the message transmissions but who has no
knowledge of the encryption keys in use. We begin by studying the standard
to identify possible vulnerabilities, and progress to study the traffic in a real
test-bed network. Unfortunately, in commercially-available equipment, low-level
access to the protocol stack is not usually available. Re-purposing commercial

P25 equipment is difficult because device programming specifications are either unavailable or available only when entering into non-disclosure agreements. This approach is further complicated because P25 equipment often employs a degree of security-through-obscurity and tamper-proofing measures. These problems motivated the investigation to adopt the use of a novel *software-defined radio* (SDR) or software radio approach. An SDR is one in which the majority of the signal processing is done in software as opposed to purpose-designed electronic circuits. This approach enables us to examine and manipulate message traffic at the physical and data-link layers of the protocol stack. The principal advantage of this technique is that the SDR is not constrained to the behaviours expected from commercial equipment and can be used to expose flaws, implement attacks and prototype countermeasures. The software radio approach can also assist in reverse-engineering protocols, which are undocumented and would otherwise not be available for analysis (an example of this is discussed in Section 5.3).

3.1   Software-Defined Radio Implementation

To facilitate the investigation we have developed software tools that allow us to create, transmit, receive and analyse P25 message traffic. The software tools are built using the GNU Radio framework [2]. This is a free software framework for writing software radios in C++ and Python and is available under the terms of the GNU Public License. The GNU Radio framework provides a large collection of signal-processing blocks which transform their input signal(s) into output signal(s) in a well-defined way. Blocks can even be combined into a functioning software radio using a graphical, direct-manipulation editor called the *GNU Radio Companion* (GRC). Using the GNU Radio framework provides a robust signal-processing framework and ensures hardware independence because GNU Radio can make use of common abstractions to communicate with a wide variety of signal sources and sinks.

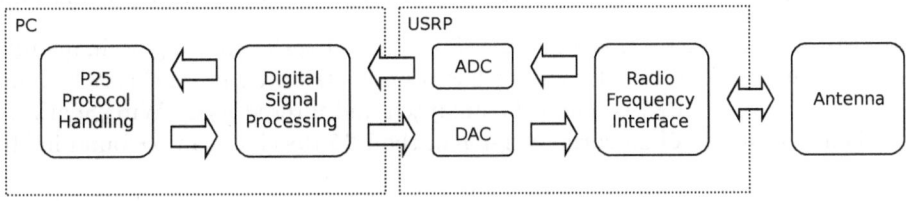

Fig. 3. Block Diagram View of Software Radio

Figure 3 shows a block diagram of the software radio. A host PC is responsible for the P25 data-link layer and the digital signal processing needed for the physical layer whilst an SDR provides the means of converting digital samples to and from radio frequency signals. The actual SDR is a *Universal Software Radio Peripheral* (USRP) [3]; this is a low-cost device that has been purpose-designed to work with the GNU Radio framework. The USRP provides for high-speed analogue/digital and digital/analogue conversion and implements a radio frequency interface that is responsible for amplification and frequency conversion from the baseband to the appropriate part of the radio spectrum. This is achieved using a daughterboard which, in this instance, provides receive and transmit capabilities for the UHF frequency bands used in public-safety communications. The digital samples are passed between the host PC and USRP via either a USB2 or a Gigabit Ethernet interface.

3.2   P25 Receiver

The USRP can process approximately 6 MHz of the radio spectrum at one time, allowing hundreds of P25 signals to be processed simultaneously. This makes it a useful tool for both security analysis and network monitoring because network traffic can be captured, monitored and analysed to assist in identifying security flaws or diagnosing operational problems. The P25 Receiver itself is a hybrid Python/C++ program that allows for message traffic to be captured off the air for storage and analysis. The P25 Receiver can be thought of as comprising four main stages:

1. Filtering to select a particular channel of interest and performing frequency translation to produce a series of baseband samples.
2. Demodulation transforms the baseband samples into a stream of dibit symbols using a *4-level frequency shift keying* (4FSK) demodulator.
3. Decoding recovers the P25 data-link frames from the symbol stream. This requires a custom signal-processing block to identify frame boundaries and re-construct the frame bodies, de-interleaving and applying forward error-correction.
4. Distribution of the resulting traffic for further processing. CAI traffic can be distributed via the Internet or intranet using a CAI-in-UDP encapsulation[1]. This traffic can be multicast or unicast to listeners that perform tasks such as audio decoding, message logging, re-transmission or detailed traffic analysis.

To assist with the inspection and analysis of P25 network traffic a plug-in module for the WireShark protocol analyzer has been contributed by Michael Ossman. This plug-in allows P25 traffic to be analyzed and filtered using WiresShark. A detailed description of an earlier version of the P25 Receiver can be found in [4].

3.3   P25 Transmitter

The P25 transmitter is also a hybrid Python/C++ program which accepts P25 data-link frames as its input and produces a P25 radio signal as its output. These frames are read from file and encoded into a symbol stream that is modulated and amplified before being sent to the USRP. The use of pre-prepared files for the input was chosen because message traffic can be prepared in advance and

---

[1] IANA has registered UDP port 8062 for use by the CAI-in-UDP encapsulation.

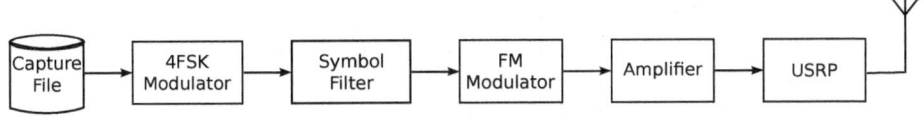

Fig. 4. Block Diagram view of P25 4-Level FSK Transmitter

offers precise control over how and when the message traffic is to be injected. The format of the P25 input file is chosen to be the same as that used by the WireShark protocol analyzer. This means that traffic captured by the P25 receiver can be re-injected with little effort. A block diagram for the transmitter is shown in figure 4 that shows how the signal-processing blocks are connected together.

4 Security Flaws in P25

Although P25 supports the use of cryptographically sound ciphers such as AES and 3DES the use of such ciphers alone is not sufficient to ensure secure operation. In this section we summarize the security flaws that we have identified in the P25 specifications.

4.1 Optional Encryption

Possibly the most important shortcoming of P25 is that the use of secure communications is optional. For *mobile radios* (MRs) an additional hardware module or firmware upgrade is usually required before encryption can be used. As we discuss later (§4.6), the security protocols of P25 do not provide an effective authentication mechanism and cannot establish the authenticity of a message. Although it is an inter-operability advantage to be able to fall back to un-encrypted or even analogue modes of operation one of the most severe consequences is that all radios must process messages that are sent in the clear. Therefore, an adversary can inject messages into the network which are in the clear and rely on network devices and infrastructure handling them as though they are legitimate. This exposes radios to the risk of "fuzzing" attacks by adversaries who can create illegal traffic that is intended to crash or otherwise compromise the integrity of radios.

4.2 Flawed Authentication and Access Control Mechanism

Authentication and access control seek to restrict access to the network to users who are suitably authorized. The original P25 standard did not mandate an authentication and access control mechanism but has been amended to include an optional authentication mechanism [5]. This a relatively recent development and has not yet been widely implemented. The result is that the vast majority of P25 systems do not have *any* means by which to prevent unauthorized access. The authentication mechanism defined by P25 uses a cryptographic challenge/response protocol to authenticate the *Mobile Radios* (MRs) and the *Fixed Station* (FS). This provides for one-way authentication (MR to FS) and mutual authentication (MR to FS and FS to MR).

The one-way *Radio Authentication* (RA) protocol is shown in protocol 1. In this protocol a unique secret key K_{MR} is shared between the MR and an *Authentication Centre* (AuC). Authentication begins in response to the MR sending a registration request to the FS. In step 1 the AuC generates an 80 bit random seed RS and 128 bit authentication key K_S and sends them to the FS. The authentication key K_S is derived from RS using the $AM1$ procedure (which zero-pads RS to the AES block size and encrypts it under K_{MR}). In step 2 the FS generates a 40 bit random challenge $RAND1$ which is sent with RS to the MR. At this point the MR can compute $RES1$ by using RS to derive K_S and encrypting $RAND1$ using the $AM2$ procedure (which zero-pads $RAND1$ to the AES block size and encrypts it under K_S). At this point the FS can compare $RES1$ against the value it has computed. If, the two values match the MR is considered to be authenticated and registered successfully; otherwise the registration attempt is rejected. An extension of this protocol allows for *Mutual Authentication* (MA).

Protocol 1. Radio Authentication Protocol

1 $AuC \rightarrow FS : K_S = AM1_{K_{MR}}(RS), RS$
2 $FS \rightarrow MS : RAND1, RS$
3 $MR \rightarrow FS : RES1 = AM2_{K_S}(RAND1)$

There is, however, a serious security flaw present in this authentication and access control mechanism. The authentication process decouples authentication and key agreement — successful authentication does *not* establish a session key but instead merely changes the state of the association to the authenticated state. This is a consequence of the the optional status of both the authentication and encryption services which can be used completely independently of each other. An adversary can monitor the channel and learn the identity of MRs that have already registered successfully and then assume those identities. The assumption that an adversary cannot discover the identities of registered stations or easily change their identity maybe valid for typical commercial systems but for a software radio it is trivial to monitor traffic and assume the identity of registered stations. As a result this mechanism provides absolutely no defence against an intruder.

4.3   Flawed Key Hierarchy

Serious security flaws are present in the design of the key hierarchy used by P25. Most importantly, the standards do not mandate a key hierarchy that ensures that individual associations have their own unique encryption key. Instead a single *traffic encryption key* (TEK) is shared by a number of MRs that are known as a cryptogroup. A single MR may belong to several cryptogroups and so a number of these TEKs can be programmed into a MR. This allows for some radios to be programmed with keys not present in others and preserves operational security between unrelated groups. The transmitter identifies which encryption key is in use by means of a sixteen-bit *key id* (KID) that is transmitted in the plain as part of the *header data unit* (HDU) and repeated as part of the *logical data unit 2* (LDU2) non-voice payload. The second level of keys in the key hierarchy are the *Key Encryption Keys* (KEKs) used by the KMF to perform an *over-the-air re-keying* (OTAR) operation in which an MR's encryption keys can be remotely re-programmed [6]. The KEKs are used by the KMF only for the distribution of encryption keys and encryption of other OTAR messages. The initial KEKs are bootstrapped into the MRs using a hardware device known as a keyloader whereas further TEKs/KEKs programmed using OTAR messages.

The use of a single TEK for many different transmissions/users means that all traffic encrypted under that key can be decrypted as the result of a successful key-recovery attack. This effect is compounded because the same traffic encryption key is likely to remain in use for an extended period of time. This is because key management can be a problem when there are many devices and key changes must be co-ordinated across many different groups. The difficulty of this task means that it tends to be performed infrequently. Australian emergency responders, for example, do not use OTAR and usually change their TEKs on an annual basis. The combined effect is that an adversary has a significant incentive to recover an encryption key because a successful key recovery will reveal the contents of a large amount of traffic. They also have a large amount of time in which to do so and, once the encryption key is discovered, have complete access to traffic in real-time.

Another serious problem with using a single key for an entire cryptogroup means that any station can masquerade as any other within the same cryptogroup. Although this is principally an insider attack it presents problems when an MR is stolen. The key plus the transmitter's station identity is assumed to be sufficient to authenticate a station. When a MR is stolen it is quite possible for an adversary to change the device's identity whilst preserving encryption keys. The theft of an MR can be mitigated in several ways. Firstly, OTAR allows for the TEKs of legitimate stations to be changed in response to a reported theft; if the stolen radio is within radio range and remains powered then OTAR permits the keys present in the stolen radio to be erased remotely. The second line of defence are the physical security and anti-tampering measures of the MR itself. It is typical for an MR to employ tamper-proofing measures that erase the encryption keys to prevent their recovery.

4.4   Weak Encryption

P25 allows for the use of several optional cipher systems including DES, 3DES and AES. Some of these cipher systems employ weak cryptographic ciphers that are subject to key-recovery attacks. At the time of writing the cipher in most widespread use is DES in OFB mode[7]. Although it is marked for "backward compatibility" by TIA several factors favour DES-OFB and militate against the use of the other, more secure, ciphers such as 3DES and AES:

- DES-OFB is the *only* cipher that manufacturers *must* implement in order to comply with the specification,
- users frequently encounter interoperability problems when using optional features of equipment from different manufacturers and
- the export of certain US-manufactured devices (such as AES-capable key-loaders) requires an export license for shipping outside of the US and Canada.

These factors entrench the use of the DES-OFB cipher system which remains in widespread use. DES has remained largely resistant to cryptographic attacks but, because of its limited key size, exhaustive key search attacks have proven to be very effective. Using specialized hardware such attacks can now be conducted very quickly using only modest resources.

4.5   No Guarantee of Message Freshness

P25 is also vulnerable to message replay attacks. The adversary can record messages and re-inject them into the system at a later time. To protect against replay attacks requires an authenticated nonce, sequence number or timing information to be included in the messages so that replayed messages can be detected by the receiver and ignored. Data frames can optionally meet these requirements using a monotonically-increasing *message number* (MN) and a MAC computed across the MN and message payload. Unfortunately, the optional nature of these protections permits an adversary to construct traffic which misrepresents its identity and indicates that no MN is present.

4.6   Flawed Message Authenticity and Integrity Mechanism

We have already alluded to the fact that there is no explicit guarantee of authenticity for voice traffic; this is a direct consequence of the optional status of the encryption protocol. Data messages are usually protected only with *cyclic redundancy checks* (CRCs) computed over the ciphertext of the frame and sent in the plain. These offer no protection against message modification and replay attacks. As an option for data traffic, P25 allows for the use of DES/CBC to compute *message authentication codes* (MACs) to authenticate the values of some data and control frames. The CBC/MAC protocol is, however, optional and can easily be bypassed (see §5.2).

5   Security Attacks and Defences in P25

The security flaws present in the P25 protocol introduce the threat of attacks and this section identifies the threats and, where possible, the proposed countermeasures. The experimental method consists of identifying security threats in the behavior of the P25 network using a simple test-bed that consists of a single P25 transceiver used together with the SDR P25 implementation. A repeater was not available for testing and so a simplex UHF radio channel is used to empirically verify the attacks.

5.1 Denial of Service - The Inhibit Attack

In all radio systems there are denial-of-service risks at the physical layer through collision jamming and other attacks. In digital and trunked systems such as P25 there are new threats from attacks directed at the network control protocol. The Inhibit attack makes use of the anti-theft measures of the P25 standard to disable legitimate nodes. The P25 protocol contains an anti-theft mechanism which is intended to prevent a stolen radio being used by an adversary. This feature is known colloquially as "stun" and is implemented by sending a special abbreviated PDU known as a *Trunk Signaling Data Unit* (TSDU) to the device. The payload of the TSDU is an "inhibit" *Extended Function Command* (XFC) the structure of which is shown in figure 5. Once a radio has been stunned by the receipt of an inhibit command the standard requires that it remains in-operational and unresponsive to the operator console or device programming interface until it receives an "uninhibit" XFC on the frequency it received the inhibit. The attack exploits the lack of any guarantee of authenticity for the frame Inhibit/Uninhibit types. The adversary simply directs "inhibit" commands towards legitimate stations causing them to become disabled without any explanation. The format of the XFC is shown in figure 5. Note that the XFC message payload may be sent either encrypted (P=1) or un-encrypted (P=0) and that there is no explicit means of authenticating the inhibit command.

The inhibit function presents a serious threat to availability and does not provide a satisfactory anti-theft measure because a thief can uninibit the radio themselves. For this reason some manufacturers allow for radios to be configured

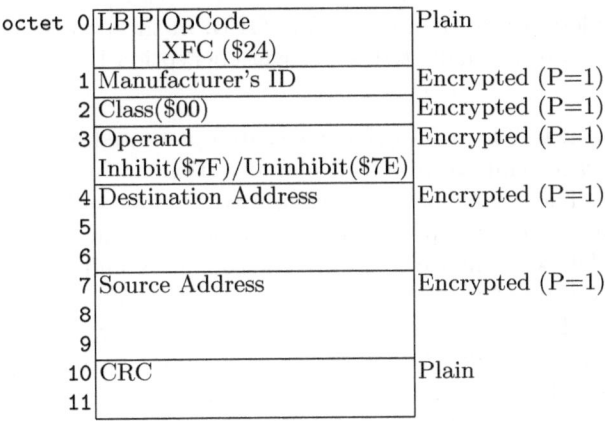

Fig. 5. Extended Function Command

to ignore inhibit commands. This is often a configuration option that can be set for each MR using the equipment's programming interface. Allowing inhibit to be disabled is intended to mitigate the threat of DoS attacks but does so at the cost of negating the anti-theft measure.

5.2   Message-Modification Attack

The weak authenticity and integrity provisions of P25 expose it to threat of message modification attacks. A message modification attack can detect the presence of MAC-protected frames, remove the MAC and substitute a CRC in its place. The receiver will accept such frames as legitimate even though they do not possess the MAC because they conform to the specification. A two-bit field is present in the frame header and indicates whether the frame has no checksum, a CRC or a cryptographic MAC. Although this field is encrypted the adversary can detect the presence or absence of the MAC based on frame size. The use of stream ciphers means that an adversary can perform a simple XOR operation to change the state of these bits. Thus messages can be modified by an adversary to remove the MAC without the receiver's knowledge and without possessing the encryption key. The only remedial measure is to make the use of MACs mandatory as the strongest authenticity and integrity mechanism available in the standard and ignore all traffic which is not suitably protected. Unfortunately such a move would still fail to protect voice traffic and would not be compatible with existing equipment.

5.3   Key Recovery by Exhaustive Key Search

The use of weak ciphers by P25 equipment makes it possible to recover the encryption key using an exhaustive search. DES is no longer regarded as secure because an exhaustive key search can be mounted to recover the encryption key. Motorola's proprietary *Advanced Digital Privacy* (ADP) cipher, which is described here for what we believe to be the first time, uses a 40 bit key and is considerably less secure than even DES/OFB. In this section we will describe how this attack can be conducted to recover encryption keys.

Known-Plaintext. The exhaustive key search presented here exploits the fact that voice messages contain a known-plaintext that occurs at known locations in the message. These arise because, when a voice message is finished but there are unused voice codewords in the current frame, the transmitter is required to complete the LDU with silence codewords [1, §8.2.3]. A similar process, known as audio muting, occurs at the beginning of voice transmissions and results in the first few voice codewords being encoded as silence Our observations have shown that audio muting provides 4 silence silence voice codewords at the beginning of a transmission. If an adversary can correctly identify a silence codeword then they can reveal 11 consecutive octets of keystream. An adversary monitoring a voice transmission can identify the first and/or last frame in a transmission and those codewords which have the highest probability of being silence. Exhaustively searching for the key which generates the appropriate keystream is possible when the key space is small enough and allows the adversary to discover the encryption key.

DES/OFB. The DES/OFB cipher system is the only cipher system which the standard declares to be a mandatory option. That is, equipment suppliers must be able to offer DES/OFB as an option on their equipment in order to pass the compliance testing. DES has a 56 bit key which means a key space of approximately 7×10^{16} unique keys. On average an adversary would search half of the key space before discovering the key. Exhaustively searching this key space is computationally intensive but modern hardware makes such a strategy possible. To conduct an exhaustive key search against DES/OFB the known-plaintext must be chosen carefully so that 16 sequential octets of keystream are revealed; these must be aligned on a 64 bit boundary and represent the input and output of a single DES/OFB encryption operation. Given these two blocks an exhaustive key search simply encrypts the input value using DES/ECB under every possible key until the actual output value is found.

When using the beginning of a captured transmission for an exhaustive key search we can use the fact that the VC1 and VC2 voice codewords at the start of the LDU 1 are silent to reveal such blocks 4 and 5 of the DES/OFB keystream. The presence of silence in the voice codewords at the start of the transmission make this the preferred choice. The situation is slightly more complex when using the codewords at the end of the LDU1 or LDU2 because they will be silent only with a given probability distribution. The uses of these latter codewords is further complicated because of the presence of two octets of non-voice payload which are unknown to the adversary. The example for an LDU1 is shown in figure 6 and a similar situation exists at the end of the LDU2. This doesn't pose a serious problem because the exhaustive key search will produce 2^{16} candidate blocks which can be verified simply by repeating the encryption and matching the resulting block to the ciphertext revealed by the known plaintext.

A commodity 2.5GHz Intel Core i7 processor can easily compute one million DES keys per second in software using the OpenSSL library. This is, however, optimized for the case of encrypting the key with large volumes of traffic and not key searching. A bit-sliced implementation carefully optimized for key searching can reach in excess of twenty-eight million keys/second. Even so, DES is not trivially defeated. Even at one hundred million keys per second it will take almost twenty-three years to search the whole key space. It is possible to achieve much better performance using dedicated hardware and many processors running in parallel. In 1998 the EFF constructed an ASIC-based device that could search the DES keyspace within 9 days at a cost of 250,000 US$ [8]. Since then the cost of computation has fallen and efficient DES cores have been developed such as the core developed by the UCL Crypto Group at the University of Lovain-la-Neuve which is optimized for such key searches [9,10]. This core has been used in COPACABANA — a recent FPGA-based device that can exhaustively search the DES key space within nine days at a cost of just 10,000 US$ [11].

64 bit DES block

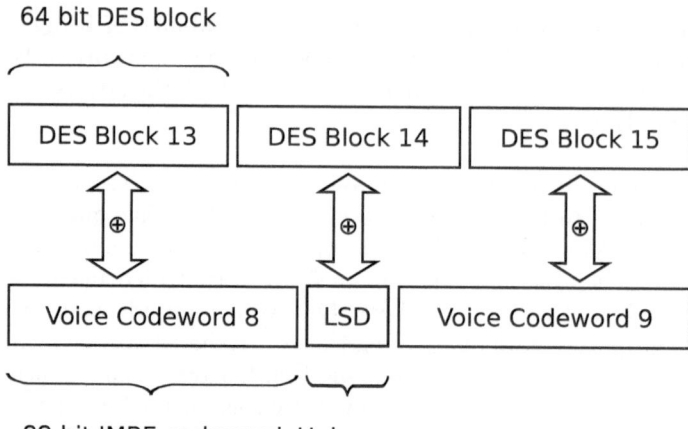

Fig. 6. Presence of Non-Voice Data in Encryption Schedule

ADP. *Advanced Digital Privacy* (ADP) is a proprietary cipher system that is available on some Motorola equipment as a firmware upgrade. There is no publicly available documentation describing the ADP and so we have reverse-engineered the cipher to discover how it operates. We know from the user interface of the radio management software that the ADP cipher has a 40 bit key. This appears to have been chosen to meet the now-defunct US export restrictions for cryptographic products. The size of the keyspace is much too small to protect traffic from an exhaustive keyspace search.

We conducted our investigation using traffic captured from a Motorola XTS 5000 hand-held radio with the ADP cipher option enabled. A transmission was made that consisted of audio silence and was sent without encryption. Inspection of the first transmission showed that the radio was correctly transmitting the silence codeword values as required by both the CAI and the IMBE vocoder specification [12]. A second transmission also of audio silence was made using ADP under a known encryption key. ADP is rumoured to make use of the RC4 cipher and so we subjected the encrypted message to a simple analysis in which different combinations of the key and IV are used to generate 2048 octets of keystream. The resulting keystream is compared with the presumed keystream from an encrypted frame and the result scored on the number of mismatches to the expected silence plaintext.

We confirmed that the cipher used by ADP is RC4 in which 40 bit secret key is combined with the 64 bit IV to form a 104 bit encryption key. The RC4 cipher is used produce 484 octets of keystream which is used to encrypt/decrypt the payload of the voice superframe. The operation of the ADP cipher is outlined in figure 7. ADP appears to makes use of RC4 in a secure fashion and:

- ADP *appends* the IV to the secret key to make the encryption key making it difficult for an observer to identify frames encoded under weak keys — one of the key flaws common to many RC4 implementations.

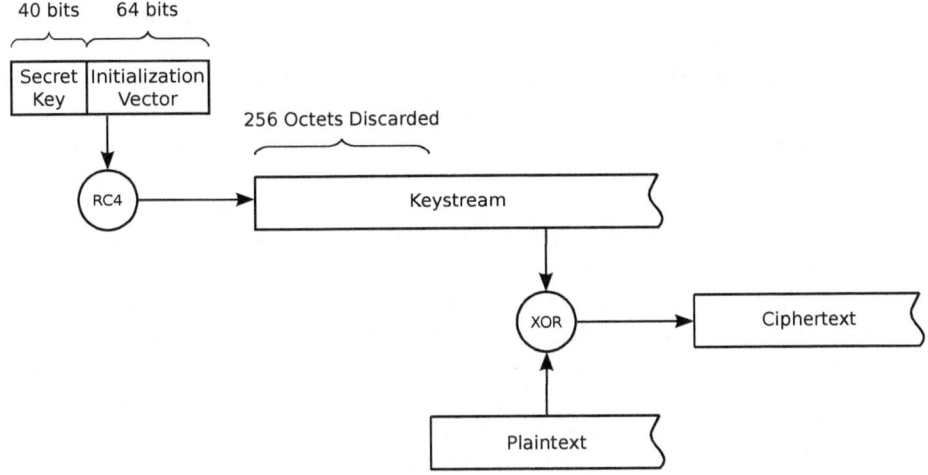

Fig. 7. ADP Cipher Encryption

- ADP discards the initial 256 octets of the keystream which have been shown to be correlated with the encryption key. In this ADP has followed the advice on the correct use of the RC4 cipher.

Exhaustive key search for ADP consists of using a silence codeword to recover the probable keystream and then using the IV for the message to search every one of the possible 2^{40} ($\approx 1 \times 10^{12}$) secret keys to find one which generates that keystream. Searching a keyspace of this size in software is well within the capabilities of ordinary commodity processors. Table 1 shows several processors and the number of millions of keystream/s that each processor core is capable of searching.

Table 1. Performance of ADP exhaustive key search

Processor	Clock Speed GHz	Cores/CPU	VC1 keys/s $\times 10^6$
Intel Core 2 Duo	1.2	2	.270
Intel Core 2 Duo	2.2	2	.475
Intel Core i7	2.6	2	.632
AMD Opteron 252	2.6	2	.375

Each of the processors identified uses an optimized RC4 implementation and generates sufficient keystream to decode the VC1 of the initial LDU1 frame. On a single core of a dual-core Intel i7 processor the search will take, on average, 10.6 days. The search time is inversely proportional to the total number of CPU cores used to conduct the search. An alternative approach is to make use of the computational capability of commonly-available GPUs which use a *single instruction/multiple data* (SIMD) architecture and can process many threads in parallel. We have investigated RC4 on GPUs and the best results improve on the performance of CPU implementations by a factor of between 3 and 5 which, allowing for hardware differences, are in general agreement with those of Li *et al.* [13]. Although this is a significant improvement these performance figures represent an extremely disappointing result and fall a long way short of the capability of the hardware. The problems in performance are explained principally by the very low occupation of the GPU by the RC4 implementation. The implementation is making use of just 6% of the available computational resources but is constrained by the memory limitations of the GPU device. RC4 implementations that are able to make more effective use of the GPU's computational resources have the potential to be much faster. Alternatively, an FPGA implementation of the RC4 cipher running on the Cube FPGA cluster can search the entire 40 bit key space in just three minutes [14]. This implementation is approximately four times faster per FPGA core than the same search running on a single CPU core.

Operational Responses to Exhaustive Key Search. A response to the threat of exhaustive key search adopted by some operators is to change the encryption keys relatively frequently. This reduces the time available for the adversary to search the keyspace, increases the amount of searching they must do and limits the amount of traffic that may be disclosed once the key is compromised. The P25 Over-The-Air-Rekeying (OTAR) protocol simplifies the key management process and allows MR equipment to be rapidly re-keyed.

Unfortunately, when using a weak cipher such as DES frequent re-keying does not significantly increase the work for the adversary. Even if an adversary can search only a small percentage of the keyspace they are likely to discover the key within a reasonable time as long as they re-start the search every time the key is changed because there is a uniform probability of picking a key within the adversary's search space. If $P(e)$ be the probability of choosing a key outside of the search space of the adversary then the probability $P(d)$ of picking a key within the adversary's search space after n re-keying attempts is given by:

$$P(d) = 1 - P(e)^n \tag{1}$$

The problem for the adversary is that searching in this way is not guaranteed to discover the key whereas searching the whole key space is. This suggests the adversary is better off storing all rekeying messages and decrypting them in turn once the original key is discovered. Unfortunately, enough of the rekeying packet is sent in the plain to allow them to be identified and stored — permitting complete decryption once the original key has been found.

A final warning relates to the use of OTAR with weak encryption keys. An adversary that can store OTAR frames can use the subsequent discovery of a TEK to provide a known plaintext and then repeat the search to recover the KEK. Once in possession of the KEK they will be able not just to monitor all traffic but to re-program the encryption keys used throughout the network.

6   Related Work

Clark *et al.* have also conducted an analysis of the security weaknesses present in the P25 protocol [15]. They identify the lack of authentication on voice and most other types of data traffic as being a significant problem, propose a novel attack against location privacy that can be used to locate a radio even when its user is not actively using the radio and discuss a physical layer jamming technique that can be used to perform denial-of-service attacks. These are all significant problems and largely complimentary in nature to those discussed here. The investigation of Clark *et al.* also makes use of the same SDR software that is presented in this paper as the basis of their investigation. The independent application of the SDR software demonstrates the utility of the approach when applied to the critical security analysis of wireless networks.

Another closely-related body of work is that of Project 54 conducted by the University of New Hampshire [16]. The focus of Project 54 is on in-car human computer interaction to provide police cruisers with an integrated environment in which communications Project 54 has implemented a P25 base station by pairing a PC with a conventional radio transceiver [17]. Ramsey *et al.* implemented this data transmitter for P25 using a conventional radio transceiver. The baseband signal is captured from the radio transceiver using the PC soundcard and the remaining signal processing stages are performed in software [18].

The RC4 cipher as used in ADP is also the basis for the flawed *Wired Equivalent Privacy* (WEP) used in IEEE 802.11. WEP does not correctly use the RC4 cipher and is subject to the weak-key attack of Fluhrer *et al.* [19] and Mantin [20]. The contrast with ADP is quite marked because ADP avoids the mistakes in the use of RC4 that were made by the designers of WEP. In other respects the P25 security protocol has similar weaknesses to the WEP flaws described by Borisov *et al.* [21]: the access control and authentication mechanism that is trivially by-passed, there are no guarantees of message freshness and the integrity controls are insufficient to protect against deliberate damage.

7   Conclusions

P25 radio systems are more secure than conventional analogue radio systems but not nearly as secure as the term "encrypted" would imply. The most serious security flaw in P25 is the optional nature of the security protocol, however even when the security protocol is used several serious security flaws present the design of P25 cryptographic protections, remain:

- Weak encryption permits an attacker to recover the encryption key, and frequent re-keying is not an effective defence.
- There is no effective authentication and access control mechanism.
- The lack of a key hierarchy means that a single key is used to encrypt traffic between many users over many sessions.
- The integrity, authenticity and freshness of traffic cannot be ensured even when the security protocol is in use.
- Serious denial-of-service threats against individual stations are possible.

The contribution of this paper is in several parts: firstly, we have applied the techniques of software-defined radio to enable the study and network security analysis. This approach has the potential to expose network traffic at all layers of the protocol stack. Secondly we have identified a number of serious security flaws that are present in the P25 protocol and described attacks which exploit them.

Acknowledgments. NICTA is funded by the Australian Government as represented by the Department of Broadband, Communications and the Digital Economy and the Australian Research Council through the ICT Centre of Excellence program.

References

1. Project 25 FDMA Common Air Interface Description. Number TIA-102.BAAA-A. Telecommunications Industry Association, 2500 Wilson Boulevard, Arlington, VA 22201, USA (September 2003)
2. GNU Radio. Project website, http://www.gnuradio.org
3. Ettus research llc, Company website, http://www.ettus.com
4. Glass, S., Muthukkumarasamy, V., Portmann, M.: A software-defined radio receiver for APCO Project 25 signals. In: IWCMC 2009: Proceedings of the 2009 International Conference on Wireless Communications and Mobile Computing, pp. 67–72. ACM, New York (2009)
5. Project 25 — Digital Land Mobile Radio — Link Layer Authentication. Number TIA-102.AACE. Telecommunications Industry Association, 2500 Wilson Boulevard, Arlington, VA 22201, USA (December 2005)
6. Project 25 Over-The-Air-Rekeying(OTAR) Operational Description. Number TIA-102.AACB. Telecommunications Industry Association, 2500 Wilson Boulevard, Arlington, VA 22201, USA (January 2002)
7. Project 25 DES Encryption Protocol. Number TIA/EIA-102.AAAA-A. Telecommunications Industry Association, 2500 Wilson Boulevard, Arlington, VA 22201, USA (2001)
8. Loukides, M., Gilmore, J.: Cracking DES: Secrets of Encryption Research, Wiretap Politics and Chip Design. O'Reilly & Associates, Inc., Sebastopol (1998), http://cryptome.org/cracking-des/cracking-des.html
9. Rouvroy, G., Standaert, F.-X., Quisquater, J.-J., Legat, J.-D.: Design Strategies and Modified Descriptions to Optimize Cipher FPGA Implementations: Fast and Compact Results for DES and Triple-DES. In: Cheung, P.Y.K., Constantinides, G.A. (eds.) FPL 2003. LNCS, vol. 2778, pp. 181–193. Springer, Heidelberg (2003), doi:10.1007/978-3-540-45234-8_19
10. Rouvroy, G., Standaert, F.-X., Quisquater, J.-J., Legat, J.-D.: Efficient uses of FPGAs for implementations of DES and its experimental linear cryptanalysis. IEEE Transactions on Computers 52(4), 473–482 (2003)
11. Kumar, S., Paar, C., Pelzl, J., Pfeiffer, G., Schimmler, M.: Breaking Ciphers with COPACOBANA –A Cost-Optimized Parallel Code Breaker. In: Goubin, L., Matsui, M. (eds.) CHES 2006. LNCS, vol. 4249, pp. 101–118. Springer, Heidelberg (2006)

12. Project 25 Vocoder Description. Number ANSI/TIA/EIA-102.BABA-1998. Telecommunications Industry Association, 2500 Wilson Boulevard, Arlington, VA 22201, USA (May 1998)
13. Li, C., Wu, H., Chen, S., Li, X., Guo, D.: Efficient implementation for MD5-RC4 encryption using GPU with CUDA. In: 3rd International Conference on Anti-Counterfeiting, Security, and Identification in Communication (ASID 2009), pp. 167–170 (August 2009)
14. Mencer, O., Tsoi, K.H., Craimer, S., Todman, T., Luk, W., Wong, M.Y., Leong, P.H.W.: Cube: A 512-FPGA cluster. In: 5th Southern Conference on Programmable Logic, SPL 2009, pp. 51–57 (April 2009)
15. Clark, S., Metzger, P., Wasserman, Z., Xu, K., Blaze, M.A.: Security weaknesses in the APCO Project 25 two-way radio system. Technical Report MS-CIS-10-34, University of Pennsylvania (2010), http://repository.upenn.edu/cis_reports/944
16. Project 54. Project website, http://project54.unh.edu
17. Kun, A.L., Thomas Miller III, W., Lenharth, W.H.: Computers in police cruisers. IEEE Pervasive Computing 3(4), 34–41 (2004)
18. Ramsey, E.R., Thomas Miller III, W., Kun, A.L.: A software-based implementation of an APCO Project 25 compliant packet data transmitter. In: 2008 IEEE International Conference on Technologies for Homeland Security, Boston, MA, May 12-13. Institute of Electrical and Electronics Engineers (2008)
19. Fluhrer, S.R., Mantin, I., Shamir, A.: Weaknesses in the Key Scheduling Algorithm of RC4. In: Vaudenay, S., Youssef, A.M. (eds.) SAC 2001. LNCS, vol. 2259, pp. 1–24. Springer, Heidelberg (2001)
20. Mantin, I.: A Practical Attack on the Fixed RC4 in the WEP Mode. In: Roy, B. (ed.) ASIACRYPT 2005. LNCS, vol. 3788, pp. 395–411. Springer, Heidelberg (2005)
21. Borisov, N., Goldberg, I., Wagner, D.: Intercepting mobile communications: the insecurity of 802.11. In: Proceedings of the 7th Annual International Mobile Computing and Networking Conference, pp. 180–189. ACM SIGMOBIL, ACM Press, New York, NY (2001)

Behavioral Mimicry Covert Communication

Seyed Ali Ahmadzadeh and Gordon Agnew

Department of Electrical and Computer Engineering,
University of Waterloo,
Waterloo, ON, Canada, N2L 3G1
{ahmadzdh,gbagnew}@uwaterloo.ca

Abstract. In this paper, the use of structural behavior of communication protocols (e.g., CSMA) in designing new covert channels is investigated. In this way, the covert transmitter adopts the communication protocol architecture to control its overt traffic flow yet with different parameters that give it enough freedom to embed the covert message in its overt traffic. A salient feature of this scheme is that its rate increases in proportion with the overt capacity of the system. In addition, the paper presents a new covert channel for the wireless environment that mimics the structural behavior of CSMA protocol. The parameters of the proposed scheme are optimized in order to maximize the channel rate, stealthiness and robustness. Finally, the performance of the proposed scheme is analyzed from security, reliability and communication rate point of view.

Keywords: Covert communication, information hiding, wireless security.

1 Introduction

Covert communication often refers to the process of communicating data through a channel that is neither designed, nor intended to transfer information [13]. The primary use of covert channels was to allow information to be leaked to an unauthorized recipient by exploiting weaknesses in conventional communication systems.

In general, two major forms of covert channels are defined in the literature. One category involves direct or indirect storage of the covert message into certain portion of the network traffic (i.e., *storage channels*) [9]. The other category (i.e. *timing channels*) [7], targets some typical characteristics of the system (e.g., inter-packet delays) to exploit normal behavior of the system and open a covert channel. In this way, the receiver can interpret the covert transmitter's message by analyzing the system behavior. This classification can be extended by identifying new channels such as *counting channels* [8] in which the number and the frequency of events come into play instead of the occurrence of an isolated event.

Kemmer [12] identified three necessary conditions for existence of a covert channel. (i) a global resource that is shared between the receiver and the sender of the covert message, (ii) ability to modify the shared resource and, (iii) a method to achieve synchronization between the sender and the receiver. The wireless environment provides all three conditions making it a perfect medium for a wide range

M. Rajarajan et al. (Eds.): SecureComm 2011, LNICST 96, pp. 134–153, 2012.
© Institute for Computer Sciences, Social Informatics and Telecommunications Engineering 2012

of covert channels, some of them are yet to be found [3,14,19]. In [1] a covert channel based on jamming over slotted ALOHA was introduced in which the covert transmitter jams specific packets in the network. The receiver decodes the covert message through the packet loss pattern of the system. A covert channel based on splitting tree algorithm was introduce in [15]. This approach exploits splitting tree collision resolution algorithm by reconfiguring the covert transmitter to choose a particular path in the splitting tree according to the covert message. The receiver on the other hand, decodes the covert message through the relative position of the covert transmitter in the tree. Later, Wang *et al.* [20] extended the above approach into an anonymous covert channel in which the receiver decodes the covert message using a specific voting mechanism that considers the probabilistic decisions of multiple covert transmitters within the collision resolution algorithm. In [10] the authors investigate the application of the covert transmitter's inter-packet arrival time patters in order to synchronize the covert transmitter and the covert receiver in the DCF mode of the IEEE 802.11 protocol. Their scheme was based on a round of training where both the transmitter and the receiver adapt themselves with the network and generate a codebook in order to embed the covert message into the transmitter's inter-packet arrival time.

Although the above covert communication schemes provide secure and stealth communication channels, they trade the achievable rate of the channel in favor of reliability and secrecy of the channel. The synchronization between the covert transmitter and the covert receiver is also a challenging issue as covert channels are often one-way channels with no universal time reference available in the channel. Moreover, wide variety of covert communication schemes [4, 5, 6, 16], focus on long-term statistical properties of the covert transmitter and aim to keep the transmitter's statistical finger prints as close as possible to a legitimate transmitter. However, to achieve this goal, the covert transmitter has to deviate from typical short-term behaviors of a legitimate source. Therefore, a system observer may be able to detect the covert transmitter and uncover the existence of the covert channel.

In this paper, we presented a new approach that systematically exploits the probabilistic nature of access control protocols in communication networks to open a covert channel in the system. To this end, we turn our attention to the structural behavior of communication protocols and design a covert transmitter that mimics not only long-term statistical behaviors of a legitimate node but also reacts to the temporal changes in the system similar to a typical transmitter. A salient feature of the proposed covert channel is that its rate increases linearly with the overt channel rate of the system.

The rest of the paper is organized as follows. In Section 2, the principles of the system under study are reviewed followed by a detailed description of the proposed covert channel in Section 3. Section 4 contains a discussion on how the proposed covert transmitter and the covert receiver are tuned in order to mimic the behavior of legitimate nodes. The performance analysis and numerical results are presented in Section 5. Section 6 concludes the paper.

2   System Model

IEEE 802.11 [11] is one of the most popular wireless communication protocols. It uses the *carrier sense multiple access / collision avoidance* (CSMA/CA) technique in order to share the wireless channel among multiple users.

In CSMA/CA, the wireless channel is divided into small time periods called time slots. Users constantly check the channel to detect transmission activities. If the channel is busy, each user selects a backoff time (measured in slot times) randomly in the interval $[0, W)$, where W is the size of the contention window. This backoff timer is decreased any time that the channel is sensed idle for a specific period of time called DIFS (i.e., Distributed Inter-Frame Space). The timer stops if the channel gets busy again and when it reached zero, a packet is transmitted and the receiver acknowledges the packet after a period of SIFS (i.e., Short Inter-Frame Space). The size of the contention window is set to W_{min} following each successful transmission, and is doubled after each unsuccessful transmission. The expansion stops when the size of the contention window reaches W_{max} and remains constant until the transmission is successful.

Through the rest of the paper it is assumed that the covert receiver is aware of the covert transmitter's identity and shares a wireless channel with several users in the system (including the covert transmitter). The terms covert receiver and receiver and also covert transmitter and transmitter are used interchangeably. It is also assumed that each packet contains the identity of its transmitter (e.g., the source address field in IEEE 802.11).

3   Behavioral Mimicry Covert Communication

In principle, the behavioral mimicry covert communication is based on adopting the structure of the medium access control protocol, in use by ordinary users in the system, and modify it in such a way that gives the covert transmitter enough freedom to embed the covert message into its overt traffic. It is noted that most access control protocols in communication networks, bring some kind of randomness into the system in order to provide each user with a fair share of resources of the system. By adopting the structure of the communication protocol, one can benefit from the aforementioned random behavior and opens a new covert channel in the system.

Inspired by this observation, in this section, a new covert communication scheme is presented which is based on mimicking the structural behaviors of CSMA/CA algorithm. The proposed scheme is primarily designed for wireless protocols such as IEEE 802.11, however it can be extended to other communication models that involve multiple access techniques and shared mediums. First, a fixed rate version of the proposed scheme is discussed in order to highlight main properties of the covert system. Then, an advanced modification of the proposed scheme is presented that adapts its rate according to the channel condition.

3.1   Fixed Rate Covert Communication (FRCC)

FRCC scheme is basically a timing covert channel that benefits from the channel activities of a subset of users in the system (i.e., the covert set) as clock ticks for a virtual clock called *covert clock*. The covert message is embedded into the covert transmitter's contention window which is controlled by the covert clock. The covert receiver also maintains its own covert clock by observing the same channel activities of members of the covert set. It is noted that due to the broadcast nature of the wireless environment, all users that share the same channel can overhear the transmitted packets. This only requires that both sides track the same set of users and are equipped with proper error correction methods in case a mismatch happens between the transmitter and the receiver. Hence, the transmitter and the receiver can observe the channel activities of the same set of users and increment their clock synchronously. In this way, upon receiving a packet from the covert transmitter, the receiver evaluates the value of its covert clock and decodes the embedded message.

Let S be the subset of network users in which their packet transmissions are considered as clock ticks. The covert set can be preset in the covert transmitter and the covert receiver or may be generated dynamically. For instance, it can be a set of users that their MAC addresses, or the hash values of their MAC addresses have certain properties. Also, a user can be included into S if its position is inside an acceptable region in the system (user position can be obtained from its signal power or using smart antenna techniques).

Figure 1 depicts how the transmitter embeds the covert message into its contention window and synchronizes the contention window with the covert clock. Let ω be a covert message from the covert message set Ω. Each covert message is associated to a unique state in the first stage of the transmitter's transmission window. Hence, the size of the message set is equal to the initial size of the transmitter's transmission window (i.e., T_0). For simplicity and without loss of generality, let's assume $\Omega = \{0, 1, ..., T_0 - 1\}$. Hence, the message $\omega \in \Omega$ corresponds to the state m_ω^0 in Figure 1. It is noted that for any message set Γ of size T_0, one can find a one-to-one mapping that transforms Γ to Ω.

For instance, suppose $T_0 = 4$ and the transmitter intends to transmit the binary sequence $\mathcal{B}$ over the covert channel. The transmitter generates the message set $\Gamma = \{00, 01, 10, 11\}$ and splits $\mathcal{B}$ into smaller items of size two, where each item is a member of Γ. It is noted that the binary to decimal conversion is a mapping that transforms Γ to Ω. In fact, one can recognize the similarity of the above example to the concept of modulation in digital communication [18].

Each communication block starts with a successful packet transmission by the covert transmitter. Then, the transmitter begins to monitor the channel to catch packets from members of S. For each packet, the transmitter's clock is incremented by one unit and it moves down one state (i.e., to the left in Figure 1) in its transmission window. The covert transmitter sends its next packet when it reaches to the last state of the transmission window to mark the value of its covert clock which is observed by the covert receiver. It is noted that the covert

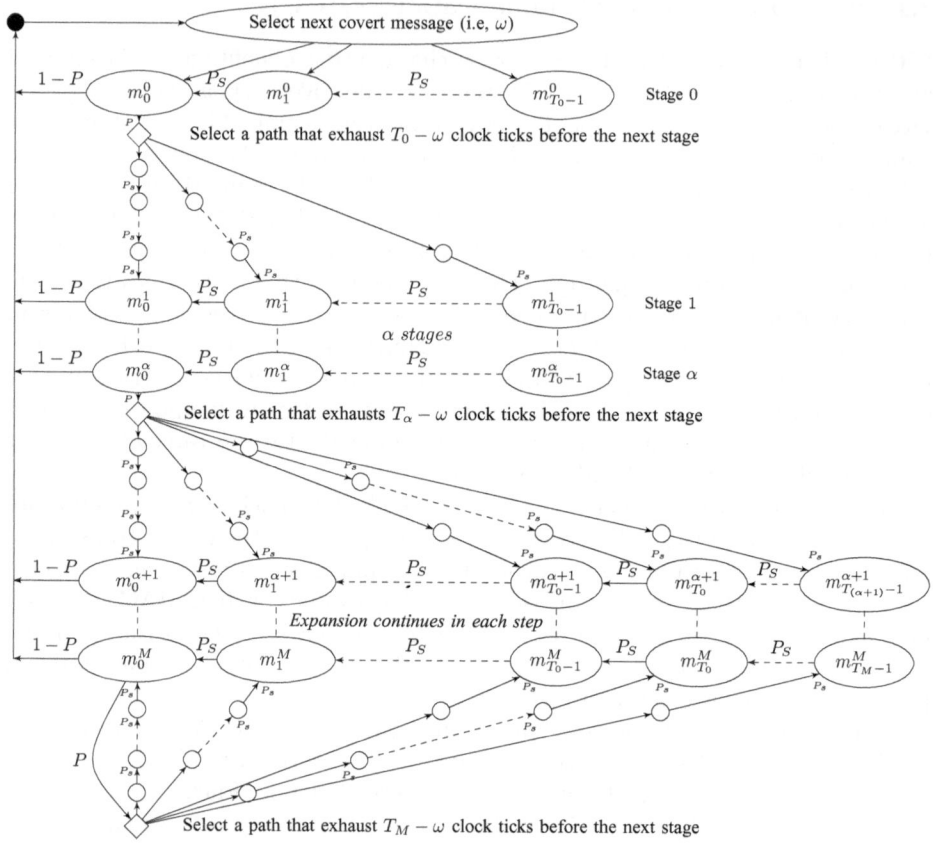

Fig. 1. Covert message transmission. P_S is the probability of a successful transmission by members of S.

transmitter can recognize multiple transmissions of a single packet using the packet's sequence number field.

Similarly, at the other end of the channel, the covert receiver monitors the channel for successful transmissions of members of the covert set and maintains the same covert clock value as the covert transmitter. In this way, when the covert receiver detects a packet from the covert transmitter, it reads the value of its covert clock and decodes the corresponding covert message. The receiver then resets its clock and monitors the channel in order to receive the next covert message. It is worth noting that this scheme does not affect the usual packet transmission of the receiver or other nodes in the system. The transmitter also is able to maintain its overt communication except that its contention window is controlled by the covert clock.

However, if the covert transmitter fails to transmit the packet on the proper time slot (e.g., due to collision with other nodes), the covert transmitter expands its contention window and selects another transmission slot to send its packet.

Algorithm 1. FRCC transmission sequence.

/* i is the covert transmitter's current stage index.
function $Success = sendpkt(T_i, message)$
$wait(message)$;
$Success = transmit\_pkt()$;
if $Success$ **then**
   return true
else
   $wait(T_i - message)$;
   return false
end if

The reason for the covert transmitter to expand its contention window is two fold. First of all, it is essential for the covert transmitter to achieve maximum stealthiness and does not behave differently as compared to other nodes in the system. In the traditional CSMA/CA protocol, each node expands its contention window and waits for a random amount of time before retransmitting its packets. The covert transmitter should not be exempted from this rule, otherwise it would be easy to detect the covert channel. Thus, the size of the covert transmitter's contention window in the ith transmission stage is calculated as follows:

$$T_i = \begin{cases} T_0 & 0 \leq i \leq \alpha \\ 2T_{i-1} & \alpha < i \leq M \\ T_M & i > M \end{cases} \qquad (1)$$

Where M is the index of the last stage in which the transmitter expands its contention window. The parameter α is a design parameter of the proposed scheme and will be explained in the Section 4. Algorithm (1) shows how the covert clock is used in order to transmit a covert message. Here, the $wait()$ function exhausts certain number of clock ticks before it returns the control to the main process, and the $transmit\_pkt()$ routine transmits the packet through the channel and returns true if the actual receiver of the packet acknowledges the reception of the packet.

In addition to achieve stealthiness, expanding the transmitter's contention window plays a major role in synchronizing end peers of the covert channel. In fact, as the covert message is embedded in the covert clock, both nodes require accurate knowledge on the current state of the covert clock if they are about to communicate effectively. To this end, following each unsuccessful packet transmission attempt, the transmitter waits for exactly $T_i - \omega$ clock ticks before expanding its contention window and moving to the next stage. Hence, the covert clock is equal to $\sum_{j=0}^{i-1} T_j$ at the beginning of the $(i)^{th}$ stage regardless of the value of the covert message. The receiver removes this offset from the value of its covert clock (i.e., C_r) in order to decode the covert message. Thus,

$$\omega = C_r \bmod T_0. \qquad (2)$$

Algorithm 2. Covert transmitter function of FRCC.

/* $PRNG(n)$ generates a random bit stream of length n.
$i = 0$; $\omega_s = \omega$; $T_{-1} = T_0$;
repeat
  if $\alpha < i < M$ **then**
    $b_i = PRNG(i - \alpha)$;
    $T_i = 2^{i-\alpha}.T_0$;
    $\omega_s = (b_i \| \omega)$;
  else
    $T_i = T_{i-1}$;
  end if
  $Success = sendpkt(T_i, \omega_s)$;
  $i = i + 1$;
until $Success$

Algorithm 3. Covert transmitter function of ARCC.

/* $getbit()$ returns extra information bits to be concatenated to the original message.

$i = 0$; $\omega_s = \omega$; $T_{-1} = T_0$;
repeat
  if $\alpha < i < M$ **then**
    $b_i = getbit(i)$;
    $T_i = 2^{i-\alpha}.T_0$;
    $\omega_s = (b_i \| \omega_s)$;
  else
    $T_i = T_{i-1}$;
  end if
  $Success = sendpkt(T_i, \omega_s)$;
  $i = i + 1$;
until $Success$

It is worth nothing that exhausting $T_0 - \omega$ clock ticks (instead of $T_i - \omega$) at the end of each stage also satisfies the synchronization criteria, however it deviates the covert transmitter's behavior from an ordinary user in the system. Hence, it is not an option for a stealth channel design.

As the size of the transmitter's contention window increases, there are more states in each stage that correspond to a particular message. For instance, if $T_i = kT_0$, there exist k states in the stage i that corresponds to the message ω (i.e., m_ω^i, $m_{T_0+\omega}^i$,...., $m_{(k-1)T_0+\omega}^i$). In FRCC scheme, the transmitter randomly picks one of the aforementioned states and moves to the next stage. Algorithm (2) depicts the transmitter's function of FRCC.

3.2 Adaptive Rate Covert Communication (ARCC)

In order to achieve stealthiness, the covert transmitter has to expand its contention window after each unsuccessful transmission attempt. In principle, by doubling the contention window in each expansion, the covert transmitter may add an additional information bit to the original message and increase the covert channel rate. ARCC scheme is designed to exploit the extra capacity and increase the covert communication rate. However, the rate increase comes at the price of reducing the reliability of the covert channel especially for the extra bits that are added to the original message. In other words, in order to decode the covert message, the receiver has to account not only for the value of the covert clock, but also it has to keep track of how many bits of information is added into the original message. Algorithm 3 depicts the transmission procedure of ARCC.

To decode the message, the covert receiver first decodes the original message according to Equation (2). Then, it checks the existence of extra information bits by removing the effect of first α stages from its covert clock. If C_r is still positive, it means that the transmitter had more than α unsuccessful re-transmission attempts, and it had to expand its contention window. The receiver counts the number of expansions by removing multiples of T_i from the value of the covert clock and decodes extra bits. Algorithm (4) depicts ARCC decoding process.

Algorithm 4. ARCC decoding at the receiver.

---

function $message = decode(C_r)$
/* First decode the original message ω_o
$\omega_o = C_r \bmod T_0;$
$C_r = C_r - \omega_o;$
/* Decode the additional message ω_a
if $C_r < \alpha T_0$ **then**
    return ω_o
else
    $C_r = C_r - \alpha T_0;$
    for $i = 1$ *to* $M - \alpha$ **do**
        if $C_r < 2^i T_i$ **then**
            $\omega_a = \frac{C_r}{T_0};$
            return $(\omega_a || \omega_o)$
        else
            $C_r = C_r - 2^i T_i;$
        end if
    end for
    $C_r = C_r \bmod 2^M T_0;$
    $\omega_a = \frac{C_r}{T_0};$
    return $(\omega_a || \omega_o)$
end if

---

4   System Parameters

In this section, different parameters of the proposed covert communication scheme are derived. The main idea is to optimize these parameters to achieve maximum stealthiness (i.e., similar characteristics as compared to other nodes in the system) and maximum channel rate. From Figure 1, it can be observed that the proposed scheme mimics the same principles as a regular CSMA/CA system. Hence, to harmonies the behavioral fingerprints of these systems, it is

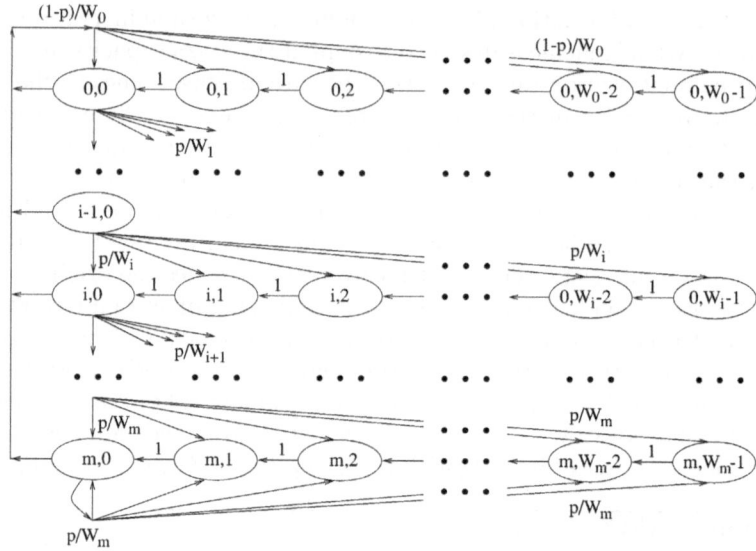

Fig. 2. Two-dimensional Markov model of the binary backoff scheme in CSMA/CA. In each stage W_i is the size of the contention window where $W_i = 2^i W_{min}$ [2]

important to derive the parameters of a regular CSMA transmitter and then adapt the covert transmitter to resemble the same characteristics.

Figure 2 depicts the two-dimensional Markov chain model for the binary back-off algorithm which is widely used for performance analysis of IEEE 802.11 MAC architecture [2]. Each state of this Markov process is represented by an ordered pair (s, b), where b represents the current state of the backoff counter and s represents the backoff stage of a given station. Using the above model, it is easy to verify that the collision probability p for a given user and the probability of transmitting a packet (i.e., q) can be written as [2]:

$$p = 1 - (1 - \sigma)(1 - q)^{N-2}, \tag{3}$$

$$q = \frac{2}{1 + W_{min} + pW_{min} \sum_{k=0}^{n-1}(2p)^k}. \tag{4}$$

Where, N is the number of users, σ is the transmission probability of the covert transmitter, and W_{min} is the minimum size of the contention window for regular users in the system. It is noted that the very first property of a transmitter is its transmission rate. Hence, if the covert transmitter has a different transmission rate as compared to a regular user in the system, it can be easily detected by a system observer. Therefore, the transmission rate of the covert transmitter is restricted to be the same as the transmission rate of regular users in the system (i.e., $\sigma = q$). Thus, one can rewrite Equation (3) as follows:

$$p = 1 - (1 - q)^{N-1}. \tag{5}$$

Let d_r^0 be the average number of time slots that each regular user has to wait before its first transmission (i.e., $i = 0$). Thus,

$$d_r^0 = \frac{W_{min} - 1}{2}. \tag{6}$$

On the other hand, the covert transmitter needs $\omega \in \{0, 1, ..., T_0 - 1\}$ successful packet transmissions from members of the covert set before it can send a packet to mark the value of the covert clock. Let π be the probability of a successful packet transmission of a user in the system. Hence, $\pi = q(1 - q)^{N-1}$ and the probability of a successful transmission by members of the covert set can be derived as:

$$P_S = |S| \times \pi. \tag{7}$$

Therefore, the average number of slots that the transmitter has to wait before its first transmission attempt (i.e., d_c^0) can be written as the average number of slots in which the transmitter observes ω packets from members of S. Thus,

$$
\begin{aligned}
d_c^0 &= \frac{1}{T_0} \sum_{\omega=0}^{T_0-1} \sum_{n=\omega}^{\infty} n \cdot \binom{n-1}{\omega-1} P_S^{\omega-1} \cdot (1 - P_S)^{n-\omega} \cdot P_S \\
&\overset{(1)}{=} \frac{1}{T_0} \sum_{\omega=0}^{T_0-1} \sum_{x=0}^{\infty} (x+\omega) \cdot \binom{x+\omega-1}{\omega-1} P_S^{\omega} \cdot (1 - P_S)^x \\
&= \frac{1}{T_0} \sum_{\omega=0}^{T_0-1} [\sum_{x=0}^{\infty} x \cdot \binom{x+\omega-1}{\omega-1} P_S^{\omega} \cdot (1-P_S)^x + \omega \cdot \sum_{x=0}^{\infty} \binom{x+\omega-1}{\omega-1} P_S^{\omega} \cdot (1-P_S)^x] \\
&\overset{(2)}{=} \frac{1}{T_0} \sum_{\omega=0}^{T_0-1} [\sum_{x=0}^{\infty} x \cdot \binom{x+\omega-1}{\omega-1} P_S^{\omega} \cdot (1 - P_S)^x + \omega] \\
&\overset{(3)}{=} \frac{1}{T_0} \sum_{\omega=0}^{T_0-1} [\frac{\omega(1 - P_S)}{P_S} + \omega] \\
&= \frac{T_0 - 1}{2 P_S}. \tag{8}
\end{aligned}
$$

Where (1) comes from $x = n - \omega$, and (2) and (3) are based on the definition of the negative binomial distribution [17].

In order to emulate an ordinary user in the system, the covert transmitter has to spend, on average, the same number of slots before its first transmission attempt as compared to any regular user in the system. To this end, by combining Equations (6) and (8), the proper value of the initial transmission window of the covert transmitter can be derived as:

$$T_0 = P_S(W_{min} - 1) + 1. \tag{9}$$

Hence, the covert transmitter and regular users in the system, on average, wait for the same number of slots prior to their first packet transmission attempt.

On the other hand, in order to maintain synchronization with the covert receiver, following each unsuccessful transmission, the transmitter resets the covert clock to $\sum_{j=0}^{i-1} T_j$ where i is the number of unsuccessful transmission attempts for the current packet (Figure 1). This re-synchronization task accounts for additional delay for the transmitter as compared to regular users in the system. Thus, if the transmitter doubles the size of its contention window after each unsuccessful transmission, the number of slots that the covert transmitter waits between consecutive packet transmissions may deviate from the same parameter of ordinary users. This difference in behavior can be detected by a system observer exposing the existence of the covert channel.

To combat this problem, the transmitter postpones expanding its transmission window for α stages. Where α is selected such that *the average number of slots between the last successful packet transmission and the αth re-transmission attempt to send a new packet converges for both ordinary users and the covert transmitter.* Hence, the covert transmitter controls the delay between retransmission attempts in order to compensate for the additional delay due to the synchronization process.

Since the transmitter does not expand its transmission window up to the stage α, the average number of slots between the last successful transmission and the ith re-transmission attempt for a new packet ($i \leq \alpha$) can be written as the average number of slots to observe $iT_0 + \omega$ packets from members of S. Thus, similar to the calculation of Equation (8):

$$d_c^i = \frac{1}{T_0} \sum_{t=iT_0}^{(i+1)T_0-1} \sum_{n=t}^{\infty} n.\binom{n-1}{t-1} P_S^{t-1}.(1-P_S)^{n-t}.P_S$$
$$= \frac{(2i+1)T_0 - 1}{2P_S}. \tag{10}$$

Similarly, a regular user, on average, spends $\frac{W_i-1}{2}$ slots in the stage i before retransmitting the packet. It also spends one slot trying to transmit the packet at the end of each stage. Hence, the average number of slots between the last successful transmission and the ith retransmission attempt for a new packet is:

$$d_r^i = \sum_{j=0}^{i} \frac{W_j - 1}{2} + i = \frac{W_{min}(2^{i+1} - 1) + i - 1}{2}. \tag{11}$$

Therefore, α can be derived as the index of the last stage in which the transmitter spends more slots, on average, trying to transmit a packet as compared to a regular user. Thus,

$$\alpha = \max_{i>0} \ \{i|\ d_r^i \ \leq \ d_c^i\}$$
$$= \max_{i>0} \ \{i|(\frac{2^{i+1} - 2i - 2}{i} \leq \frac{2 - 3P_S}{P_S W_{min}})\} \tag{12}$$

Table 1. System PHY Parameters

Parameters	Selected Values
Slot Time	20 μs
SIFS	10 μs
DIFS	50 μs
Transmission Rate	1 $Mbps$
Payload Size	1500 $Bytes$

5   Performance Analysis

In this section the performance of the proposed covert communication scheme is analyzed from security, reliability and achievable rate point of view. Table 1 contains the basic parameters of the system under study in this section. The performance analysis is performed on four distinct scenarios to cover networks with different sizes and system parameters. For each scenario, the parameters of the covert system are calculated based on the discussion in Section 4. Table 2 contains the corresponding parameters of each scenario.

Table 2. Covert Communication Simulation Scenarios

Parameter	SC1	SC2	SC3	SC4
Number of users (N)	25	35	50	15
Size of the covert set $(|S|)$	16	21	33	10
Covert transmitter min window size (T_0)	4	7	8	4
Expansion postpone parameter (α)	1	1	1	1
Regular user min window size (W_{min})	16	32	32	16
Number of back off stages (M)	6	5	5	6

5.1   Detection and Stealthiness of the Covert Channel

As the covert receiver is a complete passive entity in the proposed scheme, it is undetectable even if the covert channel is detected. Indeed, since the transmitter does not need to know the receiver's identity, the receiver is safe in case that the transmitter's information is revealed to a system observer.

There are several different statistical tests to detect a covert channel and distinguish abnormal behaviors of a covert transmitter. One of the most well known approaches is the Kolmogorov-Smirnov test (KS-test) [17]. This test has been used in detecting the watermarked inter-packet delays and is a major tool in detecting timing covert channels [6].

Let $S(x)$ and $F(x)$ be the distribution of inter-packet delays of the covert transmitter's traffic and the legitimate traffic of the same system respectively. The KS-test is defined as:

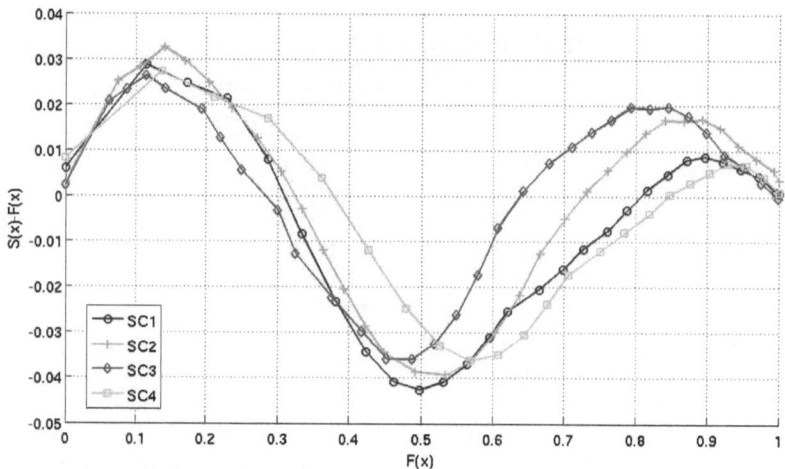

Fig. 3. Kolmogorov-Smirnov test for different scenarios

$$H_s = \sup_x |S(x) - F(x)|. \tag{13}$$

The difference between the distribution of inter-packet delays of the traffic originated from a regular user and the covert transmitter is depicted in Figure 3. According to the graph, the difference between two parameters is less than 5% at its peak which is an acceptable margin for the KS-test [16]. Such a small difference, makes it extremely difficult for an observer to detect any abnormal behavior in the system based on first level statistical tests such as the KS-test.

In addition, Figure 3 highlights how the transmitter systematically adapts its behavior in order to emulate the transmission pattern of ordinary users in the system. It is noted that the transmitter postpones its transmission window expansion for α stages in order to compensate for the extra delay caused by the synchronization process. Hence, the transmitter experiences lower inter-packet delays during the first α stages of the transmission process (i.e., the first peak of the graph). As the transmitter begins expanding its transmission window, the inter-packet delay of the transmitter's traffic increases faster than the delays of the regular traffic of the system (i.e., the second extreme point of the graph). This ends when the contention window of ordinary users are large enough such that the waiting times of the transmitter and regular users converge.

Another widely used statistical measure to detect timing covert channels is the *regularity test* [4] . In principle, the variance of the inter-packet delays changes over time due to different conditions of the network. In fact, regular users in the system have the same reaction to sudden events in the system such as packet loss or collision. However, as the covert transmitter is committed to transmit a particular covert message, it may not be able to react to network events similar to other nodes in the system. The regularity test is meant to detect such a behavior and track covert activities. To calculate the regularity test score, samples of the inter-packet delays are collected and then spread into multiple sets of size γ. The regularity score (i.e., H_r) is derived as follows:

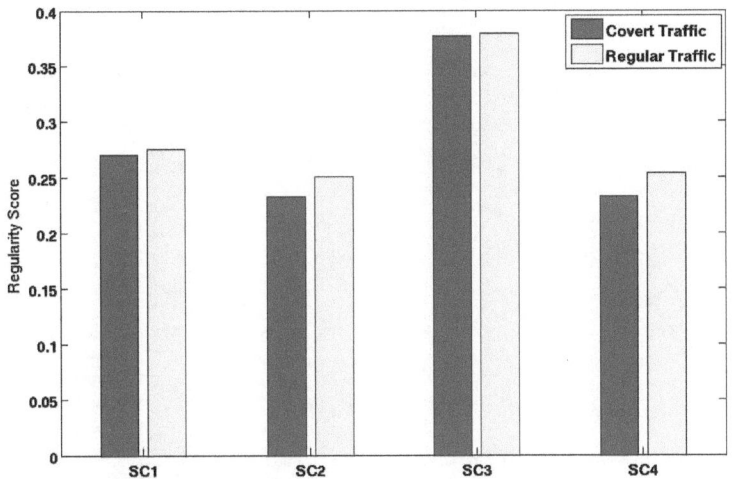

Fig. 4. Regularity test for different scenarios

$$H_r = std(\frac{|\sigma_i - \sigma_j|}{\sigma_i}), \quad \forall i, j, i < j. \tag{14}$$

Where std is the standard deviation operation and σ_i is the standard deviation of the ith set of inter-packet delays. High regularity scores means large variance in inter-packet delays of each set while the low value of H_r depicts a set of regular inter-packet delays that is likely to carry covert information.

Figure 4 shows the regularity score of the covert transmitter and also ordinary users for $\gamma = 50$. According to the graph, the covert transmitter's regularity score is extremely close to the regular users' score in all four scenarios. In other words, the covert transmitter has managed to blend itself into the crowd well enough that a simple regularity test can not detect the existence of the covert channel.

The key in maintaining the regularity score is the packet transmission mechanism of the covert transmitter and the covert clock. It is noted that the covert clock increases based on activities of other nodes in the system. Hence, if the channel condition changes in a way that other users have to wait for a longer period of time between consecutive transmissions (e.g., reduction of channel capacity, high error rates, etc), the covert clock advances with a slower paste leading to larger inter-packet delays for the covert transmitter as well. Such an adaptive behavior is an advantage of the proposed scheme as compared to other similar techniques that aim to artificially increase their regularity score by switching the transmission mode after a certain amount of time [16] or replaying a part of previously sampled legitimate traffic and switch from one sample to another periodically [4].

5.2   Reliability

Two independent packet loss events are considered in order to evaluate the robustness of the proposed scheme. The first error event is due to failure in detecting packets from members of the covert set. Such an event directly affects the value of the covert clock in one side of the channel leading to erroneous decoding

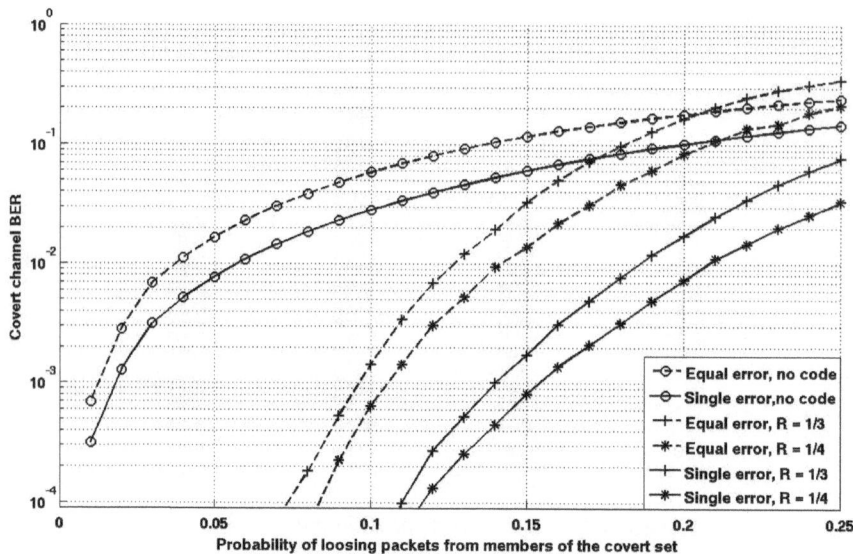

Fig. 5. Covert channel bit error rate based on the packet loss ratio of the packets from members of the covert set. Results are presented for the first scenario in Table 2, using FRCC scheme.

at the receiver. The second error event is caused by loosing the transmitter's packet at the covert receiver. If this happens, the covert receiver continues on incrementing its clock value while the transmitter resets its covert clock for the next round of transmission. Hence, the transmitter and the receiver loose synchronization and the covert channel becomes noisy.

There are several methods to reduce the effect of the aforementioned packet loss events on the performance of the proposed scheme. First of all, in most communication protocols, each packet is acknowledged by the actual receiver of the packet where the Ack message contains the sequence number and the source of the original packet. Thus, the receiver or the transmitter can learn about a packet by detecting either the packet or the corresponding Ack message.

Channel coding [18] is an alternative approach to combat the mismatch in the covert clocks of the transmitter and the receiver. In this way, the covert transmitter encodes the original message (e.g., a binary sequence B) into a coded message which is more resilient against channel errors. Then, the coded message is modulated into covert messages based on the approach explained in section 3 to be transmitted over the covert channel using FRCC or ARCC schemes. In this section, a rate $1/3$ convolutional code with the generator matrix $[47; 53; 75]$ and a rate $1/4$ convolutional code with the generator matrix $[17; 13; 13; 15]$ are used in order to analyze the effect of channel coding on the performance of the proposed scheme. Due to the space limitation, the numerical results are presented for the first scenario in Table 2 using FRCC scheme.

Figure 5 depicts the covert channel bit error rate (BER) based on the ratio of the packet loss from members of the covert set. For each coding scheme, the graph depicts two extreme scenarios from packet loss view point. (i) the transmitter

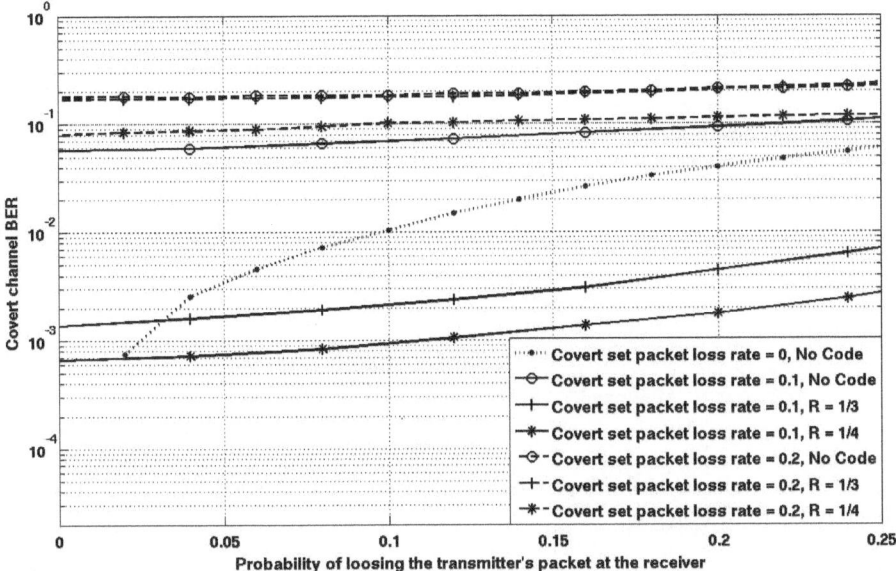

Fig. 6. Covert channel bit error rate due to the loss of transmitter's packets at the receiver. Packets from members of the covert set are subjected to error with packet loss rate 0 for dotted lines, 0.1 for solid lines, and 0.2 for dashed lines. Results are presented for the first scenario in Table 2, using FRCC scheme.

and the receiver have the same chance of loosing a packet from members of the covert set (i.e., equal error case). It is noted that the packet loss events for the receiver and the transmitter are assumed to be independent. (ii) only one of the receiver or the transmitter experiences packet loss from members of S (i.e., single error case). It is easy to verify that picking either the receiver or the transmitter in this case, does not change BER of the covert channel. In this way, all other possible scenarios are covered as their corresponding BER is bounded by the aforementioned extreme cases. The graph also illustrates that the channel coding can effectively improve the robustness of the proposed scheme against packet loss from members of the covert set. For instance, if both the receiver and the transmitter experience 15% packet loss from members of the covert set (i.e., equal error case), the BER of the covert channel drops from 0.1 (for the uncoded scenario) down to 0.035 for the rate 1/3 channel code and even further to 0.015 if the rate 1/4 code is used.

Figure 6 depicts the BER of the covert channel when the covert transmitter's traffic is also subject to error. Loosing the transmitter's packet at the receiver affects the synchronization between the two end points of the covert channel. It is noted that the covert receiver can learn about lost packets and re-synchronize itself with the transmitter when it gets a new packet from the transmitter (e.g., using the sequence number field of the new packet). However, the covert messages that were transmitted between the last received transmitter's packet and the new packet from the covert transmitter would be lost.

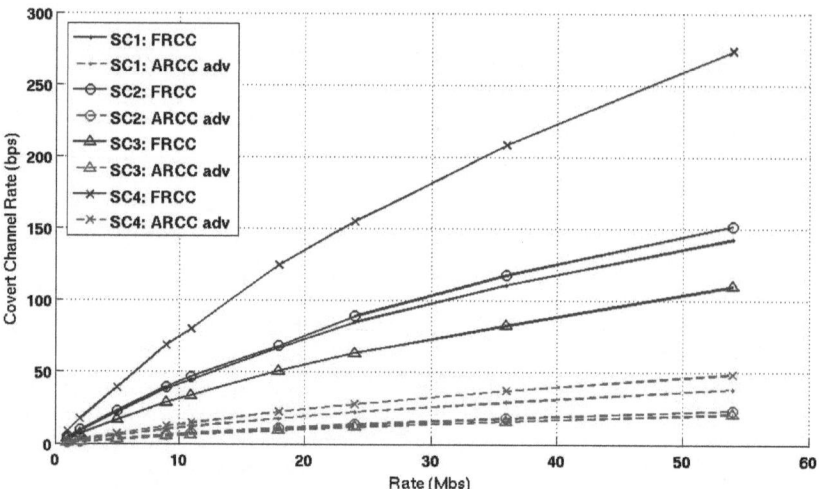

Fig. 7. Achievable rate of the proposed covert channel. Dashed lines show the extra capacity of ARCC scheme.

Plots in Figure 6 are grouped based on the ratio of the packet loss from members of the covert set. In all groups, it is assumed that the covert transmitter and the covert receiver experience the same packet loss ratio from members of the covert set (equal error case). Each group consists of three plots (one for the uncoded scenario, and two for the rate 1/3 and the rate 1/4 convolutional codes). Remarkably, if the receiver and the transmitter enjoy lossless channels from members of the covert set, the selected channel codes are strong enough to correct all errors caused by missing the transmitter's packets at the receiver. Hence, those plots are not reported in the graph.

By comparing the plots in Figure 5 and Figure 6, it can be observed that the BER of the covert channel increases much faster with the error from members of the covert set as compared to the error caused by loosing the transmitter's packet at the reviver. The flat plots of Figure 6 confirms this observation proving that the dominant factor in the reliability of the proposed scheme is in fact the packet loss from members of the covert set. This is due to the fact that the covert receiver can learn about the exact position and the number of lost packets from the covert transmitter (e.g., using the sequence number field of the transmitter packets), and use this information in order to improve the performance of the channel coding schemes that are being used in the system

5.3   Communication Rate

Figure 7 shows the achievable rate of the proposed scheme. The graph also illustrates that the channel rate increases linearly with the capacity of the communication channel. In fact, the covert channel is capable of achieving relatively high covert rates without compromising the security of the channel. The graph also depicts that it is possible to boost the capacity of the covert channel even further using ARCC scheme.

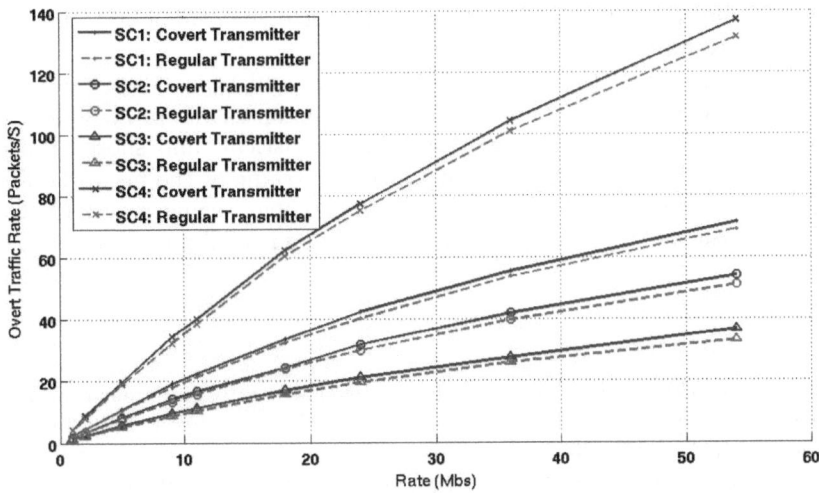

Fig. 8. Overt traffic communication rate of the system

Figure 8 depicts the overt communication rate of the transmitter and regular users in the system. According to the discussion in Section 4, the parameters of the proposed scheme are calculated based on the assumption that the covert transmitter has the same transmission probability as other users in the system. This assumption is crucial in order to prevent a system observer from tracking the transmitter based on its overt traffic rate. Figure 8 confirms the validity of this assumption as in all scenarios, the transmitter conveys the same overt transmission rate than other nodes in the system.

6   Conclusion

In this paper the concept of behavioral mimicry covert communication was introduced. In this way, it is possible to adopt a communication protocol and modify it in such a way that gives the covert transmitter enough freedom to embed a covert message into its overt traffic with minimum deviation from characteristics of a regular user of the same protocol. The paper also presents a new covert channel which is based on mimicking the structural behavior of CSMA/CA algorithm in the wireless environment.

The covert transmitter adopts CSMA/CA protocol so that the transmitter's contention window is controlled by a virtual clock called the *covert clock*. The covert clock is linked to the channel activities of all or a subset of regular nodes in the system using the broadcast nature of the wireless environment. These activities are observed by the covert transmitter and the covert receiver in order to synchronize their covert clocks and communicate through the covert channel. One important feature of the proposed scheme is that its rate linearly increases with the overt rate of the communication channel. Moreover, the covert transmitter and the covert receiver can maintain their overt channel rate like typical users in the system.

The performance of the proposed covert communication scheme is analyzed from stealthiness, reliability and communication capacity aspects showing that the proposed scheme has similar long term (statistical) and short term (temporal) characteristics as compared to legitimate traffic of the network. The numerical results also verify that the proposed scheme achieves relatively high communication rates with outstanding security and reliability scores.

References

1. Bhadra, S., Bodas, S., Shakkottai, S., Vishwanath, S.: Communication Through Jamming Over a Slotted ALOHA Channel. IEEE Transactions on Information Theory 54(11), 5257 (2008)
2. Bianchi, G., et al.: Performance analysis of the IEEE 802.11 distributed coordination function. IEEE Journal on Selected Areas in Communications 18(3), 535–547 (2000)
3. Butti, L., Veysset, F.: Wi-Fi Advanced Stealth. In: Proc. Black Hat, US (August 2006)
4. Cabuk, S., Brodley, C., Shields, C.: IP covert timing channels: design and detection. In: Proceedings of the 11th ACM Conference on Computer and Communications Security, pp. 178–187. ACM (2004)
5. Calhoun Jr., T., Cao, X., Li, Y., Beyah, R.: An 802.11 MAC layer covert channel. Wireless Communications and Mobile Computing
6. Gianvecchio, S., Wang, H.: Detecting covert timing channels: an entropy-based approach. In: Proceedings of the 14th ACM Conference on Computer and Communications Security, pp. 307–316. ACM (2007)
7. Girling, C.: Covert channels in LAN's. IEEE Transactions on Software Engineering 13(2), 292–296 (1987)
8. Gray III, J.: Countermeasures and tradeoffs for a class of covert timing channel. Hong Kong University of Science and Technology Technical report (1994)
9. Handel, T., Sandford, M.: Hiding Data in the OSI network Model. In: Anderson, R. (ed.) IH 1996. LNCS, vol. 1174, pp. 23–38. Springer, Heidelberg (1996)
10. Holloway, R.: Covert DCF - A DCF Based Covert Timing Channe. 802.11 Networks. Master's thesis, Georgia State University, Atlanta, Georgia (2010)
11. IEEE: IEEE Standard for Wireless LAN Medium Access Control (MAC) and Physical Layer (PHY) Specifications (1997)
12. Kemmerer, R.: Shared resource matrix methodology: An approach to identifying storage and timing channels. ACM Transactions on Computer Systems (TOCS) 1(3), 277 (1983)
13. Lampson, B.: A note on the confinement problem. Communications of the ACM 16(10), 613–615 (1973)
14. Li, S., Ephremides, A.: A Network Layer Covert Channel in Adhoc Wireless Networks. In: 1st IEEE Conference on Sensor and Ad Hoc Communications and Networks (SECON), pp. 88–96 (2004)
15. Li, S., Ephremides, A.: A covert channel in MAC protocols based on splitting algorithms. In: 2005 IEEE Wireless Communications and Networking Conference, pp. 1168–1173 (2005)

16. Liu, Y., Ghosal, D., Armknecht, F., Sadeghi, A.-R., Schulz, S., Katzenbeisser, S.: Hide and Seek in Time — Robust Covert Timing Channels. In: Backes, M., Ning, P. (eds.) ESORICS 2009. LNCS, vol. 5789, pp. 120–135. Springer, Heidelberg (2009)
17. Papoulis, A., Pillai, S., Unnikrishna, S.: Probability, random variables, and stochastic processes. McGraw-Hill, New York (2002)
18. Proakis, J., Salehi, M.: Digital communications. McGraw-Hill, New York (2001)
19. Szczypiorski, K.: HICCUPS: Hidden communication system for corrupted networks. In: International Multi-Conference on Advanced Computer Systems, pp. 31–40 (2003)
20. Wang, Z., Deng, J., Lee, R., Princeton, P.: Mutual anonymous communications: a new covert channel based on splitting tree MAC. In: 26th IEEE International Conference on Computer Communications, IEEE INFOCOM 2007, pp. 2531–2535 (2007)

Defense against Spectrum Sensing Data Falsification Attacks in Cognitive Radio Networks

Chowdhury Sayeed Hyder, Brendan Grebur, and Li Xiao

Department of Computer Science and Engineering
Michigan State University
East Lansing, MI 48823, USA
{hydercho,greburbr,lxiao}@cse.msu.edu

Abstract. IEEE 802.22 is the first standard based on the concept of cognitive radio. It recommends collaborative spectrum sensing to avoid the unreliability of individual spectrum sensing while detecting primary user signals. However, it opens an opportunity for attackers to exploit the decision making process by sending false reports. In this paper, we address security issues regarding distributed node sensing in the 802.22 standard and discuss how attackers can modify or manipulate their sensing result independently or collaboratively. This problem is commonly known as spectrum sensing data falsification (SSDF) attack or Byzantine attack. To counter the different attacking strategies, we propose a reputation based clustering algorithm that does not require prior knowledge of attacker distribution or complete identification of malicious users. We compare the performance of our algorithm against existing approaches across a wide range of attacking scenarios. Our proposed algorithm displays a significantly reduced error rate in decision making compared to current methods. It also identifies a large portion of the attacking nodes and greatly minimizes the false detection rate of honest nodes.

Keywords: Cognitive Radio Network, SSDF attack, 802.22.

1 Introduction

As wireless devices are dominating the methods in which people communicate with one another, the necessary resources to support these conveniences are being ever harder to obtain. In contrast, licensed bandwidth spectrums often go underutilized as demands for those services shift temporally or spatially. Static spectrum allocation cannot efficiently support the demand of such pervasive wireless devices. To combat this salient impedance, the concept of Cognitive Radio Networks (CRN) has been proposed [9].

In order to maximize radio spectrum usage, CRNs utilize an opportunistic approach to allocate frequencies. Under the scheme, two types of users exist: primary users (PU) and secondary users (SU). Individuals who have obtained a license to broadcast in a fixed spectrum range are classified as primary users. On

M. Rajarajan et al. (Eds.): SecureComm 2011, LNICST 96, pp. 154–171, 2012.
© Institute for Computer Sciences, Social Informatics and Telecommunications Engineering 2012

the other hand, secondary users attempt to "fill in the gaps" by utilizing unused spectrums. The users complement each other allowing maximal utilization of a specified spectrum.

Naturally, complications arise as secondary users must release a spectrum when the primary user for that channel starts to transmit. Several research groups are working to develop standards to meet these requirements. 802.22, the first CR based network standard, defines a centralized, single hop, point to multi-point communication standard for wireless regional area network (WRAN). This standard defines the implementation of opportunistic spectrum sharing (OSS) by outlining how/when wireless devices are able to utilize temporarily idle bands in a licensed radio spectrum. The proposal also defines the cellular like communication interface between a base station (BS) and secondary users called Consumer Premise Equipments (CPE). The BS is responsible for controlling the spectrum usage and channel assignment to CPEs. All CPEs in a cell must periodically monitor primary user signals and leverage the distributed sensing power of CPEs through continual spectrum reports obtained from secondary users.

To coordinate the process, a centralized BS collects sensing information from the secondary users residing in the cell. Each user submits a hypothesis regarding whether they suspect the primary user is transmitting. As radio waves are affected by physical barriers or environmental conditions, the detection accuracy of any node within sensing range of the PU's signal varies from time to time. Malfunctions associated with the sensing equipment may also influence the node's observed measurements. From the hypotheses supplied by the secondary users, the BS must decide on the actual state of the associated spectrum. Once a decision is made, the base station can inform SUs and revoke permission for those users currently transmitting on that spectrum.

Due to its unique characteristics, CRNs face new security threats in addition to the common existing security challenges in wireless network. One typical type of attack is the Spectrum Sensing Data Falsification (SSDF) attack or Byzantine attack. During such an assault, the malicious user compromises one or more of the secondary users and may begin sending modified sensing results to the BS. In this way, an attacker tries to influence the BS into producing a wrong decision about the channel status. Compromised nodes may work independently or may collaborate to reduce spectrum utilization and degrade overall performance of the network.

Constructing a decision-making strategy that mitigates the impact of both types of attackers will prove invaluable as the reach of CRNs expands into more places. By strengthening the base station against malicious or malfunctioning users, the interference produced from CRNs will be minimized, potentially expediting the implementation of such network alternatives. Ultimately, both users and businesses can reap the benefits of efficient radio spectrum usage through CRNs.

There are very limited research works that address SSDF attack and related security problems. Existing approaches like [1], [8], [10] mainly consider independent malicious attack. However, these approaches either require prior information of attackers (e.g. number of attackers [10], attackers' distribution, attacking strategy [8] etc.) or depend on careful threshold selection [1]. For instance, algorithm in [10] does not work in presence of multiple attackers. Similarly, performance of the algorithm proposed in [1] degrades significantly if incorrect threshold is chosen. To our best knowledge, we find only one paper [2] that handles both independent and collaborative attacks. This approach uses a reputation based method to limit the error rate in deciding channel status and in identifying attackers. Although its identification rate of attackers is high, it also misdetects a large number of honest users as attackers. Additionally, this approach fails to defend against collaborative attack and error rate (i.e. number of incorrect decision) increases almost linearly with number of attackers.

On the contrary, we propose an adaptive reputation based clustering algorithm to defend against both independent and collaborative SSDF attack that does not require any prior information about number of attackers or attacking strategies. The whole process goes through a sequence of steps in each time step. To start with, the algorithm clusters the nodes based on the sensing history and initial reputation of nodes. Each cluster takes its decision about the channel status according to the relative closeness of nodes from the median of that cluster. Finally, channel status is decided on majority of clusters' decision. At the end of the time step, the final decision is propagated back to the clusters and then to the individual nodes. Each node is assigned a share (positive or negative) of the final decision and the reputation of each node is adjusted based on its participation in the decision making process. The adjusted reputation of nodes is used to adjust the number of clusters for the next step. In this way, the algorithm works through several steps in forward and backward direction in each time step and recursively updates the clusters and the reputation of nodes. We compare performance of our algorithm with that of the algorithm proposed in [2] under different attacking scenarios. Our algorithm handles SSDF attack significantly better than the one in [2] and minimizes error in deciding channel status. Our algorithm also identifies a significant number of attackers while keeping the misdetection rate to a minimum level.

The next section explores various approaches currently proposed and specifically identifies their limitations in the problem domain. Section 3 formally defines the problem area including the setup used to measure each method. Section 4 describes a high-level overview of our proposed method mainly focusing on design choices. Section 5 covers a detailed description of the algorithm. Section 6 compares the results with current methods and Section 7 concludes with contributions and future work.

2   Related Work

Until recently, security issues in CRN have not been addressed well in research works. However, in this section, we present existing solutions to combat against SSDF attack into three categories - reputation-based, neighborhood distance based, and artificial intelligence approaches.

2.1   Reputation Based Approaches

Wang et al. [8] propose an onion peeling approach based on bayesian statistics to assign suspicion levels for all nodes in the network. If the suspicion level of any node exceeds a certain threshold, it is marked as malicious and removed from decision making. They tested their heuristic based approach for false alarm attacks, miss detection attacks, and combinations thereof. However, they assume that base station has prior knowledge about the activities of attackers which is not very common. Without such information, the thresholds are approximated, resulting in significant false detections of attackers.

Chen et al. [3] propose a hybrid method named weighted sequential probability ratio test (WSPRT) that combines reputation and a sequential probability ratio test to identify malicious or faulty units. This method outperforms standard fusion center decision making strategies, including OR, AND, and SPRT during simulations in both minimizing missed detections and maximizing the correct sensing ratio. However, WSPRT was only tested against attackers utilizing an always-false or always-free response. Such methods represent an unsophisticated attack strategy that is not likely to reflect encountered attackers. The method also requires an additional number of secondary user sensing reports to generate the final fusion center hypothesis, which can impede the overall performance of the system and potentially cause primary user interference.

Recently, Rawat et. al. in [2] explores independent and collaborative SSDF attacks. They determined optimal attacking strategies for collaborating attackers where the fusion center cannot possibly discriminate between honest and attacking CRs. A mathematically rigorous analysis of detection performance is carried out using the Kullback-Leibler divergence (KLD). According to their result, in presence of 50% independent attackers, fusion center cannot differentiate the difference between the honest users and the attackers. However, for collaborative attack, this ratio reduces to 35%. Furthermore, they proposed a simple reputation-based method to identify attackers. A major weakness of the method stems from its massive misdetection of attackers during the identification stage. The proposed method uses a relatively small sensing window for analyzing reporting patterns to identify attackers. Under such limited time spans, temporary sensing errors of honest users cause their sensing signatures to deviate from the consensus. As more honest users are removed from the voting process, the method leaves the responsibility of final decision making up to only a few users. In such scenarios, the system is left in an extremely fragile state. Any attack on the remaining users causes the entire cell to be compromised. In addition, the method's probability of error increases dramatically when as little as 35% of the nodes are collaborating in attacks.

2.2   Data Mining Approaches

In [1], a new approach based on K-neighborhood distance algorithm is presented to detect independent malicious users. The approach does not need any prior knowledge of attacker distribution and exposes attackers across multiple sensing rounds. However, when attackers collaborate and have secondary user data, they can successfully evade detection.

Further work has been done by [6] in establishing a more robust fusion center decision algorithm. Specifically, particular pieces of sensing information are used to validate the primary user hypothesis presented by each secondary user. Information regarding PU positioning and path loss to the secondary user can corroborate the hypothesis. The compiled set of sensory reports are analyzed using a biweight estimate and median absolute deviation to calculate magnitudes, which are then compared against thresholds to identify the attackers.

The proposed method dramatically increases misdetections when using incorrect static thresholds. Inaccurately identified secondary users could be excluded from the decision making process, resulting in a PU signal being ignored. Ultimately, the correct setting of the detection thresholds can only be achieved with prior knowledge of attacker distribution. Again, the information is unlikely to be available.

2.3 Artificial Intelligence Approaches

Clancy et al. [4] take a practical look into devising security for the physical transport layer of CRNs, focusing on CRs with artificial intelligence. When implementing such schemes, the CRs are highly susceptible to short-term and long-term manipulations caused by corrupted sensory data, altered node statistics, and inaccurate beliefs regarding the current environment. The paper addresses a series of steps to combat these sensitive areas by assuming a noisy environment, implementing levels of common sense, and programmatically resetting learned values to avoid extended corruption from attackers. They offer up the use of swarm behavior in determining a global decision on whether a sensed signal was actually generated by a primary user, along with a trust-based scheme. The proposals on how these CRs should operate in the field are presented without details for verification. They also did not address how to incorporate this new information into the current 802.22 system.

The current state of research holds very few proposals that work on realistic knowledge of the operating environment. Approximating these values fundamentally skews the proposed approaches' effectiveness. Furthermore, misidentification of attackers could also severely impact the effectiveness of strategies. Such considerations must be respected to develop a truly robust scheme. Ultimately, the approaches will need to face real attacks while producing acceptable error rates. In this paper, we explore strategies that exhibit these characteristics without being hindered by any assumptions of the operating environment or attacker strategy.

3 System Model

In this section, we briefly describe the topology of the CR network. We explain how the BS operates and takes decision regarding channel status from collective sensing reports. We also formulate different attacking models and analyze how they exploit the decision mechanism of BS.

The BS is the central authority to coordinate and control the operation of all secondary nodes in its cell. BS instructs SUs to sense a channel according to the standard. Each node uses the same spectrum sensing technique for PU detection. Spectrum sensing itself is an ongoing research topic and is out of the scope of this paper. For simplicity, we assume that secondary users use the threshold based energy detection technique for spectrum sensing and all nodes use the same threshold provided by the BS. All nodes prepare their reports based on sensing and send their sensing results. However, different sensing techniques offer different levels of detection accuracy and may affect the sensing decision. Later in the results section, we perform simulation with varying sensing accuracy. BS then decides the channel status considering the sensing results from all the nodes. We also assume that users have no knowledge about the actual channel status.

We consider two types of users in the network - honest users and dishonest users. In each time slot, honest SUs sense the channel, compare the sensed energy with the threshold, and decide independently about the channel status. Finally, they report their sensed status to the BS without any alteration.

On the other hand, the dishonest users alter their sensed results and send it to BS. They can be selfish or malicious based on their intention. We commonly term them as 'attackers'. A selfish attacker has a different perspective from a malicious one. From a selfish attacker's point of view, the goal is to make the base station take a wrong decision about the idle channel so that it may utilize the spectrum opportunity. As a result, spectrum utilization will be significantly reduced. On the contrary, a malicious attacker's goal is not only to minimize the spectrum utilization, but also degrade the network performance. The latter one is more harmful than the former since it will also increase the interference with primary users.

Base stations usually take decisions based on an OR rule (if any of the nodes sense channel busy, BS decides a busy channel). This approach is very conservative in the sense that one single attacker or even a malfunctioning node can reduce the spectrum utilization. Another common approach is to decide according to majority voting. This resolves the spectrum underutilization problem but significantly increases the misdetection rate. Also, it becomes vulnerable when attackers collaboratively decide their attacking strategy.

3.1 Honest User Model

We assume that even an honest user cannot detect PU presence 100% accurately. We define false alarm as the probability of sensing presence of PU when it is actually not transmitting and we define misdetection as the probability of not sensing PU when it is operating. Let us assume that the probability of false alarm and misdetection rate of a user are P_{fa} and P_{md} respectively.

$$P_{fa} = P(u_i = 1|H_0), P_{md} = P(u_i = 0|H_1)$$

where H_0 and H_1 denote the channel idle and busy status and u_i represents the sensed result by user i.

As explained, honest users do not change their sensing results. Let us assume that v_i represents the report sent to BS by user i.

$$P(v_i = 1|u_i = 1) = 1, P(v_i = 0|u_i = 1) = 0$$
$$P(v_i = 0|u_i = 0) = 1, P(v_i = 1|u_i = 0) = 0$$

Accordingly, we can calculate the detection probability of an honest user using Equation 1.

$$P_d = P(v_i = 0|H_0)P(H_0) + P(v_i = 1|H_1)P(H_1)$$
$$= (1 - P_{fa})P_I + (1 - P_{md})P_B \tag{1}$$

Here, P_d denotes the probability of accurate detection of channel status by any honest user and P_I and P_B denote the idle and busy rate of the channel respectively.

3.2   Attack Model

We assume that there exist at most M $(\alpha = M/N \le 50\%)$ attackers and the remaining users are honest, completely unaware of the presence of attackers. We do not consider the number of attackers more than 50% because it is not productive to study a network where a majority of nodes are attackers. We consider attackers devise their plan independently or collaboratively.

Independent Attack. Each attacker node changes its sensing result with probability P_{mal}. As a result, the detection probability of an attacker changes.

$$P_d^m = [(1 - P_{mal})(1 - P_{fa}) + P_{mal}P_{fa}]P_I$$
$$+ [(1 - P_{mal})(1 - P_{md}) + P_{mal}P_{md}]P_B \tag{2}$$

Here, P_d^m denotes the detection probability of an attacker while working independently. Similarly, we can find the false alarm probability of an attacker (P_{fa}^m).

Collaborative Attack. In case of a collaborative SSDF attack, attackers exchange their sensing information and decide their response collaboratively. We study different collaboration strategies to see their impacts on decision making of BS. Let us assume that Q_d^m and Q_{fa}^m denote the detection probability and false alarm probability of attackers. To start with, we follow the same collaboration strategy used in [2]. Attackers follow 'L out of M' rule to decide their final decision where 'L' is determined according to [2]. In this case, Q_d^m and Q_{fa}^m will be

$$Q_d^m = \sum_{i=L}^{M} \binom{M}{i} (P_d^m)^i (1 - P_d^m)^{M-i}$$

$$Q_{fa}^m = \sum_{i=L}^{M} \binom{M}{i} (P_{fa}^m)^i (1 - P_{fa}^m)^{M-i} \qquad (3)$$

Here, L is defined in [2]

$$L = min(M, \left\lceil \frac{M}{1 + \beta} \right\rceil) \text{ where } \beta = \frac{\ln \frac{P_{fa}}{P_d}}{\ln \frac{1 - P_d}{1 - P_{fa}}}$$

The second attacking strategy we consider here is termed as 'Going Against MAjority (GAMA)'. Each attacker shares its true sensing result and in collaboration with other attackers decides against the majority sensing result with a certain probability. For example, if 2 attackers sense the channel idle and 1 user senses the channel busy, all 3 attackers report the busy status of the channel to the BS. The idea behind this attacking strategy is that sensing results of majority nodes may reflect the actual channel status. So, when the attackers collaborate, they change the sensing result of the majority and go against that. It may help them manipulate BS taking a wrong decision. In this case, $L = M/2 + 1$ and the collaborative detection probability will be

$$Q_d^m = \sum_{i=L}^{M} \binom{M}{i} (1 - P_d)^i (P_d)^{M-i}$$

$$Q_{fa}^m = \sum_{i=L}^{M} \binom{M}{i} (1 - P_{fa})^i (P_{fa})^{M-i} \qquad (4)$$

Third, we also investigate the impact of collaboration among subgroups. In this approach, we assume that attackers exist in small groups, and each group changes their sensing result according to the first approach. Finally, one group is chosen randomly and all the attackers in that group report the same sensing result. This approach tries to attack in small groups without exposing all collaborators at a time.

4   Algorithm Design - Attackers vs BS

In this section, we discuss the viewpoints of attackers and BS and explain the defense mechanism taken by BS to defend against different attacking strategies. As stated in Section 3, attackers' detection rate varies with their strategy and is different from that of honest users. So, if the attackers can successfully manipulate the decision making process, detection rate will be significantly low, error rate in decision making will be high and spectrum utilization will be degraded.

From the attackers' point of view, the more error they make in decision making, the more successful they are. So, the most common attacking strategy is to falsify about channel status in every time step and send it to BS. In collaborative attack, since attackers share their information, they may have better idea about the actual channel status and devise their attacking plan in a more effective way. The collaboration makes it easier to manipulate the BS decision mechanism than independent attack and increases their success rate. However, if the malicious users try to strengthen their attacks and continuously send false channel status, the pattern of their sensing report will be almost the same. In this way, their sensing history will be significantly different from honest users and will be easily identifiable. So, the best attacking strategy is to attack occasionally or try to behave like an honest user otherwise. In summary, attackers' success depends on attacking frequency (i.e. when to attack) and how long they can attack without being identified. Together, all attackers can follow the same plan and can make the decision making process more complicated.

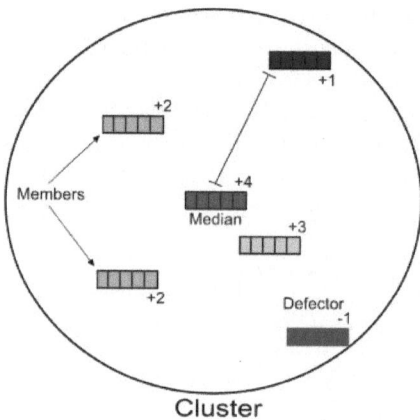

Fig. 1. Reputation Distribution

Now, from BS's point of view, its decision mechanism should be robust and capable of defending against any attacking strategy adopted by any number of malicious users. However, BS does not have any exact information about the attacking strategies or number of attackers. The only information available to BS is the sensing reports sent by users. So, the defense mechanism should be able to nullify (or at least reduce) the impact of collaboration of attackers, identify them and quarantine them from the decision process.

Accordingly, we design an adaptive reputation based clustering (ARC) algorithm to defend against both types of SSDF attack. The algorithm works against the intention and motivation of malicious users and tries to nullify their influence on the final decision. To reduce the impact of attackers, we create clusters so that nodes with similar sensing history will be in the same cluster. Then, each cluster has only one vote to cast and channel status is decided based on majority voting of clusters. The idea behind this defense mechanism is that if the attackers attack frequently, attackers and honest nodes will be in separate clusters due to their different sensing reports. Also, collaboration of attackers will not help to increase the error rate since each cluster has only one vote.

The key to attackers' success is to avoid being in the same cluster and take control of the majority of the clusters. To handle these issues, we introduce distance weighted voting in a cluster and a feedback component in each node's reputation. Voting power of each node in the cluster is inversely proportional to its distance from the median of that cluster. Similarly, each node gets reputation inversely proportional to its distance from the median of that cluster. By distributing the reputation based on distance from the median, nodes are only impacted relative to their 'confidence' of that group (see Figure 1). Furthermore, from the next round, nodes' modified reputation is also used to cluster nodes in addition to sensing history. In this way, even if an attacker and an honest user incorrectly fall in the same cluster, attackers cannot establish their decision. Furthermore, as time goes, the distance between an honest user and an attacker will be amplified due to the joint consideration of reputation and sensing history.

5   Adaptive Reputation Based Clustering (ARC) Algorithm

In this section, we explain our adaptive reputation based clustering (ARC) algorithm in detail. The algorithm goes through a sequence of phases to reach the final decision. The phase sequences are illustrated in Figure 2. In the first phase, the BS collects the sensing result from all the nodes. BS maintains sensing history of all nodes for last d time steps. In the next phase, partitioning around medoids (PAM) algorithm is applied on the sensing reports to create k equal sized virtual clusters. In the third phase, each cluster makes its decision based on the response of each individual node and their relative distance from the median of that cluster. Then the final decision is made based on majority voting of clusters. The final result is then used to adjust the number of clusters and to update the reputation of all nodes.

One of the key features in our algorithm is how we reach the final decision and use that decision recursively to update the clustering. The information flow of our algorithm from one step to another in each time step is depicted in Figure 3. The BS considers the most recent d sensing reports of each node in addition to their reputation during cluster formation. To enable this recursive approach, we

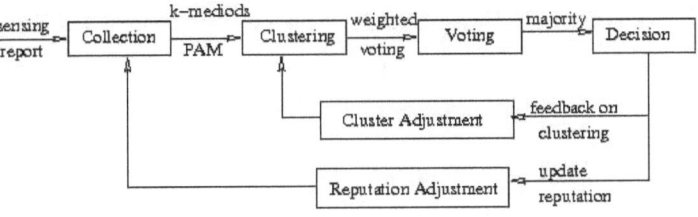

Fig. 2. Different Phases of the Algorithm

add an extra dimension to the sensing report of all nodes. This extra dimension represents the current reputation of that node (see Figure 3). So, each node provides a $d+1$ dimensional vector ($X_1 = [r_{1,1}, x_{1,1}, ... x_{d,1}]$) for cluster formation where the first dimension represents reputation and the remaining ones represent sensing report of last d time steps. Initially, all nodes are assigned the same reputation value.

Each cluster then finalizes its decision about channel status in a unique way. Only last round sensing report of each node in the cluster is considered. However, each response is weighted with an impact factor that is inversely proportional to the distance between the node and the median of that cluster. The impact factor of a node j at time t denoted by $I_j(t)$ is defined as

$$I_j(t) = \frac{1}{d_t(j, m_i)}$$

where m_i is the median of the cluster i and $d_t(j, m_i)$ denotes the distance between node j and median m_i of the same cluster at time t. Nodes closer to median have higher influence in decision making than the far ones. Accordingly, the cluster voting $v_i(t)$ at time t is determined by Equation 5.

$$v_i(t) = \frac{\sum_{j=1}^{N/k} I_j(t) * y_j(t)}{\sum_{j=1}^{N/k} I_j(t)} \tag{5}$$

Here, $y_j(t)$ is the sensing report of node j at time t which takes value from $\{0,1\}$.

After each cluster finalizes its decision, the BS makes the final decision $v(t)$ on the basis of majority voting among the valid clusters. If the reputation score of a cluster goes below a threshold, they cannot vote and all the nodes are marked as attackers. Therefore, $v(t) = \lceil 2 * \sum_{i=1}^{k} v_i(t)/k \rceil$.

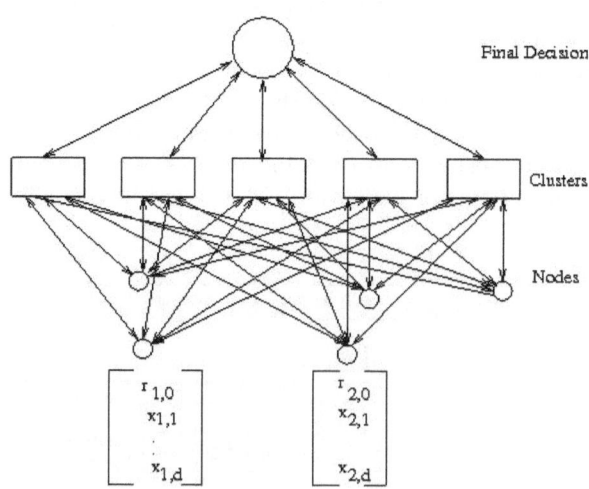

Fig. 3. Cluster Voting and Reputation Propagation

At the end of every time step, the base station updates number of clusters and reputation of all nodes according to the algorithm. The final result is propagated back to the clusters, and then to the individual nodes. If the final decision matches with the cluster decision, the cluster gets a positive feedback, and it gets negative feedback otherwise. Similarly, if a node's decision matches with its cluster decision, it gets positive feedback while it receives negative feedback for a mismatch. Each node's reputation is then adjusted according to Equation 6.

$$r_j = r_j + \Pi(v_i(t), v(t)) * \frac{\sum_{j=1}^{N/k} \Pi(v_i(t), y_j(t)) * I_j(t)}{\sum_{j=1}^{N/k} I_j(t)} \tag{6}$$

where r_j denotes the reputation of node j and $\Pi(a, b)$ is an indicator function that returns 1 if a equals b, it returns -1 otherwise.

The final result is also used to adjust the number of clusters. Initially, we start with 5 clusters with 5 random medoids. After each step, if all clusters pass the validation (i.e. reputation score exceeds threshold ϵ), we increment the number of clusters and continue the same process. Otherwise, we remove all the nodes in the cluster that fails the test.

6   Results

In this section we discuss results from the implementation of our proposed method, specifically comparing its effectiveness against a previously proposed method in [2]. We compare the two across both independent and collaborative attacks, as well as various probabilities of attack under a range of sensing conditions.

For each test, the methods are run over the same number of time steps, in this case 80 frames. For each time frame, the methods must produce a final

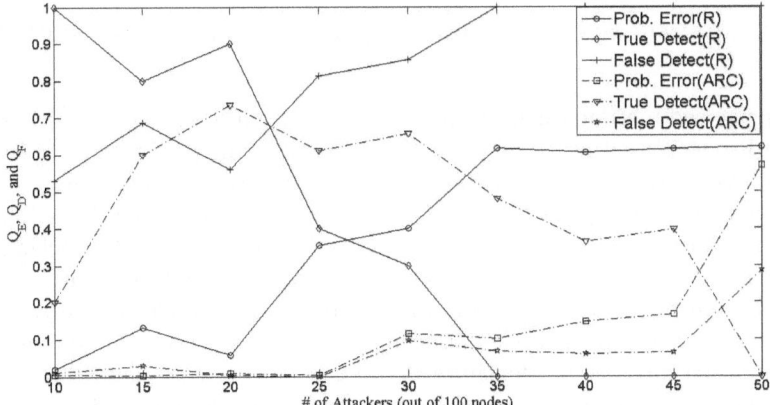

Fig. 4. Q_E, Q_D, Q_F with varying number of attackers (Collaborative SSDF Attack)

hypothesis, which is compared against actual transmission state of the primary user to determine the method's probability of error (Q_E). Rates for the correct detection of attacking nodes (Q_D) and the incorrect detection of honest users as attackers (Q_F) are also reported at the end of the test. Each test is then repeated 10 times with an average of the values displayed in the graphs. A test consists of randomly generated reports for each secondary user, adhering to labeled probability distributions. For validation test, we consider $\epsilon = 0.5$.

6.1   Collaborative Attack

First, we tested each method against a collaborative byzantine attack (see Figure 4), where the number of malicious users range from 10 to 50 out of 100 total secondary users. The byzantine attackers utilize the decision-making algorithm defined in [2]. Malicious users attack with $P_{mal} = 1$. Sensing probabilities for correctly detecting a signal and falsely detecting a signal were set to $P_d = 0.9$ and $P_{fa} = 0.1$ respectively.

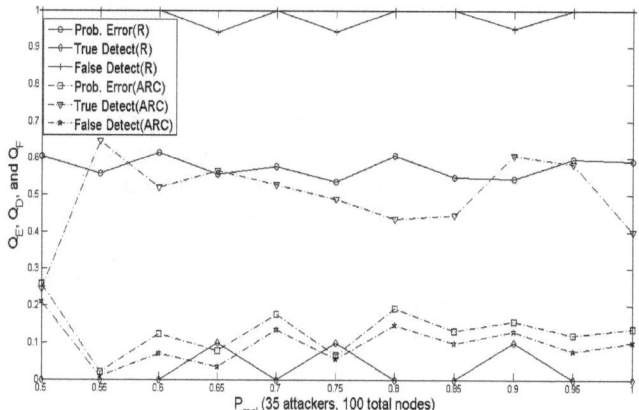

Fig. 5. Q_E, Q_D, Q_F with varying attacking probability (Collaborative SSDF Attack)

Our proposed method outperforms consistently with respect to (Q_E) showing a markedly decreased error rate until roughly 50% of the population becomes attackers. Once the population contains a majority of malicious users, it is impossible for any sensing strategy to sustain an error rate under 50%. The base stations are incapable of distinguishing between honest users and attackers. They can only resort to a blind guess for each sensing round. The Rawat method shows a high Q_D initially but quickly diminishes after 20% of nodes are attackers. At approximately the same attacker concentration, our method exceeds and maintains a marked increase in identifying attackers. Conversely, the Rawat method begins with a significant false detection rate (Q_F) while our method minimizes this rate across the entire range of attackers. Maintaining a low misdetection rate

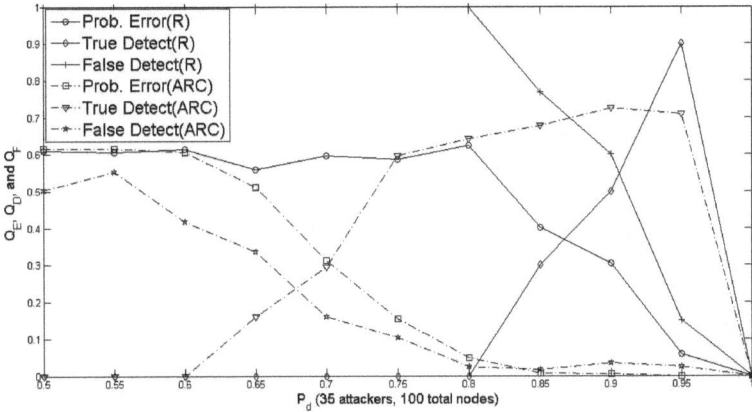

Fig. 6. Q_E, Q_D, Q_F with varying detection probability (Collaborative SSDF Attack)

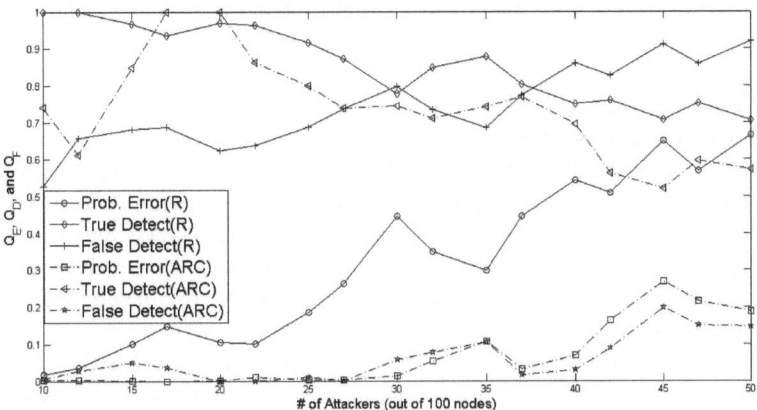

Fig. 7. Q_E, Q_D, Q_F with varying detection probability (Subgroup SSDF Attack)

allows our method to maximize honest user reports and mitigate the impact of attackers even under heavy attacks. A second set of measurements observed the impact of collaborating malicious users when varying their probability of attack. Malicious users can utilize this technique to escape detection from high dimensional clustering methods. In Figure 5, attackers produce on average less than 20% error rates while the Rawat method sustains significant errors. Regardless of attacking rate, our method consistently identifies 50% of the attackers. The Rawat method exhibits an unusually high attacker misdetection rate, which likely leads to the high error rate.

Depending on environmental conditions, the achievable sensing rates of primary user signals can vary dramatically. The next test looks at consequences of

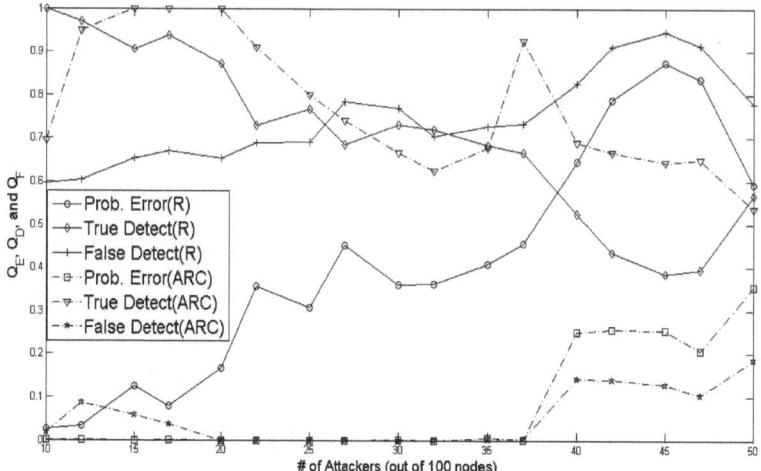

Fig. 8. Q_E, Q_D, Q_F with varying detection probability (GAMA SSDF Attack)

variable sensor accuracy (see Figure 6). Here, 35 collaborating malicious users attack during each sensing frame, and we can see the impact these sensing conditions have on the overall effectiveness of a byzantine attack. Both methods begin with relatively high error rates, as the sensing reports of honest users resemble that of attackers due to the inaccurate sensor readings. Once sensing errors fall below 65%, our proposed method shows a linear decrease in the Hypothesis error rate. The Rawat method takes significantly longer, approximately 80% detection rates, before error rates begin to decline.

We also test our algorithm in case of subgroup collaborative attack (see Figure 7). As the number of attacker increases, Q_E increases slightly in our algorithm while Q_E reaches almost 40% in the reputation method. As expected, both their true detection and false detection rate is high. On the other hand, Q_D is about 65% and Q_F is almost negligible in our algorithm.

We find interesting results for attackers with GAMA strategy. In case of our algorithm, Q_E is 0 and only increases when the number of attackers exceeds 37. On the other hand, Q_E increases almost linearly with the number of attackers in reputation based method. We get similar results in true and false detection rate. The results are plotted in Figure 8.

6.2   Independent Attack

In the next step, we compare the performance of our algorithm with reputation based scheme in [2] for independent SSDF attacks. In this attack, attackers do not collaborate to exchange their reports. Each attacker works independently to maximize its goal. Figure 9 shows the error rate of two algorithms with varying number of attackers. We keep the attacking probability $P_{mal} = 1$. Also, probabilities for true and false detection of a signal are set to $P_d = 0.9$ and $P_{fa} = 0.1$.

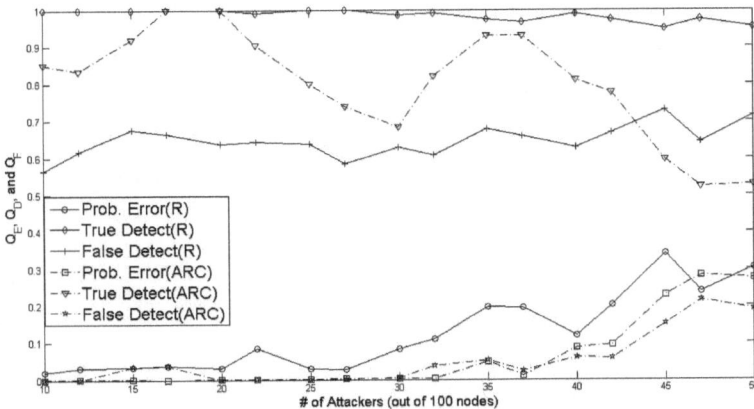

Fig. 9. Q_E, Q_D, Q_F with varying number of attackers (Independent SSDF Attack)

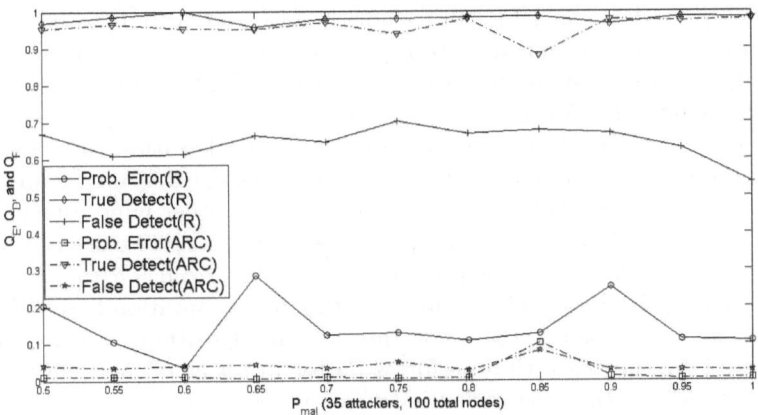

Fig. 10. Q_E, Q_D, Q_F with varying attacking probability (Independent SSDF Attack)

Our algorithm performs better up to 45 attackers and then slightly degrades its performance over their algorithm. On the other hand, our algorithm performs moderately to detect malicious attackers while their algorithm consistently identifies attackers with high precision. However, their algorithm eliminates a large number of honest users incorrectly. Figure 9 shows that about 40% honest users are miss identified as attacker. On the other hand, false detection rate of our algorithm is almost negligible. Although the reputation based algorithm performs better in detecting attacker than our algorithm, they misidentified a large number of honest users as attackers making their algorithm less effective.

Similarly, we run the simulation for independent SSDF attacks with varying attacking probability. We vary the attacking probability from 0.5 to 1 and

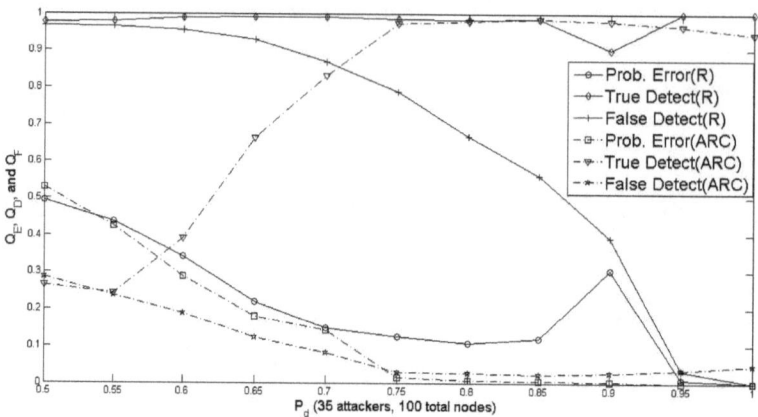

Fig. 11. Q_E, Q_D, Q_F with varying detection probability (Independent SSDF Attack)

plot Q_E, Q_E, and Q_F in 10 for our algorithm and reputation based algorithm proposed in [2]. Again, our algorithm performs better in decision making (see Figure 10). Error rate of our algorithm is almost negligible while their algorithm makes approximately 20% incorrect decisions about the channel status. The true attacker detection rate is almost the same for both algorithms. However, their algorithm constantly eliminates 60% of honest nodes as attackers for any attacking probability ranging between 0.5 and 1.0. On the other hand, our algorithm performs significantly better and keeps a false detection rate close to zero.

Next, we vary the detection probability of nodes from 0.5 to 1.0 and plot Q_E, Q_D and Q_F in Figure 11 for our algorithm and reputation based algorithm proposed in [2]. As usual, the error rate of our algorithm outperforms their algorithm. Also, our algorithm performs better in terms of misidentification of attackers. However, their algorithm identifies almost all attackers irrespective of the detection probability. On the other hand, our algorithm gradually increases the true detection rate with the increase of detection probability.

7   Conclusion

In this paper, we discussed one of the major security problems afflicting CRNs and proposed a reputation based clustering algorithm to defend against these attacks. We use reputation of nodes in addition to their sensing history to form clusters and then adjust reputation based on the cluster output. This recursive approach is tested in the presence of independent and collaborative spectrum sensing data falsification attacks. We compared the performance of our algorithm with existing approaches. With respect to current approaches, our algorithm significantly reduces the error rate in the final decision making process, thus increasing spectrum utilization. The false detection rate by our algorithm is almost negligible, while true attacker detection rate performs reasonably well.

However, the initial number of clusters plays an important role in overall performance of the algorithm. Also, it will be interesting to analyze the performance of the algorithm if attackers can overhear the honest users and decide accordingly. We will address these issues in future.

References

1. Li, H., Han, Z.: Catching Attackers for Collaborative Spectrum Sensing in Cognitive Radio Systems: An Abnormality Detection Approach. In: IEEE Symposium on New Frontiers in Dynamic Spectrum, pp. 1–12 (2010)
2. Rawat, A.S., Anand, P., Chen, H., Varshney, P.K.: Collaborative Spectrum Sensing in the Presence of Byzantine Attacks in Cognitive Radio Networks. IEEE Transactions on Signal Processing 59(2), 774–786 (2011)
3. Chen, R., Park, J.-M., Bian, K.: Robust Distributed Spectrum Sensing in Cognitive Radio Networks. In: INFOCOM: The 27th Conference on Computer Communications, pp. 1876–1884. IEEE (2008)
4. Clancy, T.C., Goergen, N.: Security in Cognitive Radio Networks: Threats and Mitigation. In: Cognitive Radio Oriented Wireless Networks and Communications (CrownCom), pp. 1–8 (2008)
5. Bian, K., Park, J.-M.J.: Security vulnerabilities in IEEE 802.22. In: Proceedings of the 4th Annual International Conference on Wireless Internet, WICON 2008, pp. 9:1–9:9 (2008)
6. Kaligineedi, P., Khabbazian, M., Bhargava, V.K.: Malicious User Detection in a Cognitive Radio Cooperative Sensing System. IEEE Transactions on Wireless Communications 9, 2488–2497 (2010)
7. Chen, R., Park, J.-M., Hou, Y.T., Reed, J.H.: Toward secure distributed spectrum sensing in cognitive radio networks. IEEE Communications Magazine 46, 50–55 (2008)
8. Wang, W., Li, H., Sun, Y., Han, Z.: CatchIt: Detect Malicious Nodes in Collaborative Spectrum Sensing. In: Global Telecommunications Conference, GLOBECOM 2009, pp. 1–6. IEEE (2009)
9. Akyildiz, I.F., Lee, W.-Y., Vuran, M.C., Mohanty, S.: A survey on spectrum management in cognitive radio networks. IEEE Communications Magazine 46, 40–48 (2008)
10. Wang, W., Li, H., Sun, Y., Han, Z.: Attack-proof collaborative spectrum sensing in cognitive radio networks. In: 43rd Annual Conference on Information Sciences and Systems (March 2009)

On Detection of Erratic Arguments

Jin Han, Qiang Yan, Robert H. Deng, and Debin Gao

Singapore Management University, Singapore
{jin.han.2007,qiang.yan.2008,robertdeng,dbgao}@smu.edu.sg

Abstract. Due to the erratic nature, the value of a function argument in one normal program execution could become illegal in another normal execution context. Attacks utilizing such erratic arguments are able to evade detections as fine-grained context information is unavailable in many existing detection schemes. In order to obtain such fine-grained context information, a precise model on the internal program states has to be built, which is impractical especially monitoring a closed source program alone. In this paper, we propose an intrusion detection scheme which builds on two diverse programs providing semantically-close functionality. Our model learns underlying semantic correlation of the argument values in these programs, and consequently gains more accurate context information compared to existing schemes. Through experiments, we show that such context information is effective in detecting attacks which manipulate erratic arguments with comparable false positive rates.

Keywords: Intrusion detection, system call argument, diversity

1 Introduction

Host-based anomaly detection techniques based on behaviors of programs in terms of system call sequences were first proposed by Forrest et al. [8], and improved and extended by a number of research work [7,9,13,14,19,23]. The normal-behavior models of the applications are learnt from the behaviors observed during a training phase; while during detection, any deviations from the established models are interpreted as attacks to the programs monitored. Later research [2,17,20,24] further enhanced the behavioral model by capturing the information of system call arguments.

Early schemes [17,20,24] model the argument behavior at the granularity of different system calls, i.e., each system call (e.g., open, read, write) is assigned with a profile. The granularity is then improved by differentiating the instances of the same system call when their call stacks are different [2]. For example, the legitimate arguments of open@callstack1 and open@callstack2 are assigned with different profiles so that they can be tested differently in the detection phase. However, since other context information is not captured during the training, an adversary is able to evade the detection of these existing schemes. Consider the following example code which assumes to contain a buffer overflow vulnerability:

M. Rajarajan et al. (Eds.): SecureComm 2011, LNICST 96, pp. 172–189, 2012.
© Institute for Computer Sciences, Social Informatics and Telecommunications Engineering 2012

```
int uid = geteuid();
char buf[128];
char* filename;
...
if (uid == 0)
    filename = "/www/admin/configure.ini";
else
    filename = "/www/user/configure.ini";
int fd = open(filename, O_RDWR);
write(fd, buf, sizeof(buf));
```

As illustrated in the example code, the system call **open** accepts two different parameter values in the training phase, both of which correspond to the same call stack. According to the existing schemes [2,17,24], both of these strings will be treated as legitimate values during detection. Thus, an attack which overflows **buf** and changes **uid** to 0 will be able to get the administrator privilege while evading detection. Such a situation is more common in modern software applications where code modules are extensively reused. Call stack is not able to tell a difference in the privilege in different executions.

The fundamental difficulty in detecting such attacks stems from the *erratic property* of function arguments. More formally, all legitimate values observed in different normal program executions are not necessarily legitimate at a particular execution. In a particular execution context, only a subset of the values (possibly one) is legitimate while others could potentially be malicious.

This problem seems deceptively simple. The fine-grained context information, which is required to differentiate the legitimate values at run-time, is difficult to gather when training merely one program [2,17,24], especially when the source code is not provided. Even for schemes which utilize two diverse applications, their model cannot be simply extended to detect such attacks. For example, hidden Markov models used in [10,11,12] (to train the normal-behavior profiles of the system call sequences) are only able to handle finite states, while the space of argument values is usually infinite.

In this paper, we propose an intrusion detection scheme which builds on two diverse programs providing semantically-close functionalities. Our model learns the underlying semantic correlation of the argument values in these programs to detect attacks manipulating erratic arguments, which are recognized as normal inputs by existing schemes. Specifically, we make the following contributions:

- We provide a formal approach of detecting attacks utilizing erratic arguments, by learning relations of the function arguments between programs providing semantically-close functionalities.
- We utilize taint analysis to further refine the detection model, which eliminates the coincident relations to decrease the false positive rates.
- We implement a prototype of our scheme and present a detailed experimental evaluation. The evaluation demonstrates that a number of real attacks which are hard to detect by existing schemes can be effectively detected using our technique. Specifically, it is shown that our detection model not only

detects sophisticated attacks on security-critical data, but also detects some Denial-of-Service attacks which are not addressed by existing techniques, with comparable false alarm rates.

2   Diversity Detection Model

In this section, we first introduce the framework of our detection approach, which is followed by the definitions of the argument relations. Different algorithms are then provided to train the behavioral model for different types of arguments.

2.1   Overview

Figure 1 illustrates the basic idea of how our intrusion detection system (IDS) is constructed. We regard two diverse software having *semantically-close functionalities* if they provide same services. Examples of such diverse software could be web servers like Apache and Lighttpd, or office software like Adobe PDF Reader and Foxit PDF Reader. Similar to existing diversity-based intrusion detection techniques, the framework in Figure 1 utilizes two diverse software providing semantically-close functionalities to build the behavioral model, base on the observations that these software cannot be successfully exploited by the same attack [15].

In this paper, we focus on building a normal-behavior model by extracting the function arguments of both applications. Since these applications provide semantically-close functionalities, there are semantic relations between the behaviors of these applications when they process the same input. **Such semantic relations will exhibit as the relations between the related function calls and their argument values.** For example, two web servers processing the same HTTP request need to access the same local file on the disk. Thus, consequently, there should be functions in both applications whose argument values contain the same file name. In the following, we will briefly introduce how our model captures the argument relations between the two diverse applications.

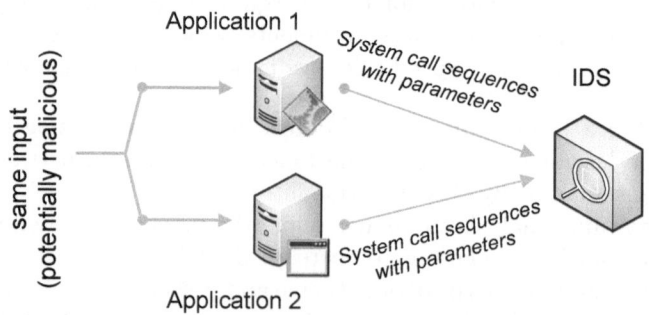

Fig. 1. Our diversity IDS framework

Once the argument relations are trained, they will be utilized to detect attacks that attempt to fool traditional IDS with erratic function arguments.

In the model of Figure 1, the same inputs, which are assumed to be free of attacks in the training phase, are passed to both of these applications (app$_1$, app$_2$). In order to process the input, each of these applications will invoke a series of system calls (for each input):

$$S_1 = \langle s_{1,1}, s_{1,2}, ..., s_{1,l_1} \rangle \qquad S_2 = \langle s_{2,1}, s_{2,2}, ..., s_{2,l_2} \rangle \qquad (1)$$

Each system call $s_{i,j}$ has a vector of arguments. In the training phase, all information for each $s_{i,j}$ will be recorded by corresponding monitor module of app$_i$, and is used to extract the information of the arguments. Specifically, in our model, each argument is identified by:

$$\text{arg}_{i,x} \text{ where } i \in \{1,2\},$$
$$x = \langle \text{index, type, s\_name, callstack} \rangle.$$

In the above representation, i in arg$_{i,x}$ indicates this argument appears in the trace of app$_i$. index is the position of this argument in the corresponding system call, whose name is s_name; type is the type of the argument (e.g. *string* or *integer*); callstack stores the call stack information of the corresponding invocation of this particular system call.

In the training phase, we first obtain a pair of system call traces (S_1, S_2) for each input. With all pairs of the system call traces, we then get a set of argument pairs. For each argument pair (arg$_{1,p}$, arg$_{2,q}$), arg$_{1,p}$ is an argument in app$_1$, which is identified by a unique set of $\langle \text{index, type, s\_name, callstack} \rangle$ appearing in the training set, and arg$_{2,q}$ is defined similarly. From the training data, we collect a set of value pairs Value$_{p,q}$ for each argument pair, where Value$_{p,q}$ = $\{(v_1, v_2)|$ arg$_{1,p}$ = v$_1$, arg$_{2,q}$ = v$_2\}$. According to Value$_{p,q}$, we then produce a database of relations $\mathbb{R}$ = $\{\langle \text{arg}_{1,p} \text{ R arg}_{2,q} \rangle\}$. This relation set $\mathbb{R}$ is finally utilized to detect whether there is any violation for each pair of parameter values. If the relation of a pair of parameter instances ($\langle \text{arg}_{1,p} = v_x \rangle$ and $\langle \text{arg}_{2,q} = v_y \rangle$) does not satisfy the corresponding $\langle \text{arg}_{1,p} \text{ R arg}_{2,q} \rangle$ in $\mathbb{R}$, the IDS will raise an alarm.

2.2   Relationships of the Arguments

In our model, we focus on two most common types of system call arguments – *string* and *integer*, the definitions of which follow the standard definition in programming language: a *string* is a sequence of zero or more characters followed by a NULL ("\0") character; while an *integer* is a numeric variable holding whole numbers.

We define binary relation R that captures the relationship between two system call arguments in the diverse applications. The relation between two arguments is expressed as $\langle \text{arg}_1 \text{ R arg}_2 \rangle$, where arg$_1$ is a particular argument in the first application, and arg$_2$ is a particular argument in the second application. Different sets of candidate relations are given to *string* and *integer* since these two argument types have different characteristics.

We provide the following basic relations for *string* arguments:

- **equal** captures equality relation of the given two arguments, e.g., the file name passed to an `open` system call in app_1 could be the same as the file name passed to another `open` (or `stat64`) system call in app_2.

- **samePrefix(n)** indicates that the two string arguments have the same prefix, the length of which is at least n. For example, if $arg_1 = $ "`/home/usr/xyz`" and $arg_2 = $ "`/home/usr/abc`", then $\langle arg_1$ samePrefix(10) $arg_2 \rangle$ holds.

- **sameSuffix(n)** indicates that the two string arguments have the same suffix substring with length at least n.

- **contain** means that the second argument is a substring of the first argument.

- **partOf** is the reverse of **contain** relation, in which the first argument is a substring of the second argument.

Note that for the same pair of arguments, more than one of the above relations may hold. For example, if $arg_1 = $ "`/home/configure.ini`" and $arg_2 = $ "`/home/conf.ini`", then both $\langle arg_1$ samePrefix(10) $arg_2 \rangle$ and $\langle arg_1$ sameSuffix(4) $arg_2 \rangle$ hold. The above five relations defined are sufficient to cover the binary relations of string arguments proposed in existing approaches, which are defined for modeling the binary relations of arguments in a single program, such as isWithinDir, hasSameDirAs, hasSameExtensionAs [2].

For *integer* arguments, we use a polynomial equation to represent the relation of the two arguments. That is, let $x = arg_1$ and $y = arg_2$ (or $x = arg_2$ and $y = arg_1$), the following equation holds:

$$y = c_m x^m + c_{m-1} x^{m-1} + ... + c_1 x + c_0 \tag{2}$$

For example, for the two `malloc` calls which create a memory region to store the `uri` string parsed from the same request, the parameter values of these two `malloc` could have the form $y = 1 \cdot x + c_0$. The value of c_0 may not be 0 because the internal structures which store the `uri` are different in these two programs. Note that in Equation (2), when $c_1 = 1$ and $\forall i \neq 1, c_i = 0$, then $arg_1 = arg_2$. In our model, this equal relation between numeric arguments is able to capture most relations of flag arguments (such as `O_RDONLY` and `O_RDWR`), because they usually appear as the same in the diverse software providing semantically-close functionalities.

Polynomial relation does not cover all the binary relations between two integer arguments, e.g., exponential relation or bitwise relation may also exist under some circumstances. In our current model, we only preserve polynomial relation for integer parameters as it is the most common relation we observed in real applications.

2.3   Training Algorithms

The training procedure can be generally divided into three stages: argument pair extraction, relation acquisition and relation refinement.

Argument Pair Extraction. In this first stage, our purpose is to extract a set of $\text{Value}_{p,q}$ for each pair of $\langle \text{arg}_{1,p}, \text{arg}_{2,q} \rangle$. Each $\text{Value}_{p,q}$ set will contain all the value pairs occurred in the whole training procedure. All the sets of $\text{Value}_{p,q}$ will then be used to train the relation R between $\langle \text{arg}_{1,p}, \text{arg}_{2,q} \rangle$. The algorithm of extracting each pair of arguments and its corresponding values are given in Algorithm 1, after which a set $\mathbb{PV}= \{(\text{arg}_{1,p}, \text{arg}_{2,q}, \text{Value}_{p,q})\}$ will be collected. This $\mathbb{PV}$ set will then be used as input in Algorithm 2 and Algorithm 3.

Algorithm 1. Argument-pair extraction

1: **for** each (S_1, S_2) pair in the training set **do**
2:     **for** each $s_{1,j}$ in S_1 and each $s_{2,k}$ in S_2 **do**
3:         **if** *comparable*$(s_{1,j}, s_{2,k})$ **then**
4:             **for** each $\text{arg}_{1,p}$ belonging to $s_{1,j}$, and each $\text{arg}_{2,q}$ belonging to $s_{2,k}$ **do**
5:                 v_1 = value of $\text{arg}_{1,p}$
6:                 v_2 = value of $\text{arg}_{2,q}$
7:                 **if** $(\text{arg}_{1,p}.\text{type} = \text{arg}_{2,q}.\text{type})$ **then**
8:                     **if** $(\text{arg}_{1,p}, \text{arg}_{2,q}, \text{Value}_{p,q})$ already exists in $\mathbb{PV}$ **then**
9:                         add (v_1, v_2) to $\text{Value}_{p,q}$ if $(v_1, v_2) \notin \text{Value}_{p,q}$
10:                     **else**
11:                         $\text{Value}_{p,q} = \{(v_1, v_2)\}$
12:                         add $(\text{arg}_{1,p}, \text{arg}_{2,q}, \text{Value}_{p,q})$ to $\mathbb{PV}$
13:                     **end if**
14:                 **end if**
15:             **end for**
16:         **end if**
17:     **end for**
18: **end for**

This step is critical to the rest of the training procedure. The amount of all the combinations of $\langle \text{arg}_{1,p}, \text{arg}_{2,q} \rangle$ could be huge, however, we only consider argument pairs which appear in `comparable` function calls (as shown in line 3 of Algorithm 1). We define *comparable* function calls as those who have the same function names or whose functionalities are semantically related. For example, system calls `open` and `stat64` are comparable, and library calls `malloc`, `calloc` and `realloc` are comparable. System calls like `setuid` and `open` are not comparable since their functionalities are not semantically related. Our current implementation of Algorithm 1 reads in a configuration file that specifies which function calls are comparable. This configuration file is carefully constructed according to the platform on which the target applications are running. Our current implementation only considers the Linux operating system with GNU C library.

Relation Acquisition. The next step is to learn the relations between each pair of arguments gained by Algorithm 1. Here we introduce two algorithms for learning the relations: Algorithm 2 is used to learn the relations between two *string* arguments; while Algorithm 3 is for *integer* arguments. We use $\emptyset$ to denote that there is no relation between two arguments ($\text{arg}_1 \; \emptyset \; \text{arg}_2$).

Algorithm 2. String-relation learning

Require: set $\mathbb{PV}$.

1: **for** each $(arg_{1,p}, arg_{2,q}, Value_{p,q})$ in $\mathbb{PV}$ **do**
2:    **if** $arg_{1,p}.type = arg_{2,q}.type = string$ **then**
3:       **for** each (v_1, v_2) in $Value_{p,q}$ **do**
4:          calculate $R \in \{equal, samePrefix(n), sameSuffix(n), contain, partOf, \emptyset\}$, which satisfies $v_1\ R\ v_2$.
5:          **if** $R \neq \emptyset$ **then**
6:             **for** each R_c that $\langle arg_{1,p}, R_c, arg_{2,q} \rangle \in \mathbb{R}$ **do**
7:                **if** R conflicts with R_c **then**
8:                   remove all $\langle arg_{1,p}, R_c, arg_{2,q} \rangle$ in $\mathbb{R}$
9:                   add $\langle arg_{1,p}, \emptyset, arg_{2,q} \rangle$ to $\mathbb{R}$
10:               **else**
11:                  add $\langle arg_{1,p}, R, arg_{2,q} \rangle$ to $\mathbb{R}$
12:               **end if**
13:            **end for**
14:         **else if** $\langle arg_{1,p}, \emptyset, arg_{2,q} \rangle \notin \mathbb{R}$ **then**
15:            add $\langle arg_{1,p}, \emptyset, arg_{2,q} \rangle$ to $\mathbb{R}$
16:         **end if**
17:      **end for**
18:   **end if**
19: **end for**

Note that there is an update procedure in the learning process of Algorithm 2 for the relation of samePrefix(n) and sameSuffix(n), which is not shown in the algorithm. Take samePrefix(n) for example, suppose the existing relation for arg_1, arg_2 in $\mathbb{R}$ is $samePrefix(n_{old})$ and the new learnt relation is $samePrefix(n_{new})$. The new relation of arg_1, arg_2 in $\mathbb{R}$ will be updated as $samePrefix(\min(n_{old}, n_{new}))$.

Another important detail not shown in Algorithm 2 is that, a threshold N can be set for the relations samePrefix(n) and sameSuffix(n), to reduce the false positives caused by small n. During learning, if the calculated $n < N$, then set $R = \emptyset$. And different N should be assigned for samePrefix(n) and sameSuffix(n). Also note that a set of confliction rules for the relations is needed in Algorithm 2 (at line 7). Generally, $\emptyset$ conflicts with other relations, and equal, contain, partOf conflict with each other since the equal relation will always be verified first.

In Algorithm 3, the given order m should be at least 2, and should not be too large so as to avoid the overfitting problem. m can also be dynamically adjusted according to the size of each $Value_{p,q}$. However, the value of m should be at most $Value_{p,q}.size - 1$ in order to have enough value pairs for solving the equation set and leave at least one value pair to verify the results.

The whole learning process is optimized by utilizing the $\emptyset$ relations. The $\mathbb{PV}$ set does not need to be fully computed before running Algorithm 2 and Algorithm 3. If $\langle arg_{1,p}\ \emptyset\ arg_{2,q} \rangle$ already appears in $\mathbb{R}$, then the remaining instances of $\langle arg_{1,p}, arg_{2,q} \rangle$ do not need to be added into $\mathbb{PV}$. The $\emptyset$ relations will be dropped at the end of the training.

Algorithm 3. Integer-relation learning
___

Require: set $\mathbb{PV}$, order m.

1: **for** each $(\mathsf{arg}_{1,p}, \mathsf{arg}_{2,q}, \mathsf{Value}_{p,q})$ in $\mathbb{PV}$ **do**
2: **if** $\mathsf{arg}_{1,p}.\mathrm{type} = \mathsf{arg}_{2,q}.\mathrm{type} = integer$ **then**
3:   **if** $\mathsf{Value}_{p,q}.\mathrm{size} < m$ **then**
4:    add $\langle \mathsf{arg}_{1,p}, \emptyset, \mathsf{arg}_{2,q} \rangle$ to $\mathbb{R}$
5:   **else**
6:    use the first m pairs of $(\mathsf{v}_1, \mathsf{v}_2)$ in $\mathsf{Value}_{p,q}$ to solve the equation set of Equation (2) to get $(c_m, ..., c_0)$, for both $(x = \mathsf{arg}_{1,p}, y = \mathsf{arg}_{2,q})$ and $(x = \mathsf{arg}_{2,q}, y = \mathsf{arg}_{1,p})$.
7:    **if** the equation set is solvable **then**
8:     $\mathsf{R} = \{x, y, (c_m, ..., c_0)\}$
9:     **for** each $(\mathsf{v}_1, \mathsf{v}_2)$ left in $\mathsf{Value}_{p,q}$ **do**
10:      **if** Equation (2) does not hold **then**
11:       $\mathsf{R} = \emptyset$
12:      **end if**
13:     **end for**
14:     add $\langle \mathsf{arg}_{1,p}, \mathsf{R}, \mathsf{arg}_{2,q} \rangle$ to $\mathbb{R}$
15:    **else**
16:     add $\langle \mathsf{arg}_{1,p}, \emptyset, \mathsf{arg}_{2,q} \rangle$ to $\mathbb{R}$
17:    **end if**
18:   **end if**
19: **end if**
20: **end for**
___

2.4 Model Refinement

In this subsection, we include an additional training phase to refine the relations we have obtained by the above algorithms. The relations $\mathbb{R}$ gained by using previous algorithms are patterns on the values we observed. However, certain trained relations may be due to the coincidence in the training data set, which could cause false alarms in detection. Thus, it will be better if we can remove those trained patterns in $\mathbb{R}$ which are not caused by the semantic relations between the two diverse applications.

However, it is not an easy task to validate the semantic relations of arguments and refine the trained model. Even with the source code, it is difficult for a human to capture the exact semantic meaning of a given function in a complex application. Thus, to automatically capture the semantic meanings of functions without the source code is an even harder problem. One way of learning the semantic relations between arguments is to use taint analysis [22]. Since the semantics of different set of function calls vary a lot, the detailed method of carrying out taint analysis needs to be customized accordingly. It is difficult to design a universal solution to perform the taint analysis for all the function calls.

In our current work, we develop a method of mapping memory management library calls (such as `malloc`, `free`, `realloc`, etc.) of two diverse web servers, according to the semantics gained by taint analysis. The basic idea is as follows: First of all, by tainting the request stream sent from client, we gain the knowledge that which portions of the request are mapped to which heap memory regions. Since these memory regions are created by the corresponding memory library calls, each library call can be correlated with a certain portion of the request. We mapped the two memory library calls (e.g., one `malloc` in Apache and one `calloc` in Lighttpd) whose memory regions store the same part of the request (e.g. the `uri`). We then preserve the argument relations that belong to the mapped library calls, and remove other unmapped relations from $\mathbb{R}$. The implementation detail is given in Section 3, the effect of such refinement will be further evaluated in Section 4.

2.5   Detection

After the relation set $\mathbb{R}$ is trained, the detection phase is quite straightforward. During detection, for each argument pair $(\text{arg}_{1,p}, \text{arg}_{2,q})$ appears in $\mathbb{R}$, each instance of $(\text{arg}_{1,p} = v_x, \text{arg}_{2,q} = v_y)$ will be tested. If an instance does not satisfy the corresponding $\langle \text{arg}_{1,p} \ R \ \text{arg}_{2,q} \rangle$ in $\mathbb{R}$, the IDS will raise an alarm. Although the complexity of the training is relatively high, the detection only involves simple and fast computation. The main cost of detection depends on the cost of monitoring and logging the function calls.

3   Implementation

We have implemented our approach on Ubuntu 8.04 (Linux kernel 2.6.24). The implementation consists of two online components and an offline component.

The two online components are both monitor modules (referred to as tracer), one of which is used to trace system calls, the other is used to trace library calls of the monitored programs. For the system call tracer, we utilize `ptrace` to intercept each system call made by the monitored program and log the following information: (a) the PC value from where the system call was invoked, (b) values of arguments, and (c) the call stack information which contains a set of absolute return addresses. For the library call tracer, we modify the GNU C library (glibc) under Ubuntu to output similar information for a selected set of library calls. Since the `backtrace` method cannot be used within the implementation of some library calls such as `malloc`, we implement our own `backtrace` method in the glibc to log the call stack information.

Each time when the monitored program starts, all the base addresses of its loaded shared libraries are also recorded, which is retrieved from corresponding `/proc/[pid]/maps`. These addresses will be used to convert the absolute addresses in the call stack recorded by the tracer to relative addresses, in the form of `[libname+offset]`. By having relative call stacks, we are able to identify the same instance of function call across different runs of the same program.

The offline component of our implementation includes the parsers of the logged traces and the training module that implements the algorithms in Section 2. As mentioned earlier, a configuration file is also provided to the training module, which specifies the function calls that are comparable. The implementation of the offline component is about 3.5K LOC.

For the model refinement part in the training, we utilize TEMU [1] to carry out the taint analysis. Web server programs running in TEMU are provided with tainted request stream and tainted local disk files, and the instructions of the monitored web server will be recorded when processing each request. The recorded instruction traces are then translated by the `trace_reader` tool in Vine [1] and used as inputs to the trace parsers we implemented. According to the taint information in the trace files, our trace parser will be able to extract the information that each memory library calls is related to which part of the request stream (or is related to which file on the disk). Then two library calls (in two diverse servers) which are related to the same part of the request (or the same local file) are recorded as the mapped library calls as mentioned in the previous section. This TEMU trace parser is around 1K LOC.

4   Evaluation

In this section, we first investigate the effectiveness of our approach in detecting real attacks and then analyze the false alarm rates. Performance overheads for intrusion detection are also discussed. All experiments are conducted under Ubuntu 8.04 and the training and testing are performed in offline mode.

4.1   Detection Effectiveness

Since the code injection attacks have been extensively addressed in prior research [7,8,9,13,14,19,23], we focus on evaluating the detection effectiveness of our model against attacks on security-critical data utilizing erratic arguments. Table 1 lists the set of attacks tested in our evaluation. The first two attacks in Table 1 are detectable by our approach since they both violate the *string* argument relations trained in our model, while the other two attacks in Table 1 violate the *integer* argument relations.

Table 1. Selected Non-control-flow Attacks

Reference	Vulnerable Program	Attack Description	Alternative Program	Detected? (type)
S.Chen et al. [4]	Ghttpd	stack overflow to overwrite filename data	Null-httpd	Yes (string)
S.Chen et al. [4]	Null-httpd	heap overflow to corrupt cgi-bin configuration string	Ghttpd	Yes (string)
S.Chen et al. [4]	Wu-ftpd	format string attack to overwrite userid data	Pure-ftpd	Yes (integer)
CVE-2008-4298	Lighttpd	memory leak via duplicate request headers	Cherokee httpd	Yes (integer)

Detection of Anomalous String Arguments.

The first attack in Table 1 exploits a stack overflow vulnerability in Ghttpd's logging function [4], which occurs in the following code fragment in function serverconnection():

```
1: if (strstr(ptr, "/.."))
2:   reject the request;
3: log(...);
4: if (strstr(ptr, "cgi-bin"))
5:   execve(ptr, ...)
```

In the above code, ptr is a char pointer to the string of URL requested by a remote client. The first two lines in the code are used to check the absence of "/.." in the URL, before the CGI request is parsed and handled in line 4–5. The stack buffer overflow vulnerability is in function log(), where a long user input string can overrun a 200-byte stack buffer. Chen et al. [4] managed to construct a stealthy attack which changes ptr to point to a string cgi-bin/../../../../bin/sh by exploiting the vulnerability in log(). Their attack neither injects code nor alters the return address, thus, it is difficult to be detected by most of existing models.

Our approach is able to detect this attack. During training, our model learns the equal relation between the first parameter of execve in Ghttpd and the parameter of corresponding execve in Null-httpd (in function cgi_main()). Since this relation is later violated when this attack has successfully changed the value of ptr in Ghttpd, an alarm is raised by the IDS.

Although this attack is also detectable by the dataflow model [2], their mechanism is different. Their system first learns that all files executed at line 5 should be within the "cgi-bin" directory. The attack is detected when it accesses a file outside this directory. However, such isWithinDir [2] relation (trained by monitoring the program itself) may not be sufficient in practical scenarios. For example, in typical business applications, files under the same directory may have different access policies. A user x is only allowed to execute program A under the directory, but not program B. Due to the overflow attack, adversary with the privilege of user x is able to gain the access to program B. Under such a scenario, the isWithinDir relation will not be able to detect such attacks since all the programs are under the same directory, while our model is still able to detect attacks in cases like these.

The second attack in Table 1 targets on a heap overflow vulnerability exists in Null-httpd. This vulnerability is triggered when a special POST command is received by the server. This vulnerability can be used to corrupt the CGI-BIN configuration of Null-httpd and will result in root compromise without executing any external code. In the attack illustrated by Chen et al. [4], two POST commands are issued to precisely overwrite four characters in the CGI-BIN configuration so that it is changed from "/usr/local/httpd /cgi-bin\0" to "/bin\0". After the corruption, /bin/sh can be started as a CGI program and any shell command can be sent as the standard input to /bin/sh.

This attack cannot be easily detected by control-flow schemes [7,8,9,13,14,19,23], and is not addressed by the dataflow scheme [2]. However, our diversity model is able to detect such an intrusion due to the same reason in the first attack – the equal relation (of the first parameter of the two execve calls in Null-httpd and in Ghttpd) learnt during training, is violated when Null-httpd is exploited.

Note that although both of these two servers (Ghttpd and Null-httpd) have vulnerabilities, we can still use them together to build our diversity detection model because their vulnerabilities are not exploitable by the same attack code. In general, the probability that the same vulnerability exists in two diverse applications providing semantically-close functionalities is very low [15].

Detection of Anomalous Integer Arguments.

The third attack in Table 1 exploits a format string vulnerability in Wu-ftpd. The vulnerable code fragment is within the getdatasock() function:

```
1: seteuid(0);
2: setsockopt( ... );
   ...
3: seteuid(pw->pw_uid);
```

The above function is invoked when a user issues data transfer commands, such as downloading or uploading a file. It requires root privilege in order to perform the setsockopt() operation. Thus, the privilege is temporarily escalated using seteuid(0) and then changed back by the second seteuid(). The data structure pw->pw_uid is a cached copy of the user ID saved on the heap. The attack proposed in [4] exploits the format-string vulnerability to change pw->pw_uid to 0, which maintains the root privilege for the attacker so that arbitrary files can be uploaded and downloaded by the attacker as a root user.

Our model detects this attack when monitoring Wu-ftpd together with Pure-ftpd. Since the two servers have the same configurations, the parameter of seteuid()[1] function call on line 3 in Wu-ftpd always has the same value as the parameter of the seteuid() calls in function doport3() in Pure-ftpd. These *integer* parameter relations are violated when the adversary overflow the heap to change pw->pw_uid to 0.

The fourth attack in Table 1 exploits a memory leak vulnerability exists in Lighttpd. When a duplicated field appears in a request header (e.g., "User-Agent :Mozilla/4.0" and "User-Agent:MSIE/8.0" both appear in the header), the http_request_parse() method in Lighttpd will allocate a memory region to store the content of the second field (i.e., MSIE/8.0), but will not recycle this resource afterwards. An adversary can utilize this vulnerability to consume the memory of the server running Lighttpd by sending many requests with duplicate fields (with a maximum field length of 2KB).

---

[1] The underlying system call invoked is setresuid32().

Such Denial-of-Service attack cannot be directly detected by the existing approaches which train on a single server, especially when the total memory consumed is not large enough to cause any exception. The difficulty comes from the memory management behaviors of these web servers. For the most commonly used servers (such as Apache, Lighttpd, etc.), the allocated memory will be reused in processing the following requests and never be explicitly freed. Thus, for both normal request and attack request processing, only memory allocation methods (such as `malloc`, `realloc` ...) are observed, no deallocation method (such as `free`) will appear in the library call sequences obtained. This makes it difficult for an IDS to precisely model the memory behaviors, as it requires simulating the complex internal memory management of these server applications.

Our diversity IDS is able to learn the integer argument relations of the corresponding memory allocation calls in the two servers monitored. To be specific, the IDS learns that 16 pairs of the parameter values to the `malloc` and `realloc` calls of Lighttpd and Cherokee servers are equal or have fixed difference (which is actually due to the size difference of the internal structures in these two servers). In the detection phase, the IDS detects the memory leak attack immediately when the attack request causes one of Lighttpd's `malloc` parameter to increase (in `buffer_copy_string_len()` invoked by `http_request_parse()`), which violates the integer relations that have been trained in the model.

4.2   False Alarm Analysis

There are three pairs of programs in Table 1. All of them are used to evaluate the false alarm rates of our approach, as shown in Table 2. Two pairs of them are http servers (Lighttpd and Cherokee, Ghttpd and Null-httpd), which are configured to hold the same content of the web site of our university. In the training phase, the two web servers in the same pair are provided with the same series of requests (10K requests) obtained from the real log of our university's web server. In the detection phase, another set of requests (50K requests) from the logs are sent to these servers to evaluate the false alarm rates. Applications in the third pair are FTP server programs (Wu-ftpd and Pure-ftpd). Since we do not have the access to the log of large amount of real FTP requests, we configure these two FTP servers to hold the files downloaded from GNU FTP[2], and simulate the requests by randomly issuing commands (such as `put`, `get`, `dir`, `passive`, `type`, etc.) for random files or directories on the servers.

We construct two different experiments to test our false alarm rates (as shown in Table 2 and Table 3). The first experiment only focuses on monitoring the system calls and their arguments so that it can be compared with existing approaches which also utilize system call arguments [2,17] (e.g., the result of the dataflow model [2] shows the false positive rate of the tested HTTP server is 64.12×10^{-5}, and the rate for SSH server is 0.02×10^{-5}). Note that the rates shown in Table 2 are "raw" false alarm rates, i.e., the fraction of system calls that caused violations, without combining the same type of violations. For

---

[2] GNU Software FTP server, `ftp.gnu.org/gnu`

Table 2. False alarm rate

Diverse Programs		Training Trace # of **Sys calls** ($\times 10^5$)	Detection Trace # of **Sys calls** ($\times 10^5$)	False alarm rates ($\times 10^{-5}$)
Pair 1	Lighttpd	2.29	10.90	0.826
	Cherokee httpd	5.19	24.35	
Pair 2	Ghttpd	7.24	39.51	1.948
	Null httpd	20.62	98.57	
Pair 3	Wu ftpd	10.78	54.15	0.617
	Pure ftpd	4.37	12.96	

Table 3. Model refinement by taint analysis

Programs	Training Trace # of **Lib calls** ($\times 10^5$)	Detection Trace # of **Lib calls** ($\times 10^5$)	False alarm rates ($\times 10^{-5}$)	
			Original	After Refine
Lighttpd	2.31	11.06	5.286	1.762
Cherokee	0.46	2.27		

example, the false alarm rate for Lighttpd in Table 2 is 0.826×10^{-5}, which means that one false alarm will be raised for every 100K system calls processed. This indicates that one out of 10K requests will cause false alarms, as on average 10.9 system calls are invoked to process one request for Lighttpd.

The results show that the second pair of applications have much higher false alarm rate than the other two pairs, as in Table 2. We investigated the reason for this higher false alarm rate, and found that this is due to the fact that during the training, there are several coincident contain relations for the string arguments between Ghttpd and Null-httpd, which are violated in the detection phase for benign requests. Our current implementation of the training algorithm regards two string arguments as contain as long as their values satisfy this relation, even if these pair of arguments only appear once in the training. However, some rules in the training phase could be added to further decrease the false alarm rate. For example, any string relations should have at least two instances of value pairs in the training phase so that one instance of values is used to set up the relation and other values can be used to validate the relation in the training (and any argument pairs which only have one instance should be regarded as $\emptyset$ relation in $\mathbb{R}$). Such modification could reduce the false positives of our model but should be carefully designed so that it would not decrease the detection capability as well. Investigation on this trade-off is left as future work.

In the second experiment (as shown in Table 3), we investigate the false positive rate when our model monitors the memory management library calls of the diverse applications. Note that different from Table 2, only library calls are considered in Table 3. We further investigate the effectiveness on false positive reduction by refining our model using taint analysis. The result shows that after removing the library call argument patterns which are not mapped by the semantic relations, the false positive rate decreases. It is possible to refine the

Table 4. Program size and model size

Programs		Program Size (Kbytes)	String Relations	Integer Relations
Pair 1	Lighttpd	767.9	143	367
	Cherokee httpd	1165.7		
Pair 2	Ghttpd	43.6	120	342
	Null httpd	34.3		
Pair 3	Wu ftpd	385.3	171	496
	Pure ftpd	87.8		

relations of other arguments by using taint analysis. However, since the semantics of different set of library/system call arguments vary, taint analysis needs to be carefully customized accordingly.

4.3   Performance Overheads

Table 4 shows the size of the programs used in our evaluation, along with the model sizes in terms of the number of relations learnt. Note that the sizes of the programs in the first pair include some of their own shared libraries. This is because part of the functionalities of these servers are compiled as shared libraries in default (e.g., many of the commonly used functions in cherokee are compiled in libcherokee-base.so and libcherokee-server.so), which is different from standalone programs. It can be seen from the table that the size of our models are relatively small compared to the sizes of the programs.

We also studied the time cost of our model for both learning and detection phases, which is illustrated in Table 5. The original size of the training traces were between 110MB and 526MB, consisting of 0.2 to 2 million system calls. As shown in Table 5, we measure the performance overheads of monitoring the system calls and library calls, which is the dominate overhead during detection. It shows that the overheads of monitoring system calls could be quite high for web servers (up to 83.4%). The overhead is mainly due to our system call tracer. As explained in Section 3, our monitor module utilizes ptrace for system call interception with our own implementation of the backtrace which records the call stack information of each system call. Similar overhead was also reported by existing approach [2] using ptrace. This cost can be reduced to less than 6% [9], by a kernel implementation of the interceptor.

Table 5. Training time and detection overhead

Programs	Training time	Detection Overheads	
		Monitoring sys calls	Monitoring lib calls
Lighttpd & Cherokee	93.8 sec	29.10%	18.38%
Ghttpd & Null-httpd	1620.9 sec	83.39%	11.41%
Wu-ftpd & Pure-ftpd	2091.3 sec	17.56%	1.37%

5   Related Work

In this section, we summarize the related work from two perspectives: one is traditional intrusion detection schemes, the other is diversity-based detection schemes.

Traditional intrusion detection techniques [5,7,8,9,13,14,19,23,26] mainly focus on utilizing only system call sequences to detect code injection attacks. Recent works [2,17,18,20,24] further incorporate system call argument information to defend against attacks which do not modify control flows. However, these approaches have difficulties in deciding which legitimate argument value is really benign, when multiple legitimate values appear in the training phase.

Early works on software diversity construct intrusion tolerance systems [3,21] with software providing semantically-close functionalities. This architecture is then utilized for developing diversity-based intrusion detection techniques [6,10,11,16,25]. Most of these techniques use Commercial Off-The-Shelf (COTS) software to build the detection models. Among those schemes, the techniques proposed by Just et al. [16] and Totel et al. [25] are output voting schemes, which only compare the final outputs (HTTP status codes and files) of the diverse software to detect intrusions. However, as many of the intrusions may not result in observable deviation in the responses of those server software, such intrusions can evade detections of these techniques.

Behavioral Distance model by Gao et al. [10,11] was later proposed to defend against stealthy attacks which are not addressed by both the output voting schemes and traditional intrusion detection techniques which only monitor single application. However, since hidden Markov model used in their scheme (to train the normal-behavior profiles of the system call sequences) is only able to handle finite states, their model cannot be simply extended to detect attacks utilizing erratic arguments.

Our approach is the first work that captures underlying semantic correlation of the argument values in diverse programs. Our model gains more accurate context information compared to existing schemes. Such context information is critical in detecting sophisticated attacks on security-critical data utilizing erratic arguments. When deployed, our model can be combined with the existing system call sequence or control flow models to defend against a wider range of attacks.

6   Conclusions

In this paper, we propose an anomaly detection model to detect erratic-argument attacks which are recognized as normal inputs by the existing techniques. Our approach utilizes the function arguments of two diverse applications which provide semantically-close functionalities. Different from existing techniques, our model learns the relations of the function arguments between the two applications, which naturally captures more accurate context information. In the evaluation, we show that our model is able to detect real attack manipulating the value of erratic arguments, with a moderate false alarm rate. The main limitation of our scheme is the additional cost on the management of diverse software. However, such a cost could be negligible for some existing fault-tolerant system where diverse software have already been deployed to prevent simultaneous failure.

References

1. TEMU and Vine. The BitBlaze Dynamic Analysis Component,
   http://bitblaze.cs.berkeley.edu
2. Bhatkar, S., Chaturvedi, A., Sekar, R.: Dataflow anomaly detection. In: Proceedings of the 2006 IEEE Symposium on Security and Privacy, pp. 48–62 (2006)
3. Chen, L., Avizienis, A.: N-version programming: A fault-tolerance approach to reliability of software operation. In: Digest of 8th International Symposium on Fault-Tolerant Computing (FTCS), pp. 3–9 (June 1978)
4. Chen, S., Xu, J., Sezer, E.C., Gauriar, P., Iyer, R.K.: Non-control-data attacks are realistic threats. In: Proceedings of the 14th Conference on USENIX Security Symposium, p. 12 (2005)
5. Lam, L.C., Chiueh, T.-c.: Automatic Extraction of Accurate Application-Specific Sandboxing Policy. In: Jonsson, E., Valdes, A., Almgren, M. (eds.) RAID 2004. LNCS, vol. 3224, pp. 1–20. Springer, Heidelberg (2004)
6. Cox, B., Evans, D., Filipi, A., Rowanhill, J., Hu, W., Davidson, J., Knight, J., Nguyen-Tuong, A., Hiser, J.: N-variant systems: a secretless framework for security through diversity. In: Proceedings of the 15th Conference on USENIX Security Symposium (2006)
7. Feng, H.H., Kolesnikov, O.M., Fogla, P., Lee, W., Gong, W.: Anomaly detection using call stack information. In: Proceedings of the 2003 IEEE Symposium on Security and Privacy (2003)
8. Forrest, S., Hofmeyr, S.A., Somayaji, A., Longstaff, T.A.: A sense of self for unix processes. In: Proceedings of the 1996 IEEE Symposium on Security and Privacy, p. 120 (1996)
9. Gao, D., Reiter, M.K., Song, D.: Gray-box extraction of execution graphs for anomaly detection. In: Proceedings of the 11th ACM Conference on Computer and Communications Security, pp. 318–329 (2004)
10. Gao, D., Reiter, M.K., Song, D.: Behavioral Distance for Intrusion Detection. In: Valdes, A., Zamboni, D. (eds.) RAID 2005. LNCS, vol. 3858, pp. 63–81. Springer, Heidelberg (2006)
11. Gao, D., Reiter, M.K., Song, D.: Behavioral Distance Measurement Using Hidden Markov Models. In: Zamboni, D., Kruegel, C. (eds.) RAID 2006. LNCS, vol. 4219, pp. 19–40. Springer, Heidelberg (2006)
12. Gao, D., Reiter, M.K., Song, D.: Beyond output voting: Detecting compromised replicas using HMM-based behavioral distance. IEEE Transactions on Dependable and Secure Computing (TDSC) (July 2008)
13. Ghosh, A.K., Schwartzbard, A.: A study in using neural networks for anomaly and misuse detection. In: Proceedings of the 8th Conference on USENIX Security Symposium, p. 12 (1999)
14. Giffin, J.T., Jha, S., Miller, B.P.: Efficient context-sensitive intrusion detection. In: Proceedings of the Network and Distributed System Security Symposium (2004)
15. Han, J., Gao, D., Deng, R.H.: On the Effectiveness of Software Diversity: A Systematic Study on Real-World Vulnerabilities. In: Flegel, U., Bruschi, D. (eds.) DIMVA 2009. LNCS, vol. 5587, pp. 127–146. Springer, Heidelberg (2009)

16. Just, J.E., Reynolds, J.C., Clough, L.A., Danforth, M., Levitt, K.N., Maglich, R., Rowe, J.: Learning Unknown Attacks - A Start. In: Wespi, A., Vigna, G., Deri, L. (eds.) RAID 2002. LNCS, vol. 2516, pp. 158–176. Springer, Heidelberg (2002)

17. Kruegel, C., Mutz, D., Valeur, F., Vigna, G.: On the Detection of Anomalous System Call Arguments. In: Snekkenes, E., Gollmann, D. (eds.) ESORICS 2003. LNCS, vol. 2808, pp. 326–343. Springer, Heidelberg (2003)

18. Maggi, F., Matteucci, M., Zanero, S.: Detecting intrusions through system call sequence and argument analysis. IEEE Transactions on Dependable and Secure Computing (TDSC) 7, 381–395 (2010)

19. Michael, C.C., Ghosh, A.: Simple, state-based approaches to program-based anomaly detection. ACM Transactions on Information and System Security (TISSEC) 5(3), 203–237 (2002)

20. Provos, N.: Improving host security with system call policies. In: Proceedings of the 12th Conference on USENIX Security Symposium, p. 18 (2003)

21. Reynolds, J., Just, J., Lawson, E., Clough, L., Maglich, R.: The design and implementation of an intrusion tolerant system. In: Proceedings of the 2002 International Conference on Dependable Systems and Networks, DSN (2002)

22. Schwartz, E.J., Avgerinos, T., Brumley, D.: All you ever wanted to know about dynamic taint analysis and forward symbolic execution (but might have been afraid to ask). In: Proceedings of the 2010 IEEE Symposium on Security and Privacy, pp. 317–331 (2010)

23. Sekar, R., Bendre, M., Dhurjati, D., Bollineni, P.: A fast automaton-based method for detecting anomalous program behaviors. In: Proceedings of the 2001 IEEE Symposium on Security and Privacy, p. 144 (2001)

24. Tandon, G., Chan, P.: Learning rules from system call arguments and sequences for anomaly detection. In: Workshop on Data Mining for Computer Security (2003)

25. Totel, E., Majorczyk, F., Mé, L.: COTS Diversity Based Intrusion Detection and Application to Web Servers. In: Valdes, A., Zamboni, D. (eds.) RAID 2005. LNCS, vol. 3858, pp. 43–62. Springer, Heidelberg (2006)

26. Wagner, D., Dean, D.: Intrusion detection via static analysis. In: Proceedings of the 2001 IEEE Symposium on Security and Privacy, p. 156 (2001)

SA³: Automatic Semantic Aware Attribution Analysis of Remote Exploits

Deguang Kong[1,2], Donghai Tian[1], Peng Liu[1], and Dinghao Wu[1]

[1] College of Information Sciences and Technology, Pennsylvania State University,
University Park, PA 16802,
{dkong,dtian,pliu,dwu}@ist.psu.edu
[2] Dept. of Computer Science and Engineering, University of Texas at Arlington, TX, 76013

Abstract. Web services have been greatly threatened by remote exploit code attacks, where maliciously crafted HTTP requests are used to inject binary code to compromise web servers and web applications. In practice, besides detection of such attacks, attack attribution analysis, i.e., to automatically categorize exploits or to determine whether an exploit is a variant of an attack from the past, is also very important. In this paper, we present SA³, an exploit code attribution analysis which combines semantic analysis and statistical analysis to automatically categorize a given exploit code. SA³ extracts semantic features from an exploit code through data anomaly analysis, and then attributes the exploit to an appropriate class based on our statistical model derived from a Markov model. We evaluate SA³ over a comprehensive set of shellcode collected from Metasploit and other polymorphic engines. Experimental results show that SA³ is effective and efficient. The attribution analysis accuracy can be over 90% in different parameter settings with false positive rate no more than 4.5%. To our knowledge, SA³ is the first work combining semantic analysis with statistical analysis for exploit code attribution analysis.

Keywords: Remote Exploit, Shellcode, Attribution, Mixture of Markov Model.

1 Introduction

A great number of code injection attacks (e.g., buffer overflow attacks, format string attacks) are used by crafted HTTP requests to compromise different kinds of web services or web applications. From the CERT [1] and SecurityFocus [2] statistics, the remote code injection attack is still one of the major attacks these days. In (remote) code injection attacks, malicious HTTP requests/replies can be forged to inject malicious code by masquerading as normal requests/replies. Different kinds of shellcode are representatives of exploit code, which can be injected into target services or applications through network connections. Worms can take advantage of these exploit code for infections and propagations. In this paper, the exploit code we focus on is remote shellcode which can be used as the payload of a packet to spread via HTTP requests. Throughout the paper, we use the terms remote exploit code and shellcode interchangeably.

There are mainly two types of techniques used for shellcode analysis and detection: the emulation-based approach and statistics-based approach. The emulation based

M. Rajarajan et al. (Eds.): SecureComm 2011, LNICST 96, pp. 190–208, 2012.
© Institute for Computer Sciences, Social Informatics and Telecommunications Engineering 2012

approach (e.g., [3,4]) emulates the executions of instruction sequences, and thus shellcode's behaviors are exposed in the virtual running environment. However, it is antagonized by many kinds of anti-emulation techniques [5]. For example, drive-by downloads web attacks [6], which target memory corruption vulnerabilities, have to prepare the environment before their successful launch. Improper emulations of the execution context will lead to incorrect executions of instruction sequences, and thus fail to expose specific specific behaviors.

Statistical analysis is another promising method used in network intrusion detection systems including the remote shellcode detection and analysis [7,8]. The basic idea of the statistical approach is to extract the distinguished features to differentiate between the normal packets and various malicious packets. The payload of a packet and the payload header information (e.g., port number, protocol field) can be used as features for classification. The disadvantage of the statistical approach is that it usually lacks clear semantic information correlated with the packets whose contents may result in malicious behaviors, and therefore it can also be evaded by different kinds of anti-statistic approaches [7,8].

From the analysis above, we can see current exploit code detection and analysis approaches are still quite limited. Meanwhile, lots of shellcode variants appeared in the past several years according to AV-test's statistics [9]. Thus in this paper we present an automatic semantic aware attribution analysis of remote exploits. The significance of such analysis is that it provides more information about an attack in addition to detecting the attack. The attribution analysis can be used in, for example, a shellcode scanner to identify different types of shellcode variants. As far as we know, such shellcode attribution analysis is still lacking in the literature. Note that Hu et al [10] present a function-call graph based approach to index the large malware repositories, which can be viewed as a kind of malware attribution analysis. Our motivation is similar to theirs, but our work is more specific for shellcode attribution analysis. Compared with shellcode detection, our work focuses more on automatically categorizing exploits and determining whether an exploit is a variant of an attack from the past. We believe this is also important besides telling whether a piece of code is malicious or not.

Exploit code attribution poses several challenges. First, the emulation based approach cannot be directly applied to this problem because we need quantitative metrics to measure the distances of different exploit code. Second, we cannot fully rely on the statistical approach because it is deceptive once the statistical features (e.g., the number of specific instructions or system calls) fail to reflect the security-critical operations, which are probably highly related with the shellcode behaviors. Third, how to extract the semantics which determine the shellcode attribution remains an open question. The emulation based approach seems a good candidate for extracting the behaviors of different shellcode. However, it can miss trivial differences existed in the behaviors of different classes of shellcode. For example, self-contained exploit code [4] often exhibits same behaviors by following the routine of "decrypt-loop" mode. Furthermore, if specific behaviors are absent in the emulation environment, it could produce more false negatives. Also, the time cost for the emulation based approach is usually very high compared with static analysis.

Our Approach. We present SA^3, a novel automatic Semantic Aware Attribution Analysis of remote exploit code. SA^3 first makes semantic analysis on the payload of packets, and then a Markov-based model is used to model each type of shellcode. Specifically, for semantic analysis, we use static data anomaly analysis on the packet payload; for statistic analysis, we use a two-way of Mixture Markov model. The statistical model is based on the refined exploit code sequences, which are pruned from the whole code sequences in the framework of static analysis. Once the model is built, any new code can be fed into the model to get an attribution analysis result.

One important characteristic of our work is that we use the "features" acquired from semantic analysis for attribution analysis. We present SA^3 based on an observation that the attribution for a piece of exploit code has great correlations with the exploit code's semantic characteristics (e.g., the opcode sequence, the instruction sequence) and also its statistical characteristics (e.g., the number of instructions, the out-degree of control flow graph). The changes of the semantics also cause the changes of the statistic exposure in shellcode instructions. This observation motivates us to consider about the integration of semantic analysis with statistical analysis by taking advantages of both of them.

Our work stands between the semantic analysis and statistical analysis. Instead of using dynamic emulation techniques introduced before, our work uses the static data anomaly analysis by making static analysis on the instruction sequences. The advantage of this approach is to capture the semantics of the exploit code with moderate time cost. Also, it will not be attacked by anti-emulation techniques [5]. Compared with only emulation based approach, our work can also overcome some inherent defects (e.g., different shellcode may expose similar behaviors) by introducing the statistical analysis. Compared with only statistical based approach, our analysis is more robust by incorporating the semantics to avoid "black-box" learning.

Contributions. The main merits of SA^3 are listed as follows. To our knowledge, our approach is the first work to make exploit code attribution analysis by combining semantic analysis with statistical analysis. Semantic analysis is used for extracting the semantic-binding code with certain malicious intent. Statistical features can help to capture the "whole" view of a packet from macroscopic point. These two different views complement each other. Our evaluation shows that our analysis result is better than purely statistical approach, which also refutes the conclusion of "impossibility of modeling polymorphic shellcode [11]" in some degree.

The rest of this paper is organized as follows. First of all, we formalize the problem in Section 2. Next we show our approach SA^3 in Section 3, followed by evaluation in Section 4. Then we introduce the related work in Section 5. Finally, we conclude the paper in Section 6.

2   Problem Statement and Analysis

2.1   Problem Formalization

Let $I(i \in I)$ be a set of different classes of exploit code; and $D(1 \leq j \leq D)$ be the total number of instances (variants) generated from a certain class. We use S_{ij} to denote

NOP	Decoder	Encrypted Payload	Return Address	Padding

Fig. 1. A demonstration of polymorphic shellcode instance

the jth exploit code instance generated from class w_i, i.e., $S_{ij} \in w_i$. For example, in reality, a set of different types of exploit code can be generated from different polymorphic shellcode engines $I = \{\text{Clet}, \text{CountDown}, \text{Pex}, \text{Tapion}, ...\}$. Different instances of the same type of exploit code can be generated using complicated obfuscation techniques like polymorphism and metamorphism [12].

Definition 1. Exploit Code Attribution Problem

(1) For lots of exploit code instances S_{ij}, how to generate a profiling for each category w_i;

(2) For an unknown exploit code s, what is the attribution of s? That is, find i such that $s \in w_i$.

2.2 The Challenge of the Problem

According to the definition of exploit code attribution problem, Problem (1) is a training problem in shellcode classification and Problem (2) is an recognition problem after a profiling for each category of exploit code is built. Problem (1) is the key step while Problem (2) can be easily solved after the learning model is built in Problem (1). These two problems match well with the standard machine learning problem. Naturally, we refer to machine learning techniques for a solution.

From above analysis, it seems any statistical approach can work in the context of exploit code attribution analysis. However, the statistics-based approach may not produce promising results. Song et al. [11] conclude that it is impossible to model the polymorphic shellcode (See Fig. 1 for an example). Polymorphic shellcode accounts the largest part of the exploit code, and therefore, modeling all of the exploit code (e.g., for attribution analysis) is much more difficult. Next, we will briefly explain why modeling polymorphic shellcode instances is difficult. The contents of the polymorphic shellcode instances usually consist of several parts: NOP part (sled), decoder part, encrypted payload part, return address part and padding part (Fig. 1). Modeling the NOP part may amount to modeling random instructions because many instructions are semantically equivalent to "NOP." For example, for the shellcode generated by CLET [13], there are 55 kinds of sled used in the "NOP" part. In the return address part, there are also many variations of the target address by adding padding bytes before it. In the padding part, the binary code can be filled in, without influencing the execution results. For obfuscation purpose, the padding bytes may have similar distribution to the normal traffic distribution. In the decoding part, different encryption keys can generate different encrypted exploit code. Clearly, due to great varieties in each part of polymorphic exploit code, the variations for a whole exploit code packet can be even larger. These great variations may result in, (R_1) no fix patterns exposed in a whole packet; (R_2) the attribution analysis process misguided by padding bytes and noisy bytes.

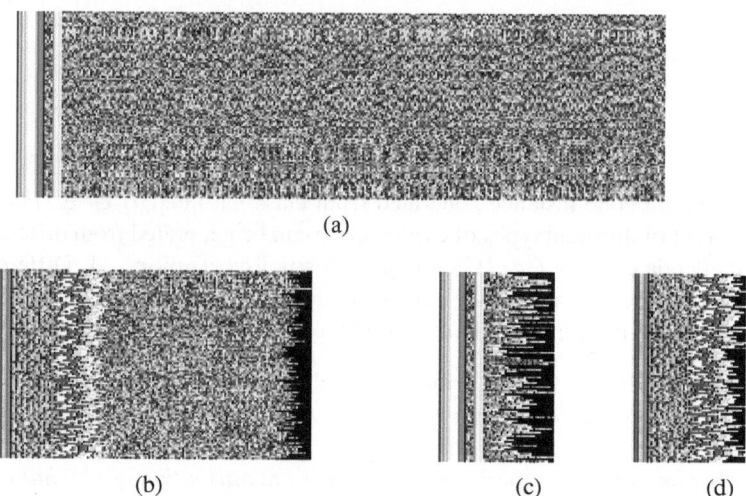

Fig. 2. Varieties of shellcode instances. (a) Pex (each of 100 instances is 344 bytes); (b) CLET (each of 100 instances is 168 bytes); (c) Pex refined shellcode after semantic analysis (corresponding to (a), each is 60 bytes); (d) CLET refined shellcode after semantic analysis (corresponding to (b), each is 60 bytes). Each pixel of the image represents a byte obtained from a shellcode instance

Fig. 2 shows two examples of shellcode varieties. Fig. 2(a) shows a spectral image, where each pixel represents a byte from a shellcode sequence generated from polymorphic engine Pex [14]. Each row is corresponding to a shellcode sequence with 344 bytes in length, and totally 100 instances form the image. Similarly, Fig. 2(b) shows the spectral image formed by 100 sequences generated from polymorphic engine CLET [13], where each row is a shellcode sequence of 168-byte in length. Clearly, these images demonstrate great varieties of different bytes in exploit code, which imply that the shellcode attribution analysis is a challenging problem.

3 Approach

In Fig. 3, we describe the framework of SA^3 . The core modules of SA^3 are *Semantic Analysis Module*, and *Statistical Analysis Module*. More detailedly, we use *Data Anomaly Analysis* in the Semantic Analysis Module and a *Two-way Mixture of Markov Model* in the Statistical Analysis Module.

The whole workflow of SA^3 can be divided into training stage (*with the real line*) and the recognition stage (*with the dashed line*). First of all, the same type of exploit code instances are fed into the semantic analysis module, and data anomaly analysis are conducted on them. We get the refined exploit code instances, which are actually the instruction sequences pruned of useless instructions. Next, a two-way Mixture of Markov Model is built on the refined input instruction sequences. We construct a mixture of Markov Model corresponding to each category of exploit code. When a new

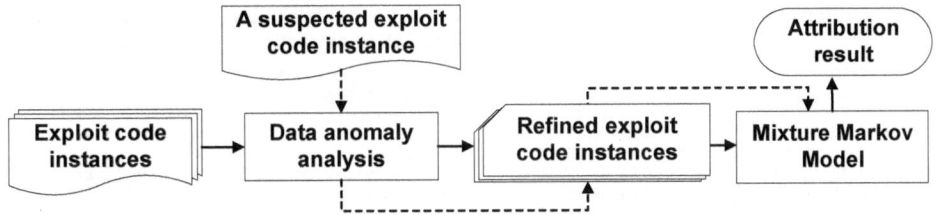

Fig. 3. SA^3 flow graph (real line for training stage, dashed line for recognition stage)

exploit code instance comes, it will be first analyzed through the data anomaly analysis module. Thus the refined code sequences are distilled as the input to the two-way mixture of Markov Model. The decision result is obtained by attributing the exploit code sequence to the one with the most fitting value.

Semantic Module. For each category of the input instruction sequences, we prune semantic-unrelated code existed in the code sequences. Data anomaly analysis is used to capture the "semantics" of the exploit code through preserving the useful instructions while pruning the useless ones which are probably containing padding and noisy bytes in the packets. This module is used for solution of R_2 presented in Section §2.2.

Statistical Module. For the pruned instruction sequences, a two-way Mixture of Markov Model is built for the solution of R_1 (Section §2.2). On one hand, it is not very clear what kind of relationship exists in the instruction sequences. On the other hand, Markov model is very suitable to model the uncertainty existed in different context. Thus, we refer to a two-way Mixture Markov model, to model relationships between the instruction sequences. The property of "two-way mixture model" makes it more robust and powerful to represent the varieties of different categories of code.

3.1 What Is the Semantics Used in Exploit Code?

Data Anomaly Analysis. We observe that certain control and data flow information remain invariable to implement certain functions in the exploit code. We call those control and data flow information as "semantic." The data anomaly analysis is used to capture those semantics, because it can preserve the useful instructions by pruning the useless ones which contain padding and noisy bytes.

First of all, we use disassemble analysis to analyze the input binary instruction sequences. In this paper, what we focus on is HTTP message flows. In an HTTP request message, malicious payload only exists in Request-URI and Request-Body of the whole flow [15]. We extract these two parts from the HTTP flows for further semantic analysis. Then we make disassemble analysis on these input sequences. If the disassemble module finds consecutive instructions in the input sequences, it generates the disassemble instruction sequences as output. An instruction sequence is a sequence of CPU instructions which has only one entry point. A valid instruction sequence should have at least one execution path from the entry point to another instruction within the sequence. Since we do not know the entry point of the code when the code is present in the byte sequences, we explore an improved recursive traversal disassemble algorithm

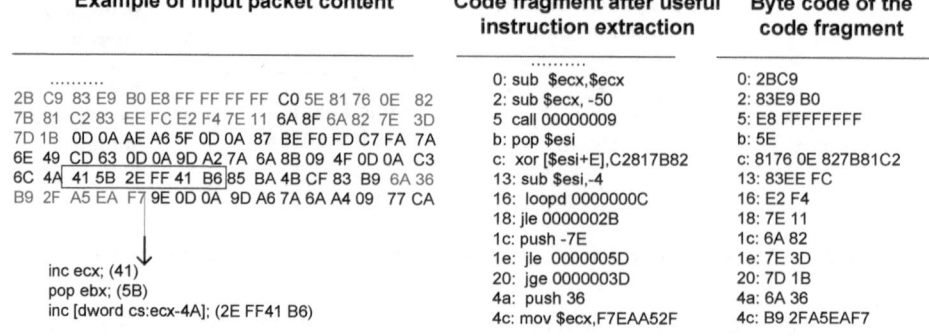

Fig. 4. A motivating example to show the procedure of semantic analysis on the input code sequence

introduced by Wang et al. [15] to disassemble the input instruction sequences. For an N-byte sequence, the time complexity of disassemble algorithm is $O(N)$.

After disassemble analysis, it may generate zero, one, or multiple instruction sequences, which do not necessarily correspond to real code. Next, we distill useful instructions by pruning useless instructions using the technique introduced in SigFree [15]. Useless instructions are those illegal and redundant byte sequences. By using the code abstraction, a static analysis technique, we can emulate the executions of instruction sequences. There are possibly 6 states in the state transition graph generated from the code sequences. State U represents undefined variable state; state D represents defined but not referenced variable state and state R represents defined and referenced variable state. The other three abnormal states are defined as follows: state DD represents abnormal state *define-define*, state UR represents abnormal state *undefine-reference*, and state DU represents abnormal state *define-undefine*. Basically, the pruned useless byte sequences correspond to three kinds of dataflow anomalies: *UR, DD, DU*. When there is an undefine-reference anomaly (i.e., a variable is referenced before it is ever assigned with a value) in an execution path, the instruction which causes the "reference" is a useless instruction. When there is a define-define anomaly (i.e., a variable is assigned a value twice) or define-undefine anomaly (i.e., a defined variable is later set by an undefined variable), the instruction that caused the former "define" is also considered as a useless instruction. Since crafted noisy bytes in the packets typically do not contain useful instructions, such irrelevant bytes in the packets are filtered out after the useful instruction extraction phase. The remaining instructions are likely to be related to the semantics of the code kept in the exploit code sequences.

Here, we further explain our motivation for useful instruction extraction. From our observations, lots of "useful instructoins" are left invariant across different shellcode instances even after complicated obfuscations (e.g., "junk insertion," "instruction replacement"). For padding and noisy bytes, they still can be assembled into code sequences. However, usually it lacks clear meanings and correlated relations for those coincidental instruction sequences. Thus, they will be pruned after rigorous data flow anomaly analysis. Moreover, we note that the remaining useful code sequences are more likely to be similar to those from the same category instead of those from the other categories.

Motivating Example. An example of polymorphic code analysis is shown in Fig. 4. Here the leftmost part is the original packet content in binary, the middle part and the right part are the disassemble code and its corresponding binary code of the useful instructions after removing useless ones, respectively. For example, the disassembly code *inc ecx* appeared in address 42 is pruned because *ecx* is defined again in address 4*c* to produce a *define-define* anomaly. In address 44, the contents in the memory cell with address *ecx-4A* is referenced without being defined beforehand. Thus we prune this instruction because it produces an *undefine-reference* anomaly.

Figs. 2(c) and 2(d) show two other examples. Fig. 2(c) gives the spectral image formed by the remaining instructions of 100 instances corresponding to Fig. 2(a). Similarly, Fig. 2(d) gives the spectral image formed by the remaining instructions of 100 instances corresponding to Fig. 2(b). In both images, each pixel represents a byte from the remaining instructions. Clearly, the lengths of the preserved code sequences are decreased. More importantly, the fixed patterns in the original code sequences are preserved while the bytes located in different positions with large varieties are cut off.

From the above polymorphic shellcode example (Fig. 4) and other instances, we find that the remaining code sequences usually consist of the following features: (F_1) getPC: the code to get the current program counter, usually contains opcode *"call"* or *"fstenv"*; (F_2) Iteration: a polymorphic exploit code usually performs iterations over encrypted shellcode using the operations like *loop*, *rep* and the variants of such instructions (e.g., *loopz*, *loope*, *loopnz*); (F_3) Jump: a polymorphic exploit code is probable to contain conditional/unconditional branch statements (e.g., *jmp*, *jnz*, *je*); (F_4) Decryption: for the encrypted shellcode, certain machine instructions (e.g., *or*, *xor*) are more often to be found in decryption routines since decryption needs to decrypt the shellcode before execution. These features are preserved after semantic analysis, which can be further used for statistical modeling. We believe these features help to capture the category of shellcode, and they may exist in most of the self-contained exploit code.

It may be attempting to use (F_2, F_4) as the only feature for category analysis. Fortunately, we also have other useful instructions preserved except for the features (F_1, F_2, F_3, F_4). This motivates us to use the statistical model for capturing the differences across various exploit codes as much as possible. For non self-contained code, not all features (e.g., F_2, F_1) exist in the shellcode (e.g, code generated from Avoid UTF8/tolower [4]) because of the absence of GetPC and self-reference operations. In these cases, the remaining instruction sequences still can be taken as good indicators for shellcode category analysis since noisy bytes are filtered. The pruned bytes are more likely to mislead the state-of-the-art statistics-based learning approaches (e.g., N-gram based learning [16], Markov Chain [8], Support Vector Machine [6]) for category analysis or detection. Note the length of code sequence can be viewed as the dimensions for the training code sequences. To prune useless instruction also means to reduce the dimension of training data This makes the machine learning module much easier and more accurate by alleviating the difficulty of "curse of dimensionality [17]".

3.2   What Is the Statistics Used for Modeling?

Why Use Markov Model? Let Y be the set of single bytes and Y^i denote the set of i-byte sequences. $X = Y \cup Y^2 \cup Y^3 \cup Y^4$ is the token set in our system because a

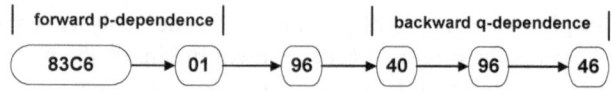

Fig. 5. Explanation of dependence in Markov Model

token in a useful instruction contains at most four bytes (e.g., "*AAFFFFFF*"), which corresponds to the word size of 32-bit systems. A Markov chain [18] is a sequence of random variables X_1, X_2, X_3, ..., satisfying the Markov property: given the present state, the future and past states are independent. More formally, probability $\Pr(X_{n+1} = x | X_1 = x_1, X_2 = x_2, ..., X_n = x_n) = \Pr(X_{n+1} = x | X_n = x_n)$, where x_i is the value for each state X_i, and $\Pr(X_{n+1} = x | X_n = x_n)$ is the conditional probability for transition from state X_n to X_{n+1}. The possible values of X_i form a countable set S called the state space of the chain. We observe that there are close relations among the code tokens in the refined instruction sequences. Markov Chain [18] is a good candidate to model uncertain dependencies in different contexts. In the context of code sequence analysis, each token in a sequence can be viewed as a state in a Markov Chain. We assume a token in a sequence is dependent on the token in front and also the token next because of the great dependencies existed in the code sequences of the nearest neighbors. To be exact, the dependency of token x_j on x_i is the co-occurance of token x_j and x_i. If x_i appeared in front of x_j in the same sequence, we call x_j is forward dependent on x_i. Otherwise, if x_i appeared after x_j in the same sequence, we call x_j is backward dependent on x_i. 1-order Markov chain requires the nth token in a chain is only dependent on the $(n-1)$th token. However, in real code segment, the nth token can be dependent on the $(n-1)$th, $(n-2)$th, ..., $(n-p)$th tokens in a sequence, and also related to $(n+1)$th, $(n+2)$th, ..., $(n+q)$th tokens. We do not know what is the value of p and q beforehand.

In our model we define two kinds of relationships to represent those bidirectional dependence. We call our Markov-derived model as a Two Way Mixture Markov (TWMM) Model. First, we define the forward dependence, i.e., nth token is depended on consecutive p tokens in front. Next, we define the backward dependence, i.e., nth token is dependent on the next consecutive q tokens. Then parameters $\pi_i (i = 1, 2)$ are used to make a balance between them, where $\pi_1 + \pi_2 = 1$. Fig. 5 shows an example, where token 96 is forward dependent on p ($p = 2$) tokens (83C6, 01) in front, and also backward dependent on next q ($q = 3$) tokens (40, 96, 46).

Model Construction. First, we construct a TWMM model for each category of code sequences. Second, after a new code sequence is fed into the model, we attribute it to the class with the highest fitting value. However, if the highest fitting value is still less than a certain threshold, we will attribute it to the normal sequence. Here the fitting value is the accumulation of probabilities, which reflects the matching score from a code sequence to the model.

Next we show how to compute the probability for a code sequence. The probability of a code sequence can be decomposed into the product of the probability of each token in a sequence. For different tokens appeared, there is a transition matrix to label the probability from one token to another. Hence, p-forward tokens' transition probability to a specific token is the probability from front p tokens' transition probability to this token. Similarly, q-backward tokens' transition probability to a specific token is the probability from next q tokens' transition to this token. In forward model, the ith token's probability is computed through product of the p-forward tokens' transition probability to this token. Similarly, in backward model, the ith token's probability is computed through the product of the q-backward tokens' transition probability to this token. Since the probability is a product of $p(L_n - p)$ values in the forward model, and a product of $q(L_n - q)$ values in the backward model, where L_n is the length for the nth code sequence. Therefore, the $p(L_n - p)$ root is needed for computing the sequence probability in forward model and $q(L_n - q)$ root is needed in backward model.

More formally, let $x_{n,i}$ denote the ith token in the nth sequence, $A_1(x_{n,i}|x_{n,j}; \theta_1)$ denote the transition probability from token $x_{n,j}$ to token $x_{n,i}$ in forward model θ_1, $A_2(x_{n,i}|x_{n,j}; \theta_2)$ denote the transition probability from token $x_{n,j}$ to token $x_{n,i}$ in backward model θ_2. Since the same token can be transferred to different tokens, the sum of such transition probability should be normalized to 1, i.e.,

$$\sum_{x_{n,i}} A_k(x_{n,i}|x_{n,j}; \theta_k) = 1 \ (k = 1, 2). \tag{1}$$

Let $g(x_n|\theta_1)$ and $g(x_n|\theta_2)$ denote the probability for the nth sequence's matching scores in the forward model and backward model, respectively. Thus we have

$$g(x_n|\theta_1) = \left(\prod_{i=p+1}^{L_n} \prod_{j=i-p}^{L_n-p} A_1(x_{n,i}|x_{n,j}; \theta_1) \right)^{\frac{1}{(L_n-p)p}} \tag{2}$$

$$g(x_n|\theta_2) = \left(\prod_{i=1}^{L_n-q} \prod_{j=i+1}^{i+q} A_2(x_{n,i}|x_{n,j}; \theta_2) \right)^{\frac{1}{(L_n-q)q}} \tag{3}$$

Next, by combing $g(x_n|\theta_1)$ and $g(x_n|\theta_2)$ in a balanced way, we have G_n to denote the matching score for nth sequence, i.e.,

$$G_n = \sum_{k=1}^{2} \pi_k g(x_n|\theta_k), \tag{4}$$

where $\pi_1 + \pi_2 = 1$. To obtain the solution for this model means to estimate the parameters in Eq. (4). Suppose we have N sequences for each category, thus the object function G to be optimized is the product of the likelihood for each sequence G_n, i.e.,

$$G = \prod_{n=1}^{N} \sum_{k=1}^{2} \pi_k g(x_n|\theta_k). \tag{5}$$

Model Solution. Here we show how to solve Eq.(5). The object function G is to be maximized to fit the model according to the principle of maximum likelihood estimation [19]. From the point view of optimization techniques, the object function is not

concave in terms of the mixture of two different Markov chains, thus directly setting
the first order derivatives on the likelihood does not work. This model is also different
from the standard mixture model which requires the same format of sub-models in a
mixture model. Thus we use the Expectation Maximum (EM) algorithm [20] to iteratively maximize the likelihood function with a gradient descent algorithm. The EM
algorithm usually takes two steps, Expectation Step and Maximization Step. At each
step, the model's likelihood function is updated in the direction of gradient ascent, and
this process is iterated until the likelihood converges. The monotonic property makes
this approach effective for the solution of many non-convex optimization problems.
Next we show how to train our model with the EM algorithm.

First, we construct the affiliated function [20]

$$W(\Theta, Q) = \sum_{n=1}^{N} \sum_{k=1}^{2} Q_{nk} \log \frac{\pi_k g(x_n | \theta_k)}{Q_{nk}}, \tag{6}$$

where Q_{nk} works as the hidden variable to denote the weight of data point n in terms
of model k, and $\sum_{k=1}^{2} Q_{nk} = 1$. Since the log function is a concave function, according
to the Jensen's inequality,[1] we have $\log(\sum x) \geq \sum \log x$. Thus $\log G \geq W(\Theta, Q)$.
The maximization of the object function G in Eq. (5) is equivalent to the maximization of Eq. (6) because Eq. (6) is the new lower bound of the likelihood function
to be maximized. Let Θ denote the parameters in the transition probability matrix
$A_k(x_{n,i} | x_{n,j}; \theta_k)(1 \leq k \leq 2)$, Q denote the hidden variable set Q_{nk}. Let Θ^t and
Q^t denote each group of parameters used in the tth iteration in the parameter estimation process. During the maximization step, the object function of Eq. (6) is required to
be monotonically increased. Based on this, we obtain

$$W(\Theta^t, Q^t) \leq W(\Theta^{t+1}, Q^t) \leq W(\Theta^{t+1}, Q^{t+1}), \tag{7}$$

which can be solved by using the Lagrange Multipliers [21] to find the stationary points
with $\arg \max_{\Theta} W(\Theta, Q^t)$ and $\arg \max_{Q} W(\Theta^{t+1}, Q)$ satisfied in each step.

Let $C(x_{n,i} | x_{n,j})$ denote the frequency of token transition from $x_{n,j}$ to $x_{n,i}$ in nth
sequence. Naturally, we use $C(\cdot | x_{n,j})$ to denote the frequency of the token transition
from $x_{n,j}$ to any tokens in the nth sequence of the model. To solve Eq.(7), we obtain
solutions in Eqs. (8–9). The complete training algorithm is shown in the table below.

$$Q_{nk} = \frac{\pi_k g(x_n | \theta_k)}{\sum_{k=1}^{2} \pi_k g(x_n | \theta_k)}, \pi_k = \frac{\sum_{n=1}^{N} Q_{nk}}{N}, \tag{8}$$

---

[1] For any concave function $f(x)$, if the balanced parameter t satisfies $0 < t < 1$, we have
$f(tx_1 + (1 - t)x_2) \geq tf(x_1) + (1 - t)f(x_2)$.

$$A_k(x_i|x_j;\theta_k) = \frac{\sum_{n=1}^{N} \frac{Q_{nk}}{L_n(L_n-\lambda_k)} C(x_{n,i}|x_{n,j})}{\sum_{n=1}^{N} \frac{Q_{nk}}{L_n(L_n-\lambda_k)} C(\cdot|x_{n,j})}, \lambda_1 = p, \lambda_2 = q. \qquad (9)$$

Algorithm 1. EM training Algorithm

Input: Instruction sequences $I_0, I_1, I_2, ..., I_n$ of each category, ε is the parameter used for convergence decision.
Output: Parameters (Θ, Q) for each category.
Procedure:
1: Initialize $\pi_k, A_k(x_{n,i}|x_{n,j};\theta_k), Q_{nk}(1 \leq k \leq 2)$
2: Compute the probability for each sequence to obtain $W(\Theta^t, Q^t)$ with Eq.(6)
3: update Q_{nk}, π_k with Eq.(8); update $A_k(x_{n,i}|x_{n,j})$ with Eq.(9)
4: **if** $W(\Theta^{t+1}, Q^{t+1}) - W(\Theta^t, Q^t) < \varepsilon$ **then**
5:    The algorithm converges, stop training
6: **else**
7:    goto Step 2
8: **end if**

The above Markov-derived model has a large state space (2^{32}), and thus it seems impractical for code sequence recognition. Fortunately, lots of tokens never or seldom appear in the state space, and this gives us the opportunity to greatly decrease the state space. First, we ignore never appeared tokens and prune seldom appeared tokens by setting a threshold. It leads to sparse items in the whole state space and very sparse transition matrices. Second, we use the data structure of hash table for storage of state transition probabilities in order to reduce the computation cost.

4 Evaluation

We test our system offline on massive polymorphic exploit code packets and on HTTP normal reply/request traces. First of all, we evaluate our approach on different kinds of exploit code in terms of false negatives and false positives, and then we compare our approach with the approach free of any semantic analysis before attribution analysis. Next, we evaluate our approach in terms of computation time cost. Finally, we discuss the advantages and limitations of our approach.

The massive polymorphic exploit code packets are generated by the metasploit [14] framework (e.g., PexFnstenvSub, Pex, ShikataGaNai), and also from polymorphic engines (e.g., CLET [13], ADMmutate [22], JempiScodes [23]). CLET, ADMmutate, JempiScodes and ShikataGaNai are advanced polymorphic engines which obfuscate the decryption routines by metamorphism such as instruction replacement and garbage insertion. CLET uses spectrum analysis to counterattack the byte distribution analysis. Opcodes of the "*xor*" and "*fnstenv*" instruction are frequently found in the decryption routine of PexFnstenvSub and also in getting the values of register of the program counter (GetPC). Pex uses *xor* decoders and relative call to get PC. The normal

HTTP traffic contains 300,000 messages collected for three weeks at seven worksta-
tions owned by seven different individuals in our lab's computers. To collect the traffic,
a client-side proxy monitoring incoming and outgoing HTTP traffic is deployed underneath the web server. Those 300,000 messages contain various types of non-attack
data including JavaScript, HTML, XML, PDF, Flash and multimedia data, which render diverse and realistic traffic typically found in the wild. We run our experiments on
a 2.4GHz Intel Quad-Core machine with 2GB RAM, running Windows XP SP2.

4.1   Attribution Analysis Results

First, we evaluate our approach in different parameter settings in terms of different
combinations of p and q. Second, we compare our approach with the approach free of
making any semantic analysis beforehand. Here we do not discuss much about data
anomaly analysis, since they have been well studied in previous researches [15,24].

Exploit Code Attribution. For each category of exploit code, we generate a corresponding TWMM Model, and then the new packets are fed into the model to evaluate the false positives and false negatives. We use 5-fold cross validation to train the
model and get the false negatives by matching the packet with the corresponding model.
During the packet attribution phase, a threshold is set to decide the attribution for this
packet. The threshold will both influence the false positives and false negatives in the
ROC curve. As is shown in Fig. 6, for different combinations of p and q, we can get
different results by setting different thresholds. Another factor to influence the attribution analysis result is the setting of the parameters p and q. There are many choices of
(p, q) combinations since p and q can be freely selected if we do not know any prior
knowledge of the structures of code sequences. It is not realistic to brute-force search all
possible (p, q) combinations. From our observations, for each token, the tokens close in
distance have much more influential power on it. That means p and q can be set to small
numbers. We do not know exactly which is the best to achieve the optimal results. In
our evaluation, tentatively, we select $p, q \in \{2, 4\}$. From the results on different datasets
in Fig. 6, we can infer that token relevances are different on different datasets. Besides
the parameters which influence the attribution results, the attribution analysis accuracy
varies depending on the "nature" of the exploit code. On all six datasets, the detection
accuracy can reach to above 90% in different parameter settings. This is a good indictor
to show the effectiveness of our approach. The false positive rate is up to 4.5% at most.
We may further bootstrap the misclassified packets to increase the analysis accuracy in
our future work. .

Comparison with Approach *without* Semantic Analysis. We compare our approach
with the approach free of any semantic analysis beforehand. The same TWMM model
is constructed for the original packets but *without* any semantic analysis before the
attribution analysis. In the approach without any semantic analysis, the tokens used are
all one-byte tokens because we do not have any prior knowledge about the minimum
semantic cell used in the whole code sequence. Note that the changes of combinations
of (p, q) do not make much difference for detection accuracy and false negative rate in
our attribution analysis, thus we set $p = 2, q = 2$ when making a comparison with the
approach without semantic analysis. The results are also shown in Fig. 6. Our semantic

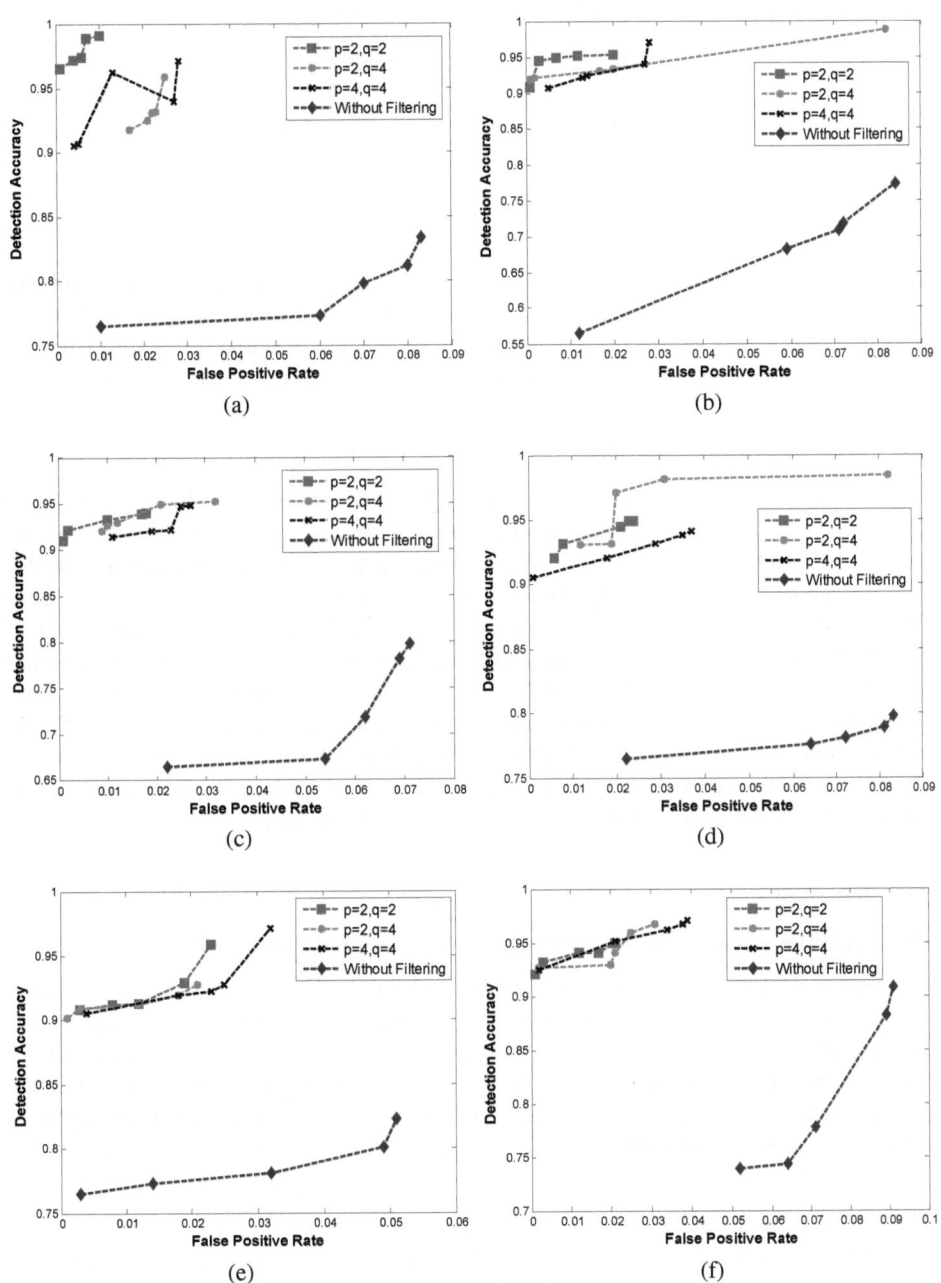

Fig. 6. Comparisons of semantic aware approach with the approach without filtering noises on six data sets: (a) CLET; (b) ADMutate; (c) PexFnstenvSub; (d) JemipiScodes; (e) Pex; (f) Shikata-GaNai

Table 1. Average Time Cost for Each Packet (millisecond)

Polymorphic engine	Training time	Decision time
CLet	5,213	7.2
Admutate	4,142	3.2
PexFnstenvMov	3,829	4.5
JempiScodes	2,487	6.8
Pex	3,152	4.1
ShiKataGaNai	7,650	4.3

aware approach outperforms the approach without semantic analysis on all six data sets, and the detection accuracy can be boosted more than 10% on all six data sets with nearly the same false positives. The promising results show that our semantic aware attribution analysis is effective and much better than the approach free of semantic analysis.

4.2   Performance Evaluation

Table 1 shows the time cost during the training phase and decision phase. The training time is the average time cost for each packet used in training, which includes the time of semantic analysis and also the time used for the training process of statistical model. The decision time is the average time cost for packet recognition, also including the time for semantic analysis. The training time cost is high due to the EM algorithm used in mixture Markov model. The EM algorithm usually needs hundreds times of iterations before convergence especially when data do not fit a model very well (e.g., exploit code instances generated from ShiKataGaNai). It also takes time in the semantic analysis module, but the time cost for semantic analysis is negligible compared with the EM algorithm in the training process. Fortunately, in order to reduce the time cost, we can conduct the training process offline before the recognition phase.

4.3   Discussion

Here we further discuss the strengths and limitations of our approach.

Strengths. First of all, our approach can filter noises through semantic analysis in the code sequences, and thus it has very good noise tolerance. Second, our approach is very robust to many different kinds of attacks (e.g., coincidental-pattern attacks [25], the token-fit attacks [26], allergy attacks [27]) due to the semantic analysis module applied. Moreover, our approach explores the semantic features to the classification process which leverages the "semantics" to increase attribution analysis accuracy. This opens a door to combine the semantic analysis with statistical analysis for practical tasks.

Limitations. First of all, since our semantic module is based on static analysis, we cannot handle some state-of-the-art code obfuscation techniques (e.g., branch-function obfuscation) in the semantic module, which may mislead the feature generations before statistical analysis. This can be solved by referring to more complicated semantic aware static/dynamic analysis techniques (e.g., symbolic execution, type inferences). Secondly, for non-self contained exploit code [4], sometimes we fail to capture the features of such code before statistical analysis. The code may mislead the classifier to make the wrong decision results. This is also a problem that state-of-the-art statistical learning techniques cannot handle. Finally, during the training phase, it may be difficult to get many (e.g., 300, 400) training data for each category in a real deployment environment. The attribution results may decay due to lack of training instances. Fortunately, compared with other models (e.g., Support Vector Machine), Markov model has stronger recognition ability even with scare training data (e.g., 10, 20). That is why we use Markov-derived model in our statistical modeling module.

5   Related Work

There is a large body of work in the area of exploit code analysis and detection. We focus on two areas most related to our work: semantics-based approaches for malware especially exploit code analysis, and statistics-based approaches for those analysis.

Semantics-Based Approaches. Malware including exploit code analysis has received considerable attention from different research views. Various kinds of semantic techniques have been explored by making static or dynamic analysis on the binary code for malware detection. Emulation-based approaches [4,28] can be used to detect polymorphic shellcode by emulating the code execution to recognize specific behaviors (e.g., decryption routines) through dynamic analysis. Libemu [3] is another attempt to achieve shellcode analysis through code emulations. Gu et al. [29] present a new malicious shellcode detection methodology by analyzing snapshots of the processs virtual memory before input data are consumed. However, these emulation-based techniques can be antagonized by many anti-emulation techniques [5]. In our work, we use the static data anomaly techniques introduced in SigFree [15] to extract the semantics from the malicious code sequences. Another similar work to the semantic module we use is STILL [24], which uses static taint and initialization analysis to detect exploit code embedded in data streams/requests targeting web services. Christodorescu et al. [30] present a dependency-graph based approach to mining the malicious behaviors present in a known malware that are not present in a set of benign programs, which can be used by malware detectors to detect malware variants. Also, Christodorescu et al. [31] use a trace semantics to characterize the behaviors of malware as well as the program being checked for infection, and use abstract interpretation to "hide" irrelevant aspects of these behaviors for malware detection/classification. The motivation of our work is very similar to these works, but ours is specific to exploit code category analysis, and more importantly, we present a novel approach for attribution analysis which combines the semantic analysis with statistical analysis. Spector [32] is a shellcode analysis system that uses symbolic execution to extract the sequence of library calls and low-level execution traces generated by shellcode. TaintCheck [33] exploits dynamic dataflow and taint analysis techniques to help find the malicious input and infer the properties of worms. Kruegel et al. [34] present a technique based on the control flow structural information to identify the structural similarities between different worm mutations. This work is close to our technique in that it analyzes the variants of worms, but they target worms, not exploit code.

Statistics-Based Approaches. Song et al. [23] study the possibility of deriving a model for representing the general class of code that corresponds to all possible decryption routines, and conclude that it is infeasible. Our work combines the semantic analysis and statistical analysis for exploit code attribution analysis, making it robust to many noise-injection attacks (e.g., allergy attack [27]). Different statistical model have been explored for intrusion detection systems, e.g., n-gram model [16] used in traffic anomaly detection, Markov chain model [8] used for web traffic anomaly detection and support vector machine [6] used for detection of drive-by-downloads attacks. A game-theoretical analysis on how a detection algorithm and an adversary could adapt to each other in an adversarial environment is introduced by Pedro et al. [35]. For exploit code attribution analysis, pure statistical approach may not produce very good results due to lack of semantic information. Recent work SAS [36] has looked at the combinations of semantic and statistical analysis to generate signatures for polymorphic worm detection. In contrast, our work is motivated for exploit code attribution analysis instead of for polymorphic worm detection, and the statistical model is also different, leading to different strategies used for classification and detection.

6   Conclusion

In this paper, we present SA^3, an automatic exploit code attribution analysis system. On the testing datasets, our approach outperforms the pure statistics-based approach with much better accuracy. To our knowledge, this is the first work that combines semantics and statistics for exploit code attribution analysis.

Acknowledgments. This work was partially supported by AFOSR FA9550-07-1-0527 (MURI), ARO W911NF-09-1-0525 (MURI), and NSF CNS-0905131.

References

1. CRET: Computer emergency response team, http://www.cret.org/
2. Securityfocus, http://www.securityfocus.com/
3. Baecher, P., Koetter, M.: Getting around non-executable stack (and fix), http://libemu.carnivore.it/
4. Polychronakis, M., Anagnostakis, K.G., Markatos, E.P.: Emulation-Based Detection of Non-self-contained Polymorphic Shellcode. In: Kruegel, C., Lippmann, R., Clark, A. (eds.) RAID 2007. LNCS, vol. 4637, pp. 87–106. Springer, Heidelberg (2007)
5. Bania, P.: Evading network-level emulation, http://packetstormsecurity.org/papers/bypass/
6. Konrad Rieck, T.K., Dewald, A.: Cujo: Efficient detection and prevention of drive-by-download attacks. In: Proc. of 26th Annual Computer Security Applications Conference, ACSAC (2010)
7. Wang, K., Cretu, G.F., Stolfo, S.J.: Anomalous Payload-Based Worm Detection and Signature Generation. In: Valdes, A., Zamboni, D. (eds.) RAID 2005. LNCS, vol. 3858, pp. 227–246. Springer, Heidelberg (2006)
8. Song, Y., Keromytis, A.D., Stolfo, S.J.: Spectrogram: A mixture of Markov chains model for anomaly detection in web traffic. In: Proceedings of the Network and Distributed System Security Symposium (2009)

9. AV-test, http://www.av-test.org/
10. Hu, X., Chiueh, T.-C, Shin, K.G.: Large-scale malware indexing using function-call graphs. In: ACM Conference on Computer and Communications Security, pp. 611–620 (2009)
11. Song, Y., Locasto, M.E., Stavrou, A., Keromytis, A.D., Stolfo, S.J.: On the infeasibility of modeling polymorphic shellcode. In: Proceedings of the 14th ACM Conference on Computer and Communications Security (CCS), pp. 541–551 (2007)
12. Collberg, C., Thomborson, C., Low, D.: A taxonomy of obfuscating transformations. In: Technical Report 148. University of Auckland (1997)
13. Detristan, T., Ulenspiegel, T., Malcom, Y., Superbus, M., Underduk, V.: Polymorphic shell-code engine using spectrum analysis, http://www.phrack.org/show.php?p=61&a=9
14. Moore, H.: The metasploit project, http://www.metasploit.com
15. Wang, X., Pan, C.C., Liu, P., Zhu, S.: SigFree: A signature-free buffer overflow attack blocker. In: 15th Usenix Security Symposium (2006)
16. Wang, K., Parekh, J.J., Stolfo, S.J.: Anagram: A Content Anomaly Detector Resistant to Mimicry Attack. In: Zamboni, D., Krügel, C. (eds.) RAID 2006. LNCS, vol. 4219, pp. 226–248. Springer, Heidelberg (2006)
17. Bellman, R.E.: Adaptive Control Processes: A Guided Tour. Princeton University Press (1961)
18. Meyn, S.P., Tweedie, R.: Markov Chains and Stochastic Stability. Cambridge University Press (2005)
19. Aldrich, J.: R.A. Fisher and the making of maximum likelihood 1912-1922. Statistical Science 12, 162–176 (1997)
20. Dempster, A., Laird, N., Rubin, D.: Maximum likelihood from incomplete data via the EM algorithm. Journal of the Royal Statistical Society, 1–38 (1977)
21. Bertsekas, D.P.: Nonlinear Programming. Athena Scientific, Cambridge (1999)
22. Macaulay, S.: Admmutate: Polymorphic shellcode engine, http://www.ktwo.ca/security.html
23. Jemiscode: Jemiscodes - a polymorphic shellcode generator, http://www.shellcode.com.ar/en/proyectos.html
24. Wang, X., Jhi, Y.C., Zhu, S., Liu, P.: STILL: Exploit code detection via static taint and initialization analyses. In: Proceedings of Annual Computer Security Applications Conference, ACSAC (2008)
25. Li, Z., Sanghi, M., Chen, Y., Kao, M.Y., Chavez, B.: Hamsa: Fast signature generation for zero-day polymorphic worms with provable attack resilience. In: IEEE Symposium on Security and Privacy (2006)
26. Newsome, J., Karp, B., Song, D.: Polygraph: Automatic signature generation for polymorphic worms. In: IEEE Symposium on Security and Privacy (2005)
27. Chung, S.P., Mok, A.K.: Advanced Allergy Attacks: Does a Corpus Really Help? In: Kruegel, C., Lippmann, R., Clark, A. (eds.) RAID 2007. LNCS, vol. 4637, pp. 236–255. Springer, Heidelberg (2007)
28. Polychronakis, M., Anagnostakis, K.G., Markatos, E.P.: Network–Level Polymorphic Shellcode Detection Using Emulation. In: Büschkes, R., Laskov, P. (eds.) DIMVA 2006. LNCS, vol. 4064, pp. 54–73. Springer, Heidelberg (2006)
29. Gu, B., Bai, X., Yang, Z., Champion, A.C., Xuan, D.: Malicious shellcode detection with virtual memory snapshots. In: INFOCOM, pp. 974–982 (2010)
30. Christodorescu, M., Kruegel, C., Jha, S.: Mining specifications of malicious behavior. In: Proceedings of the 6th Joint Meeting of the European Software Engineering Conference and the ACM SIGSOFT Symposium on the Foundations of Software Engineering (ESEC/FSE 2007), pp. 5–14. ACM Press, New York (2007)

31. Preda, M.D., Christodorescu, M., Jha, S., Debray, S.: A semantics-based approach to malware detection. In: Proceedings of the 34th Annual ACM SIGPLAN-SIGACT Symposium on Principles of Programming Languages (POPL 2007), pp. 377–388. ACM Press, New York (2007)

32. Borders, K., Prakash, A., Zielinski, M.: Spector: Automatically analyzing shell code. In: Proceedings of the 23rd Annual Computer Security Applications Conference, pp. 501–514 (2007)

33. Newsome, J., Song, D.: Dynamic taint analysis for automatic detection, analysis, and signature generation of exploits on commodity software. In: Proceedings of Network and Distributed System Security Symposium (2005)

34. Krugel, C., Kirda, E., Mutz, D., Robertson, W., Vigna, G.: Polymorphic Worm Detection Using Structural Information of Executables. In: Valdes, A., Zamboni, D. (eds.) RAID 2005. LNCS, vol. 3858, pp. 207–226. Springer, Heidelberg (2006)

35. Pedro, N.D., Domingos, P., Sumit, M., Verma, S.D.: Adversarial classification. In: 10th ACM SIGKDD Conference On Knowledge Discovery and Data Mining, pp. 99–108 (2004)

36. Kong, D., Jhi, Y.-C., Gong, T., Zhu, S., Liu, P., Xi, H.: SAS: Semantics Aware Signature Generation for Polymorphic Worm Detection. In: Jajodia, S., Zhou, J. (eds.) SecureComm 2010. LNICST, vol. 50, pp. 1–19. Springer, Heidelberg (2010)

Time-Traveling Forensic Analysis of VM-Based High-Interaction Honeypots

Deepa Srinivasan and Xuxian Jiang

Department of Computer Science
North Carolina State University
dsriniv@ncsu.edu, jiang@cs.ncsu.edu

Abstract. Honeypots have proven to be an effective tool to capture computer intrusions (or malware infections) and analyze their exploitation techniques. However, forensic analysis of compromised honeypots is largely an ad-hoc and manual process. In this paper, we propose Timescope, a system that applies and extends recent advances in deterministic record and replay to high-interaction honeypots for extensible, fine-grained forensic analysis. In particular, we propose and implement a number of systematic analysis modules in Timescope, including *contamination graph generator, transient evidence recoverer, shellcode extractor* and *break-in reconstructor*, to facilitate honeypot forensics. These analysis modules can "travel back in time" to investigate various aspects of computer intrusions or malware infections during different execution time windows. We have developed Timescope based on the open-source QEMU virtual machine monitor and the evaluation with a number of real malware infections shows the practicality and effectiveness of Timescope.

Keywords: Honeypots, Virtualization, Forensic Analysis.

1 Introduction

Honeypots have been used as an effective tool to capture and analyze computer intrusions and malware infections [29, 35]. For example, by running a commodity system, a high-interaction honeypot is typically designed to host vulnerable services (that can be remotely exploited), and in the meantime also contains additional monitoring software [4] to record intruders' behavior. By allowing intruders to completely take over the system and monitoring their behavior, we can better understand the motivations and techniques behind the intrusion. This is helpful as it will raise the awareness of network situation and lead to better design and development of next-generation intrusion detection systems (IDSs) and anti-malware software.

Forensic analysis of honeypots, though critical for the success of honeypot deployment, is still largely an ad-hoc, time-consuming process and ultimately affected by the type of data collected from honeypots. To better utilize honeypots and facilitate their forensic analysis, we argue that there is a need for a

M. Rajarajan et al. (Eds.): SecureComm 2011, LNICST 96, pp. 209–226, 2012.
© Institute for Computer Sciences, Social Informatics and Telecommunications Engineering 2012

"time-traveling" capability in existing honeypots. By doing so, a security analyst will be given an opportunity to apply a new analysis method that may not be available during the time when the honeypot was deployed. Moreover, by repeatedly "traveling back in time", multiple phases of analysis can be performed, either in parallel or sequentially. In the sequential case, one replay session can also be based on results from previous replay runs.

To "rewind" a honeypot's execution, an intuitive network-level approach would be to replay the captured network traffic targeting the honeypot system (since the honeypot is remotely compromised). However, due to inherent sources of non-determinism in modern systems and software, by simply replaying the captured network packets, we may *not* be able to obtain the same execution of the honeypot system. From another perspective, a number of system-level deterministic record and replay (R&R) approaches have been proposed for a variety of purposes, including fault tolerance [10], application debugging [1] and security analysis [13,16]. Recording and replaying a VM is well-suited for honeypots since we can capture and reproduce the entire system's execution. However, most prior VM R&R systems are not suitable for high-interaction honeypots because either they do not support commodity OSes or require extensive OS-level customization, or they heavily rely on proprietary virtual machine monitors (VMMs) [1,13]. Moreover, there is a lack of honeypot-specific forensic analysis modules that can take advantage of VM R&R capability.

In this paper, we present Timescope – a time-traveling high-interaction honeypot system designed for extensible, fine-grained forensic analysis. Leveraging previous insights from VM-level R&R systems, we have developed an open-source tool, hoping to engage the security community and benefit related research efforts that may require similar features.[1] In addition, we have extended our system by developing a number of *honeypot-specific* analysis modules: *contamination graph generator* (I), *transient evidence recoverer* (II), *shellcode extractor* (II), and *break-in reconstructor* (IV). These modules are applied only during honeypot execution replay sessions and placed externally so that the replay itself is not perturbed. By allowing the analysis modules to "travel back in time", it addresses key questions in honeypot forensic investigations, such as: "what are the contaminations or damages caused by an intrusion?"; "what intermediate evidence (e.g., files and directories), if any, has been erased by the attacker?"; "how is the attack launched?". We have implemented Timescope and these analysis modules based on the open-source QEMU VMM [8] and enabled multi-faceted, inter-related malware forensic analysis during multiple replay sessions. Our evaluation with a number of attack scenarios, including real-world worm programs and kernel rootkits, shows the practicality and effectiveness of Timescope to repeatedly and comprehensively analyze past intrusions. The experiments are enabled by repeatedly rewinding the honeypot's execution, *not* based on the log from one single run.

---

[1] The source code, to be released in September 2011, will be available in one of the co-authors' websites.

2   System Design

To better analyze compromised honeypots, our goal is to design an extensible investigation framework that is tailored for honeypot forensics. Specifically, the framework is intended to greatly facilitate an analyst to effectively reveal various aspects of honeypot intrusions. In the following, we examine two main requirements for our investigation framework.

– *Transparency.*   Our analysis framework must work with a commodity OS without requiring any changes to the OS itself. This is needed because a high-interaction honeypot will run environments that are representative of production workloads. Also, due to the potential presence of multiple vulnerabilities in various services running in the honeypot and the need for monitoring attackers' behavior after the break-in, the framework should allow for the capture of the execution of the entire honeypot system, instead of a selected few applications.

– *Extensibility and Flexibility.*   The framework needs to be extensible to support various analysis modules, each examining a particular aspect of an intrusion. In other words, it can flexibly yield itself for instrumentation during replays to enable in-depth forensic analysis. Further, any analysis module that is supported in this framework should not perturb the deterministic execution in a replay session.

Certainly, our design should also meet the basic honeypot requirement in providing a "true" computer system to attackers and reliably recording the honeypot execution for later replay. For example, to maintain the reliability of logging, we need to avoid deploying any visible logging components inside the honeypot as they can be potentially compromised once the honeypot is taken over. And the collected log should not be placed within the honeypot. Also, the presence of the framework and various analysis modules should not be exposed to an attacker.

In this paper, we assume that after compromising a honeypot, the attacker can obtain the highest privilege level inside the honeypot. We envision the scenario that an attacker exploits a vulnerability in a honeypot-hosted network daemon (or a client-side software such as the web browser) and then gains control of the system. After that, the attacker might deploy a rootkit to hide the intrusion. Due to the leverage of the virtualization layer for honeypot hosting, we assume a trusted VMM that provides necessary VM isolation (see Section 5).

2.1   Timescope Framework

The overall architecture of our system is shown in Figure 1. In essence, it involves the fundamental VM record and replay support. Note that such support can be applied at different levels in a running computer system such as for individual processes or the entire machine. Due to the need for transparently supporting honeypots on commodity hardware, we implement it at the system virtualization layer such that the execution of an entire honeypot VM can be captured and replayed. Among various virtualization techniques available (such as

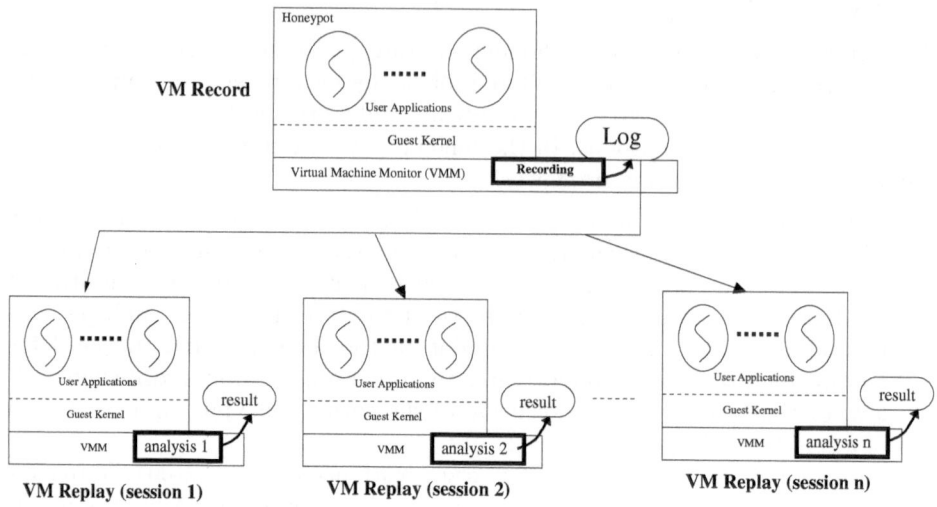

Fig. 1. Timescope enables time-traveling forensic analysis of honeypots

para-virtualization, hardware virtualization etc.), we choose *software-based full virtualization* and leverage dynamic binary translation (implemented in VMware [6], VirtualBox [5], and QEMU [8]) which offers great flexibility for implementation of analysis modules. While it introduces high overhead over native system performance, this is acceptable for honeypot purposes.

Timescope operates in two different modes: *VM record* logs the honeypot's execution and periodically takes a number of snapshots (or checkpoints that contain processor, hardware devices and memory states); *VM replay* starts from a chosen snapshot, then re-executes or rolls forward using the collected log to deterministically reproduce the execution. Note that most events in the system are deterministic (e.g. memory loads/stores and arithmetic operations). As such, they do not need to be logged. Instead, the system will just re-execute these events in the same way during replay as it did during VM record.

More specifically, if we abstract the entire guest as a simple VM process, its execution is influenced by the input it receives from external entities (such as I/O devices) and the response (including the run-time environment) from the underlying hypervisor (such as asynchronous I/O, timers, and virtual interrupts). Note that emulating guest VMs as processes will still introduce non-determinism in the VM itself and this should be addressed as shown in Section 3. To interact with external entities, it eventually uses the services also provided by the hypervisor (either through certain I/O operations or hypercalls). As a result, during a VM record phase, we can just collect these influence factors or non-deterministic inputs in a log file. During the VM replay phase, we can re-execute the same sequence of instructions with the same input from the collected log and reproduce its execution, including the detailed attack sequence in the honeypot's past execution. Certainly, when the non-deterministic inputs are collected, we also need to record the related timestamps, which is not based on wall clock time but on the virtual time lapsed since the honeypot started its initial execution. We point out that the output to external devices or peripherals will not affect VM replay and hence need not be saved. In fact, the output can be reconstructed as a by-product during the VM replay. This has the benefit of reducing the log volume – which is especially the case when the honeypot happens to run some I/O-intensive workloads.

2.2 Analysis Modules

With the development of companion analysis modules in Timescope, an analyst can travel back in time and investigate an attack when it *is happening*. Analysis sessions can be started from different snapshots to perform specific data collection within different time windows or use results from previous analysis sessions. In the remainder of this section, we describe four representative analysis modules that can be flexibly plugged into the framework during a replay session. One example attack scenario is that of a vulnerable service (e.g., the Apache web server) running in a honeypot that is compromised. After the compromise, the attacker escalates his privilege to root and installs a kernel rootkit. We assume the intrusion is observed by an administrator who notices some suspicious activity of the honeypot and denotes this detection point by *DP*. Then, we launch analysis sessions with these modules sequentially, each running in its own replay session.

Contamination graph generator (module I). The goal of this analysis module is to help obtain a high-level view of attackers' behavior by developing a contamination graph. As pointed out in [24], this graph allows us to identify which process was potentially exploited that led to the detection point. For this, the necessary logs can be collected by instrumenting the VMM's dynamic translation layer to intercept and log all system calls made by all processes running inside the honeypot. Note that these system calls are captured in the replay session, not the record session! Along with each system call, we also record the virtual CPU time to identify when the call was intercepted and the address of the instruction that is causing the system call. This analysis module helps address the question: "What time window in a honeypot's execution is interesting for further analysis?" Note the narrow-down of the time window for detailed analysis is helpful to perform targeted forensic analysis. As a result, with the generated contamination graph, we can identify a starting (ST) and ending (EN) points and the execution within [ST, EN] warrants further investigation.

Transient evidence recoverer (module II). Given a time window, this analysis module aims to recover attack evidence that may be erased during the intrusion. For example, during an intrusion, it is likely that the attack may create temporary files (that contain intermediate computation results) or manipulate some system state for various malicious purposes (e.g., opening a backdoor). As part of the investigation process, it is extremely helpful to uncover all files that may be erased or manipulated and inspect the recovered content to better understand the attacker's motivations.

Shellcode extractor (module III).   In certain attack scenarios, there is also a need to identify and extract the injected shellcode in memory. Note the shellcode is typically transient and will not be saved in the disk. Yet, it is the first attack code executed after successfully exploiting the vulnerability in the honeypot. In this analysis module, we aim to keep track of the untrusted network input and identify the set of data that is being executed as code. And this set of data is considered as the shellcode. It is also possible that a DP might be generated due to the shellcode execution, (e.g., an abnormal entry of logging a */bin//sh* process creation from the Apache web server). In our implementation, we leverage existing efforts on dynamic taint analysis [28] and more details will be presented in Section 3.2. Further, during a secondary run, this analysis module scans each incoming network message that is read by the exploited process to identify the timestamp when the shellcode is injected as well as the very moment the shellcode is about to execute. This allows us to precisely locate the time window of the code injection attack and aids in further analysis to reconstruct and understand the vulnerability that was exploited.

Break-in reconstructor (module IV).   The goal of this module is to perform fine-grained analysis to understand how the execution of malicious, injected code hijacks control flow and tampers with any system resources or objects in process and kernel memory. Specifically, in the case of kernel rootkits, when the injected malicious code executes, this module generates a log of all memory reads and writes along with the memory contents. This collected log can then be analyzed offline, in combination with the binary of the kernel being compromised, to develop a profile of the injected code's execution. With this module, we can "zoom in" to monitor and analyze the execution of the injected attack code and apply in-depth fine-grained analysis techniques. Thus, Timescope re-creates temporary memory states and enables selective application of heavyweight techniques such as execution profiling and improves their efficiency.

Finally, we note that forensic analysis is essentially an iterative process. Based on results from previous phases, it is often the case that one may want to re-run another analysis but with a different time window of the honeypot's execution. Timescope greatly facilitates such analysis with its extensible framework.

3   Implementation

We have implemented Timescope based on the open-source QEMU version 0.12.3 [8]. As mentioned earlier, due to the lack of a suitable open-source record and replay implementation, we have to implement it from scratch. On top of that, we further implement four honeypot-specific analysis modules. The dynamic binary translation architecture in QEMU and its readily available source code make it convenient for our implementation. Our development environment is a 32-bit x86 Ubuntu 9.10 running Linux kernel 2.6.31-20.

3.1   QEMU Record and Replay

In QEMU, a VM runs based on the emulated computer hardware and I/O devices. Also for each running VM, there is a corresponding user-level process on the host system. At its core, QEMU translates guest instructions in batches (basic blocks) and the resultant host instructions are known as translation blocks (TBs). The translated TBs are then executed from a "main loop". For optimized execution, it employs a technique known as "direct block chaining" [8], where TBs that have been previously translated can be re-used. When a device emulator module in QEMU requires the attention of the CPU, it asynchronously calls a function to signal that an interrupt is pending to be serviced. This causes the main execution loop to exit and service the I/O. QEMU also uses a host timer (by default, the real-time clock) to break periodically from the main loop and perform actions such as refreshing user displays and updating virtual time.

This design brings an interesting observation in our implementation: if we enable R&R for the QEMU process, we can achieve the R&R for the emulated VM. We believe this design choice is different from previous VM-based R&R frameworks [13, 16, 30]. However, from another perspective, QEMU itself is a regular but complex user-level program whose design introduces *non-determinism* in the execution of a guest OS. *This violates our requirement for a deterministic R&R!* Specifically, its execution is influenced by external sources of non-determinism such as host OS timer facilities, device interrupts and asynchronous I/O.

To make the QEMU execution deterministic, we need to capture all external inputs. For this, we use a technique known as *function interposition*. We notice that the interface to access these external inputs is the glibc library, which is loaded dynamically and all glibc symbols are resolved at run-time. As a result, we can provide a wrapper for all functions that will be used by QEMU to intercept these dependent glibc calls. During the VM record run, these function calls first invoke the corresponding function in glibc and then record the values of its output parameters and return value. During the VM replay run, the wrapper functions simply return the previously recorded output parameters and the return value from the R&R log.

There is also a subtle issue related to time in QEMU. In particular, QEMU issues the "rdtsc" instruction to read the timestamp counter from the host hardware. For our purpose, we replace the code to this instruction with an equivalent wrapper function. QEMU's default behavior is optimized for performance - the virtual CPU's instructions are executed in a highly optimized loop and exceptions (such as device interrupts) are processed asynchronously. This causes non-deterministic guest OS behavior. Instead for our implementation, we configure QEMU such that one instruction will be executed in a fixed period of virtual time. Moreover, I/O interrupts are checked and serviced only at the end of a TB's execution. With that, there is no need to rely on the host timer, which is a major source of non-determinism in the original QEMU system.

By addressing the QEMU-inherent non-determinism and logging the external input, our implementation enables deterministic VM record and replay. Also from our implementation experience, there are additional details that are worth mentioning. For example, to support R&R checkpoints, we use the built-in VM snapshot feature in QEMU, but modify it to save and retrieve VM state images to and from a separate file on the host filesystem. Also, our current implementation disables the asynchronous I/O support in QEMU which leads to additional performance penalty (Section 4), but makes our implementation easier since it only requires a single thread of execution to be recorded and replayed. Note that this limitation is not inherent in our approach and can be effectively eliminated [7]. Finally, during a replay session, all output from the virtual honeypot to the serial port is allowed to pass through, so that an analyst can "view" the honeypot's execution progress.

3.2   Analysis Modules

To demonstrate Timescope's time-traveling analysis capabilities, we have implemented four analysis modules. These modules all operate outside the virtual machine honeypot. Further, they all execute in replay sessions thus enabling time-traveling forensic analysis. The modules we developed examine different aspects of an intrusion, including contamination graph generation, transient evidence recovery, shellcode extraction, and break-in reconstruction.

Contamination graph generator   This analysis module typically runs immediately after a suspicious detection point (DP) has been identified. In particular, we replay the VM execution and apply virtual machine introspection techniques [20] to collect all system calls invoked by all processes running inside the honeypot. At a high level, whenever the honeypot executes an *int 0x80/sysenter* instruction, it indicates that a system call is being requested by a process within the honeypot. By examining the honeypot's virtual registers, the system call and corresponding arguments can be identified and reported. This process may further involve examination of the honeypot's memory and interpretation of the name of the running process that invoked the system call and other system call arguments. We point out that the interception and interpretation of guest system calls at the VMM level has been implemented in a few other systems [15,20]. It is interesting to note that all these techniques operate in a live system. Timescope instead travels back in time and operates in a replayed "live" system.

Transient evidence recoverer   As described in Section 2.2, given a starting time (ST) and ending time (EN), this analysis module aims to capture all file write activities, copy these files (including the modified content) out, and save them on the host filesystem. By doing so, one can tell the list of files that have been modified or removed by a particular process and all deleted files can still be recovered for later analysis. For this, we first keep track of the open file descriptors within the time window between ST and EN. In particular, our implementation extends the system call interception in the first analysis module: Whenever a *sys_open()* system call is being invoked within the time window, we retrieve the file name and when the corresponding call returns, we obtain the file descriptor. We also track *sys_close()* during this time window to discard file descriptors that are no longer valid. The list of file names and descriptors is maintained on a per-process basis. When a *sys_write()* is intercepted, the size and address of the buffer being written is retrieved from the EDX and ECX registers of the virtual CPU respectively. The entire buffer is then retrieved from the VM physical memory and stored to a corresponding file (referred to as *recovered file*) in a specified directory on the host file system. The name of the recovered file contains the process name that is writing to it and the file descriptor. If this file was opened within the specified time window, we store the name of the file along with the data. Thus, by looking at a recovered file, one can tell the name of the file in the honeypot that is being modified, the corresponding file descriptor and the data that was written. If the file was opened before the ST time window, our current implementation will search through the system call log generated in the first analysis module. Therefore, we are able to selectively create past states of the honeypot's execution.

Shellcode extractor Shellcode is typically the first attack code executed in an intrusion. However, the shellcode itself is not saved in the disk and hence will not be captured by previous analysis modules. In our implementation, we leverage dynamic taint analysis techniques [28,33] to extract the attack code from memory. Specifically, all incoming network packets (via the virtual NE2000 device in our current implementation) are tagged as tainted. And the taint information will be propagated based on the instructions that operate on the tainted input. Further, by instrumenting the *call, jmp,* and *ret*, we can monitor the illegal use of the tainted data. In particular, if any of the targets in call, jmp or ret are tainted, we know the attack code is about to execute. And the execution of tainted data will be collected as the shellcode for analysis. In our implementation, we extract the malicious code by collecting a trace of tainted instructions that are executed by QEMU. Using the addresses of these instructions and the running process (as per the CR3 register), we further record related context information about the shellcode, such as the name of the compromised process. Once the shellcode has been identified, this module can be re-run in a secondary analysis session to identify at which point in the exploited process' execution, this data was injected and understand how the data triggers the vulnerability. For remote code injection attacks, we monitor the returns from the *sys_read()* calls made by the exploited process and compare the buffer that is read into memory. When a match is found, the corresponding timestamp value and contents of the buffer are stored to a file on the host OS. This needs to be executed only up to the point when the first shellcode instruction is ready to execute.

Break-in reconstructor Once the injected malicious code has been identified and extracted, this module generates an instruction execution trace. The trace will be considered a working exploit against the vulnerability that leads to the honeypot break-in. In our implementation, we further perform execution profiling of the identified malicious code. For example, in our experiments with kernel rootkits (Section 4.2), we leverage it and apply the combat tracking technique described in PoKeR [34] to profile rootkit execution within a given time window ([ST, EN]). In particular, for a subset of instructions identified thus, all memory reads and writes and their contents, are recorded in a log on the host OS. Then, with the combat tracking technique, the kernel rootkit's execution profile can be obtained to reveal how kernel objects and control flow have been tampered with. Note that while the experiment is conducted in the context of kernel-level code injection, it can be readily extended to user-level code injection as well.

4   Evaluation

This section presents experimental results from our prototype implementation of Timescope. We demonstrate the accuracy of our R&R implementation and time-traveling forensic analysis capabilities. We also measure the performance overhead introduced by our framework.

4.1   R&R Accuracy

To evaluate the accuracy and effectiveness of our prototype R&R implementation, we took two measures. *First*, during a replay session, in each system call wrapper function, our prototype performs a self-check to make sure that the requested system call number and its input parameters always match the next one stored in the R&R log. Our experiments confirmed the correctness of our prototype. Note this self-checking process is costly in terms of performance and thus it is present only in debug builds of the prototype. *Second*, during several tests of VM runs and their corresponding replay sessions, we collect all instructions (organized as basic blocks) executed by the honeypot and save them in two separate log files. By literally performing a file comparison between the two, we verify that the same instructions are executed in the same order, thus yielding deterministic replay.

4.2   Time-traveling Analysis

To demonstrate the effectiveness of our prototype, we have launched four synthetic attacks. The first one intentionally tests our second analysis module by verifying the recovery of an intermediate file with randomly generated content. For the rest, we utilized real-world malware, including a worm (Slapper [11]) and two rootkits (adore-ng [26] and SucKIT [32]), to understand their behaviors and test all developed analysis modules. Here, we summarize three of them.

Experiment 1: Intermediate evidence recovery   In the first experiment, we show the ability of Timescope to re-create past, non-predictable temporary state and retrieve the content from a replay session for comparison. Specifically, we intentionally create a program that will generate an intermediate file with 1 MB random data. The file will be uploaded to a remote server and then immediately deleted. In the experiment, the run of this program is captured in a VM record session. In a replay session, we aim to uncover the content of the intermediate file using the second analysis module and compare with the copy saved in the remote server. Our manual verification indicates the uncovered file has the same *md5sum* from the server copy.

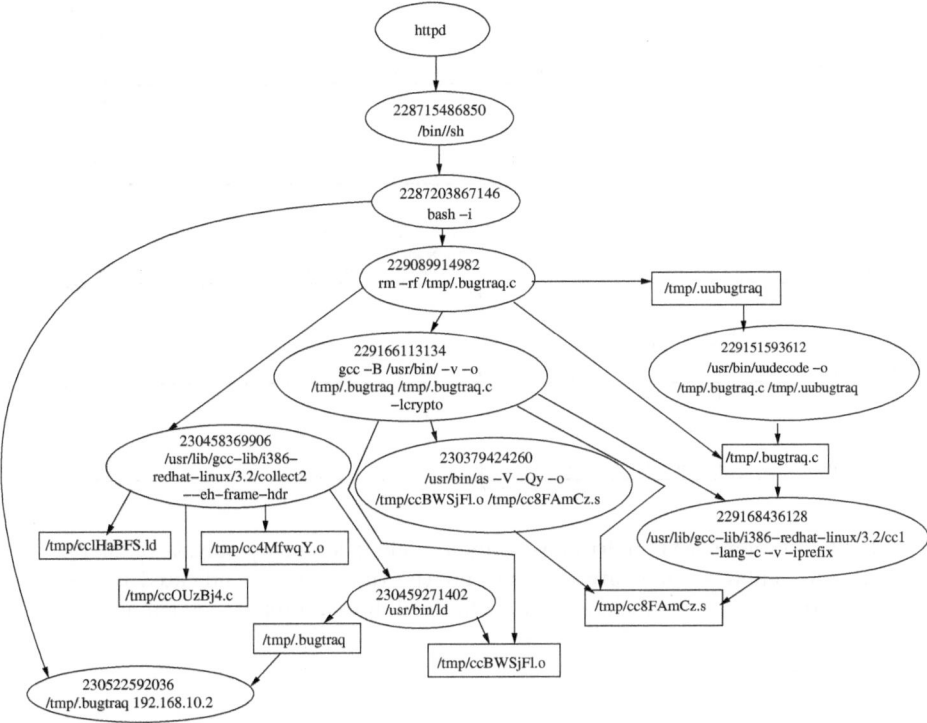

Fig. 2. The contamination graph of Slapper worm reconstructed from a Timescope-based replay session

Experiment 2: Slapper worm analysis   In this experiment, we demonstrate the time-traveling analysis capabilities of Timescope for a code injection attack (Slapper worm). Particularly, we setup a Timescope Redhat Linux 8.0 honeypot (in our isolated lab network) running a vulnerable Apache server (version 1.3.22), along with *mod_ssl* support that has a buffer overflow vulnerability exploited by Slapper. From another physical machine, we launch the Slapper worm and direct it to infect the honeypot. On the honeypot, we detect the presence of the worm by monitoring processes running and notice the process ".bugtraq". At this point, we pause the honeypot VM and retrieve the R&R log.

Our analysis is performed using multiple replay sessions using the previously described analysis modules (Section 2.2). We start a replay session with the first analysis module and using the results, we apply the backtracking algorithm [24], to generate a contamination graph (Fig. 2) of the Slapper infection. In this graph, an oval represents a process; a rectangle represents a file. The numbers in each oval represent the virtual timestamp at which the system call to execute the corresponding process was intercepted. The graph illustrates how the suspect process ".bugtraq" came to exist and shows that the *httpd* (Apache) process was compromised to spawn a shell process. We point out our analysis result is consistent with other Slapper analyses [20, 31].

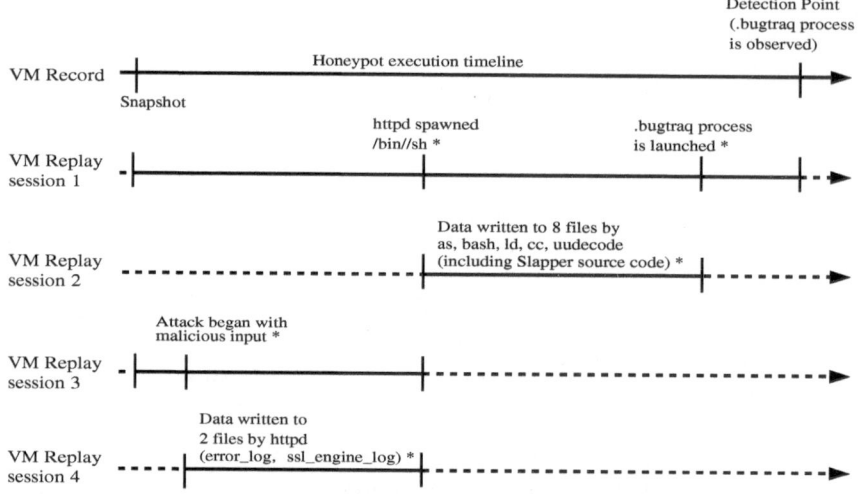

Fig. 3. Timescope-based multi-phase time-traveling forensic analysis of Slapper infection: The replay sessions are run only for the time window indicated by the solid regions in the execution timeline; results obtained during a replay session are indicated by asterisks

Next, we start another replay session with the second analysis module. This replay session focuses on a time window specified by two virtual timestamp values (ST - when the "/bin//sh" process is spawned; EN - when the ".bugtraq" process is launched). Our results show that there are 8 files that have been written to (including the entire decoded Slapper source code), and their contents are stored externally as part of analysis results. Using the third analysis module, we extract the injected shellcode in memory that invoked the "/bin//sh" process. For this, we extract the address of the instruction in the *httpd* process that caused the *sys_execve()* to spawn the shell process. We execute a Timescope replay session to collect the instruction trace of the honeypot and search for this instruction address (and the process memory layout identified by the CR3 value). Then, we can identify the basic block of instructions that causes this shell to be spawned.

Using a secondary run of the shellcode extractor, we further identify the timestamp when the malicious code was injected into the process. With that, we identify a new time window for further analysis - from the time this injection occurred in the vulnerable process until the time the shell process was spawned. With the new time window, we execute another Timescope replay session with the second analysis module and we can interestingly identify two files that are modified (including 2 log entries written to Apache's error log). As reported in [31], such behavior is related to the nature of the vulnerability exploited by Slapper. Putting it all together, Fig. 3 shows a more complete picture of the Slapper worm infection. Specifically, it depicts various events of interest along a timeline in the honeypot's execution.

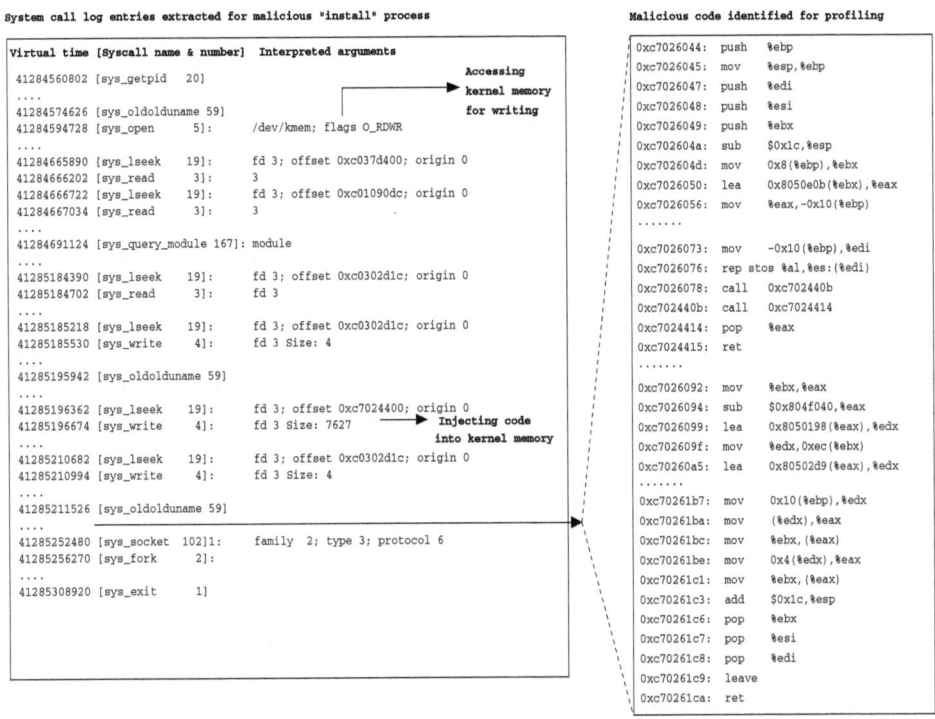

Fig. 4. SucKIT rootkit analysis using Timescope

Experiment 3: SucKIT rootkit analysis In this experiment, we aim to demonstrate how Timescope's replay-based forensic analysis techniques can be used to analyze intermediate memory states in the honeypot. For this, we use the SucKIT kernel rootkit to attack a honeypot VM. Presuming the scenario of a compromised root password, we launch this attack by logging remotely to the honeypot VM (running in an isolated lab environment), downloading the rootkit and executing a script to install it. To analyze this attack, we run a replay session with the first analysis module and notice the root login and the subsequent commands that were executed (with the *sys_execve()* system call). A subset of the log is shown in Fig. 4. In particular, we notice the command "install" run by the attacker and that it opens the file */dev/kmem* which, gives complete write access to the root user to write to arbitrary locations in the kernel memory. To highlight a subset of the execution profiling analysis, consider the lines indicating that the kernel memory is being overwritten as shown in Fig. 4. These lines indicate kernel memory being overwritten from the ranges 0xc7024400 to 0xc70261cb. Hence, to perform execution profiling, we use the fourth analysis module and generate a log of memory reads and writes and their contents for instructions fetched from addresses in these ranges when the processor is in kernel mode. Fig. 4 shows a subset of the instruction trace extracted in this range that is analyzed in detail. We can then run the log through PoKeR's combat-tracking

Table 1. Performance overhead in a VM record session

Benchmark	Configuration	Relative performance with QEMU
nbench	Default	0.97x - 1.39x
gzip	Compress 250 MB file	1.05x
ApacheBench	ab -c3 -t60	1.62x

algorithm to identify the set of kernel objects being manipulated by the SucKIT rootkit. One interesting observation we would like to note in Fig. 4 is that the "install" user process is issuing a *sys_oldolduname()* system call, when in reality, the rootkit overwrote the address of this system call handler in the kernel multiple times to use it for allocating kernel memory, injecting rootkit code in the kernel space, and hijacking kernel control flow. By combining different analysis modules in our system, we are able to understand the purposes of tampering with these data structures in the kernel memory.

4.3   Performance

After demonstrating the accuracy and effectiveness of our prototype, we then measure its performance overhead. In particular, as we are less concerned with the overhead during a replay session, we mainly measure the recording overhead. All the experiments were done with the Timescope honeypot running on a Dell Precision T1500 system with an Intel Core i7 2.8 GHz CPU and 4 GB physical memory. In our measurement, we ran three different benchmarks - Linux nbench [3], ApacheBench [2] and gzip. The configurations of these benchmarks as well as the results are summarized in Table 1. Each test was run 10 times and the averages are used to assess the overhead, compared to the default QEMU 0.12.3.

From the table, our evaluation indicates that recording introduces low overhead for the computation-intensive nbench - this is as expected, since most of the execution does not involve external interaction (or involvement of the recording layer). The slowest one in this suite is the "Assignment" test with a relative performance of 1.39x. In a couple of other tests, a minor speedup is noticed, which is due to the variation of different runs. Our evaluation indicates that recording introduces low overhead for the computation-intensive nbench (0.97x - 1.39x of the default QEMU performance). This is as expected, since most of the execution does not involve external interaction (or involvement of the recording layer). For the gzip test, we generated a 250MB file with random data and compressed it, and find that gzip performs at 1.05x of the default QEMU performance. In the case of ApacheBench, it performs at 1.62x of the default QEMU - this is a largely I/O-driven workload, hence the recording software is capturing large amounts of system activity. Though the performance overhead may seem high for normal production systems, we consider it is acceptable for honeypot purposes. From another perspective, the performance overhead is introduced due to certain simplifications we made in the implementation - e.g. disabling asynchronous I/O which could be addressed using other techniques [7].

5   Discussion

In this section, we describe current limitations in our prototype and possible solutions to mitigate them. Our honeypot framework shares certain limitations with other VM-based intrusion detection systems - the presence of the VMM can be detected by an attacker. However, recent tests have shown that only a small percentage [12] of malware currently perform such checks. Also, with the popularity of virtualized platforms, they may also appear attractive to existing malware. Moreover, recent work [7,23] shows promising ways to detect the change in a malware's execution in a virtual environment from a native one and adapt accordingly the underlying VMM layer to handle such difference. In this case, R&R could be leveraged to resume the malware's execution from the point of detection, with the VMM code now adapted to avoid detection and resume the malware analysis. Similar to other VMM-based security research efforts [16, 17, 18, 20, 21], we assume a trustworthy VMM and this is supported with recent progress in improving the hypervisor security [25, 27, 38].

Our analysis modules can also be further extended. For example, it will be helpful to develop extensions with the ability of launching a "go live" session during a replay. That is, instead of executing based on input from the log, the VM resumes real execution from a checkpoint state during a replay. Also, another example will be the development of "what-if" analysis modules that could alter certain input to the VM or its state and determine its effects. This will prove useful for developing and testing defense mechanisms. However, this will require a "live" session of the honeypot and would possibly need network packets to be replayed, depending on the kind of attack.

6   Related Work

In traditional host-based high-interaction honeypots, monitoring software (e.g., Sebek [4]) is introduced into the honeypot environment and the logs generated from it are used for forensic analysis. As another example, the Forensix [19] system targets answering various queries related to an intrusion by collecting detailed system information and enabling the resultant log for fast retrieval of queried data. Such systems are limited in re-creating past temporary state (such as memory state) and applying new data collection mechanisms. From another perspective, to address the issue of tamper-resistant forensic analysis while still collecting semantic-rich information, honeypots can be installed as virtual machines and the monitoring software operates at the VMM or hypervisor layer (e.g., by leveraging virtual machine introspection techniques [18, 20]).

Further, the use of virtualization significantly improves deployment and management of honeypots and many honeypot systems have leveraged virtualization to monitor and analyze new attacker techniques [22, 36, 37]. In Timescope, by using VM-based R&R and introducing forensic analysis modules in the VMM layer, one can rewind the honeypot's execution and examine past states of the honeypot in a transparent and non-perturbing manner.

The use of R&R has been proposed previously for a variety of purposes. For example, application cloning [9] aims to capture an application's execution and replay it to its clone on another machine. Aftersight [13] presents the general case for decoupled intrusion detection analysis so that production workloads' performance are not impacted by heavyweight analysis techniques. Similarly, Crosscut [14], allows replay logs to be "sliced" along time and abstraction boundaries. Both Aftersight and Crosscut implement the record feature based on a proprietary VMM, which significantly limits the capability to customize existing forensic analysis modules or prevents the development of new ones. ReVirt [16] presents a similar VM-based R&R system, but requires a heavily para-virtualized guest OS kernel for the R&R capability. Argos [33], originally developed for capturing zero-day attacks with system-wide taint analysis, has been extended for VM R&R. By leveraging and extending the insights from these R&R systems, we have additionally developed a number of R&R-empowered interdependent investigation modules for honeypot-specific forensic analysis (four of them have been demonstrated in the paper).

Meanwhile, it is worth mentioning that our approach to implement R&R is different from most previous ones, i.e., the host-based virtualization approach taken by QEMU will introduce non-determinism in the VM systems. Accordingly, we have to address such non-determinism to enable desirable R&R for honeypot analysis purposes. Also, our analysis modules are tailored for use in multiple-stage forensic analysis of honeypots. The development and deployment of a series of interdependent forensic analysis modules are helpful to construct a comprehensive picture of an intrusion. As a result, our system helps to address key questions in honeypot forensic analysis: "At what point in the execution of a honeypot should we retrieve its state for forensic analysis?" "Should a broader or narrower time window of the honeypot's execution be considered for further analysis?" "What data structures in memory were tampered by the intrusion?"

7 Conclusion

Honeypots are a valuable tool for intrusion and malware infection analysis. In this paper, we present Timescope, a honeypot record and replay system that greatly enhances existing ways to perform forensic analysis of honeypots. Particularly, by allowing (potentially new) analysis methods to "travel back in time", Timescope offers great flexibility in the types of intrusion analysis that can be done. We have developed a QEMU-based prototype and four representative analysis modules. Our evaluation with a number of synthetic honeypot attacks has demonstrated its effectiveness by repeatedly rewinding the honeypot's execution and comprehensively revealing various aspects of honeypot intrusions.

Acknowledgements. The authors would like to thank the anonymous reviewers for their insightful comments that helped improve the presentation of this paper. This work was supported in part by the US Air Force Office of Scientific Research (AFOSR) under Contract FA9550-10-1-0099 and the US National Science Foundation (NSF) under Grants 0852131, 0855297, 0855036, 0910767, and 0952640. Any opinions, findings, and conclusions or recommendations expressed in this material are those of the authors and do not necessarily reflect the views of the AFOSR and the NSF.

References

1. The Amazing VM Record/Replay Feature in VMware Workstation 6, http://blogs.vmware.com/sherrod/2007/04/the_amazing_vm_.html
2. Apache HTTP Server Benchmarking Tool, http://httpd.apache.org/docs/2.0/programs/ab.html
3. Linux/Unix nbench, http://www.tux.org/~mayer/linux/bmark.html
4. Sebek Project, http://projects.honeynet.org/sebek/
5. VirtualBox, http://www.virtualbox.org
6. VMware Inc., http://www.vmware.com
7. Balzarotti, D., Cova, M., Karlberger, C., Kruegel, C., Kirda, E., Vigna, G.: Efficient Detection of Split Personalities in Malware. In: Proceedings of the 17th Annual Network and Distributed System Security Symposium (2010)
8. Bellard, F.: QEMU, a Fast and Portable Dynamic Translator. In: Proceedings of the 2005 USENIX Annual Technical Conference (2005)
9. Bergheaud, P., Subhraveti, D., Vertes, M.: Fault Tolerance in Multiprocessor Systems Via Application Cloning. In: Proceedings of the 27th IEEE International Conference on Distributed Computing Systems (2007)
10. Bressoud, T.C., Schneider, F.B.: Hypervisor-based Fault Tolerance. In: Proceedings of the 15th ACM Symposium on Operating Systems Principles (1995)
11. CERT/CC: CERT Advisory CA-2002-27 Apache/mod_ssl Worm, http://www.cert.org/advisories/CA-2002-27.html
12. Chen, X., Andersen, J., Mao, Z.M., Bailey, M.D., Nazario, J.: Towards an Understanding of Anti-Virtualization and Anti-Debugging Behavior in Modern Malware. In: Proceedings of the 38th Annual IEEE International Conference on Dependable Systems and Networks (2008)
13. Chow, J., Garfinkel, T., Chen, P.M.: Decoupling Dynamic Program Analysis from Execution in Virtual Environments. In: Proceedings of the USENIX 2008 Annual Technical Conference (2008)
14. Chow, J., Lucchetti, D., Garfinkel, T., Lefebvre, G., Gardner, R., Mason, J., Small, S., Chen, P.M.: Multi-stage Replay with Crosscut. In: Proceedings of the 6th ACM SIGPLAN/SIGOPS International Conference on Virtual Execution Environments (2010)
15. Dinaburg, A., Royal, P., Sharif, M.I., Lee, W.: Ether: Malware Analysis via Hardware Virtualization Extensions. In: Proceedings of the 15th ACM Conference on Computer and Communications Security (2008)
16. Dunlap, G., King, S., Cinar, S., Basrai, M., Chen, P.: ReVirt: Enabling Intrusion Analysis through Virtual-machine Logging and Replay. ACM SIGOPS Operating Systems Review 36 (2002)
17. Garfinkel, T., Pfaff, B., Chow, J., Rosenblum, M., Boneh, D.: Terra: A Virtual Machine-Based Platform for Trusted Computing. In: Proceedings of the 19th Symposium on Operating System Principles (2003)
18. Garfinkel, T., Rosenblum, M.: A Virtual Machine Introspection Based Architecture for Intrusion Detection. In: Proceedings of the 10th Annual Network and Distributed Systems Security Symposium (2003)
19. Goel, A., Feng, W., Maier, D., Feng, W., Walpole, J.: Forensix: A Robust, High-performance Reconstruction System. In: Proceedings of the 25th IEEE International Conference on Distributed Computing Systems Workshops (2005)

20. Jiang, X., Wang, X.: "Out-of-the-Box" Monitoring of VM-Based High-Interaction Honeypots. In: Kruegel, C., Lippmann, R., Clark, A. (eds.) RAID 2007. LNCS, vol. 4637, pp. 198–218. Springer, Heidelberg (2007)
21. Jiang, X., Wang, X., Xu, D.: Stealthy Malware Detection Through VMM-Based "Out-of-the-Box" Semantic View Reconstruction. In: Proceedings of the 14th ACM Conference on Computer and Communications Security (2007)
22. Jiang, X., Xu, D.: Collapsar: A VM-based Architecture for Network Attack Detention Center. In: Proceedings of the 13th USENIX Security Symposium (2004)
23. Kang, M.G., Yin, H., Hanna, S., McCamant, S., Song, D.: Emulating Emulation-Resistant Malware. In: Proceedings of the 2nd Workshop on Virtual Machine Security (2009)
24. King, S.T., Chen, P.M.: Backtracking Intrusions. ACM SIGOPS Operating Systems Review 37 (2003)
25. Klein, G., Elphinstone, K., Heiser, G., Andronick, J., Cock, D., Derrin, P., Elkaduwe, D., Engelhardt, K., Kolanski, R., Norrish, M., Sewell, T., Tuch, H., Winwood, S.: seL4: Formal Verification of an OS Kernel. In: Proceedings of the 22nd ACM Symposium on Operating Systems Principles (2009)
26. LWN: A New Adore Root Kit, http://lwn.net/Articles/75990
27. Murray, D.G., Milos, G., Hand, S.: Improving Xen Security through Disaggregation. In: Proceedings of the 4th ACM SIGPLAN/SIGOPS International Conference on Virtual Execution Environments (2008)
28. Newsome, J., Song, D.: Dynamic Taint Analysis: Automatic Detection, Analysis, and Signature Generation of Exploit Attacks on Commodity Software. In: Proceedings of the 12th Annual Network and Distributed Systems Security Symposium (2005)
29. Northcutt, S., Novak, J.: Network Intrusion Detection: An Analyst's Handbook, 2nd edn. New Riders Publishing (2000)
30. de Oliveira, D.A.S., Crandall, J.R., Wassermann, G., Wu, S.F., Su, Z., Chong, F.T.: ExecRecorder: VM-based Full-system Replay for Attack Analysis and System Recovery. In: Proceedings of the 1st Workshop on Architectural and System Support for Improving Software Dependability (2006)
31. Perriot, F., Szor, P.: An Analysis of the Slapper Worm Exploit, http://www.symantec.com/avcenter/reference/analysis.slapper.worm.pdf
32. Phrack: Linux On-the-fly Kernel Patching without LKM, http://www.phrack.org/issues.html?id=7&issue=58
33. Portokalidis, G., Slowinska, A., Bos, H.: Argos: An Emulator for Fingerprinting Zero-Day Attacks. In: Proceedings of the 1st ACM European Conference on Computer Systems (2006)
34. Riley, R., Jiang, X., Xu, D.: Multi-aspect Profiling of Kernel Rootkit Behavior. In: Proceedings of the 4th ACM European Conference on Computer Systems (2009)
35. Spitzner, L.: Honeypots: Tracking Hackers. Addison-Wesley Professional (2002)
36. Vrable, M., Ma, J., Chen, J., Moore, D., Vandekieft, E., Snoeren, A.C., Voelker, G.M., Savage, S.: Scalability, Fidelity, and Containment in the Potemkin Virtual Honeyfarm. ACM SIGOPS Operating Systems Review 39 (2005)
37. Wang, Y.M., Beck, D., Jiang, X., Roussev, R.: Automated Web Patrol with Strider HoneyMonkeys: Finding Web Sites that Exploit Browser Vulnerabilities. In: Proceedings of the 13th Annual Symposium on Network and Distributed System Security (2006)
38. Wang, Z., Jiang, X.: HyperSafe: A Lightweight Approach to Provide Lifetime Hypervisor Control-Flow Integrity. In: Proceedings of the 2010 IEEE Symposium on Security and Privacy (2010)

Optimistic Fair Exchange of Ring Signatures

Lie Qu, Guilin Wang, and Yi Mu

Center for Computer and Information Security Research,
School of Computer Science and Software Engineering,
University of Wollongong, Wollongong,
NSW 2522, Australia
{lq594,guilin,ymu}@uow.edu.au

Abstract. An optimistic fair exchange (OFE) protocol is an effective tool helping two parties exchange their digital items in an equitable way with assistance of a trusted third party, called *arbitrator*, who is only required if needed. In previous studies, fair exchange is usually carried out between individual parties. When fair exchange is carried out between two members from distinct groups, anonymity of the signer in a group could be necessary for achieving better privacy. In this paper, we consider optimistic fair exchange of ring signatures (OFERS), i.e. two members from two different groups can exchange their ring signatures in a fair way with ambiguous signers. Each user in these groups has its own public-private key pair and is able to sign a message on behalf of its own group anonymously. We first define the security model of OFERS in the multi-user setting under adaptive chosen message, chosen-key and chosen public-key attacks. Then, based on verifiably encrypted ring signatures (VERS) we construct a concrete scheme by combining the technologies of ring signatures, public-key encryption and proof of knowledge. Finally, we show that our OFERS solution is provably secure in our security model, and preserving *signer-ambiguity* of ring signatures. To the best of our knowledge, this is the first (formal) work on this topic.

Keywords: optimistic fair exchange, ring signatures, privacy, verifiably encrypted signatures (VES).

1 Introduction

The concept of optimistic fair exchange (OFE) was first proposed by Asokan et al. [1]. By executing an OFE protocol, two parties in networks are able to fairly exchange their digital signatures with some help from an off-line trusted third party (TTP). An OFE protocol usually has at least the properties: *fairness, non-repudiation* and *optimism. Fairness* ensures that, if an honest party does not get a valid signature of the other party at the end of a fair exchange protocol, the other party cannot get that either. That is, either both two parties get each other's valid signature, or neither of them gets anything valuable. *Non-repudiation* guarantees that any party in a fair exchange protocol cannot repudiate or refute a valid signature after the protocol executed successfully. To reduce the load of the TTP, Asokan et al. proposed *optimistic* fair exchange [1].

M. Rajarajan et al. (Eds.): SecureComm 2011, LNICST 96, pp. 227–242, 2012.
© Institute for Computer Sciences, Social Informatics and Telecommunications Engineering 2012

In an OFE protocol, there is an off-line TTP, called *arbitrator*, who acts as a judge to settle the dispute between two parties and should only be involved when the protocol does not run correctly (e.g. some parties cheating or communication channel interrupted). The rare involvement of a TTP makes the fair exchange protocol more efficient and secure.

An conventional way to build optimistic fair exchange protocols is *verifiably encrypted signature* (VES), which was formally defined by Boneh et al. [2]. A VES is an ordinary signature encrypted using the public key of a TTP, together with a verifiable proof showing the validity of the encryption. Suppose Alice and Bob exchange their signatures on a message. Due to mutual distrust, neither of them wants to send his or her signature first. To solve this dilemma, Alice can send a VES generated under a TTP's public key to Bob first. Then, Bob is able to verify the validity of the VES together with a proof showing that Alice's signature encrypted in the VES can be recovered by the TTP, but cannot obtain the original signature from Alice unless Bob sends his own signature to Alice. After that, if Alice refuses to reveal Bob her signature, Bob can ask the TTP to decrypt Alice's VES and obtain her original signature.

In some cases, the anonymity of participants in fair exchange might be important in order to protect participants' privacy. For example, in the developed commercial society, the personal preferences of negotiators in business contract signing usually influence the terms of the final agreement. If a trading company A has the old contract signing records of an employee as a negotiator in another company B which is a potential trade cooperator of A, A can use these records to generalize the negotiator's trading habits, by which the company A might get advantages in the future contract negotiation with the company B. Hence it is desirable that the employees who have the right to independently sign a contract on behalf of their own company can sign contracts anonymously, which will prevent other companies from knowing the signer's trading habits. To this end, ring signatures invented by Rivest et al. [3] are the good primitive to provide the property *signer-ambiguity*, which was formally defined by Abe et al. [8]. Informally, in a ring signature scheme, the public keys of a group of users are collected spontaneously to form a public-key list. When a signer signs a message on behalf of such a ring, he uses the public-key list and adds his own private key as a glue value to issue a ring signature. A verifier cannot tell who the real signer is, because the ring signature is validated using all the public keys of the ring without revealing any information about who produced it.

In this paper, we study optimistic fair exchange of ring signatures (OFERS), in which users in each ring can fairly exchange their ring signatures with ambiguous signers for the other ring. To the best of our knowledge, this is the first work on the topic to present a formal security model of OFERS and a concrete solution with provable security. After introducing some preliminaries in Section 2, we first rigorously define the security model of OFERS in the multi-user setting under adaptive chosen message, chosen-key and chosen public-key attacks (Section 3). This is done by updating the formal models of OFE [5,6] in the scenario of ring signatures. Secondly, we present a concrete OFERS scheme (Section 4), which is constructed from verifiably encrypted ring signatures (VERS) based on Abe et al.'s scheme [8] under a TTP's public key, together with a proof of knowledge showing the validity of the original ring signature's encryption. Theoretically, any CCA2-secure [7] public-key encryption scheme can be used as such a proof of knowledge always exists (but may be not efficient). To provide practicality and high efficiency, Camenisch and Shoup's CCA2-secure encryption scheme [19] is particularly selected in the proposed scheme. Then, we formally show that the proposed OFERS solution is provably secure in our security model (Section 5). As the VES technique is employed, a notable feature of our scheme is that any holder (not necessarily the signer) of a valid ring signature can verifiably encrypt the ring signature to get a VERS without using any secret information from the signer. Due to this feature, our scheme not only preserves *signer-ambiguity* [8] of ring signatures, but also allows a signer to delegate a proxy (e.g. his/her secretary) to run OFERS after he/she produced a ring signature in advance. Finally, we discuss some extensions of our results and point out future work (Section 6).

2 Preliminaries

In this section, we introduce the technologies used in our OFERS scheme.

2.1 Ring Signature of All Discrete-Log Case

Abe et al. proposed an abstract scheme of a ring signature and several concrete examples in [8]. For the sake of simplicity, we choose the ring signature scheme of all discrete-log case in [8] as our signature scheme. And Abe et al. have proved that this ring signature scheme is unconditionally signer-ambiguous and existential unforgeability against adaptive chosen message and chosen public-key attacks. The details of the scheme are shown below:

Let p_i, q_i be large primes, $\langle g_i \rangle$ denote a prime subgroup of $\mathbb{Z}_{p_i}^*$ generated by g_i whose order is q_i. Let $y_i = g_i^{x_i} \bmod p_i$, where x_i is the secret key and (y_i, p_i, q_i, g_i) is the public key. $H_i : \{0,1\}^* \to \mathbb{Z}_{q_i}$ denotes a collision-resistant hash function. L is a list of (y_i, p_i, q_i, g_i), where $i = 0, ..., n-1$ and $n = |L|$. A signer with the secret key x_k generates a ring signature on a message m under L as follows:

1. Randomly select $\alpha \in \mathbb{Z}_{q_k}$ and compute $c_{k+1} = H_{k+1}(L, m, g_k^\alpha \bmod p_k)$.
2. For $i = k+1, ..., n-1, 0, ..., k-1$, randomly select $s_i \in \mathbb{Z}_{q_i}$ and compute $c_{i+1} = H_{i+1}(L, m, g_i^{s_i} y_i^{c_i} \bmod p_i)$, and then $s_k = \alpha - x_k c_k \bmod q_k$.
3. Send the verifier $(c_0, s_0, s_1, ..., s_{n-1})$ as the resulting ring signature on the message m under the public-key list L.

For $i = 0, ..., n-1$, the verifier computes $e_i = g_i^{s_i} y_i^{c_i} \bmod p_i$, and then $c_{i+1} = H_{i+1}(L, m, e_i)$ if $i \neq n-1$. The verifier accepts the ring signature if $c_0 = H_0(L, m, e_{n-1})$, otherwise rejects.

2.2 Zero-knowledge Proof

In [9], Ateniese introduced an underlying proof of the equality of discrete logarithms, which is used for constructing verifiably encrypted signatures. In [11], Camenisch and Michels proposed a concrete scheme to prove the equality of discrete logarithms from different groups under the strong RSA assumption [12,13]. In this paper, we modify Camenisch and Michels' proof as our zero-knowledge proof so as to build a verifiably encrypted signature scheme based on Abe et al. [8]'s ring signature introduced above. Camenisch and Michels' proof is denoted by $PK\{(\alpha,\beta) : y_1 \overset{G_1}{=} g_1^{\alpha} \wedge y_2 \overset{G_2}{=} g_2^{\alpha} \wedge \tilde{y} \overset{\mathbb{Z}_n^*}{=} h_1^{\beta} h_2^{\alpha} \wedge (-2^l < \alpha < 2^l)\}$. The details of the proof are shown below:

n is the product of two sufficiently large safe primes and must be large enough to avoid factoring. h_1 and h_2 are two random elements with large order from $\mathbb{Z}_n$. Let G_1 and G_2 be two distinct groups of orders q_1 and q_2 such that $2^{l+1} < min(q_1, q_2)$, where l is an integer, and g_1 and g_2 are the generators of G_1 and G_2 respectively. Let $y_1 \overset{G_1}{=} g_1^x$ and $y_2 \overset{G_2}{=} g_2^x$, $\epsilon > 1$ is a security parameter which controls the tightness of the statistical zero-knowledgeness. If $-2^{(l-2)/\epsilon} < x < 2^{(l-2)/\epsilon}$, the prover can convince the verifier that $\log_{g_1}^{y_1} = \log_{g_2}^{y_2}$ in $\mathbb{Z}$ by the following steps:

1. The prover randomly chooses $r \in \mathbb{Z}_n$ and computes $\tilde{y} = h_1^r h_2^x \mod n$, then randomly selects $r_1 \in \{-2^{l-2}, ..., 2^{l-2}\}$ and $r_2 \in \{-(n2^k)^\epsilon, ..., (n2^k)^\epsilon\}$, where k is the length of bits of the verifier's challenge, and computes the commitments: $t_1 = g_1^{r_1}$, $t_2 = g_2^{r_1}$, and $t_3 = h_1^{r_2} h_2^{r_1}$. After that, the prover sends (t_1, t_2, t_3) to the verifier.
2. The verifier returns a random challenge $c \in \{0,1\}^k$.
3. The prover computes the responses $s_1 = r_1 - cx$ and $s_2 = r_2 - cr$ in $\mathbb{Z}$, then sends (s_1, s_2) to the verifier.
4. The verifier accepts the proof if and only if $-2^{l-1} < s_1 < 2^{l-1}$, $t_1 = g_1^{s_1} y_1^c$, $t_2 = g_2^{s_1} y_2^c$ and $t_3 = h_1^{s_2} h_2^{s_1} \tilde{y}^c$ hold.

Note that the proof above is based on the strong RSA assumption. The prover should not know the factoring of n. Hence n, h_1, h_2 might be generated by the verifier or a trusted third party. Before executing the proof, the prover should check whether n is the product of two safe primes (see [14] for details) and whether h_1 and h_2 have large order (see [15] for details). To convert this interactive proof into a signature form on a message m, the prover can use a suitable hash function $h(\cdot)$, which is agreed by the verifier, to compute the hash value of all the public information instead of the verifier's challenge c (e.g. $c = h(m||\tilde{y}||y_1||y_2||g_1||g_2||t_1||t_2||t_3)$).

2.3 Encryption Scheme

In [9], Ateniese proposed a method to construct verifiably encrypted signatures by encrypting an ordinary signature using some specific public-key cryptosystems and giving a proof showing the validity of the signature's encryption. In such cryptosystems (e.g. Naccache-Stern [16], Okamoto-Uchiyama [17] and Paillier [18] public-key cryptosystems), computing a discrete logarithm using the secret key is an easy task, but without the secret key, it is still hard. However, all these public-key cryptosystems above do not satisfy the high level security which protects against adaptive chosen-ciphertext attacks (CCA2). In [19], Camenisch and Shoup proposed an adaptation of Paillier cryptosystem, which is proven secure against adaptive chosen ciphertext attacks under the decisional composite residuosity assumption [18]. To achieve the high level security, we use Camenisch and Shoup's scheme as our encryption scheme, which is briefly described as follows:

1. Randomly select two Sophie Germain primes p' and q', where $p' \neq q'$, and compute safe primes $p = 2p' + 1$, $q = 2q' + 1$ and $n = pq$. Then randomly select $x_1, x_2, x_3 \in_R [n^2/4]$ [1] and $g' \in \mathbb{Z}_{n^2}^*$, and compute $g = (g')^{2n}$, $y_1 = g_1^{x_1}$, $y_2 = g_2^{x_2}$, $y_3 = g_3^{x_3}$. Let $h = (1 + n \bmod n^2) \in \mathbb{Z}_{n^2}^*$, abs: $\mathbb{Z}_{n^2}^* \to \mathbb{Z}_{n^2}^*$ map $(a \bmod n^2)$, where $0 < a < n^2$, to $(n^2 - a \bmod n^2)$ if $a > n^2/2$, and to $(a \bmod n^2)$ otherwise. Obviously for any $v \in \mathbb{Z}_{n^2}^*$, $v^2 = (\mathbf{abs}(v))^2$ holds. H is a collision-resistant hash function. A label L is some public information added to the ciphertext (e.g. user's identity or expiration time). The public key is (n, g, y_1, y_2, y_3), and the private key is (x_1, x_2, x_3).
2. To encrypt a message $m \in [n]$ with a label $L \in \{0,1\}^*$, randomly select $r \in_R [n/4]$ and compute $u = g^r$, $e = y_1^r h^m$ and $v = \mathbf{abs}((y_2 y_3^{H(u,e,L)})^r)$. The triple (u, e, v) is the resulting ciphertext.
3. To decrypt a ciphertext (u, e, v), first check whether $\mathbf{abs}(v) = v$ and $u^{2(x_2 + H(u,e,L)x_3)} = v^2$. If fail, output reject, otherwise compute $\hat{m} = (e/u^{x_1})^{2t}$, where $t = 2^{-1} \bmod n$. If $\hat{m}$ is of the form h^m for some $m \in [n]$, then output m, otherwise output reject.

Recall the ring signature scheme presented in Section 2.1. Suppose the signer generates a ring signature $(c_0, s_0, s_1, ..., s_{n-1})$. In the verification of this signature, the verifier needs to compute $e_i = g_i^{s_i} y_i^{c_i}$, where $i = 0, 1, ..., n-1$. In order to convert the ring signature into a verifiably encrypted ring signature (VERS), the signer sends the verifier $w_i = g_i^{s_i}$ instead of s_i and encrypts s_i using a TTP's public key. The verifier can do the verification by computing $e_i = w_i y_i^{c_i}$ instead, but s_i is 'hidden' in w_i since in this ring signature scheme computing a discrete logarithm is hard, which means the verifier has not got the full ring signature yet. Beside that, the signer needs to give a zero-knowledge proof for convincing the verifier that the encrypted s_i is just the s_i hidden in w_i. Note that encrypting only one value in $(s_0, s_1, ..., s_{n-1})$ can also ensure the initial ring signature hidden partially, which means the verifier still cannot draw the full ring signature from the partially encrypted ring signature even though he gets the most parts of the initial ring signature. Encrypting one value makes the cost of generating a VERS does not depend on the size of the public-key list, which improves the efficiency of the generation of a VERS.

---

[1] For a positive integer a, $[a]$ denotes the set $\{0, 1, ..., a-1\}$.

To produce a verifiably encrypted ring signature, suppose the signer randomly chooses s_u, where $0 \leqslant u \leqslant n - 1$, from $(s_0, s_1, ..., s_{n-1})$ as the hidden value, and encrypts s_u using Camenisch and Shoup's encryption scheme above. Let $(\mathsf{n}, \mathsf{g}, \mathsf{y}_1, \mathsf{y}_2, \mathsf{y}_3, \mathsf{h})$ be the public key of a TTP. H is a collision-resistant hash function, and L is the public label. The signer computes s_u's ciphertext $\mathsf{u} = \mathsf{g}^\mathsf{t}, \mathsf{e} = \mathsf{y}_1\mathsf{t}\mathsf{h}^{s_u}, \mathsf{v} = \mathbf{abs}((\mathsf{y}_2\mathsf{y}_3^{\mathsf{H}(u,e,\mathsf{L})})^\mathsf{t})$, where $\mathsf{t} \in_R [\mathsf{n}/4]$. After that, by modifying the zero-knowledge proof introduced in Section 2.2, the signer gives a non-interactive proof: $PK\{(s_u, \mathsf{t}, r) : w = g_u^{s_u} \wedge \mathsf{u}^2 = \mathsf{g}^{2\mathsf{t}} \wedge \mathsf{e}^2 = \mathsf{y}_1{}^{2\mathsf{t}}\mathsf{h}^{2s_u} \wedge$ $\mathsf{v}^2 = (\mathsf{y}_2\mathsf{y}_3^{\mathsf{H}(u,e,\mathsf{L})})^{2\mathsf{t}} \wedge \hat{w} = h_1^r h_2^{s_u} \wedge -2^l < s_u < 2^l\}$ to convince the verifier that the TTP can extract s_u using its secret key and recover the original ring signature completely. Note that anyone beside the signer has the capability to convert a valid ring signature into a VERS without knowing any secret information from the signer. The property *signer-ambiguity* [8] is well preserved since the hidden value can be arbitrarily chosen in $(s_0, ..., s_{n-1})$ and no secret of the signer is needed for producing a VERS based on a given ring signature. In our verifiably encrypted ring signature scheme, for the sake of simplicity, we specify s_{n-1} as the hidden value encrypted using a TTP's public key no matter who the signer is. The details are shown in Section 4.

3   Security Definitions

In [5], Dodis et al. presented a formal security model of optimistic fair exchange under *adaptive chosen message attacks* in a *multi-user setting*, in which the optimistic fair exchange protocol can be executed between different signers and different verifiers. That is, multiple pairs of users can run the two-party fair exchange protocol without compromising security. In adaptive chosen message attacks [20], an adversary can access the signing oracle by asking for signatures on arbitrary messages. In ring signatures, there are multiple users belonging to each public-key list. So the multi-user setting is necessary for fair exchange of ring signatures. Furthermore, Huang et al. [6] extended Dodis et al.'s model by considering *chosen-key model*, i.e. an adversary may win a computational game if it is allowed to employ some public keys without knowing the corresponding private keys. By providing this extra flexibility, the chosen-key model is stronger than the certified-key model (shown in [6]). In addition, we also consider *chosen public-key attacks* in the setting of ring signatures, which is proposed by Abe et al. [8]. In chosen public-key attacks, any adversary who wants to forge a ring signature is only allowed to use arbitrary subsets of the initially considered public-key list to access the signing oracle, but cannot append new public keys to the initial public-key list. Therefore, in our security definitions specified below, all the four factors above are addressed in the setting of OFERS as a whole.

Definition 1. (Syntax) Optimistic fair exchange of ring signatures (OFERS) *consists of seven probabilistic polynomial-time algorithms.*

- **Setup^{TTP}**: *On input a security parameter **Param**, the arbitrator executes the algorithm to generate a public-private key pair (APK, ASK) and some auxiliary information if necessary.*
- **Setup^{User}**: *On input **Param** and (optionally) the arbitrator's public key with the auxiliary information, the algorithm outputs public-private key pairs (PK_i, SK_i) for every user in the ring. The public keys form a public-key list L.*
- **RSig(m, L, SK_s)**: *A signer U_s in the ring executes the algorithm by inputting a message m, a public-keys list L including PK_s and its corresponding private key SK_s, then outputs a ring signature σ.*
- **RVer(m, L, σ)**: *On input a message m, a ring signature σ on m under a public-key list L, a verifier executes the algorithm to output either 1 or 0, which means accept or reject respectively.*
- **PRSig(m, L, σ, APK)**: *On input a message m, a signer's public-key list L, a ring signature σ on m under L, and the arbitrator's public key APK, the algorithm outputs a verifiably partial ring signature θ.*
- **PRVer(m, L, θ, APK)**: *On input a message m, a signer's public-key list L, a verifiably partial ring signature θ on m under L, and the arbitrator's public key APK, the verifier executes the algorithm to output either 1 or 0, which means accept or reject respectively.*
- **Res(m, L, θ, ASK)**: *The resolution algorithm is executed by the arbitrator if the verifier does not receive the full ring signature σ from the signer ring, but has got the corresponding verifiably partial ring signature θ. On input a message m, a signer's public-key list L and a verifiably partial ring signature θ on m under L, if θ is valid and the verifier has fulfilled its obligation to the signer, the arbitrator extracts the full ring signature σ from θ using its private key ASK and reveals it to the verifier, otherwise rejects.*

Since there are three roles (*signer, verifier, arbitrator*) in OFERS, we should consider how each role may violate different aspects of security, i.e. different security properties. Here we require the arbitrator should not be able to cheat some participant by colluding with the other participant in the protocol since such a collusive adversarial arbitrator can break the fair exchange trivially. Moreover, the property *signer-ambiguity* should also be addressed as it is the heritage of ring signatures.

Security Against Signers: For the fairness to verifiers, it is required that except negligible probability, any probabilistic polynomial-time (PPT) adversarial signer $\mathcal{A}$ should be not able to generate a verifiably partial ring signature, which can be accepted by verifiers, but cannot be recovered to a valid full ring signature by an honest arbitrator. The property is formally defined by the following game:

$$\mathbf{Setup}^{\mathrm{TTP}}(\mathbf{Param}) \longrightarrow (ASK, APK)$$
$$(m, L^*, \theta) \longleftarrow \mathcal{A}^{O_{Res}}(APK)$$
$$\sigma \longleftarrow \mathbf{Res}(m, L^*, \theta, ASK)$$
$$\text{Success of } \mathcal{A} = [\mathbf{PRVer}(m, L^*, \theta, APK)=1 \wedge \mathbf{RVer}(m, L^*, \sigma)=0]$$

where O_{Res} denotes a resolution oracle, which takes as input a verifiably partial ring signature on a message m under a public-key list L, and outputs a full ring signature σ on m under L. In this game, the adversary $\mathcal{A}$ is allowed to *arbitrarily* (i.e. not necessarily following the key generation algorithm) generate public keys to form a list L^*. For each public key in L^*, $\mathcal{A}$ may not know the corresponding private key. The chosen-key model is therefore accommodated here.

Definition 2 (Security Against Signers). Optimistic fair exchange of ring signatures is said to be secure against signers *if there is no PPT adversarial signer $\mathcal{A}$ who wins the game above with non-negligible probability.*

Security Against Verifiers: The property of *security against verifiers* requires that, without help from the signer or the arbitrator, any PPT adversarial verifier $\mathcal{B}$ should not be able to extract a full ring signature from the corresponding verifiably partial ring signature with non-negligible probability. The property is formally defined by the following game:

$$\textbf{Setup}^{\textbf{TTP}}(\textbf{Param}) \longrightarrow (ASK, APK)$$
$$\textbf{Setup}^{\textbf{User}}(\textbf{Param}) \longrightarrow (SK_i, PK_i)$$
$$(m, L', \sigma) \longleftarrow \mathcal{B}^{O_{PRSig}, O_{Res}}(APK, L)$$
$$\text{Success of } \mathcal{B} = [\textbf{RVer}(m, L', \sigma)=1 \wedge (m, L', \cdot) \notin Query(\mathcal{B}, O_{Res})]$$

where L' is an arbitrary subset of the initial public-key list L consisting of all the PK_i, the oracle O_{Res} has been defined in the previous game, and the partial ring signature signing oracle O_{PRSig}, given as input a message m and a public key list L'', outputs a verifiably partial ring signature on m under L'' using the arbitrator's public key APK. The $Query(\mathcal{B}, O_{Res})$ is the set of valid queries which $\mathcal{B}$ asks to O_{Res}. In this game, $\mathcal{B}$ can ask the arbitrator for resolving any verifiably partial ring signature with respect to any sublist of L. Note that here chosen-public key attacks are considered, as the adversary $\mathcal{B}$ is only required to output a valid ring signature under L' which is a subset of L but not necessarily L. Moreover, L' does not contain any public key generated by $\mathcal{B}$. Otherwise, $\mathcal{B}$ can win the game above trivially.

Definition 3 (Security Against Verifiers). Optimistic fair exchange of ring signatures is said to be secure against verifiers *if there is no PPT adversarial verifier $\mathcal{B}$ who wins the game above with non-negligible probability.*

Security Against the Arbitrator: For the fairness to signers, the property of *security against the arbitrator* requires that except negligible probability, any PPT adversarial arbitrator $\mathcal{C}$ should not be able to produce a full ring signature without demanding the signer to generate a verifiably partial ring signatures. The property is formally defined by the following game:

$$\textbf{Setup}^{\textbf{User}}(\textbf{Param}) \longrightarrow (PK_i, SK_i)$$
$$(ASK^*, APK) \longleftarrow \mathcal{C}(L)$$
$$(m, L', \sigma) \longleftarrow \mathcal{C}^{O_{PRSig}}(ASK^*, APK, L)$$
$$\text{Success of } \mathcal{C} = [\textbf{RVer}(m, L', \sigma)=1 \wedge (m, L') \notin Query(\mathcal{C}, O_{PRSig})]$$

where the oracles O_{Res}, O_{PRSig}, the public-key lists L' and L have been described in the previous games, and ASK^* is the state information of $\mathcal{C}$, which may not correspond to the arbitrator's public key APK. $Query(\mathcal{C}, O_{PRSig})$ is the set of valid queries which $\mathcal{C}$ asks to O_{PRSig}. We remark that this game considers both chosen-key and chosen public-key attacks in the multi-user setting, as the adversary $\mathcal{C}$ (a malicious arbitrator) does not need to know the corresponding private key of the public key APK and can choose any sublist L' of the initial public-key list to forge a ring signature.

Definition 4 (Security Against the Arbitrator). Optimistic fair exchange of ring signatures is said to be **secure against the arbitrator** *if there is no PPT adversarial arbitrator $\mathcal{C}$ who wins the game above with non-negligible probability.* In [8], Abe et al. specified the security definition of *signer-ambiguity*. In our OFERS scheme, the signer should be still ambiguous in its own ring. By updating Abe et al.'s definition in the setting of OFERS, we formally define signer-ambiguity as follows:

Definition 5 (Signer Ambiguity). Let $L = \{PK_i\}$ be an initial public-key list, where each PK_i is generated by running **Setup**^{User} $\rightarrow (PK_i, SK_i)$, *and APK be the arbitrator's public key generated by running* **Setup**^{TTP} $\rightarrow (APK, ASK)$. *An OFERS protocol is called* **perfectly signer-ambiguous**, *if for any message m, any public-key list L, any public key APK of the arbitrator, any valid full ring signature $\sigma \leftarrow$ **RSign**(m, L, SK_s), and an associated verifiably partial ring signature $\theta \leftarrow$ **PRSig**(m, L, σ, APK), where SK_s is the signer's private key, given $(m, L, \theta, \sigma, APK)$, any unbound adversary $\mathcal{D}$ outputs index i such that $SK_s = SK_i$ with probability exactly $\frac{1}{|L|}$, where $|L|$ denotes the size of L.*

Remark 1. Comparing with Abe et al.'s perfect signer-ambiguity [8] for ring signatures, we also provide the verifiably partial ring signature θ of a full ring signature σ to the adversary $\mathcal{D}$, which allows $\mathcal{D}$ acquiring more information to break signer-ambiguity. In fact, this is necessary because the signer-ambiguity in ring signatures does not always guarantee the same property for OFERS (refer to the counterexample discussion in Section 5). As the unbound adversary $\mathcal{D}$ can derive all private keys from L, the above definition essentially means that for fixed (m, L, APK), the distributions of θ and σ generated by using any private key SK_i are identical. In addition, Definition 5 specifies *perfect signer-ambiguity*, and it can be easily extended to define *statistical* and *computational* signer-ambiguity, two weaker versions of ambiguity.

4   The Scheme

In our OFERS scheme, we use verifiably encrypted ring signatures (VERS) to construct verifiably partial ring signatures. In this section, we first present how to produce a VERS, and then give an optimistic fair exchange protocol of ring signatures. The generation and verification of ring signatures are similar to Abe et al.'s ring signature in all discrete-log case (see Section 2.1) except some limitation of selecting α and s_i. For the sake of simplicity, in our VERS scheme, we always encrypt the last s_i, i.e. s_{n-1}, as the hidden value. Obviously this does not affect the scheme's security since any s_i in $(s_0, ..., s_{n-1})$ can be the hidden value no matter who the signer is. Then we use Camenisch and Shoup's CCA2-secure encryption scheme and give a proof:

$$PK\{(s_{n-1}, \mathsf{t}, r) : \mathsf{w} = \mathsf{g}_{n-1}^{s_{n-1}} \wedge \mathsf{u}^2 = \mathsf{g}^{2\mathsf{t}} \wedge \mathsf{e}^2 = \mathsf{y}_1^{2\mathsf{t}} \mathsf{h}^{2s_{n-1}} \wedge \mathsf{v}^2 = (\mathsf{y}_2 \mathsf{y}_3^{H(u,e,L)})^{2\mathsf{t}} \wedge$$

$$\hat{w} = h_1^r h_2^{s_{n-1}} \wedge -2^l < s_{n-1} < 2^l\}$$

for convincing the verifier the validity of the encryption (see Section 2.3).

4.1   Verifiably Encrypted Ring Signature

The generation of a VERS consists of two steps. One is producing a conventional ring signature consisting of three algorithms denoted by **RS** = (**RKG, Sig, Ver**), the other is encrypting the ring signature consisting of three algorithms denoted by **EN** = (**Gen, Enc, Dec**) with a zero-knowledge showing the validity of the ring signature's encryption. Suppose there are two rings called R_I and R_J. U_i and U_j denote the users in these two rings respectively. A signer U_k in the ring R_I sends a VERS on a message m to a verifier in the ring R_J. L_I and L_J denote the public-key list of the ring R_I and R_J, and $n_I = |L_I|$ and $n_J = |L_J|$ denote the size of L_I and L_J respectively.

Setup[TTP]: On input the security parameter **Param**, the arbitrator executes the key generation algorithm to output the public key $(\mathsf{n}, \mathsf{g}, \mathsf{y}_1, \mathsf{y}_2, \mathsf{y}_3, \mathsf{h})$ and the private key $(\mathsf{x}_1, \mathsf{x}_2, \mathsf{x}_3)$ under Camenisch and Shoup's encryption scheme [19]. q_A denotes the order of g, and l is an integer such that $2^{l+1} < q_A$. Meanwhile, the arbitrator generates h_1, h_2 and n, which are used in the zero-knowledge proof introduced in Section 2.2 (the modulus n must be large enough to avoid factoring but does not need to depend on **Param**) and publishes $(\mathsf{n}, \mathsf{g}, \mathsf{y}_1, \mathsf{y}_2, \mathsf{y}_3, \mathsf{h}, h_1, h_2, n, l)$.

Setup[User]: The setup of users is similar to the ring signature scheme in Section 2.1. For the user U_i, let $y_i = g_i^{x_i} \bmod p_i$, where the order of g_i is $q_i > 2^{l+1}$. x_i is the secret key and (y_i, p_i, q_i, g_i) is the public key. $H_i : \{0,1\}^* \to \mathbb{Z}_{q_i}$ is a collision-resistant hash function.

RSign: The signer U_k in the ring R_I signs a message m by executing the algorithm below:

1. Randomly select $\alpha \in \mathbb{Z}_{q_k}$, and compute $c_{k+1} = H_{k+1}(L_I, m, g_k^\alpha \bmod p_k)$.
2. For $i = k+1, \ldots, n_I - 1, 0, 1, \ldots, k-1$, randomly select $s_i \in (-2^{(l-2)/\epsilon}, 2^{(l-2)/\epsilon})$, and compute $c_{i+1} = H_{i+1}(L_I, m, g_i^{s_i} y_i^{c_i} \bmod p_i)$.
3. Compute $s_k = \alpha - x_k c_k \bmod q_k$, where $s_k \in (-2^{(l-2)/\epsilon}, 2^{(l-2)/\epsilon})$. If $s_k \notin (-2^{(l-2)/\epsilon}, 2^{(l-2)/\epsilon})$, properly reselect α and run the Step 1 to 3 again until s_k lies in the right interval. The resulting ring signature is $\sigma_I = (c_0, s_0, \ldots, s_{n_I-1})$.

RVer: For $i = 0, \ldots, n_I - 1$, the verifier computes $e_i = g_i^{s_i} y_i^{c_i} \bmod p_i$, then compute $c_{i+1} = H_{i+1}(L_I, m, e_i)$ if $i \neq n_I - 1$. If $c_0 = H_0(L_I, m, e_{n_I-1})$, the verifier accepts σ_I as a valid ring signature, reject otherwise.

PRSig: The algorithm is used for converting a full ring signature σ_I to a verifiably encrypted ring signature θ_I. Let $\hat{h} : \{0,1\}^* \rightarrow \{0,1\}^\eta$ be a collision-resistant hash function and the public label $\mathsf{L} = m||L_I$.

1. Compute $w = g_{n_I-1}^{s_{n_I-1}}$ and encrypt s_{n_I-1} by computing

$$\mathsf{u} = \mathsf{g}^\mathsf{t}, \qquad \mathsf{e} = \mathsf{y}_1^\mathsf{t} \mathsf{h}^{s_{n_I-1}}, \qquad \mathsf{v} = \mathrm{abs}(\mathsf{y}_2 \mathsf{y}_3^{\mathsf{H}(\mathsf{u},\mathsf{e},\mathsf{L})})^\mathsf{t}$$

   under Camenisch and Shoup's encryption scheme.

2. Randomly select $r \in \mathbb{Z}_n$, $r_1 \in (-2^{l-2}, 2^{l-2})$, $r_2 \in (-(n2^\eta)^\epsilon, (n2^\eta)^\epsilon)$ and $r_3 \in (-(n2^\eta)^\epsilon, (n2^\eta)^\epsilon)$, compute $\hat{w} = h_1^r h_2^{s_{n_I-1}} \bmod n$ and $t_1 = g_{n_I-1}^{r_1}$, $t_2 = h_1^{r_2} h_2^{r_1}$, $\mathsf{u}' = \mathsf{g}^{r_3}$, $\mathsf{e}' = \mathsf{y}_1^{r_3} \mathsf{h}^{r_1}$ and $\mathsf{v}' = (\mathsf{y}_2 \mathsf{y}_3^{\mathsf{H}(\mathsf{u},\mathsf{e},\mathsf{L})})^{r_3}$ in their own groups.

3. Compute $\hat{c} = \hat{h}(L_I, m, w, \hat{w}, \mathsf{u}, \mathsf{e}, \mathsf{v}, g_{n_I-1}, \mathsf{g}, h_1, h_2, t_1, t_2, \mathsf{u}'^2, \mathsf{e}'^2, \mathsf{v}'^2)$ and $v_1 = r_1 - \hat{c} s_{n_I-1}$, $v_2 = r_2 - \hat{c}r$, $v_3 = r_3 - \hat{c}t$ in $\mathbb{Z}$. The resulting VERS is $\theta_I = (c_0, s_0, \ldots, s_{n_I-2}, w, \mathsf{u}, \mathsf{e}, \mathsf{v}, \hat{w}, \hat{c}, t_1, t_2, \mathsf{u}', \mathsf{e}', \mathsf{v}', v_1, v_2, v_3)$.

PRVer: The verifier first computes $\hat{c}' = \hat{h}(L_I, m, w, \hat{w}, \mathsf{u}, \mathsf{e}, \mathsf{v}, g_{n_I-1}, \mathsf{g}, h_1, h_2,$ $g_{n_I-1}^{v_1} w^{\hat{c}}, h_1^{v_2} h_2^{v_1} \hat{w}^{\hat{c}}, \mathsf{g}^{2v_3} \mathsf{u}^{2\hat{c}}, \mathsf{y}_1^{2v_3} \mathsf{h}^{2v_1} \mathsf{e}^{2\hat{c}}, (\mathsf{y}_2 \mathsf{y}_3^{\mathsf{H}(\mathsf{u},\mathsf{e},\mathsf{L})})^{2v_3} \mathsf{v}^{2\hat{c}})$, and checks whether $\hat{c}' = \hat{c}$ and $-2^{l-1} < v_1 < 2^{l-1}$. If any condition does not hold, outputs the VERS θ_I is invalid, otherwise computes $e_i = g_i^{s_i} y_i^{c_i}$ for $i = 0, \ldots, n_I - 2$ and $e_{n_I-1} = w y_{n_I-1}^{c_{n_I-1}}$, and then computes $c_{i+1} = H_{i+1}(L_I, m, e_i)$ if $i \neq n_I - 1$. If $c_0 = H_0(L_I, m, e_{n_I-1})$, the verifier accepts θ_I, reject otherwise.

Res: After the verifier shows a proof that he has fillfulled his obligation to the signer, the arbitrator decrypts the ciphertext $(\mathsf{u}, \mathsf{e}, \mathsf{v})$ using its secret key $(\mathsf{x}_1, \mathsf{x}_2, \mathsf{x}_3)$ to extract s_{n_I-1}, and reveals the full ring signature σ_I to the verifier.

4.2 Optimistic Fair Exchange of Ring Signatures

By applying the verifiably encrypted ring signature scheme above, an optimistic fair exchange protocol of ring signatures can easily be set up. Suppose two users U_i and U_j in the rings R_I and R_J respectively exchange their ring signatures on a message m. The optimistic fair exchange protocol proceeds as follows:

1. U_i computes his ring signature $\sigma_I = \mathbf{RSign}(m, L_I, SK_i)$, and converts this ring signature into a VERS $\theta_I = \mathbf{PRSig}(m, L_I, \sigma_I, APK)$ using the arbitrator's public key APK, then sends θ_I to R_J.
2. U_j checks whether $\mathbf{PRVer}(m, L_I, \theta_I, APK) = 1$. If no, U_j quits, otherwise U_j computes his ring signature σ_J and sends it to R_I.
3. U_i checks whether $\mathbf{RVer}(m, L_J, \sigma_J) = 1$, if no, U_i stops the protocol, otherwise U_i sends σ_I to R_J.

4. U_j checks whether $\mathbf{RVer}(m, L_I, \sigma_I)=1$, if yes, U_j accepts this ring signature. If σ_I is invalid or U_j receives nothing from R_I, U_j sends the arbitrator θ_I and σ_J to apply for resolution. The arbitrator first checks whether σ_J is valid, if yes, the arbitrator runs the algorithm $\mathbf{Res}(m, L_I, \theta_I, ASK)$ to recover σ_I, then sends σ_I to R_J and σ_J to R_I. If σ_J is invalid, the arbitrator will send a signal to both R_I and R_J to inform U_i and U_j that the protocol has been terminated.

Note that after Step 1, U_j can decide to carry on the protocol at any time he wants, which might give U_j some advantages. To solve this problem, before the protocol runs, U_i and U_j can set up a time point at which the protocol must be completed.

5   Security Proof

In this session, we prove that our OFE protocol for ring signatures is secure in the multi-user setting under adaptive chosen message, chosen-key and chosen public-key attacks. Let $\mathbf{RS} = (\mathbf{RKG}, \mathbf{RSig}, \mathbf{RVer})$ denote Abe et al.'s ring signature scheme, $\mathbf{EN}=(\mathbf{Gen}, \mathbf{Enc}, \mathbf{Dec})$ denote Camenisch-Shoup public-key encryption scheme, and π be a non-interactive zero-knowledge proof showing the proper encryption of a full ring signature. We have the following theorem:

Theorem 1: The proposed optimistic fair exchange of ring signatures is secure, i.e. satisfies Definitions 2-5, if the underlying $\mathbf{RS}$ is secure with signer-ambiguity and existential unforgeability against adaptive chosen message and chosen public-key attacks, $\mathbf{EN}$ is secure against adaptive chosen ciphertext attacks (CCA2), and π is a simulation-sound non-interactive zero-knowledge proof.

Proof. SECURITY AGAINST SIGNERS: In our OFERS protocol, a valid verifiably encrypted ring signature $\theta = (c_0, s_0, s_1, \cdots, s_{n-2}, w, \mathsf{u}, \mathsf{e}, \mathsf{v}, \hat{w}, \hat{c}, t_1, t_2, \mathsf{u}', \mathsf{e}', \mathsf{v}', v_1, v_2, v_3)$ consists of three parts. The first part $(c_0, s_0, s_1, \cdots, s_{n-2}, w)$ is a 'ring signature', where s_{n-1} is hidden in $w = g_{n-1}^{s_{n-1}}$. The second part $(\mathsf{u}, \mathsf{e}, \mathsf{v})$ is the ciphertext of encrypting s_{n-1} under the arbitrator's public key, where $\mathsf{u} = \mathsf{g}^{\mathsf{t}}$, $\mathsf{e}=\mathsf{y_1^t h}^{s_{n-1}}$ and $\mathsf{v}=\mathsf{abs}(\mathsf{y_2 y_3}^{H(\mathsf{u},\mathsf{e},\mathsf{L})})^{\mathsf{t}}$ for some t. The third part $(\hat{w}, \hat{c}, t_1, t_2, \mathsf{u}', \mathsf{e}', \mathsf{v}', v_1, v_2, v_3)$ provides a non-interactive zero-knowledge proof:

$$\pi = PK\{(s_{n-1}, \mathsf{t}, r) : w = g_{n-1}^{s_{n-1}} \wedge \mathsf{u}^2 = \mathsf{g}^{2\mathsf{t}} \wedge \mathsf{e}^2 = \mathsf{y_1}^{2\mathsf{t}} \mathsf{h}^{2s_{n-1}} \wedge \mathsf{v}^2 = (\mathsf{y_2 y_3}^{H(\mathsf{u},\mathsf{e},\mathsf{L})})^{2\mathsf{t}}$$

$$\wedge\ \hat{w} = h_1^r h_2^{s_{n-1}} \wedge -2^l < s_{n-1} < 2^l\},$$

which shows that the encrypted s_{n-1} is the same value hidden in w. Suppose an adversary $\mathcal{A}$ breaks the security against signers in our OFERS protocol by forging a VERS $\theta = (c_0, s_0, s_1, \cdots, s_{n-2}, w, \mathsf{u}, \mathsf{e}, \mathsf{v}, \hat{w}, \hat{c}, t_1, t_2, \mathsf{u}', \mathsf{e}', \mathsf{v}', v_1, v_2, v_3)$ w.r.t a public-key list L^* generated by himself, where $w = g_{n-1}^{s_{n-1}}$ but $\mathsf{e} = \mathsf{y_1^t h}^{s'_{n-1}}$ for

$s'_{n-1} \neq s_{n-1}$. For each public key in L^*, $\mathcal{A}$ may not know the corresponding private key. According to Definition 2, $\mathcal{A}$ wins the game of *security against signers* if and only if the corresponding full ring signature of θ is $\sigma = (c_0, s_0, s_1, ..., s_{n-2}, s_{n-1})$ and (u, e, v) is decrypted to get s'_{n-1}, where $s'_{n-1} \neq s_{n-1}$. However, this is infeasible due to the *soundness* of the zero-knowledge proof π. Hence our OFERS protocol is secure against signers if π is a non-interactive zero-knowledge proof (NIZK).

SECURITY AGAINST VERIFIERS: Suppose an adversarial verifier $\mathcal{B}$ breaks the security against verifiers in the proposed OFERS protocol. We now construct a distinguisher $\bar{\mathcal{B}}$, who can successfully distinguish the encryption of two messages with the same length of its choice from a challenger in the CCA2 game for Camenisch-Shoup encryption scheme with non-negligible probability. Note that $\bar{\mathcal{B}}$ is allowed to access the decryption oracle O_{Dec} of the encryption scheme. According to Definition 3, $\mathcal{B}$ wins the game of *security against verifiers* if $\mathcal{B}$ produces a valid ring signature σ on a message m under a public-key list L' without asking the resolution oracle O_{Res} any query (m, L', θ). As (m, L', σ) is a successful forgery of $\mathcal{B}$, the situation that $\mathcal{B}$ did not ask any corresponding VERS θ of σ via the partial ring signature signing oracle O_{PRSig} is negligible due to *security against the arbitrator* proved below. Hence we require that $\mathcal{B}$ gets θ from O_{PRSig} here. Now we show how to construct $\bar{\mathcal{B}}$ in detail.

For the given target Camenisch-Shoup encryption scheme **EN=(Gen, Enc, Dec)** with the public key APK, the distinguisher $\bar{\mathcal{B}}$ repeatedly executes Abe et al.'s key generation algorithm, **RKG** $\rightarrow \{PK_i, SK_i\}$, to form a public-key list L. Then $\bar{\mathcal{B}}$ sends (APK, L) to $\mathcal{B}$ as the input of the OFERS protocol. Let k be the total number of the queries that $\mathcal{B}$ issues to O_{PRSig}. After arbitrarily selecting j from $\{1, 2, ..., k\}$, $\bar{\mathcal{B}}$ simulates O_{PRSig}'s response to each query (m_i, L_i) issued by $\mathcal{B}$, where $i = 1, 2, ..., k$, $L_i \subseteq L$ and $n_i = |L_i|$, as follows:

1. If $i \neq j$, $\bar{\mathcal{B}}$ signs the message m_i w.r.t L_i using the private key SK_0 to generate a ring signature $\sigma_i = \mathbf{RSig}(m_i, L_i, SK_0) = (c_{i_0}, s_{i_0}, ..., s_{i_{n_i-1}})$ and returns a VERS $\theta_i = (c_{i_0}, s_{i_0}, ..., s_{i_{n_i-2}}, w_i, \varepsilon_i, \pi_i)$, where $w_i = g_{i_{n_i-1}}^{s_{i_{n_i-1}}}$ and $\varepsilon_i = \mathbf{Enc}_{APK}(s_{i_{n_i-1}})$ under Camenisch-Shoup encryption scheme, and π_i is a NIZK proof showing that ε_i encrypts the same value hidden in w_i, i.e. $s_{i_{n_i-1}}$.

2. If $i = j$, $\bar{\mathcal{B}}$ computes $\sigma_i = \mathbf{RSig}(m_i, L_i, SK_0) = (c_{i_0}, s_{i_0}, ..., s_{i_{n_i-1}})$ and chooses a proper $\hat{s}_{i_{n_i-1}}$ in the same interval of $s_{i_{n_i-1}}$ but $s_{i_{n_i-1}} \neq \hat{s}_{i_{n_i-1}}$. Then $\bar{\mathcal{B}}$ sets $\dot{s}_1 = s_{i_{n_i-1}}$ and $\dot{s}_0 = \hat{s}_{i_{n_i-1}}$ and sends $\dot{s}_1$ and $\dot{s}_0$ to its CCA2 challenger. The challenger returns a ciphertext ε_b, which equals either $\mathbf{Enc}_{APK}(s_{i_{n_i-1}})$ or $\mathbf{Enc}_{APK}(\hat{s}_{i_{n_i-1}})$. After that, $\bar{\mathcal{B}}$ returns $\theta_i = (c_{i_0}, s_{i_0}, ..., s_{i_{n_i-2}}, w_i, \varepsilon_i, \pi_i)$, where $w_i = g_{i_{n_i-1}}^{s_{i_{n_i-1}}}$, $\varepsilon_i = \varepsilon_b$, and π_i is a *simulated* NIZK proof showing that ε_i encrypts the same value hidden in w_i.

The distinguisher $\bar{\mathcal{B}}$ simulates the resolution oracle O_{Res}'s response to $\mathcal{B}$'s queries (m_i, L_i, θ_i) using the decryption oracle O_{Dec} as follows:

1. If π_i is valid and $L_i \neq L_j$, $\bar{\mathcal{B}}$ asks O_{Dec} to extract the plaintext $s_{i_{n_i-1}}$ from ε_i and returns the ring signature $\sigma_i = (c_{i_0}, s_{i_0}, ..., s_{i_{n_i-1}})$ on m_i under L_i.
2. If π_i is valid and $L_i = L_j$, $\bar{\mathcal{B}}$ checks whether $m_i = m_j$. If yes, $\bar{\mathcal{B}}$ aborts the simulation and sends a random bit to its CCA2 challenger. Otherwise, $\bar{\mathcal{B}}$ asks O_{Dec} to extract the plaintext $s_{i_{n_i-1}}$ from ε_i and returns the ring signature $\sigma_i = (c_{i_0}, s_{i_0}, ..., s_{i_{n_i-1}})$ on m_i under L_i.
3. If π_i is invalid, $\bar{\mathcal{B}}$ returns $\mathcal{B}$ a random value.

If $\varepsilon_b = \mathbf{Enc}_{APK}(\hat{s}_{i_{n_i-1}})$ (i.e. $b = 0$), θ_i looks valid but, in fact, $\sigma_i = (c_{i_0}, s_{i_0}, ..., \hat{s}_{i_{n_i-1}})$ is not a valid ring signature because of $\hat{s}_{i_{n_i-1}} \neq s_{i_{n_i-1}}$. The probability of $\mathcal{B}$ forging a valid ring signature on m_j is therefore negligible. If $\varepsilon_b = \mathbf{Enc}_{APK}(s_{i_{n_i-1}})$ (i.e. $b = 1$), ε_j is an valid encryption of $s_{i_{n_i-1}}$ which is a part of a valid ring signature on m_j. The attack environment required by $\mathcal{B}$ is perfectly simulated. Suppose (m, L', σ) is the forgery of $\mathcal{B}$, if $m = m_j$ and $L' = L_j$, $\bar{\mathcal{B}}$ outputs 1 and wins the CCA2 game by indicating that $\dot{s}_1 = s_{i_{n_i-1}}$ is the plaintext of ε_b, otherwise $\bar{\mathcal{B}}$ sends a random bit to the CCA2 challenger. Consequently, if $\mathcal{B}$ wins the game of *security against verifiers* with a non-negligible probability, $\bar{\mathcal{B}}$'s advantage against its CCA2 challenger is also non-negligible. Hence our OFERS protocol is secure against verifiers if the underlying encryption scheme $\mathbf{EN}$ is CCA2-secure.

SECURITY AGAINST THE ARBITRATOR: Suppose an adversarial arbitrator $\mathcal{C}$ breaks the security against the arbitrator in the proposed OFERS protocol. We construct a forger $\bar{\mathcal{C}}$ for Abe et al.'s ring signature scheme $\mathbf{RS} = (\mathbf{RKG}, \mathbf{RSig}, \mathbf{RVer})$ with access to a signing oracle O_{RSig}.

For the initial public-key list L given to the forger $\bar{\mathcal{C}}$, the adversarial arbitrator $\mathcal{C}$ takes L as input and then outputs (ASK^*, APK), where APK is set as the arbitrator's public key for Camenisch-Shoup encryption scheme, and ASK^* is the state information which may not correspond to APK. (ASK^*, APK, L) is the input of the OFERS protocol. After that, $\mathcal{C}$ begins to ask queries to the partial ring signature signing oracle O_{PRSig}, for which the responses can be perfectly simulated by $\bar{\mathcal{C}}$ using O_{RSig}: For any message m_i and any sublist $L'' \subseteq L$, $\bar{\mathcal{C}}$ asks its signing oracle O_{RSig} to get a ring signature σ_i, then encrypts σ_i under APK to get a VERS θ_i and generates the NIZK proof π_i. Finally, $\mathcal{C}$ outputs the forgery (m', σ') such that $\mathbf{RVer}(m', L', \sigma') = 1$ and $(m', L') \notin Query(\mathcal{C}, O_{PRSig})$, which means $\bar{\mathcal{C}}$ never asks O_{RSig} to response a valid ring signature on m' w.r.t L'. In our OFERS protocol, σ' is just the conventional ring signature on m' w.r.t L', so $\bar{\mathcal{C}}$ has succeeded for obtaining σ' as the forgery of the message m' without asking the signing oracle O_{RSig}. It is contradictory to the existential unforgeability of Abe et al.'s ring signature scheme against adaptive chosen message and chosen public-key attacks. Hence our OFERS protocol must be secure against the arbitrator.

SIGNER AMBIGUITY: Suppose that our OFERS protocol does not meet signer ambiguity, which means that there is an unbound adversary $\mathcal{D}$ can tell which private key SK_s was used to produce a given tuple $(m, L, \theta, \sigma, APK)$ with the probability not equal to $1/|L|$. Then, from $\mathcal{D}$ we now construct an adversary $\bar{\mathcal{D}}$

that breaks signer ambiguity of Abe et al.'s ring signature scheme, which thus leads to a contradiction. For a given initial public-key list L in Abe et al.'s scheme we run the key generation algorithm of Chamenisch-Shoup encryption scheme to get the arbitrator's key pair (ASK, APK). For a target (m, L, σ, APK), $\bar{D}$ runs **PRSig** algorithm to get θ, i.e. $\theta \leftarrow \textbf{PRSig}(m, L, \sigma, APK)$. By forwarding $(m, L, \theta, \sigma, APK)$ to D, $\bar{D}$ just outputs the index returned by D as its guess which private key was used to issue (m, L, σ, APK). It is easy to see that $\bar{D}$ breaks the signer-ambiguity of Abe et al.'s ring signature scheme with the exact same probability as D breaks the signer-ambiguity of our OFERS protocol. □

Remark 2. In the proofs above, we do not give the specific details about the underlying (Abe et al.'s) ring signature scheme and (Camenisch and Shoup's) encryption scheme, as our construction (specified in Section 4) can be extended to a generic scheme, i.e. based on any secure ring signature scheme and encryption scheme, the associated proofs can be obtained by simply adapting the proofs above. In addition, from our proofs we can see that a secure ring signature scheme with signer-ambiguity does not necessarily guarantee an OFERS protocol preserving the same property. The counterexample is very simple: just modify our OFERS protocol such that the VERS θ includes a public key PK_i which indicates that the private key SK_i was used to issue the corresponding ring signature σ. For this scheme, it is not difficult to see that the proofs for the first three properties still hold, but not for signer-ambiguity since, with the reminder PK_i, the adversary can tell with the probability 1 that SK_i was used to issue a tuple $(m, L, \theta, \sigma, APK)$. Further discussions on these two issues will be given in the full version of the paper.

6   Conclusion

In this paper, for achieving better privacy in optimistic fair exchange, we present the first solution of optimistic fair exchange of ring signatures (OFERS) by first formally defining its security model in the multi-user setting under adaptive chosen message, chosen-key, and chosen public-key attacks. We have also proposed a concrete scheme of verifiably encrypted ring signature (VERS) and used it to build an optimistic fair exchange protocol. The proposed scheme is proved to be *secure against signers, verifiers* and *the arbitrator* and satisfy the property *signer-ambiguity* under our security definitions. As future work, it is interesting to design efficient OFERS protocols for different types of signatures, such as Abe et al.'s RSA-based ring signatures or mixed-type ring signatures [8], and achieve other more security properties in OFERS, e.g. abuse-freeness.

References

1. Asokan, N., Schunter, M., Waidner, M.: Optimistic protocols for fair exchange. In: CCS 1997 Proceedings of the 4th ACM Conference on Computer and Communications Security, pp. 7–17 (1997)
2. Boneh, D., Gentry, C., Lynn, B.: Aggregate and Verifiably Encrypted Signatures from Bilinear Maps. In: Biham, E. (ed.) EUROCRYPT 2003. LNCS, vol. 2656, pp. 416–432. Springer, Heidelberg (2003)

3. Rivest, R.L., Shamir, A., Tauman, Y.: How to Leak a Secret. In: Boyd, C. (ed.) ASIACRYPT 2001. LNCS, vol. 2248, pp. 552–565. Springer, Heidelberg (2001)
4. Asokan, N., Shoup, V., Waidner, M.: Optimistic fair exchange of digital signatures. IEEE Journal on Selected Areas in Communication 18, 593–610 (2000)
5. Dodis, Y., Lee, P.J., Yum, D.H.: Optimistic Fair Exchange in a Multi-user Setting. In: Okamoto, T., Wang, X. (eds.) PKC 2007. LNCS, vol. 4450, pp. 118–133. Springer, Heidelberg (2007)
6. Huang, Q., Yang, G., Wong, D.S., Susilo, W.: Efficient Optimistic Fair Exchange Secure in the Multi-user Setting and Chosen-Key Model without Random Oracles. In: Malkin, T. (ed.) CT-RSA 2008. LNCS, vol. 4964, pp. 106–120. Springer, Heidelberg (2008)
7. Bleichenbacher, D.: Chosen Ciphertext Attacks against Protocols Based on the RSA Encryption Standard PKCS #1. In: Krawczyk, H. (ed.) CRYPTO 1998. LNCS, vol. 1462, pp. 1–12. Springer, Heidelberg (1998)
8. Abe, M., Ohkubo, M., Suzuki, K.: 1-out-of-n Signatures from a Variety of Keys. In: Zheng, Y. (ed.) ASIACRYPT 2002. LNCS, vol. 2501, pp. 415–432. Springer, Heidelberg (2002)
9. Ateniese, G.: Verifiable Encryption of Digital Signatures and Appliciation. ACM Transactions on Information and System Security 7, 1–20 (2004)
10. Bellare, M., Goldreich, O.: On Defining Proofs of Knowledge. In: Brickell, E.F. (ed.) CRYPTO 1992. LNCS, vol. 740, pp. 390–420. Springer, Heidelberg (1993)
11. Camenisch, J., Michels, M.: Separability and Efficiency for Generic Group Signature Schemes (Extended Abstract). In: Wiener, M. (ed.) CRYPTO 1999. LNCS, vol. 1666, pp. 413–430. Springer, Heidelberg (1999)
12. Barić, N., Pfitzmann, B.: Collision-Free Accumulators and Fail-Stop Signature Schemes without Trees. In: Fumy, W. (ed.) EUROCRYPT 1997. LNCS, vol. 1233, pp. 480–494. Springer, Heidelberg (1997)
13. Fujisaki, E., Okamoto, T.: Statistical Zero Knowledge Protocols to Prove Modular Polynomial Relations. In: Kaliski Jr., B.S. (ed.) CRYPTO 1997. LNCS, vol. 1294, pp. 16–30. Springer, Heidelberg (1997)
14. Camenisch, J., Michels, M.: Proving in Zero-Knowledge that a Number Is the Product of Two Safe Primes. In: Stern, J. (ed.) EUROCRYPT 1999. LNCS, vol. 1592, pp. 107–122. Springer, Heidelberg (1999)
15. Gennaro, R., Krawczyk, H., Rabin, T.: RSA-Based Undeniable Signatures. In: Kaliski Jr., B.S. (ed.) CRYPTO 1997. LNCS, vol. 1294, pp. 132–149. Springer, Heidelberg (1997)
16. Naccache, D., Stern, J.: A new public key cryptosystem based on higher resudues. In: 5th ACM Conference on Computer and Communications Security, pp. 59–66 (1998)
17. Okamoto, T., Uchiyama, S.: A New Public-Key Cryptosystem as Secure as Factoring. In: Nyberg, K. (ed.) EUROCRYPT 1998. LNCS, vol. 1403, pp. 308–318. Springer, Heidelberg (1998)
18. Paillier, P.: Public-Key Cryptosystems Based on Composite Degree Residuosity Classes. In: Stern, J. (ed.) EUROCRYPT 1999. LNCS, vol. 1592, pp. 223–238. Springer, Heidelberg (1999)
19. Camenisch, J., Shoup, V.: Practical Verifiable Encryption and Decryption of Discrete Logarithms. In: Boneh, D. (ed.) CRYPTO 2003. LNCS, vol. 2729, pp. 126–144. Springer, Heidelberg (2003)
20. Goldwasser, S., Micali, S., Rivest, R.: A digital signature scheme secrue against adaptive chosen-message attacks. SIAM Journal on Computing 17, 281–308 (1988)

Efficient U-Prove Implementation
for Anonymous Credentials on Smart Cards

Wojciech Mostowski* and Pim Vullers**

Institute for Computing and Information Sciences,
Digital Security group, Radboud University Nijmegen, The Netherlands
{woj,pim}@cs.ru.nl
http://www.ru.nl/ds/

Abstract. In this paper we discuss an efficient implementation of anonymous credentials on smart cards. In general, privacy-preserving protocols are computationally intensive and require the use of advanced cryptography. Implementing such protocols for smart cards involves a trade-off between the requirements of the protocol and the capabilities of the smart card. In this context we concentrate on the implementation of Microsoft's U-Prove technology on the MULTOS smart card platform. Our implementation aims at making the smart card independent of any other resources, either computational or storage. In contrast, Microsoft suggests an alternative approach based on device-protected tokens which only uses the smart card as a security add-on. Given our very good performance results we argue that our approach should be considered in favour of Microsoft's one. Furthermore we provide a brief comparison between Java Card and MULTOS which illustrates our choice to implement this technology on the latter more flexible and low-level platform rather than the former.

Keywords: anonymous credentials, smart cards, U-Prove, MULTOS, Java Card.

1 Introduction

An effort to provide citizens with electronic signature (e-signature) capable identity cards is currently in progress in many European Union countries. The first countries to introduce such cards were Belgium and Estonia. More recently (November 2010) Germany introduced a new generation identity card [8] for their citizens, which also provides a limited form of anonymous attributes for improved privacy. Although Dutch identity cards already contain a chip with personal data, like in the e-passport, there is no e-signature functionality available yet. The Dutch government is currently working on adding e-signature capability, and possibly support for attributes, to such a card.

The e-signature application on the identity cards serves two major purposes. First, what is in the name, they can be used to digitally sign documents, for

---

* Sponsored by the NL-Net Foundation through the OV-chipkaart project.
** Sponsored by Trans Link Systems/Open Ticketing.

M. Rajarajan et al. (Eds.): SecureComm 2011, LNICST 96, pp. 243–260, 2012.
© Institute for Computer Sciences, Social Informatics and Telecommunications Engineering 2012

example tax return forms. Next, and probably most, they are used to provide strong authentication of the owner of the card, mainly for logging into governmental web services. But this use of signing or authentication certificates also involves a restriction of this use case. In the Netherlands the use of the social security number, which is integrated in the identity card, is by law only allowed within the government domain.

Therefore we study methods of authentication and authorisation which preserve the privacy of the card holder and restrict linkability of card uses. For example, the card holder may wish to prove his age category (an adult over 18 or a senior over 65) without revealing his actual date of birth. One way to achieve this is to use attributes instead of identities. A number of technologies [2,6,9] have been developed based on this idea, but the main focus has been on the cryptography and less on (efficient) implementations. The implementations which have been made are mainly for ordinary computers. Our research focuses on implementing and using such technologies on smart cards. This approach offers various new use cases, but also faces difficulties due to the limited capabilities of smart card platforms and hardware.

The work that we present here targets the U-Prove technology developed by Brands [6] and now owned and marketed by Microsoft [5]. Out of the existing privacy-aware protocols [5, 7, 11], this one has not yet been implemented on a smart card in its current specification. The current U-Prove specification [22] does support the *use* of a smart card as an additional protection device. In this scenario the card performs only a fraction of the protocol run. This is motivated by the constrained resources of smart cards and was already described by Brands in 2000 [6]. In Table 1 this approach is compared with our approach which offers the full protocol implementation on a smart card. We provide the full implementation of the U-Prove protocols to solve the main disadvantage of Microsoft's approach: the smart card cannot be used independently, since it is tied to computational (and storage) resources external to the card. This means that it requires a specific, card matching terminal, like the card owner's PC, to run the protocols.

Table 1. Comparison between Microsoft's *device-protected U-Prove token* approach and our *U-Prove token on a smart card* approach

	Microsoft's approach	our approach
characteristics	add-on security measure	full protocol implementation
card stores	single device-protection attribute	all attributes, other token values
card computes	short zero-knowledge proof for the device-protection attribute	complete presentation proof
advantages	fast, lightweight, protect any number of dynamically issued tokens using pre-issued devices	independent use of the card, no need to trust the terminal
disadvantages	trusted terminal required	requires more card resources (?)

For performance our primary goal was to keep the running times of the protocol on the card sufficient for on-line use.[1] Despite the obvious efficiency concern caused by our choice to implement the full U-Prove protocols on a smart card, we managed to provide a very efficient implementation. Our worst-case execution time of the protocol on the card (with five attributes) is 0.87 seconds. Configuring the implementation for a smaller number of attributes improves this running time considerably. This makes our implementation efficient enough to be possibly considered also for the use in e-ticketing, where transactions with a card should be at or below 0.3 seconds.[2] This discards the disadvantage of our approach mentioned in Table 1, offering an overall better solution than Microsoft's approach. Thus, Microsoft is advised to change its approach to smart card support for U-Prove. Our good result is mostly due to the choice of the smart card implementation platform. Because of its more convenient API, we used a MULTOS smart card [16] in favour of the more popular Java Card platform [14]. The former has been overlooked as a prototyping platform whereas the latter exhibited questionable efficiency in some previous privacy-friendly protocol implementations [4, 25, 28].

The rest of this paper is organised as follows. Section 2 provides the necessary background on privacy-preserving protocols, related work, and open smart card platforms. We describe our MULTOS U-Prove implementation in Section 3, focusing on the implementation challenges without explaining the U-Prove protocols in detail.[3] Section 4 discusses the results of our work and compares Java Card with MULTOS. Further steps in our research on privacy-preserving protocols are presented in Section 5, and finally Section 6 concludes the paper.

2   Background

Before diving into our implementation of U-Prove we first introduce anonymous credentials and some alternatives for the U-Prove technology. Furthermore we provide some background information on smart cards and explain why we opted for the MULTOS platform instead of the more popular Java Card platform.

2.1   Anonymous Credentials

A credential is an attestation of qualification, competence, or authority issued by a third party, the *issuer*, to an individual. This individual, the *prover*, can subsequently use this credential to prove/demonstrate his qualification, competence, or authority to another party, the *verifier*. Examples of credentials are a membership certificate, such as a passport or employee card, or some kind

---

[1] The proving scenario should be fast (less then a second) whereas the less frequently run issuance scenario can take a few seconds to complete a transaction.

[2] http://www.smartcardalliance.org/resources/lib/
Transit_Financial_Linkages_WP.pdf

[3] A detailed description of the protocols can be found in the U-Prove cryptographic specification [5] and the mathematical background is addressed in Brands' book [6].

of ticket to obtain some service, such as a cinema ticket or a public transport ticket. These credentials are often bound to a specific person, by means of a name and/or picture (e.g. for a passport or public transport year pass), but this is not necessarily the case (e.g. for a paper train ticket).

Anonymous credentials have the same properties as any other credentials, except that they do not reveal the identity of the prover, i.e. they provide *authorisation without identification*. In the real world this is fairly common, think of coins or public transport tickets, but in the digital world this concept is rare. This is mostly because the authenticity of a credential is usually achieved by using digital signatures which uniquely identify the issuer and prover. It is however possible to achieve anonymous digital credentials by using more advanced cryptography, as described for the first time by Chaum [13] in 1984. In the remainder of this section we will introduce a number of recent technologies which provide anonymous credentials.

U-Prove. Stefan Brands provided the first integral description of the U-Prove technology in his thesis [6] in 2000, after which he founded the company Credentica in 2002 to implement and sell this technology. Microsoft acquired Credentica in 2008 and published the U-Prove protocol specification [5] in 2010 under the Open Specification Promise[4] together with open source reference software development kits (SDKs) in C# and Java.

The U-Prove technology is centred around a so-called U-Prove token. This token serves as a pseudonym for the prover. It contains a number of attributes which can be selectively disclosed to a verifier. Hence the prover decides which attributes to show and which to withhold (e.g. one can reveal the birth date, but not the residence address). Besides the attributes the token contains two information fields, one defined by the issuer, and one by the prover. These fields are always disclosed and can be used to provide some meta data such as a validity date of the token. Finally there is the token's public-key, which aggregates all information in the token, and a signature from the issuer over this public-key to ensure the authenticity.

A previous attempt to implement this technology on a smart card by Tews and Jacobs [28], based on Brands' description [6], resulted in a highly involved application with running times in the order of 5–10 seconds which make it not really usable in practice. Our implementation, which we describe in Section 3, not only has a much better performance but is also, except from some minimal limitations, compatible with the development kits released recently by Microsoft.

Idemix and DAA. Identity mixer (Idemix) is an anonymous credential system, based on the Camenisch-Lysyanskaya anonymous credentials scheme [9, 10, 19] developed at IBM Research in Zürich that enables strong authentication and privacy at the same time. The first prototype [11] was developed in 2002 and has been improved over the years. An open source Java implementation of Idemix was released in 2010 as part of the Open Innovation Initiative.[5]

---

[4] http://www.microsoft.com/interop/osp/

[5] http://www.zurich.ibm.com/news/10/innovation.html

Direct anonymous attestation (DAA) [7] is a technology based on Idemix. It allows a user to convince a verifier that she uses a platform that has embedded a certified hardware module.[6] The protocol protects the user's privacy: if she talks to the same verifier twice, the verifier is not able to tell whether or not he communicates with the same user as before or with a different one.

In 2009 Bichsel et al. [4] implemented Idemix on a Java Card whereas Sterckx et al. [25] did the same for DAA. They provide the first proper implementations of anonymous credentials on smart cards. The major drawback of these implementations is the running time of several seconds which is still too much for being really practical.

Self-blindable Credentials. The idea behind the self-blindable credentials by Verheul [29] is that every time a credential is used it is blinded such that two occurrences of the same credential cannot be recognised. This in contrast to the U-Prove token which is the same in each transaction, and hence serves as a pseudonym. The benefit of this approach is that the use of such credentials is untraceable. Furthermore they can be efficiently implemented on a smart card [2, 17] using elliptic curve cryptography (ECC), providing the best performance results thus far.

The drawback is that, due to the untraceable nature of this technology, incorporating revocation is hard and very costly [18]. Furthermore, ECC support on smart cards is very limited making prototyping very hard. Finally, the technology is fairly new compared to U-Prove and Idemix, and not backed by a big company which offers support for it.

German Identity Card. The protocols that we have described so far are (to the best of our knowledge) the only candidates providing anonymity by design and ones that *could* be implemented on a smart card. However, we should also shortly mention an approach of the German identity card that is actually implemented and being rolled out since November 2010, where a limited form of anonymous attribute use is achieved by altering the existing ECC based electronic identity protocols by sharing private ECC keys across large batches of cards [3]. The protocol itself provides restricted access to the card by means of the so-called card verifiable certificate mechanism [8] and allows for selective disclosure of attributes, depending on the rights specified in the certificate (e.g. an alcohol shop is only authorised to check for the "over 18" attribute). Signed attributes are partly anonymous because of the sharing of the signing keys between batches of cards, such that a signature cannot be linked to a single card.

2.2   Smart Cards

One of the goals of our research is to assess how fast privacy-friendly protocols are when run on a smart card. Hence implementing our prototypes requires an open

---

[6] DAA has been adopted in 2004 by the Trusted Computing Group in the Trusted Platform Module specification as the method for remote authentication of a hardware module.

smart card platform that also provides the necessary cryptographic hardware support – previous research [28] clearly shows that, in terms of performance, purely software based prototypes are not sufficient for realistic use. In practice that leaves us with two possible smart card platforms, Java Card and MULTOS, described below. We motivate the use of the latter one for the work presented in this paper.

Regardless of the programming technology, all smart cards provide the same external functionality. A smart card is an embedded device that communicates with the environment through Application Protocol Data Units (APDUs) – byte arrays formatted according to the ISO7816 specification. Most notably, the APDUs constrain the communication payload to roughly 256 bytes in each direction for a single APDU exchange. The permanent storage of the card (E²PROM memory) is considered highly secure, accessible only through the APDU commands offered by the application, which in turn are subject to any authentication and secure messaging requirements that the card application may impose.

Java Card. Java Card is a now well-established smart card platform based on a tailored, cut-down version of Java (hence the name) [14]. One of the main features of Java Card is software interoperability. On top of the operating system of the card resides a Java Card virtual machine, compliant with the official specification [27], that executes Java byte code. In parallel, the platform defines the Java Card API [26] that provides the developer an interface to the hardware of the smart card. In terms of the programming and deployment of applications Java Cards are (almost) fully independent of the underlying hardware and operating system of the card. Large numbers of actual smart card products are implemented on Java Cards based on a variety of chips coming from different manufactures. Precise data on the number of deployed Java Cards or MULTOS cards are hard to find, but the Java Card Forum[7] claims there are already over a billion Java Cards in use.

The Java Card API is carefully designed to support the smart card environment and has several built-in security features. For example, it provides predefined Java classes for hardware supported cryptographic key storage (with possible internal encryption). To account for different hardware profiles of a card, parts of the Java Card API implementation are made optional. For example, one card may support both RSA and ECC in hardware and expose this functionality through the API, while another card may only support RSA, in which case all API calls related to ECC are not available and report a corresponding Java exception instead.

This brings us to the main shortcoming of the Java Card platform from our point of view. The Java Card API is predefined and *closed*. Any hardware functionality that is not exposed through the imposed Java Card API, is not accessible to the developer by any other means. For example, for RSA based cryptography it is only possible to generate public and private keys of predefined

---

[7] http://www.javacardforum.org/

RSA lengths (512, 1024 bits, etc.) and perform full RSA de-/encryption or signing with these keys according to standard protocols, such as RSA-PKCS. The more primitive operations that build up RSA operations, such as modulo prime inverse or exponentiation, are not available. Since all of the protocols that we are interested in require access to such cryptographic operations (in large modulo prime and/or EC domains), this is a practical show stopper. We are not the only ones to note this. For example, in [25] similar problems regarding the development of DAA on a Java Card are reported. Even more, an efficient implementation of the e-passport standard [8] on a Java Card also requires cryptographic routines not anticipated by the standard Java Card API. In this case, due to high demand, Java Card producers decided to enrich the Java Card API with proprietary extensions to support e-passport standards [21]. But this only solves the problem for one application type and, moreover, makes the platform non-interoperable.

MULTOS. The design principles of the MULTOS platform [16, 20] are similar to those of Java Card. A hardware independent execution platform is run on top of the operating system of the card. Similarly to Java Card byte-code, a MULTOS card executes specific op-codes of the MULTOS Execution Language (MEL) and exposes smart card specific interfaces to the developers through dedicated MEL op-codes. These op-codes already provide a full and detailed API to the card's hardware. Most of the primitive operations that the hardware can possibly support are reflected in the corresponding MEL op-codes. Thus, MEL provides the full base for programming MULTOS cards, and a skilled developer can easily write programs for the card already in the MEL assembly. However, the MULTOS development tools also provide programming interfaces to C and Java. Applications in these languages are translated/compiled by the tools into MEL op-codes and can then be run on a card.

Similar to the Java Card API routines, some of the MEL op-codes are specified to be optional, mostly ones responsible for cryptographic operations. A particular MULTOS card may or may not support the optional op-codes. For our implementation we used development cards based on the SLE66 chip from Infineon. This particular MULTOS implementation [1] supports a wide range of modulo arithmetic operations, a range which is sufficient to fully support all of the U-Prove calculations. This is the main reason to choose MULTOS in the context of this work – its more low-level and flexible API as opposed to less flexible and more high level Java Card API.

Our choice is to use the MULTOS C interface to do our prototype implementation of U-Prove. For simple smart card applications the C interface seems to provide an easier programming environment than Java, and although C programming platforms are not type safe by definition (as opposed to Java), per application memory safety is guaranteed by the MULTOS platform, regardless of the high-level language used during development.

3   Implementing U-Prove for Smart Cards

U-Prove consists of two protocols. We briefly introduce these protocols here. A detailed description of the protocols and the necessary computations can be found in the U-Prove cryptographic specification [5].

During the first protocol, the issuing protocol, the U-Prove token is constructed by combining the public key of the issuer with the attributes. To authenticate this token it is signed by the issuer. However, just signing the token would allow the issuer to later recognise the resulting signed token. Therefore a blind signature scheme [12] is applied such that the issuer does not learn the exact value of the resulting signature. As a result of this protocol the prover now has a signed token containing his attributes.

The second protocol, the presenting or proving protocol, is used to present a number of attributes from the token. During this protocol the prover presents his token to a verifier together with a selection of its attributes. To verify the authenticity of the token the verifier checks the signature of the issuer. Finally the prover needs to prove that the presented attributes are actually the attributes contained in the token (and thus the signed attributes). For this purpose the prover constructs a zero-knowledge proof [15] in which he proves that he knows all the attributes contained in the token, including those not disclosed to the verifier. Due to the zero-knowledge properties of the proof the verifier does not learn anything about the attributes not disclosed to him. He is, however, able to verify, using the proof and the disclosed attributes, that the attributes actually correspond to those stored in the token.

3.1   U-Prove and Smart Cards

The use of U-Prove in combination with a smart card was already envisioned by Brands [6] and published by Microsoft in the latest release of the U-Prove cryptographic specification [22]. Their idea is to use a smart card (or even any trusted computing device) as a manner of protecting U-Prove tokens, which they then call device-protected tokens. This is achieved by having the device contribute one attribute to the token. The actual value of this attribute is, like a private key, only known by the device and will always be hidden. Therefore the device is required during the proving protocol, since a prover has to prove knowledge of *all* attributes contained in a token.

Besides adding an additional layer of protection the U-Prove technology overview [24] describes a number of other benefits gained when using device-protected tokens. For example, a device can be used to enforce dynamic policies or prevent the use of a token at a blacklisted website. It also helps to enforce non-transferability of tokens by having the prover authenticate to the device before allowing it to be used in a protocol interaction. Another option, especially interesting for smart cards, is to use the device as a carrier, or secure roaming store, for entire U-Prove tokens and not one attribute. This way the U-Prove token is always available when needed.

This last feature of a device-protected U-Prove token has one major drawback, namely one will need to trust the device that is used to perform the proving protocol. This is because the actual attribute values are used during the computation steps of this protocol. Hence the device must release all information, except its own special attribute, during a protocol run. When using a personal computer this might be acceptable, but in scenarios where the device should be used directly with a verifier, for example at a public transport gate, or at a vending machine for cigarettes, this turns out to be problematic. Since these are the areas of use which are most interesting for us, we decided to develop our own implementation of the full prover protocol specification on a smart card instead of using Microsoft's more limited approach.

3.2   U-Prove on MULTOS

A very general view of our implementation of the U-Prove technology is that it provides storage for preloaded (e.g. cryptographic domain parameters) and calculated (e.g. generated keys) values of the protocols, as well as attribute storage, and, more importantly, a sequence of hash and modulo prime arithmetic operations to execute the corresponding stages of the protocols. These arithmetic operations are the core of the performance considerations of our implementation. A few hashing operations are executed and multiple exponents over numbers in a large prime field have to be calculated during a proving protocol run. For example, the commitment a to blinding values w_i is calculated according to the following formula.

$$a = \mathcal{H}(h^{w_0} \prod_{i \in U} g_i^{w_i} \bmod p) \tag{1}$$

Here U is the set of attributes *not* to be disclosed, hence disclosing less attributes requires more exponentiation and multiplications modulo prime number p. The range of these calculations is also restricted by the limits of our MULTOS implementation platform. Namely, on our development cards we are limited to a modulus size of 1024 bits for modulo arithmetic,[8] and SHA-1 is the only built-in hashing algorithm available. Although this may sound restrictive, it also makes the choice of the U-Prove protocol configuration (protocol parameters) for our implementation easy. We have simply chosen to implement the protocols using the domain parameters fixed to the same ones as in the default configuration of the official U-Prove SDK reference implementation and official U-Prove test vectors [23], that is 1024 bits for modulus size and SHA-1 for hashing to match with the capabilities of the card.

To make the U-Prove protocol calculations efficient the smart card memory issues have be to taken into account. The first and most important aspect of developing *any* smart card application is the allocation of memory. The two rules of thumb are:

---

[8] The card actually supports up to 2048 bits, but then during exponentiation only small enough exponents can be used, a requirement which the U-Prove operations do not satisfy.

1. the total memory allocation should be optimised, and
2. to prevent memory exhaustion during operation there should be no dynamic memory allocation.

Furthermore, for any smart card platform the developer is usually offered a few kilobytes of RAM memory, which is normally used for fast "scratch-pad" computations and whose contents disappear on every power down (in MULTOS this is called session memory). The other kind of memory is the E^2PROM, which provides the permanent storage for the card (in MULTOS called static memory). Substantially more E^2PROM than RAM is usually available on a card, in the range of tens of kilobytes. However, it is slower than RAM, especially during writing. Moreover, on the hardware level E^2PROM is updated in block mode, hence repeated updating of single bytes of this memory (e.g. with a **for** loop) further hinders efficiency.

Considering the size of the U-Prove data that is used in the protocols and the requirements of the MULTOS cryptographic routines (all data for a cryptographic operation needs to be in one continuous array) the first thing to take care of is a careful split of the card data between E^2PROM and RAM. Only 960 *bytes* of RAM are available on our development cards, compared to 36 *kilo*bytes of E^2PROM. The most frequent use case of the card is the execution of the proving protocol, hence this is where good use of RAM is highly desirable. For that we limited the maximum number of stored attributes to 5 and then we ensured that all data participating in the proving protocol is allocated in RAM, as shown in Listing 1.1. After this the total RAM requirement for this protocol is 756 bytes, which just safely fits within the RAM available on the card.

Listing 1.1. Declaration of the variables residing in RAM

#pragma melsession // *These vars will sit in RAM*

union {
    ... // *Overlapping temporary storage for other parts of the protocol*
    unsigned char array[328];
} temp_ram; // *Temporary storage, 328 bytes needed in the worst case*

unsigned char UD[MAX_ATTR]; // *Attribute disclosure selection, 5 bytes*

NUMBER_QSIZE w_i[MAX_ATTR + 1]; // $w_0, \ldots, w_n$ *(total 6*21 bytes)*
NUMBER_QSIZE r_i[MAX_ATTR + 1]; // $r_0, \ldots, r_n$ *(total 6*21 bytes)*

NUMBER_QSIZE a, c; // *a and c values (2*21 bytes)*
NUMBER_PSIZE t; // *Another temporary storage (129 bytes)*

#pragma melstatic // *The following will sit in E^2PROM*
...

Listing 1.2. The function to compute commitment a from (1)

```
void computeCommitmentA(void) {
    ModularExponentiation(QSIZE_BYTES, PSIZE_BYTES,
            w_i[0].number, p.number, h.number, t.number);
    for(int i = 0; i < MAX_ATTR; i++) {
        if(UD[i]) continue; // i is in D, not interested
        ModularExponentiation(QSIZE_BYTES, PSIZE_BYTES,
                w_i[i+1].number, p.number, g_i[i+1].number, temp_ram.vars.a.number);
        ModularMultiplication(PSIZE_BYTES,
                t.number, temp_ram.vars.a.number, p.number);
    }

    // t now contains h^{w_0} ∏_{i∈U} g_i^{w_i} mod p
    int len = putNumberIntoArray(PSIZE_BYTES, t.number, temp_ram.array);

    // a = H(t) (mod q)
    SHA1(len, a.number, temp_ram.array);
    ModularReduction(QSIZE_BYTES, QSIZE_BYTES, a.number, q.number);
}
```

The initialisation and issuance protocol require more scratch-pad memory than the available RAM, hence we were forced to use E^2PROM there. Moreover, the issuance protocol makes use of E^2PROM for permanent storage of the issued U-Prove token and other permanent protocol parameters (prime numbers p, q, etc.). Because of the block mode characteristics of E^2PROM updates mentioned before, it is particularly important to use predefined MEL functionality for block operations (e.g. ADDN, COPYN, etc.). This way the E^2PROM memory is updated in block mode by the platform and execution speed can be maintained. In contrast, updating E^2PROM one byte at a time with a **for** loop causes dramatic performance loss – for updates of kilobytes of memory execution time is counted in seconds. The size of E^2PROM is not an issue – 36kB is more than sufficient to store the static data of a U-Prove token with 5 attributes each sized at the maximum of 255 bytes.

This completes the efficiency considerations for our implementation. Otherwise the implementation of the U-Prove protocols is rather straightforward in the MULTOS environment and mostly entails direct calls to the MULTOS API. An example is given in Listing 1.2, which computes formula (1).

3.3   Integration into the Microsoft U-Prove SDK

The previous section described the implementation of the U-Prove protocols which mainly concerns storage and the mathematical computations. This is, however, not sufficient to use it in combination with Microsoft's U-Prove SDK. We need to bridge between the high-level Java interfaces defined in this SDK and the low-level APDU interface of the smart card.

We designed the low-level APDU interface to be as simple as possible. Essentially it has to provide three types of functionality: (1) sending data to the card, (2) ask the card to perform the necessary computations, and (3) retrieve the results from the card. The second type of the interface functionality is easiest, we just defined an APDU instruction for each of the steps in the protocols. For transferring data to and from the card we restricted the values to the maximum amount of data that can be transferred in one APDU (255 bytes). This allows us to just define one APDU instruction per variable, parametrised only with the index if needed (for example g_i), for setting or getting a value.

Finally we need to bind this low level APDU API to the interfaces and data types provided by the U-Prove SDK. Luckily the SDK just uses byte arrays for the external access to the data types such that no additional conversion is needed. The only thing that needs to be done for a data type, for example IssuerParameters, is that the setter and getter have to be divided into the individual APDU instructions, for example the setPublicKey and setEncodingBytes instructions.

All this functionality has been combined into a single Java class which provides setters and getters for the data stored on the card as well as methods for the protocol steps. Using the Java built-in smart card library it serves as an interface between our MULTOS implementation and the Microsoft SDK.

4   Results and Performance Analysis

The two most important factors for us to test in our U-Prove implementation were correctness of the protocol calculations (obviously) and the speed. Testing the correctness was fairly easy. Since we interfaced our card to Microsoft's U-Prove SDK we could simply test it by invoking the protocol runs from the SDK and check the results. During the first stages of the development partial protocol calculations were verified with the test vectors provided with the U-Prove SDK [23]. In the whole process a few corner case problems with our calculations surfaced that required minor corrections.

As we stated in the previous section, for speed we concentrated our implementation efforts on the every day use case of the application, i.e. the attribute proving protocol. However, we also strived to optimise the rest of the protocols to maintain speed also during the initialisation and issuance parts. For the performance analysis, we executed a number of full protocol runs (initialisation, issuance, proving) on the card in various configurations. First of all we varied the number of stored attributes on the card, then within this attribute range we varied the number of (un)disclosed attributes. As shown in Figure 1 this resulted in a running time of 3.6 and 5.5 seconds for the issuance of a U-Prove token with respectively 2 and 5 attributes. The dark grey area on the graph indicates the core running time of the protocol calculations on the card, whereas light grey indicates the remaining overhead. This overhead consists of transferring data to the card and communicating the results of the protocol run between the card and PC.

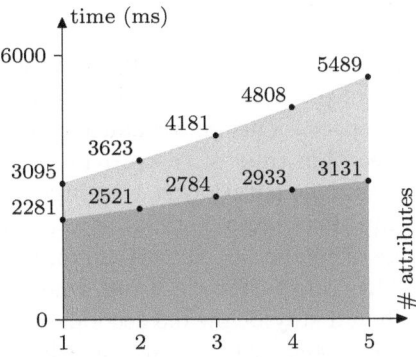

Fig. 1. U-Prove token issuance times (: computation, : overhead)

Correspondingly, the cumulative results for the attribute proving protocol are shown in Figure 2. What can be seen in these graphs is that under "full load" our implementation executes the complete proving protocol in just under 0.9 seconds (graph 2(b)). In this worst-case scenario 5 attributes are stored on the card, none of which are disclosed during the protocol run. In other words, the U-Prove token is only validated for its authenticity without revealing any attribute data. Such a scenario is not very likely to occur in reality. In a more likely scenario at least one or two attributes are going to be disclosed and we can also assume that a U-Prove token will contain less attributes (or, that a large number of attributes can be split into several separate U-Prove tokens). As the graphs show, reducing the number of stored attributes improves the running time at a rate of 100 milliseconds per attribute, and also that the performance increases along with increasing the number of disclosed attributes, roughly 50 milliseconds per each extra disclosed attribute. Overall, this brings the total

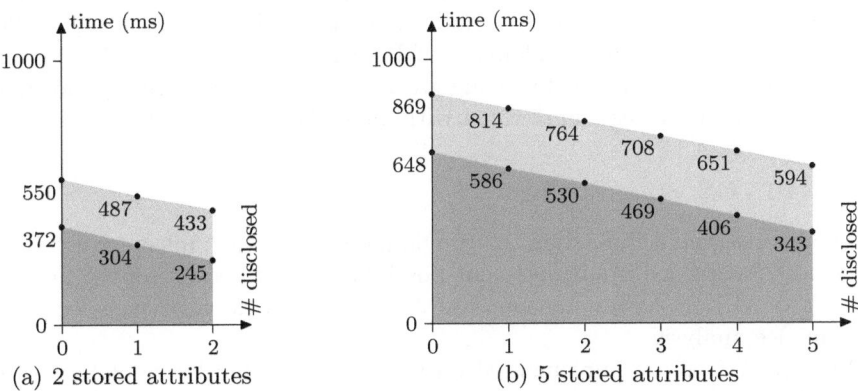

Fig. 2. Attribute proving times for different configurations (/ : same as in Fig. 1)

execution time for a two attribute token disclosing one attribute to under 0.5 seconds (graph 2(a)).

One of the reasons to justify the Microsoft's device protected approach as described in Section 3.1 are possible resource issues with smart cards (limited storage space and limited speed). Our performance results undermine this argument. The worst case execution time of the proving part is 0.87 seconds. This not only makes the card implementation fast enough to be usable in general, it also makes it usable for "field" applications, e.g. dispensing machines. Even more, for smaller numbers of smaller attributes the running times become almost acceptable for use in public transport/e-ticketing, where the commonly required card transaction times should stay below 0.3 seconds. We also see a potential to improve the running times using faster smart card hardware, we elaborate on this in the upcoming section. Overall, these good results strongly justify the idea to use U-Prove standalone on a smart card rather than to use Microsoft's device-protected token approach, which now has no obvious functional or performance advantages over our approach.

Furthermore, excluding our own previous work on implementing ECC-based self-blindable signatures on a smart card [2,17] our performance results are by far better than all the previously reported results for anonymous credentials implemented on smart cards. One of the first attempts within our group to implement a U-Prove like protocol on a Java Card [28] resulted in running times closing to 10 seconds for a setup closely corresponding to ours. The DAA protocol was also implemented on a Java Card by Sterckx et al. [25] with the running times of close to 4 seconds for the DAA signing protocol. In [4] yet another implementation of anonymous credentials on a Java Card is reported with running times of around 7–10 seconds. Our MULTOS U-Prove implementation is simply way faster.

The only limitations of our implementation are imposed by the limited resources of the MULTOS smart card. We had to limit the prime modulus size to 1024 bits, use only SHA-1 hashing, and because of the available RAM (<1kB) on the card we could only allow for the maximum of 5 attributes, each one up to 255 bytes in size. Otherwise our implementation is fully flexible and provides full U-Prove functionality, *including* the smart card features described in Section 3.1. However, it is not uncommon for modern smart cards to support up to 2048 bits for modulus size and 2 kilobytes of RAM, only no such MULTOS cards were available to us. In the following we make some speculative performance estimations based on tests performed with Java Cards that we have.

4.1   MULTOS vs. Java Card

As we already stated in Section 2.2 providing an efficient implementation of U-Prove on a Java Card is currently not possible, mainly because of the inflexible Java Card API. However, we can use Java Card to do further (speculative) performance analysis.

Our Java Cards are implemented on the SmartMX hardware platform from NXP, which provides excellent hardware cryptographic support (2048 bit RSA and 320 bit ECC), and is considered state of the art when it comes to speed.

By running comparative speed tests between our Infineon SLE66 MULTOS card and a brand new NXP SmartMX (JCOP31) Java Card we estimate two things:

1. How fast a sibling implementation, equal in terms of the supported protocol parameters, would be on the SmartMX chip?
2. How fast would an implementation supporting greater modulus size and more attributes would be on the SmartMX chip?

For this we simply compared the speed of raw SHA-1 and RSA operations between the two platforms, operating both on RAM and E^{2}PROM. The results are shown in Table 2, the running times are expressed in milliseconds for 100 iterations of each test, for example a single SHA-1 execution storing the results in RAM for the first case (MULTOS card on a contact interface) takes 51.2 milliseconds on average. More generally and roughly speaking, the JCOP31 card is 4 times faster for SHA-1, and 1.3 to 1.5 times faster for RSA-1024, depending on the target memory. Although exact estimations are not possible, we speculate that the attribute proving part with the same protocol parameters as our MULTOS implementation could be improved by a factor of 2 making the worst execution time for 5 attributes stay below 0.5 seconds. We also estimate that for the 2 attribute configuration the running times would drop below the 0.3 seconds required for public transport and e-ticketing applications. As for the implementation supporting larger modulus size and more attributes, the JCOP31 card drops its performance going from RSA-1024 to RSA-2048 by the factor of 2 to 2.5. Based on this we believe that the proving part of the protocol would be within 2 seconds realm for 2048 bit modulus size and 10 attributes. This would still be faster than any of the existing Java Card anonymous credentials implementations that only support modulus sizes smaller than 2048 with reasonable efficiency.

Yet again this stresses the Java Card shortcoming of the limited hardware interface provided by the API – had the API been more flexible, our speculative figures above would probably be factual. Although this issue has been brought up before and we know that the smart card industry is very well aware of this problem, we see hardly any improvements in this respect. The MULTOS plat-

Table 2. Performance comparison between *MULTOS on an Infineon SLE66* chip and *JCOP31 on a NXP SmartMX* chip (time in milliseconds for 100 successive operations)

	MULTOS		JCOP31	
	contact	wireless	contact	wireless
SHA-1 RAM	5120	5274	1110	1136
SHA-1 E^{2}PROM	6125	6308	1442	1466
RSA-1024 RAM	1016	1060	772	777
RSA-1024 E^{2}PROM	2936	3041	1941	1952
RSA-2048 RAM	14289	14898	1926	1950
RSA-2048 E^{2}PROM	17237	17956	3838	3865

form proved itself very strong here with its flexible API design. What MULTOS is lacking from our point of view is wider hardware support for cryptography other than RSA and DES. In our own privacy-friendly protocol designs we rely heavily on ECC, and although the MULTOS API specification supports ECC, no MULTOS cards with hardware ECC support are currently available to us for small scale development. Finally, we find the size of the RAM (960 bytes) available on the MULTOS development cards a little bit of a limiting factor to fully commit to MULTOS as our prototyping framework.

5   Ongoing Research

In our research we continue to look for efficient solutions for privacy-friendly smart card applications. For this we develop our own protocols as well as explore the existing ones. Both require prototypes for feasibility and efficiency analysis. One of the *by-products* of the work presented in this paper is the discovery of the MULTOS cards as an efficient implementation platform for this kind of protocols.

Hence, the obvious next step is to investigate the implementation of the Idemix protocol suite on a MULTOS card. Idemix has been already implemented on a Java Card [4] and despite the best effort of the implementers to maintain reasonable efficiency the running times still leave room for improvement in our opinion. Idemix has more features and is more complex than U-Prove and more involved computations are required, so clearly we do not expect an equally fast implementation as the one we just presented, but we certainly believe we can considerably improve over the current Java Card Idemix implementation.

In [2,17] we presented an efficient Java Card implementation of our own protocol based on ECC and self-blindable signatures. This protocol provides a very strong anonymity property, however our implementation, despite the achieved efficiency, still suffers from the inability to fully utilise the hardware capabilities of the card hidden beyond the Java Card API. Here, a MULTOS card with full ECC support would provide further improvement possibilities. When (if at all) such cards are available to us we will certainly investigate these possibilities.

In parallel to this protocol and speed quest we also develop case studies and a demo suite for on-line use of anonymous credentials. To this end, we are implementing a general framework in the form of a browser plug-in for smart card enabled web services. This framework will be targeted for the set of anonymity friendly protocols under our consideration and will allow us to do more practical comparative studies between the different anonymous credential approaches exemplified by suitable demos.

6   Conclusion

We have presented an efficient MULTOS implementation of the U-Prove technology that allows to run the complete prover side of the protocols on a smart card. This provides an anonymity friendly credentials mechanism for users of such a smart card, with full independence from authentication resources external to the smart card. From the user perspective, the most performance sensitive part of the protocol is attribute proving. Here, the achieved worst-case running times of 0.87 seconds for the whole set of attributes clearly establishes the practical usability of our implementation. Our performance results also strongly support our idea to use a stand-alone U-Prove smart card rather than the Microsoft device-protection approach, which seems to overlook the current capabilities of smart cards. One other thing that seems to be overlooked by scientists and smart card developers is the existence of the MULTOS smart card platform. During our work it proved itself highly flexible and reasonably fast, hence our next steps are to implement and assess the performance of other anonymity friendly protocols, primarily Idemix, in a (MULTOS) smart card setting.

Acknowledgements. We are grateful to Jaap-Henk Hoepman, Bart Jacobs, Christian Paquin, Erik Poll and the anonymous reviewers for their valuable comments which helped to improve this work.

References

1. MULTOS implementation report. Tech. Rep. MAO-DOC-TEC-010 v1.36a, MAO-SCO Limited (February 2010)
2. Batina, L., Hoepman, J.-H., Jacobs, B., Mostowski, W., Vullers, P.: Developing Efficient Blinded Attribute Certificates on Smart Cards via Pairings. In: Gollmann, D., Lanet, J.-L., Iguchi-Cartigny, J. (eds.) CARDIS 2010. LNCS, vol. 6035, pp. 209–222. Springer, Heidelberg (2010)
3. Bender, J., Kügler, D., Margraf, M., Naumann, I.: Privacy-friendly revocation management without unique chip identifiers for the German national ID card. Computer Fraud & Security (September 2010)
4. Bichsel, P., Camenisch, J., Groß, T., Shoup, V.: Anonymous credentials on a standard Java Card. In: Computer and Communications Security – CCS 2009, pp. 600–610. ACM (November 2009)
5. Brands, S., Paquin, C.: U-Prove cryptographic specification v1.0. Tech. rep., Microsoft Corporation (March 2010)
6. Brands, S.A.: Rethinking Public Key Infrastructures and Digital Certificates: Building in Privacy. MIT Press (August 2000)
7. Brickell, E.F., Camenisch, J., Chen, L.: Direct anonymous attestation. In: Pfitzmann, B., Liu, P. (eds.) Computer and Communications Security – CCS 2004, pp. 132–145. ACM (October 2004)
8. Bundesamt für Sicherheit in der Informationstechnik: Advanced security mechanisms for machine readable travel documents, Version 2.05. Tech. Rep. TR-03110, German Federal Office for Information Security (BSI), Bonn, Germany (2010)
9. Camenisch, J., Lysyanskaya, A.: An Efficient System for Non-transferable Anonymous Credentials with Optional Anonymity Revocation. In: Pfitzmann, B. (ed.) EUROCRYPT 2001. LNCS, vol. 2045, pp. 93–118. Springer, Heidelberg (2001)
10. Camenisch, J., Lysyanskaya, A.: Dynamic Accumulators and Application to Efficient Revocation of Anonymous Credentials. In: Yung, M. (ed.) CRYPTO 2002. LNCS, vol. 2442, pp. 61–76. Springer, Heidelberg (2002)

11. Camenisch, J., Van Herreweghen, E.: Design and implementation of the idemix anonymous credential system. In: Computer and Communications Security – CCS 2002, pp. 21–30. ACM (November 2002)
12. Chaum, D.: Blind signatures for untraceable payments. In: Chaum, D., Rivest, R.L. (eds.) Advances in Cryptology – CRYPTO 1982. pp. 199–203. Plemum Publishing (1983)
13. Chaum, D.: Security without identification: transaction systems to make big brother obsolete. Communications of the ACM 28, 1030–1044 (1985)
14. Chen, Z.: Java Card Technology for Smart Cards: Architecture and Programmer's Guide. Java. Addison-Wesley (June 2000)
15. Fiat, A., Shamir, A.: How to Prove Yourself: Practical Solutions to Identification and Signature Problems. In: Odlyzko, A.M. (ed.) CRYPTO 1986. LNCS, vol. 263, pp. 186–194. Springer, Heidelberg (1987)
16. France-Massey, T.: MULTOS – the high security smart card OS. Tech. rep., MAO-SCO Limited (September 2005)
17. Hoepman, J.H., Jacobs, B., Vullers, P.: Privacy and security issues in e-ticketing – Optimisation of smart card-based attribute-proving. In: Cortier, V., Ryan, M., Shmatikov, V. (eds.) Foundations of Security and Privacy – FCS-PrivMod 2010 (July 2010) (informal)
18. Hoepman, J.H., Lueks, W., Vullers, P.: Revoking self-blindable credentials (2011)
19. Lysyanskaya, A.A.: Signature schemes and applications to cryptographic protocol design. Ph.D. thesis, Massachusetts Institute of Technology (September 2002)
20. MAOSCO Limited: MULTOS Developer's Reference Manual (October 2009)
21. NXP Semiconductors: Smart solutions for smart services (z-card 2009). NXP Literature, Document 75016728 (2009)
22. Paquin, C.: U-Prove cryptographic specification v1.1. Tech. rep., Microsoft Corporation (February 2011)
23. Paquin, C.: U-Prove cryptographic test vectors v1.1. Tech. rep., Microsoft Corporation (February 2011)
24. Paquin, C.: U-Prove technology overview v1.1. Tech. rep., Microsoft Corporation (February 2011)
25. Sterckx, M., Gierlichs, B., Preneel, B., Verbauwhede, I.: Efficient implementation of anonymous credentials on Java Card smart cards. In: Information Forensics and Security – WIFS 2009, pp. 106–110. IEEE (September 2009)
26. Sun Microsystems, Inc.: Java Card 2.2.2 Application Programming Interface Specification (March 2006)
27. Sun Microsystems, Inc.: Java Card 2.2.2 Virtual Machine Specification (March 2006)
28. Tews, H., Jacobs, B.: Performance Issues of Selective Disclosure and Blinded Issuing Protocols on Java Card. In: Markowitch, O., Bilas, A., Hoepman, J.-H., Mitchell, C.J., Quisquater, J.-J. (eds.) WISTP 2009. LNCS, vol. 5746, pp. 95–111. Springer, Heidelberg (2009)
29. Verheul, E.R.: Self-Blindable Credential Certificates from the Weil Pairing. In: Boyd, C. (ed.) ASIACRYPT 2001. LNCS, vol. 2248, pp. 533–550. Springer, Heidelberg (2001)

Multi-party Private Web Search
with Untrusted Partners

Cristina Romero-Tris, Jordi Castellà-Roca, and Alexandre Viejo

Universitat Rovira i Virgili, UNESCO Chair in Data Privacy
Departament d'Enginyeria Informàtica i Matemàtiques
Av. Països Catalans 26, E-43007 Tarragona, Spain
{cristina.romero,jordi.castella,alexandre.viejo}@urv.cat

Abstract. Web search engines are tools employed to find specific information in the Internet. However, they also represent a threat for the privacy of their users. This happens because the web search engines store and analyze the personal information that the users reveal in their queries. In order to avoid this privacy threat, it is necessary to provide mechanisms that protect the users of these tools.

In this paper, we propose a multi-party protocol that protects the privacy of the user not only in front of the web search engine, but also in front of dishonest internal users. Our scheme outperforms similar proposals in terms of computation and communication.

Keywords: privacy, web search engines, private information retrieval.

1 Introduction

Search on the Internet is a frequent activity for many users throughout the world. Web search engines (WSEs) are tools which allow information retrieval from this huge repository of data. There are many WSEs in the market, such as Google, Bing, Yahoo, etc.

When a user wants to search a term in a WSE, she types the keywords and submits her query. Then, the WSE applies information retrieval techniques to select and rank the results. After that, the user evaluates the list of pages and gets the information.

Along with this process, the WSE builds a profile of this user based on her queries. For example, in its Privacy Center [1], Google states that its servers automatically record requests made by users. These "server logs" include user's query, IP address, browser type, browser language, date and time of the request and a reference to one or more cookies that may uniquely identify the user's browser.

Google uses cookies for several purposes such as identifying the users in order to improve their search results and track their trends, and also storing their preferences. Google also uses the cookies in its advertising services to help companies serve and manage the promotion of their products across the web. This is called AdSense and it represents a large source of income for Google.

M. Rajarajan et al. (Eds.): SecureComm 2011, LNICST 96, pp. 261–280, 2012.
© Institute for Computer Sciences, Social Informatics and Telecommunications Engineering 2012

Besides the financial gain for WSEs, profiling is a threat for the privacy of the user. The different logs stored by a WSE contain sensitive data that can be combined to disclose information of a certain individual. In order to do that, it is necessary to find the identity of the user. One way of doing it is to use the IP address and the cookies stored in the logs. Thus, queries that come from the same IP address or from a browser with a certain cookie are used to build the same profile. Note that users cannot rely on deleting the cookies and on the use of different IP addresses. The renewal policy of dynamic IP addresses depends on the network operator. Furthermore, some users might require static IP addresses.

In addition to IP addresses and cookies, people can reveal their personal identity in their queries. In fact, [2] indicates that 94.82% of users have searched their own name at least once. Moreover, many other queries such as the place where they live, their job, or even the car they drive, can also be a method of tracing users and revealing their identity.

Once a user is identified, the WSE can link her identity with the queries she made. According to [2], around 85% of users have searched for information that they would not want their parents or their employers to know about. For example, queries about health, sexual orientation, politics, religion, etc. can be considered extremely sensitive information for the owners. Hence, the queries of a user should be protected and never revealed to third parties.

Some incidents in the past have shown that WSEs are not capable of protecting the privacy of the users. For example, in 2006 AOL released a file with twenty million searches generated by its users [3]. This incident had serious consequences since personally identifiable information was present in many of the queries. Another example of privacy risks with WSEs is the subpoena that Google suffered in 2006 [4]. On that occasion, the Justice Department of U.S.A. tried to compel Google to provide millions of Internet search records.

Such events indicate that users should not trust the companies behind the WSEs. Therefore, it is necessary to propose alternatives that prevent the WSEs from knowing the sensitive information of the users.

2   Previous Work

The problem of private web search has been widely discussed in previous literature. In this section, the main contributions to this subject are described.

The problem introduced in this paper is similar to the Private Information Retrieval (PIR) problem [5]. However, PIR protocols are not suitable for WSEs because they assume that the server which holds the database collaborates with the user. In the WSE scenario this assumption cannot be made because WSEs have no motivation to protect the privacy of the users since it would limit its profiling objectives.

Another solution to maintain the privacy of the users is to use a proxy. There are several companies (e.g. Scroogle [6], anonymizer.com [7]) that offer a service in which the clients can redirect the traffic to their servers. As a result, requests seem to be originated by these servers and have no reference to the IP address of the client. Nevertheless, this is not the best solution to protect the privacy of the users because profiling could be done at the proxy, hence, instead of trusting the WSE, users have to trust the proxy.

Onion routing is a technique to establish anonymous channels that preserve the privacy of the users. An example of this is the Tor anonymity network which is described in [8]. The authors in [9] propose to use the anonymous channels to submit queries to the WSE. The main drawback of this scheme is that the encryption and decryption process at the onion routers make the search process too slow. According to [9], the cost of submitting one query to Google is about 10 seconds on average. This means that users would spend 25 times longer doing each query. This query delay is very high for a tool that is expected to be used quite frequently.

Another alternative is the use of a query obfuscation protocol such as GooPIR [10] or TrackMeNot [11]. These protocols generate a stream of automated queries where the real queries are blended into. As a result, the WSE is not able to create a correct profile. GooPIR uses a Thesaurus to obtain the words which are mixed with the real queries. Consequently, the fake queries are single words, while full sentences are not addressed. TrackMeNot is a plugin for Mozilla Firefox that generates dynamic queries using RSS feedback. These queries can be words or sentences, and they are periodically submitted to the WSE.

These obfuscation protocols have a major disadvantage: machine-generated queries do not have the same features as the human-generated queries. The works presented in [12] and [13] argue that it is possible to distinguish real queries from automated queries. For example, [13] develops a classifier which is very accurate in identifying TrackMeNot queries, with a mean of misclassification around 0.02%.

Another approach is to use a multi-party protocol, which is not affected by the misclassification issue of the single-party ones. Besides, they are generally faster than the schemes based on anonymous channels. In this kind of protocols, a group of users is created. Then, a user asks another component of the group to submit her query and send back the result.

In [14], the authors propose a multi-party protocol named Useless User Profile (UUP). The basic idea beneath this system is that a central node puts users into dynamic groups where they securely exchange their queries. As a result, each user submits a partner's query and not her own and, hence, she obtains a distorted profile. This protocol achieves a query delay of 5.2 seconds. This time significantly outperforms previous proposals. However, the UUP protocol has a major disadvantage. It is not secure in presence of malicious internal users. This means that a dishonest user can learn the queries of the rest of members of the group.

The authors of [15] use an scenario which is similar to the one proposed in [14]. However, they argue that the level of security of [14] is not sufficient. Hence, they modify the UUP protocol in order to be resilient against some attacks. Nevertheless, the drawback of their proposal is that it uses expensive cryptographic tools (*i.e.* double encryptions) that introduce an unaffordable query delay. In fact, the authors remark that executing their protocol is twice as expensive as in [14].

Finally, another similar approach is presented in [16] and [17]. The idea of both proposals is to minimize the role that the central node plays in the protocol. On one hand, [16] proposes to use a preestablished network with the topology of a complete graph. On the other hand, [17] proposes to employ already developed social networks (*e.g.* Facebook).

The main drawback of both proposals is that the groups are static (same members in every execution of the protocol). This means that their protocols are more vulnerable in front of an internal attack (*e.g.* the attacks proposed in [15]).

2.1   Contribution and Plan of This Paper

In this paper, we present a new multi-party protocol that protects the privacy of the users against web search engines and against dishonest internal users. Regarding similar approaches, we propose a protocol which increases the level of security of [14], and requires less computation and communication than [15].

Section 3 introduces the background and tools that the protocol uses. Section 4 describes the scenario and the privacy requirements. The protocol is detailed on Section 5. Section 6 and 7 analyze its privacy and performance respectively. Finally, Section 8 concludes the paper and reports some future work.

3   Background and Notation

3.1   *n*-out-of-*n* Threshold ElGamal Encryption

In cryptographic multi-party protocols, some operations must be computed jointly by different users. In an n-out-of-n threshold ElGamal encryption (see [18] for more details), n users have a distributed public key y and the corresponding secret key α is divided into n shares α_i, where no single party knows the entire secret. Using this protocol, a certain message m can be encrypted using the public key y and the decryption can be performed only if all n users collaborate in the decryption process. Key generation, encryption and decryption process are next described.

Key Generation. First, a large random prime p is generated, where $p = 2q + 1$ and q is a prime number too. Also, a generator g of the multiplicative group $\mathbb{Z}_q^*$ is chosen.

Then, each user generates a random private key $\alpha_i \in \mathbb{Z}_q^*$ and publishes $y_i = g^{\alpha_i}$. The common public key is computed as $y = \prod_{i=1}^{n} y_i = g^\alpha$, where $\alpha = \alpha_1 + \ldots + \alpha_n$.

Message Encryption. Message encryption can be performed using the standard ElGamal encryption function [19]. Given a message m and a public key y, a random value r is generated and the ciphertext is computed as follows:

$$E_y(m,r) = c = (c1, c2) = (g^r, m \cdot y^r)$$

Message Decryption. Given a message encrypted with the public key y, $E_y(m,r) = (c1, c2)$, user U_i can decrypt that value as follows:

Each user $j \neq i$ publishes $c1^{\alpha_j}$. Then, U_i can recover message m in the following way:

$$m = \frac{c2}{c1^{\alpha_i} \left(\prod_{j \neq i} c1^{\alpha_j}\right)}$$

This decryption can be verified by each participant by performing a proof of equality of discrete logarithms [20].

3.2   ElGamal Re-masking

The re-masking operation performs some computations over an encrypted value. In this way, its cleartext does not change but the re-masked message is not linkable to the same message before re-masking.

Given an ElGamal ciphertext $E_y(m,r)$, it can be re-masked by computing [21]:

$$E_y(m,r) \cdot E_y(1, r')$$

For $r' \in \mathbb{Z}_q^*$ randomly chosen and where $\cdot$ stands for the component-wise scalar product (ElGamal ciphertext can be viewed as a vector with two components). The resulting ciphertext corresponds to the same cleartext m.

3.3   Optimized Arbitrary Size (OAS) Benes

A Benes permutation network (PN) [22] is a directed graph with N inputs and N outputs, denoted as $PN^{(N)}$. It is able to realize every possible permutation of N elements.

A Benes PN is composed by a set of 2 x 2 switches. These switches have a binary control signal $b \in \{0, 1\}$ which determines the internal state and, hence, the output. The two possible states of a 2 x 2 switch are depicted in Figure 1(a).

The problem with a Benes PN is that the size of the network must be a power of 2. In order to have an Arbitrary Sized (AS) Benes network [23], it is necessary to introduce a 3 x 3 network like Figure 1(b) shows. Using 2 x 2 switches and 3 x 3 networks recursively it is possible to construct a network of any size.

Optimized Arbitrary Size (OAS) Benes [24] is an extension of AS Benes that reduces the number of necessary switches in the network. The way of constructing the OAS-Benes depends on the parameter N:

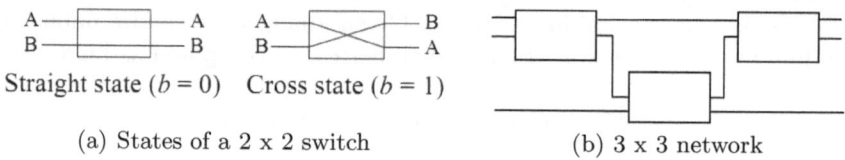

Straight state ($b = 0$)   Cross state ($b = 1$)

(a) States of a 2 x 2 switch   (b) 3 x 3 network

Fig. 1. Basic elements of an OAS-Benes

- If N is even, the OAS-Benes $PN^{(N)}$ is built recursively from two even OAS-Benes of $\frac{N}{2}$-dimension called sub-networks. The sub-networks are not directly connected to the inputs and outputs. Instead of that, they are connected to $N - 1$ input-output switches, as Figure 2(a) shows.
- If N is odd, the OAS-Benes $PN^{(N)}$ is composed by an upper $\lfloor \frac{N}{2} \rfloor$ even OAS-Benes, and a lower $\lceil \frac{N}{2} \rceil$ odd OAS-Benes. The sub-networks are not directly connected to the inputs and outputs. In this case, the first $N - 1$ inputs are connected to $\lfloor \frac{N}{2} \rfloor$ switches, and the first $N - 1$ outputs are connected to $\lfloor \frac{N}{2} \rfloor$ switches. Figure 2(b) illustrates this construction.

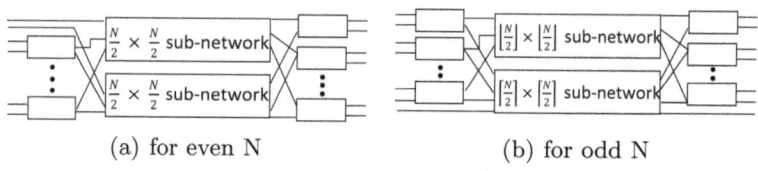

(a) for even N   (b) for odd N

Fig. 2. Construction of OAS-Benes

According to the way that an OAS-Benes is constructed, it is possible to account the minimum number of switches required to satisfy a permutation of N elements. The formula to calculate the minimum number of switches is:

$$S(N) = \begin{cases} (N - 1) + 2 * S(\frac{N}{2}) & \text{if } N \text{ is even} \\ 2 * \lfloor \frac{N}{2} \rfloor + S(\lceil \frac{N}{2} \rceil) + S(\lfloor \frac{N}{2} \rfloor) & \text{if } N \text{ is odd} \end{cases}$$

Where $S(1) = 0$, $S(2) = 1$, $S(3) = 3$

Multi-party OAS-Benes. OAS-Benes can be used to perform a joint permutation. This means that the switches of the OAS-Benes can be distributed among a group of n users trying to realize a permutation of N inputs. However, this must be done is such a way that no user knows the overall permutation between the inputs and the outputs.

According to [24], a secure permutation (where no user knows the overall permutation) requires minimally t OAS-Benes $PN^{(N)}$, where t depends on the minimum number of honest users that the system requires. The t OAS-Benes $PN^{(N)}$ are fairly divided in n adjacent stages. Then, stage i (for $i \in 1, \ldots, n$) is assigned to user i. Since the construction of the OAS-Benes is mechanical, the users can build it without any cooperation between them or from another entity.

In order to obtain a secure permutation, the condition that must be satisfied is that the honest users control, at least, $S(N)$ switches. We denote as λ the minimum number of honest users that the system requires. For example, consider a scenario with $n = 6$ users, $N = 8$ inputs and, at least, $\lambda = 3$ honest users. The number of switches of one OAS-Benes $PN^{(8)}$ is $S(8) = 17$. According to [24], the $\lambda = 3$ honest users must control 17 or more switches. This means that every user must control $\lceil \frac{17}{3} \rceil = 6$ switches. Therefore, the scheme needs at least (6 *switches per user* $\times$ 6 *users*) $= 36$ switches that will be fairly divided among the n users. Consequently, the system requires $t = \lceil \frac{36}{17} \rceil = 3$ OAS-Benes $PN^{(8)}$.

We propose the next formula in order to calculate the number of OAS-Benes required in a scheme with n users, N inputs, and λ honest users.

$$t = \left\lceil \frac{n \cdot \left\lceil \frac{S(N)}{\lambda} \right\rceil}{S(N)} \right\rceil$$

3.4 Plaintext Equivalence Proof (PEP)

PEP [25] is an honest-verifier zero-knowledge proof protocol based on a variant of the Schnorr signature algorithm [26]. The purpose of this protocol is to prove that two different ciphertexts are the encryption of the same message.

Two ElGamal ciphertexts $(c1_a, c2_a) = (g^{r_a}, m_a \cdot y^{r_a})$ and $(c1_b, c2_b) = (g^{r_b}, m_b \cdot y^{r_b})$ for some $r_a, r_b \in \mathbb{Z}_q^*$ are plaintext equivalent if $m_a = m_b$. Let:

- $\alpha = r_a - r_b$
- $k = H(y \parallel g \parallel c1_a \parallel c2_a \parallel c1_b \parallel c2_b)$, where $H(\cdot)$ is a cryptographic hash function, and $\parallel$ is the concatenation operator.
- $G = g \cdot y^k$
- $Y = \frac{c1_a}{c1_b} \cdot \left(\frac{c2_a}{c2_b}\right)^k = (g \cdot y^k)^\alpha$

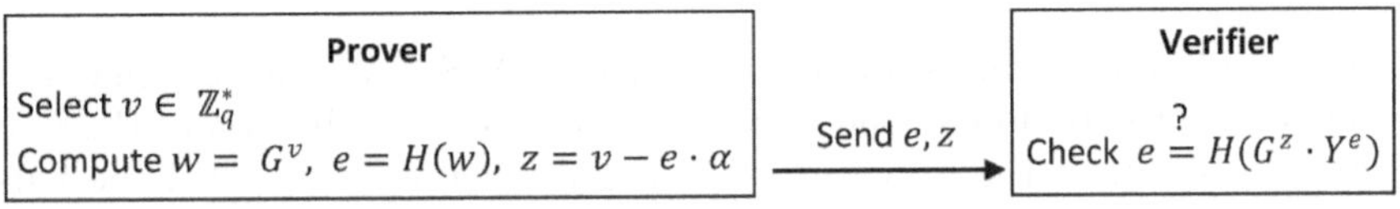

Prover		Verifier
Select $v \in \mathbb{Z}_q^*$		
Compute $w = G^v$, $e = H(w)$, $z = v - e \cdot \alpha$	Send e, z $\longrightarrow$	Check $e \overset{?}{=} H(G^z \cdot Y^e)$

Fig. 3. PEP protocol

In order to prove that $(c1_a, c2_a) \equiv (c1_b, c2_b)$, the prover must demonstrate knowledge of α by executing the protocol of Figure 3.

3.5   Disjunctive PEP (DISPEP)

DISPEP [25] is an extension of the PEP protocol. In this case, a user proves that one of two different ciphertexts is a re-masked version of another ciphertext.

Let $(c1_a, c2_a) = (g^{r_a}, m_a \cdot y^{r_a})$ and $(c1_b, c2_b) = (g^{r_b}, m_b \cdot y^{r_b})$ be two different ElGamal ciphertexts. Then, one of them is a re-masking of another ciphertext $(c1, c2) = (g^r, m \cdot y^r)$ for some $r_a, r_b, r \in \mathbb{Z}_q^*$ if $m_a = m$ or $m_b = m$. For $i \in \{a, b\}$, let:

- $\beta_i = r - r_i$
- $k_i = H(y \,\|\, g \,\|\, c1 \,\|\, c2 \,\|\, c1_i \,\|\, c2_i)$
- $G_i = g \cdot y^{k_i}$
- $Y_i = \frac{c1}{c1_i} \cdot \left(\frac{c2}{c2_i}\right)^{k_i} = (g \cdot y^{k_i})^{\beta_i}$

In order to prove whether $m_a = m$ or $m_b = m$, the prover must demonstrate knowledge of β_i by executing the protocol of Figure 4. Without loss of generality, in Figure 4, we assume that the prover is showing $m_a = m$.

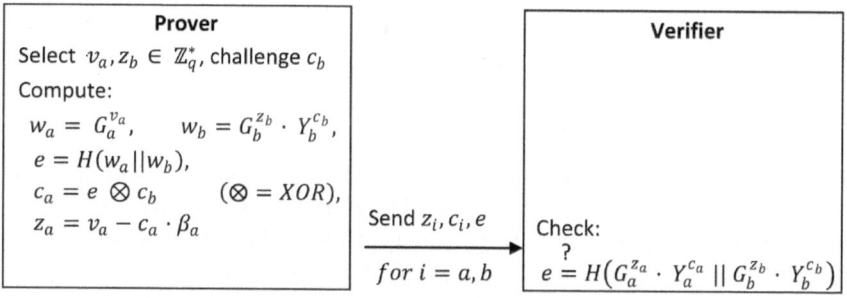

Fig. 4. DISPEP protocol

4   System Model

4.1   Entities

The protocol is executed in a scenario with three entities:

- *Users.* Individuals who submit queries to the WSE. We assume that in our scenario there are honest and dishonest users. The motivation of the honest users is to protect their own privacy. The motivation of the dishonest users is to learn the queries of the honest users.
- *Central node.* It is the entity that organizes the users into groups. Its main objective is to distribute the information that users need in order to contact the other members of the group.
- *Web search engine.* It is the server that holds the database. As previously mentioned, WSEs have no motivation to protect the privacy of their users.

4.2   Protocol Overview

The idea of the protocol is to create a group of users who collaborate in order to make searchs in a WSE. Instead of submitting her own query, a user U asks another member of the group to submit it and send the results back. At the same time, U submits the query of another user of the group. As a result, the WSE cannot create a reliable profile of any particular individual.

The protocol requires that neither the WSE nor the users of the group learn which query belongs to each user. In order to do this, the users execute a multi-party protocol that works as follows: a central node creates a group of n users. Then, the required OAS-Benes networks are fairly distributed among the n users. After that, each user encrypts and broadcasts her query. The list of encrypted queries is passed from each user to the next. In her turn, each user re-masks and permutates the list of ciphertexts at every switch that she was assigned. Furthermore, for every switch she uses PEP and DISPEP protocols to prove to the rest of users that the outputs are re-ordered and re-masked versions of the inputs.

The final result is that the users obtain a list of ciphertexts that cannot be linked to the original list. Then, each user decrypts one different query, submits it to the WSE and broadcast the result.

4.3   Privacy Requirements

In order to guarantee the privacy of the users, the scheme must fulfill the following requirements:

- The users cannot link any query with the user who generated it.
- The central node cannot link any query with the user who generated it.
- The WSE is not able to construct a reliable profile of any user.

5   Protocol Description

The protocol is composed by four phases that the users execute sequentially.

5.1   Group Setup

Every user who wants to submit a query to the WSE, contacts the central node. When the central node has received n requests, it creates a group $\{U_1, \ldots, U_n\}$. Then, the n users are notified that they belong to the same group. The users receive a message with the size of the group (n) and the position that every component has been randomly assigned $(i = 1, \ldots, n)$. Each position is associated with the IP address and the port where the user is listening. This information allows the users to establish a communication channel between them. The central node is no longer needed.

5.2   Permutation Network Distribution

As stated in section 3.3, t OAS-Benes networks are necessary to perform a secure permutation. The number of inputs of the networks equals the number of users $N = n$, which is also the same as the number of queries. Regarding the number of honest users, the parameter is always fixed at $\lambda = 2$. The reason for this choice requires a privacy analysis and, hence, is later detailed in Section 7.1.

Knowing the parameters n, N, and λ, the users calculate the value of t using the formula defined on Section 3.3. The construction of the t OAS-Benes $PN^{(n)}$ is mechanical. This means that users do not need to exchange any information. As long as they know the parameters t and n, they know the arrangement of the switches in the t OAS-Benes $PN^{(n)}$. Therefore, they can fairly divide them in n adjacent stages.

According to the positions assigned in the previous phase, user U_i is responsible for the switches that correspond to the i-th stage. Each stage is formed by d switches, where $d = \frac{t}{n} \cdot S(n)$ on average.

We denote as s_l^i the l-th switch of the i-th user for $i = 1, \ldots, n$ and $l = 1, \ldots, d$. We also define a function $\Phi(i, l)$ that, given an output of a switch, returns the input of the next switch that must follow. The result is given according to the arrangement of the switches in the PNs. Figure 5 illustrates the operation of this function.

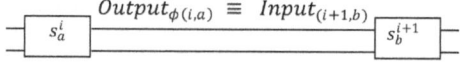

Fig. 5. Correlation between the outputs of a switch and the inputs of the next

5.3   Group Key Generation

1. Users $\{U_1, \ldots, U_n\}$ agree on a large prime p where $p = 2q + 1$ and q is a prime too. Next, they pick an element $g \in \mathbb{Z}_q^*$ of order q.
2. In order to generate the group key, each user U_i performs the following steps:
   (a) Generates a random number $a_i \in \mathbb{Z}_q^*$.
   (b) Calculates her own share $y_i = g^{a_i} \bmod p$.
   (c) Broadcasts a commitment to her share $h_i = \mathcal{H}(y_i)$, where $\mathcal{H}$ is a one-way function.
   (d) Broadcasts y_i to the other members of the group.
   (e) Checks that $h_j = \mathcal{H}(y_j)$ for $j = (1, \ldots, n)$.
   (f) Calculates the group key using the received shares:
   $$y = \prod_{1 \leq j \leq n} y_j = g^{a_1} \cdot g^{a_2} \cdot \ldots \cdot g^{a_n}$$

5.4 Anonymous Query Retrieval

For $i = 1, \ldots, n$, each user U_i performs the following operations:

1. U_i generates a random value r_i and uses the group key y to encrypt her query m_i:
$$E_y(m_i, r_i) = (c1_i, c2_i) = c_i^0$$

2. U_i sends c_i^0 to the other members U_j, for $\forall j \neq i$.

3. For every switch s_l^i ($l = (1, \ldots, d)$) with two inputs denoted as c_{i-1}^{2l-1} and c_{i-1}^{2l} received from U_{i-1} (note that the inputs for the switches of U_1 are the initial ciphertexts $\{c_1^0, \ldots, c_n^0\}$):

   (a) U_i re-masks the cryptograms c_{i-1}^{2l-1} and c_{i-1}^{2l}. She obtains a re-encrypted version e_{i-1}^{2l-1} and e_{i-1}^{2l} using the re-masking algorithm defined in section 3.2.

   (b) U_i randomly chooses $b_{i,l} \in \{0, 1\}$ to determine the state of the switch s_l^i as in Figure 1(a). According to this state, she obtains a re-ordered version of the ciphertexts $e_{i-1}^{\pi(2l-1)}$ and $e_{i-1}^{\pi(2l)}$.

   (c) U_i broadcasts $\{c_{\Phi(i,2l-1)}, c_{\Phi(i,2l)}\} = \{e_{i-1}^{\pi(2l-1)}, e_{i-1}^{\pi(2l)}\}$

   (d) Assuming:
   $$c_{i-1}^{2l-1} = E_y(m_1, r_1), \quad c_{i-1}^{2l} = E_y(m_2, r_2)$$
   $$e_{i-1}^{\pi(2l-1)} = E_y(m_1', r_1'), \quad e_{i-1}^{\pi(2l)} = E_y(m_2', r_2')$$

   U_i must demonstrate that $e_{i-1}^{\pi(2l-1)}$ and $e_{i-1}^{\pi(2l)}$ are re-masked and re-ordered versions of c_{i-1}^{2l-1} and c_{i-1}^{2l}. This is equivalent to proving the two following statements:

   I. $(m_2 = m_2') \vee (m_2 = m_1')$.
   This can be proved using the DISPEP protocol of Section 3.5.

   II. $m_1 \cdot m_2 = m_1' \cdot m_2'$.
   U_i computes $c = E_y(m_1 \cdot m_2, r_1 + r_2)$ and $c' = E_y(m_1' \cdot m_2', r_1' + r_2')$, and uses the PEP protocol (Section 3.4) to prove that c and c' are plaintext equivalent.

   All the other users U_j ($\forall j \neq i$) verify the proofs.

4. Let us denote $\{c_1, \ldots, c_n\}$ the resulting list of re-masked and re-ordered ciphertexts. At this point, each user U_i owns those n values. Then, user U_i decrypts the value c_i that corresponds to a query m^i generated by one of the group members. Note that due to the re-masking and permutation steps, probably m^i does not correspond to m_i (the query that has been generated by U_i).
   Decryption of a certain c_i requires that all n users participate by sending their corresponding shares to user U_i. According to that, U_i receives $(c1_i)^{\alpha_j}$ from U_j, for $j = (1, \ldots, n)$ and $j \neq i$. Then, U_i computes her own share $(c1_i)^{\alpha_i}$. Finally, U_i retrieves m^i by computing:

$$m^i = \frac{c2_i}{c1_i^{\alpha_i} (\prod_{j \neq i} c1_i^{\alpha_j})}$$

6   Privacy Analysis

This section analyzes the behaviour of the protocol regarding the privacy requirements that appear on Section 4.3. Basically, these requirements demand that, at the end of the protocol, no query can be linked to the user who generated it.

The system is analyzed in the presence of the three dishonest entities that may participate in the protocol: dishonest user, dishonest central node and dishonest web search engine.

6.1   Dishonest User

The ElGamal cryptosystem is sematically secure under the Decisional Diffie-Hellman assumption. This means that a dishonest user cannot know if two different ciphertexts will result into the same cleartext after decryption.

Therefore, every time that a ciphertext c_i crosses a switch, it is re-masked and permutated, and the attacker can only link the result to c_i by random guessing, with probability of success $1/2$. This probability exponentially decreases for every switch that the ciphertext crosses.

In the case of an attacker that only knows the inputs and the final outputs of the protocol, the intermediate re-maskings and permutations prevent her from finding the links between them. Hence, given a particular user, the probability of correctly linking her with a decrypted query is $1/n$.

Let us consider the case where a dishonest user successfully learns the query of another component of the group. This means that she is able to link one input of the permutation networks with one of the outputs. This attack may be conducted if one of the following conditions is fulfilled.

1. *The dishonest user knows the secret group key.* In this case, the attacker can decrypt the queries at any step of the protocol.
2. *The dishonest user ignores the key but knows the overall permutation.* In this case, the attacker waits until the ciphertexts are decrypted. Then, she can link every query with the original ciphertexts and, hence, with their sources.

Regarding the first condition, the attacker can only recover the secret key if she compromises the $n - 1$ other members of the group. The generation of the group key is distributed among the participants using the n-out-of-n threshold ElGamal key generation explained on Section 3.1. One of the characteristics of this scheme is that, if there is even a single honest user, the secret key cannot be reconstructed.

Another alternative in order to learn the secret key is to maliciously alter the key generation phase. In this phase, each user generates her share $y_i = g^{a_i}$, then she broadcasts a commitment to that share using a cryptographic function $\mathcal{H}(y_i)$, and then she sends y_i in a new message. A dishonest user may change her choice of share after receiving the shares of the other participants, before sending her own. This dishonest user calculates her share $y'_j = g^{a_j} / \prod_{i=1}^{n-1} y_i = g^{a_j - a_1 - \cdots - a_{n-1}}$ and broadcasts it. As a result, the group key is computed as $y = g^{a_j}$ and, hence, the dishonest user knows the secret group key.

In order for this attack to be successful and remain undetected, the dishonest user must be able to find collisions in the hash function. This means that she must find a value y'_j for which her previous commitment is still valid (i.e., $\mathcal{H}(y_i) = \mathcal{H}(y'_i)$). Nowadays, the probability of finding a collision in a reasonable amount of time using a cryptographic hash function such as SHA-2, is almost negligible.

Regarding the second condition, the use of OAS-Benes PNs guarantees that the permutation remains random and private. The requirement that must be satisfied is that there must be at least one permutation network controlled by honest users. This means that the proposed scheme needs a quantity of PNs that depends on the minimum number of honest users required to run the protocol. More specifically, the quantity of PNs that the scheme needs is the number that satisfies the following condition: in any possible distribution of stages among the users, the amount of switches controlled by the t honest users equals, at least, the number of switches composing one OAS-Benes PN. If this requirement is fulfilled, according to [24], the permutation is secure and remains secret to all the participants. Then, it is not possible to backtrace a permutation to find the original input.

6.2   Dishonest Central Node

The central node creates the groups of users. This entity only participates in the initial phase of the protocol, before the users exchange any message. Since it ignores any further communication between the users, the central node cannot link any query to the source.

However, consider the case where a central node is in control of at least $n-1$ machines. Then, this entity could group a single honest user with $n-1$ users in its control. In this case, even if the protocol is thoroughly followed, the privacy of the honest user is lost. This happens because, at the end of the protocol, the queries are revealed and the central node can identify which query belongs to the honest user. In a similar situation, an attacker could send many requests to the central node such that it is likely that she controls a large fraction of the group.

In order to prevent these attacks, the authors of [15] propose a solution that can be straightforwardly applied to our protocol. Their solution consists in a joint coin tossing scheme that uniformly distributes the parties controlled by the central node among all the groups executing the protocol. However, their proposal has two obstacles that may affect its practical deployment:

1. The number of parties controlled by the central node must be small in comparison with the number of users ready to execute the protocol at a certain time. In [15], the authors consider the case of millions of users running the protocol, while the dishonest central node only controls a few thousands of them.
2. Executing the joint coin tossing scheme is expensive. Therefore, [15] proposes to reuse the groups in several consecutive executions of the protocol. However, the users of the same group may not want to submit another query

at the same time. On the other hand, sharing a group several times with the same user increases the probability of learning one of her queries.

6.3 Dishonest Web Search Engine

The objective of the WSE is to gather the queries of the users in order to build their profiles. In the proposed protocol, the WSE only participates in the last phase. The WSE receives the queries from all the members of the group and returns the results.

The WSE can link each query with the user who submitted it and include that information on her profile. Since a user U_i does not submit her own query but the query of another participant, her profile is distorted. Hence, after several executions of the protocol, the profile of U_i that the WSE owns is useless.

7 Performance Analysis

The objective of this section is to analyze the performance of our proposal and to compare the results with other similar proposals. Our proposal is compared with two similar approaches: the scheme proposed by [14] and the scheme presented in [15]. Since the work presented in [15] does not include simulations nor a query delay estimation in a real environment, we decided to analyze the protocols theoretically. For this purpose, we analyze the protocol regarding the required computation time and the number of messages that need to be exchanged.

7.1 Parameter Selection

Prior to the comparisons, three parameters of the system must be defined: the size of the group (n), the key length, and the number of OAS-Benes (t).

Size of the Group and Key Length. In the proposed protocol, the privacy of the users in front of the WSE increases with the size of the group. This means that the bigger size of the group, the more privacy the members obtain.

However, in practice, the size of the group is bounded by the time that users must wait in order to create the group. In order to minimize the query delay, the creation of the group must be quick. According to [14], Google answers 1157 queries per second. The queries can be modeled using a Poisson distribution. This allows to calculate the probability of forming a group of n users in a certain amount of time. After several tests with $n = 3$, $n = 4$, $n = 5$ and $n = 10$, the authors of [14] conclude that $n = 3$ is the most realistic group size. As stated in [14], the probability of forming a group of $n = 3$ users in a hundredth of a second is close to 1.

For this reason, in the subsequent performance analysis we present the results obtained for $n = 3$ users. For a more complete comparison, we also show the results for a group size of $n = 4$ and $n = 5$ users.

Regarding the key length, according to [14] and [27], a 1024-bit key length is considered computationally safe. In addition, the work presented in [28] argues that a query is formed on average by 2.3 words and 15.5 characters. Assuming that a single Unicode character uses 2 bytes, a query would require 31 bytes on average. A key of 1024 bits can encrypt up to 128 bytes. This indicates that a system that employs a 1024-bit key length can accept queries with approximately 64 characters, a significantly higher value than the average query size.

Minimum Number of OAS-Benes PNs. The minimum number of OAS-Benes PNs, denoted as (t), is calculated according to the formula defined on Section 3.3. This formula depends on the size of the group (n), the number of inputs (N) and the minimum number of honest users (λ).

The selection of the size of the group (n) is explained above. The number of inputs equals the size of the group $(N = n)$, because the inputs are the queries that every user generates. Nevertheless, the minimum number of honest users requires a further analyis.

Our scheme must be able to provide privacy in the worst possible conditions. That is, when the number of dishonest users is large in comparison with the number of honest users. However, the smaller the parameter λ is, the more OAS-Benes PNs are required and the higher the query delay grows. Hence, the value of λ must minimize the query delay wihout sacrificing the privacy of the users.

The minimum value for the number of honest users is $\lambda = 1$. However, this value does not guarantee the privacy of the users. As stated in Section 6.2, in a scenario with a single honest user and $n - 1$ dihonest users, even if the permutation is perfectly secure, the privacy of the honest user is lost. Note that a coalition of $n - 1$ dishonest users can easily identify which of the n queries belongs to the honest user.

The next possible minimum value is $\lambda = 2$. This value defines the worst case scenario in which our scheme can provide privacy. In this case, the $n-2$ dishonest users have a probability of 0.5 of learning the query of the honest users.

In summary, we fix the parameter $\lambda = 2$ as the minimum number of honest users that our protocol requires.

7.2 Analysis of the Computation Time

Next, we analyze the computation time needed in the execution of [14], [15] and our proposal. More specifically, we focus on the amount of modular exponentiations that every user must perform in each execution of the protocol.

There are some parts of the protocol of [15] that employ a double encryption. This means that some modular exponentiations are performed modulus a 2048-bit integer value, instead of using a 1024-bit modulus like [14] and our proposal do. In order to compare the time required by a 1024-bit and a 2048-bit modular exponentiation, we executed a simulation that performed both operations.

The simulation revealed that, in the same conditions, a 1024-bit modular exponentiation takes 22 ms on average, while a 2048-bit modular exponentiation takes 172 ms on average.

Table 1 shows the theoretical computation time needed by modular exponentiations in each protocol. The τ_{1024} denotes the time required to make one 1024-bit modular exponentiation. The τ_{2048} denotes the time required to make one 2048-bit modular exponentiation.

Table 1. Modular exponentiations average time for one user

Castellà et al. [14]	$(3n + 3) \cdot \tau_{1024}$
Lindell et al. [15]	$6n \cdot \tau_{1024} + 5n \cdot \tau_{2048} - \tau_{1024} + 2 \cdot \tau_{2048}$
Our Proposal	$\left(n + 3 + \frac{25 \cdot t \cdot S(n)}{n}\right) \cdot \tau_{1024}$

Figure 6 shows the calculated times for a group size of 3, 4 and 5 users. The results indicate that [14] obtains the lowest computation time. This happens because [14] does not use any mechanism to protect the participants against dishonest users. Since [15] uses double encryptions and our proposal uses zero-knowledge proofs, the computation times are higher. However, the results indicate that, regarding the modular exponentiations cost, our proposal outperforms the protocol of [15]. For example, for $n = 3$ users, our proposal requires approximately one second more of computation time than [14], while [15] needs 3 more seconds than [14].

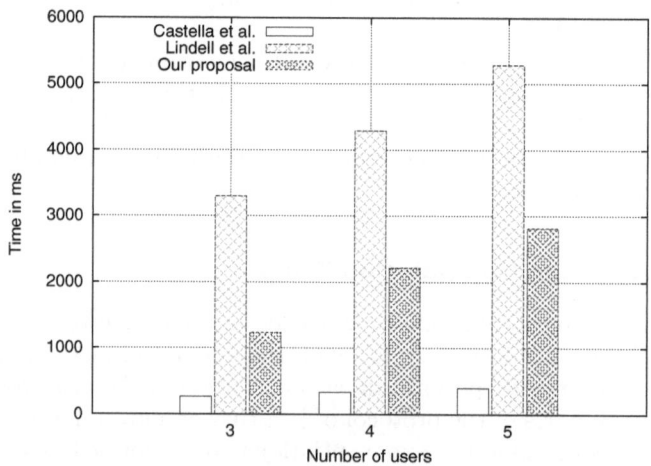

Fig. 6. Comparison of modular exponentiations times per user

7.3   Analysis of the Number of Messages

In order to analyze the performance of the protocol, another relevant parameter is the usage of the network. Table 7.3 reflects the number of messages that every user sends in each execution of the protocol.

Table 2. Average number of messages sent by each user

Castellà et al. [14]	$3n - 1 - \frac{2}{n}$
Lindell et al. [15]	$4n - 2 - \frac{2}{n}$
Our Proposal	$4n - 4$

Figure 7 represents the number of messages sent when 3, 4 or 5 users jointly execute the protocol. Although the number of messages is similar in the three proposals, the results indicate that the number of messages sent in [14] is lower than in [15] and in our proposal. The results also indicate that our proposal requires less message deliveries than [15].

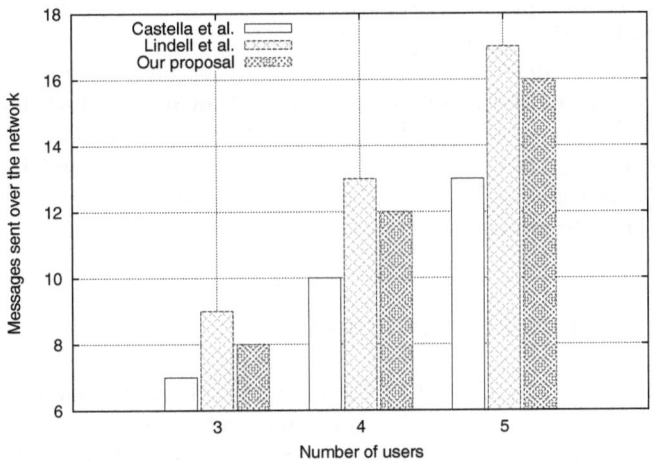

Fig. 7. Comparison of messages sent in each protocol per user

7.4   Additional Remarks

There is another difference between the protocol of [15] and our proposal that affects the performance. In [15], in order to detect a dishonest user, the participants must wait until the last phase of the protocol (i.e., when the last user broadcasts the results). At this point, if they detect any irregularity, the honest users discard the obtained results and begin a new execution with a new group.

On the other hand, our proposal is able to detect a misbehaviour earlier. For example, if the first user is dishonest, her misbehaviour can be detected immediately after she sends her zero-knowledge proofs. After the detection, the rest of users logout and start a new execution.

In conclusion, in the presence of one or more dishonest users, the users waste more time running the protocol of [15] than if they execute our proposal.

8   Conclusions and Future Work

Users frequently reveal personal information in the queries that they submit to WSEs. WSEs store this information and use it to improve the search results and for targeted advertising. In order to avoid this situation, this paper proposes a protocol that protects the privacy of the users from web search profiling.

The proposed protocol has been analyzed in terms of privacy and performance. The privacy analysis shows that the users are protected in front of the WSE and of dishonest internal users. Regarding the performance, the protocol ouperforms similar proposals with the same level of privacy.

The future work will focus on two different lines. The first line is the implementation of the proposed protocol and deployment in a real scenario. Making simulations in this scenario will allow to estimate the real query delay and compare its performance results with similar proposals. The second line of future work will focus on the search of a peer-to-peer solution that does not require the use of a central node in order to create the groups.

Disclaimer and Acknowledgments

The authors are with the UNESCO Chair in Data Privacy, but they are solely responsible for the views expressed in this paper, which do not necessarily reflect the position of UNESCO nor commit that organization. This work was partly supported by the Spanish Ministry of Science and Innovation through projects TSI2007-65406-C03-01 "E-AEGIS", CONSOLIDER CSD2007-00004 "ARES" and PT-430000-2010-31 "Audit Transparency Voting Process", and by the Government of Catalonia under grant 2009 SGR 1135.

References

1. Google Privacy Center (2011), http://www.google.com/privacy
2. Conti, G., Sobiesk, E.: An honest man has nothing to fear: user perceptions on web-based information disclosure. In: Proceedings of the 3rd Symposium on Usable Privacy and Security, pp. 112–121 (2007)

3. Barbaro, M., Zeller, T.: A Face is Exposed for AOL Searcher No. 4417749. New York Times (August 2006)
4. Hafner, K., Richtel, M.: Google Resists U.S. Subpoena of Search Data. New York Times (January 2006)
5. Ostrovsky, R., Skeith III, W.E.: A Survey of Single-Database Private Information Retrieval: Techniques and Applications. In: Okamoto, T., Wang, X. (eds.) PKC 2007. LNCS, vol. 4450, pp. 393–411. Springer, Heidelberg (2007)
6. Scroogle (2011), http://scroogle.org
7. Anonymizer (2011), http://www.anonymizer.com
8. Dingledine, R., Mathewson, N., Syverson, P.: Tor: the second-generation onion router. In: Proceedings of the 13th Conference on USENIX Security Symposium, p. 21 (2004)
9. Saint-Jean, F., Johnson, A., Boneh, D., Feigenbaum, J.: Private Web Search. In: Proceedings of the 2007 ACM Workshop on Privacy in Electronic Society – WPES 2007, pp. 84–90 (2007)
10. Domingo-Ferrer, J., Solanas, A., Castellà-Roca, J.: h(k)-private information retrieval from privacy-uncooperative queryable databases. Journal of Online Information Review 33(4), 720–744 (2009)
11. TrackMeNot (2011), http://mrl.nyu.edu/dhowe/trackmenot
12. Chow, R., Golle, P.: Faking contextual data for fun, profit, and privacy. In: Proceedings of the 8th ACM Workshop on Privacy in the Electronic Society – WPES 2009, pp. 105–108 (2009)
13. Peddinti, S.T., Saxena, N.: On the Privacy of Web Search Based on Query Obfuscation: A Case Study of TrackMeNot. In: Atallah, M.J., Hopper, N.J. (eds.) PETS 2010. LNCS, vol. 6205, pp. 19–37. Springer, Heidelberg (2010)
14. Castellà-Roca, J., Viejo, A., Herrera-Joancomartí, J.: Preserving user's privacy in web search engines. Computer Communications 32(13-14), 1541–1551 (2009)
15. Lindell, Y., Waisbard, E.: Private Web Search with Malicious Adversaries. In: Atallah, M.J., Hopper, N.J. (eds.) PETS 2010. LNCS, vol. 6205, pp. 220–235. Springer, Heidelberg (2010)
16. Reiter, M., Rubin, A.: Crowds: anonymity for Web transactions. ACM Transactions on Information and System Security 1(1), 66–92 (1998)
17. Viejo, A., Castellà-Roca, J.: Using social networks to distort users' profiles generated by web search engines. Computer Networks 54(9), 1343–1357 (2010)
18. Desmedt, Y., Frankel, Y.: Threshold Cryptosystems. In: Brassard, G. (ed.) CRYPTO 1989. LNCS, vol. 435, pp. 307–315. Springer, Heidelberg (1990)
19. ElGamal, T.: A public-key cryptosystem and a signature scheme based on discrete logarithms. IEEE Transactions on Information Theory 31, 469–472 (1985)
20. Chaum, D., Pedersen, T.P.: Wallet Databases with Observers. In: Brickell, E.F. (ed.) CRYPTO 1992. LNCS, vol. 740, pp. 89–105. Springer, Heidelberg (1993)
21. Abe, M.: Mix-Networks on Permutation Networks. In: Lam, K.-Y., Okamoto, E., Xing, C. (eds.) ASIACRYPT 1999. LNCS, vol. 1716, pp. 258–273. Springer, Heidelberg (1999)
22. Waksman, A.: A Permutation Network. Journal of the ACM 15(1), 159–163 (1968)
23. Opferman, D., Tsao-Wu, N.: On A class of Rearrangeable Switching Networks. Bell Systems Technical Journal 50(5), 1579–1618 (1971)
24. Soo, W.H., Samsudin, A., Goh, A.: Efficient Mental Card Shuffling via Optimised Arbitrary-Sized Benes Permutation Network. In: Chan, A.H., Gligor, V.D. (eds.) ISC 2002. LNCS, vol. 2433, pp. 446–458. Springer, Heidelberg (2002)

25. Jakobsson, M., Juels, A.: Millimix: mixing in small batches. DIMACS Technical report 99-33 (1999)
26. Schnorr, C.P.: Efficient Signature Generation by Smart Cards. Journal of Cryptology 4, 161–174 (1991)
27. Recommendation for Key Management, Special Publication 800–57 Part 1, NIST (2007)
28. Kamvar, M., Baluja, S.: A large scale study of wireless search behavior: Google mobile search. In: Proceedings of the SIGCHI Conference on Human Factors in Computing Systems, pp. 701–709 (2006)

v-CAPS: A Confidentiality and Anonymity Preserving Routing Protocol for Content-Based Publish-Subscribe Networks

Amiya Kumar Maji and Saurabh Bagchi

Dependable Computing Systems Lab (DCSL)
School of Electrical and Computer Engineering
Purdue University, West Lafayette Indiana, USA
{amaji,sbagchi}@purdue.edu

Abstract. Content-based Publish-Subscribe (CBPS) is a widely used communication paradigm where publishers "publish" messages and a set of subscribers receive these messages based on their interests through filtering and routing by an intermediate set of brokers. CBPS has proven to be suitable for many-to-many communication offering flexibility and efficiency in communications between a dynamic set of publishers and subscribers. We are interested in using CBPS in healthcare settings to disseminate health-related information (drug interactions, diagnostic information on diseases) to large numbers of subscribers in a confidentiality-preserving manner. Confidentiality in CBPS requires that the message be hidden from brokers whereas the brokers need the message to compute routing decisions. Previous approaches to achieve these conflicting goals suffer from significant shortcomings—misrouting, lesser expressivity of subscriber interests, high execution time, and high message overhead. Our solution, titled v-CAPS, achieves the competing goals while avoiding the previous problems. In v-CAPS, the trusted publishers extract the routing information based on the message and the brokers keep minimal information needed to perform local routing. The routing information is cryptographically secured so that curious brokers or other subscribers cannot learn about the recipients. Our experiments show that v-CAPS has comparable end-to-end message latency to a baseline insecure CBPS system with unencrypted routing vectors. However, the cost of hiding the routing vectors from the brokers is significantly higher.

Keywords: content-based publish subscribe, privacy, anonymity, message latency.

1 Introduction

With the growing demand for adaptive and intelligent communication networks, content-based publish subscribe (CBPS) has gained significant attention in the

M. Rajarajan et al. (Eds.): SecureComm 2011, LNICST 96, pp. 281–302, 2012.
© Institute for Computer Sciences, Social Informatics and Telecommunications Engineering 2012

research community over the last decade. Publish-subscribe in general is a communication technique whereby publishers "publish" messages and a set of subscribers receive these messages. This is more efficient than a publisher sending multiple point-to-point messages to each subscriber. Publish-subscribe offers a degree of decoupling between the publishers and the subscribers—a network of brokers together route the messages from a publisher to the correct set of subscribers. In traditional publish-subscribe systems, the subscribers express their interest in certain topics of messages and each message is published on one or more topics. Thus, conceptually, routing of messages to the subscribers is simple.

CBPS systems, which followed the development of traditional publish-subscribe systems, offer greater flexibility to the subscribers to express their interests. In CBPS systems, the subscriber defines a filter (a logical expression) on the content of a message, such as, a diabetic patient may be interested in availability of a drug named 'Glucotrol' where the store zip code is either '47901' or '47902' and unit price is less than '$1'. Only messages matching the filter will be delivered to our hypothetical patient. Here the brokers execute more sophisticated algorithms for matching messages with constraints on attribute values in the filter (such as sub-string, equality, inequality). Typically, a hierarchy of brokers arranged in layers perform progressive filtering of the messages till they reach the correct set of subscribers. CBPS systems have seen significant research activity over the years resulting in excellent algorithms for filter matching, filter propagation through the broker network, and minimization of delivery latency [2], [4], [5], [6], [10]. These systems have also had mature industrial deployments [1], [2].

However, CBPS systems rely heavily on the integrity of brokers. Wang *et al.* [19] have shown that achieving message confidentiality, integrity, and auditability in the presence of malicious brokers is a challenging assignment. Consider the following scenario: Our hypothetical patient Jane is infected with HIV. She wants to subscribe for drug availability and preventive care newsletters for her disease from an online health information exchange that uses CBPS for content delivery. Due to the sensitivity of her disease, Jane doesn't want the brokers to learn about her subscription. Similarly, Dr. Watson, a publisher in the health information exchange, doesn't want to divulge contents of his messages to the brokers. But normal functioning of CBPS requires that the brokers should inspect both pieces of information (notifications and subscriptions) to route messages. We term the ensuing paradoxical problem—that of computing routing decisions based on encrypted notification and subscriptions—the *secure routing problem* (P_A). To further illustrate the complexity of this problem, let us assume that we have "magically" found a solution to P_A. However, to encrypt a notification, the publisher must know the precise set of subscribers that receive a notification and share a group key with them. This violates the publisher-subscriber decoupling property of CBPS. Furthermore, the set of subscribers is a function of the notification and may change with every message. We term this problem—that of dynamic group discovery and key exchange among publishers and subscribers—*dynamic subscriber group management problem* (P_B). An anonymity-preserving solution, like Tor [9], works well for single source to single destination, but not in the case when multiple patients need to subscribe to the same information, unbeknownst to others.

In this paper, we present *v*-CAPS, a routing protocol guaranteeing **C**onfidentiality of messages and **A**nonymity of subscribers in the presence of untrusted brokers in content-based **P**ublish-**S**ubscribe networks. In essence, our protocol solves the problem P_A mentioned in the previous paragraph. Our current work assumes a solution exists for the problem P_B so that for each notification, a key can be shared with a dynamically determined group of subscribers. Candidate solutions are available in [13]. A simplistic, but workable, solution will be to have a single key shared by each publisher with all the subscribers. Our brokers are curious in that they wish to inspect the messages and the recipients of messages, but are otherwise well-behaved in that they perform their routing decisions correctly. One can argue that the adversary model we consider is more insidious of the two—clear denial of service due to dropping the messages can be detected more easily. This class of privacy-preserving CBPS systems has been motivated by others in the literature [12], [15], [16].

Several researchers have tried to address P_A by using cryptographic techniques like computation on encrypted data [15], commutative encryption [16], or homomorphic encryption [12]. However, all of these approaches have their shortcomings—false positives or misrouting [15], lesser expressivity of subscriber interests or filters [12], [15], [16], high execution time [12], [15], and high message overhead [12], [15]. We make the important observation that routing in content-based publish-subscribe networks does not necessarily require inspection of the whole message. Instead, if a trusted publisher extracts the routing information from a message before encrypting it, then the problem reduces to hiding this information from malicious brokers. In our solution approach, the publisher looks at the commonality of interests among subscribers and encodes the routing information in the form of a routing vector (hence, the letter "v" in the name of our protocol). The routing vector (RV) is added to the header of a message and it allows brokers to compute their receiver lists. We present two versions of our protocol—one where the RV is left unencrypted (termed the RV protocol), and the second where the RV is further encrypted to achieve both confidentiality and anonymity (termed Secure RV or SRV protocol). Our simple approach eliminates the need for complex cryptographic operations, thereby, making it possible to incorporate the full generality of filters in baseline CBPS systems, with low computational overhead on the brokers. Our experimental results show that RV performs nearly as fast as a baseline CBPS in terms of latency. Achieving perfect anonymity (which we do through the SRV protocol), however, is significantly more costly and practical only for medium-sized networks. Unlike earlier approaches, the choice of encryption schemes is flexible in *v*-CAPS and continuing advances in faster content matching will render *v*-CAPS more efficient. For all practical purposes, *v*-CAPS does not have false positives (subject to the non-collision guarantees of cryptographic hash functions). The concessions that *v*-CAPS makes are added execution overhead at the publisher and some loss of decoupling between publishers and subscribers. However, the partial loss of decoupling has added advantage of auditability and enforcement of access control on subscriber interests.

The rest of the paper is organized as follows. Since a major portion of our protocol is described based on terminology used in Siena [4], a baseline CBPS system (i.e., without any privacy guarantee), we present the necessary background in Section 2. In Section 3, we highlight security goals, threat model, and assumptions in the proposed scheme. Section 4 presents the design of v-CAPS, guaranteeing message confidentiality. An enhanced protocol for incorporating subscriber anonymity is illustrated next. The protocol description is followed by an experimental evaluation of v-CAPS on a wide-area deployment. Finally, we discuss some unsolved design issues and conclude the paper.

2   Background

Content-Based Publish-Subscribe (CBPS) is an asynchronous communication paradigm where a message is routed based on its content instead of a fixed destination address. Typically, three types of nodes form the backbone of a CBPS network. These are – *publishers*, the entities that send a message into the network; *subscribers*, the entities that express their intention to receive messages with certain content; and *brokers*, the intermediate nodes that route messages from the publishers to the subscribers. Typically there are multiple levels of brokers between the publishers and the subscribers. CBPS has been shown to be an effective communication stratum under various scenarios — publishers and subscribers are linked transiently, fine-grained expression of interest can be made by subscribers, and some publishers and subscribers are ephemeral. It has been shown that CBPS is capable of delivering messages with low latency and of scaling to a large number of publishers and subscribers [2], [5]. The messages generated by publishers are termed as *notifications*. A notification consists of a collection of attributes and their values. Each element in this collection is a three-tuple $<attributeName, attributeValue, attributeType>$. E.g. a sample notification regarding available appointment schedule for Dr. Watson may look as follows:

```
wardName     cardiology            string
wardId       2131                  integer
docName      Dr. Watson            string
totalSlots   20                    integer
apptSlots    list_of_slots         list_datetime
timeStamp    01/05/2011 09:00AM    datetime
```

The notification indicates that Dr. Watson in cardiology ward has 20 available appointment slots for the week (list for which is also given in the notification). The collection of attribute names and their data types define the *schema* of a notification.

A subscriber in a CBPS network may request for messages with certain attribute values. The interest of a subscriber is represented by a set of constraints over the attributes. Each *attribute constraint* is defined as a four tuple $<attributeName, operator, value, attributeType>$, where *operator* can be any boolean operator like $=$, $! =$, $>$, $<$, etc. or string operators like prefix, suffix, substring etc. For clarity of representation, we shall, however, denote attribute constraints as logical expressions in subsequent discussions and assume that the attribute type will be clear from the context. For example, an attribute constraint for the notification shown above may be `wardName="cardiology"`. A *filter* over a notification schema is defined as a conjunction of one or more attribute constraints, e.g., `(wardName="cardiology")`∧`(docName="Dr. Watson")` is a filter for receiving appointment slots for Dr. Watson in Cardiology ward. A subscriber may subscribe with one or more filters which are propagated from the subscriber to the publishers through the set of brokers. The notifications, on the other hand, are routed from the publishers to the matching subscribers through progressive filtering at different levels of brokers. We say that a notification **matches** a filter if all its attribute constraints are satisfied by the notification. Clearly, the filter `(wardName="cardiology")`∧`(docName="Dr. Watson")` matches the notification shown above.

Commonality between filters in the CBPS network is computed by a *covering relationship* as in [4]. We define that a filter F_1 **covers** a filter F_2, denoted $F_2 \prec F_1$ iff all the notifications that match F_2 also match F_1. For example, if $F_1 = $ `(wardName="cardiology")` and $F_2 = $ `(wardName="cardiology")` ∧ `(docName="Dr. Watson")`, then $F_2 \prec F_1$. Loosely speaking, filter F_2 is less permissive, i.e. stricter, than filter F_1. Notice that, in the general case, notification sets of two filters may not overlap. Hence, the covering relation imposes a partial order on the set of filters. For efficient propagation of subscriptions and notifications, each broker in the CBPS network maintains two data structures—a *filter poset* and the *subscriber list* for each filter. The filter poset is the partially ordered set of filters received by a broker from its lower level brokers or subscribers, whereas, the subscriber list stores the set of subscribers for each filter.

2.1   Filter Posets

The filter posets, which denote partial ordering between filters at a broker, are represented as a collection of directed trees. In the tree an edge is drawn from filter F_1 to F_2 ($F_1 \rightarrow F_2$), iff $F_2 \prec F_1$. The root of a tree is termed as the *root filter*. Essentially, root filters are the set of filters that are not covered by any other filter. These trees may have overlap between themselves (i.e. they share some branches). However, the overall collection of trees form a directed acyclic graph (DAG). For notification forwarding decisions, each of the filters in the filter posets is associated with a set of recipients. A recipient may be either a subscriber or a next hop broker. For example, consider the simple network shown in Fig. 1. Here P is the publisher, B_1, B_2, B_3 are the brokers and S_1, S_2, S_3, S_4 are the subscribers with filters F_1, F_2, F_3, F_4 respectively.

We assume the covering relationship between filters to be $F_2 \prec F_1 \prec F_3$ while F_4 is independent w.r.t. other filters. The filter poset and the recipient list at each of the brokers in the network are displayed alongside each broker in Fig. 1.

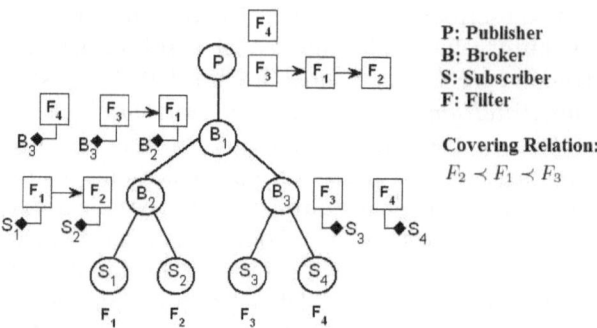

Fig. 1. An Example CBPS Network

The distinction between filter posets in v-CAPS and in baseline CBPS (Siena) lies in the content of each filter node. While each filter node in Siena contains a plaintext filter, filter nodes in v-CAPS store encrypted filters along with a unique filter ID. Additionally, each publisher in our protocol also stores the list of its filters and their covering relations in the form of filter posets. However, the publisher does *not* save recipient list for each filter. It is the responsibility of the brokers to maintain subscriber lists. The advantage of this design choice is that a publisher need not remember the topology of the network. It only remembers filters corresponding to the notifications it publishes. To avoid ambiguity, in further discussions of v-CAPS, we call the DAG representation of partially ordered list of filters at the publisher as the Publisher Filter Poset (PFPoset)and those at the brokers as Broker Filter Posets (BFPoset).

3 v-CAPS Basics

Our solution for confidentiality and anonymity preserving routing in CBPS networks, entitled v-CAPS, solves the *secure routing problem* (P_A) by introducing modified separation of duties for participating nodes (publishers, subscribers, brokers) and adding a level of indirection in filter matching. The protocol is built upon a typical publish-subscribe infrastructure, handles the full generality of baseline CBPS subscriptions, and does *not* require the presence of trusted third parties. The confidentiality and privacy goals of the proposed system are as follows:

1. *Notification Confidentiality*: No one except the publisher of a notification and its authorized subscribers can view the message content.
2. *Subscription Confidentiality*: No one except the subscriber and the publisher to whom it subscribes can know the content of a filter.
3. *Subscriber Anonymity*: A subscriber receiving notification N does not know other recipients (subscribers) of N.
4. *Filter Anonymity*: During routing, a broker can learn about matching between a notification and only those filters that are in its BFPoset. This ensures that the brokers have a very limited knowledge of which other brokers or subscribers receive a notification.

To satisfy the above security goals, we introduce two routing protocols named Routing Vector (RV) protocol and Secure Routing Vector (SRV) protocol. RV guarantees security goals (1) and (2). However, a resourceful attacker may be able to subvert goals (3) and (4) in RV. SRV, on the other hand, achieves all the security goals (1)–(4). We begin our protocol description in Section 4 by explaining RV and then highlight how we extend it to SRV in Section 5.

3.1   Threat Model and other Assumptions

We assume that the publishers and subscribers trust each other, but the subscribers do not trust each other. The brokers in the network may be malicious. We confine ourselves to an "honest but curious" model of the brokers. We assume that the brokers may try to learn the contents of a notification or subscription. It may also try to infer the mapping between a publisher and a subscriber. But the brokers follow the routing protocol correctly, i.e. it always forwards the notifications to the legitimate recipients as computed by the proposed scheme. We note that non-delivery of messages by malicious brokers can be easily detected by occasional rendezvous between publishers and subscribers. Appropriate legal actions may be taken to discourage such brokers. Similarly, notifications delivered by a malicious broker to illegitimate subscribers are unusable without the group key(s). However, "curiosity" of brokers leading to traffic analysis, etc. is challenging to detect and thwart. The threat model is, therefore, both practical and challenging. Earlier secure-CBPS schemes [11], [12], [15] are also built on this adversary model.

We assume that brokers in the CBPS network pre-compute a spanning tree connecting all the brokers and publishers. During subscription propagation, a filter is forwarded along the reverse edges of this spanning tree toward specific publishers. In case of a hierarchical broker network, the overlay network is equivalent to the spanning tree. Details of building a distributed spanning tree may be found in earlier work by Dalal and Metcalfe [8] and we omit the details in our protocol description.

3.2   Design Principles in *v*-CAPS

Our solution is motivated by two key observations. **First**, matching a notification against filters is several orders of magnitude faster in plaintext than matching on encrypted data [15], [12]. Therefore, it is desirable to compute filter matching against notifications in plaintext, rather than doing this at the brokers. **Second**, the brokers in baseline CBPS compute recipient lists of a notification based on a *match* that each broker computes. If the matching decision is added to a notification as a header, the untrusted brokers no longer need to inspect contents of notifications or filters to compute recipient lists.

4   v-CAPS Primitives

4.1   Subscribe

The subscription protocol allows subscribers to propagate their interests through-out the pub-sub network and to establish appropriate routes for receiving noti-fications. In our scheme, subscription consists of two stages. The first stage in-volves communication between the subscriber and the publisher and the second stage involves communication between the subscriber and the brokers. Details of the two stages are given below.

Stage I: *Contact Publisher*   When a subscriber (S) joins the pub-sub network, it first registers itself with its preferred publisher(s) (P) through an auxiliary channel. Publisher verifies the identity of the subscriber and provides it with an authorization token. When the subscriber wants to receive notifications matching a given filter, it contacts the publisher with its authorization token and the filter (F). On receipt of F, the publisher computes as follows:

1. Does F exist in its PFPoset?

NO: (i) Assign a unique filter ID, ID_F to F; ii) Add F to its PFPoset; (iii) Compute its parents (F_{parent}) and children (F_{child}) sets

YES: (i) Lookup ID_F; (ii) Compute F_{parent} and F_{child}

2. Compute subscription token T_{sub} as:

T_{sub} := `<parents>`F_{parent}`</parents><children>`F_{child}`</children>`
`<filter>`$ID_F|E_{k_s}(F)$`</filter>`

3. Send T_{sub} to the subscriber through an auxiliary point-to-point channel.

Note that E is any standard encryption function and k_s is the secret key used by a publisher to encrypt subscriptions and is known only to the publisher. The presence of $E_{k_s}(F)$ in the subscription request is not necessary for our content-based routing scheme. However, we store a copy of the encrypted filters at the brokers for the purpose of failure-recovery of the publisher.

Stage II: *Propagate Subscription*   In this stage, the subscription token is prop-agated upstream through the broker network such that each broker updates its filter posets. After receiving T_{sub} from the publisher, the subscriber contacts the broker (B_s) it is connected to with T_{sub}. During subscription propagation, upon receipt of T_{sub} from a downstream node x_i, every broker B_i performs the following:

1. Does ID_F exist in its BFPoset?

NO: (i) Let, local parent list, $L_{parent} = nodes(BFPoset) \cap F_{parent}$, and local children list, $L_{child} = nodes(BFPoset) \cap F_{child}$; (ii) Add ID_F to BFPoset; (iii) Update parents and children edges of ID_F; (iv) Add x_i to recipient list of ID_F

(v) If $(L_{parent} = \phi)$

Replace x_i in T_{sub} with B_i; Forward T_{sub} along the reverse edges of the spanning tree.

YES: (i) Add x_i to recipient list of ID_F

If the condition $(L_{parent} = \phi)$ in step (v) above is not satisfied, it means B_i has already propagated a more general filter than F and T_{sub} is not forwarded.

On the other hand, satisfying this condition implies F is the root of some filter chain at B_i and it needs to be forwarded along the reverse edges of the spanning tree. Note that the addition of F at some broker may lead to *compaction of filters*, which we explain with the following example.

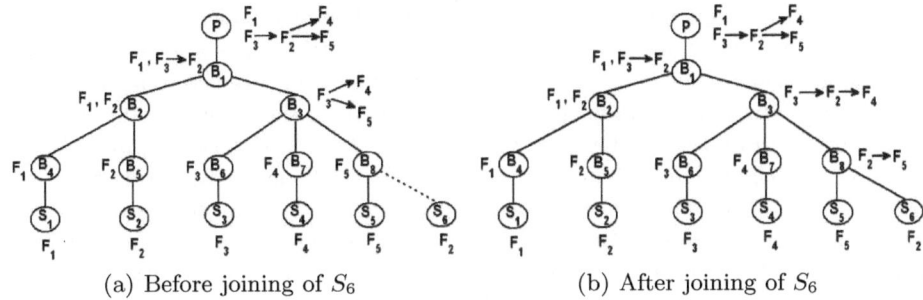

(a) Before joining of S_6 (b) After joining of S_6

Fig. 2. Subscription Forwarding: Before and After Joining of S_6

Consider the network in Fig. 2(a) consisting of a publisher (P), eight brokers $(B_1$–$B_8)$, and six subscribers $(S_1$–$S_6)$ with the given spanning tree. The filters for S_1 to S_5 are F_1–F_5 respectively. Now S_6 wants to subscribe with the filter F_2. The covering relation among the filters is assumed to be $(F_4 \prec F_2)$, $(F_5 \prec F_2)$, and $(F_2 \prec F_3)$ (readers may use the filter graph beside P in Fig. 2(a) as a quick reference). By transitivity $(F_4 \prec F_3)$, $(F_5 \prec F_3)$. The filter posets at each of the brokers and the publisher before joining of S_6 are shown in Fig. 2(a). When P receives the request it computes $F_{2_{pred}} = \{3\}$ and $F_{2_{succ}} = \{4, 5\}$ and includes these in a token T_{S_6} that it provides to S_6. When B_8 receives T_{S_6} it finds that it has no filter that belongs to $F_{2_{pred}}$ but F_5 is in $F_{2_{succ}}$. So it adds F_2 as a root filter and marks F_5 as its child. S_6 is added to the newly created recipient list of F_2. T_{S_6} is now propagated to B_3. Since $F_{2_{pred}} = \{3\}$ and F_3 is already in B_3, T_{S_6} is not propagated any further. However, F_2 is inserted into the BFPoset at B_3. Both F_5 and F_2 at B_3 have B_8 as the recipient and $(F_5 \prec F_2)$. This invokes a *compaction* of BFPoset of B_3. First, B_8 is removed from the recipient list of F_5 leaving it with no recipients. Therefore, F_5 is also removed from the filter poset at B_3. With this the routing path for S_6 is established. The final filter posets are shown in Fig. 2(b).

4.2   Publish

The publish protocol is initiated at the publisher. The publisher is responsible for extracting the *routing information* from a notification before sending it into the network. Hence, the publishers in *v*-CAPS first match a notification against the filters in PFPoset. The algorithm that we use for plaintext filter matching at publishers is the Siena Fast Forwarding (SFF) algorithm [5]. The function $M_{sff}(N, PFPoset) = F_{match}$ takes the plaintext notification N and $PFPoset$ as its inputs and produces a list of matching filter IDs (F_{match}). F_{match} is now added as a header to the notification and is termed RV. In the next step, the publisher with the help of *group manager*, computes the group key K_N for a notification N and encrypts the notification. The notification sent into the network by publisher looks as:

$$N_e = \texttt{<RV>} F_{match} \texttt{</RV><Payload>} E_{K_N}(N) \texttt{</Payload>}$$

The publisher now forwards N_e to broker B_1. The fact that the brokers do not have to do matching of filters against encrypted notifications allows us to avoid enormous performance penalties of computation on encrypted content. It may be argued that our scheme adds significant overhead on the publisher due to filter matching (as compared to baseline CBPS). But this is a practical approach considering publishers can be run on machines with sufficient computation power. Carzaniga et al. [5] have shown that even for a million subscriptions, plaintext filter matching typically takes time in the order of 10 ms on a desktop computer with 512MB of RAM. Our experiments also bear out this fact. Additionally, if filter matching is performed at each broker, this may lead to significant redundant computation as the brokers contain overlapping sets of filters.

4.3   Match

The Match() operation in v-CAPS is performed by brokers during notification delivery and its objective is to determine the list of receivers to forward the notification to. This operation is simplified by the fact that the publisher has already computed the RV and included it in the notification. The Match() operation at a broker B_i is done with the following simple steps:

Let receivers $R_{B_i} = \phi$

for each ID_F in RV
      if $(ID_F \in BFPoset)$ $R_{B_i} = R_{B_i} \cup receivers(ID_F)$
end for

B_i now forwards the encrypted notification to all the nodes in R_{B_i}. The brokers do not alter any part of the notification N_e and forwards an identical copy to all the recipients. Thus, for correct routing, a broker does not need to know either the content of a message or filters. Instead, routing may be performed using filter IDs generated by the publisher.

5   Secure Routing Vector (SRV) Protocol

The RV protocol presented in Section 4 achieves notification and subscription confidentiality (security goals 1 and 2) with the help of filter indirection and encryption. However, it does not guarantee security goals 3 (subscriber anonymity) and 4 (filter anonymity). Let us consider the following scenarios that may arise in the example in Figure 2(b):

1. S_2, a curious subscriber in our CBPS network, learns by external means that S_6 also receives notifications matching filter F_2. After receiving N_e from B_5, S_2 can easily identify S_6 as the other recipient of N_e. This violates *subscriber anonymity*.

2. B_2, a malicious broker learns by external means that B_3 subscribed to filter F_3. When, it receives N_e with RV={1, 2, 3}, it can easily identify B_3 as a recipient of N_e. Notice that filter F_3 is not even in the BFPoset of B_2. This violates *filter anonymity*.

From the examples above, let us now formulate the requirements of the SRV protocol. **First**, the RV should be encrypted in such a manner that, even if two notifications (N_1, N_2) both contain filter F_2 in the RV, it should generate different ciphertexts. This would help preserve subscriber anonymity. **Second**, the RV should be encrypted in such a manner that, a broker can only compute $\{BFPoset \cap RV_{enc}\}$. But it cannot learn which other filter IDs are in the encrypted RV_{enc}. This ensures filter anonymity. We adapt a prior solution on matching keywords in encrypted documents [18] to meet the last two requirements. The resultant solution is the *SRV protocol*. Before illustrating details of SRV, let us present a brief overview of the cryptographic technique in [18].

5.1 Background

Problem Statement: Assume, Alice has a set of secret documents D_1, D_2, .., D_k, where document D_i contains m_i words and every word is n bytes long. She encrypts these documents as Z_1, Z_2, .., Z_k and stores them on an untrusted file server Bob. Later, she wants to retrieve the documents containing an n-byte word w^*. However, Alice is reluctant to disclose either w^* or the encryption keys of Z_1, .., Z_k to Bob. So, Alice sends a query containing an encrypted keyword $x^* = E_{key}(w^*)$ to Bob. How can Bob find the precise set of encrypted documents $\mathbb{Z} = \{Z_i | D_i \text{ contains } w^*\}$ matching this query?

Solution: For clarity of representation, we abstract the encryption and match algorithms as a collection of functions. Interested readers may find the details of this algorithm in [18].

Let, $D_i = \{w_1.w_2....w_{m_i}\}$ (. denotes concatenation) is a plaintext document containing words w_1, w_2, .., w_{m_i}; w^* is a search word; and *keys* is a collection of secrets held by Alice (to be explained later). The secure search problem mentioned above can be solved by the following three functions:

- $\mathscr{E}(D_i, keys)$ is an encryption function that converts D_i to Z_i where $Z_i = \{c_1.c_2....c_{m_i}\}$ and c_j is a ciphertext for word w_j. $\mathscr{E}()$ can be used with different pseudorandom sequences to produce different encrypted versions of D_i for multiple encryptions.
- $\mathscr{F}(w^*, keys)$ is a cryptographic function that creates a search token $Q^* = \{x^*, k^*\}$ from w^*. Here, x^* is referred to as the *encrypted search word*, and k^* is referred to as the *search key* for w^*.
- $\mathscr{M}(Z_i, Q^*)$ is a match function which returns *true* **iff** w^* appears in D_i (using the above definition of Q^* which contains x^*, the encrypted keyword of w^*).

Internally, $\mathscr{E}()$, $\mathscr{F}()$, and $\mathscr{M}()$ use a standard encryption function (e.g. AES), a cryptographic hash function (e.g. SHA1), and a pseudorandom number generator as their building blocks.

Secrets Used: The algorithm uses three secrets, i.e., $keys = \{k_w, k', k_{seed}\}$. k_w is a secret key for AES, k' is a key for the cryptographic hash function, and k_{seed} is the seed for the pseudorandom number generator. All these secrets are stored by Alice and none of these is disclosed to Bob.

5.2   SRV Overview

In SRV, our trusted publishers are equivalent to Alice and the brokers to Bob. Let us first assign each of the filter nodes in PFPoset with a n-byte ID. Each notification N_i now contains n_i matching filter IDs in RV. Each RV can be considered as a document D_i that is n_i words long. We wish to restrict our brokers so that they can learn whether a filter ID_F appears in RV iff ID_F is in BFPoset. This can be achieved by encrypting RV using $\mathscr{E}$ and sharing the search token for filter ID_F with legitimate brokers. These search tokens are distributed during subscription stage of SRV. During notification forwarding, $\mathscr{M}$ is used to check the presence of filter ID_F in the encrypted RV. As in Section 5.1, publishers store the secret keys k_w, k', and k_{seed}. Let us now illustrate how we extend each of the primitives in RV for confidentiality and anonymity preserving routing. For brevity, we only highlight the additional steps needed in SRV.

5.3   Subscribe

Stage I: *Contact Publisher*   After step 1 in RV, the publisher computes as follows (here the subscriber has subscribed with filter ID_F, which has parents in the PFPoset F_{parent} and children F_{child}):

2. Compute $F'_{parent} = \mathscr{E}(F_{parent}, keys)$ and $F'_{child} = \mathscr{E}(F_{child}, keys)$
3. Compute query token for filter ID_F as:
   $$Q_{ID_F} = \mathscr{F}(ID_F, keys) = \{x_{ID_F}, k_{ID_F}\}$$
4. Compute subscription token T'_{sub} as:
   $$T'_{sub} := \texttt{<parents>}F'_{parent}\texttt{</parents><children>}F'_{child}\texttt{</children>}$$
   $$\texttt{<filter>}x_{ID_F}|k_{ID_F}|E_{k_s}(F)\texttt{</filter>}$$
5. Send T'_{sub} to the subscriber.

Note that the parents and children lists are encrypted to disallow the brokers from learning filter IDs that are not in their BFPoset. Since, subscribe is a one-time cost, the overhead of computing F'_{parent} and F'_{child} is not a performance bottleneck, however, it is essential for achieving security goals 3 and 4.

Stage II: *Propagate Subscription*   BFPoset filter nodes in SRV contain $Q_{ID_F} = \{x_{ID_F}, k_{ID_F}\}$ instead of ID_F in RV protocol. Upon receipt of T'_{sub} from node n_i, every broker B_i computes as follows:

1. Does x_{ID_F} exist in BFPoset?
   NO: i) Compute local parent list
        $$L'_{parent} = \{x_{ID_{F_i}}|\mathscr{M}(F'_{parent}, Q_{ID_{F_i}}) = true\}$$
        ii) Compute local children list
        $$L'_{child} = \{x_{ID_{F_i}}|\mathscr{M}(F'_{child}, Q_{ID_{F_i}}) = true\}$$
        iii) Add $\{x_{ID_F}, k_{ID_F}\}$ to BFPoset
        iv) Update parent and children edges using L'_{parent} and L'_{child}
        v) Follow step (iv) onwards as in RV (refer Section 4.1)

Note that the steps (i) and (ii) are necessary here since F'_{parent} and F'_{child} are encrypted.

5.4   Publish

To send a notification N into the network, a publisher first computes the matching filters $F_{match} = M_{sff}(N, PFPoset)$ as in RV. It then encrypts RV using $\mathcal{E}$ as:
$$SRV = F'_{match} = \mathcal{E}(F_{match}, keys)$$
The added overhead at the publisher, in comparison with RV, is the computation of $\mathcal{E}(F_{match}, keys)$. Our experimental results suggest that this overhead is only a small fraction of the end-to-end latency.

5.5   Match

Similar to RV, the objective of $Match()$ is to compute the recipient list for a notification N_e. However, encrypting the routing vector makes this operation significantly more complex compared to the RV protocol. Upon receipt of a notification N_e with $SRV = F'_{match}$, the broker first needs to compute the local match list L'_{match}, where
$$L'_{match} = \{x_{ID_{F_i}} | x_{ID_{F_i}} \in BFPoset \text{ and } \mathcal{M}(F'_{match}, Q_{ID_{F_i}}) = true\}$$
Hidden under the abstraction of $\mathcal{M}$, this is the most expensive part of our SRV protocol. The simple approach to compute L'_{match} would be to search for every filter in the BFPoset in every filter in the SRV. However, this would require a computation time of $m \times n$ matching operations, where $m = $ number of filter IDs in F'_{match} and $n = $ number of filter nodes in BFPoset. We reduce this cost by applying the following heuristics: (i) If a root filter with ID r_i does not match any entry in the SRV, i.e. $\mathcal{M}(F'_{match}, Q_{r_i}) = false$, then the broker does not do a search in the sub-tree of BFPoset rooted at r_i. This is based upon the observation that, if a message matches a certain filter F, then it must also match a root filter R above F. However, the performance gain of this optimization is dependent on the mix of filters in the network. If the covering between filters is high, then this heuristic would help. But, for a broker with lots of isolated filters (hence with a large number of root filters), this does not give significant improvement.
(ii) During computation of SRV match, if the broker observes that all its child brokers are already in the current receiver list, then it need not compute $Match()$ any further as all its child brokers must get that notification. This helps in reducing the SRV match times of the higher level brokers in a hierarchical broker network, which tend to have many filters and most often forward a message along all its downstream edges.

Once L'_{match} is computed by a broker B_i, the recipient list can be generated trivially. The controlled searching property of [18] ensures that a broker can only learn about the presence of its own filters in SRV and hence we are able to guarantee filter anonymity. Moreover, the encryption algorithm also ensures that if N_1 and N_2 both match filter F, the cipher IDs of ID_F in SRV_1, and SRV_2 are different. This helps us in protecting subscriber anonymity.

6   Experimental Results

We evaluated the performance of our protocols against baseline CBPS (Siena) with respect to end-to-end latency and computation time for notifications in a wide-area deployment. We implemented all the three protocols Baseline, RV, and SRV and deployed them on *PlanetLab* [14]—a worldwide computer systems testbed. Our experiments involve sending upto 100,000 subscription messages from the subscribers over a wide-area network, which, to the best of our knowledge, are the largest scale experiments on CBPS.

6.1   Experimental Setup

In our experiments, we created a hierarchical broker network with 4 levels (refer Fig. 3(a)). Each of the brokers in the top three levels were considered to have a fanout of 3, whereas, the leaf brokers were randomly connected to the subscribers. This constituted a broker network with 40 nodes. Each broker was hosted on a separate machine at Purdue University, 28 of which belonged to two clusters in our research group and the rest on public desktops in one of Purdue University laboratories. The reason for this choice of machines over PlanetLab machines is to reduce the sources of variability. We placed the less demanding subscriber processes on PlanetLab nodes.

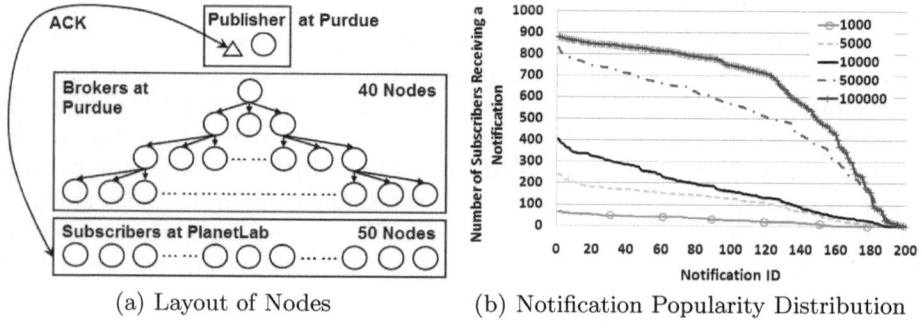

(a) Layout of Nodes   (b) Notification Popularity Distribution

Fig. 3. Experimental Setup and Workload Properties

At present, we generate notifications from a single publisher, with an interval of 3–5 seconds between successive notifications. The number of publishers can be easily increased with independent BFPoset data structures for each. The publisher was hosted on a desktop computer with 2GB RAM and 2.13GHz dual-core CPU running Ubuntu Linux 10.04. The subscribers were hosted on PlanetLab machines situated at widely varying geographical locations. We ran our experiments with upto 1000 subscribers hosted on 50 PlanetLab machines (i.e. 20 subscriber processes per machine). Each subscriber subscribed with 1–200 filters with a uniform random distribution, generating 100,000 subscriptions in our largest workload. In total, the experiments involved coordination between 1132 processes running on 91 machines over the Internet. All processes were run as user processes with default priority.

Workload Details. Since, there is no publicly available real-life workload for CBPS systems, we used *ssbg*, a component of the Siena software suite [3], to generate our workload. Attribute names for filters and notifications were chosen from a dictionary of 200 words. Each filter contained between 1 and 4 attribute constraints, while each notification contained between 1 and 9 attributes. For simplicity, all the attributes were defined to be of Integer type and their values were uniformly distributed in the range of $[1 - 100]$. Note that different subscribers may have overlapping subscriptions. We, henceforth, use the term *subscriptions* to define a set of filters from one subscriber, which may contain duplicate filters aggregated across all subscribers, and *filters* to define a set of unique filters. Using *ssbg*, we generated a total of five workloads with 100, 500, 1000, 5000, and 10000 filters respectively. Each subscriber now subscribed with a random subset of the filters, with uniform distribution in $[1-200]$. This generated the final workloads having 1000, 5000, 10000, 50000, and 100000 subscriptions respectively. Each workload contained 200 notifications. Due to the large number of subscriptions, this generated a significant number of notifications received by the subscribers (between 5459 and 125418 notifications at the subscriber end for the smallest and largest workloads respectively). Fig. 3(b) shows the popularity distribution of each notification. Based on the popularity distribution of notifications we classified them into three categories, namely, *popular*, *moderate*, and *esoteric*, where popular matches the most number of subscriptions and so on.

Latency Measurement. Latency, a simple concept in computer networks, is difficult to measure in wide-area networks. This is primarily due to coarse-grained clock synchronization accuracy over the Internet. In PlanetLab, we found that a large number of nodes had clock drifts in the range of seconds or even minutes. This compelled us to devise an alternative strategy for measuring end-to-end latency. In our experiments, prior to sending notifications, all the subscribers establish a dedicated connection to an acknowledgement server (ackServer) running on the publisher machine. After receiving a notification, the subscribers immediately forward an ACK with the notification ID and timestamp of notification. On receiving an ACK, the ackServer computes the total time spent by looking at the ACK timestamp. For future discussions, we define this closed-loop latency (from notification generation to receipt of ACK) as our *end-to-end latency*. To estimate the network RTT of PlanetLab nodes, the ackServer also periodically sends a timestamped packet to these nodes every 30 seconds which is reflected back by the subscriber nodes. We do not deduct $RTT/2$ from *end-to-end latency* as the network links were found to be asymmetric. Despite this, due to fluctuations of network latencies to and from PlanetLab nodes, we had to do some filtering of noisy points, where the estimated noise was greater than 5 ms.

Other Implementation Details. The length of filter ID was chosen to be 16 bytes as this is also the block size of AES. We used an implementation of Siena Fast Forwarding algorithm [5], as the plaintext filter matching engine in all three protocols. For cryptographic operations we used the CryptoPP library [7] and built our networking code using C++ Sockets Library [17].

6.2   Evaluating Recurring Costs

In v-CAPS, we try to achieve low computational cost for routing while guaranteeing confidentiality and anonymity. In this subsection, we present results for per notification cost.

End-to-end Latency. One of the crucial metrics for CBPS systems is to deliver notifications to the subscribers as fast as possible. In figures 4(a)–4(c), we present the end-to-end latency (as defined in 6.1) of different types of notifications for each of the protocols. The results are obtained from our experiments on the largest workload, i.e., 100,000 subscriptions. The X-axis represents various nodes on PlanetLab sorted according to their network RTT, while the Y-axis shows end-to-end latency in milliseconds. It can be seen from figures 4(a) and 4(b) that end-to-end latencies for baseline and RV are very similar. In baseline, end-to-end latency for all the nodes is within 5 ms of network RTT, whereas, in RV, this is within 10 ms of network RTT. There is no significant difference in end-to-end latencies with varying popularity type of notification. In baseline, all the three popularity types overlap on the same line and in RV, popular notifications have marginally higher latency than moderate and esoteric.

End-to-end latency in SRV, is however significantly higher than network RTT. This happens due to large matching time at the brokers. Latency also varies widely across popularity of notifications—popular notifications being the highest, followed by moderate and esoteric. The primary reason

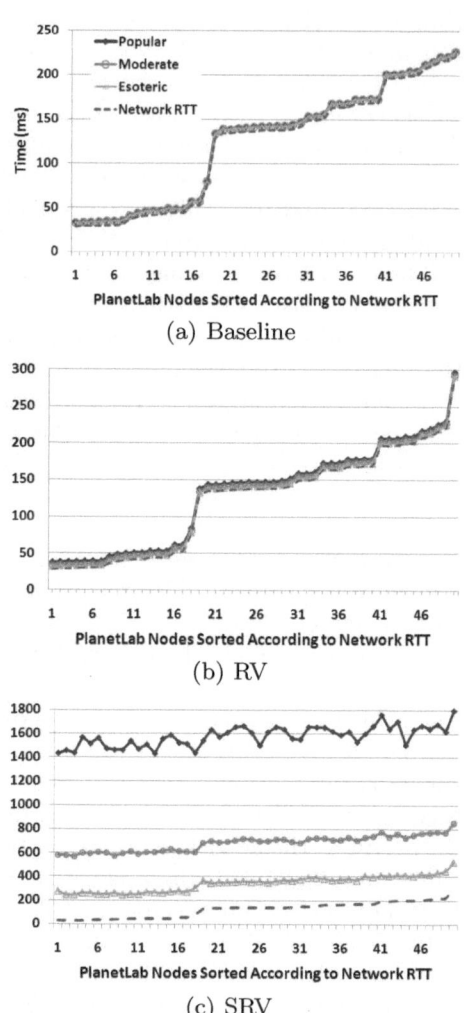

(a) Baseline

(b) RV

(c) SRV

Fig. 4. End-to-end Latency of Notification Forwarding for Different Protocols with 100,000 Subscriptions

for this is the length of SRV for these categories. One of the key findings from our results is that achieving anonymity is significantly costlier than confidentiality alone. Our current implementation of RV has only marginally higher end-to-end latency than baseline. RV can be further improved by compressing the header and thereby reducing networking overhead due to increased size.

Computation Time. In figures 5(a)–5(c), we show the total computational cost of notifications with increasing workload size. The computational cost includes both cost at the publisher (for generating RV) and at the brokers (for matching). In each plot, we compare the performance of three protocols. *The large magnitude of SRV cost necessitated use of a secondary Y-axis.* We vary workload sizes along the X-axis, while the Y-axis represents time in ms. The bars for baseline and RV follow similar pattern across all popularity types. Even with the largest workload, the difference in computational time between RV and baseline is only 3 ms.

For SRV, computation time increases with increasing workload size as expected. However, the difference in computation time across popularity types is much more prominent (~1500 ms for popular, ~560 ms for moderate, and ~220 ms for esoteric in our largest workload). This is because the number of matching filters is significantly different in the three categories (popular > moderate > esoteric) and the cost of processing at a broker for each filter is high in SRV. Contrary to a possible criticism, the cost at the publisher is quite low. Though this constituted the largest fraction of overall computation time in RV, it is only marginally higher than the computation time in baseline (within 1.5 ms) even for 100,000 subscriptions. For SRV, the cost at the publisher (~4 ms for 100,000) is three orders of magnitude lower than the cost at brokers (~1500 ms for popular at 100,000).

6.3 Evaluating One-time Costs

In this section, we evaluate the cost of registering a new subscription at publishers and brokers. At the publisher, cost of a new subscription amounts to adding the filter in PFPoset, reorganizing PFPoset edges, and computing encrypted parent and children lists. At brokers, this is the cost of evaluating local parent and children lists, reorganizing BFPoset edges, and

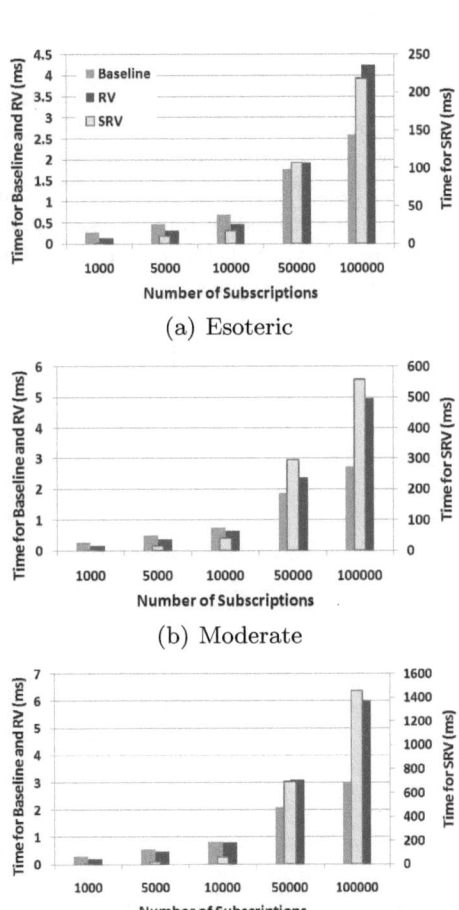

(a) Esoteric

(b) Moderate

(c) Popular

Fig. 5. Computational Cost for Notifications with Increasing Number of Subscriptions. Note the use of two separate Y-axes due to widely varying values–the left axis for baseline and RV and the right axis for SRV.

in some cases, propagating the subscription up the broker hierarchy. Notice that since subscriptions from different subscribers may contain duplication of the same filter(s), majority of the subscriptions involve only a lookup operation at publisher and brokers incurring very small overhead (in the order of a hundredth of a millisecond). In figures 6(a) and 6(b), we consider cost of adding *new* filters only. The X-axis in both the figures represent number of filters already existing at a broker or a publisher. We grouped this into buckets of size 200, i.e. when number of existing filters is (0, 200], (200, 400], etc. The point 400 represents the range (200, 400] and so on. The Y-axis represents computation time for adding a new filter in milliseconds. For brokers, the number of *filters* at a broker was upto 3400 while at the publisher it was 9400 for workload size of 100,000 subscriptions.

It can be seen from Fig. 6(a) that the cost of adding a *new* filter at a broker is much higher in SRV (~230ms for the largest workload). This is insignificant in RV (< 1ms), since, subscription propagation in RV involves only lookup operations. For baseline the cost was ~25ms for our largest workload. The RV cost is lower because the publisher has already done the processing to figure out which will be the parent and children filter nodes in the BFPoset, while in the baseline, the broker has to compute this. The slow subscription processing in SRV may not be a severe bottleneck because this is a one-time cost incurred only when a filter is entered for the first time and over time, most subscriptions result in duplicate filters.

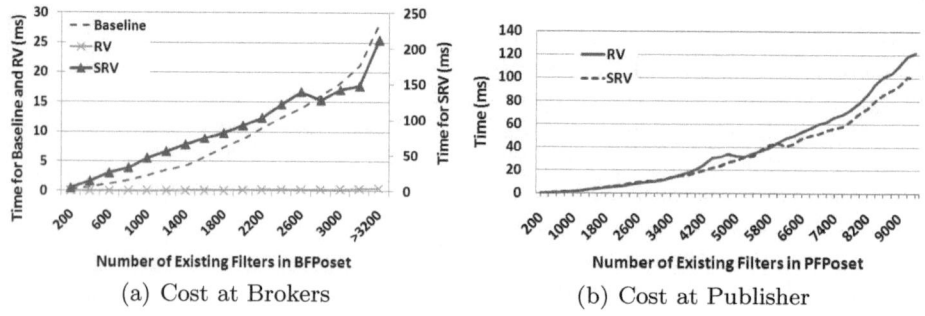

(a) Cost at Brokers   (b) Cost at Publisher

Fig. 6. Cost for Adding a New Filter at Brokers and Publishers

Fig. 6(b) shows the cost of adding a new filter in RV and SRV with increasing number of filters in PFPoset. The cost in SRV(RV) reaches upto 100(120) ms for 9200 filters. To reduce this cost, the publisher may also pre-load a set of known subscriptions in its PFPoset. The costs for RV and SRV are comparable because the same processing happens at the publisher; the slight differences (in fact SRV is faster) is explained by the different orders in which filters arrive at the publishers and the fact that different mix of existing filters affect processing time.

6.4 Message Overhead

During notification forwarding, we measured the length of RV(SRV) in each notification, where RV length is defined as the number of filterIDs in RV. This
gives us an estimate on the message overhead of v-CAPS over baseline CBPS.
Our experimental results are presented in Fig. 7. Since both RV and SRV protocol have identical header lengths, we show only one plot for both of them. The
X-axis here represents various workload sizes. Since our experiments involved
synthetic payloads for each notification, comparing the header with the payload
as a measure of overhead will be misleading. We, therefore, normalized the total header size (Num notifications×RV or SRV Length×16 bytes) by the total
number of subscribers receiving each notification. This represents the average
number of additional bytes spent per subscriber for a given class of notification.
This cost is displayed by the line plots in Fig. 7. It is encouraging to find that
the cost per subscriber is less than 4 bytes in all cases. One may argue that for
a small notification with lots of non-overlapping subscriptions (i.e. with a long
RV) message overhead is substantial. This cost is indispensable since filter IDs in
v-CAPS are equivalent to virtual "destination addresses." A possible improvement would be to add filter coverage information in the header (RV), so that,
during notification propagation, the brokers only forward relevant portions of
the RV to lower level brokers.

7 Related Work

Over the past decade and a half,
publish-subscribe has been extensively
studied as an efficient model of communication. Security in CBPS systems have been achieved under different settings—different network topologies, varying degrees of trust between
the communicating entities, and varying flexibility of subscription predi-
cates. Another significant problem—
that of key management in such a dy-

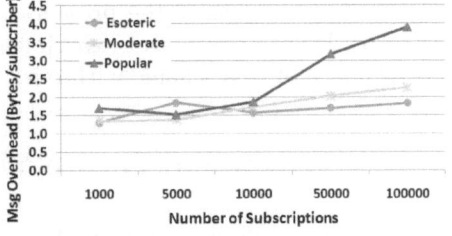

Fig. 7. Message Overhead for Routing in
RV(SRV) with Increasing Workload Size

namic environment has been studied in [13]. Majority of these approaches have
the goal of securing CBPS against the vulnerability of malicious brokers. They
balance this source of vulnerability against the common CBPS design in which
brokers need to examine the content of messages to make routing decisions. In
[15], the authors adapted the schemes presented in [18] and other techniques on
computation on encrypted data. They build a confidentiality-preserving CBPS
system that supports equality, inequality, and range matches for numeric attributes, and keyword searches for strings. The experimental results show that for
1,000 subscriptions, compared to the corresponding insecure operations, equality is 6 times more expensive, inequality is 1.7-3.0 times more expensive, and
range matching is 6 times more expensive. Apart from the computation cost,

this scheme suffers from three other significant drawbacks—restrictive filters on subscriber interests, high communication overhead (the encrypted message is 15 times the size of the plaintext message), and false positives for filter matching. On the other hand, [12] addresses privacy in CBPS by applying Paillier homomorphic encryption for equality, and inequality matches on numeric attributes. This scheme performs filter matching with two primitives—1) *blinding* the attribute value for subscriptions and notifications at the publisher, and 2) *matching* the blinded values in filters and notifications. The authors have not presented any implementation of their protocol in a publish-subscribe system. However, standalone experimental results for the cryptographic operations show that blinding **one** attribute value at the publisher takes 10-15 ms for a key length of 1024 bits and matching between one blinded attribute value and one blinded constraint takes $100\mu s$. Apart from these, complexity of key management and large message size are other drawbacks of this solution. Another research work, presented by Molva *et al.*, try to achieve confidential routing in CBPS using multiple layer commutative encryption (MLCE). The protocol computes matching between a filter and a notification by comparing their encrypted strings. As a result, this solution is limited to equality matches. Moreover, for a k-layer commutative encryption, a broker would be required to know the sender or recipient of a message at distance k from itself. Similarly, while propagating the messages downstream, a broker would be required to encrypt it separately with each of the recipients' (at distance k) keys. Ion *et al.* [11] used Attribute-based Encryption (ABE) and multi-user Searchable Data Encryption (SDE) to achieve confidentiality of notifications and filters without losing any decoupling property of CBPS. Their scheme, however, needs the presence of a trusted authority which our solution does not. Due to absence of experimental results in [11] we cannot compare the performance of this scheme with ours.

8   Discussion and Future Work

Our design and implementation of v-CAPS shows that it is possible to support privacy in CBPS. In other words, it is possible to handle the balance between the need to route by the brokers, and that the brokers are not trusted and may be curious. We achieve this without sacrificing the generality of filters in baseline CBPS. Further, we achieve this with acceptable overhead (in terms of time) over the baseline CBPS, *if* one is willing to accept a slight risk of the broker getting to know which other brokers will see a message, which may happen with the unencrypted routing vectors. However, if we want to eliminate this risk, we have to perform matching of encrypted filters with encrypted routing vectors, which is significantly more costly—for 10,000 filters, the end-to-end latency is just under 1.5 sec. However, we believe that there are two promising directions to resolve this problem. First, the matching algorithm at the broker can be easily parallelized—each entry in the secure routing vector (SRV) is matched in parallel. Thus, brokers running on multi-core machines can leverage this. Second, the publishers can send a hierarchical SRV, which will allow the broker to perform the simple optimization that if a routing vector does not match a filter, it will not match any filter in the sub-tree rooted at that filter.

Our work has not addressed the issue of fault tolerance, either at the brokers or at the publishers. A practical system needs to handle crash failures of both entities. Fault tolerance for broker failures is orthogonal to the privacy requirement of CBPS and we believe *v*-CAPS can be easily applied to a baseline CBPS that has redundancy to deal with broker failures. To handle publisher failures, the system needs to be able to recreate the publisher filter poset. This information is conceptually contained in the union of the filter posets at all the brokers. The challenge will be in gathering them in an efficient manner. The leaf brokers can potentially violate the anonymity requirement of the subscribers because they are directly forwarding messages to the subscribers. Hence, to achieve subscriber anonymity from leaf brokers, it will be required to interpose an anonymizing network between these entities. This anonymizing network will have no notion of the filters of the subscribers.

References

1. Barnett, D.: Publish-subscribe model connects tokyo highways. Web article, `http://www.industrial-embedded.com/articles/barnett/`
2. Bhola, S., Strom, R.E., Bagchi, S., Zhao, Y., Auerbach, J.S.: Exactly-once delivery in a content-based publish-subscribe system. In: DSN 2002: Proceedings of the 2002 International Conference on Dependable Systems and Networks, pp. 7–16 (2002)
3. Carzaniga, A.: Siena download. Web article, `http://www.inf.usi.ch/carzaniga/siena/forwarding/index.html`
4. Carzaniga, A., Rosenblum, D.S., Wolf, A.L.: Design and evaluation of a wide-area event notification service. ACM Transactions on Computer Systems 19(3), 332–383 (2001)
5. Carzaniga, A., Wolf, A.L.: Forwarding in a content-based network. In: Proceedings of ACM SIGCOMM 2003, Karlsruhe, Germany, pp. 163–174 (August 2003)
6. Chandramouli, B., Yang, J., Agarwal, P.K., Yu, A., Zheng, Y.: Prosem: scalable wide-area publish/subscribe. In: SIGMOD 2008: Proceedings of the 2008 ACM SIGMOD International Conference on Management of Data, pp. 1315–1318 (2008)
7. Crypto++ library - a free c++ class library of cryptographic schemes. Web article, `http://www.cryptopp.com/`
8. Dalal, Y.K., Metcalfe, R.M.: Reverse path forwarding of broadcast packets. Communications of the ACM 21(12), 1040–1048 (1978)
9. Dingledine, R., Mathewson, N., Syverson, P.: Tor: the second-generation onion router. In: Proceedings of the 13th Conference on USENIX Security Symposium, SSYM 2004, vol. 13, p. 21 (2004)
10. Eugster, P.T., Felber, P.A., Guerraoui, R., Kermarrec, A.M.: The many faces of publish/subscribe. ACM Computing Surveys 35(2), 114–131 (2003)
11. Ion, M., Russello, G., Crispo, B.: Supporting Publication and Subscription Confidentiality in Pub/Sub Networks. In: Jajodia, S., Zhou, J. (eds.) SecureComm 2010. LNICST, vol. 50, pp. 272–289. Springer, Heidelberg (2010)
12. Nabeel, M., Ning Shang, E.B.: Privacy-preserving filtering and covering in content-based publish subscribe systems. Tech. rep., Purdue University (June 2009)

13. Opyrchal, L., Prakash, A.: Secure distribution of events in content-based publish subscribe systems. In: SSYM 2001: Proceedings of the 10th Conference on USENIX Security Symposium, p. 21 (2001)
14. Planetlab: An open platform for developing, deploying, and accessing planetary-scale services. Web article, http://www.planet-lab.org/
15. Raiciu, C., Rosenblum, D.S.: Enabling confidentiality in content-based publish/subscribe infrastructures. In: Securecomm and Workshops 2006, August 28-September 1, pp. 1–11 (2006)
16. Shikfa, A., Önen, M., Molva, R.: Privacy-Preserving Content-Based Publish/Subscribe Networks. In: Gritzalis, D., Lopez, J. (eds.) SEC 2009. IFIP AICT, vol. 297, pp. 270–282. Springer, Heidelberg (2009)
17. C++ sockets library: A class library wrapping the berkeley sockets c api. Web article, http://www.alhem.net/Sockets/index.html
18. Song, D.X., Wagner, D., Perrig, A.: Practical techniques for searches on encrypted data. In: Proceedings of IEEE Symposium on Security and Privacy, pp. 44–55 (2000)
19. Wang, C., Carzaniga, A., Evans, D., Wolf, A.: Security issues and requirements for internet-scale publish-subscribe systems. In: HICSS 2002: Proceedings of the 35th Annual Hawaii International Conference on System Sciences, pp. 3940–3947 (January 2002)

Delay Fast Packets (DFP): Prevention of DNS Cache Poisoning

Shimrit Tzur-David, Kiril Lashchiver, Danny Dolev*, and Tal Anker

School of Computer Science
The Hebrew University Of Jerusalem
{shimritd,kiril,dolev,anker}@cs.huji.ac.il

Abstract. The Domain Name System (DNS) protocol is used as a naming system for computers, services, or any other network resource. This paper presents a solution for the cache poisoning attack in which the attacker inserts incorrect data into the DNS cache. In order to successfully poison the cache, the attacker response must beat the real response in the race back to the local DNS server. In our model, we assume an eavesdropping attacker that can construct a response that is identical to the legal response. The primary aim of our solution is to construct a normal profile of the round trip time from when the request is sent until the arrival of the response, and then to search for anomalies of the constructed profile. In order to poison the cache of a DNS server, the attacker has to know the source port and the Transaction ID (TID) of the request. As far as we know, all current solutions which do not change the protocol, assume an attacker that cannot see the request and therefore has to *guess* the TID. All these solutions try to increase entropy in order to make the guesswork harder. In our strict model, increasing entropy is useless. We in no way claim that our scheme is flawless. Nevertheless, this effort represents the first step towards preserving the DNS cache assuming an eavesdropping attacker.

Keywords: DNS, Cache poisoning attack, Web security.

1 Introduction

The Domain Name System (DNS) [1], [2] is a hierarchical naming system built on a distributed database for computers, services, or any resource connected to the Internet or a private network. The DNS distributes the responsibility of assigning domain names and mapping those names to IP addresses by designating authoritative name servers for each domain. Authoritative name servers are responsible for the domains in their jurisdiction. In general, the DNS also stores other types of information, such as a list of mail servers that accept email for a given Internet domain. This role of the DNS puts it in a sensitive spot. The user must trust the DNS server to return the correct result for his request. If the DNS server sends an incorrect IP address to the user, the user will access a different site while assuming he is accessing the site he intended to access. This problem becomes more severe with the DNS caching system that is used by the DNS

---
* Danny Dolev is Incumbent of the Berthold Badler Chair in Computer Science. This research was supported in part by the Israeli Science Foundation (ISF) Grant number 1685/07.

M. Rajarajan et al. (Eds.): SecureComm 2011, LNICST 96, pp. 303–318, 2012.
© Institute for Computer Sciences, Social Informatics and Telecommunications Engineering 2012

servers for speeding up the requests' processing. Attackers search for opportunities to place faulty records into the DNS's cache. Once the attacker manages to implant such a record (that is to poison the cache), every user that requests this (poisoned) record will receive an IP address of a malicious site.

The DNS protocol usually uses User Datagram Protocol (UDP) as a forth level protocol for its data communication. If for some reason the request or the response fails to reach its destination, the DNS Server simply issues another request. For such a case, the DNS Server needs to be able to handle the situation that arises from packet delays, as these may be accidently interpreted as packet losses. The DNS operates in a straightforward approach. It simply accepts and caches the first valid response (that is, a response from an authoritative server) and ignores all other responses. This is a drawback in the DNS security and a gateway for attackers to poison the cache. (See [3].)

Pharming occurs when an attacker redirects a web site's traffic to a bogus web site. Pharming is the primary risk associated with cache poisoning. Attackers employ pharming for four primary reasons [4]: identity theft, distribution of malware, dissemination of false information, and man-in-the-middle attacks.

This paper presents a *Delay Fast Packets* (DFP) algorithm which detects and prevents attempts of cache poisoning attacks. In order to successfully poison the cache, the attacker response must beat the real response (from an authoritative server) in the race back to the DNS resolver, which is the local DNS server that originated the request. In our model, we assume an eavesdropping attacker. The attacker can generate a response that is identical to the real response. Since the window of opportunity is short, the attacker tries to send a response as soon as possible and usually does so much faster than it takes the authoritative server to generate a response. Our DFP algorithm identifies that exact point by analyzing the distribution of the round trip time (RTT) from the moment the request leaves the resolver to the time the resolver gets the response. This distribution is saved for each potential authoritative server. When the algorithm identifies an anomaly in the RTT of a response, it delays the response for a short interval and waits for another response of the same request to arrive. If no additional response arrives in that interval, the delayed response is sent to the resolver.

Our contributions are two-fold. Firstly, we prevent attacks under a very strict model against a powerful adversary. To our knowledge, we are the first to introduce an engine that does not change the DNS protocol and which still assumes an eavesdropping attacker that has all the information it needs in order to generate a valid response. DNS requests and responses today are completely unencrypted and are broadcast to any attacker who cares to look. Anybody with access to the copper infrastructure can *eavesdrop*. Moreover, most of this wiring is relatively unprotected and easy to access. In fact, this strict model has a significant impact on the motivation behind solutions that encrypt the DNS packets (e.g. [5]). Existing solutions that do not change the DNS protocol do not defend a DNS server in such model (as detailed in Section 3). In addition to the strict model, our solution can be implemented as a black box that gets each request right after it leaves the resolver. Therefore, no modifications are required, neither to the DNS protocol nor to the BIND (Berkeley Internet Name Domain) server code.

The rest of this paper is organized as follows. Section 2 describes the cache poisoning attack and the common approach to prevent it. Section 3 presents the state of the art algorithms against a cache poisoning attack. Section 4 presents our algorithm. Section 5 details the considerations we examined when we chose the algorithm parameters. Section 6 presents our experimental results, and Section 7 concludes this paper.

2   Cache Poisoning

When a client waits for a DNS response, it will only accept the information returned if it includes the client's correct source port and address in addition to the correct DNS transaction ID. These three pieces of information are the only form of authentication used to accept DNS responses. Knowing the source IP is straightforward as we know the address of the name server to be queried. The source port, however, and the transaction ID present a challenge. BIND often reuses the same source port for queries on behalf of the same name server, therefore discovering the source port is not a hard task [6]. The only real obstacle that stands between the attacker and a successful cache poisoning is the transaction ID field in the DNS protocol. Therefore, the attackers look for weak spots in the protocol implementation that can allow them to make a good *guess* of the transaction ID and, in this way, interfere with the traffic. In this section we present the methods used by the attacker to overcome this obstacle.

BIND (Berkeley Internet Name Domain) [7] is the most commonly used Domain Name System (DNS) server on the Internet. The earliest BIND servers did very little to address security. In order to avoid a same transaction ID repeating at the same time in the network, the server used an "Increment by One" method. Each new query was issued with the previous *transactionID* + 1. Guessing the transaction ID in such a case is a fairly easy job. This weakness was patched and the new BIND versions issue a random transaction ID to every new query. In the new version (BIND 9), the transaction ID is a randomly generated number, or more precisely, the transaction ID is a pseudo random generated number. The algorithm that generates the IDs in each of the BIND versions is open to the public and can be easily obtained and studied. As shown in [8], in many of the BIND 9 versions, the algorithm is weak and the next random number can be derived from the previous one. This particular problem was fixed in the 9.5.0 BIND version. Here, in order to guess the correct transaction ID, an attacker can use the *birthday paradox*. The attacker first simultaneously sends a large quantity of packets to the DNS server requesting the same Domain Name. The DNS server generates the same number of queries and sends them to the authority server. The attacker generates the same amount of DNS bogus responses with a random transaction ID. The birthday paradox dictates that a few hundred packets will suffice to promise a 50% success rate where there will be a match of the transaction ID with at least one query and one bogus response. This leads to a successful poisoning of the cache to the DNS server. Such an attack was fully described in [9]. The birthday attack guaranties high chances of success with a relatively low number of packets required. In regular packet spoofing, if the attacker sends N responses for one query, the probability of success is $\frac{N}{T}$ where T is the total number of packets possible (in the DNS case $T = 2^{16} - 1 = 65535$). In the birthday paradox attack, the attacker only needs to match one of the requests to one of the responses. The probability of success can be calculated by the following formula:

$$P(success) = 1 - 1(1 - \tfrac{1}{T})(1 - \tfrac{2}{T})...(1 - \tfrac{N-1}{T}) = 1 - \tfrac{T!}{T^N(T-N)!} \cdot$$

The power of the birthday paradox attack over the regular packet spoofing attack is that it requires a relatively small number of packets in order to make a successful attack. A mere 300 packets guarantees 50% success, while 750 packets guarantees a 99% success rate. In the regular packet spoofing attack, 750 packets only guarantees a $\frac{750}{65535} = 1.14\%$ success rate. The birthday paradox attack shows that even a randomly generated transaction ID used in the latest BIND versions is vulnerable to brute-force attacks.

The big security news of Summer 2008 has been Dan Kaminsky's discovery of a serious vulnerability in DNS servers [10]. In this exploit, the attacker causes the target name server to query for random host names at the target domain. The attacker can spoof a response to the target server including an answer for the query, an authority server record, and an additional record for that server, causing the target name server to insert the additional record into the cache.

There are several solutions available for the problem of a cache poisoning attack as presented in Section 3. In our algorithm we assume the attacker knows the transaction ID, source port, or any other information from the request needed in order to generate a valid response. In contrary to other solutions, we are not trying to increase entropy, rather we assume it is known to the attacker. The presented algorithm detects anomalies in the RTT of the responses. Since in order to get into the cache, a spoofed response has to arrive before the correct one, the RTT of those responses is shorter than it usually is and therefore is considered anomalous.

3   Related Work

There are several available solutions on how to prevent cache poisoning attacks and attempts. In this section we present some of them. BIND is the most widely used DNS software over the Internet [1], [2], and therefore it is a constant target to attackers' attacks. New versions and version updates are constantly being released constantly with new updates and patches for bugs and security issues. Therefore the easiest way to enhance the security of a local DNS server is to run the most recent version of BIND.

DNS security solutions can be categorized into two categories. The solutions in the first category extend the existing DNS protocol. Solutions in the second category require massive changes and thus new DNS servers deployment. Since a large-scale deployment may not be reached in the near future, an extensive search is made in order to design solutions that do not require new deployment.

A lot of effort has been spent in trying to make the DNS transaction ID more random and less predictable [11], [12]. Ultimately, such efforts are insufficient since with only 16 bits to fight over, a determined attacker can use a purely random attack, or even a constant attack, and theoretically, eventually, and statistically speaking, break through the requestor's defenses. Most of the research these days is based on increasing the entropy of DNS queries in order to make forging a valid response more difficult. In [13] [14], the authors describe a method by which an initiator can improve transaction identity using the 0x20 bit in DNS labels. This idea uses the question section to add random bits to the query. DNS servers do not care if the question is presented in upper or lower case, and therefore a combination of the cases can provide the essential random bits to the query. In practice, all question sections in responses are exact copies of question sections from requests. The difference between lower and upper case letter is the 0x20 bit. Therefore, for any character in the domain name in the question, a request initiator can randomly choose this bit and the transaction ID can be effectively lengthened beyond 16 bits. The effectiveness of this algorithm is a function of the length of the domain. In the Random prefix [15], [16] method, the authors propose to use wildcard Domain Names to increase the entropy. For example, if a user wants to resolve the "www.example.com", the DNS server will generate a random prefix for the query and send "ra1bc3twqj.www.example.com". The authoritative DNS server returns the same domain name with the "www.example.com" IP address. This method using a prefix length of 10 will generate in the region of $\log_2 36^{10} \approx 52$ bits. In another solution, presented in [17], the authors extend the DNS query ID with up to 63 alpha-numeric characters into the query/response question name (QNAME) making the range of possible transactions IDs so large that any brute force guessing or birthday attack attempts are futile.

Most name-servers, prior to the patches released on July 2008, always sent out their queries from port 53. Therefore, another direction is to also randomize the source port [18], [19], [12]. In this method, the name server uses a random source port for his query. The name server cannot use an entire UDP port space, however, even an extra 10 or 11 bits of randomness is many times greater. A DNS source port randomization becomes vulnerable if the DNS traffic is behind NAT. NAT cancels the DNS source port randomization by translating source ports to non-random ports.

Since the DNS protocol does not include any security, Domain Name System Security Extensions (DNSSEC) [20] were developed as described in RFC 3833 [21]. DNSSEC was designed to prevent cache poisoning by having all its answers digitally signed, thereby allowing the correctness and the completeness of the data to be easily verified. DNSSEC is a new protocol and only lately have some of its critical pieces been formally defined. Using DNSSEC necessarily means deploying new servers or reinstalling the protocol in the existing ones. Consequently, deploying the protocol on large-scale networks becomes a challenging task. DNSSEC introduces new security issues such as chain of trust problems, timing and synchronization attacks, Denial of Service amplification, increased computational load, and a range of key management issues as presented in [22].

DNSCurve [5] is an alternative to DNSSEC. DNSCurve uses high-speed elliptic curve cryptography, and simplifies the key management problem that affects DNSSEC. There is not much documentation on DNSCurve, but like DNSSec, it is hard to deploy.

4   The DFP Algorithm

The primary aim of the DFP algorithm is to estimate the RTT (Round Trip Time) between the DNS Server and each of the authoritative servers it encounters and to delay the responses that are arriving *too fast* according to the approximation. Furthermore, the processing time for each service type (MX, A, AAAA, CNAME, PTR etc...) might have different lengths, such as in a case due to a more extensive database search on the authoritative side. Therefore, the DFP algorithm estimates the RTT for each service type the authoritative server can provide. For each authoritative server and service type, the estimated RTT predicts the average time needed for the next response to arrive. If for any reason, a response comes too soon, according to the DFP algorithm, the DNS Server waits for a certain amount of time before it forwards the response to the requestor. If another valid response arrives in that window of time, both responses are dropped, and a new request is generated (as is done when a regular DNS packet loss occurred). If the attacker is persistent and sends a response for each request, the user experiences DoS (Denial of Service) attack, since the DFP algorithm will not pass any of the responses back to the user. In this case, the user does not get the service, but at least he is also not exposed to more harmful attacks such as fishing and theft of critical information. Moreover, under the assumption of an eavesdropping attacker and without changing the DNS protocol, we believe that there is no solution that can also solve the DoS problem. A simple cache poisoning attack with an eavesdropping attacker is presented in Figure 1. A local name server that is deployed with the DFP engine is not vulnerable to a cache poisoning attack as shown in Figure 2.

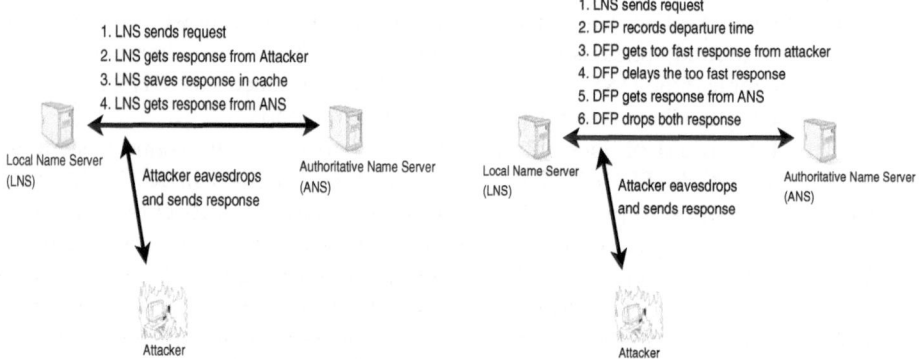

Fig. 1. Cache Poisoning Example   **Fig. 2.** DFP Operation

Algorithm 1 presents a simplified pseudo-code that demonstrates the idea of the DFP algorithm. In the case of a multiple packet attack, the algorithm *closes* the request after the first duplicate response, so any other response will not have a corresponding request and, thus, will be dropped. Another issue we have to consider is the legal *too fast* packets that might affect the RTT estimations. In the case where there are no attacks, those *too fast* packets can mark a change in the topology of the network and therefore must be considered in the RTT estimations. However, in the case of possible attacks, the algorithm should not include them in the estimations, as they may be an attempt of the attacker to lower our RTT estimations in order to make a successful attack in the near future. Therefore, *too fast* packets must not affect the RTT until the algorithm verifies their authenticity. This functionality is omitted from the the pseudo-code in order to save its simplicity.

The algorithm was tested on real traffic from the local DNS server of our university. The traffic contains 385,000 DNS requests.

Algorithm 1. DFP - Delay Fast Packets

1: *PacketDictionary.Init*() //mapping responses to request
2: *StatsDictionary.Init*() //save auth. server statistics
3: **loop**
4:     *NewPacket* $\Leftarrow$ *SniffDNSPacket*()
5:     *key* $\Leftarrow$ *GetKey*(*NewPacket.Auth* $-$ *server, NewPacket.TransactionID, NewPacket.Type*)
6:     **if** *NewPacket.isQuery*() **then**
7:         *PacketDictionaly.put*(*key, NewPacket*)
8:     **else**
9:         *RequestPacket* $\Leftarrow$ *PacketDictionary.get*(*key*)
10:        **if** *RequestPacket* == *NULL* **then**
11:         *Drop*(*NewPacket*)
12:        **else**
13:         **if** *RequestPacket.hasDelayedResponse*() **then**
14:           *Drop*(*DelayedResponse*)
15:           *PacketDictionary.clear*(*key*)
16:           *Drop*(*NewPacket*)
17:         **else**
18:           *RTT* $\Leftarrow$ *NewPacket.TimeOfArrival* $-$ *RequestPacket.TimeOfSend*
19:           *DelayTime* $\Leftarrow$ *AuthServerStats.AddSample*(*RTT, NewPacket.Auth* $-$ *Server, NewPacket.Type*)
20:           *DelayPacket*(*DelayTime*)
21:           *PacketDictionary.clear*(*key*)
22:         **end if**
23:        **end if**
24:     **end if**
25: **end loop**

AddSample(RTT, Auth-Server, Type)

1: *AuthServerStats* = *StatsDictionary.get*(*Auth* $-$ *Server* $+$ *Type*)
2: **if** *AuthServerStats* == *NULL* **then**
3:     *AuthServerStats* = *CreateStat*(*key*)
4:     *AuthServerStats.EstimatedRTT* $\Leftarrow$ *RTT*
5:     *AuthServerStats.DevRTT* $\Leftarrow$ 0
6: **end if**
7: *AuthServerStats.EstimatedRTT* $\Leftarrow (1 - \alpha) \times$ *AuthServerStats.EstimatedRTT* $+ \alpha \times RTT$
8: *AuthServerStats.DevRTT* $\Leftarrow (1 - \beta) \times$ *AuthServerStats.DevRTT* $+ \beta \times |RTT -$ *AuthServerStats.EstimatedRTT*|
9: **if** $RTT <$ *AuthServerStats.EstimatedRTT* $-$ *AuthServerStats.DevRTT* $\times$ *AuthServerStats.FactorWindow* **then**
10:     **return** (*AuthServerStats.EstimatedRTT* $+$ *AuthServerStats.DevRTT* $\times$ *AuthServerStats.FactorWindow*) $- RTT$
11: **else**
12:     **return** 0
13: **end if**

The DFP algorithm uses two hash tables. *PacketDictionary* maps between the outgoing requests and the incoming responses; *StatsDictionary* stores the statistics for each authoritative DNS server. On each packet arrival, a key is constructed from the authoritative server IP, the transaction ID, and the packet type. If the packet is a request, the packet is saved, by its key, in the PACKETDICTIONARY hash table. If the packet is a response, the corresponding DNS request is retrieved, once again, by the same key. The scenario when no matching request is found, that is, there is a response with no request, can be a result of two cases. One, the attacker sends multiple responses and the request was previously cleared. Two, there is a response without a request. In both cases, this condition can never be fulfilled unless there is an attack on (or a bug in) the DNS server; therefore, the packet is dropped. If the corresponding request has a delayed response (a *too fast* response was previously arrived to that request), the algorithm removes the request from the PACKETDICTIONARY hash table and drops both responses. In the normal case, where both the response and the request are found, the algorithm calculates the RTT between the local DNS server and the authoritative DNS server by measuring the time difference between the time the request is sent to the arrival of the response. Note that the RTT is calculated for each authoritative server and service type. It then calculates the ESTIMATEDRTT DEVRTT and estimates the normal window. If, however, the packet is *too fast*, it is delayed for d milliseconds, where d is the deviation between the RTT and the upper bound of the estimated normal window. Otherwise, the response is immediately sent to the server to be saved in the cache.

5   Design Parameters

The DFP algorithm uses the following formula in order to detect *too fast* packets: $RTT < EstimatedRTT - DevRTT \times FactorWindow$. Each DNS response that arrives too soon according to the formula is considered suspicious and delayed, thereby allowing time for another possible response with the same transaction id to arrive. The variables in the formula are controlled by three parameters: α, β and *FactorWindow*. The performance of the DFP algorithm, in terms of speed, detection accuracy, and memory consumption, depends on how well these parameters are configured. In this section we describe the considerations and the experiments that led us to choose the values for these three parameters.

5.1   The Window Parameters

The **Window** is the time interval in which response arrivals are considered normal. Each response that arrives before the window begins is considered suspicious. Each pair of authoritative server and request type has its own window. For example, for www.abc.com authoritative DNS server with type A, the window might begin 3400 ms after the request is sent, while for type MX it might begin after 3800 ms. The **Window Starting Point** is the beginning of the window. Each response arriving before the starting point is considered as a *too fast* packet. Respectively, the **Window Ending Point** is the end of the window and each response arriving after the ending point will be considered as a *too slow* packet. A false alarm occurs when a packet originated by the

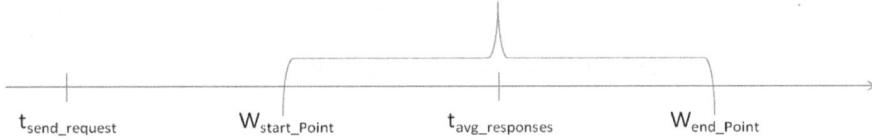

Fig. 3. The window Parameters

authoritative server arrives before the window starting point. Every false alarm causes the DNS server to store the packet in memory for a short time and release it only after it is safe. Figure 3 presents these parameters over the time axis. The sending time of a specific request is $t_{send\_request}$. The average of the arrivals times of all legal responses for the specific request type and authoritative name server is $t_{avg\_responses}$. This average has margins that define the window's starting point and ending point. Any response that arrives between $t_{send\_request}$ to W_{start_point} is considered *too fast* and any response that arrives after W_{end_point} is considered *too slow*. Some authoritative servers are infrequently requested and due to the dynamics of the network the DFP algorithm might not have enough samples in a certain point to create a distribution. The algorithm either takes the minimum values of the window starting point and window ending point, if they exist, or it takes the minimum values of an authoritative name server from the same parent domain.

The window has a very dynamic nature. Its starting point constantly changes and shifts on the time axis. This is due to the dynamic nature of the internet network and the constant changes in the RTT of the arriving requests. The window starting point dictates which packets are considered *too fast*, and which thus need to be delayed, and which packets are within the normal time boundary and can therefore immediately pass through. An attacker might try to influence the location of the window by flooding the authoritative server. In this case, the latency of the responses from the flooded authoritative server increases and the window is shifted to the right, resulting in a delayed starting point and fewer chances to successfully poison the DNS cache. In order to adjust the parameters that define the window starting point, there are two observations to consider:

– An early starting point allows more packets to pass through without a delay. The DNS server does not need to delay too many suspected packets (until it is safe to pass them on) and therefore the latency is reduced. However, the window of opportunities is increased, and a potential attacker can hit just above the starting point and pass the filter without triggering an alarm.
– A late starting point delays more packets since it considers them as *too fast* packets. This configuration hardens the attacker cache poisoning attempt since in order to avoid the DFP filter he has to compete on a small time interval. However, a late starting point forces the DNS server to delay many packets, considering them as potential threats. The major consideration of this configuration is the larger memory consumption and a slower response of the DNS server to the users.

In the following sections (5.2 and 5.3) we refer to α, β and the *FactorWindow*. We perform a set of experiments in order to demonstrate the influence of each of the parameters on the window starting point and hence on the tradeoff between the number of false alarms and the probability of detecting and preventing a potential attack.

5.2 α and β Considerations

The two parameters influencing the EstimatedRTT and the DevRTT parameters in the DFP algorithm are α and β. They determine the weight of the new RTT sample against the history, thereby influencing the window starting point. In order to find how α and β influence the number of fast packets detected by the DFP algorithm, we conducted several experiments on real traffic without any attempted attacks. In each experiment we measured the number of false positives alarms. The following figures 4, 5, 6 demonstrate the results of the experiments, using different values of α and β. In order to clearly demonstrate the results, the graphs present only 100 packets that represent the general case.

Note: The *FactorWindow* parameter is set to 2 in each of the following experiments.

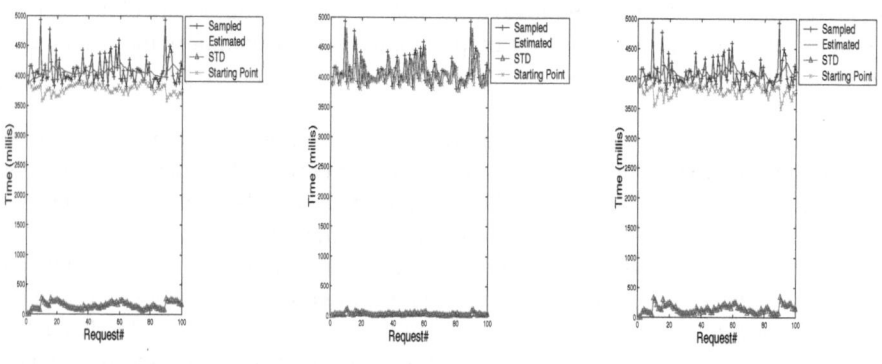

Fig. 4. α=0.125, β=0.25   **Fig. 5.** α=0.875, β=0.75   **Fig. 6.** α=0.2, β=0.4

In each of the experiments, the newest sample is given a much higher weight since it is better at predicting the future RTT. Figure 4, deals with the case of low values of α and β. Low α and β values, as in TCP RTT estimation, smooth the estimated RTT function, since more weight is given to the history of the samples rather than to the newest sample (in comparison to higher values of α and β). For each peak in the sampled RTT, the DevRTT rises. (Note, for example, the peak in the sample RTT and the rise of DevRTT at packet number 10.) As a result, the window starting point becomes low. This situation allows potentially malicious responses a wider window of opportunity to attack the DNS server. Only two packets were considered *too fast* in this configuration. The graph shows that those packets' RTT time exceeded the starting point. In Figure 5, we used high values of α and β. High values give most of the weight to the newest sample. Hence, the RTT deviation is very small and the window starting point is extremely late, making DNS attacks attempts very hard to succeed. However, this situation also creates many false alarms as any fluctuation in the RTT will probably put the new sample before the window starting point. We see that in this configuration about 20% of the packets were considered *too fast*. Figure 6 deals with the case of medium values of α and β. The values of α and β are the median of the 'Low' and 'High' configurations. As expected, the window starting point in this case is later than in the 'Low' configuration and the RTT deviation is higher than in the 'High' configuration. We see that in this configuration five of the packets were considered *too fast*.

Our experiments show that most of the time the deviation of the RTT is relatively low. Therefore the created starting point is rather high. The change in the deviation occurs when an extremely slow packet arrives. In this situation, the window starting point is lowered for a short period of time and possible attacks have a higher chance of success. However, as we can see from the results, slow packets seldom arrive. In consideration of memory consumption, it is important to prevent false alarms that might be created by valid *too fast* packets. Thus, for those, the 'Low' version should be chosen. However, if the local DNS server can afford saving more *too fast* packets, the better configuration is the one that prevents more attacks, and in that case it is better to choose the 'Medium' or even (if memory is not a problem) the 'High' configuration.

5.3   FactorWindow Considerations

After setting up the α and β parameters, the configuration of the *FactorWindow* parameter should be determined. This parameter goal is to lower the starting point created by α and β. As before, the tradeoff between the number of false alarms and the probability of a successful attack dictates which value will be chosen. Figures 7, 8 and 9 present the *FactorWindow* influence on the window starting point. As above, in order to clearly demonstrate the results, the graphs present only 100 packets that represent the general case.

Note: The α and β parameters are set to 0.125 and 0.25 respectively in each of the following experiments.

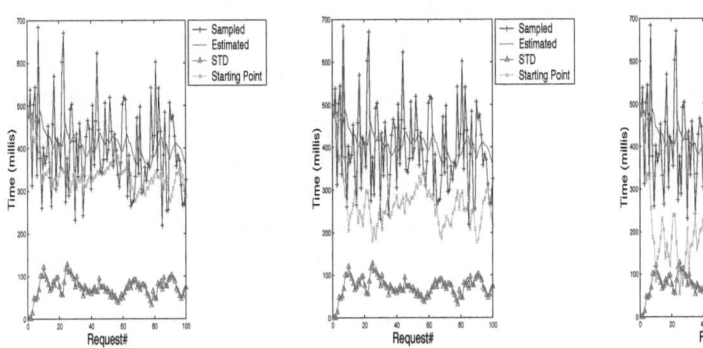

Fig. 7. Factor Window = 1   **Fig. 8.** Factor Window = 2   **Fig. 9.** Factor Window = 3

Figure 7 deals with the case where *FactorWindow* = 1. *FactorWindow* = 1 means that the window starting point is modified only by α and β. Therefore the created starting point is high and the probability for a packet to come before the starting point is respectively high. In this case, many packets will have to be delayed. We see that in this configuration, about 30% of the packets are considered *too fast* packets.

In Figure 8 we used *FactorWindow* = 2, i.e. the starting point is two estimated deviations from the estimated RTT. Using the 'Chebyshev inequality' the probability for a packet to exceed the starting point is less than $\frac{1}{4}$. However, in practice, the bound is tighter. Our experiments show that only about $\frac{1}{10}$ of the packets are considered as *too fast*.

Figure 9 deals with the case where *FactorWindow* = 3. Again, using the 'Chebyshev inequality' the probability for a packet to exceed the starting point is less than $\frac{1}{9}$, but in practice, almost no packet exceeds the starting point. The window starting point is so low that an attacker can easily intrude even without knowing that a detection and prevention DFP algorithm is running. In this configuration, only one packet is considered *too fast*.

The main consideration for choosing the configuration of the *FactorWindow* parameter is, again, the tradeoff between the number of false positives and the probability of a successful attack. By analyzing our results, we conclude that the best value for the *FactorWindow*2 is 2.

5.4   Slow Packets Consideration

The main assumption of the DFP algorithm is that the deviation from the EstimatedRTT approximates zero. This assumption was proven to be true in many experiments carried out on real traffic. But in some cases, the deviation rises for short periods of time. In those moments, the attacker gets an opportunity for a successful attack since many *too fast* packets fall after the window starting point of : $EstimatedRTT - DevRTT \times FactorWindow$ bound and are therefore considered normal.

This situation occurs after a very slow packet is received. The *too slow* packet creates a temporary increment of the deviation and lowers the starting point, as seen in Figures 10 and 11. The starting point returns to normal parameters after a few packets, when the influence of the *too slow* packet weakens. The temporary lowering of the starting point creates an opportunity for a attacker to attack the DNS server.

The way to prevent this weakness is to eliminate the *too slow* packets from the calculation of the deviation, thereby preventing the temporary lowering of the starting point. However, the DFP algorithm must take into consideration the possibility of rapid changes in the network characteristics or topology. Thus, DFP distinguishes between seldom *too slow* packets to a real tendency and the *too slow* packets are considered accordingly. An attacker cannot reduce the algorithm starting point by sending *slow* responses. The original response is likely to arrive before any spoofed slow response and therefore either the spoofed response is just dropped (if it arrives after the window ending point) or both the original and spoofed responses are dropped (if the spoofed response arrives within the window). In either case, the spoofed response is not considered when calculating the distribution parameters. Another option the attacker has is to flood a specific authoritative server in order to force *slow* responses from that server. As

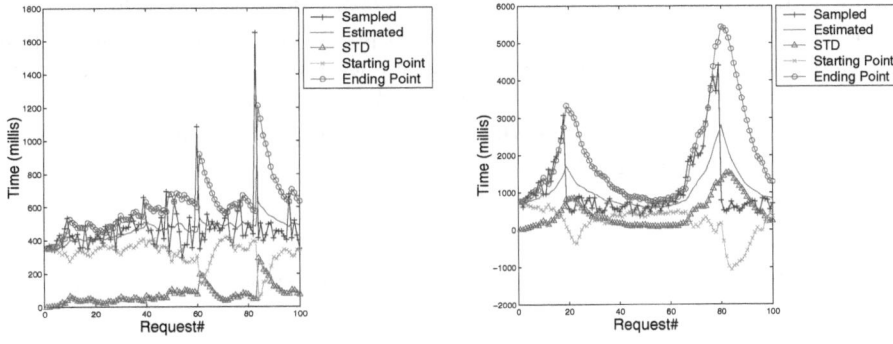

Fig. 10. Low Starting Point   **Fig. 11.** Negative Starting Point

a result, the window starting point in the local name server is reduced and the attacker can send a spoofed response without being delayed. The DFP engine does not handle these kinds of combined attacks.

5.5 Imitation of the DFP Profile

An eavesdropping attacker may adopt the DFP algorithm and imitate the same profiles. Afterwards, the attacker can apply fine control on the issuing time of forged DNS responses to make them reach the server after the starting point. In order to successfully poison the cache, the attacker's response needs to arrive before the real response. The RTTs are distributed normally, therefore, if x is the arrival time of the attacker response and $t_{get\_response}$ is the arrival time of the real response, the probability of a successful attack (after standardizing x) is

$$\int_{W_{start\_point}}^{t_{get\_response}} \frac{1}{\sqrt{2\pi}} e^{\frac{1}{2}x^2}\, \mathrm{d}x \,.$$

We can see, there are two factors that influence the odds of a successful attack, the window starting point and the arrival time of the real response. We have no control over the arrival time of the real response, but we can decrease the *FactorWindow* to narrow the window of opportunity of the attacker. This scenario demonstrates the tradeoff between memory and accuracy.

6   Experimental Results

The results are measured by two factors, memory consumption and accuracy. Usually, there is a tradeoff between these two factors. In our case this tradeoff is insignificant.

6.1   Memory Consumptions

The main consideration in choosing the best configuration for the DFP algorithms is to prevent attacks. In order to prevent attacks, the starting point should be as tight as possible to the estimated RTT. However a tight starting point might create many false alarms (as explained above). In this section we present how different starting point values affect the memory consumption. We examined three configurations. In the first one, $\alpha = 0.125$, $\beta = 0.25$; in the second, $\alpha = 0.2$, $\beta = 0.4$; and in the third configuration, $\alpha = 0.875$, $\beta = 0.75$. Figure 12 presents the percentage of packets that are considered *too fast* in each of the configurations.

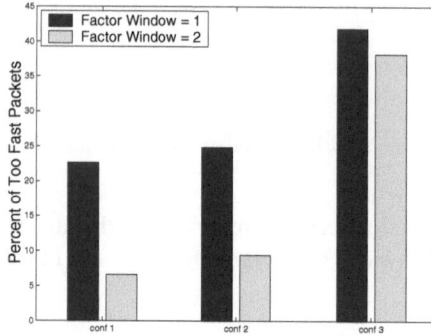 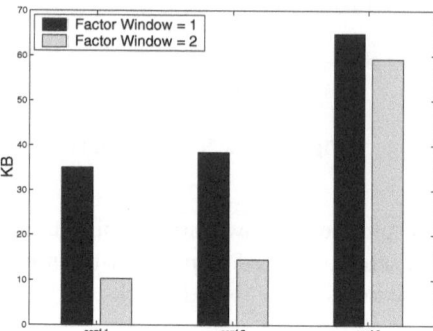

Fig. 12. Percentage of Fast Packets   **Fig. 13.** Memory Consumption

The DNS payload has a limit of 512 bytes (for IPv4). Our experiments show that an average response is about 155 bytes long. The DFP algorithm must allocate those bytes in memory for each delayed packet, usually for about few hundred ms, until the response is either released or dropped. The memory consumption depends on the inbound rate of the local DNS server. The university DNS server can only handle a few dozen responses in parallel. Since this server might not represent the general case, Figure 13 estimates how many KB the DFP algorithm consumes assuming it handles 1000 responses in parallel. As we can see, even for the most wasteful configuration, the memory consumption is no more than 65KB on average and 215KB in the worst case. Thus, memory consumption is not a limiting factor even for busier servers.

The presented algorithm was implemented and tested on real traffic collected from our university DNS Server. The traffic was sniffed and saved in pcap files that were later used for different configurations testing and analysis. The traffic was filtered to contain only DNS responses with an authoritative flag on. For each of the samples, the algorithm calculates the EstimatedRTT, the DevRTT, and with a given FactorWindow, it deduces which packets are considered to be *too fast*.

6.2   Attacks Detection

In order to test the DFP algorithm we planted a few random duplicate response packets with random arrival times in the tested traffic. The spoofed responses arrived before the real responses. The DFP algorithm with the above configuration was able to classify all of the attacks as *too fast* packets and therefore delayed them until the real result arrived. We believe that there were no real attempts to attack our university local DNS server while the samples were captured, since no duplicate packets were found beside the faked packets planted by us. Unfortunately, we cannot compare our results to other solutions since all other solutions fail to protect the DNS server from cache poisoning attack on our strict model.

7   Conclusions

This paper presents the DFP algorithm against DNS cache poisoning attacks. The algorithm assumes an eavesdropping attacker that can see the request and therefore can easily create and send a spoofed response. Our algorithm measures statistics per authoritative server and type of query in order to build a profile about the RTT distribution for these two parameters. Since, in order to get into the cache, a spoofed response has to arrive before the correct one, the RTT of those responses is shorter than it usually is and therefore, out of the constructed profile. We showed that the algorithm is scalable and its memory consumption can fit in a standard cache.

The weak spot of the DFP engine is its vulnerability to a DoS attack (in the case where the attacker repeatedly sends spoofed responses). In our future work, we will integrate the DFP engine with a mechanism that detects these repetitive spoofed responses and instead of just dropping duplicate responses, it will save a copy of each unique response and choose the correct one according to various considerations.

References

1. Dns, http://www.ietf.org/rfc/rfc1034.txt
2. Dns, http://www.ietf.org/rfc/rfc1035.txt
3. Schuba, C.: Addressing weaknesses in the domain name system protocol. Master's thesis (August 1993)
4. Hyatt, R.: Keeping dns trustworthy. The ISSA Journal, 37–38 (2006)
5. Bernstein, D.J.: Dnscurve, http://dnscurve.org/
6. Sainstitute: Attacking the dns protocol security paper (2003)
7. Terry, D.B., Painter, M., Riggle, D.W., Zhou, S.: The berkeley internet name domain server. EECS Department, University of California, Berkeley, Tech. Rep. UCB/CSD-84-182 (May 1984), http://www.eecs.berkeley.edu/Pubs/TechRpts/1984/5957.html
8. Klein, A.: Bind 9 dns cache poisoning (2007)
9. Stewart, J.: Dns cache poisoning - the next generation (2003)
10. Kaminsky, D.: The kamisky bug, http://dankaminsky.com/
11. Internet Systems Consortium, I.: "Bind 9" (2003), http://www.bind9.net/
12. Powerdns (2011), http://doc.powerdns.com/
13. Vixie, P., Dagon, D.: Use of bit 0x20 in dns labels to improve transaction identity (2008), http://tools.ietf.org/html/draft-vixie-dnsext-dns0x20-00
14. Dagon, D., Antonakakis, M., Vixie, P., Jinmei, T., Lee, W.: Increased dns forgery resistance through 0x20-bit encoding: security via leet queries. In: Proceedings of the 15th ACM Conference on Computer and Communications Security, CCS 2008, pp. 211–222. ACM, New York (2008), http://doi.acm.org/10.1145/1455770.1455798
15. Perdisci, R., Antonakakis, M., Lee, W.: Solving the dns cache poisoning problem without changing the protocol (2008)

16. Perdisci, R., Antonakakis, M., Luo, X., Lee, W.: Wsec dns: Protecting recursive dns resolvers from poisoning attacks. In: DSN, pp. 3–12. IEEE (2009),
    http://dblp.uni-trier.de/db/conf/dsn/dsn2009.html#PerdisciALL09
17. Hoy, J.G.: Measures for making dns more resilient against forged answers (2008),
    http://www.jhsoft.com/dns-xqid.html
18. Hubert, A., van Mook, R.: Anti dns spoofing - extended query id, xqid (2008),
    http://tools.ietf.org/html/draft-ietf-dnsext-forgery-resilience-10
19. djbdns (2004), http://cr.yp.to/djbdns.html
20. Dnssec, http://www.dnssec.net/
21. Atkins, D., Austein, R.: Threat analysis of the domain name system, dns (2004),
    http://www.ietf.org/rfc/rfc3833.txt
22. Ariyapperuma, S., Mitchell, C.J.: Security vulnerabilities in dns and dnssec. In: Proceedings of the The Second International Conference on Availability, Reliability and Security, pp. 335–342. IEEE Computer Society, Washington, DC (2007),
    http://portal.acm.org/citation.cfm?id=1249254.1250514

Unilateral Antidotes to DNS Poisoning

Amir Herzberg and Haya Shulman

Department of Computer Science
Bar Ilan University
Ramat Gan
Israel
{amir.herzberg,haya.shulman}@gmail.com

Abstract. We investigate defenses against DNS cache poisoning focusing on mechanisms that can be readily deployed unilaterally by the resolving organisation, preferably in a single gateway or a proxy. DNS poisoning is (still) a major threat to Internet security; determined spoofing attackers are often able to circumvent currently deployed antidotes such as port randomisation. The adoption of DNSSEC, which would foil DNS poisoning, remains a long-term challenge.

We discuss limitations of the prominent resolver-only defenses, mainly port and IP randomisation, 0x20 encoding and birthday protection. We then present two new (unilateral) defenses: the *sandwich antidote* and the *NAT antidote*. The defenses are simple, effective and efficient, and can be implemented in a gateway connecting the resolver to the Internet.

The *sandwich antidote* is composed of two phases: poisoning-attack *detection* and then *prevention*. The *NAT antidote* adds entropy to DNS requests by switching the resolver's IP address to a random address (belonging to the same autonomous system). Finally, we show how to implement the birthday protection mechanism in the gateway, thus allowing to restrict the number of DNS requests with the same query to 1 even when the resolver does not support this.

Keywords: secure dns, dns poisoning, network security.

1 Introduction

Correct and efficient operation of the DNS is essential for the operation of the Internet. However, there is a long history of vulnerabilities and exploits related to DNS; for some of the early works, see the seminal papers of Vixie [30] and Bellovin [7,8].

In the recent years, the most significant attack on the Domain Name System is *DNS poisoning* by a spoofing attacker. The spoofer tries to provide the DNS resolver with misleading mappings (e.g., map VIC-Bank.com to an IP address controlled by the attacker), by sending a fake (spoofed) response to a domain name query. The DNS poisoning scenario by a spoofing adversary typically assumes either an open recursive resolver, i.e., one that provides services to clients outside of its network, or a compromised client on the local network (LAN),

M. Rajarajan et al. (Eds.): SecureComm 2011, LNICST 96, pp. 319–336, 2012.
© Institute for Computer Sciences, Social Informatics and Telecommunications Engineering 2012

e.g., a zombie; the DNS poisoning model is in Figure 1. DNS poisoning can be used as a building block facilitating many other attacks, such as the injection of malware, phishing, website hijacking/defacing and denial of service.

When the DNS resolver receives a DNS response, it usually follows the recommendations in [18] and checks that the validation fields match the fields in one of the pending DNS requests. The DNS request contains several validation fields, e.g., transaction ID, which are also copied to the DNS response by the authoritative name server. The local DNS resolver that issued the DNS query validates that those fields appear correctly in the DNS response. If all the fields in the DNS response are correct, the response is cached and then sent to the client that issued the request. Otherwise, if one of the fields is incorrect, the DNS resolver ignores response. Once the DNS response is cached, the attacker has to wait until the TTL (time to live) expires so that it can initiate the attack again.

Although poisoning attacks on DNS were known to be devastating, this threat was believed to be impractical, since frequently accessed domain names typically reside in the cache of the DNS resolver, thus preventing the attacker from poisoning those domains of interest. Furthermore, if the legitimate response from the authentic DNS server arrives before the forgery sent by the attacker, forgery attempt fails, as the resolver will cache the first response and ignore the rest.

This situation changed when Kaminsky presented an improved attack [20,10], with two critical improvements. The first improvement was to control the time at which the resolver sends queries (to which the attacker wishes to respond), by sending to the resolver queries for a (non-existing) host name, e.g., with a random or sequential prefix of the domain name. The second improvement was to add, in the spoofed responses sent to the resolver, a type NS DNS record (specifying a new name for the domain name server) and/or a type A 'glue' DNS record (specifying the IP address of the new domain name server). These records poison the resolver's entries for a specific host in the victim's domain, e.g., the victim's name server itself. Hence, if the attack succeeds once (for one record), the adversary controls the entire name space of the victim. If the attack fails for a given host name (prefix), the attacker can repeat with new (random) prefix.

Using these two improvements attackers can often poison the DNS entry for the victim domain (e.g., VIC-Bank.com) within few seconds, when the only unpredictable field in the DNS response is the 16-bit ID field, thus allowing devastating attacks on many Internet applications (see [20,10]).

As a result of Kaminsky attack, it became obvious that changes are needed to prevent DNS poisoning. Indeed, major DNS resolvers were quickly patched to support *source port randomisation*, i.e., use and validate random source ports for each request or at least for each destination IP. Resolvers were also improved to support *birthday protection*: prevent or limit[1] duplicate concurrent requests. Both of these defenses were proposed by Bernstein already in [9].

---

[1] Complete prevention of duplicate queries may have significant overhead on popular resolver implementations, hence most implementations only limit duplicates.

However, as noted by [21,14], a determined attacker with sufficient bandwidth, e.g., controlling a large amount of compromised machines on the Internet, could still send a sufficient number of responses to have a forged DNS response accepted with high probability. Furthermore, port randomisation is often annihilated due to port-mangling by NAT devices between the resolver and the Internet [17,26,12].

Additional, easy to deploy defense requiring changes to the local DNS resolver only, RFC 5452 [18], specifies that DNS resolvers should, where possible, not only choose a random source port, but also choose a random source IP address and a random authoritative server IP address for each query. The resolver should then validate that the same IP addresses are used in the response. If the resolver uses a set of N_S IP addresses, and the authoritative name server uses a set of N_D IP addresses, then the space of identifiers is increased by a factor of $N_S \cdot N_D$. However, the impact is usually modest, as N_S is often only one, and N_D is at most three.

Indeed, recent studies, [19,16], indicate that DNS is not well protected against poisoning attacks and that the vast majority of organisations with an Internet presence are still vulnerable to DNS poisoning attacks. In particular, the ongoing attacks on DNS infrastructure, e.g., AT&T, Comcast and Rollingstone [32,11,23], motivate inspection of the 'easy-to-deploy', unilateral defenses such as those against spoofing adversaries.

Cryptographic defenses, e.g., DNSSEC [4,6,5], offer protection against a stronger man-in-the-middle adversary, and are thus a preferable alternative over defenses against spoofers. However, their deployment remains to be seen due to the significant changes that they introduce to the current DNS infrastructure. Recent survey results, [19,16], reveal that some fundamental capabilities required for adoption of DNSSEC, e.g., support of queries over TCP and support of EDNS0 [29], are not fully deployed. Furthermore, common to the defenses against MitM adversaries is the requirement for a cooperation and support of the mechanism by both parties to the DNS transaction, which is a significant overhaul. In contrast, unilateral defenses against spoofers allow an organisation or an ISP to integrate the defense, without relying on the support by the other end to the DNS transaction.

In this work, we focus on antidotes to DNS poisoning that require modification to the local DNS resolver only, which, preferably, can also be implemented in a router/firewall machine connecting the resolver to the Internet (we discuss advantages of firewall based defenses in Section 1.1).

Our proposed defenses meet all the proposed design guidelines of [24]: (1) the prevention techniques should require no change to the DNS protocol; (2) should not introduce service disruption; (3) the solution should be completely backward compatible with existing DNS servers, and transparent to users; and finally (4) it should make poisoning attacks infeasible.

Our first technique is the *sandwich antidote*, presented in Section 3. This is an efficient and simple procedure, based on a two stage defense: upon the receipt of a forged DNS response, an attack is detected; then, the attack is prevented by

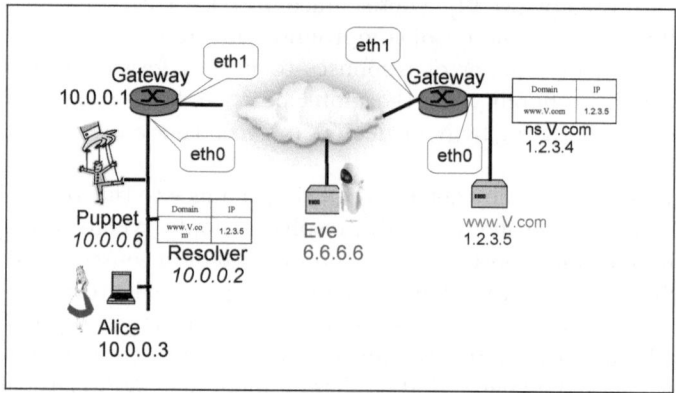

Fig. 1. Simple configuration for DNS poisoning by a spoofing adversary (Eve) on the Internet: client Alice uses a resolver connected to the Internet. The resolvers make queries to authoritative name servers, via the Internet. We consider a blind/spoofing adversary Eve, connected to the Internet. The adversary may also control some 'puppet' connected to the same local area network as Alice and the resolver.

discarding the 'malicious' DNS responses and accepting only a valid authentic DNS response.

Our second technique is the *NAT antidote*, Section 4. The NAT antidote extends the existing Network Address Translation devices and adds entropy to DNS requests, thus significantly increasing the amount of forged packets that the attacker is required to generate in order to produce the correct *forged* DNS response.

We also show how to implement the birthday protection in firewall. The mechanism restricts the number of outgoing DNS requests for the same query to 1, even if the local DNS resolver does not limit concurrent requests for the same resource record.

We implemented our proposed defenses in linux gatway, and tested their compatibility by querying the real DNS servers on the Internet. Implementing solutions in the gateway has several advantages, over implementations in the resolver itself, which we discuss in Section 3.

1.1 Firewall-Based Defense Mechanisms

Anti-poisoning defenses implemented in firewall have several advantages over defenses in the resolver:

- *Integration Challenges:* resolver software may not be amenable to modification due to complexity or due to it being proprietary, while modifications in the firewall are simpler, as firewalls already have built in tools to capture packets. The modification can be made in a small user-space program (as we did for our experimental validation of the prevention techniques), which is much simpler than modifying the resolver.

- *One Firewall Protects Many:* one firewall, e.g., of ISP, can protect all the DNS resolvers, e.g., of ISP's clients, without the need to integrate the changes in all the local DNS resolvers.
- *Modular Design:* If a DNS server is replaced, or a new server is added, there is no need to integrate the modification each time.
- *Security Feature:* for firewall vendors, adding another security feature is an important added value.

1.2   Contributions and Organisation

We present two practical and efficient defense mechanisms against DNS poisoning, that require changes only to the local DNS resolver and protect the local DNS resolver against poisoning attacks by spoofing adversaries. Our defenses can be implemented in the firewall. The *sandwich antidote* (Section 3) is simple to implement and integrate in a gateway which connects the network to the Internet, requires modest resources, and can provide sufficient entropy to make poisoning infeasible. The *NAT antidote* (Section 4) is very simple to deploy, with almost negligible overhead, and in many cases, provided a significant number of client IP addresses are available, can significantly improve defense against poisoning.

In Section 2 we discuss and compare recently proposed antidotes to DNS poisoning.

Finally, in Section 5, we show how birthday protection can be efficiently implemented in a firewall, which is significant since most existing resolvers only *limit* the amount of duplicates, e.g., to 200.

We present the implementations of our proposed defenses in Linux based firewall.

2   Proposed Antidotes to DNS Poisoning

In this section we briefly review proposed anti-poisoning defenses against spoofers, that require integration on the side of the local DNS resolver only. These techniques can be broadly categorised as follows: (1) mechanisms that increase entropy in DNS packets (subsection 2.1), and (2) mechanisms that inspect the DNS responses to detect forgery (subsection 2.2).

2.1   Entropy Increasing Mechanisms

Unilateral entropy increasing mechanisms, most notably: source port randomisation (SPR) [9], source/destination IP address randomisation (IPR) and DNS 0x20 encoding [14], add more randomness to DNS packets, in order to make it more difficult for the spoofing adversary to craft a valid DNS response, that would get accepted *and* cached by the local DNS resolver. In order to produce a successful forgery the attacker has to guess *all* the values in the validation fields correctly. The more random values pertain in the DNS requests, the lower the probability of the attacker to produce a successful guess. Entropy increasing mechanisms do not try to identify forgery attacks and respond to them, but attempt to increase the difficulty of producing a successful forgery.

Unfortunately, the number of fields in the DNS packet, that could be used to add randomness, is limited: the transaction ID field in the DNS packet, the source port, source/destination IP addresses, and the choice of upper/lower case for the query (since DNS is case-insensitive; this is the field used by DNS 0x20 encoding).

Port Randomisation. Following to Kaminsky attack, [20], the need to patch the DNS resolvers to send DNS requests from random ports became apparent. Using random source ports adds another 16 bits of entropy, resulting in a search space of $2^{16} \times 2^{16} = 2^{34}$ bits, which makes successful poisoning significantly more difficult to achieve.

Unfortunately, source port randomisation (SPR) is resource intensive, and as noted in [13,15] may be inappropriate for busy DNS servers or embedded devices. In addition, as pointed out by [14], determined attackers can overcome source port randomisation, by sending large amounts of traffic, e.g., from many zombie computers, thus covering all the search space and eventually producing a valid DNS response. Therefore, enhancing DNS security using SPR and transaction ID alone may not suffice.

Furthermore, many (or most) DNS resolvers are located behind NAT devices, and as [12,10] noted, NAT devices that use sequential assignment of external ports, may expose (even the patched) local DNS resolvers, to poisoning attacks, since NAT could reduce source port randomisation implemented by the local resolvers.

IP Randomisation. IP addresses are known to be a scarce resource on the Internet. IP address is composed of 32 bits, resulting in at most 2^{32} possible addresses. Due to this shortcoming, the DNS resolvers are often allocated a single IP address, and authority DNS servers are allocated at most 3 IP addresses. This can increase the search space of the attacker by at most a factor of 1×3, which does not offer sufficient protection. In addition, the DNS resolvers that are located behind NAT devices, which is the typical case, lose the IP randomisation, even if they are allocated several IP addresses.

DNS 0x20 Encoding. Dagon *et al.* [14] present an innovative technique, 0x20-encoding, for improving DNS defense by increasing entropy of DNS queries against poisoning by spoofed responses. The technique is based on an observation that domain names are case insensitive, however, most authoritative servers copy the string of the domain name from the incoming request to the response they send back, *exactly* as sent - preserving the case of each letter. They suggest to randomly toggle the case of letters of which the domain name consists, and validate them in response. If the domain name d contains $l(d)$ alphabetic characters, this increases the space of identifiers by factor of $X(d) = 2^{l(d)}$, e.g., $X(\text{WWW.GOOGLE.COM}) = 2^{12}$ and $X(\text{A9.COM}) = 2^4$.

Note that in Kaminsky-style attacks, the query is for a non-existing domain name chosen by the attacker, e.g., to poison addresses in the domain GOOGLE.COM, an attacker may issue a query for r.GOOGLE.COM where $r \in_R \{0, \ldots, 9\}^8$ is a random string of 8 digits, resulting in a domain name with only 9 letters, i.e., factor of only $X = 2^9$; namely, 0x20 encoding is less effective for domain names containing few letters - which are often the most important domains, e.g., the Top Level Domains (TLDs) such as .COM and .UK.

Although 0x20 encoding, as presented by Dagon *et al.*, introduces significant extra entropy to DNS requests, an attacker may still be able to poison 'high value' domain names with a rather small factor of poisoned responses. Therefore, there is need in alternative or additional technique to protect the TLDs and other domain names containing only few letters, e.g., A9.COM.

2.2 Forgery Detection Mechanisms

The 'forgery detection' mechanisms follow two approaches: the collaborative approach and techniques from machine learning. According to the collaborative approach the authenticity of a DNS response is validated by distributing the DNS requests across hosts in the system, e.g., [22,25,28], or by consulting a set of trusted peers, [31], and then, e.g., taking the majority answer. CoDNS, ConfiDNS and DoX, [22,25,31], send the requests to several peers in a peer-to-peer network and accept the first DNS response; if the first response is forged, it is still accepted. DependDNS, [28], queries several DNS resolvers, and accepts the DNS response of the majority. DependDNS relies on open recursive DNS resolvers to obtain DNS responses; open recursion DNS services are known to expose DNS to attacks. Furthermore, recently, [2] showed that DependDNS does not protect DNS against poisoning attacks. The common shortcomings of the collaborative approach are most notably the performance penalty, i.e., additional processing and communication delays, that they introduce to every DNS request, even when the system is *not* under attack, and the significant infrastructure that is required for deployment. In addition, techniques that are based on distributing the DNS request to several nodes, e.g., [22], are also exposed to cache poisoning attacks, as the first DNS response that arrives is accepted.

A recent technique, by Antonakakis *et al* [3], employs mechanisms from machine learning to identify suspicious IP addresses. Specifically, [3] designed a centralised poisoning detection system called Anax, which is based on the observation that DNS records direct users to a known set of NS records, while poisoned records redirect users to new IP addresses, outside of the victim's address space. However, deployment requires trust in one central entity that should be consulted to establish authenticity of the DNS responses. In addition, this mechanism also introduces delays and may have false positives, e.g., if an authority DNS server was moved to a new IP address for load distribution.

3   The Sandwich Antidote to DNS Poisoning

Both categories, the increasing entropy (Section 2.1) and the forgery detection (Section 2.2) mechanisms, have different shortcomings and most importantly: the DNS cache poisoning problem is not yet solved, thus motivating further investigation of anti-poisoning defenses.

In this section we present an anti-poisoning defense technique, the sandwich antidote, designated to run in a gateway (or a proxy), behind which the local DNS resolver is located, and should filter DNS traffic. The sandwich antidote is applied only to DNS packets and is based on first detecting and then activating the prevention module, to counter poisoning attempts. As a result, the mechanism does not impose performance overhead, and is only applied when DNS cache poisoning attack is detected. The sandwich antidote maintains a table that stores all outbound DNS requests, prior to forwarding them. It also keeps track of the inbound DNS responses, and matches them against the pending DNS requests. If a corresponding DNS request exists, and the DNS response is correct, i.e., all the validation fields match the corresponding values in the DNS request, then the entry is removed from the table and the response is forwarded to the DNS resolver.

A poisoning attack is detected when one of the validation fields, e.g., transaction ID, in a DNS response does not match[2] the corresponding value in the pending DNS request, in which case, the prevention module is activated. During the course of the poisoning attack many invalid DNS responses for some DNS request may arrive. Among these incorrect responses a valid response may appear, however, with high probability this can be a forged response generated by the attacker. Therefore, once an attack was detected, i.e., an incorrect DNS response was received for some pending query, the mechanism should *not* rely on that (seemingly correct) DNS response, since it can be merely a successful forgery sent by the attacker.

Once activated, the sandwich antidote issues three DNS requests, substituting the original DNS request sent by the resolver: (1) a DNS request for the requested resource record, prepended with some random string, e.g., if the original DNS request was for *x.y.com*, then after receiving an invalid DNS response for query *x.y.com*, the mechanism should issue a request for *randomString1.x.y.com*; (2) a DNS request for the original resource record, i.e., *x.y.com* as above; (3) a DNS request for *randomString2.x.y.com*, where *randomString2* is a randomly selected string, and *x.y.com* is the RR as appeared in the original DNS request.

The sandwich antidote expects to receive correct DNS responses to all three requests and in the *same order* in which the requests were sent. Specifically, it checks that the DNS responses to the above requests are correct, and arrive in the same order, in which the requests were sent. This mechanism is based on the observation that it may be possible to generate a single correct DNS

---

[2] Note that when generating a DNS response, the DNS servers copy the validation fields from the DNS request accurately, thus it is guaranteed that the validation fields should appear correct in the authentic DNS response.

response, to a potentially adversarial query. However, generating three correct DNS responses, where the first and third are random, should not be feasible, let alone ensuring that all three are received in the same order in which they were sent. The authentic responses to those three DNS requests above should be: (1) an nxdomain (i.e., with high probability the hostname $randomString1.x.y.com$ does not exist) or an NS RR, i.e., a referral to a name server lower in hierarchy, e.g., from $ns.com$ to $ns.y.com$; (2) an A RR (IP address for $x.y.com$, or an NS RR, i.e., a referral to the DNS lower in hierarchy; (3) same as (1) above, i.e., an nxdomain or an NS RR. Note that as a result of this 'order preserving' mechanism, where the original query is between two queries prepended with a random prefix, we coin this mechanism the 'sandwich antidote'.

Once correct DNS responses arrive in the required order, for all three DNS requests, the mechanism removes the pending DNS requests from the table and returns the DNS response to the DNS resolver. The sandwich mechanism ignores the responses if they arrive in an incorrect order, or if the validation fields do not match. The diagram describing the functionality of the sandwich antidote is in Figure 3. Due to length restrictions, the pseudo-code appears in the full version of the paper.

Note that similarly to other unilateral defenses, such as SPR or 0x20 encoding, the sandwich antidote does not offer protection when it is implemented in a resolver (or a firewall) which uses a higher level resolver as a forwarder, e.g., receives services from the resolver of an ISP.

In subsequent sections we present a detailed design of the sandwich mechanism. We discuss the additional overhead that our mechanism inflicts on the gateway and analyse the impact of the sandwich mechanism on the probability of the attacker to produce a successful forgery. We also show that our mechanism does not expose the DNS resolver (or its clients) to denial of service (DoS) attacks.

3.1   Detailed Design

In order to keep track of the outbound DNS requests and to record the poisoning attempts, the mechanism maintains two tables: the table T that stores all outbound DNS requests (for which a valid DNS response has not arrived yet), and the table A that maintains the DNS requests for which poisoning attempts were detected.

Table T is illustrated in Table 1. The table which is indexed by a hash function h applied on the query field of the DNS request. Upon arrival of a DNS request Req, the hash h(Req.query) is stored in table T and is mapped to the validation fields, i.e., source port $srcPort$, source/destination IP addresses $srcIP$ and $dstIP$, and DNS 0x20 encoding bits X:

T[h(Req.query)]=$(srcPort||srcIP||dstIP||X)$. Namely, the table T is composed of the indices column containing a digest of the query, and a column for each 'validation' field, and a serial number (which is used to locate the entry in T from table A). Table T can contain entries with the same index[3], i.e., when several DNS requests for the same RR were issued simultaneously.

Table A is illustrated in Table 2. Table A maintains DNS requests which were issued once forgery attempt was detected for some DNS request. Table A is composed of indices column h(Req.query), a column containing a fingerprint, i.e., the result of a PRF (pseudo-random function) f applied on the entropy fields $T[h(Req.query)]=f_K(srcPort||srcIP||dstIP||X)$, and a column containing a serial number pointing to the corresponding entry in T (required to generate the DNS response once responses for corresponding entries in A were received). Specifically, once an invalid DNS response arrives for an existing, pending DNS request, the mechanism issues three DNS requests, and stores them in A.

The diagram, in Figure 3, describes the functionality of the sandwich antidote. Upon receipt of a DNS response, in step (1), the mechanism checks if an entry for that query exists in table A, in 2, step (2).

If no matching entry exists in A, however a corresponding DNS requests is stored in T, Table 1, step (3), i.e., the DNS request was issued, the DNS response is checked (the validation fields are compared against those in the pending DNS request), step (4). If the response is correct, it is sent to resolver, and the pending DNS request is removed from table T. If the response is incorrect, e.g., the destination port in the response does not match the source port in the DNS request, attack is detected, and prevention module is triggered. Specifically, the mechanism issues three DNS requests, such that the DNS request containing the original query, is sent between two other DNS requests that contain random strings prepended to the original query: (a) $1.||Resp.query, (b) Resp.query, (c) $2.||Resp.query, s.t., request (b) contains the original query as appeared in the DNS request, and (a) and (c) contain the original request prepended with distinct random strings $1 and $2. These queries are stored in table A, and further DNS responses for that query will be processed against these entries in A.

If a matching entry exists in A, an attack was detected, i.e., at least one DNS response containing wrong values in the validation fields was received; the mechanism should not accept the DNS response as is, but should apply a special processing described next. In this case, the mechanism first checks that the validation fields match against those in the corresponding entry in A, step (5), and that the DNS response arrived in the correct order, i.e., according to the order in which the DNS requests were sent, step (6).

We implemented steps (5) and (6) as a state machine, Figure 2. The state machine is activated following to attack detection and transmission of three DNS requests (as above). The state machine transits to subsequent states following to successful receipt of the DNS response, i.e., in order and correct. The state machine halts when step 4., Figure 2, is reached. Then the DNS response, for

---

[3] Following to Kaminsky attack, DNS resolvers were patched to support birthday protection, we extend more on this in Section 5, and we also show a gateway based mechanism to restrict the number of outstanding DNS requests to 1 to prevent the birthday paradox.

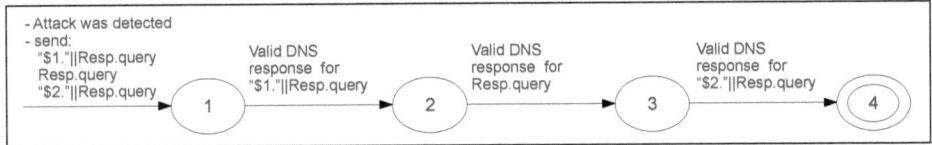

Fig. 2. The state machine of the sandwich antidote, that corresponds to steps (5) and (6) in Figure 3

Table 1. Sample entries, containing the DNS request sent by the DNS resolver, in the table T maintained by the sandwich antidote mechanism running at the gateway; for simplicity the entries are presented using ASCII characters

Index	Serial number	Transaction ID	Source IP	Destination IP	Source port	0x20 encoding
h('WWw.GOoGLe.COM')	i	12567	1.2.3.4	5.6.7.8	55555	110110110111
h('WwW.yAhOO.coM')	$i+1$	35783	1.2.3.4	7.8.9.7	61345	1010101001
h('Www.msn.COm')	$i+2$	22344	1.2.3.3	2.6.8.3	24580	100000110

Table 2. Sample entries in table A, containing the DNS request sent by the sandwich antidote mechanism, running at the gateway, once forgery attempt was detected for DNS query 'www.google.com'; for simplicity the entries are presented using ASCII characters

Index	Serial number	Fingerprint
h('wAKjfruEHa.WWw.GOoGLe.COM')	$i.1$	$f_K(12567\|\|1.2.3.4\|\|5.6.7.8\|\|44563\|\|011000011110110110111)$
h('wWw.gOOGlE.cOm')	$i.2$	$f_K(23455\|\|1.2.3.4\|\|5.6.7.8\|\|1089\|\|010011101010)$
h('OknfDEJFNa.wwW.gOogle.CoM')	$i.3$	$f_K(12577\|\|1.2.3.4\|\|5.6.7.8\|\|54333\|\|100011111000101000101)$

the corresponding DNS request stored in T, is sent to the DNS resolver, and the respective entries are removed from A and T.

3.2   Sandwich Implementation in Firewall

We implemented the sandwich antidote in C and ran it as a user-space program on Linux Netfilter (kernel 2.6) operating system. We added two rules to iptables firewall, one to capture all outbound packets destined to port 53 and another to capture all inbound packets originating from port 53. The kernel passed the captured packets to the implementation, which queued them, and applied to each packet the processing described in Section 3.1.

We tested that the sandwich antidote does not impose overhead to DNS or other traffic and that it does not 'break' the DNS functionality in two settings: without poisoning attack and when under attack.

Compatibility with DNS Infrastructure. When our resolver was configured to use a forwarder, in some cases the responses did not arrive in correct order. This is due to the fact that many domains were already in cache of the forwarder, while the two random queries did not exist. Thus the two responses for

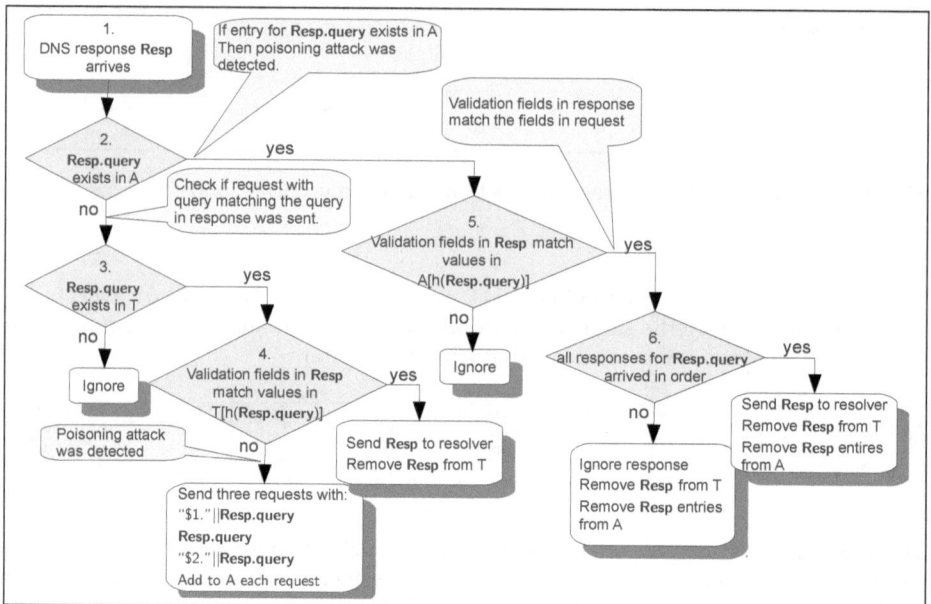

Fig. 3. A flow of the defense mechanism in firewall of the local resolver. The flow describes the steps taken by the firewall upon arrival of each DNS response.

random queries would arrive after the response to the original DNS request. To adapt the mechanism to such settings, where the local resolver uses a forwarder, we modified the implementation to issue the requests twice. Specifically, if the responses do not arrive in correct order, the same three DNS requests (random, original, random) are issued again.

Efficiency. When no attack is detected, the mechanism does not impose delays on other (non-DNS) traffic. The delays on DNS packets were in order of few microseconds. To reduce even these (negligible) delays we added a slight optimisation to our original design: we modified the firewall rule to duplicate the outbound DNS packets, then to forward, in parallel, the DNS packet to the destination (on the Internet) and a copy thereof for processing to the user-space implementation.

4   The NAT Antidote

RFC 5452 [18] recommends that when sending a query, DNS resolvers should use a random source IP address (from a list of IP addresses allocated to the resolver) and a random destination IP address (from the list of addresses of authoritative servers for the domain). Upon receiving a response, resolvers should validate it matches the query, in their source and destination IP addresses (as well as in the resolver's port, DNS query identifier, and case-sensitive query). Validation

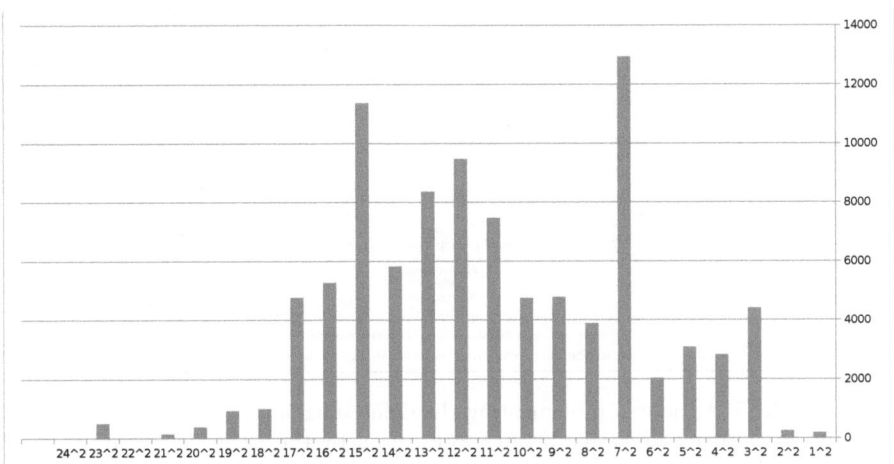

Fig. 4. Statistics of the top 100,000 domains according to Alexa, and the addresses' block range allocated to them

of IP addresses increases the entropy and makes poisoning by spoofed responses harder. Specifically, if n_R (n_A) is the number of addresses used for resolver (respectively, authority DNS), then the improvement is by factor $n_R \times n_A$.

However, typically, only a small number of IP addresses n_R, n_A are used for resolver and authority DNS; e.g., Dagon et al. [14] mention typical values of $n_R = 1$ and $n_A = 3$. Clearly, increasing n_R and n_A would improve resistance to poisoning; however, IP addresses is a scarce, expensive resource, hence allocating additional IP addresses to the DNS servers is hard to justify. On the other hand, often, a domain may have multiple IP addresses used for other purposes (not resolver), e.g., an ISP may have many IP addresses allocated to clients, and a company may have special IP addresses allocated to different publicly-available servers. The NAT antidotes takes advantage of such addresses. Specifically, we show how to add IP addresses to DNS resolver without allocating additional IP addresses. The idea is to reuse IP addresses already allocated to the network. Hence this method works for networks that have a large set of public IP addresses; fortunately, this holds for networks of many organisations and ISPs; see Figure 4 summarising the IP range blocks for top 100,000 domains according to Alexa [1], which we used in order to form a dataset. We gathered this information by running a script on the list of domains (freely available on Alexa); the script employed the whois service in order to obtain the IP address block of the domain. According to our survey the median is at 2^{11} which indicates that most domains have a sufficiently large block of IP addresses. The deployment of NAT antidote only requires modifications in the router(s) connecting the organisation to the Internet, much like commonly used network address translation (NAT) and firewall devices. Indeed, sometimes all that is required is to use existing overloading many-to-many NAT functionality.

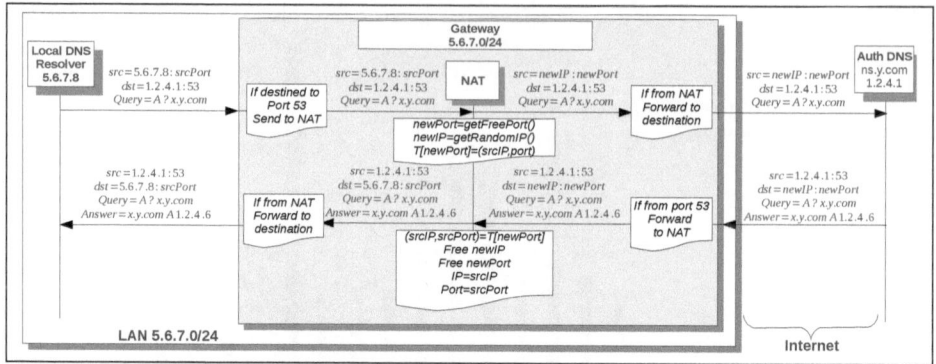

Fig. 5. The NAT Antidote, implementing the defense against DNS cache poisoning by increasing the amount of source IP addresses, used by the local DNS resolver, to the number of addresses allocated to the network. The NAT antidotes connects a network (e.g., 5.6.7.0/24) to the Internet. The NAT maps a DNS request, sent by the resolver to authority DNS, to a random IP address in the network; the NAT also changes the source port to some random, free port number, and saves this entry to a table. This allows the NAT to change the destination IP and port, in the DNS response, to the values that were originally used by the local DNS resolver.

If necessary, implementation is similar to NAT, using tools such as iptables. Figure 5 illustrates typical operation of the NAT antidote.

4.1   NAT Implementation in Firewall

The NAT antidote is a variant of many-to-many, overloading NAT functionality, i.e., mapping a set of internal IP addresses to a set of external IP address. Upon receiving a DNS request (to port 53), the firewall would perform a special type of Network Address Translation function. Specifically, it changes the IP address, of the outbound DNS requests, to a *random* IP address in the available range, stores the mapping (between the source IP, source Port, destination IP), and forwards the packet to the DNS server. When the DNS response arrives, the firewall locates the corresponding entry according to the destination IP and port, and changes the destination port and IP address to those that were used by the resolver. It then removes the stored entry and sends the DNS response; see Figure 5.

5   Birthday Paradox and Protection

Originally, DNS servers did not restrict the number of simultaneous, multiple DNS requests for the same IP address. This allowed a mathematical paradox, known as the "Birthday Paradox", to reduce the number of DNS responses required for a successful poisoning. To exploit the birthday paradox one has to send a sufficient number of queries to a DNS server, while sending an equal number of forged DNS responses at the same time. The greater the number of outgoing DNS requests, the greater the probability that the attacker will match one of those requests with a forged DNS response. As an example assume that only the transaction ID (16 bits long) is randomised in the DNS request, and that the attacker sends n responses to a DNS request; the success probability of a match of one the responses with the DNS request is $\frac{n}{2^{16}}$. If the attacker issues n requests for the same domain, and sends n responses, then the probability of a collision of one of the responses with one of the DNS request (with a random transaction ID) is: $1 - \left(1 - \frac{1}{2^{16}}\right)^{n(n-1)/2}$. For instance, for $n = 300$ there is a 50% success probability for a match and for $n = 700$ there is almost 100% success, while without the birthday paradox the success probability is $700/2^{16} = 0.01$, e.g., see [27].

Following to Kaminsky attack, many DNS resolvers were also improved to support *birthday protection*: prevent or limit [4] duplicate concurrent requests. In subsequent section we suggest a mechanism that completely prevents the birthday paradox.

5.1   Birthday Protection

Spoofing attacker can significantly increase its success probability of poisoning the cache of local DNS resolver by issuing a number of DNS requests for the same resource record, thus taking advantage of the birthday paradox. Birthday protection limits the number of concurrent DNS requests for the same record. However, not all DNS servers implement birthday protection, or sufficiently restrict the number of DNS queries. We suggest to implement the birthday protection mechanism in the firewall, without requiring modification to the local resolver itself. The idea is to limit multiple duplicate DNS requests, for the same RR (resource record) to one, by having the firewall return a single DNS response, i.e., the first one that arrives, and to ignore the rest.

The birthday protection mechanism should run at the gateway (or a proxy DNS server, through which the local resolver will issue DNS requests and receive DNS responses). The gateway should capture DNS requests and responses, by adding appropriate rules to the firewall, and should keep track of the outbound DNS requests. Specifically, when a packet destined to port 53 enters the network interface card (NIC) eth_0, (as in Figure 1), the firewall captures and queues it for processing by a waiting userspace birthday protection mechanism implementation. The mechanism maintains a table (see Table 3 for sample entries) of DNS requests and when a new request arrives it is stored in the table. The mechanism then checks if a DNS request with the same query already exists in table. If the request is new and does not exist in a table, the *first* flag is set to 1, i.e., this is the first DNS request. Then the birthday protection mechanism forwards it to the designated recipient; otherwise, the *first* is set to 0 and the request is

---

[4] Complete prevention of duplicate queries may have a significant overhead, hence many implementations only limit duplicates, e.g., to 200.

discarded. When a DNS response arrives from 53 the firewall passes it to the birthday protection mechanism. If a matching entry exists with a *flag* set to 1 the mechanism processes the response (otherwise ignores it). Taking only the response that matches the first query is important to prevent the attack exploiting the birthday paradox. For each entry in a table with a query that matches the query in the DNS response, the mechanism constructs a DNS response with the fields, e.g., port, source/destination IP, that correspond to the values in table, and uses the same *answer* field value from the DNS response that it received; it then sends the responses and removes the corresponding entries from the table. All future DNS responses for that RR will be ignored (since no matching entry exists in the table).

It may seem that the mechanism should only return the response to one of the matching DNS requests, and ignore the rest of the requests. However, depending on the implementation of the DNS resolver, when several clients make requests for the same resource record (RR), the resolver does not return the first (cached) response to the other clients, but waits for the corresponding response to arrive. Therefore, our mechanism crafts a matching DNS response to every pending DNS request. Therefore, our mechanism returns a matching DNS response to each pending entry.

Table 3. Sample entries in the table maintained by the birthday protection mechanism; for simplicity the entries are presented using ASCII characters

Index	Query ID	source IP	destination IP	source Port	0x20 Encoding	first
h('www.google.com')	12567	1.2.3.4	5.6.7.8	55555	1101101101	1
h('www.google.com')	2234	1.2.3.4	5.6.7.9	3112	1101100011	0

6   Conclusions

Currently, many DNS resolvers are still vulnerable to DNS poisoning attacks by determined adversaries, only requiring from them the ability to spoof packets. DNS poisoning can be used for a wide range of devastating attacks, hence, it is essential to develop interim solutions, to ensure security until the long-term cryptographic DNS-security mechanisms are widely deployed. Preferably, such interim antidotes to DNS poisoning should require changes only in the resolver, or, better yet, only in the gateway connecting the resolver to the Internet.

We investigated unilateral defenses against the DNS cache poisoning by spoofing adversaries, and presented new and improved mechanisms. Our central contribution is the *sandwich antidote* to DNS poisoning, which operates in two phases: detecting and then preventing poisoning attacks. We also presented the *NAT antidote*, which enhances DNS security by increasing the entropy in DNS packets for most subnets by a factor of 2^{11}, by picking a random source IP address from a pool of addresses available to the organisation. These solutions can be easily deployed in gateways (we present proof of concept code), to provide immediate defense against DNS poisoning.

References

1. The web information company, http://www.alexa.com/
2. AlFardan, N.J., Paterson, K.G.: An Analysis of DepenDNS. In: Burmester, M., Tsudik, G., Magliveras, S., Ilić, I. (eds.) ISC 2010. LNCS, vol. 6531, pp. 31–38. Springer, Heidelberg (2011)
3. Antonakakis, M., Dagon, D., Luo, X., Perdisci, R., Lee, W., Bellmor, J.: A Centralized Monitoring Infrastructure for Improving DNS Security. In: Jha, S., Sommer, R., Kreibich, C. (eds.) RAID 2010. LNCS, vol. 6307, pp. 18–37. Springer, Heidelberg (2010)
4. Arends, R., Austein, R., Larson, M., Massey, D., Rose, S.: DNS Security Introduction and Requirements. RFC 4033 (2005)
5. Arends, R., Austein, R., Larson, M., Massey, D., Rose, S.: Protocol Modifications for the DNS Security Extensions. RFC 4035 (Proposed Standard), Updated by RFC 4470 (March 2005)
6. Arends, R., Austein, R., Larson, M., Massey, D., Rose, S.: Resource Records for the DNS Security Extensions. RFC 4034 (Proposed Standard), Updated by RFC 4470 (March 2005)
7. Bellovin, S.M.: Security problems in the TCP/IP protocol suite. Computer Communication Review 19(2), 32–48 (1989)
8. Bellovin, S.M.: Using the domain name system for system break-ins. In: Proceedings of the 5th Symposium on UNIX Security, pp. 199–208. USENIX Association, Berkeley (1995)
9. Bernstein, D.J.: DNS Forgery (November 2002), Internet publication at http://cr.yp.to/djbdns/forgery.html
10. CERT. Multiple DNS implementations vulnerable to cache poisoning. Technical Report Vulnerability Note 800113, CERT (2008)
11. CNET News. Major outage hits comcast customers (2010), http://news.cnet.com/8301-1023_3-20023949-93.html
12. Cross, T.: (updated) DNS cache poisoning and network address translation. Post at IBM's Frequency X blog (July 2008), http://blogs.iss.net/archive/dnsnat.html
13. Dagon, D., Antonakakis, M., Day, K., Luo, X., Lee, C.P., Lee, W.: Recursive DNS architectures and vulnerability implications. In: Sixteenth Network and Distributed Systems Security (NDSS) Symposium. The Internet Society (2009)
14. Dagon, D., Antonakakis, M., Vixie, P., Jinmei, T., Lee, W.: Increased DNS forgery resistance through 0x20-bit encoding: security via leet queries. In: Ning, P., Syverson, P.F., Jha, S. (eds.) ACM Conference on Computer and Communications Security, pp. 211–222. ACM (2008)
15. Vixie, P., Dagon, D.: Setting dns's hair on fire (July 2008), http://www.usenix.org/events/sec08/tech/
16. Ford, B., Srisuresh, P., Kegel, D.: Peer-to-peer communication across network address translators. In: USENIX Annual Technical Conference, General Track. USENIX (2005)
17. Hubert, A., van Mook, R.: Measures for Making DNS More Resilient against Forged Answers. RFC 5452 (January 2009)
18. Infoblox. Sixth annual DNS survey (2010), http://www.infoblox.com/content/dam/infoblox/documents/press-releases/dns-survey-2010-press-release.pdf?orgSearch=google.com

19. Kaminsky, D.: It's the end of the cache as we know it. Presentation at Blackhat Briefings (August 2008)
20. Markoff, J.: Leaks in patch for web security hole. Cryptology ePrint Archive, Report 2010/449 (2008),
    http://www.nytimes.com/2008/08/09/technology/09flaw.html?r=1
21. Park, K.S., Pai, V.S., Peterson, L., Wang, Z.: CoDNS: Improving DNS performance and reliability via cooperative lookups. In: Proceedings of the 6th Conference on Symposium on Opearting Systems Design & Implementation, vol. 6, p. 14. USENIX Association (2004)
22. PCWorld: Glitch knocks rollingstone.com offline (2010),
    http://www.pcworld.com/article/189966/
    glitch_knocks_rollingstonecom_offline.html
23. Perdisci, R., Antonakakis, M., Lee, W.: Solving the dns cache poisoning problem without changing the protocol (2008)
24. Poole, L., Pai, V.S.: ConfiDNS: leveraging scale and history to improve DNS security. In: Proceedings of the 3rd Conference on USENIX Workshop on Real, Large Distributed Systems, vol. 3, p. 3. USENIX Association (2006)
25. Rosenberg, J., Weinberger, J., Huitema, C., Mahy, R.: STUN - Simple Traversal of User Datagram Protocol (UDP) Through Network Address Translators (NATs). RFC 3489 (2003)
26. Sisson, G.: DNS survey (2010),
    http://dns.measurement-factory.com/surveys/201010/
27. Stewart, J.: DNS cache poisoning - the next generation
28. Sun, H.-M., Chang, W.-H., Chang, S.-Y., Lin, Y.-H.: DepenDNS: Dependable Mechanism against DNS Cache Poisoning. In: Garay, J.A., Miyaji, A., Otsuka, A. (eds.) CANS 2009. LNCS, vol. 5888, pp. 174–188. Springer, Heidelberg (2009)
29. Vixie, P.: Extension Mechanisms for DNS (EDNS0). RFC 2671 (1999)
30. Vixie, P.: DNS and BIND security issues. In: Proceedings of the 5th Symposium on UNIX Security, pp. 209–216. USENIX Association, Berkeley (1995)
31. Yuan, L., Kant, K., Mohapatra, P., Chuah, C.N.: DoX: A peer-to-peer antidote for DNS cache poisoning attacks. In: IEEE International Conference on Communications, ICC 2006, vol. 5, pp. 2345–2350. IEEE (2006)
32. ZDay. Hd moore pwned with his own DNS exploit, vulnerable AT&T DNS servers to blame (2008),
    http://www.zdnet.com/blog/security/hd-moore-pwned-with-his-own-dns-
    exploit-vulnerable-at-t-dns-servers-to-blame/1608

Security Analysis of Leap-of-Faith Protocols

Viet Pham[1] and Tuomas Aura[2]

[1] Royal Holloway, University of London, Egham, Surrey, TW20 0EX, UK
viet.pham.2010@rhul.ac.uk
[2] Aalto University, P.O.Box 15400, FI-00076 Aalto, Finland
tuomas.aura@aalto.fi

Abstract. Over the Internet, cryptographically strong authentication is normally achieved with support of PKIs or pre-configured databases of bindings from identifiers to credentials (e.g., DNS to public keys). These are, however, expensive and not scalable solutions. Alternatively, Leap-of-Faith (LoF) provides authentication without additional infrastructure. It allows one endpoint to learn its peer's identifier-to-credential binding during first time communication, then stores that binding for future authentication. One successful application of LoF is SSH server authentication, encouraging its introduction to other protocols.

In this paper we analyze the security of LoF protocols. Various aspects are discussed to show that several proposed LoF protocols have weaker security than SSH, and that their security also depends on design and implementation details. Several protocols were analyzed, including SSH, TLS, BTNS, and HIP, revealing attacks such as impersonation, man-in-the-middle attacks, and credentials flooding. Consequently, additional mechanisms and best practices are proposed to strengthen LoF applications.

Keywords: leap-of-faith, authentication, key management, SSH, TLS, BTNS IPsec, HIP, decentralized system, infrastructureless.

1 Introduction

Due to physical separation, Internet communication suffers from identity-spoofing attacks, such as impersonation and man-in-the-middle (MitM). When two parties communicate, they need a way to name each other. Each party is represented by a *communication identifier*. For example, in `telnet` remote login, the communicating parties are the server and the client user (not the client computer). The server is identified by its DNS name or IP address, whereas the client user is identified by a username. However, since `telnet` transmits username and password in plaintext across the Internet, these identifiers could be easily spoofed.

To prevent identity-spoofing attacks, there are authentication methods based on *cryptographic credentials*. Each credential is owned by one entity and can be used to verify its identity. For instance, in public-key authentication, public keys are used as credentials. To facilitate authentication, the identifier of an entity must be mapped to that entity's credential. When someone claims to have an

M. Rajarajan et al. (Eds.): SecureComm 2011, LNICST 96, pp. 337–355, 2012.
© Institute for Computer Sciences, Social Informatics and Telecommunications Engineering 2012

identifier, the authenticator can use the corresponding credential to verify the ownership. The main problem with authentication is to maintain such kind of identifier-to-credetial mappings, or *security bindings* in our terminology.

Authentication should be strong in the sense that all bindings accepted by the authenticator are correct. In distributed systems, strong authentication is usually supported by a trusted third party (TTP) or a public-key infrastructure (PKI). For example, in TLS, each binding is represented by a certificate. Each certificate must be signed by a certificate authority (CA) within the PKI hierarchy, and its correctness could be securely verified given the public key of the root CA. Similarly, symmetric-key systems like Kerberos provides strong authentication [1] using a key distribution center (KDC) as a TTP. The strong authentication with a PKI or TTP, however, does not come without costs:

- Registration effort: correct bindings must be registered with the CA or TTP, which requires administrative effort [2]. For example, the TTP administrator must carefully perform background check on the binding owner, or otherwise attacks are possible, e.g., [3].
- Cost: as a business process, each registration incurs a cost to the registering party to have its binding certified. Most individuals and many businesses are unwilling to pay such fees especially for local or temporary IT systems.
- Scalability: with the current size of the Internet, no TTP is capable of maintaining a database of bindings for every network entity. This is especially true in peer-to-peer communication in which all endpoints are equal the their number can be very large.

These limitations have led to a search for alternative forms of authentication. One possibility is *recommendation systems* with PGP Web of Trust [4] as an early example. In these systems, the reliance on the trustworthiness of CAs is replaced by trust between people based on experiences and recommendations. As certification of bindings is decentralized to a community rather than a single PKI hierarchy, the registration and management costs could be lower. However, modelling of trust in these systems requires complicated mathematical techniques (e.g. [5]) and their applicability to non-human entities like computers is still unclear. Also, both the authenticator and the peer being authenticated must be in the same community, making it less scalable globally.

Another idea is the use of *self-certifying identifiers*. An identifier is generated by evaluating some collision-resistant function f on a credential, so that the mappings between identifiers and credentials are one-to-one, hence avoiding impersonation. As identifiers can be generated locally, no third party is needed and there is no administrative overhead. This idea works well when identifiers can include arbitrary bit strings, for instance, in the SEND protocol [6] with *cryptographically generated address* [7,8]. In contrast, user-interactive applications require human-readable identifiers, which cannot be arbitrary hash values. *Identity-based cryptography* [9] attempts to solve this, but still requires a TTP, i.e., a private key generator and thus suffers from similar problems as PKI.

In this paper, we focus on the *Leap-of-Faith (LoF)* method as an alternative to strong authentication. LoF is familiar to most university users from SSH server authentication, which can be used without pre-distributed keys or certificates. This paper is motivated by the fact that there are many proposals to imitate the SSH authentication in many other protocols. Our goal is to understand why the relatively weak LoF principle has been successful in SSH and whether it will readily extend to other protocols that operate with slightly different assumptions. This kind of analysis is important because security mechanisms often fail when they are taken outside their original operating environment.

In section 2 we describe the LoF principle in detail. Then, section 3 discusses several security considerations associated with LoF. These considerations are applied in section 4 to 7 to analyze the security of several protocols that make use of LoF. Evidently, we present a number of weaknesses on these protocols. Finally, we propose in section 8 a number of mechanisms to strengthen the security of this authentication method.

2   Leap of Faith

Due to aforementioned limitations, strong authentication is sometimes not feasible. Arkko and Nikander [10] report the emergence of new *weak or infrastructureless authentication* techniques as a workaround. The weak techniques could be used in settings where there is no sufficient information or infrastructure to establish a trust chain for strong authentication [10, 1]. One such technique is the LoF mechanism, which can be summarized as follows:

– *First communication and leap of faith*: When the authenticator and its peer communicate for the first time, the authenticator is unable to securely authenticate the peer. It takes the identifier and credential presented by the peer, checks that the identifier is new, and locally stores this identifier-to-credential binding.
– *Subsequent communication*: In any subsequent communication between the authenticator and the same peer, the communication channel is authenticated using the stored binding.

The security of LoF relies on an important assumption that the attacker is unlikely to be present during the first communication. If the accepted binding is correct, all subsequent communication will be secure. Clearly, LoF does not provide strong security and the level of assurance depends on the details of the communication network and the types of attackers that one is trying to defend against.

In the classical computer security model, LoF is unquestionably insecure. In practice, it has been applied in several contexts. The most prominent one is SSH. Another common situation is access to web sites whose TLS certificate is not signed by a recognized CA and the client user chooses to store it for future authentication. Also, when a user downloads and installs a web browser or an operating system, a list of root certificates or code signing keys is configured on that user's machine. Most users do not bother to verify offline the correctness of these certificates, and thus the LoF mechanism is applied.

It is also worth comparing LoF to a related idea, *first-come-first-serve alloca-tion* of identifiers. For example, free email service and online forums allow new users to create a name-to-credential binding for any name that has not been previously allocated. That part is similar to LoF. The difference is that, in LoF, there are some external criteria, such as the DNS hierarchy or IP address allo-cation, that could in theory be used to determine offline whether the binding is correct or not. In first-come-first-serve, there are no such external criteria and the authenticator itself allocates the names to its peers.

3   Security Considerations

The main advantage of LoF is that no third party is required. However, this implies a lack of knowledge for strong authentication. Without the LoF assump-tion, impersonation and/or MitM attacks are possible. Indeed, if the attacker appears in the first communication, he might claim the peer's identifier and give his own credential to the authenticator. Since the authenticator cannot distin-guish an attacker from a honest peer, the attacker's binding would be naively accepted. Several factors exist that influence the likelihood of this incident, as follows.

LoF scenarios. In the design of LoF protocols, two components exist: the communication initiator and the LoF maker (authenticator). We devise a num-ber of possible designs based on these components. In particular, two scenar-ios exist for the communication initiator, denoted as $Init = \{fixed, either\}$, that is, communication could be initiated by a fixed endpoint (e.g., in client-server model), or by either endpoint (e.g., in peer-to-peer model). Meanwhile, the LoF maker(s) could be one of the following: the communication initia-tor, the responder, a fixed endpoint, or both endpoints. We denote these as $LoFMaker = \{initiator, responder, fixed, both\}$. The Cartesian product $Init \times LoFMaker$ produces the set of LoF scenarios for our concern. Note that we may purge out the element $(fixed, fixed)$ as it is covered by $(fixed, initiator)$ and $(fixed, responder)$. For convenience, we denote each scenario by the initials of its components, e.g., **(FB)** stands for $(fixed, both)$.

The above two components could be used to identify potential attacks that might happen on each scenario, regardless of implementation details, purposes, or operating environments. As an example, in scenario (FI) where the LoF maker is the fixed initiator, the attacker must patiently wait for the first communication to take place before he could impersonate the responder. In contrast, scenario (FR) requires the responder to be the LoF maker, which allows an attacker to easily initiate the first communication and impersonate the honest initiator to the responder. Also in this scenario, MitM attacks are possible only if imper-sonation in the other direction could be done. This might be the case if the authentication in the opposite direction is insecure. In scenarios (FB) and (ER), however, MitM attacks are always possible because LoF is used bidirectionally. In overall, we summarize attacks on these scenarios as in Table 1.

Table 1. Attacks against scenarios in $Init \times LoFMaker$

Scenario	Potential attacks
(FI)	Intercept communication attempt $\Rightarrow$ Impersonate the responder; MitM attacks (if no strong authentication of the initiator)
(FR)	Intercept communication attempt $\Rightarrow$ Impersonate the initiator; MitM attacks (if no strong authentication of the responder) Initiate communication to the responder $\Rightarrow$ Impersonate the initiator
(FB)	Intercept communication attempt $\Rightarrow$ Impersonate both; MitM attacks Initiate communication to the responder $\Rightarrow$ Impersonate the initiator
(EI)	Intercept communication attempt $\Rightarrow$ Impersonate the responder; MitM attacks (if no strong authentication of the initiator) Initiate communication to both $\Rightarrow$ MitM attacks (if no strong authentication of the initiator)
(ER)	Initiate communication to both $\Rightarrow$ Impersonate both; MitM attacks
(EF)	Intercept communication attempt $\Rightarrow$ Impersonate the initiator Initiate communication to both $\Rightarrow$ MitM attacks (if no strong authentication of the responder)
(EB)	Initiate communication to both $\Rightarrow$ Impersonate both, MitM attacks

Binding multiple sessions. LoF follows the *temporal separation* principle [10]: using some verification techniques, a communicating party can ensure that the peer it communicates with at time t_1 is the same as that at a previous time t_0. We call the period that such t_1 may fall in as the *authenticated period*, denoted by $[t_0, t_{end}]$. Applying to LoF principle, the first communication occurs at t_0, and subsequent communication should occur within $[t_0, t_{end}]$. Thus, to avoid future attacks, the design goal is to make sure that $t_{end} \to \infty$.

To achieve this goal, LoF implementation must be able to verify credential ownership, and that ownership must be unique. Otherwise, an attacker could claim the credential and bypass the authentication, even during $[t_0, t_{end}]$. Examples include plaintext exchange of shared key as credential, since the attacker can sniff the key and becomes its second owner. Moreover, only the authenticated peer should be allowed to continue communication, or else the attacker may intercept communication at a later time. For example, some systems allow the transmission of signed session key. Although signed by the peer's credential, it can be sniffed by the attacker and used to inject valid messages.

Losses of bindings. Another threat to temporal separation is losses of security bindings, due to storage failure, accidental deletion, re-installation, etc. If this happens at the LoF authenticator side, future communication appears to be the first communication, and thus the goal $t_{end} \to \infty$ fails. Moreover, events such as storage failure often lead to the loss of many bindings, which causes many first communication sessions to occur, thus increasing chances for attackers to successfully intercept at least one session. Also, if the peer lost its credential, it would have to create a new one, causing authentication failure. This may lead to public announcement of the change to resolve failure, allowing attackers to attack at a specific time with higher chance to intercept a first communication.

Authentication failures. A failure occurs when the authenticator receives a credential that does not match the peer's binding locally stored. In many cases this implies an attack. For example, if the attacker appears only during the first communication and gives his own credential, then failures would occur on subsequent communication with the honest peer. Likewise, failures also happen if attacks are mounted on subsequent communication instead of the first one. Authentication failures may also be a result of losses of bindings. To resolve failures, the authenticator must detect which scenario is the cause. However, since the difference between these scenarios is subtle, the authenticator may either accept the new binding that allows the attacker to impersonate the honest peer, or deny the new binding of the honest peer and its legitimate communication.

Attack environment. Inherent characteristics of attack environments have certain influences on the attacker's success rate. In fact, there are several criteria that the attacker must meet in order to mount an attack, including his location, knowledge, and presence. If either route redirection or compromise of middle nodes is possible, the attacker could be anywhere in the network. Otherwise, he must be at either endpoint's local network (e.g., neighbours, university students), or on the route (e.g., ISP, intelligence agencies). The attacker might also need knowledge about an endpoint, such as its online time, or IP address that is not in the DNS and changes over time. The attacker's presence is also important for a successful attack, e.g., in MitM attacks, if an endpoint is mobile, the attacker must move along with it during the attack.

Another characteristic is the frequency of first communication sessions, which varies for each operating environment. The number of such sessions may be driven by the densities of authenticators and parties being authenticated, which is location-specific. It could also be influenced by the popularity of the LoF protocol. For example, an application-layer LoF protocol may be less used than a transport-layer LoF protocol. In addition, the dynamics of the community may as well affect the number of first communication sessions. As the community grows, or when there is churn [11], new pairs of peers and authenticators will be introduced, allowing attacks on the LoF bootstrapping process.

On the other hand, the risk of being detected is a deterrent to the attacker. This risk may be high given an effective attack detection mechanism. In certain situations, IDS techniques such as fingerprint-based misuse detection [12, 4.5] or anomaly-based detection [12, 4.4] could be used. To be feasible, these detection techniques should exploit the difference between an attacker and the honest peer, such as online time. Also, the honest peer and its authenticator may share some information through out-of-band channels, such as telephone, which the attacker is not aware of. These differences may result in the attacker's strange behaviors that make attack detection possible.

Binding multiple protocol layers. In some scenarios, the LoF protocol may be used as a transport layer carrying traffic for higher-layer applications. It is possible that these layers are not aware of each other's operation. In that case, changes at the lower layer may not be visible to applications. If the attacker could change the peer's identifier and/or credential, the application would blindly continue the communication with the wrong endpoint. This happens, for example when the application and the LoF protocol use DNS names and IP addresses as identifiers, respectively. DNS spoofing would force the LoF protocol into using a wrong peer IP address and wrong security binding. Even with higher-layer authentication, this attack may still work if a mechanism such as plaintext password authentication is used, as password sniffing is possible.

First communication detectability. The ability to detect the first communication helps the attacker avoid being caught. When the attacker hijacks a local network with many nodes, he might encounter many LoF connections. Inherently, only a small fraction of these are first communication. Attacking all connections clearly reveals the attacker's presence, as most authentication sessions will fail. Instead, selective attacks against only first communications allow the attacker to stay stealthy.

Detectability may be facilitated by different factors. As an example, a LoF protocol maybe designed with different messaging for first versus subsequent communications. Also, the timing of first communications maybe leaked through out-of-band channels, such as emails, SMS messages, or by historical statistics. We devise in Figure 1 another detection method. First, the MitM attacker passes on messages in between until (t_0) when the authenticator successfully receives its peer's credential. He then waits until the authenticator responds (t_1), and check the waiting time $t_1 - t_0$ against ϵ, the expected response time from the authenticator during a subsequent communication. If $t_1 - t_0 \gg \epsilon$, this is the first communication, as $t_1 - t_0$ is the time for the user to decide whether to accept the credential. Otherwise when $t_1 - t_0 \approx \epsilon$, no human decision is involved, and that may imply subsequent communication.

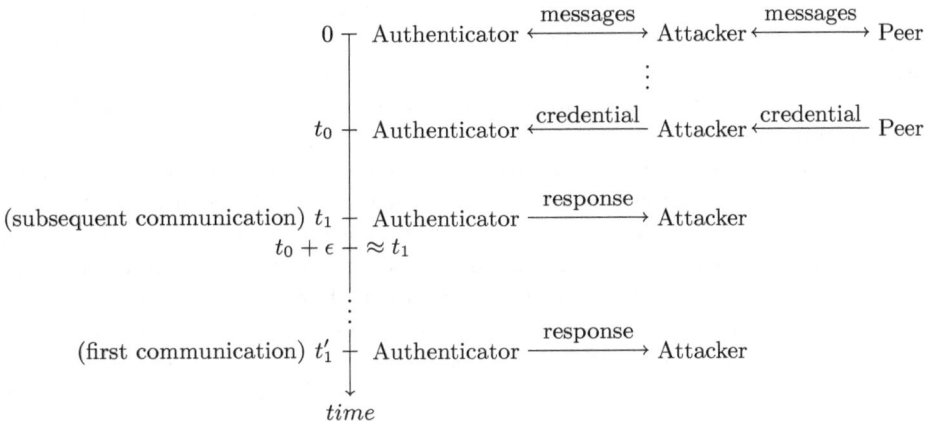

Fig. 1. Timing method to detect LoF first communication

The above attack makes use of two assumptions. Firstly, human being is involved in accepting/rejecting the credential. In fact, this applies to most LoF protocols that have been developed. Secondly, upon realization of the first communication, the attacker is able stop the authenticator from accepting the peer's credential and replace with that of his own. This attack exploits implementation defects rather than protocol issues, e.g., in certain WWW browsers as detailed in Section 5.

Performance issues. In most communication protocols, a communication state needs to be remembered by at least one communicating party. This party must store and perform lookup of state data in memory. This brings a chance for an attacker to create a massive number of sessions whose state data would either fill this party's memory or exhaust its capacity for managing the data. An early example is TCP, which suffers from SYN-flooding attacks [13]. LoF protocols are no exception, as the authenticator must store the peer's binding permanently and is thus vulnerable to resource exhaustion attacks.

4   Secure Shell (SSH)

In the early days, remote login protocols such as `telnet` and `rlogin` sendzz plaintext passwords over the networks where they could be sniffed. SSH [14] was created specifically as a response to prevalent sniffing attacks, using encrypted tunnels between the client and the server. SSH became popular because, thanks to LoF, it can be installed locally at the client and server and avoids most of the administrative overheads involved in strong server authentication.

The SSH server is identified by either its DNS name or IP address, with its public key being the credential. When the client initiates a connection, it receives the server's public key PK. The client looks in its storage of bindings, e.g., a `known_hosts` file, for a key associated with the server's identifier. If no key is found, the session is the LoF first communication, and the client user is asked whether to accept PK. If accepted, the binding from the server's identifier to PK is stored. In case the server's key is already in `known_hosts`, the server is authenticated only if this stored key equals PK. Otherwise, the user would be alerted of a potential attack and, depending on the implementation, the session may be terminated.

SSH LoF has several characteristics that make it relatively secure. It follows scenario (FI): the communication is always initiated by the client, and it is also the only LoF authenticator. Although SSH is still vulnerable to MitM attacks, these are difficult to implement. The adversary must wait for the first communication to take place to attack successfully. Meanwhile, most casual hackers are unlikely to be on the communication route at the right time. More advanced attacks that reroute the traffic via the attacker are easier to detect with an IDS and will thus not last long. Mobile clients, on the other hand, have most likely initialized their `known_hosts` before roaming into insecure networks.

In another advantage, SSH is often comes as a single piece of software comprising both the security protocol and the terminal emulator. This eliminates the problems caused by lack of application awareness to lower-layer protection: the SSH client takes care that the terminal sessions are consistently protected. The exception is with SSH port forwarding, in which case SSH carries traffic for other protocols such as SMTP, X11 or HTTP. Even then, the status of SSH is still controlled by the user with a separate interface, e.g., an SSH client.

One critical feature in the design of SSH is that a passive observer cannot distinguish between a first and a subsequent communication sessions. Thus, either the attacker ceases to attack, or he must target all connections and risks detection. In relatively static wired networks, the attacker may be able to spot new client computers or users and target them. However, the more vulnerable settings, such as open wireless networks, are actually difficult for the attacker because he cannot tell which clients are new. In such cases, an attack report policy would certainly help detect the attacker's presence. Also, the timing attack in Figure 1 would not work as its second assumption fails for most SSH implementations, such as OpenSSH and PuTTY. Upon user acceptance, these software force local storage of server's public key, without further concern. Unless the local program execution is intefered with, this storing process is unstoppable.

Despite above advantages, SSH also has some shortcomings. We recall that SSH sessions usually have two layers of authentication: LoF authentication of the server and password authentication of the client. The session key created in the key exchange will be only bound to the to server credentials but not to the user password or username. Hence, impersonation of the server is enough to learn the session key. Also, the use of plaintext password means that a successful attack against the LoF will also compromise the password. By using a challenge-response protocol for client authentication and by binding the session key to the client password these problems could be mitigated.

Another issue is that when the server private key is lost, the administrator would notify users in public. The short period following this announcement would be the best time for active attacks. The same problem may also emerge for environments with high and predictable churn rates, e.g., university networks. In such places, the attacker may know when new users appear in the network and target their first SSH logins.

5   Transport Layer Security (TLS)

Similar to SSH, TLS provides, among other things, authentication and confidentiality for peer-to-peer communication. While each peer is identified by its TLS certificate, authentication is accomplished with support from a PKI hierarchy of Certificate Authorities (CA). However, without such premises, LoF could be introduced as an alternative. While authentication in TLS can be peer-to-peer [15, F.1.1], we consider only its promient use nowadays, i.e., the client-server setting represented by scenario (FI), such as with HTTP. Thus, the similar security analysis of SSH regarding this scenario is also valid for TLS LoF.

Nevertheless, LoF TLS differs from SSH in other aspects. TLS is the transport-layer protocol, providing security services for upper layers. This implies its greater popularity than SSH which is mainly used for remote logins. For instance, many WWW servers nowadays use TLS to provide security for HTTP, however without a proper TLS certificate issued by a trusted CA. Thus, users connecting to such servers via TLS would have to make leap-of-faith on the unrecognisable certificates. Due to the inherent popularity of WWW usage, there is a high chance for successful interception of a first communication session.

The fact that TLS is a transport-layer protocol also presents multiple-layer binding issues in which users are unaware of lower layer attacks on TLS LoF. This implementation issue appears, for instance, in popular software such as Firefox and Safari, making the attack in Figure 1 feasible. In particular, when Firefox receives an unverifiable server X.509 certificate, it displays a warning to the WWW user. However, to be able to examine the certificate and accept/reject it, the user must click on an **Add exception...** button, which triggers a reconnection to the server, again asking for its certificate. This latter certificate will be presented to the user instead of the first one. With the timing method, the attacker could detect the first communication, and is able to inject his own certificate during the reconnection, thus succeed in impersonating the server. Clearly, the difference between the two certificates is visible to TLS, but not to the user.

Another concern with current implementations of TLS, most notably WWW browsers, is the temporal separation principle, which signifies that a certificate, once accepted, should be stored permanently. However, Firefox and Safari give users an option, though non-default, to accept the TLS certificate for a particular session only. Even worse, this is the default option in Google Chrome, which implies that every connection is treated as the first communication, rendering the WWW user highly vulnerable to attacks.

6   Better Than Nothing Security (BTNS) IPsec

Unlike SSH, IPsec is designed for protecting all different types of network traffic. It operates at the Internet layer and establishes secure channels for IP packets, transparent to upper layers. The main operation of IPsec is with the Internet Key Exchange (IKE) protocol. Within this protocol [16, 1.2], public-key certificates are used to facilitate peer authentication. IKE is also used to exchange a shared keying material for establishing secure channels. The security of this material is bound to the public keys of both endpoints using digital signatures.

Normally, IKE requires signed public-key certificates or a Kerberos server (in the PKInit mode of IKE) to bind the public keys to the identifiers of the end nodes. Inherently, this kind of infrastructure does not span globally. BTNS mode of IPsec [17,18] is a proposed extenstion of IPsec that supports LoF. Its goal is to perform anonymous encryption of communication and authentication within one communications session. Since the specification of BTNS is still undergoing, we have to make some assumptions in our discussion.

LoF scenarios. BTNS LoF may first appear to be similar to SSH. If used below the `telnet` application, it provides comparable security to SSH. With fixed client and server roles, it follows scenario (FI). However, generic IPsec architecture does not follow this kind of asymmetric thinking. Instead, BTNS seem to be specified with scenario (EB) in mind where either endpoint can initiate the communication and both make leaps of faith on each other. This allows the attacker to initiate a first communication to any other node, causing that node to bind any previously unbound name to the attacker's credential. This way, the attacker can hijack a server name at a client's namespace before the client connects to the server.

As a remedy, BTNS could possibly be implemented in a more restricted way. For example, the binding could be created only at the initiator, as in scenario (EI). It may first appear that this will prevent the reversal of roles and teaching the other party a false binding. However, in IPsec it is very difficult to be certain which endpoint actually initiated the communication. This is because IPsec may be triggered by another communication in opposite direction. A typical example is FTP where the server initiates connections to the client. If only the FTP data transfer is protected by BTNS IPsec, then the LoF initiator will appear to be the server. Thus, an attacker can cause the FTP server to initiate a first communication to his IP address, making attacks significantly more likely.

Similar reversals of IPsec initiator and responder roles occur in Windows implementations of IPsec where a client workstation can be configured to be in responder-only mode, i.e., to use IPsec only if the server initiates connections to it. The role reversals are perfectly acceptable in IPsec with strong authentication and fit well the symmetric design of the IPsec architecture. Authentication with LoF, however, does not fit well into this setting. This is easiest to understand in peer-to-peer protocols where there is no difference between client and server, and scenario (FI) with fixed initiator is simply nonsensical.

Binding of protocol layers. As IPsec operates at IP layer, it introduces a operation awareness problem to higher layers, causing a number of attacks [19], especially when BTNS LoF is in use. One approach to resolve this is called *connection latching* [20], which binds each upper-layer connection (e.g., TCP) to the underlying IPsec channel protecting it. This ensures that changes in the underlying IPsec channel would terminate the upper-layer connection. More importantly, an interface is provided for upper layers to monitor IPsec connections. Another approach is *channel binding* [21], which works when the higher-layer application provides strong authentication of the peer. In that case, this strong authentication is used to securely verify the public key received via BTNS. Both mechanisms solve many of the security problems that we later identify in HIP, such as the lack of binding among protocol layers.

Apart from host-to-host connections, IPsec can also be used to create tunnels between security gateways or between a host and a gateway. These are actually more common IPsec scenarios because they make up VPN tunnels. If BTNS is used, IPsec and the application-layer connections are implemented on different machines, making inter-layer binding methods such as connection latching and channel binding infeasible. Given that BTNS IPsec have yet been deployed, it is impossible to point out actual security failures. However, the possibility of

LoF-authenticated IPsec association expiring underneath a long-lived application session is an important concern when specifying BTNS-based VPNs.

Managing security bindings. The intended transparency of IPsec to application layers brings further issues when BTNS is used. Being blinded from IPsec operation, user confirmation on the correctness of security binding and offline recovery of authentication failures is typically impossible. Moreover, even if an IPsec-awareness interface is implemented on end hosts, a user behind an IPsec gateway will not be able to control the gateway and will not even know what is causing the communication failure if the gateway detects change of peer key and refuses to route further packets.

Secondly, an attacker can flood BTNS IPsec by repeating first communication sessions between a target host or gateway and presenting each time a different identifier and credential. The target will have to decide which bindings to store and which to drop, but it has not feedback from the application layer on which bindings correspond to application-layer sessions that still exist.

Thirdly, IPsec host mobility maybe problematic if BTNS authenticator, as intended, stores a binding between the peer IP address and its credential (i.e. public key). When the same IP address is reused by a different mobile device, the authenticator will see that as an attack. Similarly, hosts behind a NAT share the same IP address but have different credentials, which again will look like an attack. This makes IP addresses unsuitable identifiers for BTNS bindings.

7 Host Identity Protocol (HIP)

HIP is similar to IPsec in that it provides network authentication transparently to higher-layer applications. HIP also aims at mobility and multi-homing. To do so, it inserts a *host identity layer* into the TCP/IP model, between the IP and the transport layers. On this layer, each node is identified by a *Host Identifier* (HI), which is actually a public key. This allows each HI to be self-certifying, which avoids impersonation. Also, HIs replace IP addresses as communication identifiers for upper-layer protocols, e.g., TCP. As a result, these protocols become independent of IP address changes, thus supporting mobility and multi-homing.

The core of HIP is the base exchange [22]. It involves four messages, as shown in Figure 2. Message I1 is used by the HIP initiator to trigger the connection. It contains the hash of the responder's HI, called Host Identity Tag (HIT). Then, R1 and I2 are used to exchange the Diffie-Hellman key for the secure channel. Also, the initiator includes in I2 its HI to allow the responder to authenticate its messages. Finally, the message R2 completes the exchange.

Using HIs as identifiers, the problems mentioned in the previous section about dynamic and non-unique IP addresses are irrelevant in HIP because the IP address is only used for routing and not for security bindings. However, the problem is at the application layer where DNS names are typically used as identifiers. In this case, secure mapping from DNS names to HIs is needed. This should be solved by a secure name resolution mechanisms such as DNSSec [23]. The initiator would look up the responder HIT in DNS and send its own DNS name in

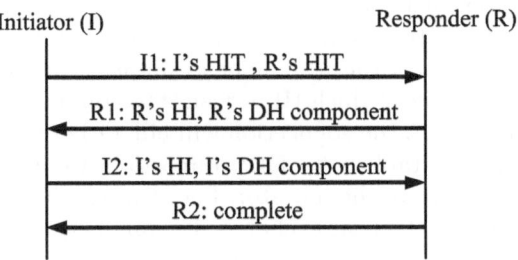

Fig. 2. A simplified operation of HIP

the I2 message, which the responder can verify from DNS. If both sides perform the lookup from secure DNS, then strong authentication is achieved.

There are several difficulties with the use DNSSec in HIP. Firstly, while DNSSec is being deployed, it still does not cover all Internet individual hosts. Secondly, not all DNS servers support HIs in DNS records. Thirdly, IP address lookup mechanisms may not necessarily support indirect mappings from DNS name to HI to IP address. This may leave a HIP host with just the knowledge of the peer's IP address rather than HI. These are the situations where LoF becomes an attractive option. The *opportunistic mode* (LoF) [24] in HIP works as follows: the initiator sends a tentative message I1 to the responder, which—if it supports HIP—responds with R1 and includes its DNS name (or other application-layer identifier) as well as its HI in the message. The initiator continues by revealing its own name in I2. Both may then store a mapping from the name to the HI.

Exploiting the Symmetric Operation. The LoF protocol described above corresponds to scenario (EB), which enables the attacker to connect to any hosts and teach them false bindings. The initiator may also choose to be anonymous, in which case the responder stores no binding. If this was taken as the only allowed mode of operation, then it would correspond to scenario (EI), which is slightly less vulnerable. There will nevertheless be the possibility of role reversal attack similar to those against BTNS because of the symmetric nature of HIP.

LoF Bootstrapping Detection. Unlike the messaging design in SSH, the HIP base exchange allows the attacker to detect the bootstrapping process (first communication). Specifically, when the initiator does not know the responder HI, it sends the I1 message with a null responder HIT. Seeing this null value, the attacker can be certain that the first communication is happening. On the other hand, with regard to the timing method in Figure 1, current implementations of HIP such as OpenHIP and HIPL are invulnerable, since the acceptance of credentials is an automatic process, i.e., it does not involve human decisions.

Problems of Transparency. HIP is designed as a general protocol operating in the middle of the TCP/IP model. Its implementation is independent of higher-layer applications. Also, HIP provides an interface for these applications to communicate across networks. Many legacy applications do not understand HIP, as well as its protection. This is the main source of problems for HIP.

In HIP, authentication of the responder is simple. The initiator originates a communication and specifies which HI it wishes to communicate with. If the responder uses a different HI, the connection will fail. Otherwise, only the owner of the HI can successfully establish the HIP connection. Conversely, the responder may not always authenticate the initiator. For example, if the initiator does not provide its DNS name in the base exchange, it cannot be authenticated, and the responder is left with an anonymous peer. Also, providing a name that cannot be resolved achieves similar effect. The problem is, upper-layer applications are not aware of this fact, and they may unintentionally use this connection. This is mainly due to bad implementation and configuration of HIP.

Weak HI-to-LSI Mappings. A problem with HIP is that legacy applications do not understand HI or HIT. HIP solves this by using Local Scope Identifiers (LSIs). Depending on the application, an LSI could be in a form of an IPv4 or IPv6 address. When the application wishes to communicate with a DNS name, HIP returns an LSI as the result of a DNS query. This LSI locally represents the actual peer, and is thus mapped to the peer's IP address and (if available) HI. When a connection is made to this LSI, HIP searches for a mapping of this LSI, and performs the base exchange with the corresponding peer.

There are currently two main methods for LSI-to-HI mapping. The first method uses a mapping list to perform lookup. When a new HI is recognized, HIP picks a free LSI from its local pool and maps the two together. Since the mapping list is bijective, authentication of LSIs is secure. In the second method, the mapping is such that the LSI is the value of a function f on the HI. If f were collision-resistant, then each LSI is a self-certifying. However, it is problematic that the range of LSIs is small. For example, a private IPv4 range such as 10.0.0.0/24 may be used as LSIs. There are only 2^{24}, or approximately 16 millions possible LSIs, and it is easy to find two HIs that map to the same LSI. Consequently, the attacker may trick the application into communicating with him instead of the honest peer, since they are represented using the same LSI.

The above weaknesses open a number of attacks on HIP. In particular, we consider impersonation attacks in a peer-to-peer model between Alice and Bob, given that they have already bootstrapped LoF. We also assume that the HI-to-LSI mapping is done using a function f instead of a mapping list. The attacker starts by computing a HI that would map to the same LSI as Bob's HI would. Then, he establishes a HIP connection to Alice, using this new HI, which results in Alice mapping this HI to the LSI she used previously for representing Bob. When Alice's higher-layer application reconnects to Bob through such LSI, HIP does not establish a new HIP connection to Bob, but simply forwards the communication to the attacker's HIP connection, making the attack successful.

In another attack variant, it may be possible to replace the underlying security association in the middle of a higher-layer session. In some implementations (e.g., OpenHIP), the HIP security association is discarded after an idle period. However, the higher-layer communication has not necessarily terminated, e.g., it could happen during long TCP idle periods. When TCP becomes active again, the HIP base exchange would again take place and the LSI would be rebound to a different HI, e.g., using the above attack. Because the upper-layer protocol is unaware of this change, an attacker may take over the connection. Also, since the attacker hijacks the upper-layer connection in the middle of it, he avoids any initial application-layer authentication that may have been initially required.

Exhausting LSI Namespace. In some HIP implementation, such as OpenHIP, acceptance of security bindings is automatic, without user confirmation. This allows potential exhaustion of the LSI space, which happens when the LoF maker is the HIP responder or the attacker manages to reverse the roles of LoF initiator and responder by triggering the target to be the initiator. In particular, the attacker may create many HIs, and uses each of them to communicate with a particular HIP responder. If this node uses a HI-to-LSI mapping list, there are two problems. As the attacker continues to generate HIs, the LSI space at the targeting HIP node will be filled up, resulting in dropping/rejecting of legitimate bindings. Even if the LSI space is large enough (e.g., IPv6-like LSI), it is questionable on how HIP manages such a large set of bindings efficiently.

8   Strengthening LoF Protocols

In previous sections, a security analysis shows that LoF brings certain security to protocols for which it is applied. However, these protocols still have some weaknesses that may lead to attacks, e.g., impersonation and MitM. The chance that these attacks occur also varies from protocol to protocol, and environment to environment. We now present several proposals that address the revealed weaknesses and thus may strengthen the overall security of LoF protocols.

8.1   Multi-path Authentication

To cope with MitM attacks, [25] introduce an idea that statistically improves the ability of detecting whether attacks are really happening. This idea is similar to the requirements on *vertex disjoint paths* between two nodes. Basically, communication between Alice and Bob is secure if there are n communication paths between them, and there are t attackers such that $n > 2t + 1$ [26, III].

The use of multiple paths could as well be applied to LoF protocols. The main concern is the requirement of disjoint paths, which maybe problematic because most network nodes have only one Internet connection. To simulate disjoint paths, Alice needs secure communication to her friends, e.g., Carol and Dave, each of which has a distinct connection to Bob. As an example, in SSH, Carol and Dave could be SSH servers whose credentials are already in Alice's known_hosts. Unlike in SSH, in other protocols such as TLS, HIP and BTNS, there might exist public infrastructures whose security bindings could be securely verified, such as public rendezvous servers in HIP, or small PKI hierarchies. These could as well be used as Carol and Dave.

8.2   Resolving Authentication Failures

As previously mentioned, the main problem with authentication failures is the difficulty in distinguishing their causes. In this section, we propose approaches that could be used to resolve failures for some specific situations.

Firstly, we distinguish two scenarios in which attacks appear during LoF first and subsequent communication, respectively. We notice that most attackers are not always active, whereas in situations like the client-server model, the server is always online. This gives a possible method: after the first communication, the LoF authenticator (e.g. the client) keeps probing the peer (e.g. the server) for its credential. These probes should be made at random times. Since the attacker cannot guess when these happen, he cannot intercept all probes. This method is especially effective with a mobile peer, because the attacker has to move along with this peer to execute attacks. If the peer always answers with the same credential, it is unlikely to be an attacker.

The second approach deals with the confusion in authentication failures caused by either loss of private keys or attacks. To resolve this confusion, the system administrator may provide information through out-of-band channels to users. For example, consider a SSH server that lost its private key and is assigned a new one. In this case, the administrator could tell a secret word to the users over the phone and the SSH server could require the client to send this word encrypted by the new public key. That way, the users are forced to contact the administrator before they can reconnect to the server, and they cannot just click ok to accept the new public key.

8.3   Best Practices for LoF Applications

Together the discussion of security considerations and the analysis of protocols reveal several principles that a LoF application should satisfy. These best practices are important for protocol designers to consider when applying LoF into their protocols. Also, they may be helpful during protocol implementation and deployment. These principles are summarized in the following list:

- To prevent attacks on LoF first communication, the LoF responder should not make any leap of faith. Note that care must be taken in determining the actual initiator, for example when one endpoint uses an external protocol to trigger LoF from the other endpoint.
- The decision to accept a security binding must be based on user confirmation. This allows out-of-band information to support verification of the binding. Also, it avoids flooding the LoF authenticator with security bindings.
- To facilitate attack detection, a credential accepted for communication must be permanently stored, or removable only by advanced users.
- Within a communication session, the secure data channel must be bound to all authentication processes. All credentials of both endpoints (e.g., keys, passwords) must be involved in creating the session key. Thus, the secure channel can only be compromised if all the involved authentication mechanisms fail.

- For application-independent LoF implementation, there should be an interface (e.g., APIs) for applications to monitor its operation. Failures to do so lead to exploitation of the application's oblivion to changes such as session restarts or policy changes.
- The LoF first communication must be made indistinguishable from the subsequent ones to sniffing attackers. This forces attackers to perform attacks on all connections, hence risking detection.
- Where possible, authentication over multiple paths should be used during LoF bootstrapping or authentication failures, which defeats MitM attackers that are not on all these paths.
- Attackers can sometimes predict the timing of the LoF first communication, e.g., after storage failures. In such cases, out-of-band channels (e.g., telephone, SMS) maybe needed to support the verification of the peer's credential.

9   Conclusion

In this paper we study the security of the LoF mechanism as it is applied to various network protocols. In principle, LoF allows the authenticator to simply accept the peer's binding during the first communication between them. This binding is used to authenticate the same peer for later communication. The security of this mechanism relies on the assumption that the LoF bootstrapping process (first communication) is attacker-free.

We investigate why this rather weak authentication mechanism has been successful in SSH. To do so, we consider different aspect of LoF protocols such as the choice of initiator and LoF authenticator, temporal separation, binding of multiple protocol layers, and performance issues. The environment where attacks might occur is also taken into consideration. Using these aspects, we pointed out some critical features that often shield SSH against attacks on the LoF first communication. We also apply the same analysis to TLS and some other protocols for which LoF has been proposed: BTNS IPsec, HIP. It turns out that the security of LoF authentication in these protocols is not comparable to SSH and that it depends heavily on the way the protocols are implemented and used.

The analysis reveals various attacks on these LoF protocols, including impersonation, MitM attacks, and flooding of credentials. We then propose several mechanisms to help reducing the success probability of these attacks, including best-practice guidelines for the design of LoF protocols that should be considered for this weak authentication to be reasonably secure.

Acknowledgements. This work was supported in part by the Academy of Finland (project no. 135230). Also, the authors thank Carlos Cid and the anonymous reviewers for helpful comments.

References

1. Kohl, J.T., Neuman, B.C., Ts'o, T.Y.: The Evolution of the Kerberos Authentication Service, pp. 78–94. IEEE Computer Society Press (1994)
2. VeriSign, Inc.: VeriSign Certification Practice Statement (2009), http://www.verisign.com/repository/CPS/
3. Potter, B.: Dangerous URLs: Unicode & IDN (2005), http://www.sciencedirect.com/science/article/B6VJG-4FVC3YD-6/2/9d0fa84d322964a8c9ac42cba2936dea
4. Abdul-Rahman, A.: The PGP Trust Model. The Journal of Electronic Commerce 10(3), 27–31 (1997)
5. Jsang, A.: An Algebra for Assessing Trust in Certification Chains. In: Network and Distributed Systems Security Symposium (NDSS 1999), San Diego, USA (1999)
6. Arkko, J. (ed.), Kempf, J., Zill, B., Nikander, P.: SEcure Neighbor Discovery (SEND). RFC 3971 (2005)
7. Aura, T.: Cryptographically Generated Addresses (CGA). RFC 3972 (2005)
8. Aura, T.: Cryptographically Generated Addresses (CGA). In: Boyd, C., Mao, W. (eds.) ISC 2003. LNCS, vol. 2851, pp. 29–43. Springer, Heidelberg (2003)
9. Baek, J., Newmarch, J., Safavi-naini, R., Susilo, W.: A Survey of Identity-Based Cryptography. In: Proc. of Australian Unix Users Group Annual Conference, pp. 95–102 (2004)
10. Arkko, J., Nikander, P.: Weak Authentication: How to Authenticate Unknown Principals without Trusted Parties. In: Christianson, B., Crispo, B., Malcolm, J.A., Roe, M. (eds.) Security Protocols 2002. LNCS, vol. 2845, pp. 5–19. Springer, Heidelberg (2004)
11. Stutzbach, D., Rejaie, R.: Towards a Better Understanding of Churn in Peer-to-Peer Networks. Department of Computer Science, University of Oregon (2004)
12. Mchugh, J.: Intrusion and Intrusion Detection. International Journal of Information Security 1, 14–35 (2001)
13. Eddy, W.: TCP SYN Flooding Attacks and Common Mitigations. RFC 4987 (2007), http://tools.ietf.org/html/rfc4987
14. Ylonen, T.: SSH - Secure Login Connections over the Internet. In: Proceedings of the 6th USENIX Security Symposium, pp. 37–42 (1996)
15. Dierks, T., Rescorla, E.: The Transport Layer Security (TLS) Protocol Version 1.2. RFC 5246 (2008), http://tools.ietf.org/html/rfc5246
16. Kaufman, C.: Internet Key Exchange (IKEv2) Protocol. RFC 4306 (2005), http://tools.ietf.org/html/rfc4306
17. Williams, N., Richardson, M.: Better-Than-Nothing Security: An Unauthenticated Mode of IPsec. RFC 5386 (2008)
18. Touch, J., Black, D., Wang, Y.: Problem and Applicability Statement for Better-Than-Nothing Security (BTNS). RFC 5387 (2008)
19. Aura, T., Roe, M., Mohammed, A.: Experiences with Host-to-Host IPsec. In: Christianson, B., Crispo, B., Malcolm, J.A., Roe, M. (eds.) Security Protocols 2005. LNCS, vol. 4631, pp. 3–22. Springer, Heidelberg (2007)
20. Williams, N.: IPsec Channels: Connection Latching. Internet Drafts (2005), http://www.ietf.org/id/draft-ietf-btns-connection-latching-11.txt
21. Williams, N.: On the Use of Channel Bindings to Secure Channels. RFC 5056 (2007), http://tools.ietf.org/html/rfc5056
22. Moskowitz, R., Nikander, P., Jokela, P. (ed.), Henderson, T.: Host Identity Protocol. RFC 5201 (2008), http://www.ietf.org/rfc/rfc5201.txt

23. Arends, R., Austein, R., Larson, M., Massey, D., Rose, S.: DNS Security Introduction and Requirements. RFC 4033 (2007)
24. Komu, M., Lindqvist, J.: Leap-of-Faith Security is Enough for IP Mobility. In: Proceedings of the 6th IEEE Conference on Consumer Communications and Networking Conference, CCNC (2009)
25. Wendlandt, D., Andersen, D.G., Perrig, A.: Perspectives: Improving SSH-style Host Authentication with Multi-Path Probing. In: Proceedings of the USENIX Annual Technical Conference, Usenix ATC (2008)
26. Desmedt, Y.: Unconditionally Private and Reliable Communication in an Untrusted Network. In: IEEE Information Theory Workshop on Theory and Practice in Information-Theoretic Security, pp. 38–41 (2005)

Secure and Practical Key Distribution for RFID-Enabled Supply Chains

Tieyan Li[1], Yingjiu Li[2], and Guilin Wang[3]

[1] Irdeto (Cloakware) Beijing, China
li.tieyan@irdeto.com
[2] School of Information Systems, Singapore Management University,
Singapore 178902
yjli@smu.edu.sg
[3] Centre for Computer and Information Security Research, School of Computer
Science and Software Engineering, University of Wollongong, Wollongong,
NSW 2522, Australia
Guilin@uow.edu.au

Abstract. In this paper, we present a fine-grained view of an RFID-enabled supply chain and tackle the secure key distribution problem on a *peer-to-peer* base. In our model, we focus on any pair of consecutive parties along a supply chain, who agreed on a transaction and based on which, certain RFID-tagged goods are to be transferred by a third party from one party to the other as in common supply chain practice. Under a strong adversary model, we identify and define the security requirements with those parties during the delivery process. To meet the security goal, we first propose a resilient secret sharing (RSS) scheme for key distribution among the three parties and formally prove its security against *privacy* and *robustness* adversaries. In our construction, the shared (and recovered) secrets can further be utilized properly on providing other desirable security properties such as tag authenticity, accessibility and privacy protection. Compared with existing approaches, our work is more resilient, secure and provides richer features in supply chain practice. Moreover, we discuss the parameterization issues and show the flexibility on applying our work in real-world deployments.

Keywords: RFID, security, privacy, key distribution, secret sharing.

1 Introduction

Radio-frequency identification (RFID) is a wireless Automatic Identification and Data Capture (AIDC) technology that has been widely deployed in many applications, especially in supply chain management. For dynamic RFID-enabled supply chains, the parties in a supply chain are usually lack of pre-existing trusted relationships. Unfortunately, almost all existing RFID *privacy-enhanced* authentication protocols such as [9,8,6], assuming a central database on managing all secret keys of the tags, may fail on delivering key information to the

M. Rajarajan et al. (Eds.): SecureComm 2011, LNICST 96, pp. 356–372, 2012.
© Institute for Computer Sciences, Social Informatics and Telecommunications Engineering 2012

correct parties when a large scale of RFID tags move along dynamic supply chains.

A practical solution to the key distribution problem is the secret sharing approach, where a tag key is split into a number of shares and the shares are stored in multiple tags. Since the tag keys are stored in the tags directly, an authorized party can collect enough shares and recover the keys, while an adversary is assumed to have limited access to the tags such that s/he cannot collect enough shares for recovering the keys. Since there is no need of distributing key information among supply chain parties, this approach is particularly useful for protecting RFID tags in dynamic supply chains.

A recent work in this direction is conducted by Juels, Pappu and Parno [4], which we call the JPP mechanism for short. In this solution, a common key for a batch of tags is split with (k, n)-Tiny Secret Sharing (TSS) scheme, and each tag stores a tiny share together with its individual (encrypted) information. A reader can recover the common key with access to at least k shares, and then decrypt the information on each tag in the batch. Since the share is tiny enough to fit in EPC tag, the proposed scheme is claimed to be suitable for practical RFID-enabled supply chains. However, the JPP mechanism poses a threat on the tags due to its *weak* adversary model, of which anyone who can scan the tags, can recover the secret. Therefore, an adversary has the intension to stay close to the tags for the convenience of scanning them, and recover the secret for easy cloning the whole batch of the tags.

On observing the hardness on designing and deploying a uniform security solution to multiple supply chain parties across geographically distinct organizations, we tackle the security problem with goods delivery in RFID-enabled supply chains from a focalized viewpoint. We look into the minimal (usually transaction-based) unit of any supply chain on processing RFID-tagged goods and focus on the security needs arisen from the involved parties. Based on the unique view, we make three major contributions in this paper.

1. We focus on any pair of consecutive parties linked by a transaction and a third party who delivers goods from one party to the other (as in common supply chain practice, usually referred to as third party logistics, or 3PL). We then identify and define the security requirements among those parties during goods delivery under a strong adversary model.
2. We propose a resilient secret sharing (RSS) scheme for key distribution among the three parties and prove its security in a formal way against both *privacy* and *robustness* adversaries.
3. We design a specific construction using the RSS scheme, so that the shared secrets are further utilized on providing additional security properties (beyond key distribution) such as tag authentication, accessibility and privacy protection.

Compared with relevant approaches, our work demonstrates a number of advantages in terms of resiliency, security and flexibility. Also, the generic scheme and the specific construction proposed in this paper, are easily extendible for their deployments in any realistic supply chain scenario.

The rest of this paper is organized as follows. In Section 2, we review secret sharing approaches in RFID security realm. In Section 3, we describe a scenario on secure goods delivery and the security properties associated with it. We elaborate on our resilient secret sharing (RSS) scheme and prove its security in Section 4. Following on, we present our construction based on the RSS scheme in Section 5, and discuss parameterization issues in Section 6. Finally, we conclude this paper and point out the future works.

2   Secret Sharing Approaches

On solving the key distribution problem in RFID-enabled supply chains, two major secret sharing based approaches [5,4] were proposed.

The first work is the "Shamir Tag" [5] proposed by Langheinrich and Marti. Based on a weak (*w.r.t.*, "hit-and-run") adversary model, the authors devised the secret sharing mechanism to distribute the *true ID* of a tag across time and space separately. The time-based mechanism splits the *ID* of a tag with Shamir's secret sharing scheme [12], and stores all the shares on the tag itself. Being queried, the shares are released gradually and once all bit values of the shares are collected, can the original *ID* of a tag be computed. However, the practicability on applying the proposed mechanisms in supply chain is questionable as it takes either too long on identifying a tag.

In USENIX Security 08, Juels, Pappu and Parno proposed a key sharing mechanism (*w.r.t.*, the JPP mechanism) [4] to enhance the practicality of the early solution [5] by removing the constraints on the period of each tag being read and the number of tags attached to each item. In the JPP mechanism, a batch of tags share the same secret key, which is split into n shares using a (k, n) tiny secret sharing (TSS) scheme, where $k < n$ is a threshold. Anyone who collects at least k shares can recover the secret. Similarly, the JPP mechanism provides two solutions for its (k, n)-TSS scheme: one is "secret sharing across space", the other is "secret sharing across time".

The JPP mechanism is particularly efficient for ownership transfer in RFID-enabled supply chains since it eliminates the need for distributing a database of tag keys among supply chain parties. The scheme is secure under the assumption that an adversary cannot get access to enough shares for recovering a tag key in the "open area" (*e.g.*, retail stores or customer homes), while legitimate supply chain parties can collect enough shares for recovering each tag key in the "closed area" of a supply chain, to which the adversary does not have access. However, the JPP mechanism works in *end-to-end* principle (regarding the starting and ending points of a tagged item moving through a supply chain) that makes intermediate supply chain parties unable to adjust the threshold of shares collected in recovering tag keys. This renders the proposal either impractical *w.r.t.*, stronger adversary or insecure due to tag cloning attack.

We realized that it could be hard to deal with the complex security needs of multiple parties (normally across multiple geographical and political regions) in a global supply chain, we thus target on two adjacent parties in any supply chain and a third party who transfers goods for these two parties. In common practice in supply chain management, assuming these parties know each other via some trust relationships such as a signed contract for their business transactions, is more reasonable. We stress that such a *peer-to-peer* view of a supply chain facilitates a more realistic and practical model than the global view, and based on what, more precise security requirements can be defined and fulfilled. We depict below such a scenario on delivering goods assisted with RFID technology.

3   Security Properties

In this section, we take for example a typical case for batch goods delivery as used in standard supply chain practice. We then define the security properties for each of the roles based on such a scenario.

3.1   Batch Goods Delivery Scenario

We consider three different roles in a simplified model: Alice, Bob and Carol. Alice, denoted by **A**, is the sender of a batch of goods (*e.g.* a manufacturer); Bob, denoted by **B**, is the receiver of the batch (*e.g.* a distributor who receives the goods from **A**); and Carol, denoted by **C**, is the Third Party Logistics (3PL) partner (*e.g.*, a transporter or carrier of the goods from **A** to **B**).

Suppose **A** and **B** (and **C**) signed contracts for the purchase and delivery of some goods beforehand. Now, the goods must be delivered securely from **A** to **B** by **C** to fulfill the contracts. If each item of the goods is attached with an RFID tag, a supply chain party can process the goods in an efficient way (by scanning all items once in a whole). It is also desirable to provide necessary security features such as anti-cloning without incurring much additional cost.

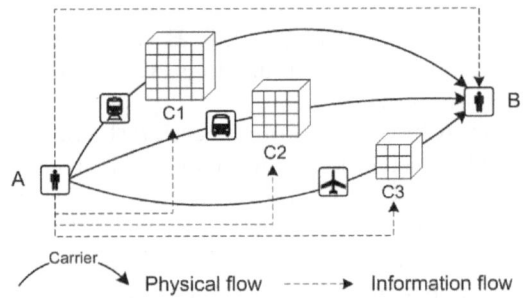

Fig. 1. Batch Goods Delivery from **A** to **B**, by **C**

As an example, Fig. 1 illustrates the scenario where a batch of 50 tags are packed into 3 cases, including a 5×5 case, a 4×4 case and a 3×3 case. These cases are delivered from **A** to **B** via different physical flows by **C** (including

C1, C2, C3, respectively). While some shared information prepared by **A** can be sent to **B** and **C** separately via the information flow. Facilitated with RFID technology, **C** can scan all RFID tags periodically during delivery, until all of them arrive at **B**. The scanning can be used to check the existence of all tags in the batch. If any adversary exists in the delivery path, however, s/he may clone some tags and thus replace authentic goods with counterfeited goods even though the adversary may not be able to know the secret keys for decrypting the tags' contents as in the JPP mechanism. To address this concern, we propose to tackle the RFID tags authentication problem in which nobody (even **C**) except **A** and **B** can access the content of tags while **C** is enabled to check the existence of all or most of the tags in the batch conveniently.

We identify two kinds of flows during the process of goods delivery. One is the physical flow in which the goods are transported by **C** through containers on ships or trucks. The other is the information flow between **A**, **B** and **C**. Intuitively, we utilize the information collected from both flows for the purpose of achieving desired security properties.

3.2 Desired Security Properties

We further identify the following security properties for guaranteeing secure goods delivery in above scenario.

- ◇ **Authenticity of tags in cases.** **C** wants to authenticate the tags case by case periodically. Other than authentication purpose, **C** has no more advantage for her to access or even clone the tags. Both group authentication (case based), and individual tag authentication are demanded for efficiency or accuracy.
- ◇ **Authenticity of tags in batch.** **B** wants to authenticate the batch of tags in a whole as the final verification. Being the new owner of the tags, **B** shall grasp all (secret) information about the tags which include the ability to update the tags.
- ◇ **Accessibility of individual tags.** Only **B** can obtain the secret information for the accessibility of individual tags. **C** or other adversaries cannot access or clone those tags.
- ◇ **Privacy protection** In the sense of protecting the tags' identifiers, all tags' IDs are encrypted by a secret key, which can only be recovered by **B**. Without necessary authorization, **C** can not even access the encrypted information, let along the decryption of such information. However, by scanning the tags, **C** or any reader can still track the tags by the unique or unchanged temporary identities. (In this paper, we consider the tracking problem a less important issue than protecting tags' identifiers themselves.)

In fact, the fundamental building block for all above listed properties is the "key distribution" problem among **A**, **B** and **C**. By designing a resilient secret sharing (RSS) scheme in next section, we can make a nice construction for above scenario so that **A** and **C** share a secret key solely for the authentication purpose, and **A** and **B** share another key for all other security properties.

4   Resilient Secret Sharing Scheme

In order to achieve all the security properties, we work on key distribution first
and design a resilient secret sharing (RSS) scheme inspired by the JPP mechanism. The proposed scheme contains the merits of the JPP mechanism in terms
of tiny shares and error-correcting code based secret sharing algorithm. It also
enhances the JPP mechanism with resiliency by collecting the shares from two
different sources (*w.r.t.*, physical flow and information flow).

4.1   Preliminaries

We recall the JPP mechanism [4]: an n-party secret-sharing scheme is a pair of
algorithms $\Pi = (\mathsf{Share}, \mathsf{Recover})$ that operates over a message space $\mathbb{X}$, where

- ◇ Share is a deterministic algorithm (if a fixed Reed-Solomon code is used, but
  a probabilistic algorithm in [12]) that takes input $x \in \mathbb{X}$ and output the
  n-vector $S \leftarrow_R \mathsf{Share}(x)$, where $S_i \in \{0,1\}^*$. On invalid input $\hat{x} \notin \mathbb{X}$, Share
  outputs an n-vector of the special ("undefined") symbol $\bot$.
- ◇ Recover is a deterministic algorithm that takes input $S \in (\{0,1\}^* \bigcup \Diamond)^n$,
  where $\Diamond$ represents a share that has been erased (or is otherwise unavailable).
  The output $\mathsf{Recover}(S) \in \mathbb{X} \bigcup \bot$, where $\bot$ is a distinguished value indicating
  a recovery failure.

Utilizing Error Correcting Code (ECC), a generalization of the secret sharing
schemes is defined as $\Pi^{ECC} = (\mathsf{Share}^{ECC}, \mathsf{Recover}^{ECC})$. An $(n, k, d)_Q$-ECC op-
erates over an alphabet Σ of size $|\Sigma| = Q$. Share^{ECC} maps $\Sigma^k \to \Sigma^n$ such that
the minimum Hamming distance in symbols between (valid) output vectors is d.
For such a share function (Share^{ECC}), there is a corresponding recover function
$(\mathsf{Recover}^{ECC})$ that recovers a message successfully with up to $(d-1)/2$ errors
or $d-1$ erasures.

In our adversary model[1], we consider two security requirements of secret sharing: *privacy* and *robustness*. Given a limited number of shares, an attack against
privacy aims to recover the secret x shared among n parties. A robustness attacker tries to tamper a number of shares such that a legal user cannot recover
the correct secret x. In formal, we give the following definitions.

Privacy. An ordinary adversary can actively attack the communication links.
In our scenario of secure goods delivery, as did in [4] we focus on underinformed
adversary, who has access to limited number of shares. Informally, privacy require
that such an underinformed adversary should not be able to recover the secret
unless he can get access to at least k correct shares. However, since we are working on *gradated*, rather than *perfect* or *computational* secret sharing schemes, an
adversary with limited number of shares may be able to get *partial* information
about the secret, though it cannot completely recover the secret itself. Moreover,

---

[1] Our adversary model is adapted from [4], which in turn is obtained by extending the
model given in [1].

the more the shares the adversary gets, the more information it reveals. In the following formal definition of privacy, oracle corrupt(S, i) is defined as a function of (S, i), *i.e.*, when the adversary submits i it will get S_i, the i-th share of a secret x.

Definition 1 (Privacy). *Formally, we say a (k, n)-RSS scheme* ($\Pi, \mathbb{X}$) *satisfies* (q_p, t_p, ε_p)-privacy w.r.t. underinformed attackers, *if for any adversary $\mathcal{A}$ who can make q_p corrupt queries to acquire q_p shares (S_p denotes the set of these q_p shares) corresponding to a shared secret x and can run within the time of t_p, $\mathcal{A}$'s advantage to win the following experiment* $\mathbf{Exp}_{\mathcal{A}}^{Pri}$, *i.e.,* $\mathbf{Exp}_{\mathcal{A}}^{Pri}$ *outputs 1, is not greater than ε_p:*

$$\mathrm{Adv}_{\mathcal{A}}^{Pri}[\Pi, \mathbb{X}] \triangleq \Pr[\mathbf{Exp}_{\mathcal{A}}^{Pri} = 1] \leq \varepsilon_p. \tag{1}$$

Experiment $\mathbf{Exp}_{\mathcal{A}}^{Pri}$
  1) $x \leftarrow_R \mathbb{X}$
  2) $S = (S_1, \cdots, S_i, \cdots, S_n) \leftarrow \mathsf{Share}(x)$
  3) $x' \leftarrow \mathcal{A}^{\mathsf{corrupt}(S, \cdot)}(S_p : S_p \subset S \wedge |S_p| = q_p)$
  4) Return '1' if $x = x'$, else '0'.

Privacy Experiment

Note that different from computational secret sharing schemes, here (as well as in Definition 2) we don't specify the adversary $\mathcal{A}$ should be a probabilistic polynomial time (PPT) algorithm. In contrast to the privacy definition given in [4], we add the running time r_p to parameterize an adversary. This makes our definition more flexible and general, though our concrete scheme is secure regardless the adversary's running time (refer to Theorem 1). Moreover, we notice that the indistinguishability game specified in Appendix B.1 of [4] is too strong to be satisfied by ECC-based secret sharing schemes. The reason is that given two secrets κ^0 and κ^1, adversary $\mathcal{A}$ can first run the encoding algorithm to regenerate the corresponding codewords S^0 and S^1, i.e. the shares for κ^0 and κ^1 respectively. As S^0 and S^1 must differ from each other for at least one index, say j, then $\mathcal{A}$ makes oracle query corrupt(S^b, j) to get S_j^b. Finally, to win the game $\mathcal{A}$ only needs to trivially guess $b = 1$ iff $S_j^b \in S^1$.

Robustness. Informally, robustness means that the original secret can be recovered even if the adversary has tampered some of the shares corresponding to such a shared secret.

Definition 2 (Robustness). *Formally, we say a (k,n) RSS scheme* ($\Pi, \mathbb{X}$) *is* (q_r, t_r, ε_r)-robust, *if for any adversary $\mathcal{A}$ who can make q_r corrupt queries to get and tamper q_r shares (those original and tampered q_r shares form sets S_r' and S_r'' respectively) of a shared secret x, which is selected by $\mathcal{A}$ itself, and has*

*running time within t_r, $\mathcal{A}$'s advantage to win the following experiment $\boldsymbol{Exp}_{\mathcal{A}}^{Rob}$,
i.e., $\boldsymbol{Exp}_{\mathcal{A}}^{Rob}$ outputs 1, is not greater than ε_r:*

$$\text{Adv}_{\mathcal{A}}^{Rob}[\boldsymbol{\Pi}, \mathbb{X}] \triangleq \Pr[\boldsymbol{Exp}_{\mathcal{A}}^{Rob} = 1] \le \varepsilon_r. \qquad (2)$$

Experiment $\boldsymbol{Exp}_{\mathcal{A}}^{Rob}$
 1) $x \leftarrow \mathcal{A}$, where $x \in \mathbb{X}$
 2) $S = (S_1, \cdots, S_i, \cdots, S_n) \leftarrow \mathsf{Share}(x)$
 3) $S_r'' \leftarrow \mathcal{A}^{\mathsf{corrupt}(S, \cdot)}$, where $|S_r''| = q_r$
 4) $x' \leftarrow \mathsf{Recover}\{S_r'' \cup (S - S_r')\}$
 5) Return '1' if $x \ne x'$, else '0'.

Robustness Experiment

4.2   RSS

Let's first review McEliece's secret sharing scheme based on Reed-Solomon (RS) codes [7]. Let $B = (b_1, b_2, \ldots, b_k)$ be the secret, where b_i is an m-bit symbol in $\mathbf{GF}(2^m)$. There exists a unique codeword D in the (k, n)-RS code $(n < 2^m)$ with $D = (d_1, d_2, \ldots, d_n)$, where $d_i = b_i$ for $1 \le i \le k$. Only the rest $n - k$ symbols $\{d_i | (k + 1 \le i \le n)\}$ are available for distribution to those sharing the secret. Of all shares, at least k shares are required to recover the secret.

On a high level, our RSS scheme aims at achieving resiliency by combining shares from both physical flow and information flow. Suppose we have only one case containing r tags in the physical flow, and a database[2] as the source of an information flow. We naturally assign one portion of the shares (typically one share for each tag) on the tags, and keep the other portion of the shares in the database. To this end, for a (k, n)-RS code, we can assign r shares to r tags and $n - k - r$ shares to the database (assuming $r < n - k$). Further on, we require that any single flow can not contribute enough shares on recovering the secret (so, $r < k$ and $n - k - r < k$). Thus, we roughly ensure the resiliency of the RSS scheme on recovering a secret with shares contributed from both flows. Such an RSS scheme can be illustrated in Fig. 2 as below.

Ideally, all r tags in a case can be scanned for sorting out all r shares. However, 100% reading is not typically guaranteed in practice as there always be some (*e.g.*, $2 - 3\%$) reading failures in realistic RFID deployments. Suppose all but δ tags are correctly scanned, we can obtain up to $r - \delta$ shares from the readings. For tolerating the reading errors, our RSS scheme allows more shares contributed from the information flow to compensate the missing shares in the physical flow. To ensure our RSS scheme having this resiliency, δ more shares are required to be stored in the database.

---

[2] Note that an online database is not required in our scenario, as a partner's database (*e.g.*, Partner **A** in Fig. 1) is only used to store the shares and pass the shares down (to **B** and **C**) all in once.

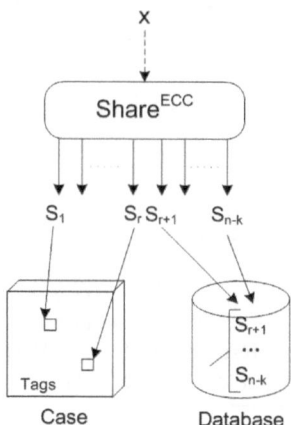

Fig. 2. RSS scheme. A secret x is shared into $n - k$ available shares, in which r shares are distributed into r tags respectively and the other $n - k - r$ shares are stored in a database.

In ECC based secret sharing scheme, a share is a symbol in a codeword (*e.g.*, in RS code), which is much shorter than the original secret. An adversary could launch a guessing attack on trying all the possibilities of a missing share. For instance, for a RS-code on $\mathbf{GF}(2^m)$, such a guessing attack needs 2^m brute force trials. To defend against the guessing attack from attackers who are able to scan all tags, the RSS scheme requires at least t shares contributed by the server in any recovery operation. Thus, a brute force guessing attack may take at $2^{t \times m}$ to recover the secret. I.e., if the system security parameter is set at 128 bits long, and $m = 16$, then we have $t = 8$.

Combining above two requirements, the RSS scheme allocates at a minimum t shares and a maximum $t + \delta$ shares to be stored in the database. Since we don't want the server to calculate the secret along by its shares, or even for brute force attack, we require that $k \geq 2t + \delta$. Our assumption is that the server may either collect all tags in a case and be able to scan $r \sim r - \delta$ tags, or collecting no tag/case at all. As we require that the combination of $r + t$ shares from the tags and database is enough to recover the original secret, so we set the threshold $k = r + t$. Also, $k \geq 2t + \delta$ implies that the number of tags $r \geq t + \delta$. Otherwise, the server is able to launch guessing attacks for guessing up to $t - 1$ shares.

Definition 3. *A $(k, n)_{m,t,r,\delta}$-RSS scheme is a tuple $(\mathbf{\Pi}^{\mathbf{ECC}}, \mathbb{X})$, satisfying $t \times m \geq \tau$ (τ is the security parameter of the system), $k = r + t$ and $r \geq t + \delta$, $n = 2r + 2t + \delta$; such that $\mathbf{\Pi}^{\mathbf{ECC}}$ distributes $n - k$ shares of a secret $x \in \mathbb{X}$, to the tags (totally r shares) and to the database (totally $t + \delta$ shares). Collecting $r - \delta \sim r$ shares from tags, and correspondingly $t + \delta \sim t$ shares from the database, suffices to recover x.*

On the security of the defined RSS scheme above, we have the following.

Theorem 1. (a) *For the* $(k, n)_{m,t,r,\delta}$-*RSS scheme* $(\mathbf{\Pi^{ECC}}, \mathbb{X})$, *any underinformed adversary* $\mathcal{A}$'s *advantage is bounded by* ε_p *such that*

$$\mathrm{Adv}_{\mathcal{A}}^{Pri}[\mathbf{\Pi}^{ECC}, \mathbb{X}] \le \varepsilon_p \le 1/2^{m(k-q_p)}, \tag{3}$$

where $q_p \le k = r + t$.
(b) *For the* $(k, n)_{m,t,r,\delta}$-*RSS scheme* $(\mathbf{\Pi^{ECC}}, \mathbb{X})$, *any adversary* $\mathcal{A}$ *with unbounded running time and making up to* $q_r \le d/2$ (*or* $q_r \le \lfloor (d-1)/2 \rfloor$) *corruptions has advantage zero to win the experiment* $\mathbf{Exp}_{\mathcal{A}}^{Rob}$. *Namely,*

$$\mathrm{Adv}_{\mathcal{A}}^{Rob}[\mathbf{\Pi}^{ECC}, \mathbb{X}] = \varepsilon_r = 0. \tag{4}$$

Proof. (a) For any underinformed adversary $\mathcal{A}$ who has made $q_p \le k = r + t$ corruptions, its total amount of information about the original secret x is upperbounded by $(2^m)^{q_p}$. More specifically, for Reed-Solomon code, the adversary $\mathcal{A}$ can only get q_p linear equations to solve the k unknown elements in field $\mathbf{GF}(2^m)$ (*i.e.*, k components of x [11]). As $q_p \le k$, regardless $\mathcal{A}$'s running time its advantage ε_p to derive the secret x is bounded by $1/2^{m(k-q_p)}$. So, Eq. (3) follows.

(b) The result on robustness comes from the nature of Reed-Solomon code, as it is an error-correcting code. Namely, an error-correcting code with design distance d can be used to correct up to $d/2$ errors. Here, the adversary $\mathcal{A}$ has tampered $q_r \le d/2$ symbols. So, using any popular decoding algorithm (*e.g.*, the decoding algorithm for alternant codes, specified on page 403 of [11]), these errors can be identified and corrected efficiently. In other words, the legal user (e.g. party **B** in our secure goods delivery scenario) is always able to recover the original secret x from shares mixed with those tampered ones. Therefore, regardless $\mathcal{A}$'s running time its advantage ε_r in the experiment $\mathbf{Exp}_{\mathcal{A}}^{Rob}$ is zero. That is, Eq. (4) holds for any $q_r \le d/2$ (or $q_r \le \lfloor (d-1)/2 \rfloor$). ∎

5   Our Construction

Above we give a generalized definition and security proof of the RSS scheme, in what follows we elaborate the constructions on applying the RSS scheme in a typical case of secure goods delivery with batch RFID tags.

In our simplified example, we suppose there are totally R tags attached on goods as a batch to be transferred from **A** to **B**, via **C**. The tags in the batch are allocated equally into l cases, each having r tags ($R = l \times r$). We assume the batch has a suitable size such that r or R is not too big to be contained, otherwise we can consider a batch as a number of blocks with suitable sizes, which are to be processed as one unit. We then discuss a tag belonging to both a case and a batch. More details are discussed in Section 6.

5.1   Secret Generation and Sharing

Before the delivery of goods, **A** generates the secrets x for the specific case and y for the whole batch such that $x, y \in \mathbb{X}$ and $|x| = |y| = \tau$, where τ is the security parameter of the system.

At the case level, **A** employs a $(k, n)_{m,t,r,\delta}$-RSS scheme according to the definition introduced in Section 4, to distribute the case secret x. For all r tags in a case, **A** assigns one share to each tag. **A** also assigns $t + \delta$ shares to **C** to facilitate the verification by **C** on such a case during delivery.

Similarly, at the batch level, **A** employs a $(K, N)_{m,t,R,\Delta}$-RSS scheme to distribute the batch secret y, assuming the security parameter and the size of the shares are not changed. For all R tags in a batch, **A** assigns one share to each tag. **A** then assigns $t + \Delta$ shares to **B** to facilitate the verification by **B** on the whole batch.

With this setting, a tag is assigned two shares: one for the case and one for the batch. Collecting the shares from the tags, **C** or **B** can recover the case secret or batch secret respectively, together with their contributed shares given by **A**. The schematic of the RSS construction is illustrated in Fig. 3.

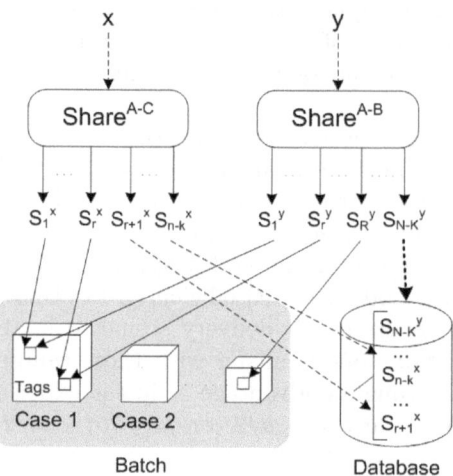

Fig. 3. Schematic of RSS construction. The case secret x is shared for Case 1, in which r shares are distributed into tags and the rest $n-k-r$ shares are stored in the database (to be assigned to **C**); the batch secret y is shared, in which R shares are distributed into all tags in the batch and the rest $N - K - R$ shares are stored in the database (to be assigned to **B**). Thus, an encoded tag carries 2 shares.

5.2   Tag Encoding

For a specific tag i, we obtain its case share $S_i^x \leftarrow \mathsf{Share}^{\mathbf{A-C}}(x)$ $(1 \leq i \leq r)$ and batch share $S_j^y \leftarrow \mathsf{Share}^{\mathbf{A-B}}(y)$ $(1 \leq j \leq R)$. As we work on $\mathbf{GF}(2^m)$, the size of a share could be $m = 16$ bits which is tiny (e.g., 32 bits in total for carrying 2 shares [4]) and suitable to be embedded into an EPC C1G2 tag. In practice, we shall prepare another 16 bits (or less) for making the shares in an ordered sequence. Thus, for an EPC C1G2 tag, we can assign 48 lower significant bits (LSBs) of the EPC memory bank for storing the sequence number and the shares. For the other 48 bits, we can either leave them untouched for classification purpose, or fill them with arbitrary random value for privacy purpose. Now we denote the current value in the EPC memory as the pseudo-ID (or PID) of a tag.

Tag ID Encryption. Suppose the original 96-bit EPC code, denoted as ID, is moved from the "EPC Memory" Bank to the "User Memory" Bank. To provide privacy protection to the EPC code, we store it in encrypted form, so that no one can decrypt and obtain the original code without a proper key. As **B** will be the next owner of the tags, we assign **B** the appropriate role of possessing the proper secret to decrypt the real IDs of those tags. Since y is the only secret shared and known between **A** and **B**, we derive the encryption key e from y such that $e = H(y)$, where $H(.)$ is a cryptographic secure hash function. Then we use e to encrypt the EPC code (in any authenticated encryption mode) and obtain the encrypted and authenticated message $\widetilde{ID} = Enc\_Auth(e, ID)$, where $Enc\_Auth(.)$ is the authenticated encryption algorithm.

Tag PIN Generation. To achieve the authentication purpose, a tag's Access and Kill PINs, denoted as $APIN$ and $KPIN$, are serving as the authenticators by **C** or **B** on performing PIN-based authentication protocol as in [3]. Slightly different from the protocol [3] on using a full (32-bit) Access PIN or Kill PIN for authentication purpose, we hereby use the two halves of Access and Kill PINs of a tag for the same purpose, such that **C** is refrained from either access or kill a tag with its knowledge on the halves of PINs. While **B** can still authenticate and access a tag individually, by deriving the full Access and Kill PINs. Apparently, we can derive the PINs using the secrets (x and y) shared between **A**, **B** and **C**. Note that various constructions are possible, we only introduce a specific construction achieving above security properties for **B** and **C**. On a high level, we generate half APIN and half KPIN with **C**'s secret x, and the other halves with **B**'s secret y. We compute $\kappa_{\mathbf{C}} = H(x||PID)$ and $\kappa_{\mathbf{B}} = H(y||PID)$ for a tag by reading its PID. We assign 16 lowest significant bits (LSBs) of $\kappa_{\mathbf{C}}$ as the 16 LSBs of $APIN$ and the other 16 most significant bits (MSBs) of $\kappa_{\mathbf{C}}$ as the 16 LSBs of $KPIN$. Also, we assign 16 LSBs of $\kappa_{\mathbf{B}}$ as the 16 MSBs of $APIN$ and the other 16 MSBs of $\kappa_{\mathbf{B}}$ as the 16 MSBs of $KPIN$. Thus, we have

$APIN = [APIN]_{31:16}||[APIN]_{15:0} = [\kappa_{\mathbf{B}}]_{15:0}||[\kappa_{\mathbf{C}}]_{15:0}$

$KPIN = [KPIN]_{31:16}||[KPIN]_{15:0} = [\kappa_{\mathbf{B}}]_{31:16}||[\kappa_{\mathbf{C}}]_{31:16}$

Note that for **C** to conduct the PIN-based authentication, we expect a positive or negative result from the tag indicating whether the correct halves of Access and Kill PINs are presented to it[3].

We are now ready to encode the tag by writing all generated codes into a tag. Again, we write on tag the shares in the EPC memory, the encrypted EPC code in the user memory, and the access and kill PINs in the reserved memory.

---

[3] Although not fully conforming with current EPC C1 G2 specification, we argue that achieving above half-PIN-based authentication on a tag is rather simple with a re-designed circuit on the PIN logic, which is practical and costless.

5.3   Secret Recovery and Verification

During delivery, **C** would verify the tags in a case from time to time. Suppose the total number of collected shares in a case is p, if $r - \delta \leq p \leq r$, **C** can recover the secret x by contributing up to $t + r - p$ shares; if not, there is no enough shares for **C** to recover the secret. Based on the secret value, **C** can generate the halves of Access and Kill PINs for each tag as described above. **C** can then authenticate each tag by performing the half-PIN-based authentication protocol described above.

When all goods are delivered to **B**, **B** would verify the tags in the batch. Similarly, suppose **B** collects P shares from all the cases. if $R - \Delta \leq P \leq R$, **B** can recover the secret y by contributing up to $t + R - P$ shares; if not, there is no enough shares for **B** to recover the secret. Based on the secret value, **B** can generate the other halves of Access and Kill PINs for each tag in the batch. **B** can obtain from **C** the halves of Access and Kill PINs of each tag based on a case, or generate by itself the half PINs by collecting all shares from **C**.

Whatsoever, **B** can access all the tags and even kill all the tags as the new owner. Suppose **B** accesses a tag and reads its encrypted ID $(\widetilde{ID})$, **B** can decrypt and authenticate it with e from y and obtain the original EPC code of the tag.

5.4   Analysis and Comparison

We summarize the desired security properties in secure goods delivery and show how they are achieved in our construction using the RSS scheme.

▶ **Key distribution.** Our RSS scheme ensures that only **B** and **C** can derive the secrets they shared with **A**. Without additional share(s) from **B** and **C**, no adversary can derive any secret by solely collecting shares from tags. **A** securely distributes the secrets to **B** and **C** via both physical and information flows.

▶ **Authenticity.** **C** can verify that most tags in a batch or case are presented, and individually, every tag can be authenticated by **C** via half-PIN-based authentication. Similarly, **B** can verify the whole batch together and authenticate individual tags one by one.

▶ **Accessibility & Anti-cloning.** Only **B** can derive full Access and Kill PINs for all of the tags in a batch, and thus can access the tags with proper PINs. No adversary, including **C**, can derive the secrets and full PINs for accessing or cloning the tags.

▶ **Privacy Protection.** Only **B** can obtain the original EPC code of a tag. The privacy of the tag identifier is protected against **C** or any adversary. As mentioned in Section 3.2, we regard the privacy problem of tracking the pseudo-ID of a tag as a less important problem.

The secret sharing approaches present a new research direction on solving the key distribution problem in RFID-enabled supply chains. Although the JPP mechanism is the first applicable solution for RFID-enabled supply chains without pre-sharing of secrets, it's security level is not sufficient as mentioned earlier.

Our RSS scheme improves the security with additional shares contributed from the information flow. Other than key distribution, our RSS construction provides more desired security properties such as anti-cloning than the JPP mechanism.

The advantages of secret sharing approaches can be clearly demonstrated by comparing with existing RFID authentication protocols [9,8,6]. These authentication protocols are designed to have different security and efficiency features with a common assumption that shared keys must exist between mutually trusted parties, and that the tag keys are stored in a central database. Another difference is that the protocol messages in these protocols are unlinkable between authentication sessions.

Basically, all of them achieves authentication on individual tags, but not on a batch of tags. Moreover, in a strong adversary model where tags can be corrupted, all except our RSS scheme fail on providing anti-cloning feature as the tags' secrets are disclosed. Table 1 lists the major security features of our scheme in comparison with traditional schemes.

Table 1. Comparison of Security Properties

	Key Storage (DB/Tag)	Authentication (Group/Tag)	Anti-Cloning (Tag Corruption)	Type of Privacy (Unlinkability/ID Secrecy)
[9][8][6]	Central DB	Tag	No	Unlinkability
TSS [4]	Tag	Group	No	ID Secrecy
RSS	Partner DB & Tag	Group & Tag	Yes	ID Secrecy

6 Parameterization

In real-world implementation, the "Philips UCODE" Gen2 tag can be employed. The tag has 512 bits of on-chip memory, containing a 96-bit EPC memory, a 32-bit TID memory, a 128-bit programmable user memory and a 64-bit reserved memory for storing Access and Kill PINs. As required by our scheme, we shall replace the original EPC code with the shares in EPC memory, and store the encrypted (and authenticated) EPC code into the user memory.

As a running example, we suppose there are totally 100 tags in a batch which are packed equally into 5 cases each having 20 tags exactly. At the case level, our RSS scheme employs a $(28, 60)$-RSS Scheme so that given a case, we need to collect at least 28 shares to recover the case secret. Our scheme works over the field $GF(2^{16})$, so a share (codeword) should have 16 bits. At the beginning, **A** generates uniformly at random a 448-bit secret x for **C**. The secret is then encoded into 60 16-bit symbols with a $(28, 60)$-RS code. From which, 32 parity symbols are ready to be shared. We assign exactly one share to each tag and 12 shares to **C**. In other words, without the shares from **C**, one can maximally collect 20 shares from the tags so that s/he is not able to recover the secret (even by brute force attacks). By contributing additional shares on recovering the secret, above scheme allows **C** tolerate up to 4 or 20% reading errors on scanning the tags in the case.

Similarly, at the batch level, **A** and **B** employ a $(108, 236)$-RSS scheme so that one needs to collect at least 108 shares to recover the batch secret. **A** generates uniformly at random a 1728-bit long secret y for **B**. Under the working field $GF(2^{16})$, the secret is extended into 236 16-bit symbols with a $(108, 236)$-RS code, of which 128 symbols are ready to be shared. Thus, we assign 28 shares to **B** and 100 share to the tags. With this setting, no one, except **B**, can collect more than 108 shares to successfully recover the secret. By contributing additional shares on recovering the secret, above scheme allows **B** tolerate up to 20 or 20% errors on scanning all the tags in the batch.

As an ECC algorithm requires the codewords be in an ordered sequence, we shall assign the sequence numbers on the tags explicitly. For this reason, we employ additional 16 bits in the EPC memory for the purpose of storing an ordered sequence number. This allows a quite long (up to 65536) sequence containing enough numbers of tags in a whole batch. To this end, we have used up 48 LSBs of the EPC memory and left the other 48 MSBs untouched. At the options of the adopters of our scheme, they can either retain these 48 MSBs serving as the EPC header for rough classification purpose, or fill this field with random values for privacy protection objective.

Moving forward, we work on encrypting the EPC code which is now set as 48 bits discarding the header. We hash the secret y with SHA-256 and take the lowest significant 128 bits of the output as the encryption key. Then we apply a block cipher (AES-128) in an authenticated encryption mode (*e.g.,* OCB [10]) on the EPC code with padding bits. The 128-bit encrypted and authenticated message is then stored in the user memory. Note that both the EPC memory and the user memory have similar physical and deployment characteristics (regarding the *PIN-based lock, unlock, permalock*, and *PIN-based write* operations on these memory banks) according to EPCglobal C1 G2 standard [2]. To allow **B** update the tags while pass the goods to some downstream players, our scheme requires *rewritable* EPC memory and user memory on a Gen2 tag. Such a *(re)write* operation is typically allowed in a **secured** state on interrogating a Gen2 tag, which is transitioned from an **open** state by providing the correct Access PIN. On implementing our scheme, we indicate that the 32-bit Access PIN and Kill PIN are derived from both the shared secrets x and y by **C** and **B** respectively. Also, it is not practical for **C** to access or kill a tag with the knowledge of the halves of its PINs, since guessing the other half of the Access PIN needs 2^{16} trials on the tag, which could be efficiently prevented by tag manufactures' disabling the tag when multiple false PINs are presented.

Moreover, in real-world deployment, one has to know the total number of tags R processed in a batch and the number of tags r in a case. Then s/he determines the threshold values k and K on recovering the secrets, together with the numbers of shares for the batch and cases respectively. In our running example above, the tags are formatted with $(28, 60)$-RSS scheme for a case and $(108, 236)$-RSS scheme for a batch. On choosing a proper threshold, k or K can be set as the smallest value (*e.g.,* $k = 28$, $K = 108$) that is a bit greater than the total numbers of tags in a case or batch to guarantee the recovery of secrets only with additional shares from **C** or **B**, instead of solely reading all tags in a case or batch. On the other hand, n or N could also be chosen properly to maximally tolerate reading errors (20% in our example) in a case or batch.

Last but not least, remind that we mentioned such a condition $r \geq t + \delta$ in the definition of our RSS scheme in Section 4. If there exists a relatively small number of tags in a case, our RSS scheme can adjust the relevant parameters in a resilient way. Without loss of security, we can put multiple shares on a tag or enlarge the size of a single share to minimize the value of t. For instance, we have no problem to deal with only 2 tags in a case with $(8, 16)_{32,4,2,0}$-RSS scheme with 2 shares on a tag or $(4, 8)_{64,2,2,0}$-RSS scheme with one big share on a tag. Pushing that to an extreme, for a case with only one tag, a $(2, 4)_{96,1,1,0}$-RSS scheme could be used for filling the EPC memory of the tag with a single share to achieve a maximum 96-bit security.

7   Conclusion and Future Work

In this paper, we worked on pairing supply chain parties and proposed a resilient secret sharing (RSS) scheme for distributing keying material in RFID-enabled supply chains. The scheme is proved to be secure in terms of *privacy* and *robustness*, and is resilient due to various access structures in sharing and recovering a secret. Particularly, our construction, which is based on a practical case study of "secure goods delivery", provides a set of desired security properties for batch RFID tags. Under proper parameter setting, our solution can be easily incorporated in standard RFID appliances and used in supply chain practice. Our future work is to implement our solution in real world deployments such as 3rd Party Logistics in which supply chain parties are inter-connected by EPCglobal Network.

References

1. Bellare, M., Rogaway, P.: Robust computational secret sharing and a unified account of classical secret-sharing goals. In: Proc. of the 14th Conference on Computer and Communications Security, pp. 172–184 (2007)
2. EPCglobal. EPC radio-frequency identity protocols class-1 generation-2 UHF RFID protocol for communications at 860 MHz-960 MHz, version 1.2.0 (October 2008)
3. Juels, A.: Strengthening epc tags against cloning. In: ACM Workshop on Wireless Security – WiSe 2005 (2005)
4. Juels, A., Pappu, R., Parno, B.: Unidirectional key distribution across time and space with applications to rfid security. In: 17th USENIX Security Symposium, pp. 75–90 (2008)
5. Langheinrich, M., Marti, R.: Practical Minimalist Cryptography for RFID Privacy. IEEE Systems Journal, Special Issue on RFID Technology 1(2), 115–128 (2007)

6. Li, Y., Ding, X.: Protecting RFID Communications in Supply Chains. In: Proceedings of the 2nd ACM Symposium on Information, Computer and Communications Security, ASIACCS 2007, pp. 234–241 (2007)
7. McEliece, R.J., Sarwate, D.V.: On sharing secrets and reed-solomon codes. Communications of the ACM 24, 583–584 (1981)
8. Molnar, D., Wagner, D.: Privacy and Security in Library RFID: Issues, Practices, and Architectures. In: Conference on Computer and Communications Security – ACM CCS 2004, pp. 210–219 (2004)
9. Ohkubo, M., Suzuki, K., Kinoshita, S.: Efficient Hash-Chain Based RFID Privacy Protection Scheme. In: International Conference on Ubiquitous Computing – Ubicomp 2004 (2004)
10. Bellare, M., Rogaway, P., Black, J.: Ocb: A block-cipher mode of operation for efficient authenticated encryption. ACM Transactions on Information and System Security (TISSEC) 6(3), 365–403 (2003)
11. Roman, S.: Coding and Information Theory. Graduate Texts in Mathematics, vol. 134. Springer, Heidelberg (1992)
12. Shamir, A.: How to share a secret. Communications of the ACM 22(11), 612–613 (1979)

Towards a Deterministic Hierarchical Key Predistribution for WSN Using Complementary Fano Plane

Sarbari Mitra, Ratna Dutta, and Sourav Mukhopadhyay

Indian Institute of Technology, Kharagpur, India
sarbarimitra@gmail.com,
{ratna,sourav}@maths.iitkgp.ernet.in

Abstract. We propose a key pre-distribution scheme based on the complementary design of a Fano plane. The nodes are arranged hierarchically in the form of a 6-nary tree. Key predistribution follows a deterministic approach. Each node in our scheme requires storing significantly less number of secret keys. Our scheme provides better resiliency compared to other existing schemes and reasonable connectivity as well. It can be found that any two nodes are connected either directly or via a key-path. Moreover, any number of nodes can be introduced in the network by assigning a few keys to the newly joined nodes only, without disturbing the existing set-up of the network.

Keywords: complementary design, Fano plane, key predistribution.

1 Introduction

Sensor nodes are small, mobile, low-cost, battery powered and resource (such as memory, power etc.)-constrained devices. They are deployed with high density in the target region to form a Wireless Sensor Network (WSN). Due to their huge application in many areas (home front to military operation), WSN has become a burgeoning field nowadays. There are two types of WSNs: Distributed and Hierarchical. In Distributed network all the nodes are assumed to be uniform whereas Hierarchical network comprised of sensor nodes with different memory, power, transmission range etc.

The sensor nodes are supposed to collect data from the environment and then transmit them to the base station by communicating with other nodes within the specified transmission range. This communication, when takes place in hostile region, is intended to be secret, for which secret keys need to be given to the nodes. One of the possible methods is online key agreement, but this is practically infeasible as this approach is highly expensive. The other approach is to store the keys to the nodes before their deployment, which is termed as key predistribution. Key predistribution can be of three types: (i) *Probabilistic-* where the keys are chosen randomly from the key pool and given to the nodes so that

M. Rajarajan et al. (Eds.): SecureComm 2011, LNICST 96, pp. 373–388, 2012.
© Institute for Computer Sciences, Social Informatics and Telecommunications Engineering 2012

any two nodes share common key with certain probability, (ii) *Deterministic-* the selection and assignment of keys to the nodes follow a certain pattern, and (iii) *Hybrid-* which is a combination of the above two approaches.

The parameters of a key pre-distribution scheme are : (i) *Scalability-* when it is required to introduce a few new nodes to the network, existing set-up should not be disturbed, i.e., key-chains of the existing nodes should not be altered; (ii) *Storage-* less number of keys should be stored in the nodes so that rest of the memory can be used for computation; (iii) *Resilience-* how robust the network is against node capture; (iv) *Connectivity-* most of the nodes should share secret keys so that they can communicate secretly.

There are two extreme key pre-distribution schemes. First, is to store one master key to all the nodes in the network. Connectivity of the resulting network is very high as any two nodes can communicate but the network is not at all resilient. Capture of any single node will reveal the secret master key. As a result, the whole network cease to work. Second is to store a secret key for each pair of nodes in the network. Then connectivity and resiliency both are optimal, but the storage requirement is too expensive which is not affordable. Hence we observe that any of the above cases is not suitable due to the fact that the parameters storage, resiliency and connectivity are contradictory in nature. To achieve a scheme which optimizes all the parameters, authors have tried to get a trade-off between aforesaid parameters. We discuss literature survey in the following subsection.

1.1 Previous Work

Eschenauer and Gligor [7] were first to use random key pre-distribution in WSN. The key distribution scheme proposed by them includes random selection of key chains from the large key-pools and then assigning the keys to the nodes. Any two nodes can communicate if they share a common key. The scheme is referred to as the *basic scheme*. Later Chan, Perrig and Song [5] proposed *q-composite scheme* which is a modified version of the basic scheme: any two nodes can communicate if they share at least q common keys.

The main disadvantage of the aforesaid probabilistic schemes is that sharing of common keys between any two nodes is not certain. On the contrary, the schemes based on deterministic approach using combinatorial designs increases the probability of key sharing between nodes to a greater extent. Naturally, *Combinatorial Design* has become a useful technique of key pre-distribution. Mitchell and Piper [11] were first to apply combinatorial design as one of the key distribution techniques whereas Camptepe, Yener [1] introduced combinatorial design for key predistribution in wireless sensor network. In this paper [1] two combinatorial designs are considered: first is the symmetric $(p^2 + p + 1, p + 1, 1)$-BIBD (or finite projective plane of order p) and the second is generalized quadrangles. The advantage of this deterministic approach is that any two nodes certainly share a common key, which improves the connectivity of the network to significantly. The authors observed that the main drawback of deterministic approach is that the scheme is not scalable as the network size N should satisfy $N \leq p^2 + p + 1$; if one wants to introduce some new nodes to the network which exceeds the bound then p has to be raised to the next prime number (as the existence of projective planes of order p is confirmed for only prime values of p), which results in a much more larger network than what is required, and the key-chains at each node have to be changed. It is also observed that generalized quadrangles induce better scalable network and provide better resilience than projective planes [2]. For the scalability, they have proposed a hybrid scheme which improves the resilience, but the probability of any two nodes sharing a common key is reduced.

In 2005, Lee and Stinson [8] proposed a scheme on group-divisible design or Transversal design. It is noticed that the expected proportion that any two nodes can communicate directly is 0.6 and almost 0.99995 portion of the nodes can communicate either directly or via intermediate nodes. Chakrabarti et al. [3] provided an example to show that out of 2401 nodes in a network 18% of the links will be destroyed if only 10 nodes are captured. This is the main disadvantage of this scheme. Later, in 2008, the authors had developed quadratic schemes [9] based on Transversal designs and referred the method described in [8] as linear schemes. Their work suggests that the quadratic scheme provides best resilience unless the number of compromised nodes is high. If the number of compromised nodes increases beyond 20, then linear scheme is preferred to quadratic scheme for better resilience. Quadratic schemes in general provide better connectivity than linear schemes. Both linear and quadratic schemes are preferred to 2-composite scheme if shared-key-discovery is taken into consideration.

In 2005, Chakrabarti et al. [3] proposed a probabilistic key predistribution scheme. Construction of the blocks were in the same manner as proposed by Lee and Stinson in [8]. The sensor nodes are then formed by random merging of the blocks, which consequently increases the probability of sharing common keys between sensor nodes. Their scheme provides better resiliency as compared to the Lee-Stinson scheme at the cost of large key-chain size in each node. Dong et al. [6] proposed a scheme by considering 3-design as the underlying design. Keys are assigned to the sensor nodes in the network by Möbius Planes. This scheme provides better connectivity than that of the scheme proposed by Lee-Stinson [9] and better storage as compared to Camptepe-Yener scheme [1]. The prime drawback of the scheme is that resiliency reduces rapidly with the increasing number of compromised nodes.

Ruj and Roy [12] proposed a deterministic key pre-distribution scheme based on Partially Balanced Incomplete Block Design. The authors claim that this scheme gives better resilience than that of [8] storing less than $\sqrt{N}$ keys to the nodes where N is the network size. But to store that many keys to the nodes, for a very large network is also expensive.

It is observed that the schemes based on deterministic approach provide high connectivity, but the storage is also very expensive and the schemes are not scalable in most of the cases. On the contrary, the probabilistic schemes are scalable but do not confirm high connectivity. Our target is to develop a scheme which gives scalability in deterministic approach and also provides better values for the other parameters.

1.2   Our Contribution

Here we present a deterministic key pre-distribution scheme. We have used the complementary design of the Fano plane, i.e., a symmetric $(7, 4, 2)$ - BIBD as our basic building block and map it repeatedly to design the whole network. The network thus formed is heterogeneous, i.e., the nodes are assumed to be placed hierarchically on the basis of computation power, the chance of getting compromised etc.

The storage requirement for this scheme is significantly less (better) than majority of the existing schemes. Storage is an important factor as we all know that once the nodes are deployed to the target region, any external source of power is not available. Moreover, increased memory consumption for storage will decrease the computation power.

We emphasize that apart from storage-efficiency, this scheme provides reasonable connectivity. The whole network is divided into 7 sub-networks each of which forms a 6-nary tree-hierarchical structure. Most of the nodes in the same sub-network are directly connected, but nodes from the different sub-networks may be connected directly or via a key-path through the *level* 1 nodes (in the worst possible case).

Apart from being cost-effective, storing significantly less number of keys leaks very less information (in the form of secret keys) when captured. This leads to improve the resilience of the network. Obtained results support the fact that our scheme provides better resilience than the other similar schemes. Unlike the existing deterministic key pre-distribution schemes, our scheme is flexible in the sense that insertion of a large number of nodes can be done by adding only a few keys to the newly joined nodes without disturbing the previously assigned nodes.

Rest of the paper is organized in the following manner. Some definitions are given in Section 2, the proposed scheme is discussed in detail in Section 3. Obtained results are included in Section 4. Section 5 and Section 6 respectively provides the connectivity and performance of the scheme following the concluding remarks in Section 7.

2   Preliminaries

Combinatorial Design is one of the mathematical tools used for key predistribution to the nodes. Some useful definitions from combinatorial designs are given below:

Definition 2.01. *A design is defined as a pair (X, A) such that (i) X is a set of points or elements, (ii) A is a subset of the power set of X (i.e. Collection of non-empty subsets of X)*

Definition 2.02. *A t-design is defined as a t - (v, k, λ) block design (with $t \leq k \leq v$) such that the following are satisfied (i) $X = v$, (ii) each block contains* *k points, (iii) for any set of t points there are exactly λ blocks that contain all these points.*

Definition 2.03. *A t-design with t = 2 is known as (v, k, λ)-Balanced Incomplete Block Design[BIBD].*

Example 2.01. *A $(10, 4, 2)$-BIBD has $X = \{0, 1, 2, 3, 4, 5, 6, 7, 8, 9\}$*
$A = \{(0, 1, 2, 3); (0, 1, 4, 5); (0, 2, 4, 6); (0, 3, 7, 8); (0, 5, 7, 9); (0, 6, 8, 9); (1, 2, 7, 8);$
$(1, 3, 6, 9); (1, 4, 7, 9); (1, 5, 6, 8); (2, 3, 5, 9); (2, 4, 8, 9); (2, 5, 6, 7); (3, 4, 5, 8);$
$(3, 4, 6, 7)\}$

Definition 2.04. *A t-design with $\lambda = 1$ is known as Steiner system.*

Example 2.02. *A $(9, 3, 1)$-design has $X = \{1, 2, 3, 4, 5, 6, 7, 8, 9\}$*
$A = \{(1, 2, 3); (4, 5, 6); (7, 8, 9); (1, 4, 7); (2, 5, 8); (3, 6, 9); (1, 5, 9);$
$(1, 6, 8); (2, 4, 9); (2, 6, 7); (3, 4, 8); (3, 5, 7)\}$

Definition 2.05. *Finite symmetric projective plane of order n is defined as a pair of set of $n^2 + n + 1$ points and $n^2 + n + 1$ lines, where each line contains $n + 1$ points and each point occurs in $n + 1$ lines.*

Definition 2.06. *The Fano Plane is the projective plane of smallest order i.e., of order 2. It is a $(7,3,1)$ BIBD and it can also be considered as a Steiner system.*

Therefore, all the projective planes are Steiner systems.

Example 2.03. *Projective plane of order 2, a $(7, 3, 1)$-BIBD, i.e.,the Fano plane is as follows: $X = \{1, 2, 3, 4, 5, 6, 7\}$*
$A = \{(1, 2, 3); (1, 4, 7); (1, 5, 6); (2, 4, 6); (2, 5, 7); (3, 4, 5); (3, 6, 7)\}$.

Example 2.04. *Projective plane of order 3, a $(13, 4, 1)$-BIBD is as follows:*
$X = \{1, 2, 3, 4, 5, 6, 7, 8, 9, 10, 11, 12, 13\}$
$A = \{(1, 2, 3, 4); (1, 5, 6, 7); (1, 8, 9, 10); (1, 11, 12, 13); (2, 5, 8, 11); (2, 6, 9, 13);$
$(2, 7, 10, 12); (3, 5, 10, 13); (3, 6, 8, 12); (3, 7, 9, 11); (4, 5, 9, 12); (4, 6, 10, 11);$
$(4, 7, 8, 13)\}$.

By complementary design we mean the design where each block is mapped to another block such that they are mutually exclusive and exhaustive. The complementary design of the Fano plane is a 2-(7,4,2) design,i.e., it is a symmetric $(7, 4, 2)$-BIBD. From the structure it is clear that the design is no longer a Projective plane and obviously not a Steiner system either, as any pair of keys is included in exactly two nodes.

Any design (X, A) can be mapped to a sensor network where the elements of the set X represent the keys and the blocks of the set A correspond to sensor nodes.

3   Proposed Scheme

3.1   Key Predistribution to Seven Nodes

In this section we will discuss a particular Steiner system that is taken as a basic building block to design our key predistribution in the hierarchical structure of nodes and then explain how it can be mapped to a sensor network. Let us consider a 2 - $(7, 4, 2)$ design where $X = \{1, 2, 3, 4, 5, 6, 7\}$. The blocks are given by the set $A = \{(4, 5, 6, 7), (2, 3, 5, 6), (2, 3, 4, 7), (1, 3, 5, 7), (1, 3, 4, 6),$ $(1, 2, 6, 7), (1, 2, 4, 5)\}$. Note that each block shares exactly two common elements with all other blocks. We map the system to the sensor network by considering X to be the key-pool i.e. all the elements to be the keys and sets (blocks) in A correspond to the key-chains of each sensor node. Here seven elements correspond to seven keys and each block represents a sensor node (key chain of the node). This assigns a set of seven keys to seven nodes such that all nodes together contain exactly seven keys and any two are connected by exactly two common keys.

3.2   Key Predistribution to the Tree Hierarchy

We label all the nodes and all the keys by $1, 2, 3, 4, \ldots$. In level 1, seven keys $\{1, 2, 3, 4, 5, 6, 7\}$ are distributed to the first seven nodes as described above. Thus the key-rings assigned to the nodes $1, 2, 3, 4, 5, 6, 7$ are respectively $\{4, 5, 6, 7\}$, $\{2, 3, 5, 6\}$, $\{2, 3, 4, 7\}$, $\{1, 3, 5, 7\}$, $\{1, 3, 4, 6\}$, $\{1, 2, 6, 7\}$, $\{1, 2, 4, 5\}$. Loosely speaking, the node-set $\{1, 2, 3, 4, 5, 6, 7\}$ of these seven nodes form a 2-$(7, 4, 2)$ design in level 1. We refer the keys $\{1, 2, 3, 4, 5, 6, 7\}$ chosen in level 1 as level 1 keys. In level 2, node 1 forms a 2-$(7, 4, 2)$ design with new six level 2 nodes $8, 9 \ldots 13$. A set of seven keys is required to complete the key set. Note that node

Table 1. Components of 2 - $(7, 4, 2)$ designs formed by level 1 nodes

Node	Node-set	Key-set
node 1	$\{1, 8, 9, 10, 11, 12, 13\}$	$\{4, 5, 6, 7, 8, 9, 10\}$
node 2	$\{2, 14, 15, 16, 17, 18, 19\}$	$\{2, 3, 5, 6, 11, 12, 13\}$
node 3	$\{3, 20, 21, 22, 23, 24, 25\}$	$\{2, 3, 4, 7, 14, 15, 16\}$
node 4	$\{4, 26, 27, 28, 29, 30, 31\}$	$\{1, 3, 5, 7, 17, 18, 19\}$
node 5	$\{5, 32, 33, 34, 35, 36, 37\}$	$\{1, 3, 4, 6, 20, 21, 22\}$
node 6	$\{6, 38, 39, 40, 41, 42, 43\}$	$\{1, 2, 6, 7, 23, 24, 25\}$
node 7	$\{7, 44, 45, 46, 47, 48, 49\}$	$\{1, 2, 4, 5, 26, 27, 28\}$

1 already contains the keys $\{4, 5, 6, 7\}$. We choose three new keys, say $\{8, 9, 10\}$ and take the key set $\{4, 5, 6, 7, 8, 9, 10\}$ for the key predistribution among seven nodes. We call the new keys $8, 9, 10$ chosen in level 2 as level 2 keys. This process is repeated for the other nodes of level 1. The 2 - $(7, 4, 2)$ designs corresponding to all the level 1 nodes are explicitly described in Table 1. In level 3, each of level 2 nodes are attached to 6 new level 3 nodes and the corresponding key chain is chosen in the same manner i.e. keeping the four keys same as the level 2 keys contained by level 2 nodes and adding three new level 3 keys. This process is repeated until keys are assigned to all the nodes in the network. We provide below the algorithm KPDistribution for assigning keys to the tree hierarchy as explained above. We consider a hierarchical structure using a 6-nary tree for key predistribution.

Let us consider a network having maximum N nodes. Let K denote the total key-pool and l denote the maximum level in the hierarchical tree structure. The four keys assigned to N[i] are stored in N[i][1], N[i][2], N[i][3], N[i][4] respectively. Choose $\{u_4, u_5, u_6\; u_7\} \in_R K$, where the symbol $\in_R$ stands for random selection.

Algorithm. KPDistribution

$i := 0$;
N $[1][1] := u_4$; N $[1][2] := u_5$; N $[1][3] := u_6$; N $[1][4] := u_7$;
procedure KPDistribution (u_1, u_2, u_3, u_4)
$X := \{u_4, u_5, u_6, u_7\}$;
Choose $\{u_1, u_2, u_3\} \in_R B$ where $B \subseteq K - X$, B is the set of unused keys
$X := X \cup \{u_1, \ u_2, \ u_3\}$;

$\quad j := 6i + 2$;
$\quad$ N[j][1] := u_2,   N[j][2] := u_3,   N[j][3] := u_5,   N[j][4] := u_6;
$\quad$ N[j + 1][1] := u_2; N[j + 1][2] := u_3; N[j + 1][3] := u_4; N[j + 1][4] := u_7;
$\quad$ N[j + 2][1] := u_1; N[j + 2][2] := u_3; N[j + 2][3] := u_5; N[j + 2][4] := u_7;
$\quad$ N[j + 3][1] := u_1; N[j + 3][2] := u_3; N[j + 3][3] := u_4; N[j + 3][4] := u_6;
$\quad$ N[j + 4][1] := u_1; N[j + 4][2] := u_2; N[j + 4][3] := u_6; N[j + 4][4] := u_7;
$\quad$ N[j + 5][1] := u_1; N[j + 5][2] := u_2; N[j + 5][3] := u_4; N[j + 5][4] := u_5;
$p := 1$; $r := 1$; $s := 0$; $m := r + s$;
while $(p < l)$ **do**
$\quad\quad r := r + 6^p$; $s := s + 6^{p-1}$;
$\quad\quad p + +$;
$\quad\quad$ **for** $i := m$ to $(r + s - 1)$ **do in parallel**
$\quad\quad\quad$ **call** KPDistribution (N[i][1], N[i][2], N[i][3], N[i][4])
$\quad\quad$ **end do**
$\quad m := r + s$;
end do
end KPDistribution

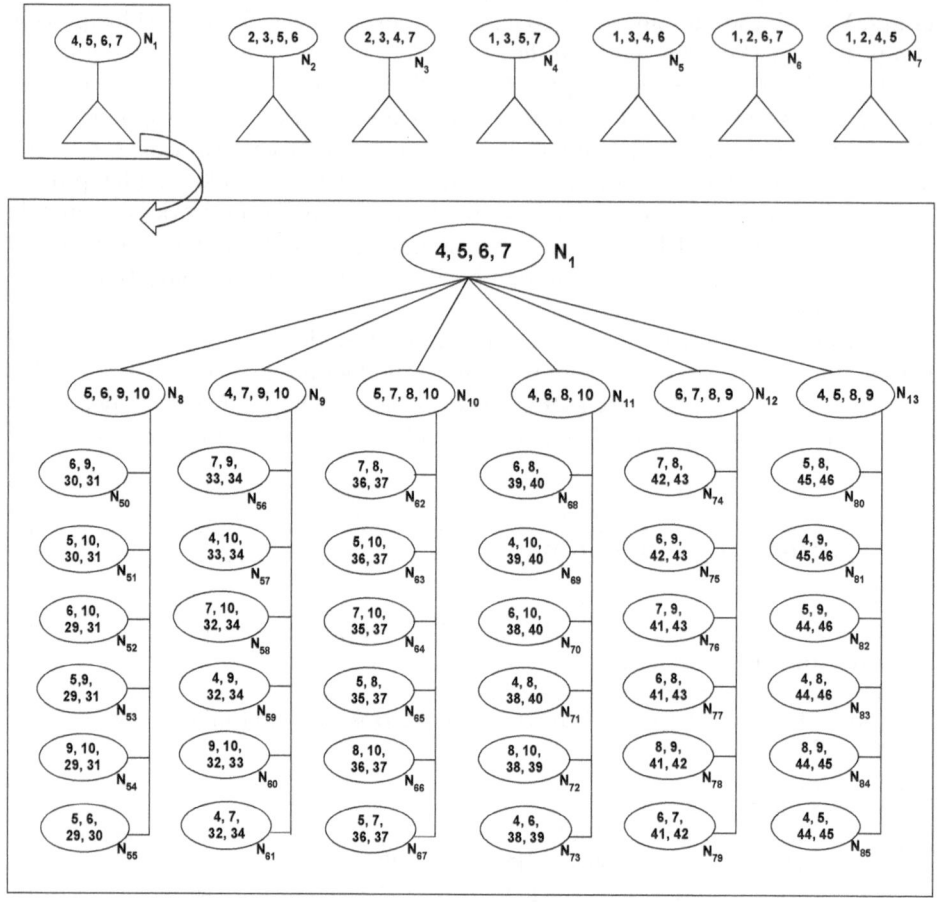

Fig. 1. Key predistribution to a sub tree upto *level* 3

4   Results

Theorem 4.01.   *(a) Number of nodes in level j is $n_j = 7 \times 6^{j-1}$, $\forall\, j \in \{1, \ell\}$
    where l denotes the total number of levels present in the network.
    (b) Total number of nodes in the network is $T_{nodes} = \frac{7}{5}(6^\ell - 1)$.
    (c) Number of keys that are used for the first time in level j is*

$$k_j = 21 \times 6^{j-2}, \; \forall j \geq 2; \quad k_1 = 7;$$

*(d) Total number of keys in the network is $K = 7\left[1 + \frac{3}{5}(6^{\ell-1} - 1)\right]$.
    (e) Number of nodes to which a level i key is assigned to, is $N_i = 2 \times \{3^{l+1-i} - 1\}$*

.

(f) The maximum level required to accommodate T_{nodes} number of nodes in the network is $l = \lceil log(\frac{5}{7}T_{nodes} - 5) \rceil$.

Proof:

(a) The result holds trivially for $i = 1$.

Let us consider the following notations:

Level 1 nodes are denoted by $N_{i_1}^{(1)}$, $i_1 \in \{1, 2, \ldots 7\}$. Level 2 nodes are denoted by $N_{i_1,i_2}^{(2)}$, $i_1 \in \{1, 2, \ldots 7\}$, $i_2 \in \{1, 2, \ldots 6\}$, where $N_{i_1,i_2}^{(2)}$ represents the i_2^{th} child at level 2 of i_1^{th} node at level 1. Level t nodes are denoted by $N_{i_1,i_2,\ldots i_t}^{(t)}$, $i_1 \in \{1, 2, \ldots 7\}$, $i_2, i_3, \ldots, i_t \in \{1, 2, \ldots 6\}$.

Clearly total number of nodes in t^{th} level is $7 \times (6 \times 6 \times \ldots \times 6)$ $(t-1$ times$)$.

Fig. 2 illustrates the detailed hierarchical tree structure upto level 5.

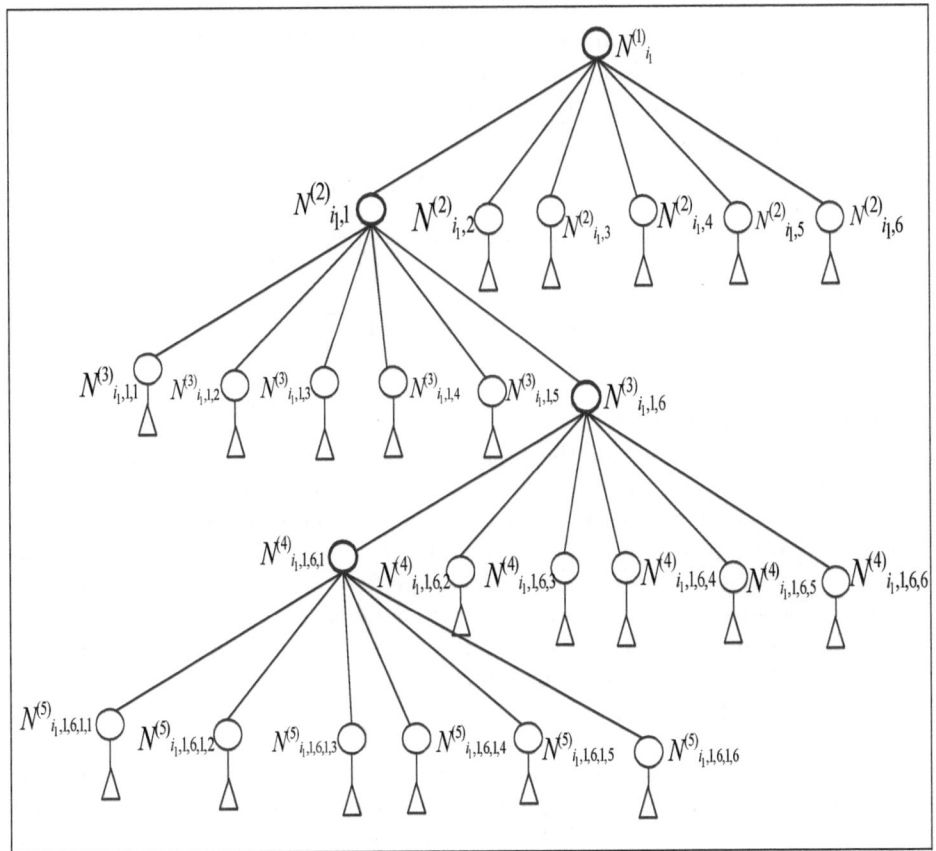

Fig. 2. Hierarchical tree structure upto level 5

(b) As the levels of the nodes are exhaustive and disjoint, we have

$$T_{nodes} = n_1 + n_2 + \ldots + n_l,$$

where l represents the total number of levels in the network. Thus

$$T_{nodes} = \sum_{j=1}^{j=t} n_j = 7 \sum_{j=0}^{l-1} 6^j.$$

Hence the result follows.

(c) $k_1 = 7$ holds trivially, as level 1 contains only one Complementary Fano plane consisting of seven keys.

Observed that, from level 2 onwards, each Complementary Fano plane in a level includes six new nodes and three new keys in the following level. Hence

$$k_j = 3 \times n_{j-1} , \ \forall \, j \, \in \, \{ \, 2 \, , \, \ell \, \},$$

where n_i denotes the number of nodes in level i. The result follows on substitution of the expression for n_i from (a).

(d) As the keys appearing for the first time in a particular level are exhaustive and disjoint, we have

$$K = k_1 + k_2 + \ldots + k_l,$$

l being the total number of levels in the network. Thus

$$K = \sum_{j=1}^{j=t} k_j = 7 + 21 \sum_{j=0}^{l-2} 6^j$$

Hence the result follows.

(e) The key that appears for the first time in level i is contained in only one Complementary Fano plane and hence goes to four nodes in level i. In $(i + 1)^{th}$ level, that key goes to each of the four Complementary Fano planes corresponding to each of the previous level nodes and in each system, the key is contained in three new nodes. Thus we observe that the nodes to which a level i key is contained, form four ternary trees with their root in level i. The number of nodes to which a level j key is assigned to is given by $\sum_{i=j}^{l} 4 \times 3^{i-j}$. Hence the result follows.

(f) Follows directly from (b)   □

The results in (b),(d) and (f) establish inter-relationship between the total number of nodes, total number of keys and the maximum number of levels required to accommodate all the nodes. Thus, when any two of them are known or given, third one can be obtained. Result(e) helps us to calculate resilience, as will be seen later in Section 6.

5   Connectivity

We now discuss how the nodes are connected by single-hop (direct) paths. From the key distribution pattern among the nodes in the network, it is observed that any two nodes can share at most 2 (i.e. 0 or 1 or 2) keys. So we summarize below the possible cases as the following: Let A be any node from level $\leq k$ in the network.

Case 0: The node B be chosen from level k. A shares **0** keys with B in level k and hence A is not connected to any of its descendants in level $\geq k$ either.

Case 1: The node B be chosen from level k. A shares **1** key with B in level k. In $(k+1)^{th}$ level, B has six children namely : B_1, B_2, B_3, B_4, B_5 and B_6. A is connected to exactly three of them by sharing only one key with each. Without loss of generality, let us assume that A is connected to B_1, B_2, B_3 and is not connected to B_4, B_5, B_6. To get the connectivity of the node A with the grand children of B, i.e. B_{ij} for $i,j \in \{1, 2 \cdots 6\}$ in level $k+2$, we observe the following subcases:

Subcase 1.1: B_1, B_2 or B_3 falls under Case 1 and same arguments hold as in Case 1 with $B := B_i$, for $i \in \{1, 2, 3\}$; $k := k+1$.

Subcase 1.2: B_4, B_5 or B_6 falls under Case 0.

Case 2: The node C be chosen from level k. A shares **2** keys with C in level K. In $(k+1)^{th}$ level, C has six children namely, C_1, C_2, C_3, C_4, C_5 and C_6. A shares only one key with exactly four of them, only one key with exactly one and no key with the remaining one. Without loss of generality, let us assume that A shares exactly one key with C_1, C_2, C_3, C_4, only one key with C_5 and does not share any key with C_6.

To observe how node A is connected with the grand children of C, i.e., C_{ij} for $i,j \in \{1, 2 \cdots 6\}$ in level $k+2$, we have the following sub cases:

Subcase 2.1: C_1, C_2, C_3 or C_4 fall under Case 1 and same arguments hold as in Case 1 with $B := C_i$, for $i \in 1, 2, 3, 4$; $k := k+1$.

Subcase 2.2: C_5 falls under Case 2 and same arguments hold as in Case 1 with $C := C_5$; $k := k+1$.

Subcase 2.3: C_6 falls under Case 0.

Example:

Let us discuss here how we observe the connectivity of a particular node. According to above discussion we assume that the network consists of 4 levels of nodes and keys.

Connectivity of a level 1 node (say N_1). All the nodes of level 1 form a 2-$(7, 4, 2)$ design, so each node is connected to the other six nodes, and each pair of nodes shares exactly two common keys. Hence, N_1 shares two keys with all other six nodes at level 1, i.e. with N_2, N_3, N_4, N_5, N_6 and N_7.

Now in level 2, N_1 is connected to all its own six children by sharing two common keys with each of them i.e. N_1 shares two keys with its children in level 2. There are exactly one child of each level 1 node with which N_1 shares two keys. Therefore, number of nodes in level 2 with which N_1 shares two common keys is 12 and the number of nodes in level 2 with which N_1 shares exactly one common key is given by 24. Out of total 42 nodes in level 2, N_1 is connected to 36 nodes.

In level 3, the number of nodes with which N_1 shares two common keys is 12 and the number of nodes with which N_1 shares exactly one common key is 120. Thus, out of total 252 nodes in level 3, N_1 is connected to 132 nodes.

Similarly in level 4, N_1 is connected to 12 nodes by sharing two common keys and 408 nodes by sharing exactly one key.

Hence out of total 1512 nodes in level 4, N_1 is connected to 420 nodes. Total number of nodes to which N_1 is connected is $= 6 + 36 + 132 + 420 = 594$. As all the level 1 nodes are uniform, any level 1 node is connected to 594 nodes out of total 1813 nodes in the network. This implies that only one level 1 node is directly connected to almost 32% of the nodes in the whole network. So, intuitively we can say that all the nodes in the network is connected to at least one level 1 node.

Connectivity of a level 2 node (say N_8). We note that out of seven nodes in level 1, N_8 shares two keys with exactly two nodes, no key with one node, and only one key with the remaining four nodes. Therefore six nodes of level 1 are connected to N_8.

N_8 is one of the child of N_1, therefore N_8 shares two keys with the other five children of N_1 in level 2. Also N_2 in level 1 shares two keys with N_8, hence, out of the six children of N_2, one shares two keys, one no key and remaining only one key with N_8. Thus number of nodes with which N_8 shares two keys in level 2 is 6 and the number of nodes with which N_8 shares only one key in level 2 is 16. Thus total 22 nodes of level 2 are connected to N_8.

Following similar arguments, N_8 shares two keys with 12 nodes in level 3 and the number of nodes with which N_8 shares a common key is given by 72. Hence N_8 is connected to 84 nodes in level 3.

In level 4, N_8 shares two keys with 12 nodes and one key with 264 nodes. Thus N_8 is connected to 276 nodes in level 4. Therefore N_8 is connected to 376 nodes in the whole network. As all the level 2 nodes are uniform, any level 2 node is connected to 376 nodes in the network.

Similarly, we can calculate these values for other level nodes also, and intuitively we can predict that this scheme has reasonable connectivity.

6   Performance

We calculate resilience by the following formula proposed by Lee-Stinson [8]

$$fail(s) = 1 - \prod_{i=1}^{l} \left(1 - \frac{N_i - 2}{N - 2} \right)^{s_i}$$

where $fail(s)$ denotes the portion of total link failure when s number of nodes are compromised; N_i denotes the number of nodes to which a level i key is assigned to, s_i is the number of compromised nodes in the ith level and s is the total number of compromised nodes. Therefore we must have $\sum_{i=1}^{l} s_i = s$.

In our scheme, the nodes are arranged hierarchically in the network, i.e., the lower level nodes (which are very less in number) are more powerful and hence are less liable of getting compromised than higher level nodes (which are much more in number).

The average values of $fail(s)$ corresponding to certain values of s has been listed in Table 2, which describes how the network collapses with increasing number of compromised nodes. This table shows that the proposed scheme provides reasonable resilience.

Table 2. Network collapses with increasing number of compromised nodes

s	$fail(s)$	s	$fail(s)$	s	$fail(s)$
10	0.017549	110	0.238873	450	0.718262
20	0.032655	120	0.252230	500	0.752019
30	0.056979	130	0.290375	550	0.800994
40	0.072504	140	0.302058	600	0.825032
50	0.112959	150	0.314306	650	0.850413
60	0.135263	200	0.396464	700	0.868336
70	0.149500	250	0.469364	750	0.884240
80	0.169968	300	0.574162	800	0.907102
90	0.207049	350	0.635533	850	0.918233
100	0.220104	400	0.679556	900	0.938538

In Table 3, we provide the comparison based on the performance of our scheme with Lee-Stinson linear scheme [8], Chakrabarti et al. scheme [3], Ruj-Roy scheme [12] and Lee-Stinson quadratic scheme [9], where T_{nodes} denotes total number of nodes in the network and T_{keys} denotes total number of keys present in each node.

The comparison between the schemes has been shown graphically in Fig. 3 and Fig. 4. In Fig. 3 we show the comparison of our scheme with Lee-Stinson linear scheme [8], Chakrabarti et al. scheme [3], Ruj-Roy scheme [12] and Lee-Stinson quadratic scheme [9] for less number of compromised nodes i.e. $1-10$ nodes. In

Table 3. Comparison with some of the existing schemes

	[8]	[3]	[12]	[9]	Ours
T_{nodes}	1849	2550	2415	2197	1813
T_{keys}	30	≤ 28	136	30	4
$fail(10)$	0.201070	0.213388	0.0724	0.297077	0.017549

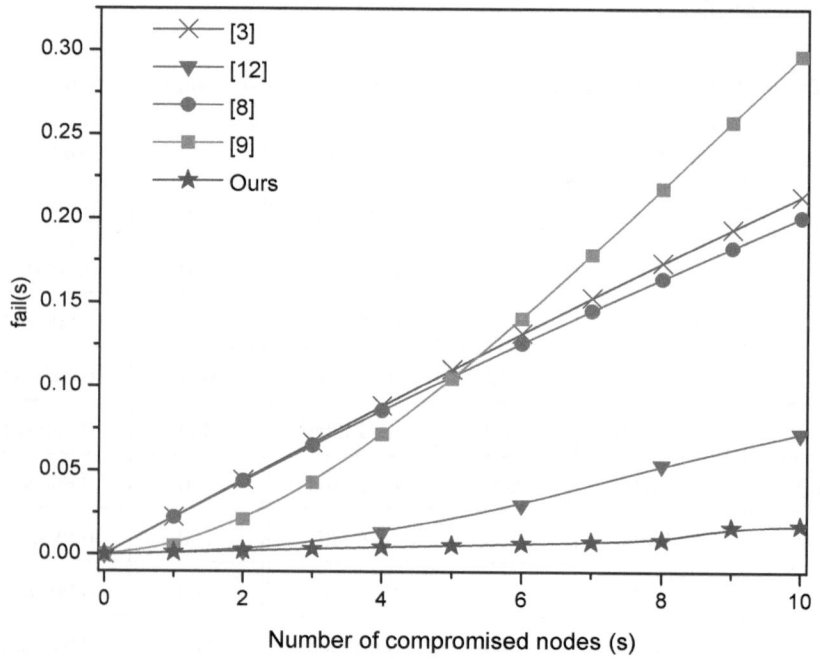

Fig. 3. Comparison of resilience for small number of compromised nodes

Fig. 4 we provide the comparison with Lee-Stinson linear scheme [8] and Lee-Stinson quadratic scheme [9] for a large number (i.e., 10-200) of compromised nodes. It is very clear from the figures that the networks based on other schemes collapses very fast compared to ours.

Remarks. *We feel that generalizing the scheme by considering the complementary design of any projective plane (instead of Fano plane) will improve the connectivity of the network. This is due to the fact that complementary design of a $(p^2 + p + 1, p + 1, 1)$ projective plane is in the form of a symmetric $(p^2 + p + 1, p^2, p^2 - p)$-BIBD, i.e., a set of p^2 keys are shared between $p^2 - p$ nodes in the network, which increases by a greater extent with increasing values*

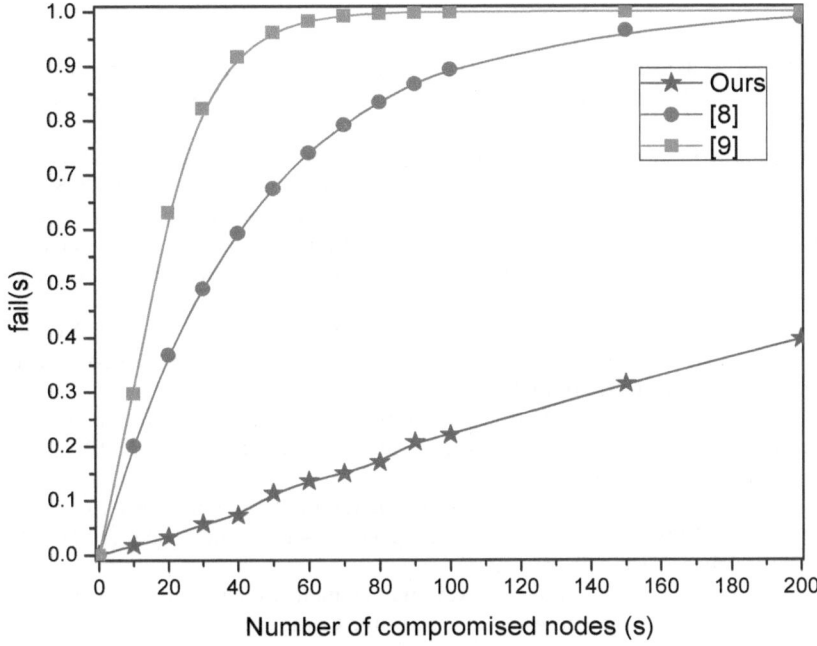

Fig. 4. Comparison of resilience for large number of compromised nodes

of p (a prime number). Thus, key-sharing between the nodes can be achieved to the desired level for complementary design of higher order projective planes. But we have to analyse the resilience of those schemes also. As our future work we would like to achieve improved connectivity with a reasonable trade off with resilience.

7 Conclusion

In this paper we have introduced a key predistribution scheme for wireless sensor network based on Complementary Fano plane. Our approach is deterministic and the sensor nodes are arranged hierarchically in the form of a 6-nary tree structure. The proposed scheme is significantly storage-efficient and has the flexibility of introducing new sensor nodes by adding only a few keys to the joining nodes without disturbing the existing set-up. We have analysed the connectivity of our scheme and it was noticed that all the nodes in the network are well-connected. It is observed that any node shares two keys with a considerable portion of the network. Obtained results support that the resilience of the resulting network is found better than some of the similar combinatorial design based schemes.

References

1. Çamtepe, S.A., Yener, B.: Combinatorial Design of Key Distribution Mechanisms for Wireless Sensor Networks. In: Samarati, P., Ryan, P.Y.A., Gollmann, D., Molva, R. (eds.) ESORICS 2004. LNCS, vol. 3193, pp. 293–308. Springer, Heidelberg (2004)
2. Camptepe, S.A., Yener, B.: Combinatorial Design of Key Distribution Mechanisms for Wireless Sensor Networks. IEEE/ACM Trans. Netw. 15(2), 346–358 (2007)
3. Chakrabarti, D., Maitra, S., Roy, B.: A Key Pre-distribution Scheme for Wireless Sensor Networks: Merging Blocks in Combinatorial Design. In: Zhou, J., López, J., Deng, R.H., Bao, F. (eds.) ISC 2005. LNCS, vol. 3650, pp. 89–103. Springer, Heidelberg (2005)
4. Chakrabarti, D., Seberry, J.: Combinatorial Structures for Design of Wireless Sensor Networks. In: Zhou, J., Yung, M., Bao, F. (eds.) ACNS 2006. LNCS, vol. 3989, pp. 365–374. Springer, Heidelberg (2006)
5. Chan, H., Perrig, A., Song, D.X.: Random Key Predistribution Schemes for Sensor Network. In: IEEE Symposium on Security and Privacy, pp. 197–213. IEEE Computer Society (2003)
6. Dong, J., Pei, D., Wang, X.: A Key Predistribution Scheme Based on 3-Designs. In: Pei, D., Yung, M., Lin, D., Wu, C. (eds.) Inscrypt 2007. LNCS, vol. 4990, pp. 81–92. Springer, Heidelberg (2008)
7. Eschenauer, L., Gligor, V.D.: A Key-management Scheme for Distributed Sensor Networks. In: ACM Conference on Computer Communications Security, pp. 41–47. ACM (2002)
8. Lee, J., Stinson, D.R.: A Combinatorial Approach to Key Predistribution for Distributed Sensor Networks. In: IEEE Wireless Communications and Networking Conference (WCNC), pp. 1200–1205 (2005)
9. Lee, J., Stinson, D.R.: On The Construction of Practical Key Predistribution Schemes for Distributed Sensor Networks Using Combinatorial Designs. ACM Trans. Inf. Syst. Secur. 11(2) (2008)
10. Lee, J., Stinson, D.R.: Common Intersection Designs. International Journal of Combinatorial Designs 14, 251–269 (2006)
11. Mitchell, C.J., Piper, F.: Key Storage in Sensor Networks. Discrete Applied Mathematics 21, 215–228 (1988)
12. Ruj, S., Roy, B.: Key Predistribution Using Partially Balanced Designs in Wireless Sensor Networks. In: Stojmenovic, I., Thulasiram, R.K., Yang, L.T., Jia, W., Guo, M., de Mello, R.F. (eds.) ISPA 2007. LNCS, vol. 4742, pp. 431–445. Springer, Heidelberg (2007)

Context-Related Access Control
for Mobile Caching

Zhi Xu[1], Kun Bai[2], Sencun Zhu[1], Leslie Liu[2], and Randy Moulic[2]

[1] Pennsylvania State University, University Park PA 16802, USA
{zux103,szhu}@cse.psu.edu
[2] IBM T.J. Watson Research, 19 Skyline Drive, Hawthorne NY 10532, USA
{kunbai,lesliu,rmoulic}@us.ibm.com

Abstract. Mobile caching is a popular technique that has been widely applied in mobile applications to reduce the bandwidth usage, battery consumption, and perceived lag. To protect the confidentiality of cached data, the data with sensitive information has to be encrypted as it is cached on mobile devices. Currently, several mobile platforms provide encryption utilities which allow mobile applications to encrypt their local caches. However, existing encryption utilities are too coarse-grained and not directly applicable to dynamically enforcing fine-grained context-related access control policies in context-aware mobile applications.

In this paper, we first show the necessity of new encryption schemes in context-aware mobile applications by examples, and then propose three encryption schemes for enforcing context-related access control policies on cached data. The proposed encryption schemes adopt different cryptographic techniques. By comparing the cache hit rate and communication gain, we analyze the impact of applying the proposed schemes to the efficiency of the existing mobile cache management algorithm in context-aware mobile applications. Further, we evaluate the performance of these schemes through extensive simulations, and suggest the suitable application scenarios for each scheme.

Keywords: Context-related access control, mobile caching, data encryption schemes, context-aware mobile applications.

1 Introduction

1.1 Mobile Caching

Mobile caching is one of the most widely used techniques in web browsers, streaming media applications, and data access applications on mobile devices [1] [2] [3]. Caching recently used data (e.g. routes, pictures of sights) on a mobile device can help the mobile device to reduce the bandwidth usage, battery consumption, and perceived lag.

As most third party mobile applications are only allowed to implement their caches in the application space, one security concern for these mobile applications is the confidentiality of cached data on mobile devices. The attacker may be

M. Rajarajan et al. (Eds.): SecureComm 2011, LNICST 96, pp. 389–408, 2012.
© Institute for Computer Sciences, Social Informatics and Telecommunications Engineering 2012

able to access the content of cached data easily if it is stored in plaintext. For example, it has been shown in [4] that, all iPhones, iTouchs, and iPads running iOS 4.0 or later versions log the user's location information in plaintext to a *consolidated.db* file. If the attacker can have access to an iPhone/iTouch/iPad or its synchronized Mac/PC, he can easily map the movement of device using the cached information in *consolidated.db* with tools, like *iPhone Tracker*.

To protect the confidentiality of cached data, the straightforward way is to encrypt the sensitive data as it is cached on the mobile device. Several modern mobile platforms provide encryption utilities which allow mobile applications to encrypt their local caches, for example the data protection features in iOS 4, the password-based encryption feature in BlackBerry OS, and the *EncryptedLocal-Store* class in Adobe AIR.

1.2   Context-Aware Mobile Applications

In context-aware mobile applications, the application interacts with the user according to its current *context*, which includes the current location of the mobile device, the current state of the user, the current time, etc. [5] [6]. With the advances in portable devices and sensors, many context-aware mobile applications have been introduced. For example, [7] proposed *Smart Signs*, a context-aware guidance and messaging system providing guests customized route information; [8] proposed a framework for *mHealth* in which the context-related policies are applied when the physician attempts to access the patient's Electronic Patient Record (EPR); and [9] presents a *mobile tourism* application, TIP, which delivers information about sights based on the user's current context.

Obviously, adopting mobile caching technique can also help improve the quality of service in these context-aware mobile applications. However, to enforce context-related access control policies on cached data, the existing encryption utilities are not directly applicable due to several unique challenges.

First, the data access policies to cached data (i.e., data file) in context-aware mobile applications are fine-grained and context-related. Briefly, each data downloaded in the cache is associated with a unique context-related access control policy. Different data may have different access control policies. The cached data accessible in the current context may no longer be allowed to access when the context changes. Mostly, existing encryption utilities are coarse-grained and all data cached in one application are encrypted with the same key. This key is usually generated basing on the application ID and user ID. Therefore, additional extensions are required to suit for context-related policy enforcement.

Second, access control policy enforcement in context-aware mobile applications must be capable of reacting dynamically to the changes of context at runtime, while keeping the efficiency of caching. Existing encryption utilities only support one single context in the cache. When the context changes, the cached data must be cleared. Especially, in mobile applications, the context of a mobile device may change frequently. Erasing cached data whenever context changes may greatly affect the efficiency of mobile caching. Otherwise, if the mobile application is compromised, all cached data downloaded in both current context and previous contexts will be leaked.

In this paper, we make the first effort to analyze the impact of enforcing context-related access control policies on cached data to the efficiency of mobile caching in context-aware mobile applications. Specifically,we present three encryption schemes using different cryptographic techniques: *Flush Scheme, Context Based Encryption (CBE) Scheme*, and *Attribute-based Encryption (ABE) Scheme*. These schemes differ in the strategy to manage the cached data according to context-related access control policies. Among these schemes, our experiment results demonstrate that the *CBE* scheme is most suitable for mobile applications in which the user is usually associated with a static set of contexts and there is little data sharing among different contexts. For example, in a mobile lab application, a scientist is assigned different data access privileges when working on different projects and the project assignment does not change frequently. The *ABE* scheme works best in mobile applications where the user's context changes frequently and some cached data are accessible in different contexts. For example, in the *mHealth* application, the context of a physician may change frequently and unpredictable depending on the patient he is treating.

2   An Example of Context-Aware Mobile Health Information Application

In this section, we present a context-aware mobile health information application, shown in Figure 1, to explain the necessity of applying context-related access control policies on cached data. Also, we show that new encryption schemes are needed to provide confidentiality protection to cached data while allowing the mobile application enjoying the benefits of mobile caching.

As shown in Figure 1, Dr. House is a physician who has a mobile device (e.g. iPad) with a context-aware mobile health information (MHI) application installed on the device. This MHI application allows Dr. House to download and read documents on the mobile device via the application's user interface. These documents are stored in the hospital's content server and protected by context-related access control policies. In this application, the context is determined the status of user, for example, the task Dr. House is performing, the current indoor location of mobile device, the patient who is being treated.

The red trace in Figure 1 shows the trace of Dr. House during a typical workday. In different contexts during the trace, Dr. House will be assigned different privileges by the authority. Here we present two types of documents with different context-related access control policies to show the necessity of applying fine-grained access control on the mobile cache in this application.

One type of documents is the patient's *Electronic Patient Record (EPR)*. To protect an individual patient's privacy, a physician is allowed to read the patient's EPR if and only if he is treating this particular patient in the patient's room. For example, in the first visit to Ellen, the MHI application downloads Ellen's EPR onto the mobile device and saves it in the cache. When Dr. House leaves

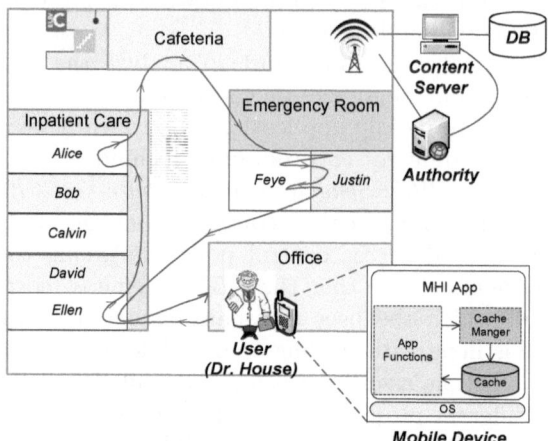

Fig. 1. A mobile health information system

Ellen's room, the Ellen's EPR may stay in the cache but can not be accessed any more because of context change. When Dr. House visits Ellen again, the MHI application can display Ellen's EPR by reading its copy in the cache.

The other type of documents is the *On-Duty Notes* which contains instructions of standardized operations in the hospital. Different to EPRs, on-duty notes are less sensitive and it can be accessed in different contexts as long as Dr. House is within the hospital. Thus, once downloaded into the cache, Dr. House is allowed to access the copy in the cache during the whole trace.

By the comparison of EPRs and on-duty notes,we show that different data cached by context-aware mobile applications on mobile devices may have different access control policies. Thus, fine-grained access control mechanisms are required to enforce their context-related access control policies on cached data.

3   Models and Assumptions

3.1   Mobile Caching Model

The *Mobile Device* (e.g. a smartphone) is connected to a *Content Server* in the client-server manner through wireless connection. In the mobile device, an *Application Cache* is implemented as a part of application. It contains two components: the *Cache* is the local storage keeping the cached data; and the *Cache Manager* is the component managing the cached data. Functions of *Cache Manager* include cache replacement [10], cache invalidation [11], etc. At the server side, we assume that an access control system has been deployed on *Content Server* to guard the data access request from mobile devices to DB. The *Authority* is in charge of user authentication as well as maintaining context-related data access policies. This generic network model has been applied in many mobile information systems, such as [12].

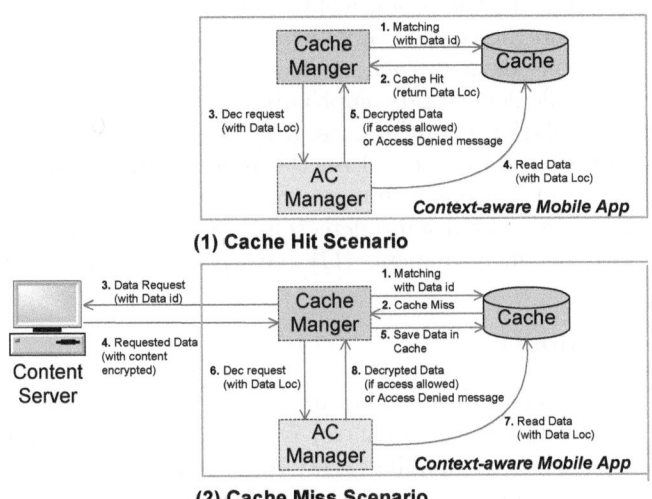

Fig. 2. Basic workflows of proposed system design

In Figure 2, we illustrate the workflow of mobile caching with enforcement of context-related access control policies. We explain the workflow as follows,

Cache Hit Scenario: If the requested data is contained in the *Cache* (i.e. Cache Hit), the *Cache Manager* will send the reference of data (i.e. the location of encrypted data in the *Cache*) to the *AC Manager* for decryption. The *AC Manager* will be able to decrypt this data if and only if the data access is allowed by the context-related access control policies associated with this requested data.

Cache Miss Scenario: If the requested data is not contained in the *Cache* (i.e. Cache Miss), the *Cache Manager* will send a data request to the *Content Server*. If access granted, the *Content Server* will encrypt the requested data and send the ciphertext back to the *Cache Manager*. The *Cache Manager* will first save the received data in *Cache* and then request *AC Manager* for decryption.

3.2   Trust Model

In this paper, we trust the integrity of mobile platform and the context-aware mobile application. Specifically, we assume that the mobile application and the mobile platform will perform correctly as required. Also, we assume that the authority is aware of the current context and the context change of mobile device. In Dr. House's example, this assumption means that the attacker (including Dr. House) can not fool the *Authority* with fake context information (e.g. the current location of device) so as to get desired data access privileges. Various location identification (e.g. GSM/3G technology [13]), location tracking [14], location verification techniques (e.g. Echo protocol [15]) can be applied.

We also assume that the compromise of mobile application or mobile platform will be detected within the context in which the compromise happened. Due to the character of mobile devices, such as easy to steal, the attacker may physically possess the mobile device and compromise not only the mobile applications but also the mobile platform. In this case, it is inevitable that the attacker will have access to all information stored on the mobile device, including the decryption keys. However, various techniques can be applied to the integrity measurement insurance and compromise detection, such as such as Trusted Mobile Platform [16], integrity measurements [17] and hypervisor based isolation [18].

3.3   Adversary Model

In this work, the adversaries are nonconforming or curious users who try to bypass the context-related access control policy enforcements and access the content of data stored in the mobile cache. As the application cache is usually implemented in application space, we assume that the adversaries can read and copy the encrypted data in the cache. For example, the adversaries may plug the smartphone to a desktop and copy all the content in the cache storage to the desktop for analysis. However, without the correct decryption key, the attacker cannot get the corresponding ciphertext.

When a data item is required and there exists a cache, the mobile application will always check if there is a copy of requested data before sending a request to the remote content server. Therefore, we assume that the attacker may attempt to access data cached in the previous context by some featured functionalities, such as the "go backward" button and "view history records" function.

3.4   Design Rationale

To enforce the context-related access control policies, one thought is to implement a reference monitor for mobile cache within the mobile application. However, implementing such a reference monitor is too complex and impractical. First of all, this reference monitor will bing a high overhead. It has to keep a detailed record of current context of mobile device, and download the associated access control policies for every data within the cache. Second, the implementation is difficult because the reference monitor at mobile application has to be the same as the reference monitor that is already deployed at content server. Third, the context-related access control policies themselves are sensitive and some companies do not allow downloading these policies from the authority.

Thus, we propose an approach that applies cryptographic techniques to enforcing context-related access control policies. Intuitively, once a data query is approved, the content server will encrypt the requested data with its associated context-related access control policy and send the ciphertext to the mobile application. The encrypted data can be cached locally on the mobile device. At the mobile application(client) side, the mobile application is given a decryption key generated basing on the current context by the authority. The mobile application will decrypt data on-the-fly. The plaintext of data only appear in the memory and will be deleted after usage.

Compared to the approach with reference monitor, the mobile application in our approach only needs to maintain a decryption key corresponding to its current context and perform decryption operations. When context changes, the mobile application simply replace the outdated decryption key by the new decryption key of the new context. Moreover, cached data will remain in the cache in the *CBE Scheme* and *ABE Scheme* with even less negative impact to efficiency of existing mobile caching schemes. Details of designs and implementations will be introduced in later sections.

4   Proposed Schemes

To enforce context-related access control policies within the *AC Manager*, we propose three cryptographic schemes: *Flush Scheme, Context Based Encryption (CBE) Scheme*, and *Attribute Based Encryption (ABE) Scheme*. These schemes differ in the strategy of policy enforcement and they perform best in different application scenarios. Briefly,

- In the first (simplest) scheme, *Flush Scheme*, the user is only allowed to cache data requested within the same context. When the context changes, all existing cached data will be erased.
- In the second scheme, *Context Based Encryption Scheme*, the cached data are encrypted basing on the context when they are downloaded from the content server. When the context of mobile device changes, existing data in the mobile cache will not be erased. If the mobile device change from context A to context B and then back to context A, the cached data downloaded previously in context A can still be accessed if it is still in the cache.
- In the third scheme, *Attribute-Based Encryption Scheme*, we adopt the *ciphertext-policy attribute-based encryption* (CP-ABE) technique to further improve the caching efficiency and flexibility by allowing possible sharing among different contexts. For example, suppose that the data m is downloaded in context A, and it is allowed to be accessed by a mobile device in both context A and B according to the context-related access control policy. If the mobile device changes from context A to context B and m is in the mobile cache, the user will be able to access the cached data m.

In the rest of section, we explain the motivation of proposed schemes and their strategies to deal with context changes. Due to the space limit, the detailed encryption and decryption procedures are not presented.

4.1   Scheme One: Flush Scheme

In *Flush Scheme*, the user is only allowed to cache data requested within the current context. The *Flush Scheme* utilizes the context-based access control enforcement at the *Content Server*. If the downloading request of a data is allowed at the *Content server*, the access to its cached copy of data should be allowed too in the same context. However, whenever the context changes, the *AC Manager* will erase all existing cached data.

The Flush Scheme can be implemented using *Secret Key Cryptography (SKC)*. For each context of a user, the *Authority* generates a random secret key K_{rand}, which will be sent to *AC Manager*. When context changes, the *AC Manager* will replace the old context's decryption key by the one of new context. In any circumstances, the *AC Manager* only keep the decryption key of current context. The cached data may be in the form of $M_{data} = (C_{data}, Time_{data\_exp}, ID_{context}, Hash())$.

4.2   Scheme Two: Context Based Encryption Scheme

In the *Context Based Encryption (CBE) Scheme*, the cached data are encrypted based on the current context of user. When the context changes, the existing data in the *Cache* will not be affected. The deletion of cached data in CBE scheme is managed by the *Cache Manger* according to ordinary cache management schemes, such as Latest Recent Used (LRU) scheme.

The decryption procedure in *CBE Scheme* involves two contexts. One is the context in which the data is encrypted at *Content Server* and delivered to the mobile cache. The other is the context in which the *AC Manager* tries to decrypt the data. In the CBE Scheme, the decryption can be performed correctly if and only if these two contexts are the same.

Here a context can be represented by a set of privileges assigned to this particular user within this context or simply an ID assigned to this context. A user may re-enter the same context multiple times. For instance, in the example of MHI application, whenever Dr. House enters Ellen's room, the context will be the same. Thus, Dr. House will be able to read Ellen's EPR directly from the cache when revisiting Ellen's room, if its encrypted copy is still in the cache.

The *CBE Scheme* can also be implemented using *SKC*. For each context of a user, the *Authority* generates a secret key $K_{context}$ based on the current context of mobile device/user. When the user enters the same context, the assigned decryption key will be the same as well. The cached data in *CBE Scheme* is in the form of $M_{data} = (C_{data}, Time_{data\_exp}, ID_{enc\_context}, Hash())$.

4.3   Scheme Three: Attribute-Based Encryption Scheme

In the third scheme, *Attribute-Based Encryption Scheme*, we adopt the *ciphertext-policy attribute-based encryption* (CP-ABE) technique [19] to further improve the caching efficiency and flexibility by allowing possible sharing among different contexts. In the *ABE Scheme*, a cached data may be accessed in different contexts as long as these contexts satisfy the data's associated context-related access control policies. For instance, in the example of MHI application, if the *On-Duty Notes* is already in the cache, Dr. House will be able to access the cached copy in different contexts during the trace. Because Dr. House is always in the hospital in this example.

Specifically, in the ABE Scheme, the privileges of a user in a context is represented by a set of attributes. In each context, the user will be assigned a decryption key generated by the attributes assigned to the current context. On the other hand, the context-related access control policy associated with one data is represented by an access structure $\mathbb{A}$ on a set of attributes. During the encryption, the encryptor (i.e. *Content Server*) encrypts the plaintext of data with $\mathbb{A}$. In the *AC Manager*, the decryption can be performed correctly if and only if the attributes of user's decryption key satisfy the access structure $\mathbb{A}$ associated with the ciphertext. Various CP-ABE schemes have been proposed, currently we adopt the CP-ABE scheme introduced in [19] to describe how we apply this scheme in our *ABE Scheme*. Specifically, the *Authority* first generates a master key MK and a public key PK. The public key PK will be given to the *Content Server* and *AC Manager* on a mobile device. The master key MK will never leave the *Authority*. When a context starts, the *AC Manager* will receive a decryption key D which is generated based on the master key MK and the set of attributes assigned to the user in this context.

When encrypting data, the *Content Server* encrypts the data content with the public key PA and an access structure $\mathbb{A}$. The ciphertext is now in the form of $M_{data} = (C_{data}, Time_{data\_exp}, ID_{context}, \mathbb{A}, Hash())$. When decrypting data, the *AC Manager* uses its current decryption key D, public key PK, and follows the access structure $\mathbb{A}$. Due to the space limit, please refer to [19] for details of the CP-ABE scheme.

5   Simulation

In this section, we study the impact on existing mobile cache management schemes when applying proposed encryption schemes to enforce context-related access control policies on cached data. Specifically, we measure the changes of efficiency of the underlying cache replacement algorithm that are caused by applying proposed schemes. Efficiency is critical to our proposed schemes. Because enforcing context-related access control policies over the cached data may neutralize the benefits gained by caching. If allowing mobile caching with access control is too costly, people would prefer disallowing caching any sensitive data on the mobile device. Each of proposed schemes has its own pros and cons in terms of efficiency. Details of cost and benefit analysis are presented in appendix.

5.1   Simulation Setup

A Query Model with Context Changes. Existing query models proposed to evaluate mobile caching algorithms do not take context into consideration. Therefore, we present a new query model to simulate the user behavior in the context-aware mobile application.

In our new query model, we use a sequence of ordered queries to represent the data queries issued by one user within a period of time. Each query consists of a data ID, a context ID, and a timestamp, representing respectively the data requested, the current context, and the current time when the query is raised. The *ThinkTime* between neighbor queries in the sequence by following an Exponential distribution. The timestamp for the first query in the sequence is zero.

To model the database protected by context-related access control policies at content server, we crate a database and divide its data items into different groups. Each group corresponds to one context. To model the case when data may be accessible in two contexts, we randomly select a portion (p) of data in each group and pair them. Those paired data will be considered as the equivalent data items. For each group/context, we generate a set of queries satisfying a zpif distribution on the data in the database. These sets of queries represent the data queries generated by the user in different contexts.

The context change mode is application-specific and is usually derived from traces of real user behavior [20] [21]. In this paper, we consider the general case of context changes. Specifically, we create a *Markov Chain model*, in which the states represent possible contexts of users and the state transitions represent the context changes. Each state has one transition to itself, representing that the next query will stay in the current context, and one transition to any other state in the model, representing the context change. We assume that, if a context change happen, the next query may be in any one state in the model with the same probability. Formally, let S ($s, s' \in S$) denotes the set of states in the model, the context of current query is at X, the context of next query is at X', and λ be the probability that the s' will state in the same context. Then,

$$Pr(X' = s' | X = s) = \begin{cases} \lambda & if s' = s \\ \frac{1-\lambda}{|S|-1} & s' \neq s \end{cases} \tag{1}$$

Parameters Selection. Four parameters are considered in simulations: *cache size, data sharing rate, context change rate,* and *time-to-live (TTL)*. *Cache size* represents the resource constraint on mobile devices. *Context change rate* represents the dynamics of user's status and the query pattern of user. *Data sharing rate* describes the characteristic of data in DB. *TTL* defines the maximum length of time a data item is allowed to cache locally. Table 1 presents the settings of other parameters in simulations.

Efficiency Measurements. The efficiency metrics in the study are the Cache Hit Rate (CHR) and the Communication Gain (CG). The cache hit rate is computed by dividing the sum of the queries that are answered using *Cache* by the sum of the total queries in the simulation. The communication gain is computed by the data transmission saved by caching minus the data transmission brought by synchronization between a mobile device and *Authority*. We compare the three proposed schemes under different cache size, expiration time (i.e. Time-To-Live), and context change frequency.

The CG is measured by counting the amount of data downloaded by mobile device with a sequence of queries. In the base case

Table 1. Simulation parameter settings

Parameter	Setting
Query sequence length	1200
Zipf distribution	θ=0.80
Number of context sets	4
Database size each context	1000
Cache size	20, ..., 400
ThinkTime (T_t)	Exponential Distribution (mean=100s)
Data item size (the same size)	1KB, 15KB, 100KB
Data sharing distribution	p=5%

(i.e. disallowing caching), the total amount of data downloaded is de-noted by $BaseAmount = (sequence\_length \times data\_size)$. So, we com-pute CG by $Syn\_Cost + Comm\_Cost - BaseAmount$. The $Synchro$-$nization\ Cost\ (Syn\_Cost)$ stands for context change information down-loaded from Authority whenever context changes. That is $Syn\_Cost = (number\_of\_context\_changes) \times (data\_downloaded\_per\_context\_change)$; The $Communication\ Cost(Comm\_Cost)$ stands for the amount of data downloaded from Content Server with the sequence of queries. That is $Comm\_Cost = |M_{data}| \times (sequence\_length) \times (1 - CHR)$.

For comparison purpose, we ignore the cost for building a secured communica-tion channel between a mobile device and authority. Also, we ignore the context change request message sent from a mobile device to Authority. We just measure the data required to transfer from Authority to a mobile device. Suppose the size of original data is $|P_{data}|$. For encryption and decryption, the Flush and CBE scheme use the AES-128, and the ABE scheme uses the $cpabe$ toolkit. In addi-tion, SHA-1 is used for the one-way hash function. For each proposed scheme, we calculate $|update|$ (i.e. the new context information downloaded per context change) and $|M_{data}|$ (i.e. the response from $Content\ Server$ with the ciphertext of requested data). Note that, in ABE scheme, the sizes of decryption key and ciphertext depend on the number of attributes associated with the decryption key and the access structure $\mathbb{A}$, respectively. In our experiments, a decryption is about 23.8 KB with 3 attributes and 94.4KB with 8 attributes. When $\mathbb{A}$ con-tains 7 attributes, the size of ciphertext will be about 14.4KB larger than the plaintext. When $\mathbb{A}$ contains 15 attributes, the size of ciphertext is about 15.2KB more than the plaintext. For our discussion, we assume that the size of decryp-tion key is 23.8KB (3 attributes case) and the size of ciphertext will increase with 14.4KB (7 attributes case).

5.2   Experiment 1: CHR vs. Cache Size and Data Sharing Rate

In this experiment, we measure the performance of our proposed schemes with different cache sizes. Considering the data sharing, we also measure its CHR with three sharing rates (Hot, Cold, and Random). By sharing, we mean a data item is allowed to be access by multiple set of contexts. As data queries follow a zipf distribution [22], popular data items are data that are queried most.

- Hot-Sharing: randomly choose 50 (i.e. 5% × 1000) from the top 20% popular data items;
- Cold-Sharing: randomly choose 50 from the 20% of least popular data items;
- Random-Sharing: randomly choose 50 from the whole DB;

As we can see from Figure 3(a), increasing the cache size may help improve the CHR in the proposed schemes. Among these schemes, the ABE scheme always achieves the highest CHR in all cache sizes, and the CBE scheme is close to ABE scheme. Both CBE and ABE scheme have much higher CHR than Flush scheme. Further, when the sharing rate increases, the ABE scheme gains more advantages. For Flush scheme, we observe that the effect of increasing cache size is affected by context changes. As shown in the Figure 3(a), when the cache size increases to a threshold point, the CHR cannot be improved any more. This is because the Flush scheme will empty the Cache whenever there is a context change. When the cache size is big enough for any single context, increasing its size will not improve the performance of CHR.

5.3   Experiment 2: CHR vs. Context Change Rate

In this experiment, we study the impact of increasing context change frequencies on the CHR with different sized cache. Specifically, we measure CHR with three cache sizes: 400(BIG), 200(MEDIUM), and 20(SMALL). The purpose is to investigate the resistance to frequent context changes in proposed schemes. The scheme resistant to frequent context changes will be suitable for applications in dynamic environments. As the context change rate reflects the user's behavior pattern, the experiment results help the application developer to choose right combination of schemes and cache sizes for different behavior patterns.

From the experiment results shown in Figure 3(b), the CBE and ABE schemes are more resistant to context changes. To both CBE and ABE schemes, the cache size is the dominating factor for CHR. To the contrary, Flush scheme highly relies on the context change rate.

Furthermore, a careful comparison between CBE and ABE schemes shows that the gap between these two are shrinking as the cache size increases. This is because ABE scheme utilizes the space in cache more efficiently than CBE scheme. Without sharing, data shared by multiple contexts may have several copies in the Cache belonging to different context sets in CBE scheme. Therefore, when the cache size is small, ABE scheme achieves more advantages. When the cache size is big, the effect of cache space utilization is reduced.

5.4   Experiment 3: CHR vs. TTL

Time-To-Live (TTL) is the duration a data item is allowed to be cached on a mobile device. TTL is determined by Authority when giving the permission assignment, and enforced at Content Server when sending the data. For Authority,

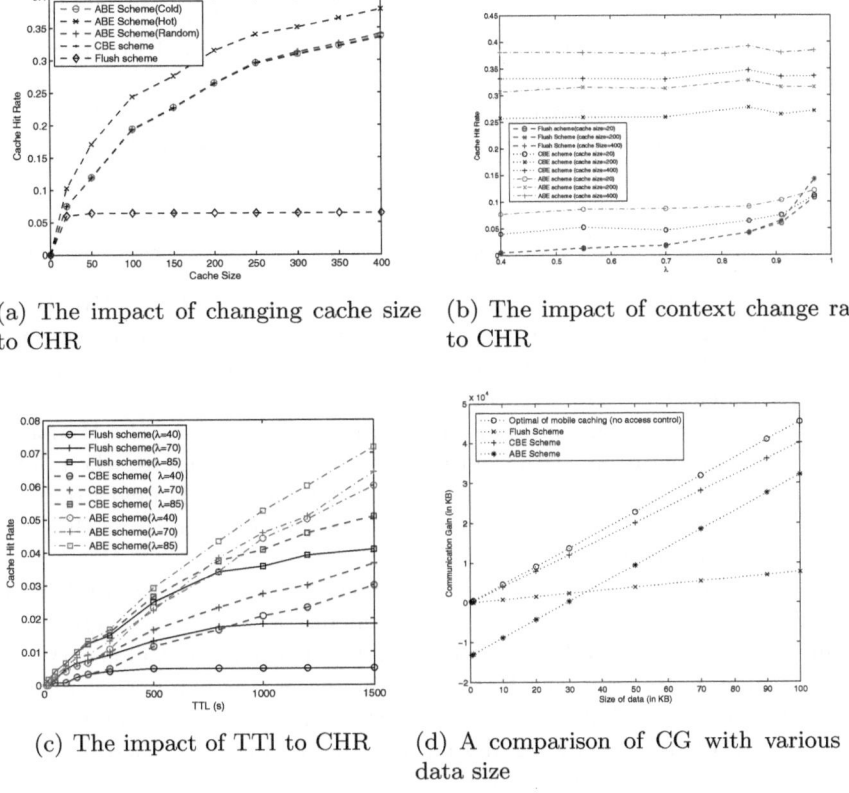

(a) The impact of changing cache size to CHR

(b) The impact of context change rate to CHR

(c) The impact of TTl to CHR

(d) A comparison of CG with various data size

Fig. 3. Evaluation of mcRBAC Schemes

he wants to assign the TTL "just long enough" for future data access. The idea is quite similar to Belady's optimal cache replacement algorithm, which always discards the data that will not be needed for the longest time in the future. But, the *Authority* sets TTL from perspective of security.

In this experiment, given a cache size, we would like to investigate how to choose TTL according to user's query pattern, i.e. the context change frequency. The result will help us (1) understand the impact of TTL with different DB access patterns in proposed schemes; (2) understand how to choose right TTL for different DB types. A comparison combining all three schemes is in Figure 3(c). From the experiment results of ABE and CBE schemes, we see that the CHR keeps increasing as the TTL increases, because both schemes allow accessing data cached in previous contexts. Therefore, keeping data in the cache for longer time will result in higher CHR.

In the Flush scheme, the CHR increases to a threshold and then stops increasing with the increase of TTL. This is because flush scheme will empty the cache when context changes. Thus, the context change rate λ determines the value of threshold in *Flush* scheme. As shown in the figure, the larger λ results in higher maximum CHR. Therefore, when applying CBE or ABE schemes, one may consider adjusting TTL as a way to improve the efficient of existing cache management schemes, similar to the idea of using Adaptive TTL approach [23] to maintain the cache coherency. when applying Flush scheme, user's query pattern (including context change pattern) should also be considered. A overly large TTL will be a waste in Flush scheme. How to set an optimal TTL for a cached data can be one of our future works.

5.5   Experiment 4: CG vs. Data File Size

In previous experiments, the ABE always achieves the highest CHR. However, the size of cipher-text in ABE scheme is larger than in the other two schemes. The purpose of this experiment is to show the tradeoff between CG and CHR in different cache sizes. We present the results in Figure 3(d).

In this comparison, the optimal results are generated using the Hypothetical Optimal Scheme with no access control. As shown in the figure, when data size increases, the CG in all schemes increases. When the CG is below 0, it means that it downloads more data than the case without caching. In such a case, it would be better not to allow caching at all.

Flush scheme has very little overhead, however, the gain from CHR is also little. When the size of data increases, the benefits of CHR become greater. CBE scheme has little overhead but moderate CHR. Therefore, its CG is very close to the optimal case. However, as the file sizes increases, the gap between these two will increase because of the differences in CHR; ABE scheme has a high overhead thus not suitable for cases when data size is small. However, when the data size increases, the benefits of CHR starts to beat the overhead. When the file size is greater than 30KB, the CG of ABE climbs to above 0. Also notice that, the gap between ABE and CBE scheme is shrinking, meaning that the advantage in CHR may be more important when the data size is big and the sharing rate is high. If the sharing rate is not high, ABE scheme may not beat CBE scheme by gaining from CHR improvement on allowing data sharing. Therefore, when the data size is small, the Flush scheme and CBE scheme may be more suitable in terms of CG. When the data size is moderate, CBE may be a better choice. When the data size is huge, one may consider the ABE scheme. Because, in this case, achieving better CHR has more direct effect to CG.

5.6   Experiment 5: CG vs. Context Change Rate

In Experiment 2, we have shown that, the ABE scheme has the best CHR when context changes frequently. In perspective of CG, things may be different because the great overhead of context changes in ABE scheme. In this experiment, we study the impact of context change rate in the same setting as Experiment 2, but now we compare schemes from the perspective of CG. The data size in this experiment is fixed as 50 KB.

The result of comparison is shown in Figure 4. From the experiment results, we can clearly see the tradeoff of applying different schemes. The Flush scheme

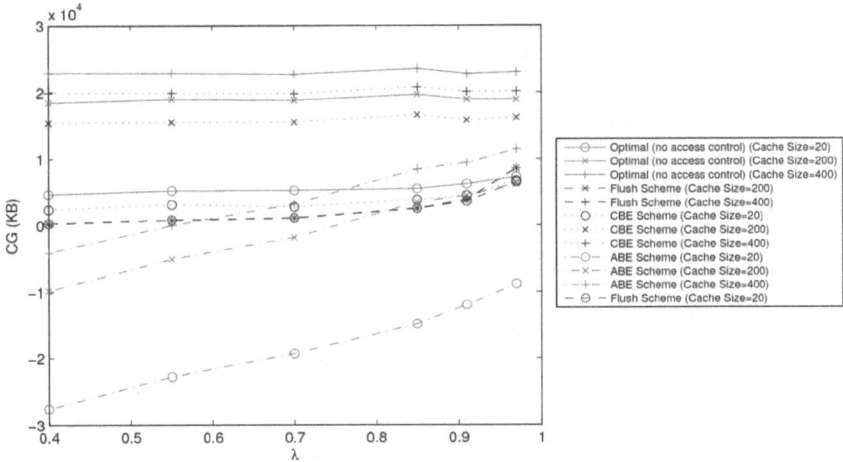

Fig. 4. The impact of context change rate to CG

has the lowest overhead, and yet its CHR is limited. To another extreme, the ABE scheme can achieve highest CHR, and yet its overhead of context change is too high. When context changes frequently or the gain from CHR is too little, the CG of ABE scheme will be much below 0. The CBE scheme provides the best CG in this experiment. As we can see from Figure 4, it is always close to the optimal case. Therefore, when the cache size is small and data file is not big, the CBE scheme would be the best choice. ABE scheme is more suitable for cases with bigger data size. Flush scheme would perform best if the cache size is big and the data sharing rate is small.

6   Related Work

6.1   Context-Related Access Control for Mobile Computing

In [24], a system called *CRePE* (Context-Related Policy Enforcing) is proposed, which extends the permission checking of Android to support enforcing context-related security policies at run-time. Differently, no permission checker is required in the proposed schemes. Instead, we rely on cryptographic techniques and enforcing context-related security policies by carefully assign the user different decryption keys according to their contexts.

Also, in many research works, such as [25, 26], the authors consider context as environment roles and propose context-related access control approaches by extending the RBAC model with spatial and temporal information. For example, [25] proposes a Spatial Role-based Access Control (SRBAC) model which allows the authority to use location information in security policy definitions. [26] proposes a GEO-RBAC model which allows securing the access to spatial data in location-aware applications.

Different to these extended RBAC models, first of all, our work is more data-oriented and focuses on enforcing the access control policy at the mobile device side. Second, we rely on the deployed access control system to detect and enforce the context change (i.e. updating the decryption key). The *AC Manager* does not run as a reference monitor. Third, our focus is not about how the context of mobile device changes. Instead, our proposed schemes focus on mechanisms of enforcing context-related access control policies when the context changes.

6.2   Distributed Data Management

Many cryptographic techniques have been applied to enforce access control policies on distributed data. For example, [27] proposes a Fine-grained Distributed data Access Control (FDAC) Scheme which applies Key-Policy Attribute-Based Encryption (KP-ABE) to protect distributively stored sensed data in wireless sensor networks. Different from the FDAC scheme in [27], the mobile device in our design does not allow to encrypt or publish data. The mobile device only has the decryption function and is limited by decryption key assigned. In addition, [28] and [29] introduce the Attribute Based Messaging (ABM) system which allows the message sender to specify allowed recipients with attribute-based access control policies. Specifically, [29] discusses employing CP-ABE to provide end-to-end confidentiality for ABM. [30] applies the ABM to secure the first response coordination in mobile environment. Different from the push model in ABM, we adopt the pull model in which the data request is generated by the mobile device and responded by the server. Moreover, [29] focuses on recipients classified by attributes. Differently, our focus is the same recipient with changing contexts.

6.3   Access Control on Mobile Devices

Some research works have been done to design access control systems for mobile devices. For example, [31] proposes a mandatory access control (MAC)-based mechanism on cellphone with the purpose of controlling the program accesses to important system resources. [32] proposes the design of a trusted subsystem which can be used to enforce MAC on mobile devices. [33] proposes a *TaintDroid* system, which tracks the information-flow of privacy sensitive data through third-party applications. [34] proposes a *Porscha* system, which enforces Digital Rights Management policies on smartphones. Both TaintDroid and Porscha require to implement a reference monitor within the kernel of Android platform.

In this work, we focus on enforcing context-related access control policies on the application cache only. All components of access control are within the mobile application space and implemented by the developer of context-aware mobile app. Thus, our proposed schemes can be easily implemented on commodity mobile devices with little modification and overhead.

7   Conclusion

We study the problem of enforcing context-related access control on cached data in mobile devices. Specifically, we propose the design of three encryption schemes adopting different cryptographic techniques. We present a quantitative comparison of proposed schemes through analysis as well as simulations. We show an application on commodity smart phones.

In our future work, we are planning to work on two directions: one direction is to apply the proposed schemes to other context-aware mobile applications. The other direction is to look for best cryptographic implementations suitable for proposed schemes on different smartphone platforms.

References

1. Jiang, Z., Kleinrock, L.: Web prefetching in a mobile environment. IEEE Personal Communications 5, 25–34 (1998)
2. Höpfner, H., Wendland, S., Mansour, E.: Data caching on mobile devices - the experimental mymidp caching framework. In: Proc. of the 4th International Conference on Software and Data Technologies (2009)
3. Apple, "Safari developer library: Storing data on the client", http://developer.apple.com/library/safari/
4. Allan, A., Warden, P.: Got an iphone or 3g ipad? apple is recording your moves (2011), http://radar.oreilly.com/2011/04/apple-location-tracking.html
5. Schilit, B.N., Adams, N., Want, R.: Context-aware computing applications. In: Proc. of The Workshop on Mobile Computing Systems and Applications, pp. 85–90. IEEE Computer Society (1994)
6. Abowd, G.D., Dey, A.K., Brown, P.J., Davies, N., Smith, M., Steggles, P.: Towards a Better Understanding of Context and Context-Awareness. In: Gellersen, H.-W. (ed.) HUC 1999. LNCS, vol. 1707, pp. 304–307. Springer, Heidelberg (1999)
7. Lijding, M., Meratnia, N., Benz, H.: Smart signs show you the way. IO Vivat 22(4), 35–38 (2007)
8. Kyriacou, E.C., Pattichis, C., Pattichis, M.: An overview of recent health care support systems for eemergency and mhealth applications. In: Proc. of 31st Annual International Conference of the IEEE EMBS (2009)
9. Hinze, A., Buchanan, G.: Context-awareness in mobile tourist information systems: Challenges for user interaction. In: Proc. Workshop on Context in Mobile HCI, in Conjunction with Mobile HCI (2005)
10. Johnson, T., Shasha, D.: 2q: a low overhead high performance buffer management replacement algorithm. In: Proc. of the 20th International Conference on Very Large Databases (1994)
11. Cao, G.: A scalable low-latency cache invalidation strategy for mobile environments. IEEE Trans. on Knowl. and Data Eng. (2003)
12. Ferraiolo, D.F., Barkley, J.F., Kuhn, D.R.: A role-based access control model and reference implementation within a corporate intranet. ACM Trans. Inf. Syst. Secur. 2, 34–64 (1999)
13. Ardagna, C.A., Cremonini, M., Damiani, E., di Vimercati, S.D.C., Samarati, P.: Supporting location-based conditions in access control policies. In: Proc. of the 2006 ACM Symposium on Information, Computer and Communications Security, ASIACCS 2006, pp. 212–222 (2006)

14. Priyantha, N.B., Chakraborty, A., Balakrishnan, H.: The cricket location-support system. In: Proc. of the 6th Annual International Conference on Mobile Computing and Networking, MobiCom 2000, pp. 32–43 (2000)
15. Sastry, N., Shankar, U., Wagner, D.: Secure verification of location claims. In: Proc. of the ACM Workshop on Wireless Security (WiSe 2003), pp. 1–10 (2003)
16. N. DoCoMo, IBM, I. Corporation: Trusted mobile platform: Hardware architecture description (2004)
17. Muthukumaran, D., Sawani, A., Schiffman, J., Jung, B.M., Jaeger, T.: Measuring integrity on mobile phone systems. In: Proc. of the 13th ACM Symposium on Access Control Models and Technologies, SACMAT 2008, pp. 155–164 (2008)
18. Cox, L.P., Chen, P.M.: Pocket hypervisors: Opportunities and challenges. In: Proc. of the Eighth IEEE Workshop on Mobile Computing Systems and Applications, HOTMOBILE 2007, pp. 46–50 (2007)
19. Bethencourt, J., Sahai, A., Waters, B.: Ciphertext-policy attribute-based encryption. In: Proc. of the 2007 IEEE Symposium on Security and Privacy, SP 2007, pp. 321–334 (2007)
20. Chen, G., Kotz, D.: A survey of context-aware mobile computing research, Hanover, NH, USA, Tech. Rep. (2000)
21. Kim, M., Kotz, D., Kim, S.: Extracting a mobility model from real user traces. In: Proc. of the IEEE International Conference on Computer Communications (IEEE INFOCOM 2006) (2006)
22. Breslau, L., Cao, P., Fan, L., Phillips, G., Shenker, S.: Web caching and zipf-like distributions: Evidence and implications. In: Proc. of the Conference on Computer Communications (IEEE Infocom 1999) (1999)
23. Cate, V.: Alex-a global file system. In: Proc. of USENIX File System Workshop 1992, pp. 1–12 (1992)
24. Conti, M., Nguyen, V.T.N., Crispo, B.: CRePE: Context-Related Policy Enforcement for Android. In: Burmester, M., Tsudik, G., Magliveras, S., Ilić, I. (eds.) ISC 2010. LNCS, vol. 6531, pp. 331–345. Springer, Heidelberg (2011)
25. Hansen, F., Oleshchuk, V.: Srbac: A spatial role-based access control model for mobile systems. In: Proc. of 7th Nordic Workshop on Secure IT Systems (2003)
26. Damiani, M.L., Bertino, E., Catania, B., Perlasca, P.: Geo-rbac: A spatially aware rbac, vol. 10. ACM (2007)
27. Yu, S., Ren, K., Lou, W.: Fdac: Toward fine-grained distributed data access control in wireless sensor networks. In: Proc. of the IEEE International Conference on Computer Communications (IEEE INFOCOM 2009), pp. 963–971 (2009)
28. Bobba, R., Fatemieh, O., Khan, F., Gunter, C.A., Khurana, H.: Using attribute-based access control to enable attribute-based messaging. In: Proc. of the 22nd Annual Computer Security Applications Conference, pp. 403–413 (2006)
29. Bobba, R., Fatemieh, O., Khan, F., Khan, A., Gunter, C.A., Khurana, H., Prabhakaran, M.: Attribute-based messaging: Access control and confidentiality. ACM Transactions on Information and Systems Security, TISSEC (2010)
30. Weber, S.G.: Securing first response coordination with dynamic attribute-based encryption. In: Proc. of World Congress on Privacy, Security, Trust and the Management of e-Business 2009 (2009)
31. Xie, L., Zhang, X., Chaugule, A., Jaeger, T., Zhu, S.: Designing system-level defenses against cellphone malware. In: Proc. of the 28th IEEE International Symposium on Reliable Distributed Systems, pp. 83–90 (2009)
32. Zhang, X., Seifert, J.-P., Sandhu, R.: Security enforcement model for distributed usage control. In: Proc. of the IEEE International Conference on Sensor Networks, Ubiquitous, and Trustworthy Computing, Sutc 2008 (2008)

33. Enck, W., Gilbert, P., Chun, B.-G., Cox, L.P., Jung, J., McDaniel, P., Sheth, A.N.: Taintdroid: An information-flow tracking system for realtime privacy monitoring on smartphones. In: Proc. of the USENIX Symposium on Operating Systems Design and Implementation, OSDI (2010)
34. Ongtang, M., Butler, K., McDaniel, P.: Porscha: Policy oriented secure content handling in android. In: Proc. of the 26th Annual Computer Security Applications Conference, ACSAC (2010)
35. Bethencourt, J., Sahai, A., Waters, B.: The cpabe toolkit in advanced crypto software collection, http://acsc.cs.utexas.edu/cpabe/

A Appendix

A.1 Security Analysis

Inter-Context Compromise Resistance. In both CBE and ABE schemes, data downloaded in previous contexts may remain in the cache. If the mobile application is compromised, the attacker may possess the decryption key of current context. The content of cached data accessible in current context will be leaked inevitably. However, in both schemes, the data leakage is limited to only cached data that are accessible in the current context. Because the compromise will be detected by the authority within the current context, only the decryption key of current context is stored in the mobile application. Therefore, the attacker can only possess the decryption key of current context.

Collusion Resilience. According to the adversary model, the attacker may possess multiple mobile devices. In this case, it is critical for access control schemes to be resilient to collusion attacks. That is, the attacker should not be able to derive new decryption keys by keys he possessed. To defend against collusion attacks, in the *Flush Scheme*, the context's secret key $K_{context}$ is randomly chosen for each context thus collecting multiple keys will have no use at all. Similarly, in the *CBE Scheme*, the keys are randomly generated basing on a set of contexts instead of for every single context. Thus, the attacker will not be able to use multiple decryption keys of different users or the same user to generate a new decryption key. In the *ABE Scheme*, the collusion resilience is provided by the CP-ABE scheme. For example, [19] adds randomness in the data encryption and decryption key generation to prevent collusion attacks.

A.2 Computation Overhead Analysis

The major computation overhead is caused by performing decryption by *AC Manager*. If there is a cache hit and the data is allowed to be accessed, both *Flush Scheme* and *CBE Scheme* need one round decryption operation with a secret key. If there is a cache hit by data id but the access is denied, both *Flush Scheme* and *CBE Scheme* result in access denied by a simple value-based comparison. More expensively, *CBE Scheme* requires a decryption attempt to reveal the feasibility of decryption. Because the *ABE Scheme* requires to perform a series of decryption operations following the access structure $\mathbb{A}$. According to the measurements in [19], the decryption workload depends greatly on the particular access tree A and the set of attributes involved in the decryption. From the perspective of decryption algorithm implementation, the efficiency of elliptic curve based operations is the key for the decryption speed.In [27], the author presented an efficient implementation of elliptic curve based operations on sensors with low computational capacity. Currently, the implementation we are using is the *cpabe* toolkit implemented at *Advanced Crypto Software Collection (ACSC)* developed by John Bethencourt, et al. [35].

A.3 Implementation Complexity Anslysis

Flush Scheme and *CBE Scheme* depend on SKC based decryption which is easy to implement and has many efficient implementations already. The *CP-ABE*, on which *ABE Scheme* relies, is relatively new compared to SKC and only have several implementations provided by research groups.

A.4 Efficiency Metrics

Efficiency is critical to our proposed schemes. Because enforcing context-related access control policies over the cached data may neutralize the benefits gained by caching. If allowing mobile caching with access control is too costly, people would prefer disallowing caching any sensitive data on the mobile device.

Cache Hit Rate (CHR). The Cache Hit Rate (CHR) is represented by the percentage of data accesses that results in mobile cache. It is computed by dividing the sum of the queries that are answered using *Cache* by the sum of the total queries in the simulation. Other performance metrics, such as query delay, throughput, and data communication cost, all have a strong relation with CHR.

Communication Gain. Communication Gain (CG) measures the benefits of applying a proposed scheme in terms of data downloaded. Applying access control may require extra data downloaded, because of the synchronization between the *Authority* and the mobile device. To measure CG of a proposed scheme, we count the overall data downloaded with a sequence of queries and then compare it with that in the case without caching (i.e. *base case*). If the CG of a scheme is negative, it means that applying this scheme will need to download even more data than the base case.

Anonymity for Key-Trees with Adaptive Adversaries[*]

Michael Beye[1] and Thijs Veugen[1,2]

[1] Information Security and Privacy Lab, Faculty of Electrical Engineering,
Mathematics and Computer Science, Delft University of Technology,
The Netherlands
m.r.t.beye@tudelft.nl
[2] Security Group, TNO, The Netherlands
thijs.veugen@tno.nl

Abstract. Hash-lock authentication protocols for Radio Frequency IDentification (RFID) tags incur heavy search on the server. Key-trees have been proposed as a way to reduce search times, but because partial keys in such trees are shared, key compromise affects several tags. Buttyán [4] and Beye and Veugen [3] devised trees to withstand such attacks, but assumed adversaries to be non-adaptive, without access to side-channel information. We illustrate how in practice, side-channel information can be used to attack the system. We also describe adaptive attacks that are easy to mount and will significantly reduce tag anonymity. Theoretical analysis of the implications on anonymity in key-trees leads to new requirements and a new tree construction. Simulation is used to test its performance, the results showing an improved resistance to adaptive attacks.

Keywords: RFID, Hash-lock protocol, key-tree, anonymity, anonymity set, adaptive adversaries.

1 Introduction

We consider the problem of authenticating many Radio Frequency IDentification (RFID) tags through hash-lock protocols, in an efficient way. The tags are authenticated towards the reader through a challenge-response mechanism. Each tag authenticates itself using some secret key combined with a random value. To authenticate the tag, the reader will have to check the keys of all tags combined with all possible random values, in order to find a match. Since this task is very intensive for the reader, a key-tree is used. Each leaf of the tree represents a tag, and each edge corresponds to a specific key. Every tag is assigned the keys that lie on its path from the root of the tree (see Fig. 1). During the authentication protocol, a tag is authenticated step by step, i.e. edge by edge, such that the computational load of the reader, and thus the total authentication time, is lowered.

---

[*] Part of this research was performed at TNO for a master's thesis for the University of Utrecht (UU). Special thanks go to Gerard Tel (UU) for his advice, and to Harry Fluks (TNO) for his work on the simulation code.

M. Rajarajan et al. (Eds.): SecureComm 2011, LNICST 96, pp. 409–425, 2012.
© Institute for Computer Sciences, Social Informatics and Telecommunications Engineering 2012

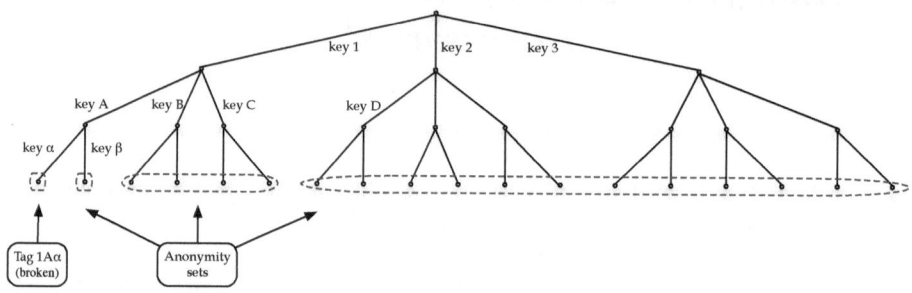

Fig. 1. Key-tree with a single broken tag

However, the authentication mechanism should still remain secure. If hardware level tampering is taken into account, keys that were assigned to compromised tags can become known to the adversary. Because partial keys are shared between neighboring tags in the tree, several additional tags may be partially broken as well. How to construct the tree such that the impact to an average tag's anonymity will be minimal in case of one or more compromises?

In existing work on tree optimization [4, 3], adversaries are assumed not to mount adaptive or side-channel attacks. However, we argue that in practice side-channel information may be readily available, and we show how adaptive attacks on the system can be mounted with minimal effort.

The main contribution of this paper is twofold. First, the effects of adaptive and side-channel attacks on anonymity in key-trees are studied and distilled into a new tree optimization problem. Because this problem is diametrically opposed to Buttyán's original optimization problem, a hybrid defense strategy is devised and tested, to provide protection from both naive *and* adaptive / side-channel attacks.

The layout of this paper is as follows: Section 2 will outline related work, with a brief explanation of most relevant concepts. Section 3 will focus on side-channel information, adaptive attackers and targeted attacks. Section 3.1 considers the impact of such attacks on key-tree anonymity, and proposes a novel type of tree as defence. Section 4 will evaluate the performance of this new construction by means of simulations, and finally, conclusions are drawn in Section 5.

2   Related Work

Molnar was the first to propose using a *tree of secrets* for RFID tags [9]. Although originally used for a system built around exclusive-OR and a pseudo-random function, it can be applied to other challenge-response building blocks. Damgård and Østergaard Pedersen [5] use the same concept, but speak of *correlated keys*. Nohara et al. in their "K-steps protocol" ([10], also dubbed NIBY) propose to apply trees to the hash-lock setting. They use the term *group IDs* rather than correlated keys, and their trees are unconventional (being of non-uniform depth). Note that all these approaches use a sequence of group- and sub-group IDs to narrow down a tag's identity. As Molnar mentions, *partial keys in such a tree should be chosen independently and uniformly from a key space of sufficient entropy*. Failure to do so would make the system vulnerable to attack. If partial keys are chosen properly, the adversary will have a large key space to search, while the owner of the system can efficiently search through a limited subspace (the actual tree).

The trade-off that exists between efficiency and security in tree-based protocols was already pointed out by Avoine [2], with respect to Molnar's original trees. Because tags share their partial keys, if one tag is compromised (i.e. has its memory probed through invasive tampering), an adversary learns partial keys for several other tags as well. This will enable him to decipher some of their responses, resulting in reduced anonymity and facilitating tracking. Nohl and Evans [11] try to quantify this more precisely. They distinguish between scenarios where compromised tags are chosen in a *selective* or a *random* way, and compute the *information leakage measured in bits*. Their work is one of the few that considers adaptive adversaries (those that selectively choose tags), although not related to the construction of optimal key-trees.

A paper of particular interest is by Buttyán et al. [4], where the concept of trees with *variable branching factors* is introduced, to better preserve anonymity in case of attack. Anonymity in key-trees is expressed in terms of anonymity sets (see Section 2.2). An optimization problem is formulated and solved, and the performance of its solution is evaluated.

In [1], Buttyán et al. attempt to further improve the balance between complexity and privacy in a new "group-based" authentication protocol. However, because the first stage of this protocol includes an encryption of the tag's personal ID, compromise of a group key would result in complete loss of anonymity for all group members. In short, we believe that the results in [1] are flawed, and that merging authentication steps into one step makes for more efficient search, but by definition reduces preservation of anonymity (as follows from results in [4]).

Beye and Veugen [3] also suggest improvements upon [4], by generalizing Buttyán's optimization problem. The resulting trees are provably optimal, and greatly outperform Buttyán trees for some inputs. Beye and Veugen's trees tend to be slightly larger than required, allowing for future system expasion or tag replacement. The results of [4] and [3] are summarized in Section 2.2.

2.1 Notation

This paper bases its notation on that of Buttyán in [4], but makes minor extensions for adaptive adversaries:

- $T = \{t_1, \cdots, t_N\}$: set of all tags in the system
- N: size of T, or actual number of tags in the system
- N': number of leaves in the tree ($\prod(B)$), or maximum number of tags in the system, $N' \geq N$

- c: number of compromised tags
- $P(t_i)$: helper function that returns the anonymity set to which tag t_i belongs
- P_j: anonymity set j, $0 \le j \le \ell$
- S: size of a given anonymity set
- $\mathcal{T}$: the set of targeted tags, $\mathcal{T} \subseteq T$
- $\bar{S}(\mathcal{T})$: average size over all anonymity sets for the members of $\mathcal{T}$, in a given configuration
- $\bar{S}_{\langle - \rangle}(c, \mathcal{T})$: $\bar{S}(\mathcal{T})$, averaged over all configurations of c compromised tags across T (Definition 2)
- $\bar{S}_0(c, \mathcal{T})$: lower bound for $\bar{S}(c, \mathcal{T})$, in the worst-case configuration of c compromised tags across $\mathcal{T}$ (see Definition 3)
- $B = (b_1, \ldots, b_d)$: a "branching factor vector" (or tuple), representing a tree of depth d; furthermore, $B \backslash \{b_1, \cdots, b_x\}$ denotes the vector $(b_{x+1}, \ldots, b_d)$
- $R(B)$: resistance to single member compromise for a tree with branching factor vector B. $R(B) \equiv \frac{\bar{S}_{\langle - \rangle}(1, T)}{N} \equiv \frac{\bar{S}_0(1, T)}{N}$
- $R_c(B)$: resistance to c member compromise for a tree with branching factor vector B, $R_c(B) = \bar{S}_{\langle - \rangle}(c, \mathcal{T})/N$
- $\sum(B)$: shorthand for $\sum_{i=1}^{d} b_i$, or the sum over all elements in B
- $\prod(B)$: shorthand for $\prod_{i=1}^{d} b_i$, or the product over all elements in B

Sometimes $\mathcal{T}$ is left out of the notation, e.g. in $\bar{S}(c)$, when $\mathcal{T} = T$. Similarly, c is omitted in case of single member compromise ($c = 1$).

2.2   Key-Trees

Buttyán et al. noted that a time-anonymity trade-off exists, where *narrow, deep trees allow faster search, while wide, shallow trees provide more anonymity*. Obviously, if many tags share the same partial keys, many tags can be excluded from the search space after each authentication stage, implying faster search. The increased anonymity can be intuitively explained by the fact that when partial keys are shared between fewer tags, the amount of information gained by compromising a single tag is limited. Buttyán uses the concept of *anonymity sets* (Pfitzmann and Köhntopp [12], Díaz [6]) to quantify matters.

Definition 1. *Assume a tag t_i sends a given message m (or participates in a protocol execution). For an observer O, the anonymity set $P(t_i)$ contains all tags that O considers possible originators of m. Because all tags in $P(t_i)$ are indistinguishable to O, t_i is anonymous among the other tags in the set.*

Anonymity sets provide a sliding scale for anonymity, where belonging to a larger set implies a greater degree of anonymity. Total anonymity holds if the set encompasses all possible originators in the whole system (one is indistinguishable among all N tags in T), and belonging to a singleton set implies a complete lack of anonymity.

To measure the level of anonymity offered by a tree, the level of anonymity provided to a randomly selected member is used. This *expected size of the anonymity set that a randomly selected member will belong to* is denoted $\bar{S}$ by Buttyán and equals $\bar{S}(c, T)$ in our notation. One could also view it as *the average anonymity set size over all tags*, as shown in Equation 1. Note that $\bar{S}$ can be computed for any given scenario where a tree is broken into anonymity sets.

$$\bar{S} = \sum_{i=1}^{N} \frac{|P(t_i)|}{N} = \sum_{j=1}^{\ell} \frac{|P_j|}{N} |P_j| = \sum_{j=1}^{\ell} \frac{|P_j|^2}{N} \ , \tag{1}$$

where $P(t_i)$ is a function that returns the anonymity set to which tag t_i belongs, P_j denotes an anonymity set and ℓ is the number of sets. Set P_0 is defined as the set containing the compromised tag, e.g. in Figure 1 $P_0 = \{t_{1A\alpha}\}$. The sets P_i, $1 \leq i \leq \ell$, form a partitioning of T.

Buttyán then defines R, the *resistance to single member compromise*, as $\bar{S}$ computed for a scenario where *a single tag* is broken, and then normalizing the result (as in Díaz [6]). Note that because we can freely order the anonymity sets, $c = 1$ leads to a single unique configuration. With its range of $[0, 1]$, R is independent of N, allowing for easy comparison between systems of different sizes.

$$R = \frac{\bar{S}}{N} = \sum_{j=1}^{\ell} \frac{|P_j|^2}{N^2} \ , \tag{2}$$

where P_j denotes an anonymity set, ℓ is the number of sets, d denotes tree depth, and $\bar{S}$ *is computed for the (unique) scenario resulting from single member compromise*. Verify that, in this scenario, the number of sets ℓ is indeed equal to $d + 1$.

Buttyán proposes the use of trees with different, independent branching factors on each level, sorted in descending order (as shown in Figure 1). We will refer to such trees as *"Buttyán trees"*, and to trees with a constant branching factor as *"Classic trees"*.

Trees will be described by their branching factor vectors $B = (b_1, \ldots, b_d)$, where the variables b_i ($1 \leq i \leq d$) are positive integers denoting the branching factor at level i.

Buttyán et al. in [4] reach the conclusion that the branching factors near the root contribute more to $\bar{S}$ and R. For trees with variable branching factors this means that a deep, top heavy Buttyán tree can potentially outperform a shallow classic tree.

We rephrase Buttyán et al.'s optimization problem as:

Problem 1. *Given the total number N of members and the upper bound D_{max} on the maximum authentication delay, find the lexicographically largest vector $B = (b_1, \ldots, b_d)$ subject to the following constraints:*

$$\prod (B) = \prod_{i=1}^{d} b_i = N, \ and \ \sum (B) = \sum_{i=1}^{d} b_i \le D_{max} \ . \tag{3}$$

Buttyán et al. provide a *greedy* algorithm that solves this problem recursively. It starts with the prime factorization of N and tries to combine prime factors as long as the sum (authentication time) remains acceptable.

However, Buttyán recognizes that trees need to stand up to more than single tag compromise. Without going into mathematical detail, Buttyán suggests to express $\bar{S}$ for the general case in two different ways:

Definition 2. $\bar{S}_{\langle - \rangle}(c)$ *expresses* $\bar{S}(c)$ *as the average over all* $\binom{N}{c}$ *possible distributions of c compromised members across the tag set T.*

Our notation is a natural extension of Buttyán's $\bar{S}_{\langle - \rangle}$, directly incorporating c. Depending on how each successive member is picked from the tree, different anonymity sets are broken down. Buttyán notes that computing $\bar{S}_{\langle - \rangle}$ is hard, and therefore suggests an alternative measure:

Definition 3. $\bar{S}_0(c)$ *represents the* worst-case *value of* $\bar{S}(c)$ *for all* $\binom{N}{c}$ *possible distributions of c compromised members across the tag set T.*

Although not stated explicitly in [4], this worst-case value is attained in (any of) the most uniform distributions of c compromised tags across T.

Proof. Assume that we are allowed to choose tags to be compromised sequentially, with the aim to minimize the average anonymity set size. The first compromised tag leads to a unique configuration. Each subsequent compromised tag leads to a new configuration, with more anonymity sets (of varying, decreasing size). To minimize the average set size in the *resulting* configuration, the next tag to be compromised should be chosen from (one of) the largest anonymity set(s) in the *current* configuration. When sorting anonymity sets in ascending order, we observe that this is equivalent to chooseing tags (as) uniformly (as) possible given the tree structure) across T. By induction, our claim holds for any c. □

Again, Buttyán's notation $\bar{S}_0$ is generalized to directly incorporate c. Buttyán correctly remarks that $\bar{S}_0(c)$ is far easier to compute, and acts both as a lower bound and an accurate approximation for $\bar{S}_{\langle - \rangle}(c)$.

A different tree construction was proposed by Beye and Veugen [3], who modify Buttyán's optimisation problem to:

Problem 2. *Given the total number N of members and the upper bound D_{max} on the maximum authentication delay, find the vector $B = (b_1, \ldots, b_d)$ that maximizes $R(B)$ subject to the following constraints:*

$$\prod (B) = \prod_{i=1}^{d} b_i \ge N, \ and \ \sum (B) = \sum_{i=1}^{d} b_i \le D_{max} \ . \tag{4}$$

The main idea is that the condition $\prod(B) = N$ is too strict and could lead to inferior solutions. It is shown in [3] how key-trees can be optimized for Problem 2, and that they indeed better retain anonymity when tags are compromised. The number of leaves in the tree, $N' = \prod(B)$, will generally be larger than the actual number N of current tags in the system, and therefore gives an additional buffer of tag IDs which is useful when expanding the system, or replacing compromised tags. Note that because a key-tree only needs to be constructed once (and as a pre-computation stage), the efficiency of the tree-building algorithm is not critical. However, both Buttyán's algorithm, as that of Beye and Veugen are sub-linear in the size of inputs N and D_{max}.

The difference in output can be illustrated with the help of the examples in Table 1:

- Set 1, borrowed from [4], shows that Buttyán's algorithm is not optimal in the setting of Problem 2. The output of Beye and Veugen's algorithm is lexicographically larger, although not much.
- In Set 2, the input contains relatively large primes. Buttyán's algorithm cannot improve upon the Classic tree at all, leaving much room for improvement by Beye and Veugen's algorithm. The difference in performance is about as large as between the Classic and Buttyán trees in Set 1.
- For Set 3, Buttyán's algorithm performs similarly and provides the same output as Beye and Veugen's algorithm. Set 3 is a relatively small example to test whether a large b_d has a positive effect on the entire tree.

Table 1. Test cases

Input	Classic	Buttyán	Beye and Veugen	Hourglass
Set 1: $N = 27000$, $D_{max} = 90$	$(30, 30, 30)$	$(72, 5, 5, 5, 3)$	$(73, 5, 3, 3, 3, 3)$, $N' = 29565$	$(70, 3, 3, 3, 2, 9)$, $N' = 34020$.
Set 2: $N = 24389$, $D_{max} = 100$	$(29, 29, 29)$	$(29, 29, 29)$	$(84, 4, 3, 3, 3, 3)$, $N' = 27216$	$(80, 4, 3, 3, 10)$, $N' = 28800$
Set 3: $N = 1728$, $D_{max} = 36$	$(12, 12, 12)$	$(24, 4, 3, 3, 2)$	$(24, 4, 3, 3, 2)$	$(20, 4, 3, 9)$, $N' = 2160$

3   Adaptive Adversaries

Buttyán et al. in [4] and Beye and Veugen in [3] assume their adversaries to be *non-adaptive* and to select tags at random (naively). Their aim is to provide optimal defense (by maximizing $\bar{S}_{\langle - \rangle}(c, T)$) in the *expected average case* – a uniformly random distribution of compromised tags.

We would like to model other possible lines of attack and see what is required to best preserve anonymity in those cases. First of all, we wish to distinguish the following two goals that an adversary may have:

1. *Universal tracking:* an attacker wants to track *any and all* tags in the system.
2. *Targeted tracking:* an attacker wants to track *certain* tags in the system.

In both scenarios, naive attacks can be mounted by breaking tags at random, thus reducing the expected anonymity set size of the average tag ($\bar{S}_{\langle-\rangle}(c, T)$ and $\bar{S}_{\langle-\rangle}(c, \mathcal{T})$, respectively).

However, clever adversaries may employ additional knowledge to expedite matters. In cryptographic literature, a *side-channel attack* is commonly defined as "any attack based on information gained from the physical implementation of a crypto-system, rather than theoretical weaknesses in the algorithms, which is the aim of cryptanalysis." The following formal definition is based on that of Köpf and Basin's [8]:

Definition 4. *Let K be a finite set of secret inputs, M be a finite set of messages, and D be an arbitrary set. We model cryptographic systems as (consisting of) functions of type $F : K \times M \to D$, where we assume that F is invoked by two collaborating callers. One caller is an honest agent that provides a secret argument $k \in K$ and the other caller is a malicious agent (the attacker) that provides the argument $m \in M$. We assume that the attacker has no access to the values of k and $F(k, m)$, but that he can make physical observations about F's implementation I_F that are associated with the computation of $F(k, m)$ (side-channel information). The malicious agent performs an attack in order to gather (side-channel) information for deducing k or narrowing down its possible values. Such an attack consists of a sequence of attack steps, each with two parts: A query phase in which the attacker decides on a message m and sends it to the system, and a response phase in which he observes I_F while it computes $F(k, m)$.*

In the setting of RFID key-trees, the most obvious example of *side-channel information* is *serialized issuing*. RFID tags are delivered in batches and companies often implement systems in a structured way. Adversaries that are interested in breaking the keys belonging to a particular company, departement or person, will often be able to easily learn some additional information about the RFID tags, and consequently about the construction of the key-tree. Choosing keys from the tree and assigned them to tags in such an orderly fashion can give rise to strong correlations between date of issuing, physical location and key material.

Using this information, an attacker could mount the following attacks:

Ad 1. Universal tracking: to track all tags efficiently, an attacker will aim to make the average anonymity set size over all tags ($\bar{S}$) as small as possible. Assuming that tags are distributed and compromised at random (no known side-channel information can be exploited), the expected remaining anonymity after an attack is equal to $\bar{S}_{\langle-\rangle}(c, T)$ (by definition). In some cases, an unknown order in the tree (i.e. serialized issuing) can work against this adversary's goals, by making the spread of his compromised tags less uniform than he expects. However, if the adversary manages to exploit such an underlying source of side-channel information, it can help him to select his compromised tags *with a more uniform distribution*. This will shift the results closer to the worst-case value $\bar{S}_0(c, T)$.

Ad 2. Targeted tracking: when attacking a specific subset of tags $\mathcal{T} \subset T$, without side-channel information, the expected result $\bar{S}_{\langle - \rangle}(c, \mathcal{T}) = \bar{S}_{\langle - \rangle}(c, T)$; tags in $\mathcal{T}$ are no different from the average tag. However, if the attacker is able to exploit side-channel information, his efforts can be focussed on breaking tags in $\mathcal{T}$ (or in branches that contain members of $\mathcal{T}$). Note that breaking other tags does have *a limited impact*: it reduces the set size for those tags (if any) in $\mathcal{T}$ which have not had any of their keys revealed yet (and are thus in the same anonymity set). Still, breaking tags in $\mathcal{T}$ itself has by far the largest impact.

Even worse, we argue that a stronger and more readily available source of side-channel information exists, when considering *adaptive attacks*:

Definition 5. *In an adaptive attack, the attacker can use the observations made during his first n queries to I_F to choose his message m for the $n + 1$st query.*

The most obvious adaptive attack in the current setting would be to test target tags before deciding whether to compromise them or not. Because we already assumed that our attacker has the capability to interrogate a tag and observe its response (for the purpose of tracking), this type of attack would be almost trivial to mount in practice. By simply interrogating a candidate tag, the adversary can determine how many (and even which) keys it shares with his set of "already known keys".

An adaptive adversary has the ability to compromise only those tags that best suit his purposes (i.e. do the most harm with a minimal c), making the following attacks possible:

Ad 1. Universal tracking: if a candidate tag shares too many of its keys with previously compromised tags, it can already be tracked to some extent. It does not form a worthy target for actual compromise, because it would not yield enough new keys. Only tags from unknown parts of the tree, that (mostly) use unknown keys, will be compromised. The resulting distribution is *more uniform than the expected case*, and more closely resembles the fully-uniform worst-case distribution. The rapid breakdown of remaining large anonymity sets will push anonymity metrics towards their worst-case value $\bar{S}_0(c, T)$.

Ad 2. Targeted tracking: if a candidate tag replies with partial keys that are known, it is located in a known part of the tree, and the tag is selected for compromise. This focusses the efforts in a particular sub-tree and rapidly breaks down the anonymity of this subset of tags. Although it would be hard for the attacker (without additional knowledge) to choose *which* part of the tree to attack, a (randomly selected) subset $\mathcal{T}$ can be attacked in particular. Attacks that combine adaptive strategies with other side-channel information (e.g. exploitation of serialized issuing) would have a serious impact the anonymity in *specifically chosen* target sets.

To keep the input to our simulations manageable, we assume that tags in $\mathcal{T}$ are adjacent tags in the tree. We believe this will fit (most) real-world sources of side-channel knowledge. However, to model adversaries trying to track a subset

$\mathcal{T}$ of a different shape (e.g. adaptive testing in a tree with no internal order), a different model would be required.

We generalize $\bar{S}(c, T)$ to represent the anonymity provided to a randomly selected tag $t_i \in \mathcal{T}$, for some target set $\mathcal{T} \subseteq T$.

$$\bar{S}(c, \mathcal{T}) = \sum_{i \in \mathcal{T}} \frac{|P(t_i)|}{|\mathcal{T}|} \; , \tag{5}$$

where $P(t_i)$ is a function that returns the anonymity set to which tag t_i belongs.

Definition 6. $\bar{S}_{\langle - \rangle}(c, \mathcal{T})$ *expresses* $\bar{S}(c, \mathcal{T})$ *as the* average *over all* $\binom{N}{c}$ *possible distributions of c compromised members across the tree T.*

Definition 7. $\bar{S}_0(c, \mathcal{T})$ *represents the* worst-case *value of* $\bar{S}(c, \mathcal{T})$ *for all* $\binom{|\mathcal{T}|}{c}$ *possible distributions of c compromised members across the (sub-)tree containing* $\mathcal{T}$.

The worst case for tags in $\mathcal{T}$ is attained for those scenarios where all c tags fall into those branches containing members of $\mathcal{T}$, and the spread of these tags is (as close as possible to) uniform. If $c \geq |\mathcal{T}|$, then the remaining tags are spread uniformly (so far as possible) over the remaining branches of the tree.

3.1   Theoretical Impact of Targeted Attacks

Buttyán notes that his result graph for $\bar{S}_0(c, T)/N$ seems to "become a constant" when $c = b_1$. The same trend was observed in the simulation results in [3]. Buttyán mainly uses it to support his claim that the preservation of anonymity relies mostly on the first element of the branching factor vector [4], while we use this observation as our foundation for a better defense against targeted attacks. First we expand upon the informal explanation of this observed behaviour given in [3], which will clearly illustrate the impact of side-channel attacks.

Definition 8. *We define a* turning point *of function* $\bar{S}_0(c, T)/N$ *as a point where its second derivative exhibits a* jump discontinuity. *In specific, the rate of decline of* $\bar{S}_0(c, T)/N$ *suddenly slows down by an order of magnitude.*

Corollary 1. *Let* c_i *be the number of compromised tags for which* $\bar{S}_0(c, T)/N$ *reaches its i-th turning point. Then* $c_i = \prod (b_1, b_2, \cdots, b_i)$ *(product of the first i branching factors of B). The value of* $\bar{S}_0(c_i, T)/N$ *will equal* $R(B \backslash \{b_1, b_2, \cdots, b_i\})$, *in other words is determined only by the remaining branching factors, further down in B.*

Proof. Assume the worst-case scenario, where the distribution of broken tags across T is always at its most uniform (by definition of $\bar{S}_0(c, T)$). This implies that each subsequent tag to be broken, *must come from (one of) the largest remaining anonymity set(s)*. For $c \leq b_1$, each newly compromised tag will thus come from a top-level branch containing zero compromised tags. Each compromise reveals one new top-level key, which was previously unknown to the adversary. This key is shared with a whole top-level branch containing $\frac{N}{b_1}$ tags, and its compromise has a large impact on $\bar{S}_0(c, T)/N$.

For $b_1 < c \leq b_1 \cdot b_2$, targets will again fall in the *largest remaining sets*, but these are now housed in the second-level sub-trees and are much smaller than before. All top-level and b_1 of the second-level keys are known, so the following $b_1 \cdot b_2 - 1$ compromised tags each yield one new *second-level* key as the most significant result. These keys are shared among less tags ($\frac{N}{b_1 \cdot b_2}$). Thus, each additional compromise has a smaller impact on $\bar{S}_0(c, T)$. Although $\bar{S}_0(c, T)/N$ does not actually become a constant, the speed of its decline changes drastically.

Such a turning point will occur whenever all keys *from a given level ℓ* have become known to the adversary. There are $\prod(b_1, \cdots, b_\ell)$ such keys, so to reveal them requires (in this worst-case) an equal amount of compromised tags. This means that $c_1 = b_1$, $c_2 = b_1 \cdot b_2$, $\cdots$, $c_d = \prod(B)$. In these cases, all sub-trees (τ_j for $1 \leq j \leq \prod(b_1, \cdots, b_\ell)$) suspended below the branches on level ℓ are identical, and each contains exactly 1 broken tag. From the fact that all tags are housed in an identical subtree, it follows that $\bar{S}_0(c, T)/N$ for the whole tree is equal to the *local* $\bar{S}_0(1, \tau_j)/N'$ for any j. By definition, $\bar{S}_0(1, \tau_j)/N$ (for a tree τ_j containing 1 broken tag) equals $R(B')$ (from Equation 2, also verified by observing a subtree with one compromised member in Figure 1). However, the *local* $\bar{S}_0(1, \tau_j)$ and $R(B')$ are based on τ_j's local $B' = B\backslash\{b_1, b_2, \cdots, b_\ell\}$ and $N' = \prod(b_{\ell+1}, \cdots, b_d)$.

By induction on ℓ, it follows that $\bar{S}_0(c, T)/N$ for the whole tree T assumes the values $R(B\backslash\{b_1\})$ (for $c = c_1$), $R(B\backslash\{b_1, b_2\})$ (for $c = c_2$),$\cdots$,1 (for $c = c_d$) at its turning points. Hence, the remaining anonymity of the remaining tags is dependent only on the remaining branching factors $b_{\ell+1}, \cdots, b_d$ further down in the tree.   □

We expect a similar situation to hold for $\bar{S}_{<->}(c, T)$, although we cannot offer a formal description. According to the *Coupon Collector's Problem* [7], one would need to break approximately $b_1 \cdot \log(b_1)$ tags to hit each top-level branch once (assuming branches contain sufficiently many tags, such that breaking tags does not change the probabilities for each branch significantly). However, because tags picked from other branches also (slightly) impact $\bar{S}_{(-)}(c, T)$, we expect a *turning trajectory* rather than an exact turning point. Still, we expect the rate of decline for $\bar{S}_{<->}(c, T)$ to depend on the same factors as $\bar{S}_0(c, T)$.

We have seen that given side-channel information, a target subset T can be rapidly broken down into small anonymity sets. With a Universal Attack based on side-channel information, attackers can cause $\bar{S}_0(c, T)$ and $\bar{S}_{(-)}(c, T)$ to reach their *turning points* and associated low anonymity values prematurely. Beye & Veugen's Optimized Buttyán trees [3] remain the best defense in this case.

For Targeted Attacks, the situation in the branches containing T will strongly resemble the one described in the previous paragraphs. Given enough side-channel knowledge, directed attacks inside a smaller sub-tree ignore the top-level branching factor(s). Because the adversary can pick tags from the right branches accurately, the remaining branches offer little to no protection. We therefore postulate that *the values reached by $\bar{S}_0(c, T)$ and $\bar{S}_{(-)}(c, T)$ after the turning points are most important*, not when the turning points are reached.

These values mostly depend on the tail end of B, not the head. Also, *we feel that the difference between belonging to a large and a medium anonymity set is less critical than the difference between belonging to a small anonymity set, and having no anonymity at all.*

3.2 Hourglass Trees

Based on the conclusions of the previous section, we arrive at two conflicting optimization problems. Maximizing the top branching factor is key in defending against Universal and naive attacks, while the lower branching factors play a central role in defending against Targeted Attacks. Without making further assumptions about real-world adversaries, an optimal way of allocating weights cannot be found. To test our hypotheses experimentally, we propose the *"Hourglass"* tree shape. It is top-heavy like Buttyán or Beye & Veugen trees (to provide defense against naive and Universal Attacks), but some weight has been shifted to the *lowest* branching factor to defend against heavy Targeted Attacks. We expect this tree shape to perform better in such scenarios, without sacrificing too much of their strength versus Universal or naive attacks.

Without being able to formulate exact requirements for the tree shape, designing a new tree-building algorithm is not possible. For the purpose of our experiments we will manually adjust B as follows. The bottom branching factor b_d of Beye & Veugen's Optimized Buttyán trees is normally between 2 and 4. We will increase it to a value of around 9, by moving weight from the other b_i, which we expect will provide noticeable results. Note that in some cases, such modification allows for the merging of other branching factors, resulting in a more shallow tree (see Table 1).

4 Simulation

It has already been shown in [3] that Beye & Veugen's trees can yield a lexicographically larger B than Buttyán's approach. We now want to evaluate our Hourglass trees and compare them to Classic and Beye & Veugen trees. To do this, we will compute anonymity measures for each of these tree shapes, under different circumstances.

$\bar{S}_0(c, T)$, $\bar{S}_{\langle - \rangle}(c, T)$ and $\bar{S}_0(c, \mathcal{T})$ will be computed by iterating over all possible scenarios in an efficient way, and taking the (weighted) average and minimum. We will estimate $\bar{S}_{\langle - \rangle}(c, \mathcal{T})$ by means of random sampling, for reasons of tractability. Where applicable, anonimity measures for trees with $N' > N$ tags will be scaled by a factor $\frac{N}{N'}$ as discussed in [3].

Side-channel knowledge (or adaptive behavior) is modeled by a probability P for successfully applying knowledge to select a tag from $\mathcal{T}$, where a higher P represents more side-channel knowledge. In case of failure (probability $1 - P$), a random tag is selected from the entire (uncompromised) population. Hence, the total probability of selecting the $(c+1)^{th}$ tag from $\mathcal{T}$ equals $P + \frac{|\mathcal{T}| - c}{N - c}(1 - P)$, excluding the c tags that were previously compromised.

In our experiments, $|\mathcal{T}| = 100$, while $P = 0.1$, 0.5 and 1.0. To approximate $\bar{S}_{\langle-\rangle}(c, \mathcal{T})$, 10,000 random samples were taken and averaged. This resulted in a smooth graph for all inputs, except where $P = 0.1$, for Sets 1 and 2. In these cases 100,000 samples were taken, leading to better results. Running all calculations for $0 \leq c \leq 100$ was still feasible on the hardware used (Pentium-IV 2.0GHz running Windows XP).

Table 1 shows the three input sets for which we have evaluated the Classic, Beye & Veugen and Hourglass trees.

4.1   Graphs for Naive Attacks

Figures 2, 3 and 4 show the performance of the different trees, in the case of naive attacks (compromise at random, without side-channel knowledge). The datasets are selected by relevance, and we discuss how these results relate to our hypotheses and claims.

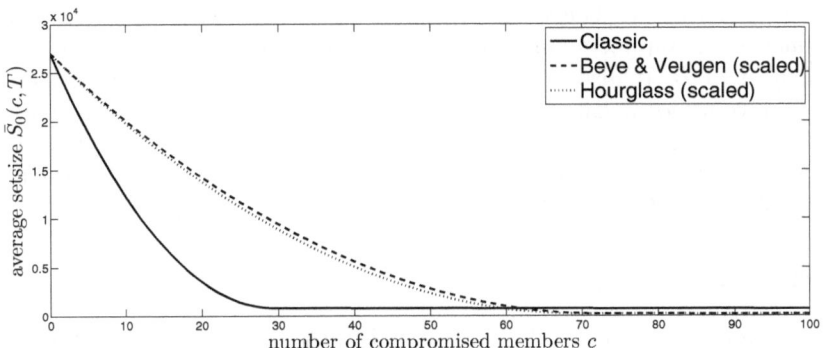

Fig. 2. $\bar{S}_0(c, T)$ for Set 1

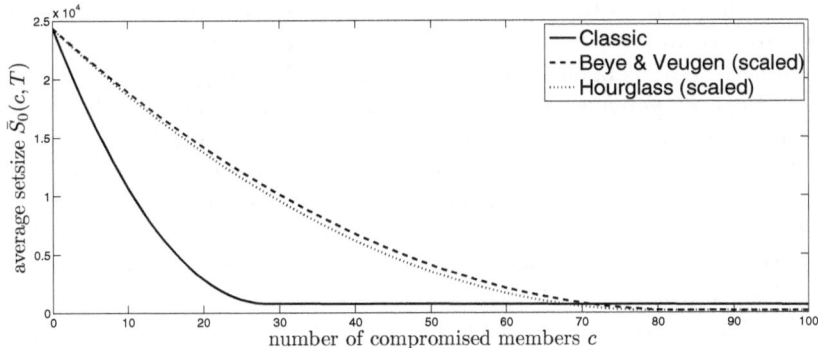

Fig. 3. $\bar{S}_0(c, T)$ for Set 2

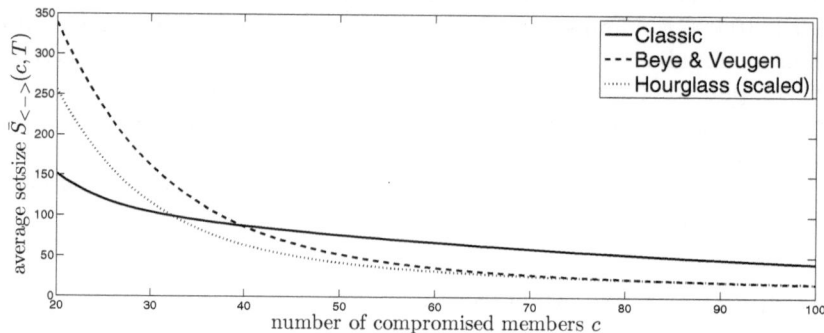

Fig. 4. $\bar{S}_{\langle - \rangle}(c, T)$ for Set 3

Figure 2 shows the Beye & Veugen and Hourglass trees performing similarly for Set 1, in terms of $\bar{S}_0(c, T)$. The same trend was observed for Set 2 (Figure 3), and for $S_{\langle - \rangle}(c, T)$ in Set 3 (Figure 4). The fact that *the differences between Hourglass and Beye & Veugen trees is not large in the absence of side-channel knowledge*, again supports our claim that the value of $\bar{S}$ depends mostly on the first element of B. It also confirms our hypothesis that a small decrease in b_1 does not have major negative impact on the anonymity in case of naive attacks.

The Hourglass tree shape seems to offer no benefit in the non-adaptive (naive) scenario's (as expected), and performs only slightly worse than the other trees in terms of $S_{\langle - \rangle}(c, T)$ (as in Figure 4).

4.2 Graphs for Targeted Attacks

Figures 5 and 6 show the results in case of Targeted Attacks (on a target subset T of size 100, with the aid of side-channel knowledge or adaptive testing). Again, a selection of result datasets is shown, based on relevance.

It is interesting to observe Classic trees performing very well in these scenario's, which is due to their large value of b_d. As expected, superior results for $\bar{S}_0(c, T)$ are attained with Hourglass trees, second only to Classic Trees. They outperform Beye & Veugen's Optimized Buttyán trees significantly (Figure 6). However, Beye & Veugen's trees can perform better in terms of $\bar{S}_{\langle - \rangle}(c, T)$ at low c values, as was the case for Set 3 ($0 \leq c \leq 20$) in Figure 5.

For $\bar{S}_{\langle - \rangle}(c, T)$, Hourglass trees under perform in scenarios with low side-channel knowledge ($P = 0.1$). Although we did not expect this, it can be explained by the fact that the expected average distribution will remain closer to uniform than in cases with more side-channel knowledge – in other words, we remain close to a naive attack. For low P values, $\bar{S}_{\langle - \rangle}(c, T)$ behaves much like $\bar{S}_{\langle - \rangle}(c, T)$, for which we have seen that Hourglass trees degrade performance (slightly).

In case of higher side-channel knowledge, the strength of Hourglass trees becomes more apparent. An intersection point exists (see Figure 5), where

Hourglass trees start outperforming Beye & Veugen trees. This point arises ear-lier when stronger side-channel knowledge is available. Indeed, for the worst-case $\bar{S}_0(c, \mathcal{T}), P = 1.0$, the turning point comes very early ($c = 20$), and the Hourglass tree performs significantly better than its competitor (see Figure 5).

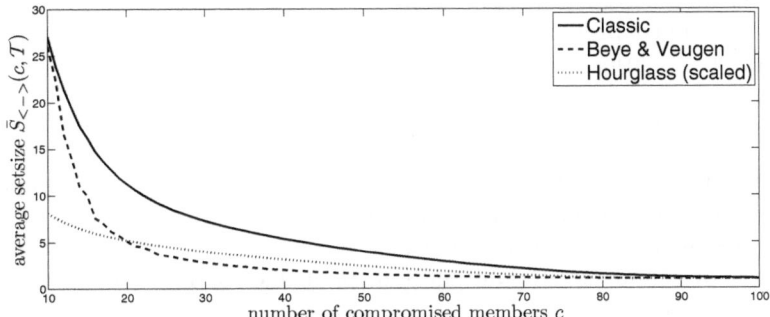

Fig. 5. $\bar{S}_{\langle - \rangle}(c, \mathcal{T})$ for Set 3, $P = 1.0$

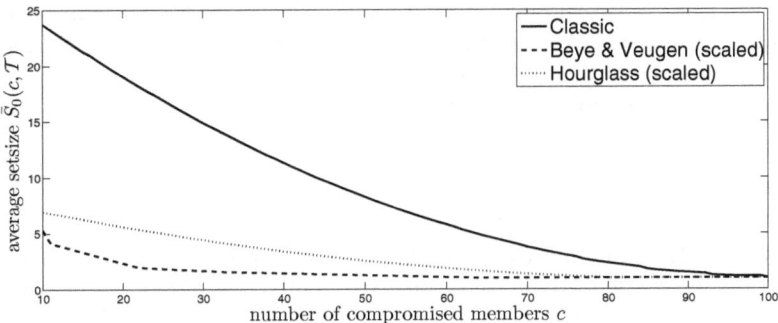

Fig. 6. $\bar{S}_0(c, \mathcal{T})$ for Set 2

5   Conclusions and Future Work

Simulation results support our intuition with regards to our proposed anonymity measures $\bar{S}_0(c, \mathcal{T})$ and $\bar{S}_{\langle - \rangle}(c, \mathcal{T})$. They represent the anonymity in a target subset $\mathcal{T}$ in the same way that $\bar{S}_0(c, T)$ and $\bar{S}_{\langle - \rangle}(c, T)$ do for the whole tree T. Their rate of decline is directly related to the branching factors. As anticipated, the remaining anonymity in case of Targeted Attacks depends heavily on the branching factors located in the tail of B. This means that maximizing $\bar{S}(c, T)$ and $\bar{S}(c, \mathcal{T})$ are indeed contradicting goals, and real-world assumptions regarding attackers will dictate where the emphasis should lie.

The Beye & Veugen trees perform well in terms of $\bar{S}_0(c, T)$ and $\bar{S}_{\langle-\rangle}(c, T)$, but not for $\bar{S}_0(c, \mathcal{T})$ and $\bar{S}_{\langle-\rangle}(c, \mathcal{T})$ with high side-channel knowledge and c values, as we expected.

The proposed *Hourglass* trees perform best in terms of $\bar{S}_0(c, \mathcal{T})$ and $\bar{S}_{\langle-\rangle}(c, \mathcal{T})$, but only with high side-channel knowledge and c values. Their performance in terms of $\bar{S}_0(c, T)$ and $\bar{S}_{\langle-\rangle}(c, T)$ is only slightly below that of Beye & Veugen trees. To summarize: if we expect heavy Targeted Attacks, Hourglass trees will provide prolonged protection, at only a small "cost" in overall anonymity in other attack scenarios.

Some possible directions for future work are:

- Better simulation of real-world scenarios, specifically side-channel knowledge and adversarial behavior. For example modeling non-continuous target sets, and realistically estimating the size of target sets, minimum and maximum values for c, and the amount and nature of side-channel knowledge available to adversaries.
- Given the trade-off between maximizing $\bar{S}(c, T)$ and $\bar{S}(c, \mathcal{T})$, find a way to prioritise between defending against targeted and general attacks, and design an algorithm to optimize trees accordingly.
- Look into new measures for anonymity which do not show absolute declines, but the ratio between current anonymity set size and the decline caused by the next tag being compromised. This would fit the idea that a decline in set size from 1,000 to 999 does not have the same impact as going from a set of size 2 to having no anonymity at all.

References

1. Avoine, G., Buttyán, L., Holczer, T., Vajda, I.: Group-based private authentication. In: IEEE International Symposium on a World of Wireless, Mobile and Multimedia Networks, pp. 1–6 (2007)
2. Avoine, G., Dysli, E., Oechslin, P.: Reducing Time Complexity in RFID Systems. In: Preneel, B., Tavares, S. (eds.) SAC 2005. LNCS, vol. 3897, pp. 291–306. Springer, Heidelberg (2006)
3. Beye, M., Veugen, T.: Improved Anonymity for Key-trees. Cryptology ePrint Archive (2011)
4. Buttyán, L., Holczer, T., Vajda, I.: Optimal Key-Trees for Tree-Based Private Authentication. In: Danezis, G., Golle, P. (eds.) PET 2006. LNCS, vol. 4258, pp. 332–350. Springer, Heidelberg (2006)
5. Damgård, I., Pedersen, M.Ø.: RFID Security: Tradeoffs between Security and Efficiency. Cryptology ePrint Archive, Report 2006/234 (2006)
6. Díaz, C.: Anonymity Metrics Revisited. In: Dolev, S., Ostrovsky, R., Pfitzmann, A. (eds.) Anonymous Communication and its Applications. Dagstuhl Seminar Proceedings, vol. 05411, Internationales Begegnungs- und Forschungszentrum fuer Informatik (IBFI), Schloss Dagstuhl (2006)
7. Flajolet, P., Gardy, D., Thimonier, L.: Birthday paradox, coupon collectors, caching algorithms and self-organizing search. Discrete Appl. Math. 39(3), 207–229 (1992)

8. Köpf, B., Basin, D.A.: An information-theoretic model for adaptive side-channel attacks. In: ACM Conference on Computer and Communications Security, pp. 286–296 (2007)

9. Molnar, D., Wagner, D.: Privacy and security in library RFID: issues, practices, and architectures. In: CCS 2004: Proceedings of the 11th ACM Conference on Computer and Communications Security, pp. 210–219. ACM, New York (2004)

10. Nohara, Y., Nakamura, T., Baba, K., Inoue, S., Yasuura, H.: Unlinkable identification for large-scale rfid systems. Information and Media Technologies 1(2), 1182–1190 (2006)

11. Nohl, K., Evans, D.: Quantifying Information Leakage in Tree-Based Hash Protocols (Short Paper). In: Ning, P., Qing, S., Li, N. (eds.) ICICS 2006. LNCS, vol. 4307, pp. 228–237. Springer, Heidelberg (2006)

12. Pfitzmann, A., Köhntopp, M.: Anonymity, Unobservability, and Pseudonymity - A Proposal for Terminology. In: Federrath, H. (ed.) Designing Privacy Enhancing Technologies. LNCS, vol. 2009, pp. 1–9. Springer, Heidelberg (2001)

Analyzing the Hardware Costs of Different Security-Layer Variants for a Low-Cost RFID Tag*

Thomas Plos and Martin Feldhofer

Institute for Applied Information Processing and Communications (IAIK),
Graz University of Technology, Inffeldgasse 16a, 8010 Graz, Austria
{Thomas.Plos,Martin.Feldhofer}@iaik.tugraz.at

Abstract. Radio-frequency identification (RFID) technology is the enabler for the future Internet of Things (IoT) where security will play an important role. In this work, we evaluate the costs of adding different security-layer variants that are based on symmetric cryptography to a low-cost RFID tag. In contrast to related work, we do not only consider the costs of the cryptographic-algorithm implementation, but also the costs that relate to protocol handling of the security layer. Further we show that using a tag architecture based on a low-resource 8-bit microcontroller is highly advantageous. Such an approach is not only flexibility but also allows combining the implementation of protocol and cryptographic algorithm on the microcontroller. Expensive resources like memory can be easily reused, lowering the overall hardware costs. We have synthesized the security-enabled tag for a 130 nm CMOS technology, using the cryptographic algorithms AES and NOEKEON to demonstrate the effectiveness of our approach. Average power consumption of the microcontroller is 2 µW at a clock frequency of 106 kHz. Hardware costs of the security-layer variants range from about 1100 GEs using NOEKEON to 4500 GEs using AES.

Keywords: Low-cost RFID tag, 8-bit microcontroller, AES, NOEKEON, security layer, low power consumption.

1 Introduction

Over the last years, radio-frequency identification (RFID) technology has found its way into many applications of our daily life. The integration of RFID functionality into the latest smart phones (*e.g.* Nexus S, Blackberry Bold 9900) emphasizes the relevance of this technology. An upcoming application that relies on RFID technology is the Internet of Things (IoT). The vision of the future IoT is that every object has communication capabilities by equipping it with

---

* This work has been supported by the Austrian Government through the research program FIT-IT Trust in IT Systems under the Project Number 820843 (Project CRYPTA) and by the European Commission through the ICT programme under contract ICT-2007-216676 (ECRYPT II).

M. Rajarajan et al. (Eds.): SecureComm 2011, LNICST 96, pp. 426–435, 2012.
© Institute for Computer Sciences, Social Informatics and Telecommunications Engineering 2012

an RFID tag. An important aspect of the IoT is security [5]. Equipping every object with a tag presumes that they are cheap in price, making the integration of security a challenging task.

A typical RFID system mainly consists of three components: a back-end database, a reader, and one or more tags. The reader is connected to the back-end database and communicates with the tags contactlessly by means of a radio-frequency (RF) field. A tag is a small microchip attached to an antenna that receives its data and probably the clock signal from the RF field emitted by the reader. So-called passive tags also receive their power from the RF field.

The emergence of the IoT will not only pave the way for new applications but will also require to have additional functionality available on the tags. Such additional functionality comprises for example file management and security features, which increases the control complexity on the tag. Today's RFID tags use state machines fixed in hardware for handling their control tasks. As soon as the control complexity increases, the state-machine approach is no longer practical and even inefficient. Using a microcontroller approach instead that is more flexible seems to be favorable [13, 14]. Having a microcontroller on the tag for handling the control tasks, allows reusing it for computing cryptographic algorithms that are necessary for the security features.

Our contribution in this paper is twofold and deals with the integration of security on low-cost RFID tags. Firstly, we analyze the benefits of having a combined implementation of protocol handling and cryptographic algorithm on a microcontroller. We demonstrate this by using a synthesizable 8-bit microcontroller that is optimized for low-resource usage. Secondly, we define three different security-layer variants using the block ciphers AES and NOEKEON and evaluate the hardware costs introduced by them. In contrast to related work, not only the costs of the cryptographic-algorithm implementation alone are considered, but also the costs that arise from protocol handling of the security layer. Our results underline that protocol handling constitutes a significant cost factor and must not be neglected.

The remainder of this paper is structured as follows. In Section 2 we present a system overview of our low-cost tag. Section 3 gives details about the deployed security-layer variants and Section 4 describes the concept for realizing them on the tag. The implementation results are provided in Section 5. Conclusions are drawn in Section 6.

2   System Overview

RFID tags consist of a small microchip attached to an antenna. The microchip contains an analog front-end and a digital part. Complexity of the digital part ranges from simple state machines with a small EEPROM for storing its unique identifier (UID), to contactless smart cards with powerful microcontrollers and special coprocessors. Powerful microcontrollers as they are found in contactless smart cards are not suitable for our low-cost tag. They consume too much power and require too much hardware resources. Hence, we are using a self-designed

8-bit microcontroller for our tag that is optimized for low-resource usage. A preliminary version of the microcontroller has been published in [12].

Our tag uses the ISO14443 standard for communication and operates in the high frequency range at a carrier frequency of 13.56 MHz. Low-level functionality is implemented according to ISO14443-3 [6]. High-level functionality is implemented according to ISO14443-4 [9] and uses a block-transmission protocol for exchanging application data as specified in ISO7816-4 [7]. The digital part of our tag mainly consists of five components: the framing logic, the low-resource 8-bit microcontroller, the bus arbiter, the EEPROM, and the true-random number generator (TRNG). The framing logic is connected to the analog front-end and provides a byte interface to the microcontroller. Low-level commands that are time critical are directly handled by the framing logic, commands on higher level are forwarded to the microcontroller. The 8-bit microcontroller is the central part of our security-enabled tag and controls all other components of the digital part through an Advanced Microcontroller Bus Architecture (AMBA) Advanced Peripheral Bus (APB) [1]. The APB is managed by the bus arbiter.

High-level protocol functionality of the tag, including commands for security and file-management operations, as well as the cryptographic algorithm itself are entirely implemented in the program memory of the microcontroller. Hence, there is no dedicated coprocessor that handles encryption or decryption of data as typically found in the design of security-enabled tags. Random data that is required for security operations is generated within the TRNG and transferred to the memory of the microcontroller over the APB. The EEPROM is divided into files and is used for storing configuration data of the tag, the UID, the cipher key, and user data. Files are handled through file-management operations that allow selecting a file, reading from a file, or writing to a file. Depending on the file, different access rights are granted.

3   Security Layer

Two security services have been selected for implementation on our tag to quantify the costs of adding security functionality. The two security services are tag authentication and reader authentication. Tag authentication ensures originality of the tag to prevent simple cloning of. Reader authentication ensures originality of the reader to restrict access to certain resources on the tag.

The security services are based on a challenge-response protocol using symmetric cryptography as defined in ISO9798-2 [8]. We have selected two different cryptographic algorithms for the security services: AES [11] and NOEKEON [2]. Both algorithms are block ciphers with a block size of $n = 128$ bits. Selecting two different block ciphers allows analyzing their influence on the overall implementation costs. AES has been chosen because it is standardized and provides high security. NOEKEON has been selected since it provides a good trade off between security and resource usage (encryption and decryption function of NOEKEON can be implemented with very little overhead). Using symmetric cryptography requires that reader and tag share a secret key K. The key can be stored on

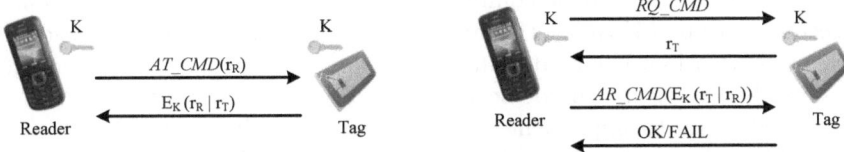

Fig. 1. Tag authentication   **Fig. 2.** Reader authentication

the tag, for example, during a personalization phase that is performed within a protected environment (*i.e.* it can be assumed that there is no adversary).

Tag Authentication. The basic principle of tag authentication is illustrated in Figure 1. The reader sends a randomly-selected challenge r_R with a length of $\frac{n}{2}$ bits through a tag-authenticate command (AT_CMD) to the tag. After receiving r_R from the reader, the tag generates itself a random number r_T of the same length, and encrypts the concatenation of the two random numbers $r_R \mid r_T$ under the secret key K. The encrypted value is then sent to the reader, which can decrypt it with its secret key. If both reader and tag use the same secret key, the decrypted value will contain the random number r_R that has initially been selected by the reader, and the tag is treated as authentic.

Reader Authentication. The second security services is reader authentication, which is depicted in Figure 2. The reader sends a request command (RQ_CMD) to the tag, which in turn generates a random number r_T with a length of $\frac{n}{2}$ bits that is transmitted to the reader. It is important to note that the tag has to store r_T internally to be able to verify later whether the reader is authentic or not (consumes $\frac{n}{2}$ bits of memory). After receiving r_T the reader generates its own random number r_R (also with a length of $\frac{n}{2}$ bits), and encrypts the concatenation of the two random values $r_T \mid r_R$ (position of random numbers is interchanged compared to tag authentication) using its secret key K. As next step, the encrypted value is transmitted through a reader-authenticate command (AR_CMD) to the tag, which decrypts the value using its secret key. When both reader and tag use the same secret key K, the decrypted value will contain the random number r_T initially selected by the tag, and the reader is treated as authentic. Alternatively, the reader can also decrypt $r_T \mid r_R$ instead of encrypting it. This has the advantage that the tag only needs to support encryption and not encryption and decryption, which makes for block ciphers like AES a significant difference in terms of resource usage. The tag finalizes the authentication step by sending a message to the reader with the status of the authentication process (OK or $FAIL$).

Security-Layer Variants. For a detailed analysis of the costs caused by adding a security layer to our tag, three security-layer variants are considered. The first variant (named *Variant 1* in the following) only supports tag authentication. Thus, the tag needs to implement the encryption function of the block cipher and to handle one additional command. This is the least-expensive scenario. The second variant (*Variant 2*) realizes both services tag authentication and reader authentication. For reader authentication, the alternative method previously described is used, where the reader decrypts the value $r_T \mid r_R$. Hence, the tag needs only to implement the encryption function of the block cipher. Three additional reader commands have to be handled by the tag and memory for storing r_T inside the tag has to be provided. The third security-layer variant (*Variant 3*) is the most expensive one. Tag and reader authentication are supported. As in case of *Variant 2*, three additional reader commands need to be handled and memory inside the tag has to be reserved for storing r_T. However, the important difference to *Variant 2* is that the reader-authentication approach is used that requires the tag to support also the decryption function of the block cipher. In order to prevent potential attacks on protocol level such as reader-impersonation, every tag should use a different secret key K. Further, the tag accepts an *AR_CMD* only if it directly follows a *RQ_CMD* (*i.e.* using an *AT_CMD* after the *RQ_CMD* aborts the reader-authentication process).

4   Concept for Implementing the Security-Layer Variants

The way we implement the security-layer variants on our tag differs from the traditional approach typically found in related work, where protocol handling and cryptographic algorithm are implemented separately. There, protocol handling is implemented in a control state machine fixed in hardware and the cryptographic algorithm is implemented within a coprocessor that is highly optimized for low-resource usage. A schematic view of this approach is given in Figure 3. As already shown in various publications, for example in the work of Yan *et al.* [13] and Yu *et al.* [14], using a programable controller for handling complex control tasks on RFID tags is advantageous. The design becomes more flexible, easier to maintain, and faster to adapt.

Our tag uses also a programable approach for handling the complex parts of the protocol (high-level protocol). Complex parts of the protocol include for example: reconstructing chained reader commands, handling file-access commands, and managing configuration-parameters of the tag. Moreover, when adding a security layer, control complexity further increases. Generation of random values has to be triggered and the values have to be transferred to concerning locations in memory. Encryption and decryption of data has to be initiated and results have to be checked. Combining the security layer with existing tag functionality like handling file-access commands and managing configuration parameters also increases control complexity. Hence, we only use a fixed state machine in hardware (called framing logic) for time-critical commands that require low control complexity (low-level protocol) and whose functionality is typically fixed. Complex protocol parts are processed by an 8-bit microcontroller optimized for low-resource usage, which can be reused for computing cryptographic algorithms as well. A schematic view of this combined approach is presented in Figure 4. The program code of the microcontroller contains both the implementation of

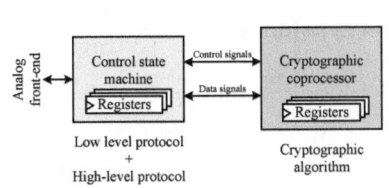

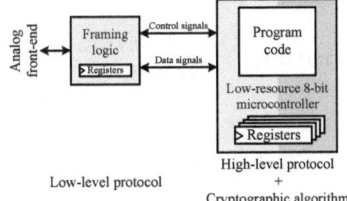

Fig. 3. Traditional approach where protocol handling and cryptographic algorithm are implemented separately

Fig. 4. Combined approach where high-level protocol and cryptographic algorithm are handled by a low-resource microcontroller

the high-level protocol and the cryptographic algorithm. Another benefit of this combined approach is the easier and more efficient reuse of costly resources like memory (registers of the microcontroller).

5   Implementation Results

We have implemented the three security-layer variants previously described using the block ciphers AES and NOEKEON, respectively. For each block cipher, various versions with different optimization targets are used. Implementation results are given for a 130 nm CMOS process technology [3] after place and route using Cadence RTL compiler and involve all components of the tag's digital part excluding TRNG and EEPROM.

Central element of our tag is a synthesizable 8-bit microcontroller optimized for low-resource usage. The microcontroller is based on a Harvard architecture using an 8-bit wide data memory (register file) and a 16-bit wide program memory (program ROM). Depending on the targeted application, up to 64 registers can be included into the register file (specified during synthesis). The program ROM is realized as look-up table and contains the instructions that the microcontroller should execute. Size of the program ROM is also flexible and can be at maximum 128 kB. Synthesizing the microcontroller core (control unit, program counter, and arithmetic-logic unit (ALU)) without register file and program ROM for a 130 nm process technology results in a chip area of 1067 GEs. A preliminary version of the microcontroller has been published in [12] to which we refer for more details.

5.1   Implementation Results of AES and NOEKEON

The two block ciphers AES and NOEKEON have been used for realizing the security-layer variants described in Section 3. For each cipher, three different optimization targets have been used: *fast*, *balanced*, and *small*. The target *fast* aims for shortest execution time of the cipher by using techniques like code duplication and loop unrolling, *balanced* provides a good trade off between execution

Table 1. Implementation results of the block ciphers AES and NOEKEON

Algorithm	Optimization target	Encryption	Decryption	Code size	Utilized registers
		[clock cycles]	[clock cycles]	[bytes]	-
AES	fast	3149	4570	2034	39
	balanced	3369	5101	1816	39
	small	5104	8286	1602	39
AES (encr. only)	fast	3070	n/a	1050	39
	small	4270	n/a	858	39
NOEKEON	fast	3817	3785	980	35
	balanced	5839	5824	532	25
	small	7563	7546	414	23
NOEKEON (encr. only)	fast	3805	n/a	652	35
	small	7553	n/a	382	23

time and code size, and *small* is optimized for minimal code size where as many operations as possible are handled through function calls that can be reused. Encryption function and decryption function of both ciphers are implemented. Moreover, for security-layer variants *Variant 1* and *Variant 2*, also encryption-only versions of the two algorithms are realized (with targets *fast* and *small*). Data that needs to be encrypted or decrypted is located in the register file of the microcontroller. The cipher key is stored in the EEPROM and has to be loaded each time during processing of data.

A summary of the implementation results is presented in Table 1. The AES implementations used in this work are similar to the ones published in [12]. In contrast to AES, NOEKEON requires only bit-wise Boolean operations and cyclic shifts which can be implemented with compact code size. No large look-up tables are required. We are using NOEKEON in indirect mode that applies an additional key schedule to increase resistance against related-key attacks. The key schedule in indirect mode can be precomputed, since the operation is independent of the processed data and all rounds use the same key. Hence, a lot of computation time can be saved when storing the precomputed working key in the EEPROM instead of the original cipher key.

5.2   Implementation Results of the Security-Layer Variants

Adding security to our tag influences mainly register-file size and ROM size of the microcontroller. For simplification, costs introduced by the TRNG and through storing additional data like the cipher key in the EEPROM are neglected. These costs are independent of the selected security-layer variant and the chosen block cipher.

Our tag with advanced file-management functionality utilizes 45 8-bit registers in the register file and 2214 bytes of code in the ROM for high-level protocol handling. Synthesizing the microcontroller with this configuration for our 130 nm target technology results in a chip size of roughly 9 kGEs (after place and route).

Only 9 of the 45 registers are permanently used for handling the protocol (*e.g.* to store status of tag and parameters). The remaining 36 registers are used for temporarily storing data (*e.g.* to reassemble chained reader commands) and can be reused when computing cryptographic algorithms. Since the computation of AES on our microcontroller requires 39 registers, only 3 additional registers are necessary when combining the computation of protocol and cryptographic algorithm. When using NOEKEON, no additional registers are necessary. Even the "largest" NOEKEON version consumes only 35 registers and fits within the 36 registers that can be reused from protocol handling.

When selecting a security layer based on *Variant 2* or *Variant 3* that involves reader authentication, additional registers are required for storing the random number r_T. Since r_T has a length of $\frac{n}{2} = 64$ bits, 8 additional registers are necessary. As a result, the total number of utilized registers increases to a maximum of 56 registers when reader authentication is supported and AES is used, and 53 registers when NOEKEON is used.

For determining the overall costs of the different security-layer variants, not only the size of the register file but also the size of the ROM has to be considered. ROM size is influenced by the security-layer variants through two parameters: the implementation of the block cipher and handling of the additional reader commands. Information about the code size of the different block-cipher implementations have already been given in Section 5.1. The required code size for handling the additional reader commands depends on the security-layer variant and ranges from 250 bytes for *Variant 1* to 460 bytes for *Variant 2*.

Synthesizing our tag with the different security-layer variants for a 130 nm process technology gives actual numbers about the area requirements in hardware. The register file of the microcontroller is built up with latches to minimize chip area. The ROM of the microcontroller is implemented as look-up table which gets mapped by the synthesis tool to an unstructured mass of standard cells. Detailed synthesis results after place and route obtained with Cadence RTL compiler are provided in Table 2. The least-expensive security-layer variant, which is *Variant 1* with the code-size optimized version of NOEKEON, results in an area overhead of 1074 GEs. The most-expensive security-layer variant, which is *Variant 3* with the speed-optimized version of AES, leads to an overhead of 4465 GEs.

When considering only the area requirement of the block-cipher implementation, AES encryption function and decryption function can be realized with 2772 GEs. Implementing the encryption-only version costs less than 1600 GEs. This is a consequence of heavily reusing registers that are normally utilized for handling the protocol. The so far smallest AES coprocessor implementation has been reported by Feldhofer *et al.* [4] and consumes about 3400 GEs. The smallest encryption-only version of AES, recently published by Moradi *et al.* [10], has a size of 2400 GEs. NOEKEON comes at much lower costs. The smallest version of NOEKEON containing encryption and decryption function counts 751 GEs. Comparison with related work is difficult since we could not find any published low-resource hardware implementation of NOEKEON.

Table 2. Overhead costs introduced by the different security-layer variants

Security layer		Protocol costs			Block-cipher costs			Total costs
Variant	Algorithm	Regi-sters	Code size	Total	Regi-sters	Code size	Total	
		-	[bytes]	[GEs]	-	[bytes]	[GEs]	[GEs]
	AES							
Variant 1	fast	0	250	**500**	3	1050	**1614**	**2115**
	small	0	250	**500**	3	858	**1517**	**2017**
Variant 2	fast	8	460	**1257**	3	1050	**1678**	**2935**
	small	8	460	**1257**	3	858	**1615**	**2872**
	fast	8	452	**1165**	3	2034	**3300**	**4465**
Variant 3	balanced	8	452	**1165**	3	1816	**2981**	**4146**
	small	8	452	**1165**	3	1602	**2772**	**3937**
	NOEKEON							
Variant 1	fast	0	250	**500**	0	652	**887**	**1387**
	small	0	250	**500**	0	382	**574**	**1074**
Variant 2	fast	8	460	**1283**	0	652	**1041**	**2323**
	small	8	460	**1283**	0	382	**660**	**1943**
	fast	8	452	**1191**	0	980	**1545**	**2736**
Variant 3	balanced	8	452	**1191**	0	532	**883**	**2074**
	small	8	452	**1191**	0	414	**751**	**1942**

Costs introduced by handling the additional reader commands and potentially storing the random number r_T range from 500 GEs to 1283 GEs. Although often neglected in related work, handling the protocol part of the security layer constitutes a significant portion of the overall costs and can even be the dominating factor. An example is *Variant 2* with the code-size optimized version of NOEKEON, where 66 % of the overhead costs are caused by the implementation of the protocol.

Simulating our microcontroller with the most-expensive security-layer variant (*Variant 3* with speed-optimized version of AES) gives an average power consumption of 2 μW at a clock frequency of 106 kHz and a voltage of 1.2 V. This value is very low since the microcontroller is highly optimized for low power consumption. Another advantage that arises from the combined implementation of protocol handling and cryptographic algorithm on the microcontroller is that no additional power is consumed for handling the security layer. When using a dedicated coprocessor, additional power would be required during computation of the cryptographic algorithm.

6   Conclusion

In this work we have evaluated the hardware overhead that arises from integrating different security-layer variants into a low-cost RFID tag. The security-layer variants are based on the cryptographic algorithms AES and NOEKEON.

We have used a combined implementation of high-level protocol handling and cryptographic algorithm on a low-resource 8-bit microcontroller. This combined approach provides high flexibility and allows reusing registers of the microcontroller that are only temporarily used during protocol handling. In that way AES encryption function can be implemented with an overhead of about 1600 GEs and NOEKEON encryption function with an overhead of about 600 GEs when using a 130 nm CMOS technology. The microcontroller has a power consumption of 2 μW at a clock frequency of 106 kHz. Total costs of the security-layer variants range from 1100 GEs to 4500 GEs and consider also the protocol handling of the security layer. Protocol handling can make up a significant part of the total costs and must not be neglected.

References

1. ARM Ltd. AMBA Advanced Microcontroller Bus Architecture Specification (1997), http://www.arm.com
2. Daemen, J., Peeters, M., Assche, G.V., Rijmen, V.: Nessie proposal: NOEKEON (2000), http://gro.noekeon.org/Noekeon-spec.pdf
3. Faraday Technology Corporation. Faraday FSA0A_C 0.13 μm ASIC Standard Cell Library (2004), http://www.faraday-tech.com
4. Feldhofer, M., Wolkerstorfer, J., Rijmen, V.: AES Implementation on a Grain of Sand. IEEE Proceedings on Information Security (1) (October 2005)
5. Giusto, D., Iera, A., Morabito, G., Atzori, L.: The Internet of Things - 20th Tyrrhenian Workshop on Digital Communications. Springer, Heidelberg (2010)
6. International Organization for Standardization (ISO). ISO/IEC 14443-3: Identification Cards - Contactless Integrated Circuit(s) Cards - Proximity Cards - Part3: Initialization and Anticollision (2001)
7. ISO/IEC. 7816-4: Information technology - Identification cards - Integrated circuit(s) cards with contacts - Part 4: Interindustry commands for interchange (1995)
8. ISO/IEC. 9798-2: Information technology – Security techniques – Entity authentication – Mechanisms using symmetric encipherment algorithms (1999)
9. ISO/IEC. 14443-4: Identification Cards - Contactless Integrated Circuit(s) Cards - Proximity Cards - Part4: Transmission Protocol (2008)
10. Moradi, A., Poschmann, A., Ling, S., Paar, C., Wang, H.: Pushing the Limits: A Very Compact and a Threshold Implementation of AES. In: Paterson, K.G. (ed.) EUROCRYPT 2011. LNCS, vol. 6632, pp. 69–88. Springer, Heidelberg (2011)
11. National Institute of Standards and Technology (NIST). FIPS-197: Advanced Encryption Standard (November 2001)
12. Plos, T., Groß, H., Feldhofer, M.: Implementation of Symmetric Algorithms on a Synthesizable 8-Bit Microcontroller Targeting Passive RFID Tags. In: Biryukov, A., Gong, G., Stinson, D.R. (eds.) SAC 2010. LNCS, vol. 6544, pp. 114–129. Springer, Heidelberg (2011)
13. Yan, H., Jianyun, H., Qiang, L., Hao, M.: Design of low-power baseband-processor for RFID tag. In: International Symposium on Applications and the Internet Workshops (SAINT 2006). IEEE Computer Society (January 2006)
14. Yu, Y., Yang, Y., Yan, N., Min, H.: A Novel Design of Secure RFID Tag Baseband. In: RFID Convocation (2007)

Preventing Secret Data Leakage from Foreign Mappings in Virtual Machines

Hanjun Gao[1], Lina Wang[1,2], Wei Liu[1], Yang Peng[1], and Hao Zhang[1]

[1] School of Computer Science, Wuhan University, Wuhan 430072, China
ghjwhu@sina.com
[2] The Key Laboratory of Aerospace Information and Trusted Computing,
Ministry of Education, Wuhan, 430072, China

Abstract. The foreign mapping mechanism of Xen is used in privileged virtual machines (VM) for platform management. With help of it, a privileged VM can map arbitrary machine frames of memory from a specific VM into its page tables. This leaves a vulnerability that malware may compromise the secrecy of normal VMs by exploiting the foreign mapping mechanism. To address this privacy exposure, we present a novel application's memory privacy protection (AMP^2) scheme by exploiting hypervisor. In AMP^2, an application can protect its memory privacy by registering its address space into hypervisor; before the application exists or cancels its protection, any foreign mapping to protected pages will be disabled. With these measures, AMP^2 prevents sensitive data leakage when malware attempts to eavesdrop them by exploiting foreign mapping. Finally, extensive experiments are performed to validate AMP^2. The experimental results show that AMP^2 achieves strong privacy resiliency while incurs only 2% extra overhead for CPU workloads.

Keywords: Direct Foreign mappings, Virtual machine, Hyprevisor, Privacy, Secrecy, Data leakage.

1 Introduction

In recent years, virtual machine monitors (VMMs, or hypervisor) have been widely adopted in modern computing systems, such as Xen[1], VMware[2] and KVM[3] etc. The distinguishing security features of hypervisor, especially in VM introspection (VMI), have aroused many researchers' attentions. For example, Livewire[4] proposes the concept of VM introspection and applies it in the field of intrusion detection. AntFarm[5], Xenprobes[6], XenAccess[7] and VMwall[8] incorporates VM introspection to monitor real-time memory status and disk activity of Guest OS, and consequently infer guest-internal events, such as running processes, file-system operation and network connections etc. VMwatcher[9] is implemented for detecting malwares and kernel rootkits, which are difficult to be done in conventional methods. SBCFI[10] is used to protect the control flow integrity of guest OS and improve its reliability and security. With the help of hypervisor, Lycosid[11], Patagonix[12] and Manitou[13] can effectively detect and

M. Rajarajan et al. (Eds.): SecureComm 2011, LNICST 96, pp. 436–445, 2012.
© Institute for Computer Sciences, Social Informatics and Telecommunications Engineering 2012

identify hidden processes.These efforts effectively exploit the fact that hypervisor can easily fetch memory pages from the target guest OS.

Related Work. In spite of various managemental gains as illustrated above due to the privileged ability in Xen hypervisor, we observe that it is also desirable to enforce some restrictions to this privilege to avoid misuse and/or abuse. In Xen hypervisor, any software running in the Dom0 use-space can obtain arbitrary memory pages by making direct foreign mappings. This non-restricted memory sharing mechanism may potentially undermine the privacy of guest OS. For instance, when a user logs in his bank account, his account's password will be temporarily stored somewhere in the memory, and malware residing in Dom0 may eavesdrop the password by performing direct foreign mappings. Murray*et al.* [14] suggested to remove all uses of the direct foreign mapping operation from Dom0 user-space to protect the privacy of virtual machine. Unfortunately, Dom0 is designed to serve as a managing domain, and a simple removal of all uses may undermine its availability and corrupt other security measures such as VM introspection which has been widely used to solve system security problems (e.g.,[4,5,6,7,8,9,10,11,12,13,15]).

Several efforts have been devoted to privacy protection of virtual machines without significantly undermining their availability. Yang and Shin proposed SP^3[16] which exploits hypervisor to prevent application information from unauthorized exposure and does not require the operating system to be trustable. And Chen et al[17] also proposed their scheme to protect the privacy and integiety of application data based on the same assumptions. However, if malware resides in Xen's privileged domain, it can still eavesdrops the application data by foreign mapping. Borders *etal.* proposed Storage Capsules [18] which allow users to view and edit sensitive files in a compromised machine without leaking confidential data. The key technique is to take a checkpoint of current system state and disable device output. When editing files and re-encrypting are done, the system is restored to original state and device output is resumed. However, this methodology leaves the gap that if storage capsules are equipped in Xen, malware residing in Dom0 can steal confidential data by foreign mapping.

Our Contributions. In this paper, we propose a novel scheme to protect application's memory privacy in DomU even when there are malwares attempting to eavesdrop them by direct foreign mappings. The scheme is called application's memory privacy protection (AMP^2) which is designed to mainly protect data resided in memory, such as decrypted secrets, password entered to login bank account etc. Whereas files stored on disk are out of our concern, because they can be properly protected via encryption. Compared to the SP^3 [16], the Overshadow[17] and the Storage Capsules [18] proposals, our methodology makes special efforts to protect secret data in the case that malware resides in privileged domain(Dom0) in Xen, which enables our scheme to be complementary to these above three proposals and to provide stronger privacy protection.To keep availability, instead of removing the foreign mappings as in the Murray *et al.* solution [14], our scheme restricted them in a way such that a memory page allocated to protected application is unable to be mapped by Dom0 or any other privileged domains. To this end, we present a kernel module to accept the request from the user-space and created a hypercall to send the protection request to the hypervisor. Also, we carefully strengthen the page table updating handler to intercept any mapping operation so that it can dynamically protect application's memory pages.

2 AMP^2 Scheme

In AMP^2, when an application needs to be protected, it issues the request to hypervisor. Hypervisor maintains a protected applications memory page counter table (AMPC table) which is used to keep the page counters registered by the application.[1] When foreign mapping to DomU's pages occur, hypervisor will look up AMPC table to get the counters and decide whether the foreign mapping can be done. At the same time, AMP^2 also maintains a foreign mapping tracking table (FMT table) to record all foreign mapping operations. If a memory page which has been mapped by foreign mapping is dynamically allocated to a protected application, the previous foreign mapping will be redirected to some other public page, such as shared info page etc, and the relevant entries in FMT table will be cleared too. Finally, AMP^2 must be aware of the events of application exiting, memory protection canceling and DomU destroying, and consequently update AMPC table lest legitimate foreign mapping cannot be performed.

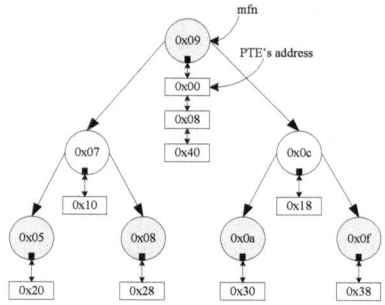

Fig. 1. Foreign mapping tracking table, FMT table

In the following, we illustrate with an example how AMP^2 works. It is assumed that Dom0 has first 4 page out of a total 16 ones and the rest belongs to DomU. AMP^2 intercepts all foreign mapping operations and maintains a FMT

---

[1] In our scheme, the AMPC table's size is proportional to that of machine memory, and one memory page correspond one entry in AMPC table. When a memory page is registered, the corresponding entry in AMPC table is increased by 1. It is possible that multiple processes sharing the same memory pages register its memory space for protection. In this case, the values of some entries are larger than one.

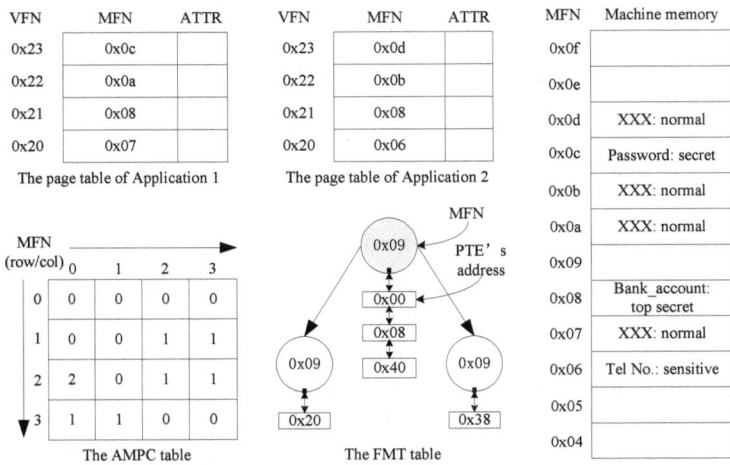

Fig. 2. AMP^2 example

table to record these operations, as shown in Figure 1. This FMT table shows that seven machine page frames in DomU have been mapped by Dom0 and these records are stored in a red-black tree, where the key of node represents the foreign mapped machine frame number (mfn). Taking the root as an example, the page frame 0x09 has been foreign mapped 3 times by Dom0, and the corresponding PTEs' machine addresses are 0x00, 0x08 and 0x40 respectively, all at page frame 0x0.Figure 2 shows the process that AMP^2 protects applications' memory pages when they apply protection to hypervisor. In the figure, there are two applications applying protection to the hypervisor. They occupy seven pages in total, the mfn of which are 0x6, 0x7, 0x8, 0xa, 0xb, 0xc and 0xd respectively. The corresponding entries in AMPC table are increased by 1, except 0x8, which is increased by 2 because it is occupied by two applications simultaneously. Then, AMP^2 look up FMT table to check whether these pages have been recorded. In our example, there are four pages having been foreign mapped, the mfn of which are 0x7, 0x8, 0xa, and 0xc, respectively. Base on the mfns, AMP^2 can quickly locate the target nodes and remove them from FMT table. Meantime, AMP^2 can easily get corresponding PTE's address and modify PTE to redirect to public page, such as shared info page etc.

3 AMP^2 Design

3.1 Restricted Foreign Mapping

When a foreign mapping opeartion occurs, AMP^2 captures it and parses the mapped machine page frame number (mfn) and the corresponding PTE's address. Then it checks whether the mapped page's counter in AMPC table is above zero or not, which shows that whether some applications have applied protection. If the counter is more than zero, AMP^2 fails this mapping request. Otherwise the mapping can be performed and the operation is recorded in FMT table. The reason to maintain FMT table is that, with FMT's help, AMP^2 can effectively redirect previous established foreign mappings when an application, which is not protected before, requests for protection.

3.2 Application Applying for Protection

In the hypervisor-based implementation, we define a hypercall for applications to issue protection requests.When AMP^2 is aware of the protection request, it firstly obtains the head of the list virtual memory area (that is mmap) and the page global directory (pgd) base on the PID of the application, and then parses the mfn of the occupied pages,including page directory, page table, and currently occupied machine frames. Secondly, AMP^2 updates AMPC table according to these mfns (The index of AMPC table is mfn, and the value of the table entry represents the counters). Because the request is for protection, the value of corresponding enntries is increased by 1.

In morden OS, the memory page is allocated to a process until it is actually needed. Therefore, AMP^2 will capture all the events of normal pages mapping in DomU, retrieve the page allocated to the protected application, and eventually register it for protection in the application's runtime. The detail is illustrated in section 4. At last, AMP^2 looks up FMT table to check whether there exists any recorded mapping. If a mapping is found in FMT table, AMP^2 will modify the mapping to redirect to the public page, such as shared info page which is designed for share infomation between Dom0 and DomU. Furthermore, any child process created by the protected application will also be automatically protected.

3.3 AMP^2 Page Table Updating

AMP^2 page table updating extends the interface of Xen's. We implement our checking logic by intercepting all Xen's page table updating routines. In these routines, the eventual control structure to be handled is a simple pair:$\langle ptr, val \rangle$,the ptr is machine address of PTE, and the val is new contents (the key is mfn) of PTE. Figure 3 illustrates the AMP^2 page table updating framework. It first checks the P (present) bit of val to determine that the updating is mapping or unmapping. If it is a mapping operation, and even is a foreign mapping operation, AMP^2 will ensure that the counter of entry whose index is val.mfn in AMPC table is equal 0. Only in this case, the foreign mapping can be performed and meantime the operation will be recorded in FMT table.(In the opposite case, the foreign mapping failed.) Otherwise, if it is a normal guest domain page mapping, AMP^2 will check whether the ptr (that is machine address of PTE) locates in a protected process's address space or not. If it does, AMP^2 will increase the page's counter by 1 in AMPC table based on the val.mfn. In the meantime, AMP^2 checks against FMT table to redirect previous foreign mapping to a public page if this memory page had been foreign mapped before.

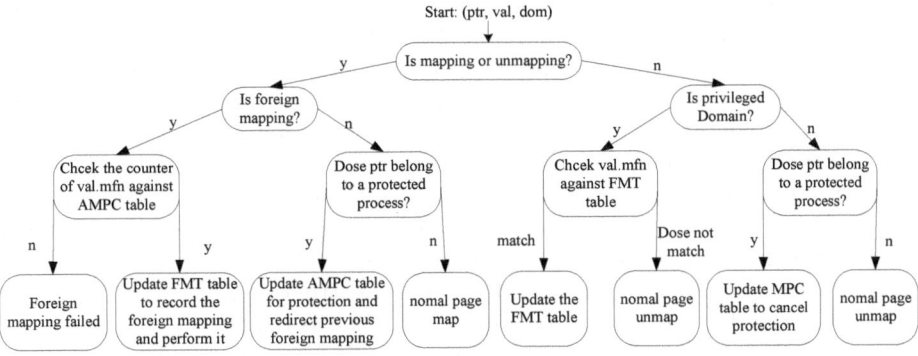

Fig. 3. AMP^2 page table updating

On the other hand, if the updating is an umapping operation, and it is from a privileged domain, AMP^2 will check the val.mfn against FMT table. If a record is found, it is shown that this is a foreign unmapping operation. And AMP^2 will clear the relevant entry in FMT table based on the mfn. Otherwise, if the unmapping is from the guest domain and the address of PTE belongs to a protected application, AMP^2 will update AMPC table to cancel the memory page's protection.

4   AMP^2 Implementation

In order to accept the request for protection from the application, we provide a hypercall and a kernel module. User explicitly issues a register request, which triggers the kernel module. Handler in the module parses corresponding page tables based on the pid, wraps up all mfns as a request, and invokes the hypercall to pass the request to AMP^2. It increases the corresponding entries in AMPC table and check whether the pages for protection have been mapped by Dom0 in the past. If it is, AMP^2 will redirect the foreign mapping to other public page such as shared info page in read-only mode for security.

Due to on-demand paging, it is insufficient to only protect the pages which the application actively registers. We add codes into the Xen's handler responsible for PTE updates to protect the memory page which is dynamically allocated to the application. In the para-virtualization, OS can update a PTE either by using hypercall, or with the help of writeable page table. Either way, the hypervisor can intercept PTE updates. It is no doubt that hypercall always trap into hypervisor by definition. Meantime, a modification to a PTE incurs a page fault which always traps into hypervior too. Therefore, we modify the Xen's handler for PTE updates to achieve our goal. The relevant modified handlers include do_mmu_update, do_update_va_mapping, and ptwr_emulated_update.

In AMP^2, besides explicitly canceling its protection by issuing a hypercall, the exit of a protected application also results in canceling protection. Therefore,

AMP^2 needs to intercept page unmaping events for lifting the page's protection. Unfortunately, normal page unmapping goes through a fast path for the sake of optimization and never traps into hypervisor. The only exception is that the page unmapping caused by foreign mappings. The reason is that Xen modifies the mm_struct.context of an application to add a has_foreign_mappings field in it. When the page unmapping occurs, the system call will check whether the field is set. If it not, hypervisor will unpin the page table. It means that modifying the page table will not trigger any page fault. If it is set, clearing the PTE will arouse the page fault and the hypervisor will emulate this direct page table write. Therefore, we also add an is_protected filed in that structure (mm_struct.context) and modify the do_exit handler to implement our check logic.

Finally, when a domain exits, the relevant resources allocated to it will be recycled, and the protection about an application in the very domain will also consequently be lifted. Therefore, we modifiy the resources recycling routine, especially the memory pages recycling handler: relinquish_memory, to clear corresponding entries in AMPC table to lift protection when a domain exit.

5   Evaluation

In this section, we first analytically examine the security guarantees provided by AMP^2. Then we measure the performance overhead. The machine used in our evaluation has a 3.0 GHZ Core 2 processor with 1GB of RAM. The version of hypervisor is Xen 3.3.0, and the kernel's version is XenoLinux 2.6.18. There are two virtual machine instances(one is Dom0, the other is DomU). Xen allocates 512 MB of RAM to Dom0, and the rest is allocated to DomU.

5.1   Security Analysis

As memtioned above, FMT table and AMPC table are key data structures to achieve our goal. Therefore, the integrity of them(including codes of AMP^2) should be guaranteed. According to our design, all of them are kept in hypervisor space, which runs in the highest privileged level. And there is no supported method to modify the Xen code in runtime even taking control over Dom0. In other words, it is difficult to bypass AMP^2 by patching out its check codes or tampering data structures without recompiling the Xen. Although there was a backdoor to subvert hyperviosr by overwriting Xen code and data structures by conducting DMA to Xen's memory[19], and it is indeed a real threat to AMP^2. Fortunately, however, Wang[20] proposed HyperSafe that endows Xen hypervisors with a unique self-protection capability to provide lifetime controlflow integrity. With the help of HyperSafe, the integrity of AMP^2 can be effectively protected.

In real usage, whenever an application needs to make sensitive operations, it just applies a protection request to AMP^2. And before the application exists or cancels its protection, any foreign mapping to protected pages will be disabled. And the pages which are foreign mapped before will be redirected. Therefore, AMP^2 don't detect whether malware is running in Dom0 or hides its presence.

5.2   Performance Evaluation

To evaluate the performance overhead introduced by AMP^2, we measured the runtime overhead with some CPU and memory intensive workloads, including two programs from the SPEC CPU 2000 integer benchmarks, and two other real world applications.

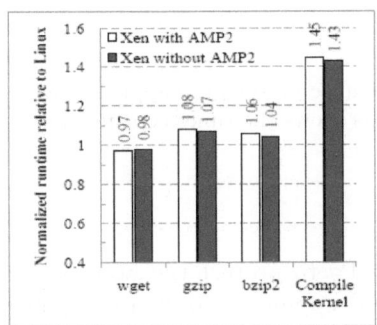

Fig. 4. Applications performance normalized to native Linux. (The numbers on top of bars represent runtime of applications normalized to native Linux without Xen).

We tested the application's performance in the guest OS in three scenarios: native Linux, Xen with and without AMP^2. First, we executed these applications in native Linux and measured the runtime. Then, these applications were executed in Xen without AMP^2. Last, we measured the runtime overhead in the Xen with AMP^2. The final performance result is shown in Figure 4. The performance overhead is presented as a relative runtime normalized to native Linux. Since these applications run in the guest OS, the mainly performance penalty comes from PTE updating, maintaining AMPC table and checking against FMT table. Therefore, the performance of an application with a frequent page table updating will be influenced dramatically. Overall, AMP^2 increases applications execution time by only 2% CPU workloads.

Another possible performance penalty may exist in the foreign mapping in Dom0. When the foreign mapping request is sent to hypervisor, AMP^2 will search FMT table, and decide whether the mapping can be performed. And if the mapping is valid, AMP^2 will record the pair of pte's address and target mfn. Figure 5 shows the times consumed to execute foreign mapping in Dom0. We tested 16 sets of data in total, ranging from two pages to thirty-two pages, and compared the consumed time. As the mapped pages increase, the size of FMT table and the time consumed to manipulate it increase too. However, using foreign mapping to map large amount pages is not always needed except for security reasons, so we can tolerate the performance penalty in most circumstances.

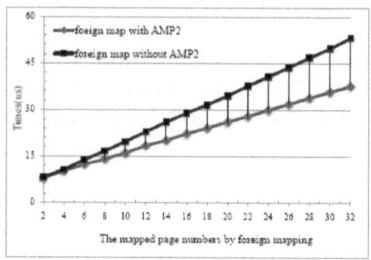

Fig. 5. Normalized performance of foreign mapping (The x-axis shows the page numbers mapped, and the y-axis shows the times consumed to complete foreign mappings)

6   Conclusion

This paper proposed AMP^2 to protect the application's memory data privacy from malware's evil eavesdropping via foreign mapping. When foreign mappings to DomU pages occur, hypervisor will decide whether the mappings can be done based on security requirements. We detailed the modifications and extensions made to hypervisor. To protect the target application, we presented a kernel module to accept the request from the user-space and created a hypercall to send the protection request to hypervisor. Finally, we strengthened the page table updating handler to intercept any mapping operation so that it can dynamically protect application's memory pages. Extensive practical experiments were carried out and the results shows that AMP^2 can successfully protect the memory data privacy without significant performance penalties.

Acknowledgement. The authors would like to thank my colleagues and the anonymous reviewers for their insightful feedback. This work is supported by National Natural Science Foundation of China under Grant No. 60970114.

References

1. Barham, P., Dragovic, B., Fraser, K., et al.: Xen and the Art of Virtualization. In: 19th ACM Symposium on Operating Systems Principles (SOSP), Bolton Landing, pp. 164–177 (2003)
2. Waldspurger, C.A.: Memory resource management in VMware ESX Server. In: 5th Symposium on Operating Systems Design and Implementation (OSDI), New York, pp. 181–194 (2002)
3. Kivity, A., Kamay, Y., Laor, D., Lublin, U., Liguori, A.: kvm: the Linux virtual machine monitor. In: The 2007 Ottawa Linux Symposium, Ottawa, pp. 225–230 (2007)
4. Garfinkel, T., Rosenblum, M.: A Virtual machine Introspection-Based Architecture for Intrusion Detection. In: 10th Network and Distributed System Security Symposium (NDSS), San Diego, pp. 191–206 (2003)

5. Jones, S.T., Arpaci-Dusseau, A.C., Arpaci-Dusseau, R.H.: Antfarm: Tracking processes in a virtual machine environment. In: Proceedings of the 2006 Annual USENIX Technical Conference, Boston, pp. 1–14 (2006)
6. Quynh, N.A., Suzaki, K.: Xenprobe: A lightweight user-space probing framework for xen virtual machine. In: USENIX Annual Technical Conference, San Diego (2007)
7. Payne, B.D., Carbone, M., Lee, W.: Secure and Flexible Monitoring of Virtual machines. In: The Annual Computer Security Applications Conference (ACSAC), Miami Beach, pp. 385–397 (2007)
8. Srivastava, A., Giffin, J.: Tamper-Resistant, Application-Aware Blocking of Malicious Network Connections. In: Lippmann, R., Kirda, E., Trachtenberg, A. (eds.) RAID 2008. LNCS, vol. 5230, pp. 39–58. Springer, Heidelberg (2008)
9. Jiang, X., Wang, X., Xu, D.: Stealthy Malware Detection through VMM-based "out-of-the-box" Semantic View Reconstruction. In: 14th ACM Conference on Computer and Communications Security (CCS), Alexandria (2007)
10. Petroni, N.L., Hicks, M.: Automated Detection of Persistent Kernel Control-Flow Attacks. In: 14th ACM Conference on Computer and Communications Security, CCS, Alexandria (2007)
11. Jones, S.T., Arpaci-Dusseau, A.C., Arpaci-Dusseau, R.H.: VMM-based hidden process detection and identification using Lycosid. In: International Conference on Virtual Execution Environments (VEE), New York, pp. 91–100 (2008)
12. Litty, L., Lagar-Cavilla, H.A., Lie, D.: Hypervisor support for identifying covertly executing binaries. In: 17th Conference on Security Symposium (USENIX SECURITY), San Jose, pp. 243–258 (2008)
13. Litty, L., Lie, D.: Manitou: A layer-below approach to fighting malware. In: The Workshop on Architectural and System Support for Improving Software Dependability (ASID), pp. 6–11, San Jose (2006)
14. Murray, D.G., Milos, G., Hand, S.: Improving Xen Security through Disaggregation. In: 4th International Conference on Virtual Execution Environments (VEE), New York, pp. 151–160 (2008)
15. Jiang, X., Wang, X.: "Out-of-the-Box" Monitoring of VM-Based High-Interaction Honeypots. In: Kruegel, C., Lippmann, R., Clark, A. (eds.) RAID 2007. LNCS, vol. 4637, pp. 198–218. Springer, Heidelberg (2007)
16. Yang, J., Shin, K.: Using hypervisor to provide Data Secrey for User Applications on a Per-Page Basis. In: Proc. of the 4th International Conference on Virtual Execution Environments (VEE), New York, pp. 71–80 (2008)
17. Chen, X., Garfinkel, T., Lewis, E.C., Subrahmanyam, P., Waldspurger, et al.: Overshadow: A Virtualization-Based Approach to Retrofitting Protection in Commodity Operating Systems. In: Proc. of the 13th Conference on Architectural Support for Programming Languages and Operating Systems (ASPLOS), Seattle (2008)
18. Borders, K., Weele, E.V., Lau, B., Prakash, A.: Protecting Confidential Data on Personal Computers with Storage Capsules. In: 18th USENIX Security Symposium (USENIX SECURITY), Montreal (2009)
19. Wojtczuk, R.: Subverting the Xen Hypervisor. In: Black Hat, USA (2008)
20. Wang, Z., Jiang, X.: HyperSafe: A Lightweight Approach to Provide Lifetime Hypervisor Control-Flow Integrity. In: Proc. of the 31st IEEE Symposium on Security & Privacy (SSP), Oakland (2010)

Winning with DNS Failures: Strategies for Faster Botnet Detection*

Sandeep Yadav and A.L. Narasimha Reddy

Department of Electrical and Computer Engineering, Texas A&M University
sandeepy@tamu.edu, reddy@ece.tamu.edu

Abstract. Botnets such as Conficker and Torpig utilize high entropy domains for fluxing and evasion. Bots may query a large number of domains, some of which may fail. In this paper, we present techniques where the failed domain queries (NXDOMAIN) may be utilized for: (i) Speeding up the present detection strategies which rely only on successful DNS domains. (ii) Detecting Command and Control (C&C) server addresses through features such as temporal correlation and information entropy of both successful and failed domains. We apply our technique to a Tier-1 ISP dataset obtained from South Asia, and a campus DNS trace, and thus validate our methods by detecting Conficker botnet IPs and other anomalies with a false positive rate as low as 0.02%. Our technique can be applied at the edge of an autonomous system for real-time detection.

Keywords: Botnet, Domain-fluxing, DNS, Failures.

1 Introduction

Botnets have been used for spamming, phishing, DDoS (Distributed Denial of Service) attacks. Some botnets such as Kraken/Bobax, Torpig [8], and Conficker [6] utilize *fluxing* techniques, where the domain name of a C&C server changes rapidly (*domain fluxing*) or the IP address for a domain name is altered (*IP fluxing*). To automate the domain name generation for fluxing, botnet owners rely on generating domain names algorithmically. The domain names thus formed, comprise of alphanumeric characters chosen randomly, and which thus exhibit high *information entropy*. As the domain names for the C&C servers are short lived, and as only a fraction of this large set of domains may be used for actual DNS use, blacklisting techniques prove ineffective in countering such fluxing botnets.

Reverse engineering of bot executables may yield the domain name generation algorithm and subsequently the domain names that a bot may query in the future. These domain names may be blacklisted or pre-registered in advance by security researchers. Domain fluxing botnets overcome this vulnerability by choosing to generate a large number of names, where only a few of them may host the C&C server. The large number of domain names is expected to overwhelm the pre-registration by others and potentially provide a cover for the actual name of the C&C server used by the botnet.

---

* This work is supported in part by a Qatar National Research Foundation grant, Qatar Telecom, and NSF grants 0702012 and 0621410.

M. Rajarajan et al. (Eds.): SecureComm 2011, LNICST 96, pp. 446–459, 2012.
© Institute for Computer Sciences, Social Informatics and Telecommunications Engineering 2012

Botnets that employ domain fluxing can be characterized by the following two important features: (a) The alphanumeric distribution or entropy of the domain names for C&C servers is considerably different from human generated names. (b) The bots generate many failed DNS queries as many of the algorithmically generated domain names may not be registered or not available as C&C servers. We exploit these two important properties to detect botnets with very low latency, where we define latency as the number of domain names required for successful anomaly detection (or the time taken to collect those domains).

With our approach, we analyze successful DNS queries, and the failed DNS queries within the vicinity of the successful queries, thus exploiting their features to not only detect the C&C servers of those botnets faster, but also simultaneously detect bots within the network. While our detection mechanism is designed specifically to detect domain fluxing botnets by utilizing DNS failures, previous approaches relying only on domain entropy analysis can still be used in the event that there are no DNS failures. By analyzing the failed queries along with the successful queries, we increase the data available for analysis and hence speed up the detection process. While our technique can be used online (or in real-time), we focus on a trace-driven evaluation methodology here to keep the explanation simpler. Additionally, our analysis is based only on DNS network traffic, thereby reducing resource requirements, in comparison to techniques relying on general network traffic analysis.

When individual clients/hosts query a resolver, the failed queries can potentially be attributed to the presence of bots on that client and the successful queries close to the failures can be assumed to be related with high confidence. However, when queries are forwarded to a resolver from another local resolver or a DNS query aggregator, the queries from many clients can be grouped together and relating failed queries to other successful queries in the query stream becomes problematic. Our approach is cognizant of this difficulty and is capable of producing accurate results in the presence of aggregated query streams.

The main contributions of this work are:

- We utilize the failures around successful DNS queries and the entropy of the domains belonging to such queries, for *detecting* botnets with lower latency compared to previous techniques.
- We propose and evaluate a *speeding* technique which correlates DNS domain query failures for faster detection of domain fluxing botnets' C&C server IPs. We utilize temporal correlation between DNS queries and entropy-based correlation between domain names, for speedier detection.
- We show through a trace driven analysis that the proposed techniques can considerably speed up the detection of botnets that generate many DNS query failures. This in turn will constrain the domain name generation algorithms further if they want to evade detection by techniques such as proposed here.

We apply our techniques to two datasets. The first is a Tier-1 ISP dataset obtained from South Asia, captured for a period of approximately one day. Additionally, we analyze a university campus DNS trace captured over a month. The datasets consist of botnets validated through previous techniques applied to the trace [11]. Based on our analysis, we detect the presence of the recently discovered *Conficker* botnet. Our experiments indicate a false positive rate as low as 0.02% with a high detection rate. Our evaluation also yields how different features characterizing botnets can be varied, to assist a network administrator in tuning these parameters for their network(s).

The rest of this paper is organized as follows. Section 2 discusses the related work on botnet detection. In section 3, we discuss our methodology for *detection* of domain-fluxing botnets, as well as propose an alternate correlation criteria for *speeding* the state-of-the-art detection techniques. The results have been outlined in section 4 followed by the discussion on the limitations and security loopholes that attackers may exploit, in section 5. Finally, we draw the conclusions and highlight the future work in section 6.

2   Related Work

Alphabet entropy measures to detect algorithmically generated botnets by using successful domain name queries mapping to IP addresses, are proposed in [11]. Jiang et. al. [4] use DNS failures to determine suspicious activity within the local autonomous system. Their technique analyzes bipartite graphs between failed DNS domain names and querying clients, to determine connected components with anomalous activity. Our approach, additionally, analyzes related successful queries and detects the botnet C&C servers along with the bots. The authors in [13] analyze unproductive network traffic of multiple protocols to classify malicious hosts based on features such as rate of failed traffic generation, entropy of ports used etc. In our work, we do not require training of data, and only rely on DNS based features for botnet detection.

Botnet identification using DNS has been explored in [9] where the authors utilize query rates based features of successful and failed DNS queries, to identify botnet anomalies. [10] detects new bots based on the similarity in querying behavior for known malicious hosts. Our technique does not rely on query rates and can detect botnets even if each bot queries for an independent botnet C&C server's domain names. Previous work on botnet detection has also examined the correlation of network activity between time and space as exhibited by users within a network [3]. We, however, use only the DNS traffic for detecting botnet activity, drastically reducing the resource requirements. Also, DNS security has been investigated in a number of recent studies [12] which have focused on DNS indirection and cache poisoning prevention.

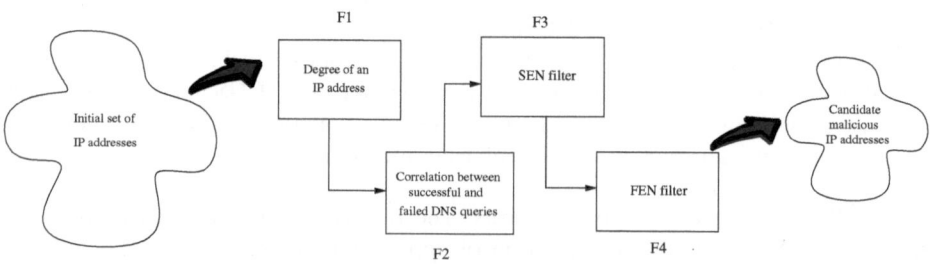

Fig. 1. Filtering steps

3   Methodology

In this section, we describe our technique for detecting botnets through DNS traffic analysis using successful and failed DNS queries. We also highlight correlating failed domains, for speedier detection of malicious IP addresses. Our primary goal is to detect the IP address of a domain fluxing botnet's C&C server. As a consequence of our analysis, we obtain the bots within the local network, and the domain names belonging to the botnet, thus exposing the botnet altogether. To discover anomalous IP address(es), we exploit multiple features such as the botnet structure and the temporal correlation between DNS query patterns of participating bots. Prior to analyzing the DNS traffic, we use a white-list for filtering out known benign DNS queries (details in section 4), leveraging a more accurate analysis.

3.1   Filtering Steps

Figure 1 demonstrates the steps involved in narrowing down the set of IP addresses that are returned in DNS response packets (post white-listing), to a relatively smaller list of anomalous IP addresses. With each filter, we select a fraction of the input supplied by the previous filter, reducing the subsequent work. In the following subsections, we describe each filter applied for a candidate C&C IP address (denoted by $cncip$) resulting in $cncip$ being discarded as legitimate or subject to additional filters. The measures employed by each filter, are either computed using select or all the time windows in which the candidate IP address occurs. The typical time bin/window length used in our trace is subjective to the dataset in consideration. For evaluation presented in section 4, we typically use a 128 sec window (64 sec symmetric about $cncip$). The following subsections detail how each measure is computed.

Degree of an IP Address (D_{cncip}). Domain fluxing is characterized by multiple domain names mapping to an IP address. We define the degree of an IP address as the number of domain names that map to a $cncip$. As a first filter, we use the degree (F_1 in Figure 1) to separate a set of IP addresses more likely to exhibit botnet like domain fluxing. For a given IP address, this number may vary based on the length of the trace analyzed. For instance, an IP address analyzed for an hour may have five domain names mapping to it. However, if analyzed for two hours, eight domain names may map to it, which includes previously expired domain names. While we consider the IPs which have a degree of at least two, we vary D_{cncip} to evaluate how quickly we detect anomalies. For a typical analysis, we use a degree threshold of eight, independent of the time for which a candidate IP address is analyzed. Thus, the filter F_1 can be bypassed if an IP has less than eight domain names mapping to it. However, this puts a constraint on the fluxing that a botnet server can exhibit. It should be noted that, Content Distribution Networks (CDNs) also have a high degree. However, CDNs get separated through additional filters as described ahead.

Correlation Metric ($Corr_{cncip}$). As introduced earlier, bots generate burst of DNS queries, a fraction of which may fail. Thus, we exploit the temporal correlation between DNS successes and failures to identify malicious behavior. On observing a time window of DNS queries for a bot, we may observe the presence of failures, more frequently, than for legitimate clients. It is represented by filter F_2 in Figure 1.

The correlation metric ($Corr_{cncip}$) for a candidate IP address is computed as the probability of observing at least one failed DNS query in a time bin, given that $cncip$ was returned as an answer to a successful DNS query in the same bin. For detection, we heuristically choose the threshold as 0.5 implying that majority of windows in which a $cncip$ appears, should also have failures for it to be considered a meaningful anomaly. In section 4, we study how the false positives decrease on increasing this threshold or when the correlation metric changes upon restricting our analysis to windows with more failures.

We use the following equation to compute this metric:

$$Corr_{cncip} = \frac{\sum \text{Time bins with } (S_{cncip} \cap F_{client})}{\text{Time bins with } S_{cncip}} \tag{1}$$

where S_{cncip} denotes the boolean condition of whether $cncip$ occurs in a time bin. F_{client} refers to the boolean variable indicating the presence of at least one failure in the corresponding time bin for the *client*. The correlation metric is computed with the time series of all clients which receive $cncip$ as the DNS response address. This metric may not be sufficient in topologies comprising of DNS aggregators where the temporal co-occurrence of DNS failures and successes is more frequent. Further developed measures limit the errors produced due to DNS aggregators.

Succeeding Domain Set Entropy (SEN_{cncip}). We use *edit distance* as a metric for determining the similarity between a pair of domain names. Algorithmically generated domains exhibit a high value for this metric, owing to limited similarity between a given pair of domains. However, domain names observed for a legitimate entity, frequently have repeated occurrence of certain characters, which lower the computed normalized edit distance (or the entropy associated with the entity), as substantiated by [11]. For instance, a pair of domain names such as *www.google.com, ns.google.com* have a lower normalized edit distance than a pair like *jswrts.ws, yvqcbtvztpm.cc*, as observed for Conficker.

Edit distance is defined as an integral value indicating the number of transformations required to convert a given string to the other. The type of eligible transformations include addition, deletion, and modification of a character. We use the normalized edit distance measure computed as the Levenshtein edit distance [5] between a pair of strings normalized by the length of the longer string. The entropy of domains mapping to an IP address (and hence successful DNS queries), SEN_{cncip}, is determined by computing the normalized edit distance between every pair of domains that map to $cncip$ (taken from set with cardinality $|D_{cncip}|$), and averaged over all such pairs. Therefore, the complexity of entropy calculation is $O(n^2)$ where n is the number of domain names successfully mapping to an IP address over the duration of analysis. This duration is defined either in terms of a pre-determined time, or the first few successful domains encountered for a given $cncip$. Once SEN_{cncip} is computed, if it exceeds a threshold (reserved for highly domain fluxing entities), we consider it for further analysis. Our evaluation shows that while high SEN_{cncip} IPs may be detected easily, even enitities with relatively low entropy are detected with small false positive rates, making it difficult for botnet owners to improve their domain generation algorithm (DGA).

Failing Domain Set Entropy (FEN_{cncip}). For a botnet, the domain name generation algorithm for failed domain names is no different than the domain names successfully resolved. The features expressed through alphanumeric characters composing the failed and successful DNS queries generated by a botnet, are therefore very similar. Thus, the failed domain names can help reduce the latency of analysis and improve detection since many more names can be analyzed in a shorter period of time, when associated with the succeeding queries.

To compute the entropy of failed domain names (denoted as FEN_{cncip}), we analyze the failing queries that occur in the vicinity of a successful DNS query. Our hypothesis is as follows. *For a bot issuing a burst of DNS queries to determine the C&C server address, the entropy of failed DNS queries present in the burst, is of the same order as the entropy of the successful queries.* We again use the normalized edit distance for determining the entropy of failed domain names present in a time bin containing successful query resolution. It is symmetric about the time instant where $cncip$ was observed. It is noteworthy that all failed DNS queries present in the time bin, may not be related to the successful DNS query. Such queries deviate the output. The noise is especially amplified at DNS *aggregators* which query on behalf of several individual local clients. Thus, choosing an appropriate time window length is critical for accurate analysis. During evaluation, we show how changing window size affects the performance.

To compute the failed domain entropy (FEN) for a candidate C&C IP address, we use the following equation:

$$FEN_{cncip} = \frac{\sum(FEN_{client})}{\text{Number of clients}} \qquad (2)$$

where FEN_{client} is the FEN value computed by examining *client's* time series of query generation, with respect to $cncip$. To elaborate, the failed query entropy for a client is computed between pairs of strings (failed domain names) present within every time window in which $cncip$ occurs. Subsequently, all such FEN values are averaged thus giving FEN_{cncip}. The computation of this entropy requires at least two failed domain names within the window of consideration. A higher number of failures increase the confidence in the computed FEN value for that window implying that botnets are detected more accurately. Alternately, individual failed queries can be directly compared with the candidate successful domain names to compute the edit distance relevant to each failed domain name. We have evaluated both approaches and obtained similar results. Owing to space constraints, we only report on one of the approaches.

To further filter the candidate set of anomalous IP addresses, we consider only those addresses with FEN_{cncip} greater than a threshold. We choose a conservative threshold to avoid ignoring genuine anomalies. To apply our hypothesis of the proximity of SEN_{cncip} and FEN_{cncip}, we use the following inequality to further eliminate false positives:

$$(SEN_{cncip} - \delta) \leq FEN_{cncip} \leq (SEN_{cncip} + \delta) \qquad (3)$$

where δ represents a small bound or the *proximity* within which FEN_{cncip} and SEN_{cncip} are expected to lie. To choose an appropriate δ, we compute the standard deviation σ of entropy for domains belonging to the known botnet IPs present in our dataset. Thereby, we choose δ as 3σ.

From the above description, the temporal correlation and entropy related parameters are analyzed and IPs satisfying the outlined malicious criteria, help in identifying bots within the network as well. In an autonomous system, where the DNS queries are observed from local clients and DNS aggregators, our technique may be applied recursively at the aggregator, yielding the bots which use the aggregator as their DNS recursive resolver.

3.2   Correlating Failures for Improved Latency

Here, we present an alternate strategy for *speeding* up the detection technique which relies only on successful queries. The work in [11] emphasizes upon applying statistical techniques such as K-L divergence, Jaccard Index, and Edit distance, to the set of successful domains for a *cncip* (SQ_{cncip}). Through evaluation, it is shown that a large set improves the accuracy of anomaly detection. However, accumulating a larger set requires a considerable amount of time. Therefore, we propose supplementing the set SQ_{cncip} with failed queries that occur within the vicinity of successful DNS queries. The resulting set is accumulated faster, decreasing the latency of analysis by an order of magnitude.

The detection technique proposed in this work provides the basis for associating the queries with successes viz. temporally. In addition to temporal characteristics, to improve the quality of failed domain name set, we propose considering only those failing domains within the time window, whose entropy characteristics are similar to the successful domain set. Such similarity parameters for entropy can help identify a DGA. Here, we explore supplementing SQ_{cncip} with these two main features. Additional features as described for detection can also be used.

To realize the faster accumulation of relevant domains, we compute the entropy (normalized edit distance) between a failed domain name and each of the successful DNS domain names discovered under analysis. A domain yielding an entropy value close to the average SEN (or the entropy of successful domains) is considered relevant. The measure of closeness is defined using eqn. 3 as described above. For this particular experiment, we choose $\delta = \sigma$. We note that such marginally expensive computation for identifying relevant domains may improve latency *and* accuracy. We evaluate this

Table 1. Trace description

	ISP trace	Campus trace
Trace collection period	Nov 03-04, 2009	Aug 22 - Sep 22, 2010
Total number of DNS sessions	1.61 M	112.7 M
White-listed sessions	770.23 K	54.4 M
Total number of failed DNS packets after white-listing	57.72 K	1.28 M
IP addresses analyzed for maliciousness	9948	74.7 K (per segment avg.)
Number of clients (or aggregators)	8472	1735 (per segment avg.)

correlation strategy for Conficker's C&C server addresses in section 4. Note that the analysis of discarded failed domain names identifies irrelevant queries belonging to services like *qq.com* and *ask.com* while few excluded domains belong to Conficker, strengthening our confidence in the new set.

4   Results

We validate our technique using the DNS datasets described below. For our analysis, we consider only DNS type A records. Several DNS blacklist based services utilize the A record to verify whether an IP address, domain name, or an executable (a feature used by McAfee) is present in the blacklists. To exclude these queries from analysis, we white-list a total of 31 trusted second-level domain names including several blacklist services, Content Distribution Network services (such as *akamai.net, cloudfront.net*) and popular domains (such as *google.com, facebook.com*). The white-list helps us focus on other potentially malicious domains, in addition to refining the failed domains set used for analysis. Additionally, we avoid processing answers with RFC 1918 (private) addresses [7].

4.1   Data Sets

Table 1 details the traces used for analysis. The 20-hour long ISP trace contains known malicious IPs belonging to the Conficker botnet. Using a blacklist, we obtain a set of 100 odd IPs labelled malicious, which we further verify manually by checking against exhaustive databases such as *robtex.com* and *mywot.com*. We believe that these two sources provide us with the most recent information concerning the queried domains or IP addresses. The 19 IPs obtained post verification with the above sources, contain two IP addresses hosting adult websites. We disregard these as non-fluxing behavior. One C&C address apparently belongs to the domain-fluxing Kraken/Bobax botnet (based on the domain names we see). However, the Kraken C&C address has a degree of only two. The 16 remaining IPs belong to Conficker, some of which are sinkhole servers [1]. Nonetheless, we consider them as anomalous as they help keep the botnet alive. As a result, we consider the remaining 9931 IPs as legitimate. Note that all IPs considered for ground truth evaluation, have a degree of at least two.

    We also use a DNS trace captured at a primary recursive resolver of a university network. We divide the month-long trace into approximately week-long segments and present our results on randomly chosen segments. Each segment contains an average of 295K IP addresses returned as DNS responses (after white-listing). As table 1 shows, approximately 75K IP addresses have degree $D_{cncip} > 2$. For the campus trace, we use the C&C server information from the ISP trace to obtain 29 IP addresses (out of 75K), labelled as malicious. Since the ground truth information for the ISP trace is relatively old, we again verify this set manually. As a result, we are left with *four* Conficker C&C addresses which are common with those present in the ISP trace.

4.2   Latency Comparison

The latency of detection is expressed in terms of the number of successful domain names required to analyze and detect a rogue server accurately. Figure 2(a) shows the

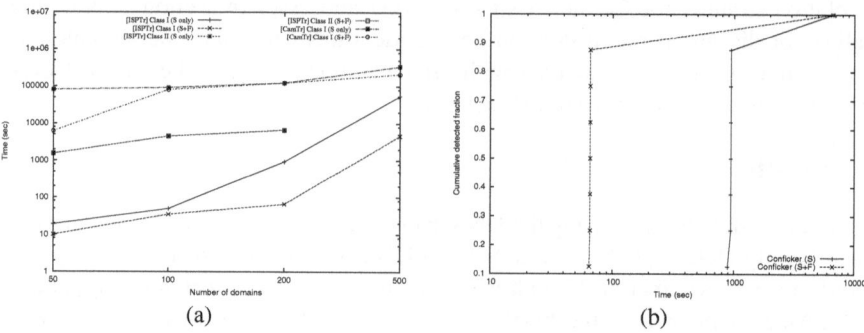

Fig. 2. Latency comparison (a) for different number of domain names. (b) for 200 domain names.

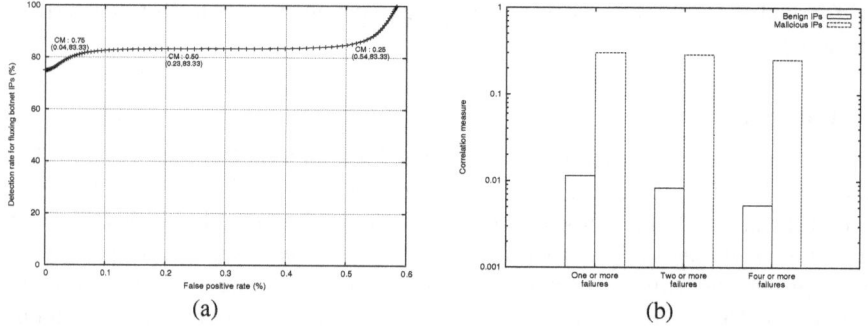

Fig. 3. (a) ROC curve for changing correlation thresholds. (b) Correlation comparison for changing flux behavior.

gain obtained in terms of time taken to collect a set of botnet domain names. The figure shows two classes of botnet IPs that we observe. Class I represents those C&C server addresses where domain fluxing yielded both successful and failed queries. However, for the C&C server in Class II, the bots issued none or very few failed DNS queries. In our ISP trace with more than 50 domain names mapping to it, we find eight C&C server addresses belonging to Class I and two belonging to Class II. Also, we observe that all four C&C addresses in the analyzed campus trace segment belong to Class I.

Figure 2(a) shows the improved latency for the average time taken by Class I or II addresses. From the figure, we observe that when failed domain names are correlated with successful DNS domains, the time taken to collect 50, 100, 200 or 500 domain names is considerably reduced. Especially, for 500 domain names, we see a gain of an order of magnitude when the time of collection reduces from approximately 54000 secs to only 4600 secs. With Class II, however, we do not observe any gain since no failures help in supplementing the set of successful botnet domains. Thus, we infer that in context of applying statistical techniques for anomaly detection, the proposed correlation mechanism can significantly reduce the time to collect input required for analysis of Class I C&C addresses. Note that we do not obtain 500 successful domains for the Class II address. The analysis with the campus trace follows analogous behavior. However, we plot the latency observed when correlating failures with successes, using the criterion highlighted in section 3.2. We also note a higher initial latency for domain name collection, owing to slower traffic seen for a campus (Tier-4) as compared to a Tier-1 network trace. Although, the time of collection is reduced considerably even with the campus trace. For instance, we observe 100 domains are collected 10K seconds faster than when using only successful DNS traffic.

While figure 2(a) shows average time taken for Class I and II anomalous entities, figure 2(b) shows the pace at which those anomalies are detected, for the specific case of 200 domain names. From the figure, we see that using the both successful and failed DNS domains, we can detect more than 80% of the total IP addresses, an order of magnitude faster than when using only the successful ones. We note that the cumulative detection reaches 100% because of the presence of Class II address.

From the figures, we conclude that considering failed domain names assists in speeding up detection of domain-fluxing botnet. While speeding up the detection through methods presented in [11], the worst case detection latency is same as the original latency where only domains from SQ_{cncip} are used. We also transform botnet detection to a real-time detection approach through the speeding mechanism presented above, as well as through the detection strategy.

4.3   Effect of the Correlation Parameter

We evaluate the significance of using the correlation as a feature for anomaly detection. Figure 3(a) represents the Receiver Operating Curve (ROC) curve for changing thresholds for correlation between DNS successes and failures. The ROC curve shows a decrease in false positive rate with a decreasing detection rate, when increasing $Corr_{cncip}$ thresholds. A higher threshold requirement would imply that failures coincide with the successful queries more frequently. We would expect benign IP addresses to have a low correlation value. Hence, increasing the threshold results in decreasing false positives. For this particular experiment, we note detecting a maximum of 12 (out of 17 C&C IPs) as the remaining IPs do not have enough domain names for analysis (at least eight domains). We also note a maximum false positive rate of only 0.6% which primarily comprises of legitimate IPs with relatively lower entropy than seen for fluxing botnets and few failures within the window of analysis (that is, a correlation value just above the threshold). In contrast, fluxing botnets usually have a high number of failed domain names within the corresponding bin. Note that the false positives include ISP's intra-AS DNS resolution queries where the hosts have been assigned random-appearing domain names.

4.4   Correlation vs Number of DNS Failures

Through this experiment, we aim to study the behavior seen for malicious IPs, in terms of the number of failed domain names generated. Figure 3(b) shows the correlation observed for malicious and benign IPs. We compute the correlation for three cases where we expect at least one, two or four failures to occur within the same window, as the *cncip*. The figure shows a decrease in correlation, for both benign and legitimate IPs, though the correlation reduces only slightly for the malicious set. Such a study implies that the correlation criteria may be adapted towards highly fluxing botnets while keeping fewer false positives.

4.5   Variation in Entropy

We evaluate the impact of information entropy expressed by the domains which map to a candidate *cncip* (that is, SEN_{cncip}). The effect of changing the entropy thresholds for considering a *cncip* is shown through an ROC curve as in Figure 4. The figure shows an increase in the detection rate and the false positive rate as the threshold for entropy is decreased. This is in line with the observation that for a low threshold, several sets of domain names, and in particular those for CDNs satisfy the filters used for detection. Analogous to the performance with varying correlation threshold, the maximum false positive rate observed is 0.52%. Analysis of false positives reveals DNSBL services (*redcondor*), popular websites (*sina.com.cn* which offer multiple services), DNS and HTTP servers providing service to multiple entities, blogging services (*blogspot*) and CDN addresses. For instance, we observe *redcondor* IPs labelled malicious when the entropy thresholds are 0.35 or lower, indicating that even though correlation may be high for this DNSBL service, the entropy helps distinguish it from actual anomalies, when using higher thresholds. In section 5, we discuss how botnets may attempt to fool our detection approach into generating domains with low entropy. Note that we determine the detection rate over the 12 detectable botnet IPs, as discussed previously.

4.6   Size of Time Bin

The impact of varying the size of time bins is shown in Table 2. In all experiments, we observe that false positives increase with larger time bins. The wider bins allow a higher possibility of inclusion of failures within the corresponding *cncip* bin, resulting in an increased $Corr_{cncip}$ value. Thus, more candidate IP addresses meet the criteria set by filter F_2 (in figure 1) and the ones with high entropy may be incorrectly labelled

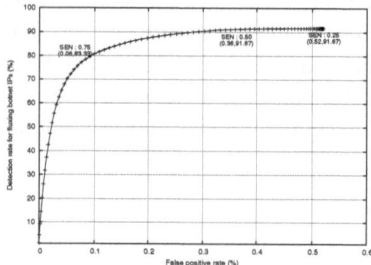

Table 2. Impact of changing time bin size

Window size (sec)	4	8	16	32	64	128	256
	ISP trace						
FPR (%)	0.022	0.043	0.043	0.097	0.173	0.259	0.302
TPR (%)	75.0	75.0	75.0	75.0	75.0	83.33	83.33
	Campus trace						
FPR (%)	0.021	0.039	0.084	0.120	0.209	0.434	0.752
TPR (%)	100.0	100.0	100.0	100.0	100.0	100.0	100.0

Fig. 4. Performance with changing entropy thresholds

malicious. From the table, we also observe that smaller window sizes result in fewer IP addresses being detected within the ISP trace. An inference of this observation is that bots spread their DNS queries making temporal correlation between failures and successes difficult. The false positive rate, however, is less than 0.3% for ISP trace (and 0.75% for campus trace) for all experiments making the choice of larger windows possible. However, the marginal or no increase in detection rate and false positive rate, for the change in window size from 4 secs to 128 secs implies that a window as small as 4 secs may be sufficient for detecting a domain-fluxing botnet like Conficker. Note that the false positives for the campus trace are higher when compared to the ISP trace, as we frequently observe DNSBL based NXDOMAIN failures within the campus dataset. Such DNSBL failures affect the correlation/entropy parameters resulting in more benign IPs classified as malicious.

Dyndns is a service for generating customizable/random temporary domain names. In the ISP trace, we observe several random sub-domains for *dyndns* which exhibit high entropy characteristics, with several failures belonging to this service. Our detection mechanism designates these IP addresses as benign owing to presence of temporally distant failures, reinforcing our hypothesis of utilizing temporal correlation of failed domains for anomaly detection through the use of small time bins. We also limit our study to a maximum bin size of 256 seconds as fast-fluxing botnets have low DNS Time-To-Live (TTL) values.

5 Discussion

In this work, we detect Conficker C&C addresses which exhibit high entropy owing to randomized distribution of alphanumeric characters composing the domain names. However, to evade our detection mechanism, botnet owners may alter the way domain names are composed. For instance, our separate study has observed combination of dictionary words being used as an alternate way of domain-fluxing. Some example domain names that we observe for a botnet are *haireconomy.ru, greedycake.ru* and *empirekey.ru* [2]. The information entropy computed for a set of such domain names indicates that owing to high edit distance values, such domain names can still be distinguished through entropy analysis.

To validate the robustness of our approach, we artificially inject domain queries as observed above, with some of them failing and some domain names successfully mapping to a reserved address. We randomly choose clients to insert such DNS queries. Based on our study, we still detect the simulated anomalies with similar experiment parameters as used previously for evaluation. Also, in future if botnet owners formulate a DGA where the observed entropy is lower than that observed for fluxing botnet detected in this work, our detection mechanism can detect them with low false positives, as hinted by figure 4.

A direct weakness of our detection strategy is reliance on failed domain names. Our experiments are based on analyzing the first few successful domain names and thus correlating failures that are present in their vicinity. In the event that no failures are present, or failures that occur right after the window of analysis, our detection strategy may fail in which case switching to the algorithm for correlating failures to *supplement* the set SQ_{cncip} would help. Thus, a combination of both the strategies presented in this work may be useful for fast anomaly detection. It is possible to generate DNS queries slowly such that the failed queries are outside the time window considered in our scheme. Such an approach, however, will slow down the bot in identifying its C&C server and hence constraining the botnet writer again.

Our technique for detection can be mapped back to detect individual bots that issued the queries for a malicious $cncip$. For instance, with our campus trace analysis, we observe 12 hosts within our AS querying for three of the four C&C addresses, and 10 hosts (subset of the 12 above) querying for the remaining C&C address. While the Tier-1 ISP trace may not have individual clients (we would mostly observe aggregators), the mechanism applied for a smaller-sized network or when applied recursively, may result in more accurate detection of anomalies and bots, owing to a better DNS failure signal.

6   Conclusion

In this paper, we proposed methodologies for utilizing failed domain names in the quest for rapid detection of a fluxing botnet's C&C server, the bots within the local network, and the related domain names, and thus revealing the botnet infrastructure. Utilizing only DNS traffic, we reduce the resource requirement for botnet detection. We also considerably reduce the latency of detection when compared to previous techniques. For faster detection, we utilize not only the entropy of the domain names successfully mapping to an IP address, but also that of the correlated failed DNS queries occurring within the vicinity of the succeeding DNS query. With our technique, we achieve a false positive rate as low as 0.02% with a high detection rate. As a future work, we plan to utilize SERVER FAILURE based DNS failures, or failures related to the name servers, as a means for detecting botnets which exhibit double fast flux.

References

1. Conficker Working Group,
   http://www.confickerworkinggroup.org/
   wiki/pmwiki.php/ANY/FAQ#toc5
2. New Technique Spots Sneaky Botnets,
   http://mobile.darkreading.com/9292/show/
   4711c9403b772e7281ae08cee69758cc&t=
   461a4a89abc0a0c761234d11086f5003
3. Gu, G., Porras, P., Yegneswaran, V., Fong, M., Lee, W.: BotHunter: Detecting Malware Infection Through IDS-Driven Dialog Correlation. In: Proc. of the 16th USENIX Security Symposium (Security 2007) (August 2007)
4. Jiang, N., Cao, J., Jin, Y., Li, L.E., Zhang, Z.-L.: Identifying Suspicious Activities Through DNS Failure Graph Analysis. In: IEEE Conference on Network Protocols (2010)
5. Manning, C.D., Raghavan, P., Schutze, H.: An Information to Information Retrieval. Cambridge University Press (2009)
6. Porras, P., Saidi, H., Yegneswaran, V.: Conficker C Analysis. Technical report,
   http://mtc.sri.com/Conficker/addendumC/
7. Rekhter, Y., Moskowitz, B., Karrenberg, D., de Groot, G., Lear, E.: Address Allocation for Private Internets (1996), http://www.ietf.org/rfc/rfc1918.txt

8. Stone-Gross, B., Cova, M., Cavallaro, L., Gilbert, B., Szydlowski, M., Kemmerer, R., Kruegel, C., Vigna, G.: Your Botnet is My Botnet: Analysis of a Botnet Takeover. In: ACM Conference on Computer and Communications Security (CCS) (November 2009)
9. Villamarín-Salomón, R., Brustoloni, J.C.: Identifying Botnets Using Anomaly Detection Techniques Applied to DNS Traffic. In: Consumer Communications and Networking Conference (2008)
10. Villamarín-Salomón, R., Brustoloni, J.C.: Bayesian Bot Detection Based on DNS Traffic Similarity. In: Proceedings of the 2009 ACM Symposium on Applied Computing, SAC 2009, pp. 2035–2041. ACM, New York (2009)
11. Yadav, S., Reddy, A.K.K., Reddy, A.L.N., Ranjan, S.: Detecting Algorithmically Generated Malicious Domain Names. In: Internet Measurement Conference (2010)
12. Yadav, S., Reddy, A.N.: MiND: Misdirected dNs packet Detector. In: IASTED Computer and Information Security (2010)
13. Zhu, Z., Yegneswaran, V., Chen, Y.: Using Failure Information Analysis to Detect Enterprise Zombies. In: Chen, Y., Dimitriou, T.D., Zhou, J. (eds.) SecureComm 2009. LNICST, vol. 19, pp. 185–206. Springer, Heidelberg (2009)

Trading Elephants for Ants: Efficient Post-attack Reconstitution

Meixing Le, Zhaohui Wang, Quan Jia, Angelos Stavrou,
Anup K. Ghosh, and Sushil Jajodia*

Center for Secure Information Systems,
George Mason University, Fairfax, VA
{mlep,zwange,qjia,astavrou,aghosh1,jajodia}@gmu.edu

Abstract. While security has become a first-class consideration in systems' design and operation, most of the commercial and research efforts have been focused on detection, prevention, and forensic analysis of attacks. Relatively little work has gone into efficient recovery of application and data after a compromise. Administrators and end-users are faced with the arduous task of cleansing the affected machines. Restoring the system using snapshot is disruptive and it can lead to data loss.

In this paper, we present a reconstitution framework that records inter-application communications; by logging only inter-application events, we trade our capability for data provenance and recovery *within* an application, for performance and the capability to recover long after the intrusion. To achieve this, we employ novel algorithms that compute the data provenance dependencies from the application interactions while minimizing the required state we maintain for system reconstitution. Our experiments show that our prototype requires two to three orders of magnitude less storage for recovery.

Keywords: Data Provenance, Causal Dependency, System Recovery.

1 Introduction

Computing has evolved into a necessary component for business, government, and military environments. Logistics, transportation, finance, intelligence, modern combat systems all depend on the correct operation of computer systems. Despite intense efforts towards improving software and network security, computers continue to be routinely compromised and exploited. Moreover, even when intrusions are detected, recovery happens long after the actual attack takes place.

---

* This work is sponsored in part by US National Science Foundation (NSF) grant CNS-TC 0915291 and AFOSR MURI grant 107151AA "MURI: Autonomic Recovery of Enterprise-wide Systems After Attack or Failure with Forward Correction." Sushil Jajodia and Meixing Le were partially supported by the National Science Foundation under grants CCF-103987 and CT-20013A, and by the Army Research Office DURIP award W911NF-09-01-0352. The views and conclusions contained herein are those of the authors and should not be interpreted as necessarily representing the official policies or endorsements, either expressed or implied, of the U.S. Government.

M. Rajarajan et al. (Eds.): SecureComm 2011, LNICST 96, pp. 460–469, 2012.
© Institute for Computer Sciences, Social Informatics and Telecommunications Engineering 2012

Administrators and end-users spend considerable time and effort "cleaning up" after the attacks. The standard practice consists of little more than re-formatting the disk, re-installing the operating system, and recovering user data from the most recent backup[1]. This is a time-consuming, error-prone process that is disruptive to end-users and enterprise operations.

The most recent work on system recovery is Retro [20]. Similar to Taser [5] and Solitude [7], Retro maintains an action history graph to capture the dependencies among system actor and objects (files) at multiple levels of abstraction. Contrary to all of these process-level recording approaches, our goal is to recover but also minimize the maintained system state by abstracting the low-level activities in the system trading-off recovery granularity. Instead of maintaining a voluminous log of low-level system activity including the input and return values of system calls, we attempt to simplify the causal dependencies which determines the log size. Our provenance graph maintains relations between objects only when those relations are necessary for potential future recovery. Last but not least, containers[2] abstract the execution of applications on physical machines.

Our approach attempts to lay a strong foundation to prevent cross-application contamination and provide efficient system reconstitution. To accomplish this, we designed a two-pronged architecture: on one hand, we record the data exchanged between contained applications; on the other hand, we leverage these logs to compute the application and user data provenance and use that information to recover. A challenging trade-off is the choice of the monitoring granularity. Using the finest possible granularity, the execution of every function call can be inspected and logged to obtain the most detailed knowledge of information flow. However, the computation and storage cost of recording and analyzing these events is prohibitively high for many applications and especially so over long periods of time. In contrast, many administrators rely solely on system and application logs for recovery. These logs usually offer a coarse-grain view that lacks sufficient information for analysis. Moreover, they are susceptible to tampering by attackers. To avoid these pitfalls, we only record application activities as container data exchanges. Therefore, we trade our capability for taint-tracking and recovery *within* a container for far lower processing and storage overhead.

As shown in experimental results, our system does not impose prohibitive logging or storage requirements: by selectively storing information based on data provenance, we provide better recovery for less storage when compared to pure versioning file systems, interval based backup or system snapshots. Finally, our recovery algorithm is able to reconstitute a typical desktop system even after the launch of hundreds of application instances long after the initial corruption. We demonstrate through different user studies, that the hourly temporary recovery log for a typical Desktop remains below 250MB and the persistent state is only

---

[1] For example, CERT's instruction on recovering compromised Unix and Windows NT systems: `http://www.cert.org/tech_tips/root_compromise.html`

[2] We use VEEs, VEs, and containers as abbreviations for Virtualized Execution Environments.

12MB for over 65 hours of collected data. This is between two to three orders or magnitude less information collected and stored compared to all prior research.

2   Related Work

The use of virtualization technologies for system monitoring and recovery has received a lot of attention [2,15]. In Revirt [2], a virtual machine snapshot encapsulates the entire system. By recording VM-to-host interactions the system stored a full OS-level replay of the entire duration of the attack. To enhance forensic analysis of intrusions, Goel *et al.* introduced Forensix [4], a system for forensic discovery and history reconstruction by monitoring a selected set of system calls. The Taser [5] recovery system was more geared towards tracking the propagation of an intrusion in a system, and it did not use virtualization to isolate processes. This allows intrusions quickly spreading in the entire system. Moreover, having to track all OS events, they generate enormous amounts of event data that have to be stored and analyzed. Solitude [7] used chroot jails that are limited mostly on the file system level. It cannot provide any strict kernel enforced isolation guarantees so that taint propagation through other channels such as memory, IPC is still possible. Contrary to Solitude, our approach enforces kernel-level separation so that isolate application instances bottom up in terms of memory, network, file system isolations.

Retro [20] re-executes the suspect actions to restore legitimate actions. It uses an action history graph to capture the dependencies among system actor and objects (files) at multiple levels of abstraction. Compared to Retro, we uses lightweight virtualization to encapsulate each application instance, and our aim is to minimize the maintained system state by abstracting the low-level activities in the system trading-off recovery granularity. We trade the recovery granularity for better performance compared to the 4-150GB per day for log storage. Apiary [12] used isolation on the file system and display layer to seamlessly isolate processes.

Taint analysis and system recovery using dependencies were also studied in [8,6,10,17]. There are other works [3,19] provide more accurate and efficient taint analysis, but all of them either incur high analysis overhead. Finally, researchers have used file versioning systems [13,11,18] to create file snapshots at block level to support recovery.

3   Threat Model and Isolation

3.1   Threat Model

Software vulnerabilities and the increasing installation of new applications and browser plug-ins are at the root of security risks. Malicious programs stealthily download and execute foreign code corrupting other files, sending out confidential information, etc. Most of these attacks are detected long after the initial intrusion take place. In our system, we use containers to isolate applications and track their data communications over the entire duration of their life-cycle. We assume the attacks cannot break out of the container and corrupt the underlying system kernel as loading an kernel module in a container is prohibited. Furthermore, we assume that the point of intrusion (a tainted input) is provided to us by an external entity which can be an anti-virus or an intrusion detection system. We are also very conservative in marking tainted entities: containers become tainted after reading malicious files or receiving malicious network messages. All the output files and messages of a tainted container are considered tainted.

3.2   Container-Based Isolation

A container is a group of processes running on top of the same kernel as host within the same isolation zone. Starting up with a container template, an empty container will have all the necessary system processes of a working OS. These are all virtualized processes which is different from those on the host OS. This isolation is enforced by OpenVZ at kernel level. In our system, we put each application instance in a dedicated container. Process in one container can not communicate with or even be aware of the processes running in another container. The only allowed ways of data communication between containers is through networking or file sharing, and we record these events in our logs.

Inter Process Communication (IPC): For IPCs in our system, most of them such as *dbus* can be done within the isolated container. For X11 service IPCs, we choose to convert them to socket communications while all other inter-container IPCs are disabled. Therefore, for all IPCs in our system, either we do not trace them since they occur within one container, or we record them if they are the network events across containers. Without such isolation, it is easier for a process to taint another through IPCs, and it will be even worse if there is no mechanism to monitor these events on such a system.

Networking: Lightweight virtualization shares the same network processing code among containers but tags network related data (*i.e. packets, socket objects in kernel*) to achieve namespace isolation. Therefore, each VEE has its own independent network namespace. Namespace checks are enforced by kernel before any packet processing. Thus, network attacks that target applications or services running in one VEE won't affect the services running in the rest of the VEEs. With network isolation, each application instance has its own IP address.

Stackable File System: Unionfs [21] is a stackable file system service so that allow us to create one base template and share it among all containers, and this lowers the disk requirement. The base template is mounted to each container as read-only root "/" while a dedicated write-enabled layer is mounted on top of the root allowing each container to store its state in a separate directory. All the containers share one "shared_directory", therefore our system has the same functionality as the normal desktop systems. Whereas, all the interactions with this directory are monitored, and it is expected that containers only store persistent user data in this directory and all system related and temp files are stored within the containers' isolated file systems.

4   System Architecture

The overall system architecture is illustrated in Figure 1. Each application instance is running inside a VEE. We adopted the kernel probe [9] on the host OS to log system calls, and we monitor all the system call that can convey data between containers, which includes most file system related operations and network operations. The logs cannot be tampered by any process running in the containers.

4.1   Computing Provenance from Logs

The recorded system call logs offer a low-level view of all the container communications and data exchange including those with the host OS. Such view, however, does not immediately reveal the high-level and semantic dependencies among the containers. To produce the high-level view, we summarize and distill the raw system call entries into semantic objects (VEEs, files) and actions (read, write, overwrite, send via network). The summarized logs expose the logical events happening across the containers. We do the log summarization on the fly, and only keep the provenance information which will be discussed next as a high-level view of system events for recovery purpose. By doing this, we largely reduce the storage requirement for logs.

Here, we use the term **provenance** [16,1,14] to refer to the process of tracing and recording the origin of data and its propagation in the system. To be more precise, here we clarify what provenance means for file versions and the container states. The provenance of a file (at a certain version) is defined to be all the actions that modified any **present** portion of this file from its initial version. Modifications of sections that are not currently present (*i.e. discarded*

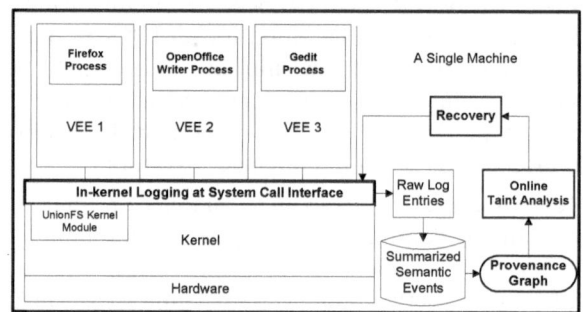

Fig. 1. Overall system architecture: application instances are confined inside containers. Logging, analysis, and recovery are performed on the same host.

or overwritten) are not part of the file provenance. On the other hand, the provenance of a container is the union of the provenance of all the input (files, network, and user input) of this container.

Intuitively, the inputs of containers can be categorized into three types: reading shared files, receiving network messages, and user input. We assume that user input can be implicitly trusted since our protection is geared towards desktop users that have no incentive in harming themselves. We monitor the other two types of inputs.

4.2   Modeling States Using Provenance

By examining the provenance of files and containers, we can quantify a container's life-cycle into states. We use these states to track the containers' provenance set and create new file versions. To avoid unnecessary versioning, we further divide each container state into Input Sub-state and Output Sub-state. Each container state can only begin with new input, and output does not cause state transition. If the container receives continuous input events, it remains the Input Sub-state. The state of a container is changed only when the container is in the Output Sub-state and receives **new** input. An input is considered "old" if it has been already read in the past (for example, reading the same unmodified file twice). In case of old input, the provenance set does not need updating.

All containers are initiated from the same clean template. The container can become tainted only after it is potentially contaminated by some malicious or tainted input(s). Any tainted input causes a container to transit from the clean state to a tainted state. Since we do not know which input is malicious in advance, we treat all **new** inputs as the start point of a potential malicious input. For an input event, we check the provenance of this event given the state of the container. If all the previous information contributed to the event is already included in the container's provenance set, the container will not change its state since the provenance set will not change. If the input is a new event to the container, its state may be changed depending on whether the container is in Output Sub-state.

Traditionally, a new file version is generated whenever a container updates a file. Contrary, in our system, even if the container writes to the same file several times under the same state, we will only keep one version of this file. This is because, while we remain in the same container state, all file versions generated under this container state are either clean or tainted.

4.3   Recovery Using Provenance Graphs

Using the above model, the provenance of each file version is associated with a set of container states that have contributed to the content of that file. Therefore, files inherit the provenance of the container at that state. For the provenance of a container, subsequent states inherit the provenance set of previous states (in terms of time). Using these states, as well as the inherited relationships among them, we can construct the provenance graph of the system. In the provenance graph G=<V,E>, each node $v \in V$ represents a state of a container or a version of a file or a network message. Each edge $e \in E$ represents an input/output or state transition relation between the two nodes, which indicates a taint propagation path. Different states of the container are represented by the nodes in the graph, and they are connected by edges indicating the state transition. Each version of a file is a separate node also, and so are different messages. By traversing the graph in the opposite direction of the arrows, we can easily get the provenance of a file or message.

Because of the strong isolation provided by our system, the only possible ways of cross-container communication is through shared files and network communications. The provenance graph provides a concise representation of the container interactions enabling recovery even long time after the intrusion. The main idea is that, when given an initial intrusion point, we traverse the provenance graph to identify files and containers that have been tainted and require reconstitution from the latest recorded clean version.

5   Performance Evaluation

We implemented a fully working prototype of our system with OpenVZ. We performed several experiments in order to quantify the storage requirements of our system and the gains of using provenance for both storage and the capability to recover files when compared our system to both interval-based backup and pure file versioning. Our evaluation platform consisted of a 2.0GHz Pentium 4 CPU and 1GB of memory. The host OS was running CentOS 5 with a customized 2.6.24 kernel. OpenVZ containers are created from an Ubuntu 8.04 template.

5.1   User Study Using Real Deployment

We tested our prototype system under the load generated from typical desktop users. Five students were selected for the user study over a period of 7 days. The tested applications in VEEs include two web browsers (Firefox and Opera), two text editors (gedit and emacs), PDF reader (evince), and the Open Office suite (including writer, calc, impress, draw, math). In total, 218 VEEs were created in the experiments: 104 web browser VEEs, 47 Open Office VEEs, 40 text editor VEEs, and 27 PDF reader VEEs.

Our system transparently monitors the shared files without having to keep versions of files that are intermediate or non-persistent. For all the 87 shared files in our experiment (73 of which were downloaded from Internet), the total file size is about 52MB. Our system created 152 backup files for the 10 days operations, with a total size of 43MB. The size of raw system logs with

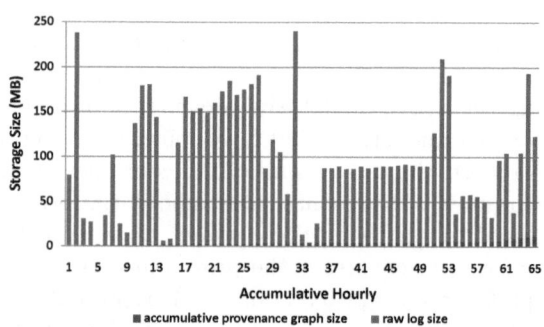

Fig. 2. Hourly Provenance Graph Generation

all the system calls which is comparable to other systems is 13.1 GB. After preserving only the log entries about the shared directory and Internet activities, the log size is only 604MB. Finally, we only need 12MB of storage to maintain provenance information for recovery after 10 days operation. This is less than

1/1000 of the original size. In this experiment, we generated the provenance graph from the non-summarized 604MB logs offline, it took 36 seconds to finish, which is mostly used to read the logs.

5.2 Hourly Provenance Graph Generation

In this experiment, we picked 65 hours of raw system logs in our user study. At the end of each hour, we ran our provenance generation algorithm, and updated the existing provenance graph with the new hourly information. Figure 2 depicts the storage space needed for hourly provenance graph generation. The maximum size of raw logs for one hour was less than 250MB. After each hour the analyzed raw logs were discarded, therefore, the total storage space for logs needed by our approach for 65 hours was still below 250MB. In addition, the bottom columns show the accumulative size of the provenance graph. As time pass, the size of the graph increased, however, even after 65 hours, the total size of the provenance graph was just around 10MB. From this figure, we can see the benefits of our approach in terms of state we have to maintain for recovery. For a typical system, it possible for us to recover data from an attack many days after the initial incident.

5.3 Versioning FS and Timed Backups

Here, we measured the storage overhead and the ability to recover information among interval-based backup systems, pure versioning file systems and our provenance-based approach. Interval-based backup approach takes periodic system snapshots, but the application and file information is lost from the last known good snapshot point. Pure versioning file systems keep every versions of files, so they require an enormous storage space. Our approach can always restore a corrupted file to the most recent clean version, if such exists. In contrast, interval-based backup can only partially recover files because it cannot differentiate between tainted and clean files after infection. Of course, the comparison of versioning and interval-based backup systems depends a lot on the system

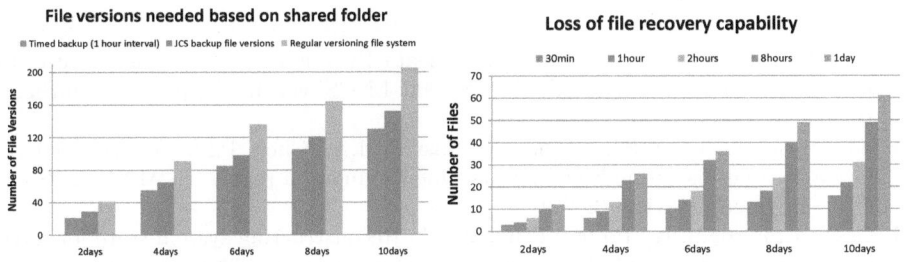

Fig. 3. Comparison of storage overhead for different backup approaches

Fig. 4. Loss of file recovery capability for interval-based backup

usage but it is always the case that the versioning file system requires at least as much storage as the time-interval system. Both systems do not keep provenance information and thus cannot identify the proper versions of files to restore.

We compare the versioning storage overhead of shared files in terms of number of file versions. Figure 3 depicts the corresponding storage overhead comparison among interval-based backup, our approach, and regular versioning file systems. Using the provenance information, after 10 days, we can eliminate 53 versions of files compared to regular versioning file systems without losing any recovery information. The time interval based approach (1 hour interval) stored 22 versions less. Unfortunately, this difference in storage has an impact on the ability to recover files: Figure 4 shows the recovery ability lost in interval-based approach. We varied the backup time intervals to cover different backup scenarios. Although we were fairly aggressive in keeping data, for a 30 minutes interval, after 10 days, this approach lost 16 versions files, which means there are 16 possible cases that a tainted file can not be restored to the most recent clean version. Our results show that as we increase the time interval, less storage is required for backup. However, this diminishes the ability to recover data.

6   Conclusions

We presented a reconstitution framework that aims to provide fast and consistent recovery long after a corruption has taken place. We chose to log application events at the container level rather than the process-level offering a trade-off between finer-grain data recovery within an application for lower state requirements. We show through user studies, that the hourly temporary recovery log for a typical Desktop remains below 250MB and the persistent provenance graph is only 12MB for over 65 hours of collected data. To achieve this state reduction, we proposed a new method for generating data provenance graphs based on the state of the containers and interactions using files and network events. Recovery is feasible even after the launch of hundreds of desktop applications instances following the initial corruption.

References

1. Buneman, P., Khanna, S., Tan, W.-C.: Data Provenance: Some Basic Issues. In: Kapoor, S., Prasad, S. (eds.) FST TCS 2000. LNCS, vol. 1974, pp. 87–93. Springer, Heidelberg (2000)
2. Dunlap, G.W., King, S.T., Cinar, S., Basrai, M.A., Chen, P.M.: Revirt: Enabling intrusion analysis through virtual-machine logging and replay. ACM SIGOPS Operating Systems Review (2002)
3. Goel, A., Farhadi, K., Po, K., Feng, W.-C.: Reconstructing system state for intrusion analysis. ACM SIGOPS Operating Systems Review (2008)
4. Goel, A., Feng, W.-C., Maier, D., Walpole, J.: Forensix: A robust, high-performance reconstruction system. In: 25th IEEE International Conference on Distributed Computing Systems Workshops (2005)

5. Goel, A., Po, K., Farhadi, K., Li, Z., de Lara, E.: The taser intrusion recovery system. In: SOSP 2005: Proceedings of the 20th ACM Symposium on Operating Systems Principles (2005)
6. Hsu, F., Chen, H., Ristenpart, T., Li, J., Su, Z.: Back to the future: A framework for automatic malware removal and system repair. In: ACSAC 2006: Proceedings of 22nd Annual Computer Security Applications Conference (2006)
7. Jain, S., Shafique, F., Djeric, V., Goel, A.: Application-level isolation and recovery with solitude. In: Eurosys 2008: Proceedings of the 3rd ACM SIGOPS European Conference on Computer Systems (2008)
8. King, S.T., Chen, P.M.: Backtracking intrusions. In: SOSP 2003: Proceedings of the Nineteenth ACM Symposium on Operating Systems Principles (2003)
9. Krishnakumar, R.: Kernel korner: kprobes a kernel debugger. Linux Journal (2005)
10. Liu, P., Ammann, P., Jajodia, S.: Rewriting histories: Recovering from malicious transactions. Distributed Parallel Databases 8, 7–40 (2000)
11. Peterson, Z., Burns, R.: Ext3cow: a time-shifting file system for regulatory compliance. Transactions on Storage 1, 190–212 (2005)
12. Potter, S., Nieh, J.: Apiary: Easy-to-use desktop application fault containment on commodity operating systems. In: ATC 2010: USENIX 2010 Annual Technical Conference (2010)
13. Santry, D.S., Feeley, M.J., Hutchinson, N.C., Veitch, A.C., Carton, R.W., Ofir, J.: Deciding when to forget in the elephant file system. ACM SIGOPS Operating Systems Review 33, 110–123 (1999)
14. Seltzer, M., Muniswamy-Reddy, K.-K., Holland, D.A., Braun, U., Ledlie, J.: Provenance-aware storage systems. In: USENIX ATC 2006: Proceedings of the USENIX Annual Technical Conference (2006)
15. Sharif, M., Lee, W., Cui, W., Lanzi, A.: Secure in-vm monitoring using hardware virtualization. In: CCS 2009: Proceedings of the 16th ACM Conference on Computer and Communications Security (2009)
16. Simmhan, Y.L., Plale, B., Gannon, D.: A survey of data provenance techniques. Technical report, Computer Science Department, Indiana University, Bloomington IN 47405 (2005)
17. Sriranjani, S., Venkatesan, S.: Forensic analysis of file system intrusions using improved backtracking. In: IWIA 2005: Proceedings of the Third IEEE International Workshop on Information Assurance (2005)
18. Soules, C.A.N., Goodson, G.R., Strunk, J.D., Ganger, G.R.: Metadata efficiency in versioning file systems. In: FAST 2003: Proceedings of the 2nd USENIX Conference on File and Storage Technologies (2003)
19. Suh, G.E., Lee, J.W., Zhang, D., Devadas, S.: Secure program execution via dynamic information flow tracking. In: ASPLOS 2004: Proceedings of the 11th International Conference on Architectural Support for Programming Languages and Operating Systems (2004)
20. Taesoo Kim, N.Z., Wang, X., Kaashoek, M.F.: Intrusion recovery using selective re-execution. In: OSDI 2010: Proceedings of the 9th Symposium on Operating Systems Design and Implementation (2010)
21. Unionfs, http://www.am-utils.org/project-unionfs.html

Privacy-Preserving Online Mixing of High Integrity Mobile Multi-user Data

Akshay Dua, Nirupama Bulusu, and Wu-chang Feng

Portland State University
{akshay,nbulusu,wuchang}@cs.pdx.edu

Abstract. Crowd-sourced sensing systems facilitate unprecedented insight into our local environments by leveraging voluntarily contributed data from the impressive array of smartphone sensors (GPS, audio, image, accelerometer, etc.). However, user participation in crowd-sourced sensing will be inhibited if people cannot trust the system to maintain their privacy. On the other hand, data modified for privacy may be of limited use to the system without mechanisms to verify integrity. In this paper, we present an interactive proof protocol that allows an intermediary to convince a data consumer that it is accurately performing a privacy-preserving transformation mixing inputs from multiple expected sources, but without revealing those inputs. Additionally, we discuss privacy transformation functions that are compatible with the protocol, and show that the protocol introduces very little overhead, making it ideal for real-time crowd-sourced data collection.

Keywords: privacy, integrity, interactive proofs, participatory sensing.

1 Introduction

Crowd-sourced sensing systems must protect the privacy of all data sources, whilst also providing integrity guarantees for the collected data. Data obtained from the crowd can enable novel people-centric applications in health care, traffic, and environmental monitoring systems [17,15,13]. User contribution of sensitive data such as location may be inhibited due to privacy concerns. One way to protect user privacy is to perform a privacy-preserving transformation, such as mixing, on the raw data collected from mobile users. But this may engender reluctance to trust the integrity of the transformation in the consumer. The conundrum here is that it is difficult to prove the transformation's integrity without revealing the raw data and compromising the privacy of data sources. Thus, integrity and privacy wind up as dueling goals of a crowd-sourced sensing system.

Most prior approaches have either proposed novel transformation functions to provide privacy [8,16], or proposed mechanisms to verify data integrity [7], but have not addressed both problems simultaneously. VPriv [14] is the only prior work that attempts to offer both integrity and privacy using an additive homomorphic commitment scheme, for the application scenario of computing tolls over paths taken by vehicles. But its integrity is limited to additive functions, while its privacy is limited by the need for random spot checks.

M. Rajarajan et al. (Eds.): SecureComm 2011, LNICST 96, pp. 470–479, 2012.
© Institute for Computer Sciences, Social Informatics and Telecommunications Engineering 2012

Our previous work [6] provided a mechanism to verify the integrity of privacy-preserving transformations of data from an individual source without revealing the raw data. But it did not address the problem of verifying the integrity of privacy-preserving transformations that *mix* data from *multiple* data sources. Mixing data from multiple users, as opposed to performing transformations on data from a single user, is essential to ensuring better privacy for all users [8]. However, simultaneously achieving privacy and integrity with mixing is not trivial. It is reasonable to assume a user's vested interest in her own privacy, but not necessarily in the privacy of others. Thus, the integrity verification must now be robust to any privacy threats that stem from a collusion between a data source and the data consumer.

In this paper, we address the problem of privacy-preserving online mixing of mobile multi-user data. Our work uses the system model illustrated in Fig. 1. It assumes that multiple independent *data sources or producers* forward their raw data to a trusted *privacy proxy*. The proxy then performs a *privacy-preserving transformation* on the received data and forwards the result to a *data consumer*. Here, the proxy is analogous to a Tor mix-node [5], which mixes data from multiple sources to provide anonymity. Note that the proxy is trusted by the sources but not by the consumer.

Our goal is to enable the privacy proxy to assure the data consumer that, the result it publishes is indeed the output of a given privacy-preserving transformation on data from multiple expected sources as input (integrity guarantee), without having to provide that input to the consumer (privacy guarantee). The contributions of this paper include:

- An interactive proof protocol [10], using which, only an honest privacy proxy can convince a data consumer that it is correctly computing a given privacy-preserving transformation that mixes data from multiple users. Most importantly, the proof requires the proxy to send the consumer only the output of the transformation. Since the inputs — sensitive data contributed by participants — are never sent to the consumer, each participant's privacy remains protected (Section 4).
- Demonstrating privacy-preserving transformations whose integrity can be proved using our interactive proof protocol (Section 5).
- Deriving the overhead introduced by the protocol. We show that the overhead is a fraction of the complexity of the privacy-preserving transformation being computed by the proxy (Section 6)

2   Problem Statement

Only an honest privacy proxy P should be able to convince a data consumer C that it is indeed publishing the result of a privacy-preserving transformation function f_{priv} on data $D_j = \{d_{1j}, d_{2j}, ..., d_{nj}\}$ received from a set of sources $S = \{s_1, s_2, ..., s_n\}$ in interval j (Fig. 1). C receives the result $p_j = f_{priv}(D_j)$, but never the data D_j. Essentially, the following must be satisfied:

- **Integrity requirement.** C must be convinced with high probability that $p_j = f_{priv}(D_j)$ only if P is honest
- **Privacy requirement.** C must not be able to learn or verify that $D_j = \{d_{1j}, d_{2j}, ..., d_{nj}\}$

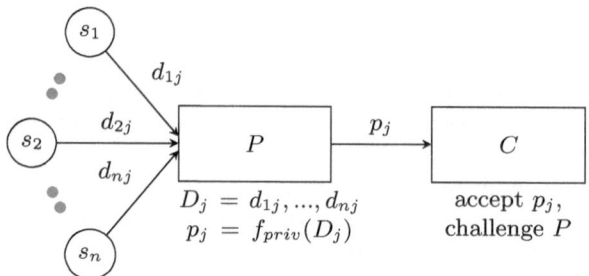

Fig. 1. System model

3   Threat Model

The design of our protocol aims to both prevent a malicious data consumer C from discovering any raw data D contributed by any of the sources S, and prevent a malicious privacy proxy P from using either alternate transformation functions besides f_{priv}, or data besides D, or both.

Insiders pose significant risks to the system. We assume that the data consumer is an adversary of privacy, but not of integrity. This is reasonable because the data consumer C has a vested interest in the integrity of the privacy-preserving transformation. Further, we assume that the privacy proxy P is an adversary of integrity, but not of privacy. The reason being, that the data sources trust P to protect their privacy, but the consumer may not trust P to preserve data integrity. An implication of the above adversarial model is that P and C do not collude in any way. Since sources could contribute bogus information to skew the collected data, they are considered adversaries of integrity. Our proof protocol alone, however, is not designed to address the threat of fabricated data from the sources. The proof only guarantees that the output of a privacy transformation was computed using inputs from S, but the integrity of those inputs — the sensory data collected by S – cannot be guaranteed by our protocol. Our earlier work [7] describes the design and implementation of a trusted sensing platform that can be used to address this issue.

We do not consider denial-of-service attacks in which communicating parties P, C, and S can potentially suppress responses that are expected by others. Nor do we consider threats from eavesdropping adversaries that can be mitigated by standard network security protocols, like TLS.

Our work focuses on the integrity and privacy of *content* rather than their *origin*. Thus, attacks that could reveal or alter the origin of a message are not

Table 1. Normal Operation

s_i	P
interval j: sense d_{ij}	
if j mod $h = 0$,	
choose random m from $[0, h-1]$	
set $m = m + j$	
if $j = m$,	
save $[d_{ij}, j]$	
$s_i \to P$: d_{ij}	$P \to C$: $p_j = f_{priv}(d_{ij})$
...	...

considered. Directing traffic from S through a mix network like Tor [5] and using anonymous group signatures [3] for authentication can mitigate such attacks.

Finally, we assume that C and sources in S honestly execute the protocol since C has a vested interest in collecting high-integrity data, and S has a vested interest in protecting personal privacy. Nevertheless, C is free to perform offline privacy attacks on the data received from P. Mitigation strategies for such attacks have been addressed in the security analysis of our prior work [6], and are not discussed in this paper.

4   Interactive Proof Protocol

As shown in Fig. 1, after receiving p_j, C may randomly choose to issue a challenge that will require P to prove that it is honestly computing f_{priv} using inputs from sources S. This challenge message marks the beginning of the interactive proof protocol. After the proof, C will be convinced about the integrity of the data with *high probability* only when P is honest, but not otherwise.

4.1   Preliminaries

For the protocol to work, we require a shared symmetric key k_{ic} between the source s_i and the data consumer C, a key k_{ip} between s_i and privacy proxy P, and a buffer at s_i that is large enough to store data collected in b distinct intervals. Where encryption/decryption is necessary, the notation $Enc_{k_{ic}}$ and $Dec_{k_{ic}}$ indicate a symmetric encryption and decryption algorithm (e.g. AES) using key k_{ic}. Additionally, we need the privacy-preserving transformation function f_{priv} to satisfy the following condition: given an *obfuscation function* $g(r, x)$ that obfuscates input x using random number r that we call the *obfuscation key*, we require that

$$f_{priv}(g(r, x_{1j}), ..., g(r, x_{mj})) = g(r, f_{priv}(x_{1j}, ..., x_{mj})) \qquad (1)$$

So for example, let $g(r, x) = r \cdot x$, and $f_{priv}(x_{1j}, ..., x_{mj}) = mean(x_{1j}, ..., x_{mj})$ then,

$$f_{priv}(g(r, x_{1j}), ..., g(r, x_{mj})) = mean(r \cdot x_{1j}, ..., r \cdot x_{mj})$$
$$= r \cdot mean(x_{1j}, ..., x_{mj})$$
$$= g(r, f_{priv}(x_{1j}, ..., x_{mj}))$$

Here, the privacy-preserving transformation is simply a mean of its inputs (raw data from sources) and we can see that this particular transformation satisfies Equation (1). What is significant, is that Equation (1) establishes a relationship between the *transformed value*, and *obfuscated raw data* from sources. This relationship is fundamental to the success of our protocol because it gives us the ability to check the integrity of the published data without requiring the potentially sensitive raw data from sources.

Data sources must, however, provide obfuscated data to the consumer during the protocol. Fortunately, without the obfuscation key, the consumer may have no way to extract the correct raw data, especially because the key changes every interval. Further, even if there was a way, say by using an oracle, the consumer could only ever extract raw data for half the number of intervals in which it challenges the proxy. So, if C challenges 4 out of 10 intervals, then using the oracle it could extract raw data for 2 intervals.

4.2   Protocol Details

Table 1 shows the normal operation of source s_i, which, continuously picks a random interval j from every h, and saves the corresponding data in its buffer. Once the buffer is full, s_i is ready to participate in the interactive proof protocol. We explain later how each source s_i picks the same j.

The interactive proof protocol begins once C randomly issues one of two challenges to P (via S, see Tab. 2). On receiving a response, C performs one of two different tests to check the response's integrity.

Both tests are performed using obfuscated raw data from sources in S or from their chosen leader s_{lead} (more on this later). Note that P *does not know* which test will be performed until it has responded. Thus, P's initial response acts as a bit commitment [2]. The tests serve three purposes:

1. Allow an honest P to pass either test with the same response, but force a dishonest P to create a different response for each. Since a dishonest P does not know which test is going to be performed, its chances of passing are $1/2$. If P repeatedly passes, then C has more confidence in P's honesty.
2. Make sure that obfuscated raw data from S and the corresponding obfuscation key are not simultaneously available to C during any given challenge. If that were the case, C could extract the raw sensitive data from the obfuscated values. We can see, that during Challenge 1, C has the obfuscation key but not the obfuscated data. Where as in Challenge 2, its vice versa.
3. Use one test to check that a published transformed value was indeed computed using raw data from s_i, and the other to check that the privacy-preserving transformation computed by P was indeed f_{priv}. Test 1 does

Table 2. Interactive proof protocol

Sources $S = \{s_1, ..., s_n\}$	**C**
	for each $s_i \in S$,
	With probability $1/2$:
	$C \to s_i$: $Enc_{k_{ic}}$(**Challenge 1**)
	OR, $C \to s_i$: $Enc_{k_{ic}}$(**Challenge 2**)
at each $s_i \in S$,	
decrypt challenge	
Pick random number r	
randomly choose saved interval l, $l \le j$	

Sources $S = \{s_1, ..., s_n\}$	**P**
at each $s_i \in S$,	
$s_i \to P$: $M_{i0} = Enc_{k_{ip}}(g(r, d_{il}))$	
	$O_l = Dec_{k_{1p}}(M_{10}), ..., Dec_{k_{np}}(M_{n0})$
	$P \to C$: $p = f_{priv}(O_l)$

Sources $S = \{s_1, ..., s_n\}$	**C**
if Challenge 1,	
$s_{lead} \to C$: $M_1 = Enc_{k_{lead,c}}(r, l)$	
else,	
at each $s_i \in S$,	
$s_i \to C$: $M_{i2} = Enc_{k_{ic}}(g(r_i, d_{il}))$	
	M_1 OR $M_{12}, ..., M_{n2}$
	Test 1 (if **Challenge 1**):
	$r, l = Dec_{k_{lead,c}}(M_1)$
	if $p \ne g(r, p_l)$,
	reject
	Test 2 (if **Challenge 2**):
	$O_l = Dec_{k_{1c}}(M_{12}), ..., Dec_{k_{nc}}(M_{n2})$
	if $p \ne f_{priv}(O_l)$,
	reject

the former while Test 2 does the latter. Test 1 compares $f_{priv}(O_l) \overset{?}{=} g(r, f_{priv}(D_l))$, where O_l is obfuscated sensory data, and D_l is raw sensory data for a past interval l. This will be true only if source s_i created O_l by obfuscating D_l. Test 2 compares the transformed value sent by P with $f_{priv}(O_l)$ computed by C. Since C is computing f_{priv} on data received directly from the sources, this comparison will be true only if P computed f_{priv} as well.

Once the interactive proof is complete, s_i purges the respective interval of data from its buffer, thus making room for more. In the interest of clarity, we have omitted the use of digital signatures for authentication.

One question remains: how does one get all the sources to pick the same saved interval j, same challenge interval l, and random number r? With the correct r, j, and l, each source can obfuscate and forward its own data to C as shown in Tab. 2.

Table 3. Initialization phase

Sources $S = \{s_1, ..., s_n\}$
establish shared group key k_g
establish leader $s_{lead} \in S$
s_{lead} broadcasts $M_{init} = Enc_{k_g}(r_{seed}, b, h)$
at each $s_i \in S$,
set $r_{seed}, b, h = Dec_{k_g}(M_{init})$
initialize PRNG with r_{seed}
allocate buffer for b intervals of data

We can get all the sources to pick the same random numbers if each one uses the same Pseudo-Random Number Generator (PRNG) with the same random seeds. The random seed could be securely communicated (via P) to each source by another that is picked to be the leader (s_{lead}). For secure communication among sources, a group key will need to be established [12]. To reliably elect a leader, a communication-efficient stable leader election protocol can be used [1].

Once the secure communication channels are established, the elected leader can broadcast (via P) the protocol's various parameters — the random seed, size of the buffer b, and sampling frame size h — to the rest of the sources during an initialization phase (Table 3).

5   Privacy-Preserving Transformations

We do not attempt to define what precisely is a privacy-preserving transformation. Rather, we claim that if such a transformation satisfies Equation (1), then the entity computing the transformation can provide proofs of integrity for the result without disclosing the inputs. The question is, what privacy-preserving transformations satisfy Equation (1)?

While providing an exhaustive list (or category) of privacy-preserving transformations satisfying Equation (1) is out of the scope of this paper, we present one whose computational integrity can be proven using our protocol. The privacy-preserving transformation in question is a *cloaking* algorithm similar to the one by Gruteser and Grunwald [11] intended for use in Location Based Services (LBS). The idea is to spatially cloak a set of GPS coordinates published by participants, and return an area (e.g., a quadrant) that includes at least

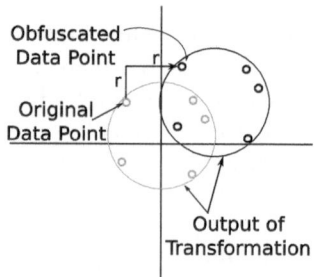

Fig. 2. Spatial Cloaking

k_{min} of them. Here, k_{min} quantifies the amount of anonymity desired. Specifically, it enforces the fact that each participant's location cannot be distinguished from at least $k_{min} - 1$ others.

The privacy-preserving transformation f_{priv} is the function that takes the GPS coordinates as input and returns the respective area (see Fig. 2) as output. Unlike the original algorithm, where the f_{priv} returned a quadrant, we define an f_{priv} that returns a circular area (x, y, u), where (x, y) is the center of that circle, and u is its radius. Formally, we define f_{priv} as:

$$f_{priv}((x_1, y_1, 0), ..., (x_n, y_n, 0)) = (x_c, y_c, u_c) \tag{2}$$

Intuitively, the privacy transformation above returns a circle large enough to cover all the circles provided as input. A participant's coordinates are thus expressed not as points, but as circles whose radii are zero. We now define the obfuscation function g as: $g(r, (x, y, u)) = (x + r, y + r, u)$.

Intuitively again, the obfuscation function moves the input circle by r units in the x and y dimensions. Using the above definitions for f_{priv} and g in the left and right hand side of Equation (1) we have: Since f_{priv} and g satisfy Equation

$$
\begin{aligned}
&f_{priv}(g(r, (x_1, y_1, 0)), ..., g(r, (x_n, y_n, 0))) &&g(r, f_{priv}((x_1, y_1, 0), ..., (x_n, y_n, 0))) \\
=&f_{priv}((x_1 + r, y_1 + r, 0), ..., (x_n + r, y_n + r, 0)) &&=g(r, (x_c, y_c, u_c)) \\
=&(x_c + r, y_c + r, u_c) &&=(x_c + r, y_c + r, u_c)
\end{aligned}
$$

(1), our interactive proof protocol is applicable in this LBS scenario.

6   Overhead

We now present an analysis of the overhead imposed by our protocol. We will show that the introduced overhead is a fraction of the complexity of the privacy-preserving transformation computed by the proxy P. Our baseline is a data collection system like PoolView [8], where privacy guarantees are provided without integrity guarantees. The overhead then, is due to all computations and message exchanges required to perform the interactive proof of integrity while preserving privacy (Table 2). Also, note that we are mainly interested in the overhead of the more expensive challenge where in addition to P, C must also compute f_{priv}. Our result, therefore, is the worst case bound for overhead as it assumes that every challenge from C is the more expensive one, when in reality that will only be true during approximately half the challenges.

We define t_b as the time it takes for baseline operation: sources in S send data to P, which computes f_{priv} over that data and forwards the result to C. We define t_c as $t_b + t_{proof}$ where t_{proof} is the time it takes to complete the interactive proof. Then, overhead $t_o = t_c - t_b = t_{proof}$. Now,

$$t_b = t_{fpriv} + \frac{rtt_{SP}}{2} + \frac{rtt_{PC}}{2}$$

where, t_{fpriv} is the time it takes to compute the privacy transformation, and rtt_{ij} is the round-trip time between i and j. We have excluded minor computations such as a data source randomly choosing and saving an interval of data in its buffer. Also,

$$t_c = 3\, t_{fpriv} + 2\, rtt_{SP} + 2\, rtt_{PC} + \delta$$

where δ includes symmetric encryption or decryption operations performed on raw data values, and the computation of the simple obfuscation function $g(r, x)$.

Subtracting t_c from t_b we get overhead:

$$t_o = 2\, t_{fpriv} + \frac{3\, rtt_{SP}}{2} + \frac{3\, rtt_{PC}}{2} + \delta$$

Note that the overhead t_o is applicable only in those intervals in which the data consumer issues a challenge. The probability $P(challenge)$ with which the consumer issues a challenge during any given interval is $1/h$ (Section). Further, if the round-trip, encryption, and decryption times are negligible compared to the privacy transformation f_{priv}, then $t_o \approx 2\, t_{fpriv}$. With this in mind, the expected overhead of our protocol after I intervals of data collection is,

$$E(overhead) = I \times t_o \times P(challenge) = \frac{2I\, t_{fpriv}}{h}$$

It is important to note that if the data publishing interval is larger than $E(overhead)$, then the entire proof will finish before the sources disseminate the next interval of data. Thus, causing no perceptible delay in data publication.

7   Conclusion

Crowd-sourced sensing can revolutionize applications from intelligent transportation to health care monitoring, but confronts the challenge of maintaining user privacy to encourage contribution of data, while maintaining data integrity to encourage governmental and citizen use of that data. We have proposed the first solution using interactive proofs that allows an intermediary to convince a data consumer that it is accurately performing a privacy-preserving transformation that mixes inputs from multiple data sources, without providing those inputs to the consumer. The proposed protocol preserves the privacy advantages of mixing data from multiple sources, while being robust to privacy threats that arise from collusion between a data source and a consumer during integrity verification. The key idea is that unlike traditional interactive proofs with one prover (privacy proxy) and one verifier (data consumer), ours involves a collaboration between the verifier and all additional parties that wants to protect their privacy (data sources) to keep the prover in check. We have analyzed the protocol overhead and discussed compatible privacy-preserving transformations.

Acknowledgments. This work was supported by the National Science Foundation under grants CISE-0747442 and CNS-1017034. We would like to thank Tom Shrimpton for his feedback on the interactive proof protocol.

References

1. Aguilera, M.K., Delporte-Gallet, C., Fauconnier, H., Toueg, S.: Stable Leader Election (Extended Abstract). In: Welch, J.L. (ed.) DISC 2001. LNCS, vol. 2180, pp. 108–122. Springer, Heidelberg (2001)

2. Chaum, D., Damgård, I.B., van de Graaf, J.: Multiparty Computations Ensuring Privacy of Each Party's Input and Correctness of the Result. In: Pomerance, C. (ed.) CRYPTO 1987. LNCS, vol. 293, pp. 87–119. Springer, Heidelberg (1988)
3. Chaum, D., van Heyst, E.: Group Signatures. In: Davies, D.W. (ed.) EUROCRYPT 1991. LNCS, vol. 547, pp. 257–265. Springer, Heidelberg (1991)
4. Consolvo, S., McDonald, D., Toscos, T., Chen, M., Froehlich, J., Harrison, B., Klasnja, P., LaMarca, A., LeGrand, L., Libby, R., et al.: Activity sensing in the wild: a field trial of ubifit garden. In: Proceeding of the Twenty-Sixth Annual SIGCHI Conference on Human Factors in Computing Systems, pp. 1797–1806. ACM (2008)
5. Dingledine, R., Mathewson, N., Syverson, P.: Tor: The second-generation onion router. In: USENIX Security, p. 21. USENIX Association, Berkeley (2004)
6. Dua, A., Bulusu, N., Feng, W.: Catching Cheats with Interactive Proofs: Privacy-preserving Crowd-sourced. Data Collection Without Compromising Integrity (2010)
7. Dua, A., Bulusu, N., Feng, W., Hu, W.: Towards Trustworthy Participatory Sensing. In: HotSec 2009: Proceedings of the 4th USENIX Workshop on Hot Topics in Security. USENIX Association, Berkeley (2009)
8. Ganti, R., Pham, N., Tsai, Y., Abdelzaher, T.: PoolView: stream privacy for grass-roots participatory sensing. In: Proceedings of ACM SenSys, Raleigh, North Carolina, pp. 281–294. ACM (2008)
9. Gentry, C.: Fully homomorphic encryption using ideal lattices. In: Proceedings of the 41st Annual ACM Symposium on Theory of Computing, pp. 169–178. ACM (2009)
10. Goldwasser, S., Micali, S., Rackoff, C.: The knowledge complexity of interactive proof-systems. In: Proceedings of the Seventeenth Annual ACM Symposium on Theory of Computing, p. 304. ACM (1985)
11. Gruteser, M., Grunwald, D.: Anonymous usage of location-based services through spatial and temporal cloaking. In: Proceedings of the 1st International Conference on Mobile Systems, Applications and Services, pp. 31–42. ACM (2003)
12. Katz, J., Yung, M.: Scalable protocols for authenticated group key exchange. Journal of Cryptology 20(1), 85–113 (2007)
13. Paulos, E., Honicky, R., Goodman, E.: Sensing atmosphere. In: Workshop on Sensing on Everyday Mobile Phones in Support of Participatory Research. Citeseer (2007)
14. Popa, R., Balakrishnan, H., Blumberg, A.: VPriv: Protecting privacy in location-based vehicular services. In: Proceedings of the 18th USENIX Security Symposium (2009)
15. Reddy, S., Parker, A., Hyman, J., Burke, J., Estrin, D., Hansen, M.: Image browsing, processing, and clustering for participatory sensing: lessons from a DietSense prototype. In: ACM SenSys, Cork, Ireland, pp. 13–17. ACM (2007)
16. Shi, J., Zhang, R., Liu, Y., Zhang, Y.: PriSense: Privacy-Preserving Data Aggregation in People-Centric Urban Sensing Systems. In: IEEE INFOCOM (2010)
17. Thiagarajan, A., Ravindranath, L., LaCurts, K., Madden, S., Balakrishnan, H., Toledo, S., Eriksson, J.: VTrack: accurate, energy-aware road traffic delay estimation using mobile phones. In: Proceedings of the 7th ACM Conference on Embedded Networked Sensor Systems, pp. 85–98. ACM (2009)

Symbolic Analysis for Security of Roaming Protocols in Mobile Networks
[Extended Abstract]

Chunyu Tang, David A. Naumann*, and Susanne Wetzel

Stevens Institute of Technology, Hoboken NJ 07030 USA

Abstract. Both GSM (2G) and UMTS (3G) wireless standards are deployed worldwide. Like the 4G standard now appearing, these standards provide for mobile devices with differing capabilities to roam between providers or technologies. This poses serious challenges in ensuring authentication and other security properties. Automated analysis of security properties is needed to cope with the large number of possible scenarios. While some attacks exploit weaknesses in cryptographic functions, many attacks exploit flaws or other features of the protocol design. The latter attacks can be found using symbolic (Dolev-Yao) models. This paper demonstrates the use of a fully automatic tool to exhaustively analyze symbolic models of GSM, UMTS, and the respective roaming protocols. The results include the demonstration of known attacks as well as the confirmation of expected properties.

Keywords: Mobile networks, GSM, UMTS, roaming protocols, security, authentication, secrecy, symbolic modeling, automated analysis.

1 Introduction

Starting in the early 90s, the Global System for Mobile Communications (GSM)—also referred to as second generation (2G) technology—became a main standard for mobile telecommunication. Recently, phone carriers have started to build fourth generation (4G) networks. Given the evolution of the telecommunication standards and devices, enabling secure roaming and handover is at the core of providing service to mobile subscribers.[1] This includes roaming and handover within one technology as well as across technologies.

While Universal Mobile Telecommunications System (UMTS)—also called third generation (3G)—allows for the interoperation with GSM, its successor is to support many more options. Analyzing the security of all possible combinations of interoperating scenarios by hand is a rather tedious undertaking. While for the interoperation between GSM and UMTS six different scenarios had to be investigated, this number grows an order of magnitude for 4G.

---

* Tang and Naumann were supported by US NSF award CCF-0915611.

[1] The term *handover* refers to mechanisms for mobility of an ongoing phone call or data exchange; *roaming* refers to mobility while no such service is currently active.

M. Rajarajan et al. (Eds.): SecureComm 2011, LNICST 96, pp. 480–490, 2012.
© Institute for Computer Sciences, Social Informatics and Telecommunications Engineering 2012

This paper explores an approach that allows for a structured exploration of specified security properties in the various contexts. The first contribution is to provide formal models of the main security components of both the GSM and UMTS standards (Sects. 3 and 4), together with the specification of required authenticity and secrecy properties. The second contribution is to show that one can automate the checking of the various (roaming) scenarios to see whether or not specified security properties hold—thus replacing the tedious checking of all possible combinations by hand (Sect. 5). The automated analysis finds several known attacks, and does not miss known attacks except those that exploit weaknesses in cryptographic functions. The feasibility study in this paper lays the basis for a formal modeling and automated analysis of 4G and its manifold associated roaming and handover scenarios.

2   Related Work

The security of the mobile communication standards has been studied extensively both in the context of the standardization efforts [19] and outside by the greater research and user community. For example, [8] noted that GSM is susceptible to a false base station attack. Recently, Nohl et al. demonstrated that it is possible to eavesdrop on GSM communication in practice with rather little effort. Attacks on GSM ciphers were devised by, for example, Golic [9], and Dunkelman et al. [6]—the latter of which is also of relevance in the context of UMTS security. Aside from general assessments of UMTS security (e.g., [16]), or works focusing on UMTS encryption and integrity mechanisms (e.g., [16,11]), one main focus in UMTS is on security in the context of roaming and handover (e.g., [14,15,13]).

In this paper we focus on the analysis of protocols in the *symbolic* or Dolev-Yao model, which assumes perfect cryptography: an encrypted message can be decrypted only with the appropriate key, hash functions do not have collisions, etc. The attacker has complete control over the network: it can introduce, alter, replay, and delete any message. Several open-source protocol analyzers have seen extensive use; we mention selected examples. Taha et al. [17] analyze the handover schemes and the pre-authentication handover protocol in IEEE 802.16e standard (Mobile WiMAX) using the Scyther tool. They find the attacker can obtain the keys in both protocols. Taha et al. [18] analyze the privacy and key management protocol in IEEE 802.16 (PKMv1) and 802.16e (PKMv2) using Scyther. They find a pseudonymity attack in both protocols, and an attack violating the data secrecy in PKMv1. Lim et al. [12] propose a handover protocol for WLAN, WiBro and UMTS, and verify it using AVISPA. Bouassida et al. [4] analyze the key management architecture for hierarchical group protocols using AVISPA, and find an attack on the members promotion protocol. Other relevant tools are LySa [3] and protocol analyzers of Meadows et al. [7].

In this work we use the ProVerif tool (PV for short). Chang and Shmatikov [5] use PV to analyze the Bluetooth device pairing protocols; They confirm the offline guessing attack [10] and discover an attack scenario for a then-proposed

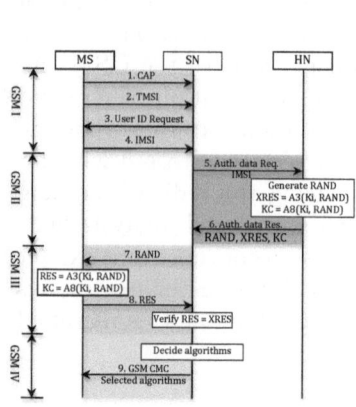

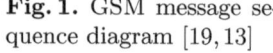

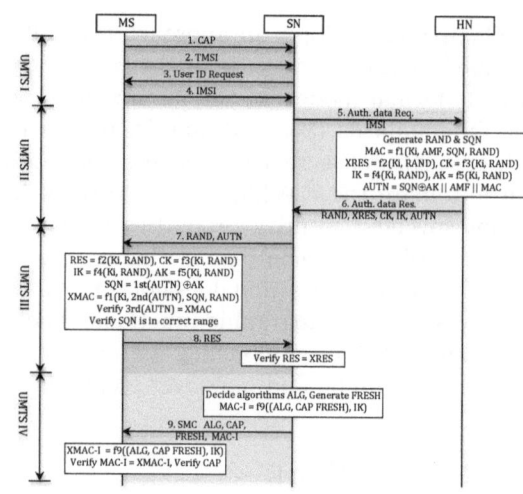

Fig. 1. GSM message sequence diagram [19, 13]

Fig. 2. UMTS message sequence diagram [19, 13]

Simple Pairing protocol. Abadi et al. use PV to analyze the Just Fast Key protocol [1]. Blanchet and Chaudhuri [2] use PV to analyze a protocol for secure file sharing on untrusted storage.

3 Review of GSM, UMTS, and Roaming

3.1 GSM

When connecting to a *Base Station* (BS) of a *Servicing Network* (SN), a *Mobile Station* (MS) first transmits its *Temporary Mobile Subscriber Identity* (TMSI) as well as its *CAPabilities* (CAP), i.e., the encryption algorithms it supports to the SN. In case the SN does not recognize the TMSI (i.e., the SN cannot resolve the received TMSI to a unique *International Mobile Subscriber Identity* (IMSI), the SN will require the MS to send its unique IMSI. A SN may be the MS's wireless service provider, i.e., its *Home Network* (HN) or a *Foreign Network* (FN). A MS might receive service from a FN in areas where its HN does not provide service. Based on the IMSI, the SN will then request an authentication vector from the MS's HN (see Message 5 in Fig. 1).

The MS and HN share a long-term symmetric secret key K_i. Using this pre-shared secret key K_i and a random nonce $RAND$, the HN generates an authentication vector consisting of the three components $RAND$, $XRES$, and a session key K_c. (The details of the algorithms A3 and A8 [19] which are used to compute the $XRES$ and K_c are not important in the context of this paper.) Upon receiving the authentication vector (Message 6), the SN starts a challenge-response type exchange with the MS. Specifically, the SN sends the challenge $RAND$ to the MS (Message 7). Based on the received $RAND$ and the pre-shared key K_i stored on its SIM card, the MS computes the session key K_c as well as a response RES to the received challenge $RAND$. Subsequently, the MS sends the computed response RES to the SN. If RES matches the response $XRES$ (which the SN received from the HN as part of the authentication vector) then the MS has successfully authenticated itself to the SN. Then the SN moves on to decide which encryption algorithm will be used to encrypt the communication on the air interface between the SN and the MS (based on the CAP it received from the MS earlier). The SN informs the MS of its choice (Message 9) and starts the (possibly encrypted) communication.

Security in GSM: The protocol described above assures the SN of the *authenticity* of the MS in case the response RES received from the MS matches $XRES$ received from the HN. Only an MS holding the pre-shared key K_i will be able to compute the correct result RES in response to the random challenge $RAND$ (assuming the security of algorithms A3 and A8). However, GSM does not provide any assurance for the MS that it is in fact connected to a legitimate BS of the SN. The *false base station attack* is a *man-in-the-middle attack* [8], i.e., the false BS sits in between the MS and the legitimate BS, pretending to be a legitimate BS when communication with the MS and pretending to be a legitimate MS when communicating with the actual BS. Since the MS sends its capabilities CAP in the clear, it is possible for a false BS to intercept and modify that information before forwarding it to a legitimate BS. In particular, it can change the capabilities CAP it received from the MS so that the legitimate BS will believe that the MS cannot support encryption. Consequently, the false BS will be able to listen in and arbitrarily modify the unencrypted communication between the MS and the legitimate BS.

3.2   UMTS

Establishing a connection to a BS of a SN in UMTS follows the same principles as those in GSM. The main differences lie in that those specified in UMTS are intended to provide mutual authentication of the MS and the SN and they also include mechanisms to support integrity protection and to establish freshness guarantees. Specifically, upon receiving an authentication request from the SN (Message 5 in Fig. 2), the HN computes an authentication vector that is more extensive than the one issued in GSM. In addition to determining a challenge response pair $RAND$ and $XRES$, in UMTS the HN also computes a *Message Authentication Code* (MAC), a *Ciphering Key* (CK), an *Integrity Protection Key* (IK), an *Anonymity Key* (AK), a *Sequence Number* (SQN) as well as an *Authentication Management Field* (AMF).

Upon receiving the authentication vector (Message 6), the SN initiates the challenge response exchange with the MS. Unlike in GSM, the MS receives the *Authentication Token* (AUTN) as part of Message 7 which allows the MS to determine whether or not this is a *fresh* authentication challenge. Upon receiving the response RES from the MS (Message 8), the SN checks whether or not it matches $XRES$. If so, then the MS has successfully authenticated to the SN. The SN then proceeds to deciding on the encryption algorithm. In contrast to GSM, in UMTS the SN includes the CAP (MS's encryption and integrity protection capabilities) in its message to the MS as it received them as part of Message 1.

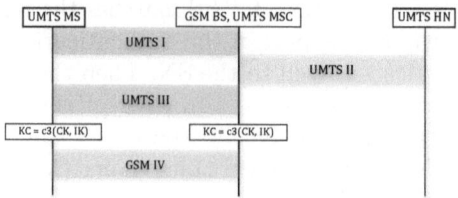

Fig. 3. UMTS subscriber roams into mixed network (blocks GSM I–IV, UMTS I–IV are protocol components in Figs. 1, 2) [19, 13]

Message 9 is integrity protected. Based on Message 9, the MS can verify that the SN received the CAP as the MS sent them. In addition, the integrity protecting as part of Message 9 allows the SN to authenticate itself to the MS.

Security in UMTS: The MS has correctly authenticated to the SN if *RES* matches *XRES*. The authentication of the SN to the MS requires two components to be present: the freshness of AUTN (sent in Message 7)—preventing the replay of authentication data—and a correctly integrity protected Message 9.

3.3 Roaming between GSM and UMTS

The UMTS standard defines roaming mechanisms to allow a GSM MS to connect to a UMTS infrastructure as well as for a UMTS MS to connect to a GSM infrastructure. The assumptions are that the respective MSs support both the GSM and UMTS radio interfaces and provide for both the GSM and UMTS encryption and integrity protection mechanisms.

For the discussion of roaming scenarios it is necessary to distinguish two components of the SN: the BS and the *Mobile Switching Center* (MSC). Depending on whether the BS and MSC are of GSM or UMTS technology, they are referred to as GSM/UMTS MSC and GSM/UMTS BS. There are six roaming scenarios:

1. A UMTS MS roams to a SN with a UMTS BS and UMTS MSC. This case is equivalent to regular UMTS operation.
2. A GSM MS roams to a SN with a GSM BS and GSM MSC. This case is equivalent to regular GSM operation.
3. A UMTS MS roams to a SN with a GSM BS and GSM MSC.
4. A GSM MS roams to a SN with a UMTS BS and UMTS MSC.
5. A UMTS MS roams to a SN with a GSM BS and a UMTS MSC. See Fig. 3.
6. A GSM MS roams to a SN with a GSM BS and a UMTS MSC. This case is equivalent to regular GSM operation. I.e., the UMTS MSC will act as a GSM MSC.

Security in Roaming: Scenarios (3) and (5) are prone to the false base station attack as the GSM cipher command is not integrity protected and does not include the MS's CAP. Furthermore, as shown in [13, 14] it is possible to mount an *asynchronous* man-in-the-middle attack in an all UMTS environment.

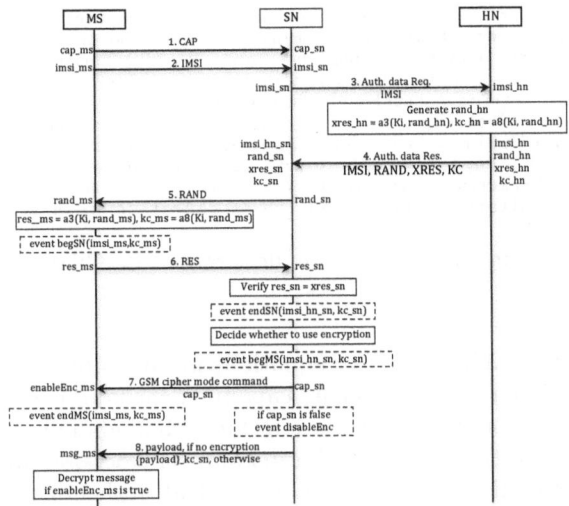

Fig. 4. GSM annotated in accord with our model, omitting TMSI/ID Request and adding a first message of data traffic

4 Modeling and Analyzing GSM and UMTS in ProVerif

4.1 GSM Model

Fig. 4 augments the protocol diagram of Fig. 1, as a guide to our model. The TMSI and ID request messages are omitted. When a MS first roams into a FN, an IMSI is always requested. Labels, like cap_ms and cap_sn for the first message, are the names of the relevant variables in the processes that model protocol roles. Besides variable names, the other augmentation is the addition of *events* (the dashed boxes). These are instrumentation used in order to specify authenticity properties as so-called *correspondence assertions*, which are the standard technique for formal specification of authenticity properties. Such properties take the form "if event E happens then event F must have happened previously". For example, whenever the SN decides to proceed with communication, using a particular K_c, because it successfully verified the response to a challenge, then that MS must indeed have sent the response and computed K_c for itself. An event is like a message—sent to an omniscient observer—with a tag indicating what kind of event, together with parameters like the specific IMSI and K_c. Events are not visible to the attacker, nor can they be generated by the attacker.

The HN, SN, and MS communicate over two shared channels declared in line 1 in Fig. 5. Traffic on the **private** channel is not accessible to the attacker; in our model, this channel is used by the SN and HN. Messages on a non-**private** channel can be copied, deleted, and fabricated by the attacker. We declare additional types and define a number of (distinct) constant values in lines 2–3. In lines 4–7, the cryptographic functions are declared and their algebraic properties are

```
1   free pubChannel: channel.   free secureChannel: channel [private].
2   type key. type ident. type nonce. type msgHdr. type resp. type sessKey.
3   const CAP: msgHdr. const ID: msgHdr. const AV_REQ: msgHdr.  ...
4   fun a3(nonce, key) : resp. fun a8(nonce, key): sessKey.
5   fun sencrypt(bitstring, sessKey): bitstring.
6   reduc forall m: bitstring, k: sessKey; sdecrypt(sencrypt(m, k), k) = m.
7   reduc encCapability() = true; encCapability() = false.
8   table keys(ident, key). (* Tables are not accessible to the attacker. *)
9   free payload: bitstring [private]. (*not initially known to attacker*)
10  free secretKc: bitstring [private].  (*a secret to be protected by Kc*)
```

Fig. 5. Excerpts from declarations for GSM

defined by equations. There are two equations in line 7 for encCapability so that the MS process can choose whether its capability includes encryption or not.

The main process forks multiple sessions for each kind of process. Fig. 6 shows the complete code of the processes. An instance of processMS models the initial activation of a MS followed by a single attempt at authentication. In lines 3–4, MS generates a fresh IMSI and a fresh K_i; in line 5 these are inserted in the table. Fresh values (keyword **new**) are unguessable by the attacker. In line 6, the MS decides on its encryption capability. The analysis will consider all possible executions, which thus include those where MS has encryption and those where it does not. In lines 8–9 the MS sends its capability and IMSI. Notice that the channel itself is not typed. The message in line 8 is the header literal CAP paired with boolean cap_ms; the one in line 9 pairs the ID header with a value of type ident. In line 10, the process waits until a message is available on the public channel. The message must match the designated format or the process terminates prematurely. PV statically checks types, which helps the user avoid modeling errors. However, PV ignores types during analysis. This enables PV to detect type flaw attacks. The events in lines 13 and 16 instrument the process to facilitate specification of security properties.

To be able to specify secrecy of data traffic following authentication, the model includes message *payload* declared in line 9 in Fig. 5. The SN encrypts payload, or not, based on the choice received in line 22 in Fig. 6. If encryption is not chosen, an event in line 34 records that fact. In line 41, HN uses the **get** operation on the private table of IMSI/K_i pairs for registered MSs.

Specifying and Analyzing Authenticity and Secrecy: We will consider in detail the following specifications:

```
1   query attacker(payload).
2   query attacker(payload) ⤳ event(disableEnc).
3   query attacker(secretKc).
4   query id: ident, k: sessKey; event(endSN(id, k)) ⤳ event(begSN(id, k)).
5   query id: ident, k: sessKey; event(endMS(id, k)) ⤳ event(begMS(id, k)).
```

Line 1 says that payload remains secret. This is not a requirement for GSM; the attacker can certainly obtain payload, e.g., if the MS is not capable of encryption. PV finds such attack trace. The conditional property in line 2 does express a requirement: if the attacker obtains the secret payload then the event disableEnc must have previously taken place in the SN. This query is indeed proved by PV.

```
 1   let processMS =
 2       (* registration and setup *)
 3       new imsi_ms: ident;
 4       new ki: key;
 5       insert keys(imsi_ms, ki);  (* pre−shared identity and key*)
 6       let cap_ms: bool = encCapability() in  (* choose capability*)
 7       (* the protocol *)
 8       out(pubChannel, (CAP, cap_ms));                (* [Message 1]*)
 9       out(pubChannel, (ID, imsi_ms));                (* [Message 2]*)
10       in(pubChannel, (=CHALLENGE, rand_ms: nonce));  (* [Message 5]*)
11       let res_ms: resp = a3(rand_ms, ki) in  (* compute response*)
12       let kc_ms: sessKey = a8(rand_ms, ki) in
13       event begSN(imsi_ms, kc_ms);  (*MS is authenticating itself to SN*)
14       out(pubChannel, (RES, res_ms));                (* [Message 6]*)
15       in(pubChannel, (=CMC, enableEnc_ms: bool));    (* [Message 7]*)
16       event endMS(imsi_ms, kc_ms);
17       in(pubChannel, (=MSG, msg_ms: bitstring));     (* [Message 8]*)
18       out(pubChannel, sencrypt(secretKc, kc_ms));
19       if enableEnc_ms = true then
20           let msgcontent: bitstring = sdecrypt(msg_ms, kc_ms) in   0.
21   let processSN =
22       in(pubChannel, (=CAP, cap_sn: bool));    (* [Message 1]*)
23       in(pubChannel, (=ID, imsi_sn: ident));   (* [Message 2]*)
24       out(secureChannel, (AV_REQ, imsi_sn));   (* [Message 3]*)
25       in(secureChannel,                        (* [Message 4]*)
26       (=AV, imsi_hn_sn: ident, rand_sn: nonce, xres_sn: resp, kc_sn: sessKey));
27       out(pubChannel, (CHALLENGE, rand_sn));   (* [Message 5]*)
28       in(pubChannel, (=RES, res_sn: resp));    (* [Message 6]*)
29       if res_sn = xres_sn then    (* Check response*)
30           event endSN(imsi_hn_sn, kc_sn);
31           event begMS(imsi_hn_sn, kc_sn);
32           out(pubChannel, (CMC, cap_sn));      (* [Message 7]*)
33           if cap_sn = false then
34               event disableEnc;
35               out(pubChannel, (MSG, payload))  (* [Message 8]*)
36           else
37               out(pubChannel, (MSG, sencrypt(payload, kc_sn))).  (* [Message 8]*)
38   let processHN =
39       in(secureChannel, (=AV_REQ, imsi_hn: ident));  (* [Message 3]*)
40       new rand_hn: nonce;  (* Generate a fresh random number*)
41       get keys(=imsi_hn, ki_hn) in  (* attempt to look up key*)
42       let xres_hn: resp = a3(rand_hn, ki_hn) in  (* compute XRES and Kc*)
43       let kc_hn: sessKey = a8(rand_hn, ki_hn) in
44       out(secureChannel, (AV, imsi_hn, rand_hn, xres_hn, kc_hn)).  (* [Message 4]*)
```

Fig. 6. Processes for GSM, with reference to Fig. 4

Another requirement is that K_i and K_c remain secret—regardless of whether encryption is enabled. We declare another secret in line 10 in Fig. 5 and specify that the attacker does not obtain it. Then we introduce an extra message in line 18 of the MS process, and it is sent regardless of whether encryption is enabled. The query in line 3 is successful, which implies that K_c remains secret since otherwise the attacker would obtain secretKc. The property is unconditional: the key remains secret regardless of whether encryption is chosen. Furthermore, because K_c is computed as a function of $RAND$, which is sent in the clear, and K_i, secrecy of K_c implies secrecy of K_i.

Line 4 says that whenever the event endSN occurs with some arguments id and k, there must have been a prior occurrence of event begSN with the same arguments. The former event happens only following successful check of the expected response from MS. This query says that if the SN believes it has established a session key K_c associated with an MS using this particular IMSI, for which the HN has provided a challenge and expected response, then indeed there is a MS that reached that stage of its protocol role, for that IMSI and K_c. The event endSN occurs only following successful verification in the SN, as that is the step that is intended to establish authentication. The event begSN is placed in the MS process just before it sends the response, i.e., after it has computed the K_c to which the event refers. The event should not be placed later in the MS process, because successful verification by the SN does not give the SN evidence that MS has progressed any further.

The protocol is not intended to authenticate the SN to MS (see Sect. 3.1). However, to gain confidence in our model we check that property. For the query in line 5 above, PV does find a trace that violates the property.

A more interesting man-in-the-middle scenario is the one PV finds in violation of the first secrecy condition above, **query attacker**(payload). The MS sends out its encryption capability and identification. The attacker intercepts the capability message and changes it to no-encryption, so the SN receives the modified capability. The HN generates the authentication vector and sends it to the SN. The one-way challenge-response between the SN and MS succeeds. Since the SN receives no-encryption from the attacker, it decides not to use encryption.

4.2   Modeling and Analyzing UMTS

As with GSM, we omit the TMSI and ID Request messages. We also abstract from the SQN and AMF. UMTS authentication establishes the CK and the IK, so these are included in the parameters of the events. The secrecy and authentication properties are specified similarly as in the GSM model. The simple secrecy property, **attacker**(payload), fails: as in GSM, the MS can choose no-encryption, and regardless of the choice the attacker can modify the capability message to claim the MS has no encryption. However, if the MS chooses the capability of encryption and the attacker modifies that, this will be detected by the MS which will stop responding. PV proves the conditional secrecy property **attacker**(payload)⤳**event**(disableEnc) as well as secrecy of CK and IK (using the idiom explained in Sect. 4.1). It also proves authentication in both directions:

```
query  d : ident , c : cipherKey , i : integKey ; event ( endSN ( d , c , i ) ) ⤳ event ( begSN ( d , c , i ) ).
query  d : ident , c : cipherKey , i : integKey ; event ( endMS ( d , c , i ) ) ⤳ event ( begMS ( d , c , i ) ).
```

5   Modeling and Analyzing GSM/UMTS Roaming

As described in Sect. 3.3, there are six different roaming scenarios, three of which are basically the same as GSM or UMTS from the perspective of security. Of the other three cases, numbers (3–5), case (5) is the most interesting.

In case (5), to support GSM BS, the SN converts the UMTS keys into a GSM session key. The CMC message does not include the received encryption capability and is not integrity protected. To communicate with GSM BS, the

MS converts the UMTS keys into a GSM session key. Then the MS performs the steps in GSM block IV. The HN is modeled exactly the same as in UMTS.

Since the SN authenticates the MS as in UMTS authentication, the events begMS and endMS use UMTS keys in the authentication property specification:

```
1   query attacker(payload).
2   query attacker(payload) ↝ event(disableEnc).
3   query d:ident, c:cipherKey, i:integKey;
4        event(endSN(d,c,i)) ↝ event(begSN(d,c,i)).
5   query d:ident, k:sessKey; event(endMS(d,k)) ↝ event(begMS(d,k)).
```

The query of secrecy of payload in line 1 fails and PV finds a trace similar to the one we describe for the same query against GSM. The required properties in lines 2–4 are proved, as is key secrecy.

What is interesting is that the required authentication property in line 5 is violated. In the attack trace, the attacker first acts as a BS to intercept the CAP message and replace it with no-encryption. The attacker forwards the challenge and response. The MS receives the CMC message which is forged by the attacker.

References

1. Abadi, M., Blanchet, B., Fournet, C.: Just Fast Keying in the Pi Calculus. In: Schmidt, D. (ed.) ESOP 2004. LNCS, vol. 2986, pp. 340–354. Springer, Heidelberg (2004)
2. Blanchet, B., Chaudhuri, A.: Automated formal analysis of a protocol for secure file sharing on untrusted storage. In: IEEE Symp. on Sec. and Priv. (2008)
3. Bodei, C., Buchholtz, M., Degano, P., Nielson, F., Nielson, H.R.: Automatic validation of protocol narration. In: IEEE CSFW, pp. 126–140 (2003)
4. Bouassida, M.S., Chridi, N., Chrisment, I., Festor, O., Vigneron, L.: Automated verification of a key management architecture for hierarchical group protocols. Annals of Telecommunications (2007)
5. Chang, R., Shmatikov, V.: Formal analysis of authentication in Bluetooth device pairing. In: FCS-ARSPA (2007)
6. Dunkelman, O., Keller, N., Shamir, A.: A Practical-Time Related-Key Attack on the KASUMI Cryptosystem Used in GSM and 3G Telephony. In: Rabin, T. (ed.) CRYPTO 2010. LNCS, vol. 6223, pp. 393–410. Springer, Heidelberg (2010)
7. Escobar, S., Meadows, C., Meseguer, J.: State Space Reduction in the Maude-NRL Protocol Analyzer. In: Jajodia, S., Lopez, J. (eds.) ESORICS 2008. LNCS, vol. 5283, pp. 548–562. Springer, Heidelberg (2008)
8. Fox, D.: Der IMSI catcher. In: DuD Datenschutz und Datensicherheit (2002)
9. Golić, J.D.: Cryptanalysis of Alleged A5 Stream Cipher. In: Fumy, W. (ed.) EUROCRYPT 1997. LNCS, vol. 1233, pp. 239–255. Springer, Heidelberg (1997)
10. Jakobsson, M., Wetzel, S.: Security Weaknesses in Bluetooth. In: Naccache, D. (ed.) CT-RSA 2001. LNCS, vol. 2020, pp. 176–191. Springer, Heidelberg (2001)
11. Mitchell, C.J., Knudsen, L.R.: An analysis of the 3GPP-MAC scheme. In: WCC (2001)
12. Lim, S.-H., Bang, K.-S., Yi, O., Lim, J.: A Secure Handover Protocol Design in Wireless Networks with Formal Verification. In: Boavida, F., Monteiro, E., Mascolo, S., Koucheryavy, Y. (eds.) WWIC 2007. LNCS, vol. 4517, pp. 67–78. Springer, Heidelberg (2007)

13. Meyer, U.: Secure Roaming and Handover Procedures in Wireless Access Networks. PhD thesis, Darmstadt University of Technology, Germany (2005)
14. Meyer, U., Wetzel, S.: A man-in-the-middle attack on UMTS. In: ACM WiSec, pp. 90–97 (2004)
15. Meyer, U., Wetzel, S.: On the impact of GSM encryption and man-in-the-middle attacks on the security of interoperating GSM/UMTS networks. In: IEEE Symposium on Personal, Indoor and Mobile Radio Communications (2004)
16. Niemi, V., Nynberg, K.: UMTS Security. Wiley (2003)
17. Taha, A., Abdel-Hamid, A., Tahar, S.: Formal analysis of the handover schemes in mobile WiMAX networks. In: Conf. on Wireless and Optical Comm. Net. (2009)
18. Taha, A., Abdel-Hamid, A., Tahar, S.: Formal verification of IEEE 802.16 security sublayer using Scyther tool. In: IFIP N2S 2009, pp. 1–6 (2009)
19. 3GPP The mobile broadband standard, `http://www.3gpp.org/specifications`

CloudSeal: End-to-End Content Protection in Cloud-Based Storage and Delivery Services

Huijun Xiong[1], Xinwen Zhang[2], Wei Zhu[2], and Danfeng Yao[1]

[1] Computer Science Department, Virginia Tech, Blacksburg, VA, USA
{huijun,danfeng}@cs.vt.edu
[2] Huawei Research Center, Santa Clara, CA, USA
{xinwen.zhang,wei.zhu}@huawei.com

Abstract. Recent years have seen the trend to leverage cloud-based services for large scale content storage, processing, and distribution. Security and privacy are among top concerns for public cloud environments. Towards the end-to-end content confidentiality protection, we propose *CloudSeal*, a scheme for securely sharing and distributing data via cloud-based data storage and content delivery services (e.g., Amazon S3 and CloudFront). CloudSeal ensures the confidentiality of content stored in public cloud storage services, by encrypting it before sharing at the cloud. To achieve flexible access control policies, CloudSeal further adopts k-out-of-n secret sharing and broadcast revocation mechanisms to renew shared secrets, e.g., when a user joins or leaves a content sharing group. Most importantly, CloudSeal leverages proxy re-encryption algorithm to transfer part of stored cipher content in the cloud, which can be decrypted by a valid user with updated secret keys. We achieve this property without modifying most of the encrypted content. This feature is critical for the efficiency of content distribution.

Keywords: Cloud computing, content delivery network, proxy-based re-encryption, secret sharing.

1 Introduction

Security issues have been one of the top concerns for cloud computing [1], despite the increase in cloud usage. Among them, how to maintain the confidentiality and privacy of outsourced content in the public cloud remains a challenging task. The issue becomes more difficult with flexible content processing and sharing among Internet users through cloud-based services. For confidentiality, a content provider should encrypt her content with keys that are out of the reach of the cloud provider. Content accessible to different users should be encrypted with different keys to distinguish their privileges. Key management may be complex when the content is shared by many users with different privileges. Previous work has studied such problems in conventional distributed environments [2,3]. For large scale cloud-based content sharing and distribution services, there are additional new requirements besides key management as explained in the following. First, the accessible content of a user may change dynamically, e.g., based

M. Rajarajan et al. (Eds.): SecureComm 2011, LNICST 96, pp. 491–500, 2012.
© Institute for Computer Sciences, Social Informatics and Telecommunications Engineering 2012

on the content provider's security policy or the user's subscription information. Each piece of content may be shared by different users or groups, and users may belong to multiple groups. Second, encrypting the same content with different keys not only results in multiple redundant copies of the content in the cloud storage, but also diminishes the efficiency of content delivery via the distribution network.

Multicast security [4] aims to address the confidentiality of content sharing. However, in conventional multicast and broadcast settings, there are only two types of entities involved: multicast/broadcast center and users, and the center is the content provider or is fully trusted by the content provider. Their setting differs from our new cloud-based content delivery model, which requires a semi-honest cloud provider to assist the content provider and the users.

In cloud-based content storage and delivery services, the cloud provider provides two cloud-based services: *content storage service* and *content delivery network service*. By using them, the content provider is able to provide large-scale content sharing services to groups of subscribers through the public cloud. Subscribers consume the content by software installed on their host machines, such as a video player to play a digital movie file. It has been widely recognized that content security should be mainly relied on content providers who use the cloud-based services, instead of cloud service providers [5].

In this paper, we propose *CloudSeal*, an end-to-end solution for content confidentiality protection in the storage and delivery via cloud computing. By end-to-end, we mean that content is encrypted at cloud-based storage and delivery channels, and only authorized end users can decrypt it. We uniquely leverage several algorithms to achieve flexible security and efficient storage and distribution, including proxy re-encryption, k-out-of-n secret sharing, and broadcast revocation schemes. By proxy re-encryption algorithm, a content provider can transfer its initially encrypted content to the ciphertext so that only authorized subscribers can decrypt. To reduce the workload of content re-encryption, the content provider employs a proxy running at cloud side to perform content re-encryption in the cloud. The content provider generates new re-encryption keys upon user joining or leaving.

In CloudSeal, when there is a request from a subscriber, the proxy first checks if the content in the cloud storage is encrypted with the latest re-encryption key from the content provider. If yes, the content can be downloaded via the content delivery service interface; otherwise, the proxy first invalidates any encrypted form of the target content via the delivery service, re-encrypts the content with the latest re-encryption key, and then authorizes the access. Therefore, there is only one encrypted copy of the content stored in cloud storage, and delivery network only serves contents encrypted with the latest re-encryption key. CloudSeal efficiently splits the ciphertext of the content into two parts. The re-encryption operation is only performed on a very small part, and the massive part remains unchanged. This feature enables efficient cache mechanism during content distribution.

The access control in CloudSeal is enforced by distributing a shared secret key to authorized users, with which re-encrypted content can only be decrypted. CloudSeal separates the distribution of the shared secret key from that of the content and re-encryption keys. Therefore, it supports flexible authorization policies. Only authorized users can obtain the shared secret key, and the content provider maintains the control of issuing new keys whenever needed. CloudSeal leverages k-out-of-n secret sharing and broadcast revocation mechanisms to renew the shared secret key to achieve scalability. Due to space limits, We refer the readers to the full version of our paper for more details on the implementation and evaluation of CloudSeal [6].

2   Model and System Goals

Threat Model Three types of parties are involved in our system: content provider, cloud provider, and subscriber. CloudSeal trusts the content provider and subscribers. Specifically, only the content rendering application or agent running on a subscriber's device is trusted, e.g., it does not release the content decryption key and any clear content to unauthorized parties, and it physically removes decryption key when the user leaves a group or is revoked by the content provider. We consider the cloud service provider to be *honest but curious* or semi-honest; that is, it follows the protocol and operations defined in CloudSeal, but it may actively attempt to gain knowledge of cleartext of the content. The content delivery service is also semi-trusted: it is curious to sniff content distributed and cached in the network, but it honestly performs all the operations and satisfies the quality of services, e. g., specified in service level agreement between the content provider and the delivery service provider. In addition, the cloud infrastructure (hardware and software) may be exploited by attackers who aim to expose the stored content [7].

We summarize the security and system objectives of CloudSeal as follows.

- CloudSeal should ensure data confidentiality when stored in cloud even under the collusion between the cloud provider and subscribers.
- CloudSeal should support dynamic system state, i. e., a user may choose to join or leave a group, or be revoked from a group by the content provider at any time.
- CloudSeal should support forward and backward security. For *backward security*, a user who leaves the group or is revoked from the group cannot access any data published after leaving or revocation. For *forward security*, a user cannot access any content that is published before she joins.

Beyond these security objectives, CloudSeal aims to achieve the following performance requirements. CloudSeal should preserve the efficiency of content delivery network. In particular, it is desirable for the network to store a single copy of encrypted content at each state for content integrity and distribution efficiency. Content decryption should not affect user experience at the device side, e. g., the speed of decrypting the video streaming should not be significantly lower than that of decoding.

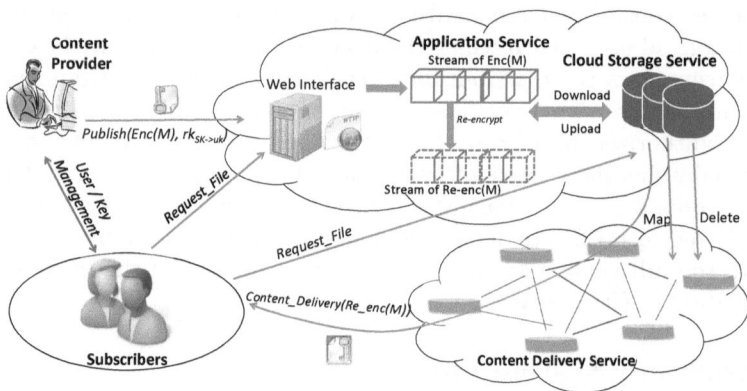

Fig. 1. CloudSeal overview

3   CloudSeal Scheme Details

In this section, we first give an overview of CloudSeal, and then present details of the operations for content distribution and user management. Security properties of CloudSeal are then discussed.

3.1   Overview

Figure 1 shows the architecture of CloudSeal with three main parties: *cloud provider*, *content provider*, and *subscribers*.

- *Cloud Provider* provides two public cloud services: *storage service* for content storing and *content delivery network* for content distribution. It also provides virtual infrastructure to host application services, which can be used by the content provider to manipulate content stored in the cloud, or by content subscribers to retrieve content.
- *Content Provider* provides content to groups of subscribers, as well as user management. It uses cloud-based service from the cloud provider to store and distribute content.
- *Subscriber* is able to access to the content stored in the cloud if she successfully subscribes to the content provider. The subscriber can decrypt delivered content and consume it with local software.

Operations of CloudSeal are across two planes: data plane and control plane. In the *data plane*, we describe the implementations of content operations, including *system setup*, *content publishing*, *proxy re-encryption*, and *content retrieving*, along with involved cryptographic algorithms; in the *control plane*, we describe user management including *user subscription* – when a new user joins a group, and *user revocation* – when a user leaves or is revoked from a group. Our scheme utilizes the proxy re-encryption scheme proposed by Ateniese *et al.* [8] and the secret sharing scheme in [9].

3.2   Preliminary

Bilinear Maps [10,11]: Let $\mathbb{G}$, $\mathbb{G}_T$ be two multiplicative cyclic groups of prime order p, we say e is a bilinear map if: (1) computative actions in $\mathbb{G}$ and $\mathbb{G}_T$ are efficient; (2) for all $\alpha, \beta \in \mathbb{Z}_r$ of prime order r, we have $e(g^\alpha, g^\beta) = e(g, g)^{\alpha\beta}$; (3) for any $g \in \mathbb{G}$, e is non-degenerate, i.e., $e(g, g) \neq 1$.

Secret Sharing [12,9]: A k-out-of-n threshold secret sharing scheme is that a secret $S \in \mathbb{Z}_r$ shared by n users can be recovered, if the number of the secret shares exceeds the threshold k. The scheme utilizes a random polynomial P of degree $k - 1$, where $P(x) \in \mathbb{Z}_r$ and $P(0) = S$. Given any k shares $< x_0, P(x_0) >$, ..., $< x_{k-1}, P(x_{k-1}) >$, one can use Lagrange interpolation formulas as follows to recover $P(0)$:

$$P(0) = \sum_{i=0}^{k-1} \lambda_i P(x_i), \text{ where } \lambda_i = \prod_{j \neq i} \frac{x_j}{x_j - x_i} \tag{1}$$

Proxy Re-encryption [8]: A proxy re-encryption algorithm transforms ciphertext c_{k1} to ciphertext c_{k2} with a key $rk_{k1 \to k2}$ without revealing the corresponding cleartext, where c_{k1} and c_{k2} can only be decrypted by different key $k1$ and $k2$, respectively, and $rk_{k1 \to k2}$ is a re-key issued by another party, e.g., the originator of ciphertext c_{k1}.

3.3   CloudSeal Operations

Our cryptographic operations are described below. Our notation used in this paper is shown in Table 1.

Table 1. Notation

Term	Notation	Term	Notation
PK	content provider's public key	P	polynomial formula
SK	content provider's secret key	x_i	user i's ID
uk	shared secret key for a group	$P(x_i)$	polynomial value of user i
$rk_{SK \to uk}$	re-encryption key	M	original content
k	number of shares to recover uk	h	a temporary secret of content provider

System Setup is called by the content provider to prepare the cryptographic system for content encryption and re-encryption. The content provider first chooses system public parameters $params$, namely $g \in \mathbb{G}$ and a bilinear map e. It chooses a secret key $SK \in \mathbb{Z}_r$ and public key $PK = g^{SK} \in \mathbb{G}$. The content provider keeps SK secret. This setup is performed by the content provider for each group of users. The content provider chooses an integer k and a list L of polynomials of degree $k - 1$ with coefficients randomly chosen from $\mathbb{Z}_r$, which are kept secret. The number of users who can be revoked at the same time is $k - 1$.

Content Publishing is followed by the content provider to publish its content to the public cloud. The content provider encrypts the content M before publishing it to public cloud with the secret key SK and *params* as shown in Algorithm 1. The resulting encrypted content has two components (u_{SK}, v), both are stored in the content storage service by the application service via cloud APIs. u_{SK} depends on the random secret h and content provider's secret key SK, while v depends on both h and the content. Usually, u_{SK} is much smaller than v.

Algorithm 1: *Enc(params, M, SK)*

---

step1: Choose a random secret $h \in \mathbb{Z}_r$; let Z denote $e(g, g)$;

step2: Compute $Z^h = e(g, g^h) = e(g, g)^h \in \mathbb{G}_T$, $u_{SK} = g^{SK \cdot h}$; erase h;

step3: Output ciphertext of content M: $(u_{SK}, v) = (g^{SK \cdot h}, MZ^h)$.

Content Retrieving is for subscribers to access content stored in the public cloud. Two algorithms – *Re_Key* and *Re_Enc* – are involved in this process. The *Re_Key* algorithm is where content provider generates a content re-encryption key $rk_{SK \to uk}$ with its secret key SK and the current decryption key uk. Details are shown as follows.

Algorithm 2: *Re_Key(params, SK, uk)*

---

step1: Given $params, SK, uk$, the content provider computes $rk_{SK \to uk} = g^{uk/SK}$.

Upon request, the application service re-encrypts the target cipher content (u_{SK}, v) with the following *Re_Enc* algorithm.

Algorithm 3: *Re_Enc((u_{SK}, v), params)*

---

step1: Obtain the newest $rk_{SK \to uk}$ from the content provider;

step2: Calculate $u_{uk} = e(rk_{SK \to uk}, u_{SK}) = e(rk_{SK \to uk}, g^{SK \cdot h}) = e(g, g)^{uk \cdot h} = Z^{uk \cdot h}$;

step3: Output re-encrypted content (u_{uk}, v).

The application service stores u_{uk} in the content storage service and allows the download of the cipher content. u_{uk} and v can be cached in the content delivery network for download. The re-encryption is only performed on u_{SK}. Because u_{SK} is independent of the content M, CloudSeal saves the processing time and storage I/O cost between the application service and storage service.

When the system state is changed, i.e., the shared secret key is updated from uk to uk'. Once the new secret key is updated to authorized users (explained next), the content provider generates the re-key $rk_{SK \to uk'}$ by running *Re_Key* algorithm and sends the key to the application service for content re-encryption with *Re_Enc* algorithm. The new cipher content is $(u_{uk'}, v)$. The user can then download $u_{uk'}$ from the cloud storage service, and v from the content delivery network. u_{uk} is invalidated from the content delivery network by the application service before the download for backward security.

After a user obtains the encrypted content (u_{uk}, v), she follows Algorithm 4 below to decrypt the cipher with her current secret key uk. The user either obtains the secret key uk from the content provider when she first joins or computes it (described in User Subscription next).

Algorithm 4: *Decrypt((u_{uk}, v), uk)*

step1: Given u_{uk} and uk, compute $u_{uk}^{1/uk} = (Z^{uk \cdot h})^{1/uk} = Z^h$;

step2: Calculate $M = v/Z^h = (MZ^h)/Z^h = M$;

step3: Output original content M.

User Subscription happens when a user join a group. Successful subscription authorizes a user's access to protected content. To prevent a new user from accessing content published before joining (forward security), a new key is generated and distributed to the new user. To update remaining users' secret key, a share of secret of the new user is generated and broadcasted to the entire group as follows. For the ease of description, we assume that $k = 2$ in what follows. Our algorithm can be generalized for any arbitrary k values.

- Upon receiving a join request from a new user, the content provider obtains the first polynomial $P' = ax + b$ on list L, and calculates key $uk' = P'(0)$; uk' is sent to the new user in a secure channel.
- The content provider assigns the new user a unique identity $x_i \in \mathbb{Z}_r$ and her share of secret from polynomial $P'(x_i)$, along with x_i's values for the other polynomials on list L. The content provider sends these polynomial values, except for $P'(x_i)$, to the new user for future key updating. P' is removed from the list L.
- The content provider broadcasts $< x_i, P'(x_i) >$ to the current group members for new key generation.
- For each current group member x_j, upon receiving $< x_i, P'(x_i) >$ from the content provider, she calculates the new key with her share of secret $P'(x_j)$ for P' that was received when x_j joined earlier. This user can recover the new secret key $uk' = P'(0) = b$ by calculating $P'(0) = \frac{x_j}{x_j - x_i} P'(x_i) + \frac{x_i}{x_i - x_j} P'(x_j)$ according to Equation 1.

User Revocation happens when a subscriber leaves a group or is revoked by the content provider. Our revocation scheme is based on k-out-of-n threshold secret sharing scheme.

- *Case I:* There are $k-1$ users to be revoked at one time. The content provider revokes $k - 1$ users with shares $P(x_1), P(x_2), ..., P(x_{k-1})$, respectively. The content provider broadcasts the shares of secrets and identities of these users $< x_1, P(x_1) >, < x_2, P(x_2) >, ..., < x_{k-1}, P(x_{k-1}) >$ to the entire group. Each user x in the group combines her share of secret $< x, P(x) >$ with these $k-1$ shares, to interpolate the new secret key $uk' = P(0)$. The content provider uses uk' as the new shared secret key to generate re-encryption key for non-revoked users.

– *Case II:* There are t users to be revoked, where $t < k - 1$. The content provider performs the revocation by sending the t shares of secret and additional $k - t - 1$ shares of the secret of polynomial P. These additional shares are values different from any existing users.

Polynomial P is then removed from the list L. If the list L is empty, the content provider adds new polynomials, as well as computes and distributes corresponding secret shares to current subscribers (for future interpolation purposes).

3.4 Security Analysis

Because published content is encrypted before being stored in the cloud storage service, and the system secret key SK is never released from the content provider, CloudSeal achieves the confidentiality of data in the public cloud. Furthermore, in any system state, with received re-encryption key $rk_{SK \to uk}$, the cloud service provider or an attacker cannot decrypt the cipher content. CloudSeal ensures that for any content access, the application service always uses the latest re-encryption key derived from the latest user secret key by the content provider, therefore only authorized users can decrypt the cipher content in any system state. By controlling the issuing of secret keys to authorized users, the content provider maintains the control of security policies.

Our re-encryption algorithm utilizes the proxy re-encryption proposed in [8], which has been proven to be secure against the Decisional Bilinear Diffie-Hellman Inversion problem. Besides, this re-encryption algorithm is resistant against collusion between users and the cloud provider according to. This guarantees that the secret key of content provider is safe even either the user or the cloud provider obtains both re-encryption key and user's decryption key.

CloudSeal is able to protect content forward and backward security by integrating proxy re-encryption and k-out-of-n secret sharing scheme. When an user joining or leaving event happens in the group, CloudSeal clears old content stored in content delivery network and alters content to be delivered with updated decryption key. Therefore, new users can not decrypt the old content by the new key; revoked users can not decrypt the new content with their old keys.

Leveraging content delivery network, CloudSeal uniquely achieves content protection and distribution efficiency. When the system state changes, only a small part of a cipher content needs to be re-encrypted, such that most of the content object can be cached in cloud and shared by users. The separation of content operations (data plane) and user management operations (control plane) further enables flexible and scalable deployment of CloudSeal in the cloud and highly distributed environment.

4 Related Work

Several security solutions have been recently developed for securing the cloud [13, 14, 15, 16], including secure data access, data privacy, and operations on encrypted data. With similar security concerns in cloud service, Yu et al. [15]

proposed an attribute based access control policy to securely outsource sensitive user data to the cloud. CloudSeal is different from their approach in that: Cloud-Seal only allows a content provider to perform the Re_Key operation, and our proxy re-encryption is performed directly on part of the cipher content. Therefore, directly applying their approach in the problem that we target here is not practical, as their ciphertext data is customized for different users. Essentially, efficient data distribution with common ciphertext that can be cached in content delivery network is not the goal of [15].

Secure storage system is an important application of proxy re-encryption [8, 17]. CloudSeal is based on the scheme proposed in [8], where the authors build an encrypted file storage with an access control proxy in charge of data access according to their proxy re-encryption methods. In comparison, we deploy the re-encryption algorithm in a unique cloud-based content delivery application. CloudSeal also supports the k-out-of-n secret sharing for efficient user-revocation purposes.

Secure multicast communication [18, 4, 19, 20] and conditional access systems [21] address similar security problems as ours in distributing content to dynamic user groups and key management. Proxy re-encryption and k-out-of-n mechanisms are also used to solve these problems. The problem solved by CloudSeal is different from them due to the cache properties in content delivery network, which requires more efficient and flexible secure content delivery and user management mechanisms.

5   Conclusion and Future Work

We design CloudSeal, an end-to-end content confidentiality protection mechanism for large-scale content storage and distribution systems over public cloud infrastructure. By leveraging advanced cryptographic algorithms including proxy re-encryption, threshold secret sharing, and broadcast revocation, CloudSeal addresses unique challenges of efficient cipher content transformation, cipher content cache in delivery network, and scalable user and key management. We have implemented a prototype of CloudSeal based on Amazon EC2, S3, and Cloud-Front services. Our initial evaluation results demonstrate that CloudSeal can provide efficient and scalable secure content storage and delivery in cloud-based storage and content delivery network. The details of our implementation and evaluation can be found in [6]. For future work, we plan to investigate practical and scalable browser-based methods for distributing secret information from the content provider to the subscribers.

References

1. Cloud Computing, an IDC update (2010),
   http://www.slideshare.net/JorFigOr/cloud-computing-2010-an-idc-update
2. Koglin, Y., Yao, D., Bertino, E.: Secure Content Distribution by Parallel Processing from Cooperative Intermediaries. IEEE Transactions on Parallel and Distributed Systems 19(5), 615–626 (2008)

3. Yao, D., Koglin, Y., Bertino, E., Tamassia, R.: Decentralized Authorization and Data Security in Web Content Delivery. In: Proc. ACM Symp. on Applied Computing (SAC), pp. 1654–1661 (2007)

4. Canetti, R., Garay, J., Itkis, G., Micciancio, D., Naor, M., Pinkas, B.: Multicast Security: A Taxonomy and Some Efficient Constructions. In: Proceedings of INFOCOM (March 1999)

5. AWS Customer Agreement (2011), http://aws.amazon.com/agreement/

6. Xiong, H., Zhang, X., Zhu, W., Yao, D.: CloudSeal: End-to-End Content Protection in Cloud-based Storage and Delivery Services. Technical report, Huawei Research (2011)

7. Ristenpart, T., Tromer, E., Shacham, H., Savage, S.: Hey, You, Get Off of My cloud! Exploring Information Leakage in Third-Party Compute Clouds. In: Proceedings of ACM Conference on Computer and Communications Security (2009)

8. Ateniese, G., Fu, K., Green, M., Hohenberger, S.: Improved Proxy Re-encryption Schemes with Applications to Secure Distributed Storage. ACM Trans. Inf. Syst. Secur. 9, 1–30 (2006)

9. Naor, M., Pinkas, B.: Efficient Trace and Revoke Schemes. In: Frankel, Y. (ed.) FC 2000. LNCS, vol. 1962, pp. 1–20. Springer, Heidelberg (2001)

10. Boneh, D., Franklin, M.: Identity-Based Encryption from the Weil Pairing. In: Kilian, J. (ed.) CRYPTO 2001. LNCS, vol. 2139, pp. 213–229. Springer, Heidelberg (2001)

11. Boneh, D., Lynn, B., Shacham, H.: Short Signatures from the Weil Pairing. In: Boyd, C. (ed.) ASIACRYPT 2001. LNCS, vol. 2248, pp. 514–532. Springer, Heidelberg (2001)

12. Shamir, A.: How to Share A Secret. Commun. ACM 22 (November 1979)

13. Li, M., Yu, S., Cao, N., Lou, W.: Authorized Private Keyword Search over Encrypted Personal Health Records in Cloud Computing. In: Proceedings of The 31st Int'l Conference on Distributed Computing Systems, ICDCS 2011 (2011)

14. Wang, C., Wang, Q., Ren, K., Lou, W.: Privacy-Preserving Public Auditing for Data Storage Security in Cloud Computing. In: Proceedings of INFOCOM (2010)

15. Yu, S., Wang, C., Ren, K., Lou, W.: Achieving Secure, Scalable, and Fine-grained Data Access Control in Cloud Computing. In: Proceedings of INFOCOM (2010)

16. Zarandioon, S., Yao, D., Ganapathy, V.: K2C: Cryptographic Cloud Storage With Lazy Revocation and Anonymous Access. In: Rajarajan, M., et al. (eds.) SecureComm 2011. LNICST, vol. 96, pp. 59–76. Springer, Heidelberg (2012)

17. Kallahalla, M., Riedel, E., Swaminathan, R., Wang, Q., Fu, K.: Plutus: Scalable Secure File Sharing on Untrusted Storage. In: Proceedings of FAST, Berkeley, CA, USA (2003)

18. Wong, C.K., Gouda, M., Lam, S.S.: Secure Group Communications Using Key Graphs. IEEE/ACM Trans. Netw. (2000)

19. Briscoe, B.: MARKS: Zero Side Effect Multicast Key Management Using Arbitrarily Revealed Key Sequences. In: Rizzo, L., Fdida, S. (eds.) NGC 1999. LNCS, vol. 1736, pp. 301–320. Springer, Heidelberg (1999)

20. Briscoe, B.: Nark: Receiver-based Multicast Non-repudiation and Key Management. In: Proceedings of ACM Conference on Electronic Commerce, EC 1999 (1999)

21. Traynor, P., Butler, K.R.B., Enck, W., McDaniel, P.: Realizing Massive-Scale Conditional Access Systems Through Attribute-Based Cryptosystems. In: NDSS (2008)

Call Behavioral Analysis to Thwart SPIT Attacks on VoIP Networks

Hemant Sengar[1], Xinyuan Wang[2], and Arthur Nichols[1]

[1] Technology Development Dept., Windstream Communications, Greenville,
SC 29601
{Hemant.Sengar,Arthur.Nichols}@windstream.com
[2] Dept. of Computer Science, George Mason University, Fairfax, VA 22030
xwangc@gmu.edu

Abstract. The threat of voice spam, commonly known as Spam over Internet Telephony (SPIT) is a real and contemporary problem. If the problem remains unchecked then it may become as potent as email spam today. In this paper, we present two approaches to detect and prevent SPITting over the Internet. Both of our approaches are based on the anomaly detection of the distributions of selected call features (i.e., day and time of calling, call durations etc.). The first approach uses *Mahalanobis Distance* as a summarization tool and it is able to reliably detect individual spam VoIP calls at a microscopic level. The second approach is designed to detect groups of (potentially collaborating) VoIP spam calls at a macroscopic level. By computing *entropy* of call durations of groups of calls, we are able to build profile of normal calls and reliably detect the deviation from normal human call behavior that are caused by bulk spam calls. We empirically validate our VoIP spam call detection approaches with real VoIP call traces obtained from a VoIP service provider network. Our experimental results show that call feature distributions can be used to build a fairly general and effective anomalous call behavior detection framework.

Keywords: Voice Spam, SPIT, VoIP, Behavioral Analysis.

1 Introduction

In Japan where the VoIP market is more mature than USA has witnessed some recent voice spam attacks. The SoftbankBB, a VoIP service provider with 4.6 million users, has reported 3 incidents of spam attacks within its own network [9]. Similarly, Columbia University at New York experienced voice spam attack, with someone accessing the SIP proxy server and "war dialing" a lot of IP phone extensions [10]. Technically, it is easier for the spammer to generate unsolicited bulk VoIP calls and target multiple VoIP subscribers than generating spam calls over PSTN. As the number of VoIP subscribers hits a critical mass, it is expected that VoIP spam will emerge as a potentially serious threat. If the SPIT problem is not effectively addressed, it may become as rampant as email spam today and hinder the deployment of IP telephony.

M. Rajarajan et al. (Eds.): SecureComm 2011, LNICST 96, pp. 501–510, 2012.
© Institute for Computer Sciences, Social Informatics and Telecommunications Engineering 2012

The *Internet Engineering Task Force* (IETF)'s RFC [7] analyzed the voice spam problem in SIP environment and examined various potential solutions for solving the email spam problem. Unfortunately, many of the anti-spam solutions that have been proposed or deployed are either heavily influenced by or directly inherited from the email spam world. For example, the anti-spam solutions based on *computational puzzles* [7] try to frustrate the VoIP spam call generator by requiring it to solve some computational puzzles. While such methods require modification of the underlying signaling protocol, they are not effective against distributed VoIP spam call generation where multiple powerful PCs are compromised into zombies and used for generating bulk spam calls. The *Turing tests* [7, 11] based approaches, on the other hand, require manual and active involvement of callers, which is not intuitive and may scare away many potential users. The solutions relying on *social network* [2, 14] and *caller's reputation value* [8, 5, 1] require infrastructure changes and modifications of SIP UAs, yet they are susceptible to malicious reputation poisoning. The anti-spam solutions based on a *trusted third party* [4] are not scalable. Similarly, it is hard to apply the *content based filtering* [3] to voice spam since the real-time voice content analysis and is exceedingly difficult. Recently, Wu et al. [13] proposed a spam detection approach involving user-feedback and semi-supervised clustering technique to differentiate between spam and legitimate calls. However, the current generation of telephone sets do not provide an option to give feedback of a call to service provider's system. In summary, voice spam problem can not be effectively addressed by simple adaption of existing email spam solutions or asking for overhauling of network infrastructure and signaling protocols.

In this paper, we propose two approaches for detecting VoIP spam calls. Both approaches build normal call behavior upon distribution of selected call characteristics (e.g., day and time of the call, call duration) and neither of them requires callee's feedback or modification of the underlying signaling protocol. Compared with existing VoIP spam defenses, our proposed approaches have the following advantages:

- They are transparent to end users, and they do not require any explicit feedback from the end users or modification of the underlying signaling protocols or UAs.
- They are designed to detect both sporadic and bulk VoIP spam calls. The proposed approach is able to suppress VoIP spam calls from local, authenticated callers.

We empirically evaluated our VoIP spam detection approaches using real VoIP call traces, and our results show that our approaches are effective in detecting both individual and bulk VoIP spam calls.

The remainder of the paper is structured as follows. In section 2, we establish the baseline of normal VoIP call behavior. In section 3, we present our first approach to detect individual local misbehaving callers. In Section 4, we discuss how to distinguish normal human generated calls from bulk machine generated spam calls based on entropy measurement of call duration. Section 5 concludes the paper.

2   Baseline of Normal VoIP Call Behavior

In this section, we establish the baseline of normal VoIP call behavior. Specifically, we used the call logs collected from a VoIP network of NuVox Communications, a voice service provider in Southeast and Midwest regions of the USA [6]. The seven days (July 21 - 25, July 28, and August 04' 2009) call logs were collected from a Class-V switch located at Winter Haven, Florida. The call logs correspond to VoIP calls made by subscribers of Orlando and Tampa cities in Florida. Figure 1 shows the call arrivals and the distribution of call duration characteristics of two days (21st-22nd July'09). Each of the call logs are of 24 hours duration starting at the midnight. The logs of 21st and 22nd July contain 56259 and 51625 successfully completed calls, respectively.

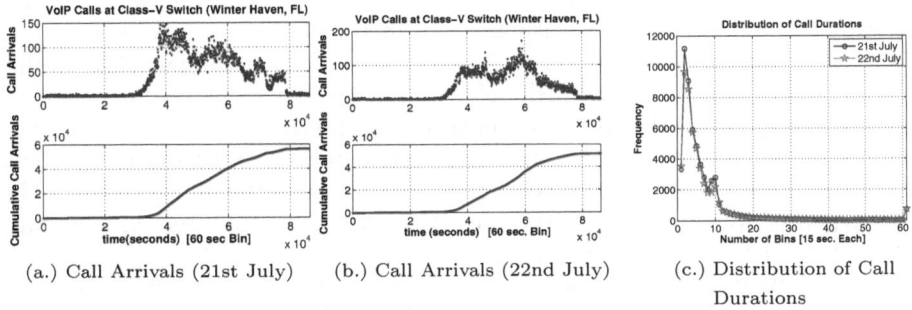

(a.) Call Arrivals (21st July)   (b.) Call Arrivals (22nd July)   (c.) Distribution of Call Durations

Fig. 1. Call Arrivals and Distribution of Call Durations

Call Duration Probability Distribution.   The call logs for VoIP traffic traces are analyzed to obtain call duration distribution. As shown in Figure 1 (c.), we observe that $\approx 50\%$ of the calls complete within a minute. The measured call durations are used to calculate the mean μ and standard deviation σ. The mean and standard deviation pair (μ, σ) [in seconds] for the 21st-22nd July VoIP traces are found to be $(111.87, 264.04)$, and $(115.83, 283.58)$, respectively.

3   Detecting Individual Misbehaving Subscriber

In this section, we focus on detecting individual misbehaving VoIP subscribers who are local and authenticated to the protected VoIP network. A VoIP caller can be classified as local or external subscriber based on the following attributes: 1) the source IP and the status of REGISTER message – the successfully completed REGISTER transaction lets us know that this particular subscriber is local (i.e., subscriber account is maintained by the service provider) and also from where to expect next outbound call request; 2) the SIP URI and the source IP of INVITE call requests that do not have corresponding REGISTER messages – these inbound call requests represent external unauthenticated subscribers and the source IP determines whether the request is from one of the peering partners or known business SIP trunking customers.

Discriminant Analysis Based on Mahalanobis Distance: The spam detection module (collocated with the session border controller) detects abnormal call behavior of individual local subscribers in the collection of past calling data points, going through a process consisting of two phases: the *training phase* and the *testing phase*. During the training phase, for each of the local subscribers we collect *day, time of calling,* and *call duration* for successfully completed calls. Since each subscribers calling behavior is quite different, we need a common base to make comparison and find out how individual subscribers deviate from the base. This common base is known as a *reference pattern.*

Later, the whole day is divided into small time periods of ΔT ($= 15$ min.) where individual subscriber's call behavior is compared with common *reference pattern*. The common reference pattern can be assumed to belong to a *virtual user* generating exactly 5 calls within each time window. The call arrivals are assumed to be poisson distributed with mean of 180 sec., and the call durations are exponentially distributed with mean talk time of 60 sec. Within a time window if a subscriber has less than 5 calls, we ignore that time window as this low call-rate cannot be a spam call behavior. Otherwise, using the *Mahalanobis distance*, we measure the distance between two multivariate data sets. In the training phase, the measured distances are used to derive a threshold i.e., an upper bound of distance values considered to be a normal call behavior. In the testing phase, we determine if the measured distance of a time window falls beyond a threshold value raising an alarm.

More formally, now assume that on a particular day of the first week and within a particular time window we have observed n realizations of a $d-$dimensional random variable. From the data set we get a data matrix $\chi(n \times d)$

$$\chi = \begin{pmatrix} x_{11} & \cdots & x_{1d} \\ \vdots & \vdots & \vdots \\ x_{n1} & \cdots & x_{nd} \end{pmatrix}$$

The row $x_i = (x_{i1}, \ldots, x_{id}) \in \mathbb{R}^d$ denotes the ith observation of a d-dimensional random variable $\chi \in \mathbb{R}^d$. The *center of gravity* of the n observations in $\mathbb{R}^d$ is given by the vector $\overline{x}$ of the means $\overline{x}_j$ of the d variables:

$$\overline{x} = \begin{pmatrix} \overline{x}_1 \\ \vdots \\ \overline{x}_d \end{pmatrix} = n^{-1} \chi^T 1_n$$

The dispersion of the n observations can be characterized by the covariance matrix of the d variables:

$$S = n^{-1} \chi^T \chi - \overline{x}\,\overline{x}^T$$

This matrix can equivalently be defined by

$$S = \frac{1}{n} \Sigma_{i=1}^n (x_i - \overline{x})(x_i - \overline{x})^T$$

Now our task is to compare the observed data matrix $\chi_p(n \times d)$ with the reference data matrix $\chi_q(m \times d)$ and find out how calls within a particular time window is correlated with the reference. We use Mahalanobis distance to measure the similarity between two data matrix [12]. The Mahalanobis distance between two populations p and q is defined as:

$$d_{pq} = \{(\overline{x}_p - \overline{x}_q)^T \Sigma^{-1}(\overline{x}_p - \overline{x}_q)\}^{\frac{1}{2}}$$

where Σ is pooled unbiased covariance matrix

$$\Sigma = [(n-1)S_p + (m-1)S_q]/(n+m-2)$$

Threshold Determination. In the training phase, the distribution of measured Mahalanobis distances are used to calculate the mean μ of all observed distances. To set an upper bound on distance values that may act as a threshold, we use $d_{thresh.} = \mu + n * \mu$, where $n \geqslant 0$. The value of n defines a confidence band where subscriber's calls falling in the region are treated as normal calls. Beyond this normal region, the observed distances are abnormal raising an alarm. The lower value of n governs the detection sensitivity, however at the cost of more false alarms.

White Listing to Suppress VoIP Spam Calls From Local, Authenticated Callers. Based on the normal call profile and the determined threshold, we can determine if an outgoing call from local caller is normal or not. We can further put any active local caller into a dynamic white list if most of its calls are determined normal. This would allow us to suppress VoIP spam calls from those local callers that are not in the dynamic white list. This suppression should only be used when it is determined local callers have issued bulk spam calls.

Empirical Validation: To demonstrate the applicability of the proposed method, we analyzed the call behavior of ≈ 50 subscribers. As a representative sample, from the 21st July call log we randomly selected six local subscribers of varying call rate. The per subscriber data set derived from the successfully completed calls within a particular time window is used to calculate the Mahalanobis distance.

Each individual subscriber is compared with the reference data set to get a whole day's distribution of Mahalanobis distance. This comparison is a part of training phase where we determine as how far a subscriber's legitimate call behavior may deviate from the reference data set as shown in Figure 2. The average of all distance values is found to be 1.21. It is used to derive an upper bound (i.e., $d_{thresh.} = 1.21 + 4 * 1.21 = 6.05$) beyond that calls are assumed to be abnormal. In our experiments we observe that the confidence band of $4 * \mu$ (i.e., $n = 4$) achieves high detection sensitivity with no false alarms. The so obtained threshold value is used to detect misbehavior of callers in the testing phase. The call logs of July 28 and August 04 are used as testing data set. Figure 3 a.), b.) and c.) plot the two whole day's data points for subscribers *User4*, *User5*, and *User6*, respectively. In the testing phse, for each individual time windows where

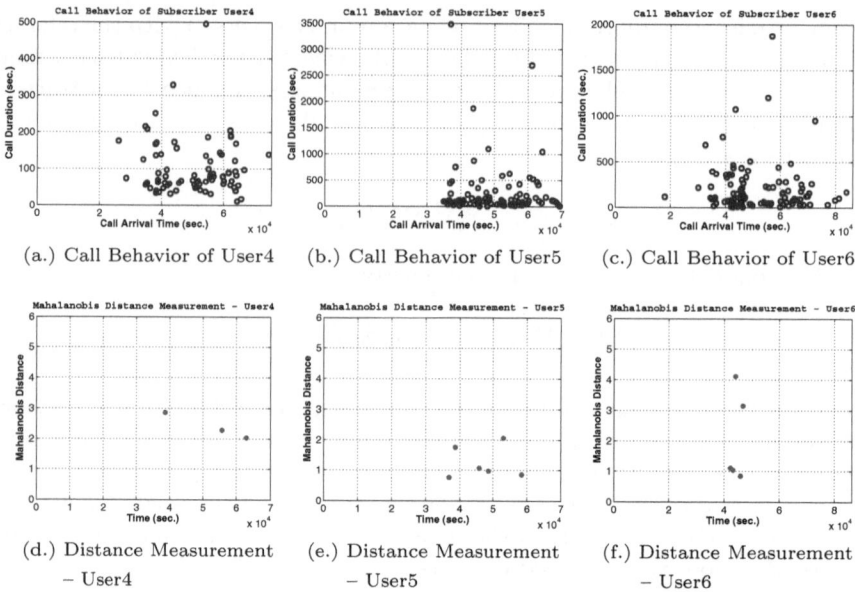

(a.) Call Behavior of User4   (b.) Call Behavior of User5   (c.) Call Behavior of User6

(d.) Distance Measurement   (e.) Distance Measurement   (f.) Distance Measurement
– User4   – User5   – User6

Fig. 2. Distance Measurement To Determine Threshold Value [Training Phase]

we observe at least 5 calls is compared with the common reference data set to
compute a similarity value using Mahalanobis distance as shown in Figure 3 c.),
d.) and e.). We observe that for both of these days, the distance values remain
well below the threshold value.

Now we mix 20 attack instances (each at an hour apart) within the 28th July
call log and each attack instance consists of 20 spam calls. The call arrivals
are assumed to be poisson distributed with mean of 30 sec., and the call durations are exponentially distributed with mean talk time of 15 sec. The measured
effectiveness of Mahalanobis distance classifier is summarized in Table 1.

4   Detecting Groups of Misbehaving Calls

The proposed scheme in the previous section is to detect abnormal call behavior of authenticated (i.e., local) callers at an individual level. In this section, we
develop an entropy-based approach to detect unusual call behavior at an aggregated level irrespective of being local or external subscribers. The basic insight is
that if a number of callers misbehave by performing low-rate attacks, it is possible
that at an individual level the call behavior may seem benign, however at aggregated level, the entropy-based approach sums up these individual low-rate spam
attacks leading to an efficient and easier detection mechanism without maintaining call behavior profiles for unknown and unauthenticated external callers and
thus avoiding unnecessary lookups and excessive entries in the database.

Few Observations. In the case of spam attacks, the machine generated bulk
calls will either be answered by subscribers (i.e., humans) or end up at the

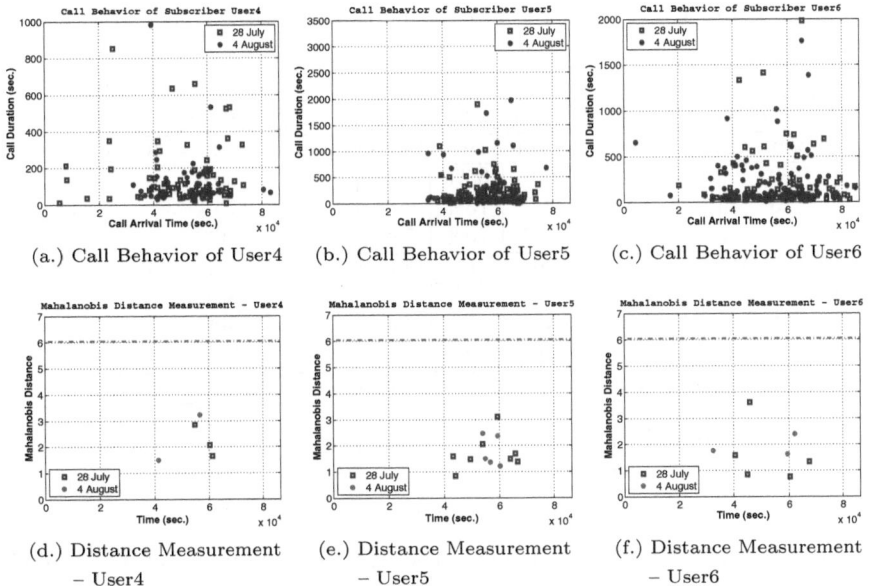

(a.) Call Behavior of User4   (b.) Call Behavior of User5   (c.) Call Behavior of User6

(d.) Distance Measurement   (e.) Distance Measurement   (f.) Distance Measurement
    – User4   – User5   – User6

Fig. 3. Distance Measurement To Detect Unusual Calling Behavior [Testing Phase]

voicemail system. If the spam calls are answered by subscribers then the average of call durations is expected to be short compared to other regular calls. Therefore, during the attack, the average of call durations will fall. Further, if the spam calls are answered by a voicemail system, still we are expected to observe unusual behavior. Generally, a voicemail system allows voice recording of only few minutes (a typical value is of $2-3$ minutes). At the expiration of voice recording timer, the voicemail system terminates the call. Hence, many of the calls will be having a constant call duration.

Entropy Classifier. The entropy classifier component makes spam attack detection based on entropy measurement of call durations. The call durations are binned into N contiguous bins (of varying lengths). We can interpret the bins as the states x_i of a discrete random variable X, where $p(X = x_i) = p_i$. The entropy of the random variable X is then

$$H[p] = -\sum_i p(x_i)\ln p(x_i) \tag{1}$$

Distributions $p(x_i)$ that are sharply peaked around a few bins will have a relatively low entropy, whereas those that are spread more evenly across many bins will have higher entropy. For example, if the entropy is low for our selected attribute of *call duration* then it indicates predictable patterns of the abnormal call behavior. It could be due to short call durations are skewed toward few selected lower-side bins or may be constant call durations have filled up one (or few) particular bin(s). However, if the measured entropy is high (i.e., call durations

Table 1. Performance of Mahalanobis Distance Classifier*

20 Attack Instances Introduced in the Whole Day Traffic of 28th July						
Calls/ΔT	User1	User2	User3	User4	User5	User6
Spam Attack Detection Probability [Poisson arrival mean = 30 sec.]						
20	100%	95%	100%	95%	95%	90%
15	100%	85%	90%	75%	80%	75%
10	100%	80%	85%	70%	75%	70%
Spam Attack Detection Probability [Poisson arrival mean = 20 sec.]						
20	100%	85%	95%	80%	85%	80%
15	100%	80%	90%	80%	75%	80%
10	100%	70%	80%	70%	75%	75%
Spam Attack Detection Probability [Poisson arrival mean = 15 sec.]						
20	100%	80%	90%	80%	80%	80%
15	100%	80%	90%	80%	75%	75%
10	100%	80%	85%	65%	75%	75%

* Without removing the outlier data points.

are distributed across bins), it indicates the irregular or unpredictable behavior of human conversations.

Entropy Measurement of Call Durations. In our experiments, the binning of call duration data points use 61 contiguous bins. The first 60 bins are of 15 sec. each and the last 61th bin is a default bin to capture all call durations that are longer than 15 minutes. However, it should be noted that the choice of fine granular bins is more accurate in classifying the attacks since it leads to a better estimate of the entropy. In our study of call duration entropy, we divide the whole day in three separate time zones based on the observation of call arrival rate. The first time zone starts at midnight and ends at 9:00 AM. In this time zone the call arrival rate is very low (e.g., see Figure 1).

The entropy estimation is based on 30 minutes time window to make sure that we collect enough data points. As the time increases, the call rate also increases resulting in the growing trend of entropy. The second time zone represents usual

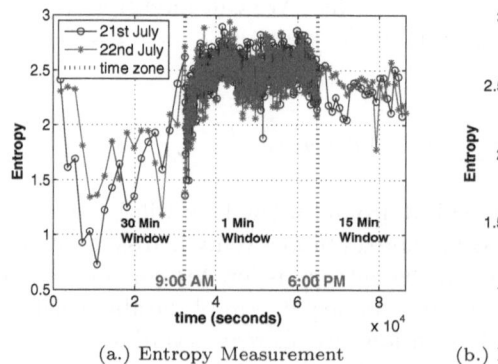

(a.) Entropy Measurement

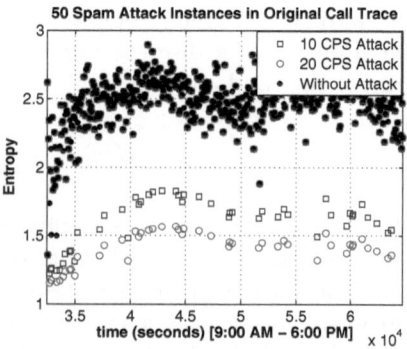

(b.) Entropy Measurement Under Spam Attack

Fig. 4. Entropy Measurement

working hours between 9:00 AM and 6:00 PM where call rate is usually high. In this time zone we use 1 minute time window for entropy estimation. In our analysis, we find that the busy hour entropy remained confined between 2.0 and 3.0 as shown in Figure 4 (a). The third time zone starts at 6:00 PM and ends at midnight. In this time zone, we use 15 minutes time window for entropy measurement that generally varies between 2.0 and 2.5. The off-peak hour entropy is more unpredictable (especially between midnight to 9:00 AM).

Determination of Entropy Cutoff Scores. To use entropy measures for spam attack classification, based on previous collected data during the training period, we build a entropy profile of call durations with respect to time. The measured entropy is used to set a cutoff score and if the test score (during the testing period) is greater than or equal to the cutoff score, the call requests are classified as human generated. If the test score is less than the cutoff score, the call requests are classified as malicious spam calls. The cutoff score and its relation with time is an important parameter in determining the false positive and true positive rates of the entropy classifier. Since in the first time zone the call rate is very low so to avoid detection, most of the attacks are expected to occur during the busy hour of call traffic where malicious calls can easily hide among legitimate call traffic. Our focus is mainly on this time segment. Note that with the proper setting of threshold values, there will be no false alarm (i.e., false positive) under normal conditions. However, to balance both false positives and false negatives, we set our entropy threshold at 1.75. In two day's call log analysis we observed that out of 1082 observations, 4 observations had entropy value below the threshold value of 1.75. Therefore, 0.37% times the entropy value falls below the threshold value and thus giving us false alarms.

Empirical Evaluation of the Entropy Classifier: Now we empirically evaluate the effectiveness of the proposed entropy classifier in terms of its spam detection accuracy. In our experiments, we made the following three assumptions: 1.) during busy-hour spam attack, 95% calls are answered by humans and the remaining 5% by the voicemail system; 2.) for simplistic reason we assume that the human answered call durations are exponentially distributed with mean talk time of 15 sec.; and 3.) the voicemail system's recording time limit is of 2 minutes. After 2 minutes of recording, the voicemail calls are terminated by the voicemail system.

In our experiments, the call logs are used to generate call requests and used as the normal background traffic. Later, this traffic is randomly mixed with the spam traffic of varying call rates. For example, during the busy hour between 9:00 AM to 6:00 PM, we introduce 50 individual spam attack instances of 10, 20, 30, 40 and 50 calls per second. Each of these attack instances lasts for a small time period of 30 seconds and thus introducing 300, 600, 900, 1200, and 1500 spam calls per attack instances. Figure 4 (b) shows 50 individual attack instances (three times two individual attack instances fell within the same time window). These attack instances belong to two different call rates of 10 and 20 CPS. Under spam attack, we could observe as how entropy drops from those representing the normal call behavior. To measure false negatives, we use detection probability that is defined as the percentage of the successful identified attack instances over the total launched attacks in one set of experiments. The results demonstrate that our proposed entropy classifier is able to reliably detect aggregated ($\geq$ 20 calls per second) VoIP spam calls with no more than 0.37% false positive rate.

5   Conclusion

SPIT is touted as the next biggest spam threat after email spam. To mitigate the potential threat of voice spam, this paper proposed two complementing and yet practical schemes. The first scheme, which is based on Mahalanobis distance, can detect unusual call behavior at the individual subscriber level. The second approach utilized entropy of call durations to detect spam attack at an aggregated level. It can detect spam attacks when a group of subscribers misbehave. The empirical results of our study show that it is feasible for a VoIP service provider to detect VoIP spam attacks irrespective of whether it is launched from within an enterprise network, peering partners or from subscribers.

References

1. Balasubramaniyan, V., Ahamad, M., Park, H.: CallRank: Combating SPIT Using Call Duration, Social Networks and Global Reputation. In: The Fourth Conference on Email and Anti-Spam (2007)
2. Dantu, R., Kolan, P.: Detecting spam in voip networks. In: Proceedings of the Steps to Reducing Unwanted Traffic on the Internet on Steps to Reducing Unwanted Traffic on the Internet Workshop (2005)
3. Graham-Rowe, D.: A Sentinel to Screen Phone Calls (2006), http://www.technologyreview.com/communications/17300/?a=f
4. Kayote Networks. The Threat of SPIT (2007), http://www.kayote.com/
5. Niccolini, S., Tartarelli, S., Stiemerling, M., Srivastava, S.: SIP Extensions for SPIT identification. draft-niccolini-sipping-feedback-spit-03, IETF Network Working Group (2007) (work in progress)
6. NuVox Communications. Service Provider (2009), http://www.nuvox.com
7. Rosenberg, J., Jennings, C.: The Session Initiation Protocol (SIP) and Spam. RFC 5039, IETF Network Working Group (2008)
8. SIPERA. Sipera IPCS: Products to Address VoIP Vulnerabilities (April 2007), http://www.sipera.com/index.php?action=products,default
9. VOIPSA. Confirmed cases of SPIT. Mailing list (2006), http://www.voipsa.org/pipermail/voipsec_voipsa.org/2006-March/001326.html
10. VOIPSA. VoIP Attacks in the News (2007), http://voipsa.org/blog/category/voip-attacks-in-the-news/
11. Wikipedia. Turing test (2009), http://en.wikipedia.org/wiki/Turing_test
12. Wikipedia. Mahalanobis distance (2010), http://en.wikipedia.org/wiki/Mahalanobis_distance
13. Wu, Y.-S., Bagchi, S., Singh, N., Wita, R.: Spam Detection in Voice-Over-IP Calls through Semi-Supervised Clustering. In: IEEE Dependable Systems and Networks Conference (DSN 2009) (June-July 2009)
14. Rebahi, Y., Al-Hezmi, A.: Spam Prevention for Voice over IP. Technical report (2007), http://colleges.ksu.edu.sa/ComputerSciences/Documents/NITS/ID143.pdf

T-CUP: A TPM-Based Code Update Protocol Enabling Attestations for Sensor Networks

Steffen Wagner[1], Christoph Krauß[1], and Claudia Eckert[2]

[1] Fraunhofer Research Institution AISEC, Garching, Germany
{steffen.wagner,christoph.krauss}@aisec.fraunhofer.de
[2] TU München, Dpt. of Computer Science, Chair for IT Security, Garching, Germany
claudia.eckert@in.tum.de

Abstract. In this paper, we propose a secure code update protocol for TPM-equipped sensor nodes, which enables these nodes to prove their trustworthiness to other nodes using efficient attestation protocols. As main contribution, the protocol provides mechanisms to maintain the ability of performing efficient attestation protocols after a code update, although these protocols assume a trusted system state which never changes. We also present a proof of concept implementation on IRIS sensor nodes, which we have equipped with Atmel TPMs, and discuss the security of our protocol.

Keywords: Wireless Sensor Network, Security, Node Compromise, TPM, Attestation, Secure Code Update.

1 Introduction

Wireless sensor networks (WSNs) [1] can be used for various security-critical applications, such as military surveillance. Sensor nodes with embedded sensing, computation, and wireless communication capabilities monitor the physical world and send data through multi-hop communication to a central base station. The resources of a sensor node are severely constrained since they are mainly designed to be cheap and battery-powered.

Since sensor nodes are often deployed in unattended and even hostile environments, node compromise is a serious issue. By compromising a sensor node, an adversary gets full access to data such as cryptographic keys stored on the node. Especially sensor nodes which perform special tasks for other sensor nodes (e.g., key management) are a valuable target. One approach to protect the cryptographic keys on such nodes is the use of a Trusted Platform Module (TPM) [15]. The TPM is basically a smartcard and can be used to create a secure storage and execution environment. The TPM additionally provides mechanisms to realize attestation protocols where the sensor nodes can prove that no adversary has tampered with their components.

However, previously proposed attestation protocols for WSNs, e.g., in [9], rely on a trusted system state which never changes. The main idea is to use the TPM to cryptographically bind certain attestation values (e.g., symmetric keys) to a trusted initial platform configuration. The platform configuration is validated

M. Rajarajan et al. (Eds.): SecureComm 2011, LNICST 96, pp. 511–521, 2012.
© Institute for Computer Sciences, Social Informatics and Telecommunications Engineering 2012

during each boot process by calculating hash values for bootloader (acting as Core Root of Trust for Measurement (CRTM)), operating system (OS), and all installed applications and comparing them with references values protected by the TPM. Only if they match, access to the attestation values is possible. Thus, any code update, which might be necessary to patch security vulnerabilities or add new functionalities, would result in a different system state which prevents successful attestations.

In this paper, we present T-CUP, a secure code update protocol which enables TPM-based attestation protocols and provides mechanisms to validate the authenticity, integrity, and freshness of the wirelessly transmitted code update. We also present a proof of concept implementation and security discussion.

2   Related Work

Existing over-the-air programming (OTAP) protocols, such as Deluge [7], Infuse [2], or MNP [10], mainly focus on the (efficiency of the) update procedure, but do not consider security. In [4,3,12,13,8], code update protocols with security mechanisms have been proposed which are often based on an existing OTAP protocol, mostly Deluge. Secured hash chains are used to ensure authenticity and integrity of the individual parts of the code update. Because of the chaining, only the first hash needs to be protected by some cryptographic mechanism. However, the key used to protect this hash value must not be accessible by an adversary since this would enable him to create false code updates. In [4,3,12,14], digital signatures are used for this purpose which have much higher computational costs than symmetric approaches. The protocols proposed in [13,8] are solely based on symmetric (hash-based) mechanisms. However, all previously proposed protocols are not directly applicable to update TPM-equipped sensor nodes while maintaining the ability to perform attestations.

The use of a TPM for attestation protocols in hybrid WSNs where only a minority of special sensor nodes are equipped with a TPM has initially been introduced by Krauß et al. [9]. They propose two attestation protocols which either enable a single node (including the base station) or multiple sensor nodes to simultaneously verify the trustworthiness of a TPM-equipped sensor node. The main idea is to use the Sealing function of the TPM to bind certain attestation values (symmetric keys or values of a hash chain) to an initial trustworthy platform configuration. However, code updates are not considered.

Using the TPM in WSNs has been also proposed in [5] and [6] where all sensor nodes of a WSN are equipped with a TPM to perform public key cryptography.

3   Setting and Notation

In this section, we explain the setting and define the notation for our protocol.

3.1   Setting

We consider a hybrid WSN consisting of a large number of common cluster sensor nodes (CNs) and very few TPM-equipped cluster head (CH) nodes. CHsperform special tasks and services for a certain number of CNs. Data is sent via multi-hop communication to one central base station (BS) which is assumed to be trustworthy, i.e., cannot be compromised.

Before node deployment, BS and all CHs are initialized in a trusted environment. The TPM of each CH is initialized by generating asymmetric key pairs which are only used within the TPM and marked as "non-migratable", i.e., the private key cannot be extracted from the TPM. These asymmetric keys are used by the sealing function of the TPM to cryptographically bind shared symmetric keys between BS and the CHs to an initial trusted system state. Likewise, a timestamp which indicates the current version of the system software is also bound to the trusted system state.

Furthermore, we assume an adversary which tries to compromise a CH by attacking the code update protocol. The adversary can either try to physically compromise a CH or by performing attacks via the wireless channel. In the first case, the adversary directly tries to read out stored data such as cryptographic keys or tries to re-program the node with his own malicious code. In the latter case, the adversary can perform attacks such as eavesdropping on the wireless communication, manipulate transmitted packets, inject new or replay old packets. However, we assume that an adversary is not able to break cryptographic algorithms, e.g., decrypting encrypted messages without knowing the key or inverting hash functions. The adversary is also not able to access cryptographic keys which are protected by the TPM or reset the TPM.

3.2   Notation

Cluster heads are denoted as CH_i with $i = 1, \ldots, a$ and the cluster nodes as CN_j with $j = 1, \ldots, b$, where $b \gg a$ (cf. [9]).

A symmetric key K between the BS and the CH_i is referred to as K_{BS,CH_i}. Since the current version of the TPM does not support symmetric cryptographic operations internally, we allow this key to be stored in RAM for a short time.

Applying a cryptographic *hash function* H on data m is denoted with $H(m)$. A one-way *hash chain* [11] stored on a CH is denoted with $C^{CH} = c_0^{CH}, \ldots, c_n^{CH}$. A hash chain is a sequence of n hash values, each of fixed length l, generated by a hash function $H : \{0,1\}^* \rightarrow \{0,1\}^l$ by applying the hash function H successively on a seed value c_0, such that $c_{\nu+1} = H(c_\nu)$, with $\nu = 0, 1, \ldots, n-2, n-1$.

A specific system state of a TPM-equipped cluster head CH_i is referred to as *platform configuration* $P_{CH_i} := (PCR[0], \ldots, PCR[p])_{CH_i}$ and stored as *integrity measurement values* μ in the *platform configuration registers* (PCRs) of the TPM. To store the value of a measured (software) component in a PCR, the existing value is not replaced, but combined with the new value using $PCRExtend(PCR[i], \mu)$, which is specified as $PCR[i] \leftarrow SHA1(PCR[i] \,\|\, \mu)$ [15].

For our protocol, we define two platform configurations referred to as *full* and *reduced platform configuration*. The full platform configuration $P_{CH_i}^{(0,\ldots,p)}$ uses at least two PCRs and must consider all software layers up to the OS and application layer (cf. Fig. 1, left). Similarly, we denote the reduced platform configuration as $P_{CH_i}^{(0,...,r)}$, which uses $r < p$ registers and only considers the static trusted components up to the bootloader (cf. Fig. 1, right).

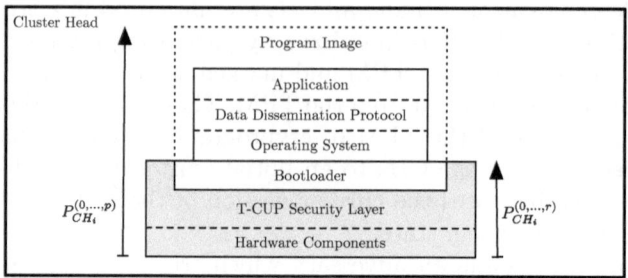

Fig. 1. T-CUP Security Layer on Cluster Head

Data m can be cryptographically bound to a specific platform configuration P by using the TPM_Seal command, which we call *Seal* for the sake of simplicity. Using the TPM_Unseal command (or simply *Unseal*), the TPM decrypts m only if the platform configuration has not been modified. Given a non-migratable asymmetric key pair (e^{CH_i}, d^{CH_i}) we denote the *sealing* of data m to the platform configuration P_{CH_i} with $\{m\}_{P_{CH_i}}^{e^{CH_i}} = Seal(P_{CH_i}, e^{CH_i}, m)$. For *unsealing* the sealed data $\{m\}_{P_{CH_i}}^{e^{CH_i}}$, it is necessary that the current platform configuration P'_{CH_i} is equal to P_{CH_i}: $m = Unseal(P'_{CH_i} = P_{CH_i}, d^{CH_i}, \{m\}_{P_{CH_i}}^{e^{CH_i}})$.

4   Protocol Description

In this section, we describe the concept of our proposed code update protocol.

4.1   The T-CUP Header

The code update is divided into pages $pg0$ to pgT, i.e., $upd = (pg0 \| \ldots \| pgT)$, as depicted in Fig. 2. To ensure the authenticity of such a code update, we define a *T-CUP Header*, which is shown in detail on the right of Fig. 2. This header includes the number of pages T, a timestamp ts, a chain of hashes and an HMAC ($hmac\_upd$) for the complete code update.

The cryptographic values of the T-CUP Header are calculated as follows: First, the HMAC $hmac\_upd$, which allows to verify the authenticity and integrity of the complete code update, is calculated using the shared symmetric key K_{BS,CH_i} between BS and CH_i (here simply K):

$$hmac\_upd = HMAC(K, upd) = HMAC(K, (pg0 \| \ldots \| pgT)) . \qquad (1)$$

After that, the chain of hashes is then generated in reversed order as shown in Fig. 2 (right): For page $T-1$, the hash is created as $h_T = H(pgT \| hmac\_upd)$, i.e., by concatenating the data of page T with the HMAC of the complete code

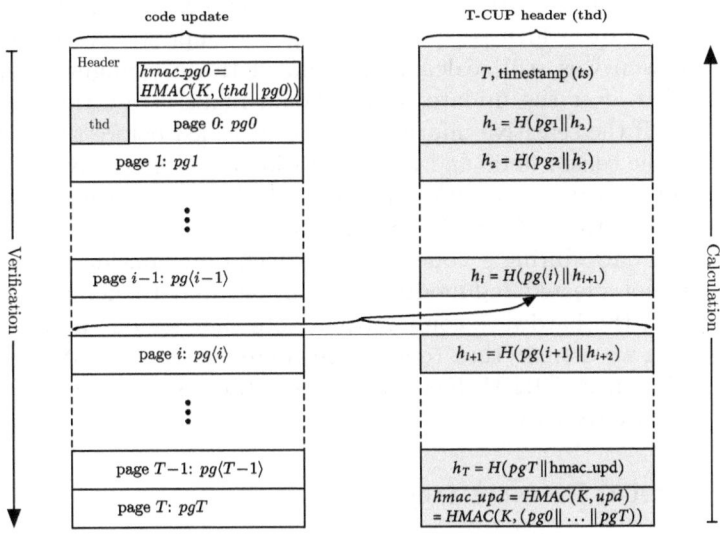

Fig. 2. Code update and T-CUP Header with chained hashes

update and hashing the result using a one way-hash function H. Starting from page $T-2$, the hash value h_i is created by concatenating the data of page i with the previously cacluated hash h_{i+1} and hashing the resulting value:

$$h_i = H(pg\langle i\rangle \,\|\, h_{i+1}) \,. \tag{2}$$

Finally, a second HMAC, which is referred to as $hmac\_pg0$ and includes the T-CUP Header (particularly, hash h_1 and the timestamp) as well as the first page (with index 0), is generated (and stored in the code update header):

$$hmac\_pg0 = HMAC(K, (thd\,\|\,pg0)) \,. \tag{3}$$

For the verification of the code update (cf. Fig. 2, left), we start with checking the HMAC $hmac\_pg0$, which authenticates the T-CUP Header. The timestamp is compared with the sealed reference value to check the freshness. With the hash chain, we are able to validate the authenticity and integrity of the following parts of the code update page by page (cf. Section 4.3).

4.2   The T-CUP Security Layer

In addition to the *T-CUP Header* that protects the wirelessly transmitted code update, we also specify a *T-CUP Security Layer* beneath the OS (cf. Fig. 1). This layer protects the sensitive information stored on the CHs during a code update and maintains the ability to access sealed data even after the code update.

   The general idea behind the *T-CUP Security Layer* results from the need to protect the sensitive information during a code update and preserve the trusted system state in order to access these information after the code update. The reason for preserving the trusted state is that the data is sealed to the initial trusted system state, which is changed by the code update. As a consequence, if the information was still sealed to the old platform configuration, it could not be unsealed after the update, which would make attestations impossible. But obviously, if the sensitive information was unsealed before the code update is performed, the sensor node and the attestation could be easily compromised. That is why all sensitive information need to be sealed even during a code update.

Thus, we define the *T-CUP Security Layer* as a reduced platform configuration for sealing data during a code update, which only considers those components that are not affected and modified by the code update, i.e., the CRTM, the bootloader, and the hardware components. Note that for our proof of concept implementation we assume that (one of the components of) TOSBoot is trustworthy since it acts as CRTM. For real implementations, we suggest a hardware CRTM to increase security

4.3   The T-CUP Protocol Steps

In this section, we describe the protocol steps of T-CUP in detail. The T-CUP protocol can be divided into three phases: (P1) Initialization and Dissemination, (P2) Validation and Preparation, and (P3) Verification and Processing. In the first phase, the code update is generated on the base station and distributed to CHs. In the second and third phase, CHs checks the authenticity, integrity, and freshness, prepares for the necessary reboot, and processes the code update after an additional verification. During the code update, all sensitive information is sealed to the security layer. It is resealed to the new full platform configuration after the code update is installed.

In Phase 1 (cf. Table 1), the base station first generates the program binary (P1.1) and then creates the T-CUP Header as described in Section 4.1 by setting the number of pages and timestamp in the T-CUP Header (P1.2) and by calculating the HMAC for the complete code update $hmac\_upd$, the hash chain for the code update pages, and the HMAC for the first page $hmac\_pg0$ (P1.3 – P1.5). After that, the code update is disseminated in the network (P1.6).

In Phase 2 (cf. Table 2), the cluster head validates the code update (P2(a)) and prepares for the reboot (P2(b)). Thus, when the dissemination is initiated by the base station, CH eventually receives $hmac\_pg0$ and page 0 (P2.1). To verify the HMAC for the first page, CH first unseals the shared key K_{BS,CH_i} (P2.2), which is only possible if the node is still in a trustworthy system state:

$$K_{BS,CH_i} = Unseal(P_{CH_i}^{(0,\dots,p)}, d^{CH_i}, \{K_{BS,CH_i}\}_{P_{CH_i}^{(0,\dots,p)}}^{e^{CH_i}}) \ . \tag{4}$$

With the unsealed key, the cluster head can recalculate the HMAC and compare it with the reference value $hmac\_pg0$ from the global header (P2.3):

$$hmac\_pg0 \stackrel{?}{=} HMAC(K_{BS,CH_i}, thd \,\|\, pg0) \ . \tag{5}$$

If the values are identical, the authenticity and integrity of page 0, the head of the hash chain, and the timestamp in the T-CUP Header is successfully validated.

Table 1. Phase 1: Initialization on Base Station

Step	Node	Data	Action/Description
P1(a): Initialization			
P1.1	BS	*binary code*	creates program binary
P1.2	BS	*#pages, timestamp*	sets number of pages and time-stamp
P1.3	BS	*hmac_upd* $= MAC_{upd}^{K_{BS,CH_i}}$	creates a HMAC for the complete code update with the symmetric key K_{BS,CH_i}
P1.4	BS	h_i	creates hash values for each page
P1.5	BS	*hmac_pg0*	creates a HMAC for page 0
P1(b): Dissemination			
P1.6	$BS \rightarrow CH_i$ *upd*		disseminates code update

Otherwise, the code update protocol stops. To verify the freshness of the code update, the CH extracts the authenticated timestamp in step P2.4 and compares it with the sealed reference value. If the extracted timestamp indicates a more recent program binary, the current reference value is replaced with the timestamp from the code update (after sealing it). Otherwise, the protocol aborts since the code update is outdated.

After the validation of the T-CUP Header, CH requests the complete code update page by page and verifies the elements of the hash chain (P2.5), which ensure the integrity and authenticity of the included pages, by recalculating each value and comparing it with the expected result (cf. Section 4.1).

After CH has received the complete code update, it starts preparing for the reboot in order to program the new image by sealing the shared key K_{BS,CH_i} to the security layer in step P2.6:

$$\{K_{BS,CH_i}\}_{P_{CH_i}^{(0,...,r)}}^{e^{CH_i}} = Seal(P_{CH_i}^{(0,...,r)}, e^{CH_i}, K_{BS,CH_i}) \,. \tag{6}$$

CH also seals the HMAC for the complete code update to the reduced platform configuration (P2.7) to be able to verify the image after the reboot:

$$\{hmac\_upd\}_{P_{CH_i}^{(0,...,r)}}^{e^{CH_i}} = Seal(P_{CH_i}^{(0,...,r)}, e^{CH_i}, hmac\_upd) \,. \tag{7}$$

The second HMAC *hmac_upd* allows for an efficient verification of the complete code update again after the reboot, because it 1) is already implicitly authenticated, 2) requires only one calculation instead of calculating again all values of the hash chain, and 3) occupies less space. Thus, *hmac_upd* effectively preserves the effort already invested in authenticating and verifying the complete hash chain page by page.

As the final step of the preparation, CH reseals all sensitive information m, e.g., the attestation values such as a symmetric key, to the security layer (P2.8):

Table 2. Phase 2: Validation and Preparation

Step	Node	Data	Action/Description
P2(a): Validation			
P2.1	CH_i	$hmac\_pg0$, page 0	receives page 0 and $hmac\_pg0$
P2.2	CH_i	K_{BS,CH_i}	unseals the symmetric key
P2.3	CH_i	$hmac\_pg0$	checks the HMAC
P2.4	CH_i	$timestamp$	checks timestamp
P2.5	CH_i	upd	receives complete upd page by page and validates each hash value
P2(b): Preparation			
P2.6	CH_i	$\{K_{BS,CH_i}\}^{e^{CH_i}}_{P^{(0,\dots,r)}_{CH_i}}$	reseals the symmetric key to the security layer
P2.7	CH_i	$\{hmac\_upd\}^{e^{CH_i}}_{P^{(0,\dots,r)}_{CH_i}}$	seals the HMAC for the complete code update to the security layer
P2.8	CH_i	$\{m\}^{e^{CH_i}}_{P'^{(0,\dots,p)}_{CH_i}}$ $\rightarrow \{m\}^{e^{CH_i}}_{P'^{(0,\dots,r)}_{CH_i}}$	reseals the sensitive information to the security layer

$$\{m\}^{e^{CH_i}}_{P^{(0,\dots,r)}_{CH_i}} = Seal(P^{(0,\dots,r)}_{CH_i}, e^{CH_i}, m)$$
$$= Seal(P^{(0,\dots,r)}_{CH_i}, e^{CH_i}, Unseal(P^{(0,\dots,p)}_{CH_i}, d^{CH_i}, \{m\}^{e^{CH_i}}_{P^{(0,\dots,p)}_{CH_i}})) . \tag{8}$$

After resealing, CH reboots and executes the bootloader.

In Phase 3 (cf. Table 3), CH verifies the code update again to check if it is still unmodified (P3(a)) and processes the verified update (P3(b)). For the verification, the CRTM starts with measuring the security layer to create a reduced platform configuration $P'^{(0,\dots,r)}_{CH_i}$ (P3.1). This platform configuration has to match the platform configuration, which has been specified to seal the shared key before the reboot, in order to unseal it (P3.2):

$$K_{BS,CH_i} = Unseal(P'^{(0,\dots,r)}_{CH_i}, d^{CH_i}, \{K_{BS,CH_i}\}^{d^{CH_i}}_{P'^{(0,\dots,r)}_{CH_i}}) . \tag{9}$$

That is only the case if the security layer is still unmodified, i.e., if the equation $P'^{(0,\dots,r)}_{CH_i} = P^{(0,\dots,r)}_{CH_i}$ holds. CH also unseals the HMAC for the complete update (P3.3), where the same condition applies:

$$hmac\_upd = Unseal(P'^{(0,\dots,r)}_{CH_i}, d^{CH_i}, \{hmac\_upd\}^{d^{CH_i}}_{P'^{(0,\dots,r)}_{CH_i}}) . \tag{10}$$

For the verification of the code update stored in memory, a fresh HMAC is calculated and compared with the unsealed HMAC reference value:

$$hmac\_upd = MAC^{K_{BS,CH_i}}_{upd} \stackrel{?}{=} HMAC(K_{BS,CH_i}, upd) . \tag{11}$$

Once the trustworthiness of the security layer and the code update is verified, the bootloader copys the binary to the program memory (P3.5). After that,

Table 3. Phase 3: Verification and Processing

Step	Node	Data	Action/Description
P3(a): Verification			
P3.1	CH_i	$P'^{(0,\ldots,r)}_{CH_i}$	measures the security layer
P3.2	CH_i	K_{BS,CH_i}	unseals the symmetric key
P3.3	CH_i	$MAC^{K_{BS,CH_i}}_{upd}$	unseals the HMAC
P3.4	CH_i	$upd, MAC^{K_{BS,CH_i}}_{upd}$	uses the symmetric key to compare the unsealed MAC with a freshly calculated HMAC of the upd
P3(b): Processing			
P3.5	CH_i	upd	copies update to program memory
P3.6	CH_i	$P'^{(0,\ldots,p)}_{CH_i}$	measures remaining components for a full platform configuration
P3.7	CH_i	$\{K_{BS,CH_i}\}^{e^{CH_i}}_{P^{(0,\ldots,p)}_{CH_i}}$	CH_i seals K_{BS,CH_i} to the new trusted full platform configuration
P3.8	CH_i	$\{m\}^{e^{CH_i}}_{P'^{(0,\ldots,r)}_{CH_i}} \to \{m\}^{e^{CH_i}}_{P'^{(0,\ldots,p)}_{CH_i}}$	reseals the sensitive information to the new trusted full platform configuration P'

it measures the remaining software components and creates the full platform configuration, which includes the OS and application components. Using this new trusted full platform configuration, CH finally reseals the shared symmetric key (P3.7) as well as all other sensitive information (P3.8).

5 Implementation

As proof of concept, we implemented T-CUP on IRIS sensor nodes, which we connected with Atmel *AT97SC3204T* TPMs via I^2C, by extending the current de-facto standard code dissemination protocol *Deluge* [7] and the boot loader *TOSBoot* from TinyOS [16]. The *T-CUP Image Format* extends the specification of a Deluge image with the cryptographic information of the T-CUP Header to enable the verification of the authenticity, integrity, and freshness of the distributed code update. Based on the T-CUP Image Format specification, we have implemented the T-CUP protocol as (1) an interface script for the base station and (2) T-CUP components for CHs. The new T-CUP interface script *tos-tcup* is based on the Deluge interface script *tos-deluge* and can be used to initialize CHs prior to deployment, i.e., the cryptographic keys are generated and symmetric keys and initial timestamps are sealed to the initial trusted platform configuration. The T-CUP components for CHs consists of the TPM driver and extended Deluge and TOSBoot components for the dissemination and reprogramming.

6 Security Discussion

In this section, we evaluate the security of T-CUP. We first discuss an adversary performing attacks via the wireless channel and then an adversary that physically tampers with a CH (cf. Section 3.1).

To compromise a CH via wireless channel, an adversary can try to send his own malicious code update to CH. Lets assume that an adversary is able to do this. A code update which is accepted by CH must contain a valid *hmac_upd*. Since we assume an adversary is not able to break cryptographic algorithms (cf. Section 3.1), the adversary must be in possession of the symmetric key shared between BS and CH. To get access to the required key, the adversary must have either compromised BS or CH. However, this is a contradiction to the assumption that BS is trustworthy and that all keys on a CH are protected by the TPM. Thus, an adversary cannot inject his own malicious code update. The same applies to manipulations of eavesdropped valid code update sent by BS.

An adversary could also try to replay and install a valid old code update which is known to possess certain weaknesses, e.g., possible buffer overflows. However, CH verifies the freshness by comparing the timestamp in the header, which is protected by *hmac_pg0*, with the sealed reference value. Thus, an adversary would have to manipulate that timestamp and create a valid *hmac_pg0* which is a contradiction to our assumptions already mentioned above.

Now we consider the case where an adversary has physical access to CH and tries to compromise it. The adversary can try to manipulate the software components of a CH (cf. Fig. 1) to get access to the cryptographic keys. However, we assume that runtime attacks such as buffer overflows are not possible. Thus, an adversary has to install his malicious code and reboot CH. But after the reboot, the platform configuration has changed and the TPM denies access to the sealed cryptographic keys preventing a successful compromise.

Instead of manipulating the installed software, the adversary might tamper with a code update stored in the flash memory before it gets installed. However, CH verifies *hmac_upd* before the code update is installed. Thus, an adversary would have to forge the correct HMAC for the manipulated code update. But this would also require the adversary to break cryptography, compromise BS, or access TPM-protected keys which is contradictory to our assumptions.

The adversary might also try to exploit the (re)sealing to different platform configurations and the security layer. First, keys are sealed to the initial platform configuration which is assumed to be trustworthy. Thus, an adversary cannot perform successful manipulations during the unsealing and resealing of the keys to the security layer before a new update is installed. After a reboot, only the integrity of the security layer, including the CRTM and all necessary security services such as the HMAC engine, is checked. Thus, an adversary could theoretically manipulate the other software components above the security layer, i.e., OS and application components. However, this would have no effect, because the new trusted code update (since *hmac_upd* is valid) is installed by the security layer and overwrites the malicious code. Thus, also the resealing to the new platform configuration is performed when CH is in a trustworthy state.

7   Conclusion

In this paper, we presented T-CUP, a TPM-based code update protocol to secure distributed program images while still enabling attestation protocols based on binding keys to a trusted initial platform configuration. T-CUP provides mechanisms to validate the authenticity, integrity, and freshness of the wirelessly transmitted code update. To enable attestations, we introduced a new "virtual" security layer beneath the OS where attestation values are temporarily bound to during an update. Our protocol is based on efficient cryptographic primitives such as hash functions and MACs to avoid computational intensive digital signatures and unnecessary large messages. We also presented the feasibility of T-CUP in a proof of concept implementation and discussed the security of our protocol. T-CUP can handle an adversary attacking via the the wireless channel as well as an adversary which directly tampers with a CH using physical access.

References

1. Akyildiz, I.F., Su, W., Sankarasubramaniam, Y., Cayirci, E.: A survey on sensor networks. IEEE Communications Magazine 40(8), 102–114 (2002)
2. Arumugam, M.U.: Infuse: a TDMA based reprogramming service for sensor networks. In: SenSys (2004)
3. Deng, J., Han, R., Mishra, S.: Secure code distribution in dynamically programmable wireless sensor networks. In: IPSN (2006)
4. Dutta, P.K., Hui, J.W., Chu, D.C., Culler, D.E.: Securing the Deluge Network Programming System. In: IPSN (2006)
5. Hu, W., Corke, P., Shih, W.C., Overs, L.: secFleck: A Public Key Technology Platform for Wireless Sensor Networks. In: Roedig, U., Sreenan, C.J. (eds.) EWSN 2009. LNCS, vol. 5432, pp. 296–311. Springer, Heidelberg (2009)
6. Hu, W., Tan, H., Corke, P., Shih, W.C., Jha, S.: Toward trusted wireless sensor networks. TOSN 7(1) (2010)
7. Hui, J.W., Culler, D.: The dynamic behavior of a data dissemination protocol for network programming at scale. In: SenSys (2004)
8. Kim, D.H., Gandhi, R., Narasimhan, P.: Castor: Secure code updates using symmetric cryptosystems. In: Real-Time Systems Symposium (2007)
9. Krauß, C., Stumpf, F., Eckert, C.: Detecting Node Compromise in Hybrid Wireless Sensor Networks Using Attestation Techniques. In: Stajano, F., Meadows, C., Capkun, S., Moore, T. (eds.) ESAS 2007. LNCS, vol. 4572, pp. 203–217. Springer, Heidelberg (2007)
10. Kulkarni, S.S., Wang, L.: MNP: Multihop Network Reprogramming Service for Sensor Networks. In: ICDCS (2005)
11. Lamport, L.: Password authentication with insecure communication. Communications of the ACM 24(11), 770–772 (1981)
12. Lanigan, P.E., Gandhi, R., Narasimhan, P.: Secure dissemination of code updates in sensor networks. In: SenSys (2005)
13. Lee, S., Kim, H., Chung, K.: Hash-based secure sensor network programming method without public key cryptography. In: Worksh. on World-Sensor-Web (2006)
14. Liu, A., Oh, Y.-H., Ning, P.: Secure and dos-resistant code dissemination in wireless sensor networks using seluge. In: IPSN (2008)
15. Trusted Computing Group. Trusted Platform Module (TPM) Specifications, https://www.trustedcomputinggroup.org/specs/TPM
16. University of California Berkeley: TinyOS, http://www.tinyos.net/

Build and Test Your Own Network Configuration

Saeed Al-Haj, Padmalochan Bera, and Ehab Al-Shaer

University of North Carolina Charlotte, Charlotte NC 28223, USA
{salhaj,bpadmalo,ealshaer}@uncc.edu

Abstract. Access control policies play a critical role in the security of enterprise networks deployed with variety of policy-based devices (e.g., routers, firewalls, and IPSec). Usually, the security policies are configured in the network devices in a distributed fashion through sets of access control lists (ACL). However, the increasing complexity of access control configurations due to larger networks and longer policies makes configuration errors inevitable. Incorrect policy configuration makes the network vulnerable to different attacks and security breaches. In this paper, we present an imperative framework, namely, *ConfigLEGO*, that provides an open programming platform for building the network security configuration globally and analyzing it systematically. The *ConfigLEGO* engine uses Binary Decision Diagram (BDD) to build a Boolean model that represents the global system behaviors including all possible interaction between various components in extensible and scalable manner. Our tool also provides a C/C++ API as a software wrapper on top of the BDD engine to allow users in defining topology, configurations, and reachability, and then analyzing in various abstraction levels, without requiring knowledge of BDD representation or operations.

Keywords: Imperative analysis, BDDs, Formal methods, Network configuration.

1 Introduction

The extensive use of various network services and applications (e.g., telnet, ssh, http, etc.) for accessing network resources forces enterprise networks to deploy policy based security configurations. However, most of the enterprise networks face security threats due to incorrect policy configurations. Recent studies reveal that more than 62% of network failures today are due to security misconfiguration. These misconfigurations may cause major network failures such as reachability problems, security violations, and introducing vulnerabilities. An enterprise LAN consists of a set of network *domains* connected through various interface routers. The security policies of such networks are configured in the security devices (like, routers, firewalls, IPSec, etc.) through set of access control lists (ACLs) in a distributed manner. The global network configuration may contain several types of conflicts (redundancy, shadowing, spuriousness, etc.) in different levels (intra-policy, inter-policy) [1] which may violate the end-to-end

M. Rajarajan et al. (Eds.): SecureComm 2011, LNICST 96, pp. 522–532, 2012.
© Institute for Computer Sciences, Social Informatics and Telecommunications Engineering 2012

security of the network. Moreover, there may exist several reachability problems depending on flow-, domain-, and network-level constraints. Thus, the major challenge to the network administrators/developers is to comprehensively build and analyze the security configurations in a flexible and efficient manner.

In this paper, we present an imperative framework, namely, *ConfigLEGO* that allows users to comprehensively specify, implement, and diagnose network configurations based on user requirements. *ConfigLEGO* internally uses an efficient binary decision diagram (BDD) structure to compactly represent the network configuration and further uses the configuration BDDs for analysis. On the other hand, *ConfigLEGO* provides a C/C++ programming interface that acts as a software wrapper on top of the BDD engine to selectively compose different BDDs for systematic evaluation. *ConfigLEGO* is named after the famous Lego toy. In a Lego toy, one can build a complex design from a set of basic components. *ConfigLEGO* provides all basic components to design a network, and allows the user to build and test his own network by putting all components together and by writing the queries he needs to check the validity of configuration properties. *ConfigLEGO* hides BDDs complexity and allows users to analyze the network without requiring previous knowledge about BDD representation or operations.

Compared to other declarative modeling languages/systems, *ConfigLEGO* is the first BDD-based engine that provides a generic C/C++ programming interface for configuration modeling, abstraction, and analysis in usable and scalable manner. Compared to other network management tools like COOLAID [2], *ConfigLEGO* provides libraries for comprehensively creating and analyzing network configurations based on user requirements.

In terms of diagnosability, *ConfigLEGO* can evaluate various configuration problems such as follows:

- Network reachability, intra- and inter-firewall misconfigurations, flow-level, path-level and domain-level network traffic reachability.
- Inferring configuration problems using a sequence of evaluation results.
- Analyzing network configuration and testing whether the current configuration meets the provided risk requirements.

The remaining sections of the paper are organized as follows: Section 2 describes the architecture of *ConfigLEGO*; Section 3 introduces different examples verified using *ConfigLEGO*. This section also describes the formalization of the examples in Boolean logic using efficient BDD representation; Section 4 discusses the evaluation and experimental results; Section 5 is the related work; Finally, conclusion and future work have been presented in Section 6.

2   Architecture of ConfigLEGO

The presented *ConfigLEGO* system (refer Figure 1) consists of two major modules: Internal Module and User Program Module. The Internal Module is the core of the system which has two components; *ConfigLEGO* Engine and the *ConfigLEGO* API. *ConfigLEGO* Engine is responsible for modeling the device

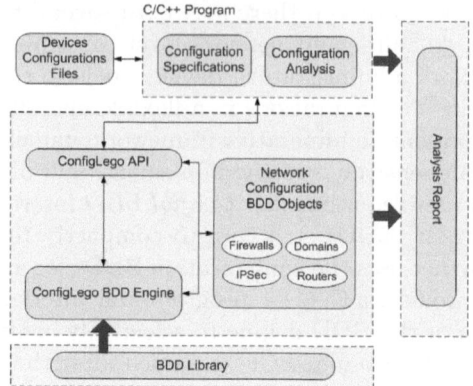

Fig. 1. *ConfigLEGO* System Architecture

configuration (behavior of each device such as, domains, routers, firewalls etc.), topology, and the network using efficient BDD representation. The engine builds a BDD for each device and each path in the network. It can also provide a BDD for the entire network depending on user requirement. A complete set of functions for managing internal module is defined in *ConfigLEGO* API. It provides an interface to the User Program Module to use *ConfigLEGO* system.

The user only needs a basic knowledge of the available functions in the API to write his/her program for analyzing/diagnosing a network.

2.1   ConfigLEGO Internal Module

ConfigLEGO parses the device configuration files and builds a BDD structure for each device. Then, it allows to define the links between the device BDDs and different access paths depending on the network topology specification. This network configuration can be formalized as a network access model.

Definition 1 [Network Access Model]: A network access model is defined as a 3-tuple $NG = \langle N, I, F \rangle$, where,

- N is a finite set of network devices. Network devices (N) can be of three types: NR- network routers; NF- firewalls and NE- end point devices (hosts/domains) represented as an IP address block. Each device is associated to several connecting interfaces which are identified by an IP address.
- $I \subseteq N \times N$ is a finite set of network links between devices, such that for every physical link between N_1 and N_2 there is a pair of lines or channels: $I_{12} = \langle N_1, N_2 \rangle$ and $I_{21} = \langle N_2, N_1 \rangle$.
- F is a finite set of access control lists (ACL) associated to different devices.

Modeling Network Configuration. Each device configuration in the network has to be modeled in BDD for modeling the network configuration. More details about modeling devices configuration can be found in [3]. After modeling devices configuration, we model the complete network considering the topology and the combined effect of the routing and firewall rules. *ConfigLEGO* allows users to specify the topology using C/C++ programming constructs. It is represented as a formal network access model, $NG\langle N, I, F\rangle$ as described in the last section. Then, we formalize the combined effect of firewall rules along different access routes between source and destination. In this process, the notion of *Access Routes* and *Access Route Policy* have been introduced.

Definition 2 [Access Route]: An *Access Route* $AR_i^{(S,D)}$ is defined as a sequence of devices $(N_1, N_2, ..., N_k)$ from source S to destination D in the network where, each $\langle N_i, N_{i+1}\rangle \in I$ and D is reachable from S through $S, N_1, N_2, ..., D$. This corresponds to the physical topology of the network.

Definition 3 [Access Route Policy]: An *Access Route Policy* $(ARP^{(S,D)})$ between a source S and destination D is a combined model of the distributed policy rules along all possible access routes $(AR_1^{(S,D)}, ..., AR_n^{(S,D)})$ between a source S and a destination D. It is represented as a Boolean function:

$$ARP^{(S,D)} = (P_{AR_1^{(S,D)}} \vee P_{AR_2^{(S,D)}} \vee \ldots \vee P_{AR_n^{(S,D)}})$$

such that $P_{AR_i^{(S,D)}} = \bigwedge_{N \in AR_i} P_a^N$. This represents the logical access path.

Here, $P_{AR_i^{(S,D)}}$ (along the route AR_i) is represented as the conjunction of policies for all devices in that route. Then, we represent the complete access route policy $ARP^{(S,D)}$ between a source S and a destination D as disjunction of all $P_{AR_i^{(S,D)}}$ for access route AR_i. We describe the modeling of logical access paths between a specified pair of source and destination. However, depending on user requirement, *ConfigLEGO* is also capable of generating the combined network model considering all possible source and destination pairs in the network. For basic reachability analysis, the presented *ConfigLEGO* framework checks the conjunction of the BDDs along the access route as specified. On the other hand, for imperative analysis, it uses the sequence of reachability results. Section 3 shows the verification of such analysis with different examples.

　　ConfigLEGO Engine in Figure 1 utilizes the compact canonical format that BDDs provide to encode the device configuration file into a BDD representation. This will be used later by the *ConfigLEGO* API for providing a convenient interface to the user writing his own program. A partial set of the functions provided by *ConfigLEGO* API are shown in Table 1. The functions support three phases of network's design: (1) Components Installation, (2) Components Connection, and (3) Testing and Validation.

2.2   User Program Module

In this module, the user can provide network specifications in C/C++ programming language. The *ConfigLEGO* API supports user's program module by providing a set of functions that will be used by a user to construct a network. For

Table 1. ConfigLEGO API Functions

Definitions and Function Names	Description
Network N	To create a new network N
Firewall F("policy.txt")	creates a firewall that has policy defined in *policy.txt* text file
Router R("rtable.txt")	creates a router that has routing table defined in *rtable.txt* text file
IPSec G("policy.txt")	creates an IPSec device that has policy defined in *policy.txt* text file
Domain D("domain.txt")	creates a domain D that has an address and a network mask defined in *domain.txt* test file
Host H("host.txt")	creates a host H that has an address defined in *host.txt* test file
Rule r	creates a BDD representation for a firewall rule
link(C1, interface1, C2, interface2)	links components C1 and C2 through interface1 and interface2 respectively
buildDeviceBDD()	builds a BDD for each device in the network
buildGlobalBDD()	builds a BDD for the network
checkFlow(S, source-port, D, dest-port)	checks flows between source and destination using specified ports and returns a BDD that represents the computed flows
printFlows(B, n)	print the first n flows that satisfy the BDD B
getPathObjects(src, dst, vec, TYPE)	returns a vector *vec* of objects of type *TYPE* along the path between source *src* and destination *dst*, TYPE can be FIREWALL, ROUTER, IPSEC, or IDS
policy()	returns the BDD representation for a firewall/router

a firewall, it contains the policy rules and two interfaces while it contains a routing table and up to 16 interfaces for a router. The configuration file is assigned logically to the proper device in the initialization statement in the program. To give a clear explanation how *ConfigLEGO* system works, we provide several code segments throughout the paper, where each segment solves a specific problem.

Any user program starts with initializing a network N stated as follows:

```
Network N;
```

Given a configuration file for each device, it can be added to the network N. A firewall $F1$ with configuration file *"f1.txt"* can be defined firewall as follows:

```
Firewall F1("f1.txt");
```

Other devices (routers, IPSec, etc.) can be added to the network similarly. After adding all components in the network N, the next step is to connect the components by introducing links between them. The connections between components are installed. *Link(...)* function is used to link two components as follows:

```
N.link(D1, ANY_IFACE, F1, 1);
```

Here, domain *D1* (any interface) is linked to firewall *F1* (interface 1).

After linking all components in network *N*, a BDD for the network and each device are generated by invoking the statements:

```
N.buildDeviceBDD(); N.buildGlobalBDD();
```

3 Verification Examples

In this section, we provide examples for showing the usability of *ConfigLEGO*. The examples are categorized as: Basic Analysis and Imperative Analysis.

3.1 Basic Analysis

ConfigLEGO can perform various security analysis, such as, reachability, intra-policy conflicts, and inter-policy conflicts. Due to the space limitation, we will show an example on reachability verification.

A traffic *C* is reachable to a distention node/domain *D* from a source node/domain *S* along an access route $\langle S, R_i, F_k, D \rangle$, iff the traffic is allowed by the routing table rule T_i^j [BDD for router R_i and port j] and the firewall policy F_k along that route. It can be formalized as follows:

$$reachable(C, S, D) : (C \Rightarrow \bigwedge_{(i,j)\in P} T_i^j) \wedge (C \Rightarrow \bigwedge_{(i,k)\in P} F_k).$$

ConfigLEGO checks the reachability by analyzing the BDDs for routers and firewalls along an access route between specified source and destination domain. This can be checked by the following statement:

```
T = N.checkFlow(src, src-port, dst, dst-port);
```

CheckFlow(...) returns a BDD, *T*, that represents the computed flows between a source *src* and a destination *dst* considering source and destination ports as provided in the function call. If the resultant BDD *T* is *bddfalse*, then there is no flow between source and destination. Flow computations are performed based on the *AccessRoute* and *AccessRoutePolicy* defined in section 2.1. *ConfigLEGO* can analyze the reachability between all source hosts and a single destinations or between all sources and all destinations by calling checkFlow(...) function inside a loop. The following example checks the reachability between all source hosts and a single destination D1:

```
// hSize is the number of hosts
int hSize = allHosts.size();BDD T, TC=TRUE;
for(i = 0; i < hSize; i++ ){
  T = N.checkFlow(*allHosts[i], ANY, D1, ANY);
  TC = TC | T;
  if( T != bddfalse )
    cout<<"Reachable from Host "<<i; }
```

Here, two BDDs, T and TC, are computed. T represents all flows from a host to a destination D1, and TC is the BDD for the complete representation from all hosts to the destination D1. An example of further analysis is to compare two hosts in term of the incoming traffic. Here, the BDD TC is the disjunction of all BDDs T, the operator | is overloaded to perform BDD "OR" operation.

3.2   Imperative Configurations Analysis

The *ConfigLEGO* system is capable of analyzing different imperative cases using sequence of evaluation steps which is one of the unique features of the system. The use of *loops* and *conditional statements* allows the users to comprehensively analyze these imperative queries.

Path Conflict Analysis for Firewalls. First, we introduce the formalization of *shadow-free* and *spurious-free* relations based on inter-policy firewall conflicts.

Lemma 1: Shadow-free and spurious-free are *transitive relations*. Assume S_a^i, S_a^j and S_a^k are upstream to downstream firewall policies in a path P, the following is always true:

$$[(\neg S_a^i \wedge S_a^j) = false] \bigwedge [(\neg S_a^j \wedge S_a^k) = false] \Rightarrow [(\neg S_a^i \wedge S_a^k) = false]$$

We formalize *Path Conflicts* using *path-shadowing* and *path-spuriousness*.

Definition 4 [Path Conflict]: Assuming S_a^i to S_a^n are the firewall policies from upstream to downstream in the path from x to y, a *path conflict(x,y)* between any two firewalls is represented as follows:
   Path Shadowing(x,y):

$$\bigvee_{i=1..(n-1) \ and \ i \in path(x,y)} (\neg S_a^i \wedge S_a^{i+1}) \neq false$$

   Path Spuriousness:

$$\bigvee_{i=1..(n-1) \ and \ i \in path(x,y)} (S_a^i \wedge \neg S_a^{i+1}) \neq false$$

ConfigLEGO checks this type of path conflicts as a sequence of steps (under a *loop*), where each step checks the conflicts between a pair of BDDs. The following code finds path shadowing between a source and a destination.

```
N.getPathObjects(src, dst, fwVec, FIREWALL);
for(i = 0 ; i < fwVec.size()-1 ; i++)
  if(!fwVec[i].policy() & fwVec[i+1].policy()){
    cout<<"Path Shadowing"; break; }
```

Here, getPathObjects(...) function returns a vector, *fwVec*, of all firewall objects between a source *src* and a destination *dst*. A pair of consecutive firewalls is checked for shadowing. The conflict is reported once found, the loop is stopped.

Reachability Requirement Verification. In large networks, some subnets are restricted to communicate with others, which is known as least privilege principle. For example, in a university network, student subnet is not allowed to use resources allocated for staff subnet. Network administrator can enforce least privilege by defining a reachability requirement matrix. Requirement matrix tells for each subnet which subnets are allowed to reach which signifies the soundness of the system. The soundness of a configuration can be defined as:

Definition 5 [Soundness]: a network configuration $\mathcal{C}$ is *sound* if, for all domains x and y, all possible paths from x to y are subset of the requirement matrix REQ. Formally, soundness can be defined as follows:

$$\forall x \forall y (reachable(x, y) \wedge src(x) \wedge dest(y)) \rightarrow REQ[x][y] = true$$

The following example verifies connection requirements between domains:

```
int domSize = allDomains.size();
int Req[domSize][domSize]; BDD T;
for( int i = 0; i < domSize; i++ )
 for( int j = 0; j < domSize; j++ )
  if( i != j ){
   T=N.checkFlow(*allDomains[i], ANY, *allDomains[j], ANY);
   if(   (T != bddfalse && Req[i][j] == 0) ||
          (T == bddfalse && Req[i][j] == 1)   )
     cout<<"Reachability Violation";  }
```

Here, *Req* is the requirement matrix. If Req[i][j] is *ZERO*, then subnets i and j are not allowed to communicate.

4 Performance Evaluation

The various modules of *ConfigLEGO* framework have been implemented in C/C++ programming language using BuDDy2.2 package [4] and tested on a machine with a 1.8 GHz core 2 CPU and 2GB memory. Parsers have been developed for device configuration files. For evaluating imperative examples, *ConfigLEGO* analyzes a combination of device's BDDs (using loop and conditional statements) and infer about the configuration issues under consideration.

ConfigLEGO is evaluated with respect to time and space requirements. The framework has been tested under 100 different network configurations in more than 20 different test networks with up to 5000 nodes and 50 thousands of policy rules under each configuration. Table 2 shows the experimental results with different test cases. We have thoroughly analyzed the impact of network size and policy rules on network building time and configuration diagnosis time.

Impact of Network Size and Policy Rules on Space Requirement and Network Building Time: The space requirement basically covers the total BDD size for the network. *ConfigLEGO* framework creates a BDD for each

Table 2. Evaluation Results

Network Size	Total No. of Rules	BDD Size (Mb)	Network Building Time (sec)	Configuration Analysis and Diagnosis Time (sec)		
				Reachability	Flow analysis	Distributed Path Conflict
500	5000	1.6	0.665	0.235	0.65	0.37
1000	8500	3.2	1.325	0.43	1.32	1.33
1500	15000	4.6	1.95	0.65	1.89	3.2
2000	22500	6.3	2.67	0.885	2.5	5.32
3000	32500	9.65	3.92	1.38	3.78	11.27
4000	40125	12.7	5.12	1.82	5.25	21.5
5000	48755	15.8	6.34	2.33	6.52	32.12

network device by parsing the associated policy rule file. Thus, BDD size is linearly dependent on both network and policy size. Table 2 shows that space requirement lies within 15 MB for 5000 nodes and total of 50000 policy rules which is reasonably good for large networks.

Network model building time is almost linearly dependent on both network and policy rule size. It can be observed that this time lies within 7 seconds for 5000 nodes with 50000 policy rules.

Impact of Network Size and Policy Rules on Configuration Diagnosis Time: *ConfigLEGO* framework evaluates different configuration problems using Boolean satisfiability analysis of the network and device BDDs. The impact of network size on the evaluation time varies based on the problem complexity.

Reachability Analysis: ConfigLEGO checks the conjunction of all BDDs along a specified access. Thus, the reachability analysis time is linearly dependent on the number of nodes along that access path.

Flow Level Reachability: ConfigLEGO checks flow level reachability under a specific traffic flow C_k by evaluating BDDs for all routers (in a *loop*) and the destination firewall along the specified path P. For path level unreachability, *ConfigLEGO* analyzes all possible flows in a path P from node i to node j. Thus, the complexity of flow level reachability problem can be represented as $O(T_{pathreachability} * k)$, where, $T_{pathreachability}$ indicates the flow level reachability analysis time (for a specific flow) and k indicates the total flows. Table 2 shows the average flow level analysis time which lies within 6.5 seconds for 5000 nodes and 50000 policy rules.

The space and time requirement shows that the framework is scalable for large scale networks. The uniqueness of *ConfigLEGO* framework lies in comprehensive use of C/C++ programming language features and use of efficient BDD representation for systematically diagnosing different configuration problems.

5   Related Work

Researchers proposed different high level security policy languages and frameworks for automated management and modeling network configurations. *FLIP* [5], is a high level conflict-free firewall policy language for enforcing access control based security and ensuring seamless configuration management. In *FLIP*, security policies are defined as high level service oriented goals, which can be translated automatically into access control rules. However, it limits in comprehensively specifying and analyzing the global network configuration with imperative queries. Chen et al. present a framework called COOLAID [2] for comprehensive management of network configurations by embedding knowledge bases from different network users. COOLAID uses a declarative framework for integrating explicit knowledge bases derived from low level network configurations and then reason about misconfigurations based on high level intents. However, this work does not provide the libraries for performing fine-grained security analysis and applications on top of the network configurations. This is an important requirement for providing diagnosability and provability of network configurations. Secondly, the scalability of network configuration management and automation have not been analyzed in these tools. Al-shaer et al. proposed a BDD based framework, ConfigChecker [3], for end-to-end verification of network reachability. Narain et al. [6] proposed a SAT-based approach for security configuration analysis. However, none of the earlier approaches provide an open interface for security configuration analysis.

The literature survey reveals the need of a framework that allows users to build the network configuration comprehensively as well as systematically analyze various configuration problems with imperative queries. Towards this goal, we develop the *ConfigLEGO* system exploiting the advantages of C/C++ programming language features and efficient BDD structure. The *expressiveness*, *composability*, and *reusability* features of *ConfigLEGO* allows user to comprehensively specify the network configuration and diagnosis requirements.

6   Conclusion and Future Work

In large scale networks, it is hard to find and debug misconfigurations and analyze security requirements manually. Thus, there is a need of an automated tool for finding and reasoning such misconfigurations in an abstract and comprehensive way. In this paper, we presented an imperative framework for comprehensively analyzing and diagnosing the network configurations. The framework is implemented in a tool called *ConfigLEGO*. It allows users to write C/C++ program that captures network specifications and implement the required analysis. This makes *ConfigLEGO* a convenient tool to use. For the purpose of analysis and diagnosis, *ConfigLEGO* uses an efficient BDD engine, this engine hides BDDs complexity and does not require previous knowledge about BDDs representation and operations. The efficiency of the framework has been evaluated rigorously with different network and policy rule sizes. In future, the *ConfigLEGO* framework can be extended for finer-grained security analysis like, role based access control and risk based policy configuration in enterprise networks.

References

1. Al-Shaer, E.S., Hamed, H.H.: Discovery of Policy Anomalies in Distributed Fire-walls. In: Proceedings of IEEE INFOCOM 2004, Hong Kong, China, pp. 2605–2626 (March 2004)
2. Chen, X., Mao, Y., Mao, Z.M., Van der Merwe, J.: Declarative Configuration Management for Complex and Dynamic Networks. In: Proceedings of ACM CoNEXT (2010)
3. Al-Shaer, E., Marrero, W., El-Atway, A., AlBadani, K.: Network Configuration in a Box: Towards End-to-End Verification of Network Reachability and Security. In: Proceedings of ICNP 2009, Princeton, NY, USA, pp. 123–132 (2009)
4. Lind-Nielsen, J.: The BuDDy OBDD package,
   `http://sourceforge.net/projects/buddy/`
5. Zhang, B., Al-Shaer, E.S., Jagadeesan, R., Riely, J., Pitcher, C.: Specifications of A High-level Conflict-Free Firewall Policy Language for Multi-domain Networks. In: Proceedings of ACM SACMAT 2007, France, pp. 185–194 (June 2007)
6. Narain, S., Levin, G., Malik, S., Kaul, V.: Declarative Infrastructure Configuration Synthesis and Debugging. Journal of Network and Systems Management 16, 235–258 (2008)

PP2db: A Privacy-Preserving, P2P-Based Scalable Storage System for Mobile Networks

Manuel Crotti, Diego Ferri, Francesco Gringoli,
Manuel Peli, and Luca Salgarelli⋆

University of Brescia - Italy
{firstname.lastname}@ing.unibs.it

Abstract. Reputation-based systems that handle millions of users face the problem of simultaneously supporting privacy and trust in an efficient way. In order to scale, often existing systems either sacrifice privacy to preserve trust, or vice versa. The introduction of advanced cryptographic techniques such as Group Signatures might offer a solution, but their applicability to large, distributed systems such as P2P-based ones has yet to be proved. In this paper we introduce PP2db, a privacy-preserving, scalable and distributed storage system targeted at mobile networks, specifically designed to support the anonymous but trusted exchange of Quality of Experience (QoE) information. In such case-study, QoE data is exchanged among users so as to make informed decisions on which network to select at any given time. We demonstrate that by enriching a P2P database with Group Signatures it is possible to create distributed storage mechanisms that guarantee privacy-preserving features, while offering strong trust at the group level. Furthermore, we demonstrate that the resulting architecture can scale in a realistic mobile network scenario to handle millions of users.

Keywords: Trust, anonymity, secure P2P, databases, mobile networks.

1 Introduction

Reputation-based systems have been recently proposed to drive the deployment of next-generation mobile communication services, where users with multi-interface terminals dynamically select the best available network service based on the evaluation of historical Quality of Experience (QoE) data, saved by the community [1]. QoE is an indication of how well the system meets the end user's needs, providing a measure of the end-to-end performance at the service level from the end user's perspective [2].

Two major building blocks are at the base of such vision: a storage system for historical QoE data that can scale to millions of users, typical of modern wide-area mobile networks; and a mechanism that while protecting the user's privacy when posting relevant QoE data to the community, guarantees that only people belonging to the community itself can indeed provide such data. The last issue

---

⋆ This work was funded in part by the E.U. FP7 project "PERIMETER".

M. Rajarajan et al. (Eds.): SecureComm 2011, LNICST 96, pp. 533–542, 2012.
© Institute for Computer Sciences, Social Informatics and Telecommunications Engineering 2012

is almost an oxymoron, expressing the need for two colliding requirements: on one hand, protecting the user's privacy, possibly through anonymization, while on the other hand ensuring the community that the QoE data provided by each user can be trusted, therefore requiring some form of identification.

In this paper we present the design and evaluation of PP2db – Privacy-Preserving, Peer-to-Peer (PP^2) distributed Data Base: a mobile, distributed storage system for QoE data with privacy preservation features that aims at solving the issues described above. Besides defining the general architecture, we analyze its scalability, showing how it can scale to millions of users, making it applicable to current and future mobile networks.

While we designed PP2db with QoE-based mobile networks in mind, its flexible, scalable, P2P-based architecture makes it amenable to different applications, wherever large communities share data that needs to be trusted, while preserving the privacy of the users. Therefore PP2db can easily find applications in fields such as social networking, community networks, Internet of Things, and any large scale feedback-based application. We make our software freely available for download under an Open Source license at [3].

The rest of this paper is organized as follows. Section 2 describes the high-level requirements and goals pursued by our architecture. Section 3 introduces the two main building blocks which we used to design and implement PP2db. Section 4 describes the PP2db architecture internals, while we analyze its scalability in Section 5. Finally, Section 6 concludes the paper.

2   Rationale, Goals and Design Choices

The mobile telecommunication market is very diverse in its offerings to final users. Consumers can choose among large sets of service providers, technological means (WiFi, UMTS in its many incarnations, second generation technologies, etc.), subscription plans and add-on services. The recent introduction of community networks makes the selection of the "right" service even more complex, especially in large cities.

Several research projects have proposed in the recent past approaches to solve this issue by letting end users make informed decisions through their multi-interface devices so as to be always best connected: one example can be found in [4] or, more recently, in [1]. Most of these technologies require users to share with other users information about their Quality of Experience, i.e., indication of how well each service met their specific needs. Through the analysis of QoE data made available by other users, terminals should then be able to automate their service-selection process, always obtaining the service that better suits their needs.

Such an infrastructure to store and share QoE data must satisfy several high-level requirements. The storage system should be **scalable** enough to handle the growing numbers of mobile users, where a regional service must sustain tens of millions of users. Feedback collected from users should be **protected from pollution**: for example, a malicious network operator should not be able to alter in their favor QoE data in order to bias the users' choices. Finally, the **privacy of end users should be preserved**, both against operators and other users. In fact, posting QoE data together with identity-related information could open the door to retaliation from network operators, in case the QoE feedback is negative with respect to the services they offer. It could also expose private details: for example, stating that "the free WiFi service under the Eiffel tower in Paris is very good on Fridays" would expose one's location at a specific time.

The first and second requirements call for a distributed, scalable storage architecture. The architecture we propose is based on a Peer-to-Peer storage system.

The second and third requirements are in conflict with each other: while some form of identification is necessary to satisfy the second requirement, anonymization is paramount to achieve the third one. In order to strike a balance between the two, PP2db relies on the use of a somewhat recent set of cryptographic authentication techniques, called Group Signatures.

In the following Section we briefly describe the basics of these two fundamental building blocks we used in designing PP2db.

3   Background

3.1   XPeer

XPeer [5] is a P2P distributed database based on a hybrid P2P architecture. In XPeer data is stored and managed in XML format, and can be retrieved using XQuery [6]. The system automatically redistributes the workload over its overlay network by means of self-organizing algorithms, therefore providing for scalability.

The overlay network of the XPeer system is a tree structure. The leaf nodes are called *peers* and the inner nodes are called *superpeers*. Each peer stores a portion of the distributed database in XML format and each superpeer stores indexes for data retrieving. Figure 1 (left) depicts a two-levels overlay network. Peers, after registering with a superpeer, retrieve data following two steps: query compilation and query execution.

The **query compilation** phase involves a peer $P1$ that submits a query to superpeer $SP1$, which in turn returns to $P1$ the list of peers that possess the

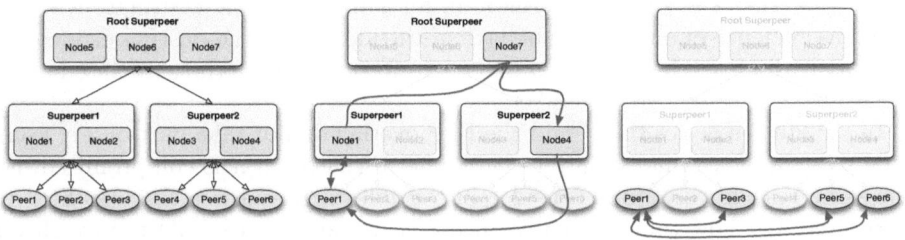

Fig. 1. XPeer Overlay Network (left), query compilation (center), query execution (right)

requested data. At this point $P1$ starts **executing the query**, which is split into sub-queries that are sent to the corresponding peers Pi. Once the results arrive, $P1$ joins them generating the requested response.

Each peer stores and maintains its own data: whenever a change is committed to the local XML, the peer sends a TreeGuide update message to the superpeer it is connected to, so that the relevant indexing information can be updated in the entire XPeer overlay.

3.2   Group Signatures

A *group signature scheme* (GS) is a relatively new digital signature scheme with enhanced privacy features [7]. Only *group members* can sign messages anonymously on behalf of the group, each one using a private and non disclosable *member secret key* ($\mathcal{MSK}$). On the contrary, everyone having access to the *group public key* ($\mathcal{GPK}$) can verify the validity of the produced *group signatures*. A trusted *group manager* holds the *group secret key* ($\mathcal{GSK}$), and is responsible for setting up the group, adding new members, revoking their membership, etc.

The first *Provably–Secure* and *Dynamic* GS scheme was introduced by Ateniese et al. [8]. From here on we will simply refer to it as ACJT. After ACJT, *Membership Revocation* received a good deal of attention. One of the most popular techniques that offer this capability has been consolidated by Camenisch and Groth [9] and we will refer to it as CG in the following.

4   The PP2db Architecture

PP2db realizes a highly scalable, distributed storage architecture with privacy-preserving capabilities, amenable by design to support the sharing of QoE-information as described in Section 2.

A schematic representation of PP2db is given in Figure 2 (left). The P2P network at the center of the picture is accessed by users in a given group that either want to 1) anonymously upload new group data or 2) collect existing records and verify that they have been inserted by authorized users belonging to the same group. To this end the information in the P2P network is made of entangled pairs of (record, signature): thanks to this approach anyone can verify and trust a record; furthermore if, for some reason, a legitimate record is found as evidence of a user's misbehaving, the identity of the posting user can be eventually disclosed by the group manager after "opening" the associated group signature.

In PP2db the nodes that build the P2P overlay do not take part of any users' group, i.e., a SP can not add data to the network even if it is compromised. For the same reason we do not consider in the following analysis the way SPs are connected and how they mutually authenticate, and we exclude the overheads due to this kind of traffic from our investigation.

A peer connects to PP2db via a *power-up signaling* procedure. Once connected, the it can carry out the following operations, as shown in Figure 2 (left):

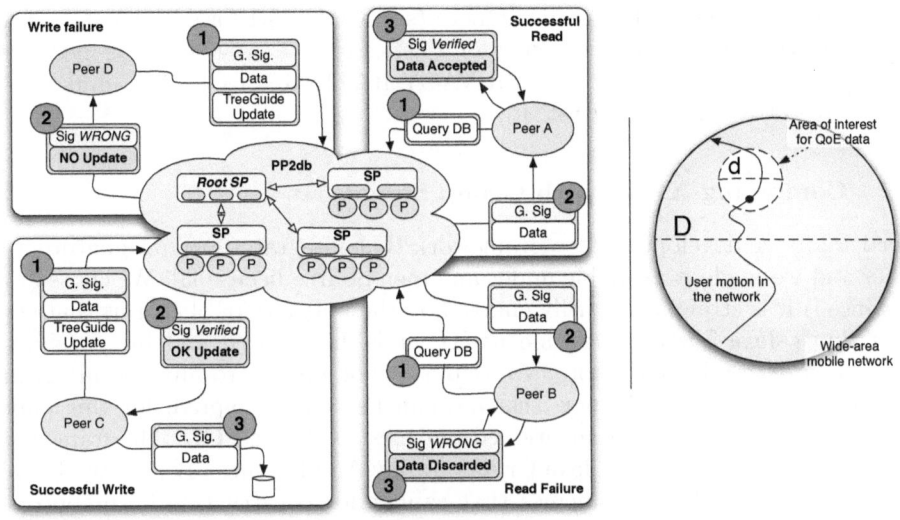

Fig. 2. Left: Schematic model of the PP2db architecture. – **Right**: QoE-enabled mobile network model adopted for PP2db.

READ. Peer A (upper right) queries the PP2db network for a given record/group, executing a *PP2db MetaSearch* operation and receiving back *PP2db Meta-SearchAnswer messages*. After following the procedure outlined in Section 3.1, the network returns (record, signature) pairs within *PP2db QueryResult messages*. The Peer will keep the data only if the group signature is valid, discarding it otherwise (lower right).

WRITE. Peer C (lower left) signs a message with its private group key and sends the pair (record, signature), together with the group name and the TreeGuide update, to a SP through the *PP2db MetaUpdate* procedure. Upon successful verification of the group signature, the SP makes the data available to the PP2db network, otherwise the TreeGuide update is discarded (upper left).

4.1   XPeer-Based Storage Module

The storage module of PP2db is based on XPeer for the collection and sharing of QoE data. Feedback coming from participating user terminals is converted in XML and stored in the local PP2db database of the same terminals. Each of the QoE fields that will be shared with community users is paired with its corresponding group signature that is stored in a properly reserved field of the XML schema. After each change of the local database, a TreeGuide update message is spread through the XPeer network in order to update the tree-guide of superpeers [5].

Data can be retrieved through XQuery (see Section 3.1 for details) and a user can query the XPeer network asking for a list of service providers that meets her quality standards (e.g., "PRIVACY_RATING=SECURE and not COST_RATING=EXPENSIVE").

4.2 Combining XPeer with Group Signatures

For PP2db we developed a new framework that integrates group signature services and we made it available under an Open Source license [3]. We chose Java because i) it is straightforwardly enabled on the majority of platforms that support Sun's Java Virtual Machine ii) XPeer is Java based and iii) no similar framework was released before. We opted to not bind it to any specific group signature scheme, so that new schemes can be easily adapted: for this paper we integrated the two aforementioned schemes ACJT and CG. The framework was designed to extend the Java Cryptography Architecture (JCA) [10]. To this end we reviewed the GS schemes that cannot for construction be mapped to the services already offered by the JCA and we implemented two different protocols: one for "signature" operations (**sign**, **verify**, **open**); another for group "maintenance" operations (**setup**, **join**, **revoke**).

We then reviewed the codebase of XPeer and we changed the way data is read and written: for each write operation a signature is added by the client that is pushing the data; the same signature will be verified against the group certificate for each following read operation.

5 Performance of PP2db: Scalability

The scalability of PP2db is affected by two main factors: the amount of computational resources required by each terminal that participates in the system, and the amount of network traffic generated by the architecture while in use. We start by describing the reference scenario for our evaluation, which we derived from the QoE-enabled mobile network architecture defined in [1].

5.1 Application of PP2db to a Mobile Network Scenario: A QoE-Enabled Mobile Network

Our scenario models a QoE-enabled wide area mobile network, albeit with some simplifications. We assume that users are uniformly distributed in a circle of diameter D, as shown in Figure 2 (right). While in this circle, users are randomly moving of uniform motion.

Every time a terminal powers up, its PP2db instance connects to a superpeer and gets access to the distributed storage system. Users are regularly asked to rate their mobile service experience. Such ratings are injected into PP2db in the form of Quality of Experience (QoE) reports, which represent a moving average of the ratings expressed by the user for a given service at a given location over time.

At the same time, terminals collect through PP2db both past and present QoE reports relevant for their location and produced by other users in the same geographic area. We define this "area of interest" as a circle of radius d and the user's location as the centre of this smaller circle. With this information, users are able to decide which connection is best suited to their needs, for example, whether to prefer lower price or higher reliability.

We imagine for our analysis a very simple PP2db scenario, where the hierarchical tree is made of one *Root* superpeer on top of a single layer of superpeers. All peers are then clustered around them. In accordance with our model, both peers and superpeers are uniformely distributed in the network.

Table 1. Network and system parameters used in our PP2db mobile network scenario

Symbol	Description	Value
P, SP, R	Peer, superpeer, Root	
K	# of SP whose father is R	100
D	Network diameter	1000 (Km)
$d(\leq D)$	Diameter of network portion of interest to current user for QoE purposes	1 (Km)
N	Total number of users in the mobile network	120 (Million)
P_a	Fraction of active users (powered-on terminals)	50%
n	Active users in area of interest d	60
T	Interval between two subsequent QoE writes	60 (s)
h	Fraction of users in area of interest that have relevant QoE data to share	5%, 20%, 50%

In Table 1 we show the symbols of the parameters we adopted for our model, and the values we assigned to them.

Several of the values we assigned to the parameters were derived using the statistical data for modern 3G networks taken from [11]. We consider in our model a relatively large country ($D = 1000km$) with four operators, each of them with 30 million subscribed users (total $N = 120M$). At any given time, half of the users are active. As we have already noted, the users are uniformly distributed in the network circle, and move of randomly uniform motion at a speed uniformly distributed between 0 and $30km/h$ ($0 - 8.3m/s$). A couple of simple formulas let us derive the number of active users in each "area of interest" at any given time ($n = 30$), and the number of powerups/downs in such area ($694 \cdot (d/D)^2$).

We conservatively assume that each user writes to the PP2db storage system updated QoE data every $T = 60sec$, regardless of where they are. Each user will request QoE data any time it crosses a new area of interest. In our experiments, we consider three cases regarding the fraction of users in each area of interest that can respond with relevant QoE data to a query. We identify such parameter with h, and consider for it values of 5, 20 and 50%.

Table 2. PP2db message size and overheads for each basic operation

Symbol Description		Value
M_1	PP2db power-up/down signalling message size	1.5 (kB)
M_2	PP2db MetaUpdate message size	36 (kB)
M_3	PP2db MetaSearch message size	3.7 (kB)
M_4	PP2db MetaSearchAnswer message size	2 (kB)
M_5	PP2db QueryResult message size	5 (kB)
	Power up and connect to SP	$8 \cdot M_1 + 2 \cdot M_2$
	Power down	$2 \cdot M_1 + M_2$
	TreeGuide update	$2 \cdot M_1 + 2 \cdot M_2$
	Query Compilation	$(K+1) \cdot M_3 + K \cdot M_4$
	Query Execution	$h \cdot (2 \cdot M_1 + M_5)$

Messages exchanged among PP2db-enabled nodes are either for signalling or exchanging meta-data. We classify them according to the procedures defined in Section 4. We computed their size by tracing an active PP2db network in our laboratory, and report them with symbols M_1 through M_5 in Table 2. Finally, simple formulas link the parameters and message sizes expressed above to the total traffic generated by the QoE storage system for each of the read/write operations defined in Section 4.

5.2 Computational Overheads

We have analyzed all the primitives that we implemented in the PP2db Group Signature Java framework to profile their computational costs. The space allowed for this paper does not allow us to report on our findings. In extreme summary, all operations that are executed by mobile terminals are independent on the number of users in the system, therefore **PP2db can scale indefinitely in size with respect to the computational burden imposed on each mobile terminal**. Please refer to [12] for more details.

5.3 Network Traffic Overheads

The characterization of the message overheads introduced by the various group signatures schemes that PP2db implements is fully described in [12]. Here, for space constraints, we just use the numerical values that were derived in that technical report.

For group signatures we suppose that every mobile user belongs to the same GS group, because we are interested in the study of the performance of our system in the whole network of a particular mobile operator. For this evaluation, we used signatures of 1024 bits equivalent security. In terms of revocation (GC signature scheme), we considered a base value of 5% of users revoked in a solar year, i.e., 5% of the subscribers to a given operator will switch to another one each year.

Table 3. Scalability of PP2db in three privacy-preserving configurations

Privacy protection	$h = 5\%$	$h = 20\%$ Bandwidth Mb/s (overhead)	$h = 50\%$
PP2db with no security	1.79	1.93	2.22
PP2db with ACJT GS	1.81 (1.18%)	1.98 (2.59%)	2.30 (3.60%)
PP2db with CG GS	1.82 (1.68%)	1.98 (2.59%)	2.30 (3.60%)

Applying the message overhead of [12] to the parameters and formulas described in Tables 1 and 2, we obtain the amount of bandwidth occupied by PP2db messages in any given QoE area of interest (diameter d), as shown in Table 3.

The first result worth commenting is that the overhead introduced by PP2db alone is quite sustainable by modern mobile networking infrastructures, generating only up to 2.22 Mb/s of traffic in a network area of a 1km radius when no privacy protection scheme is activated. When 5% of users have relevant QoE data, this value drops to 1.79 Mb/s.

Quite surprisingly, such an overhead remains well under control even when privacy protection is enabled and a large fraction of users ($h = 50\%$) responds to PP2db queries: in this case the use of group signatures introduces an extra 3.60% overhead, generating 2.3 Mb/s of PP2db traffic. Note that in the case of CG, the impact of handling revocation for 5% of the users is next to null, amounting to an extra 0.5% of overhead only in the case of $h = 5\%$. Note that such sustainable bandwidth figures were obtained by forcing users to rate QoE every minute ($T = 60\text{sec}$), which is really an inflated estimate.

The system presents no other visible limits since all relations in the model are linear. Therefore, **PP2db introduces manageable network overheads when used in privacy-preserving QoE storage architectures for modern mobile networks.**

6   Conclusions

In this paper we presented PP2db, a privacy-preserving, scalable storage system for mobile networks. We designed it to support an emerging requirement of modern multi-operator, multi-interface mobile network architectures, such as the one described in [1], where there is the need to store QoE data in a scalable and privacy-preserving way, while ensuring trust at the group level.

Our analysis shows that PP2db scales quite well to support such requirements in modern mobile networks with millions of users, even when its overhead are evaluated in highly dynamic ($h = 50\%$) and densely populated environments. As far as we know, PP2db is the first system to combine strong trust at the group level through Group Signatures, anonymity and distributed storage systems in a highly scalable architecture.

Although PP2db was designed with these expressed targets in mind, its features make it amenable to many other scalable storage applications where privacy must be coupled with trust, such as online social services, community services, media-sharing applications, and, in general, new distributed applications in contexts such as the Internet of Things.

We make PP2db available under an Open Source license at [3].

References

1. PERIMETER - User-centric paradigm for seamless mobility in future internet. STREP, EU FP7 Grant No. 224024, http://www.ict-perimeter.eu/
2. Architecture & Transport Working Group. Tripleplay Services Quality of Experience (QoE) Requirements. TR-126, DSL Forum (December 2006)
3. PP2db: A Privacy-Protected, P2P-based Scalable Storage System for Mobile Networks, http://www.ing.unibs.it/ntw/tools/pp2db
4. Andersson, K.: Always Best Served and Managed. Technical report, Lulea Univ. of Technology (2007)
5. Sartiani, C., Manghi, P., Ghelli, G., Conforti, G.: XPeer: A Self-Organizing XML P2P Database System. In: Lindner, W., Fischer, F., Türker, C., Tzitzikas, Y., Vakali, A.I. (eds.) EDBT 2004. LNCS, vol. 3268, pp. 456–465. Springer, Heidelberg (2004)
6. XQuery 1.0: An XML Query Language, http://www.w3.org/TR/xquery
7. Chaum, D., van Heyst, E.: Group Signatures. In: Davies, D.W. (ed.) EUROCRYPT 1991. LNCS, vol. 547, pp. 257–265. Springer, Heidelberg (1991)
8. Ateniese, G., Camenisch, J., Joye, M., Tsudik, G.: A Practical and Provably Secure Coalition-Resistant Group Signature Scheme. In: Bellare, M. (ed.) CRYPTO 2000. LNCS, vol. 1880, pp. 255–270. Springer, Heidelberg (2000)
9. Camenisch, J., Groth, J.: Group Signatures: Better Efficiency and New Theoretical Aspects. In: Blundo, C., Cimato, S. (eds.) SCN 2004. LNCS, vol. 3352, pp. 120–133. Springer, Heidelberg (2005)
10. Sun Microsystem. Java Cryptography Architecture Reference Guide for JavaTM Platform Standard Edition 6
11. Tonesi, D., Salgarelli, L., Sun, Y., La Porta, T.F.: Evaluation of signaling loads in 3GPP networks. IEEE Wireless Communications 15(1), 92–100 (2008)
12. Ferri, D.: Secure P2P Storage Systems: Techniques and Architectures. Technical report, University of Brescia, M.Sc. Thesis (2010)

NetFlow Based Network Protection

Vojtech Krmicek[1] and Jan Vykopal[2]

[1] Faculty of Informatics, Masaryk University, Brno, Czech Republic
vojtec@ics.muni.cz
[2] Institute of Computer Science, Masaryk University, Brno, Czech Republic
vykopal@ics.muni.cz

Abstract. Protecting network perimeter against adversaries both from inside and outside is a crucial task for nowadays network administrators. Inspecting all network traffic by traditional deep packet inspection is very resource intensive task in high speed networks and scalable solutions are needed. In our work, we describe network protection system based on NetFlow data. It uses hardware accelerated monitoring center (HAMOC) for inspecting network traffic, generating NetFlow data and also for active filtration/blocking of malicious traffic. Active network protection use case against brute force dictionary attacks is presented and also other network protection use cases are discussed. Main contribution of this work are: (i) scalable solution suitable for current high-speed networks (10 Gbps and more), (ii) use of hadrware accelerated HAMOC platform performing both monitoring and traffic filtering, (iii) light-weight alternative using software tools instead of hardware platform suitable for protection of networks with lower amount of traffic.

Keywords: active network defense, NetFlow, flow monitoring, HAMOC.

1 Motivation

Information and communication infrastructure is an integral part of nowadays IT world and provides a wide set of crucial services used in everyday life. Therefore it is necessary to use, study and develop new technologies securing this infrastructure, especially against frequent network attacks from Internet world. Such technologies include firewalls, intrusion detection/prevention systems, vulnerability scanners, network access control systems, honeypots, etc. Although it is necessary to provide security also inside monitored network, we will focus on securing observed network against network threats from outside in the following.

Network-based intrusion detection and prevention systems are deployed to serve for this purpose. The malicious traffic is traditionally detected by deep packet inspection: the payload is searched for signatures of known attacks. However, this is very resource-intensive task and scalability is a growing problem in present large and multigigabit networks. On the contrary, intrusion detection based on an analysis of network flows scales well and is capable to capture some kinds of attacks [3]. So we are focused on research of NetFlow monitoring and intrusion prevention.

M. Rajarajan et al. (Eds.): SecureComm 2011, LNICST 96, pp. 543–546, 2012.
© Institute for Computer Sciences, Social Informatics and Telecommunications Engineering 2012

2   Used Technologies

2.1   NetFlow Monitoring

A network flow (NetFlow) is defined as unidirectional sequence of packets with some common properties that pass through a network device, e. g., IP addresses, protocol and ports [2]. These flow statistics were originally generated by routers and switches for accounting and management purposes only. Nowadays there are many network devices (including stand-alone probes) exporting NetFlow for network behaviour analysis and anomaly detection too. Using flow-based approach the detection is feasible even in 10 gigabit networks without any packet loss because the flow exporting process inspects only packet headers, not the entire payload. In our experience of deploying and running many NetFlow probes at campus network, NetFlow monitoring is very usable and powerful tool.

2.2   Hardware-Accelerated Monitoring Center

In our work, we use *Hardware-Accelerated Monitoring Center* (HAMOC) platform [1] to perform both network traffic monitoring (NetFlow/IPFIX acquisition and deep packet inspection) and network traffic filtering at high speed networks (10 Gbps). This platform provides hardware acceleration to already available and well-known monitoring applications.

The HAMOC is based on commodity PC platform. The lack of computing power for high-speed network applications is solved by COMBO hardware accelerator performing time critical operations. Used FPGA technology enables flexible firmware changes according to specific demands in particular tasks.

A set of network monitoring tools was tuned and tested with HAMOC platform to be able to proceed 10 Gb/s traffic at line rate, including traffic analysis tools (*tcpdump, tcpreplay, Wireshark*) and deep packet inspection tools (*Snort, Bro, Sucirata, OpenDPI*). The HAMOC platform provides also filtration capability with possibility to change filtration rules without packet loss and traffic distribution among multiple processors to increase computational power.

2.3   Light-Weighted Alternative

An alternative suitable for deployment in the lower speed networks (up to 1 Gb/s) is a usage of software probe (*fProbe*[1], *nProbe*[2]) for NetFlow acquisition and Linux *iptables* as traffic blocking tool instead of hardware platform HAMOC. This software variant is also able to protect observed network against network threats, but it is limited by various factors, e.g., incomplete traffic statistics during heavy attacks ((D)DoS) and inaccurate timestamps of network flows.

---

[1] http://fprobe.sourceforge.net/
[2] http://www.ntop.org/nProbe.html

3   Active Network Protection Scenarios

NetFlow based network protection can be built up from various components. In our research we focus on the following scenarios:

1. NetFlow probe(s) + collector + RTBH – Several probes exports NetFlow to the central collector where the analysis is done, the detection module can set *Remotely Triggered Black Hole Filtering* (RTBH) [4] at routers.
2. HAMOC running NetFlow probe and firewall – NetFlow acquisition, storage and detection as well as attack prevention is done at the HAMOC center.
3. HAMOC running quarantine – To protect users from phishing, all traffic destined to the known phishing websites is redirected to quarantine by HTTP proxy running at the HAMOC center.
4. HAMOC running NetFlow probe, collector and attack tools – Similar to the second scenario, but HAMOC is capable of conducting a counterattack.
5. HAMOC running NetFlow probe, collector and traffic limiter – Similar to the second scenario, but HAMOC is capable of limiting traffic incoming from the attack source.

The second scenario is described in a detail in the following section.

4   Use Case: Active Protection against Network Attacks

One of a possible application of the HAMOC platform is a network protection against various types of network threats and attacks. HAMOC is deployed as a NetFlow probe and packet filter (see Figure 1) at the borders of network. Acquired NetFlow data are sent to the NetFlow collector where are stored and analyzed by a detection tool. If an attack is found, the detection tool sends an event to the control center. The center assesses the severity of the event and issues a command to the packet filter running in HAMOC.

An example scenario of network protection against SSH brute-force attack follows:

1. the attacker probes the protected network for SSH servers by TCP SYN scanning,
2. the attacker starts brute-force attack against the SSH service running at the hosts that responded in the previous step,
3. TCP SYN scans and the brute-force attack are found by detection tool (plugin for the NetFlow collector), which processed acquired NetFlow data; these events are sent to the control center,
4. the control center processes the events, and as a result, instruments HAMOC to block all TCP traffic from the attacker's IP address to the TCP/22 port in the protected network,
5. the attacker continues with the brute-force attack but all SSH packets incoming to the protected network are dropped.

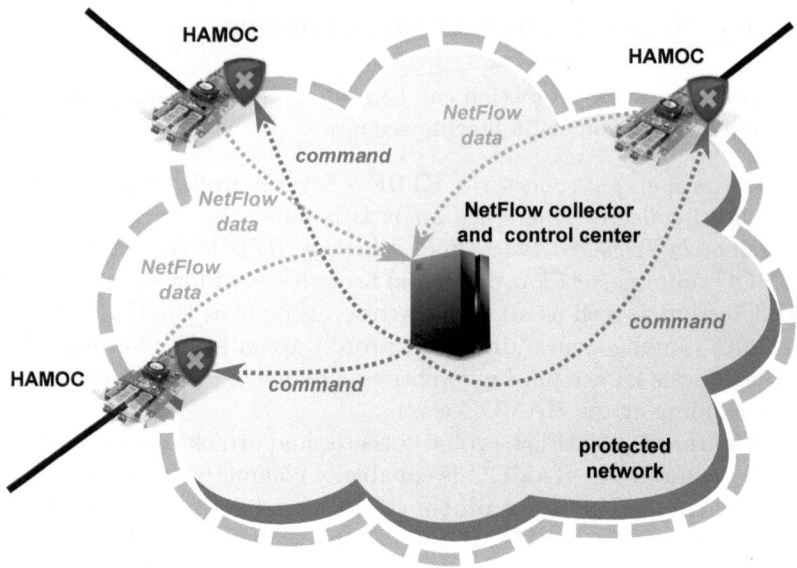

Fig. 1. NetFlow based network protection using HAMOC platform

5   Conclusion

In this work, we have presented NetFlow based active network protection. Network protection system was implemented in high-speed networks by using NetFlow monitoring and hardware accelerated monitoring center (HAMOC). Current work is focused on detailed system evaluation in both laboratory testbed and real network. The quality of network protection, system performance during heavy attacks and protection against new network threats are subjects of future research.

References

[1] Celeda, P., Krejci, R., Bariencik, J., Elich, M., Krmicek, V.: Cesnet technical report 9/2010 (2010), http://www.cesnet.cz/doc/techzpravy/2010/hamoc/
[2] Claise, B.: Cisco Systems NetFlow Services Export Version 9. RFC 3954 (Informational) (October 2004), http://www.ietf.org/rfc/rfc3954.txt
[3] Sperotto, A., Schaffrath, G., Sadre, R., Morariu, C., Pras, A., Stiller, B.: An Overview of IP Flow-Based Intrusion Detection. IEEE Communications Surveys & Tutorials 12(3), 343–356 (2010), http://doc.utwente.nl/72752/
[4] Cisco Systems. Remotely triggered black hole filtering, Whitepaper (2005), http://www.cisco.com/en/US/prod/collateral/iosswrel/ps6537/ps6586/ps6642/prod_white_paper0900aecd80313fac.pdf

Author Index